THE DIARY OF EDWARD BATES
1859–1866

EDITED BY

HOWARD K. BEALE

UNITED STATES
GOVERNMENT PRINTING OFFICE
WASHINGTON : 1933

For sale by the Superintendent of Documents, Washington, D.C. - - - - - Price $1.50 (Cloth)

PREFACE

" Notes &c." was the title which Edward Bates himself applied to his diary. The portion here printed is the property of Miss Helen Nicolay, but has been deposited by her in the Manuscripts Division of the Library of Congress. It consists of five volumes. The first one is large but only half filled, and covers the period from April 20, 1859, when Mr. Bates was already seriously discussing the possibility of his nomination for the Presidency, to February, 1861, when he was about to depart for Washington to enter Lincoln's Cabinet. The second volume, smaller in size, contains " Notes of Business in Cabinet " from February, 1861, to November 5, 1862, when Mr. Bates apparently abandoned entirely the idea of describing the proceedings of Cabinet meetings, which he had found time to do only spasmodically at best. The third and fourth volumes are small, closely written, leather-bound books including the period from November 1, 1861, to June 4, 1862, and that from November 7, 1862, to September 30, 1863. The final volume is a large one badly worn and bulging with newspaper clippings and other insertions. There is an earlier portion of Mr. Bates's diary in the possession of the Missouri Historical Society covering the years 1846 to 1852 which could not be secured for inclusion in this publication.

Unlike Gideon Welles and John Quincy Adams, Mr. Bates was not a tireless penman. There were long periods when he made no entries. But even when he was most faithfully keeping notes of events, he frequently did not describe a piece of news or an opinion at length as Mr. Welles or Mr. Adams would have done; but, instead, he clipped an item from a newspaper and then pasted it into his diary. Sometimes he inserted these clippings without comment, but more often he carefully noted the date and source, and then commented at length, varying from a sentence to several paragraphs. Usually Mr. Bates pasted these items in where they belonged and commented upon them at the time. Sometimes he crowded his remarks in later. At other times he left a space for discussion, but never found leisure to return and write down his ideas. Not infrequently he left a space and later pasted a relevant clipping into it. Occasionally he could not find room for a clipping where it belonged and hence had to insert it several pages out of place. These clippings created not only confusion but a serious editorial problem, since the comments of Mr. Bates upon them, which comprise an important portion of the diary, lose significance if the clippings are omitted.

Besides the clippings, Mr. Bates included in his "notes" opinions read by himself in Cabinet, an occasional letter of his own or of some one else to him, several interesting broadsides, election handbills, a military pass, two or three printed pamphlets (one with detailed comments of his own upon it), occasional passages copied out of books that interested him, and numerous quotations from memory of verse or prose. To have included all of these items would have been impossible; to have excluded all but the usual diary material would have meant extracting much of the most interesting matter and would have left some of the remainder unintelligible. After all, Mr. Bates himself labeled each volume "Notes &c." The editor finally decided to print: (1) everything in Mr. Bates's own hand, whether his own composition or quotations of others which he had copied because he regarded them as relevant; (2) a mere notation of clippings which have no accompanying comment—because they often contain valuable material which could be used by reference to the manuscript diary, or because they indicate Mr. Bates's tastes and interests; (3) a brief summary of all clippings upon which Mr. Bates commented, including whatever is requisite to an understanding of Mr. Bates's remarks; (4) a full quotation of a few printed items such as, for example, editorials about Mr. Bates, a printed letter of Mr. Bates's which he obviously meant to make a part of the diary, and a broadside reprint of a very cocky secession poem written in Richmond in 1862. Because it is not available save in obscure places, the editor has reproduced in full one significant letter on reconstruction which Mr. Bates pasted into his diary. It was written by General Sherman in January, 1865, and then printed as a broadside and presented to Mr. Bates in September. Finally, one letter of Mr. Bates's printed in the *New York Tribune* of 1859, one printed in the *National Intelligencer* of 1860, and one preserved in the Johnson Manuscripts of 1866, have been included because of Mr. Bates's diary references to them and their own inherent significance in a study of Mr. Bates's political views. In the "Appendix" are printed the series of six letters to the people of Missouri which Mr. Bates wrote in 1865 and to which he frequently refers in the diary. All passages by Mr. Bates himself are printed in roman type without brackets. The editor's descriptions of clippings and inserts are italicized and inclosed in brackets. Actual reprints of these clippings and also letters not written by Mr. Bates are set in smaller roman type and inclosed in brackets.

Omissions are indicated wherever made, but nothing has been omitted save countless comments on the weather, almost equally numerous references to the state of the Bates garden, a few details of Mr. Bates's ill-health of a particularly private nature, and one story—the only one—of a private scandal. The weather has been included in cases where it affected what followed, such as the movement of armies or the state of Mr. Bates's health. A few descriptions of a St. Louis garden of the 1860's have been included as possibly interesting to the social historian. One or two descriptions of drunkenness of public figures were after deliberation included because the present editor found similar *unprinted* items in the Welles MS. Diary important in the establishment of Johnson's sobriety, and hence historically significant. Several items describing the escapades of one of Mr. Bates's sons were included, again after deliberation, because the father's reaction to them was particularly illuminating to anyone seeking to know Mr. Bates's character. The many petty local or family entries have been printed, partly because once omissions were begun, no logical stopping place could be found, and partly because the diary will be used not only by the political historian of the period in which Mr. Bates lived, but also by the social historian who is interested in the environment of a typical Missouri figure of the Civil War period.

The diary has been reproduced as accurately as possible. Mr. Bates was individual in his spelling and punctuation. These have been preserved save where they would interfere with intelligent reading. Then the necessary period or comma or the correction in spelling has been added in brackets. Because too many textual corrections would have made fluent reading difficult, Mr. Bates's frequent misspellings of proper names have not been indicated or remedied in the text. The correct form has been supplied in the footnote instead, except in place names so familiar that both the place and its approved spelling are generally known. The abbreviations have been retained in simple words like " cd.," " brot.," " ansd.," in such titles as " Gen.," " Atty. Gen.," " Sec.," etc., and in the names of most states. But in longer words such as " comee." and " admn." where abbreviation might impede fluent reading, in proper names, and in cases such as " S. C." which is used for both " Supreme Court " and " South Carolina," the missing letters have been supplied in brackets. Superior letters have been brought down and a period supplied in place of raising the letter as in " Mr." Otherwise, the period after abbreviations, which more often than not Mr. Bates omitted, has not been inserted where he did not use it, since the necessary bracketed periods would needlessly have cluttered the text; but the manuscript form of each abbreviation has been meticulously reproduced. Mr. Bates's capitalization is erratic, and in many cases it is impossible to be certain of " C's," " S's," and " M's," but the editor has followed as closely as he could Mr. Bates's form. A few of Mr. Bates's dates are centered above the first paragraph of the day. For the sake of uniformity the editor has brought these down to the beginning of the paragraph. Almost none of Mr. Bates's dates are underscored; for the sake of clarity in reading the editor has italicized the date for each day. More often than not the date is not separated from the first sentence of the paragraph; the editor has supplied the period in every such case. Otherwise the dates have been left as Mr. Bates wrote them.

Mr. Bates sometimes made explanatory comments which he labeled " Note " as he made the entry. He frequently went back and made additions either on an unused part of a page or in the margin. These " Notes " are usually so labeled, often dated; and sometimes they clearly indicate from the context whether they were added at the time the entry was made or later. Where only the manuscript evidences a later addition, the editor has indicated this, and he has labeled all marginal entries. Mr. Bates used brackets not only in quoted passages but sometimes in his own comments. These brackets of Mr. Bates's are represented thus < > whereas the editor's own are the more usual type [ ].

In Mr. Bates's quotations he rarely copied or remembered accurately. Where possible the passage has been corrected in brackets to its original form. Where this could not be done, the inaccuracy has been noted. Because they throw so much light on Mr. Bates's tastes and intellectual background, the references to books and verse which he was reading or knew well enough to quote have been supplied whenever the editor could cite them.

In the footnotes, references that were not entirely clear in the text have been explained. Places, events, court decisions, not generally known, have been briefly described. Where persons are mentioned, the editor has supplied information on their occupation, the offices they held, their party affiliations, their ideas on public questions, and necessary dates. Five classes of persons were not thus described in footnotes: a large number of friends or acquaintances of Mr. Bates who were so obscure that no information about them survives; the numerous members of the Bates family and their relatives who enter and reënter the picture constantly and who are described in the " Introduction "; a group of contemporary Americans so prominent that comment would be superfluous, namely, Presidents Fillmore, Pierce, Buchanan, Lincoln, Johnson, Jefferson Davis, and Generals Grant and Lee; a group of well-known Americans of other periods, like Washington, Madison, Clay, Calhoun, and John Brown; and finally leaders in other countries like Cæsar, Cardinal Wolsey, Cromwell, John Evelyn, Robespierre, Napoleon, and John S. Mill. Lesser people of other periods or other countries have been described. Presidential candidates like Douglas, Bell, Breckinridge, and McClellan, Generals McClellan, Frémont, and W. T. Sherman, and the two Chief Justices, Taney and Chase, have been footnoted only when first mentioned; Lincoln's cabinet officers, only at the time when they were appointed to office. Breckinridge and Montgomery Blair, however, have been given a footnote wherever they might be confused with others of the same name. But, except in the above enumerated cases, cross references guide the reader from each subsequent mention of a man back to the original description of him. Obviously, to many readers these notes will be superfluous when they deal with leading figures of the day like Sumner and Wade. But the editor found it impossible to draw any logical distinction that would satisfy the purposes of all readers once he began to omit certain senators, for instance, and include others. It is hoped that readers who do not need information about some of the men mentioned will not regard the notes as insults to their intelligence but will consider them useful reminders of dates for those whose memories do need refreshing and as information for the reader who has not yet attained their fortunate familiarity with the period. It is hoped, too, that the diary may prove useful and enjoyable reading for advanced undergraduates and graduate students who are only beginning to know this period. The editor believes that source material such as this diary, sufficiently annotated to be intelligible to these students, will prove an interesting and effective means of learning American History.

A debt of appreciation is due several who have assisted in the task of editing. Miss Helen Nicolay, the owner of the diary, supplied the manuscript and has been most gracious in allowing the American Historical Association full freedom in publishing it. The Manuscripts Division of the Library of Congress has provided facilities for working on the manuscript. Dr. E. Wilder Spaulding, assistant to the historical adviser of the State Department, and Miss Olive M. Jack of the Law Division of the Library of Congress have given valuable aid in finding diplomatic and legal material. Dr. Leo F. Stock of Catholic University gave useful suggestions on the technique of editing. Mrs. Mary Parker Ragatz is preparing a comprehensive index for the diary. And to my father, Frank A. Beale, my mother, Nellie K. Beale, my friends, T. Eliot Weil, Jane Kline, Mrs. Jane Ruby, Mrs. Enid F. Gilluly, and Mrs. Gertrude Working, and my secretary, Miss Freya Torrey, I am deeply indebted for painstaking and patient assistance in collation, checking of footnotes, and proofreading.

HOWARD K. BEALE.

WASHINGTON, D. C., *June 23, 1932.*

INTRODUCTION

When Edward Bates began this portion of his diary he was living in political retirement in St. Louis. But he was already being discussed as a candidate for the Presidency. And in the troubled times of 1860 he was unusually "available." He was born in Goochland County, Virginia, west of Richmond and north of the James River, in 1793, the son of Thomas Fleming Bates, a planter and merchant. He brought with him to Missouri many of the traditions of Virginia planterdom. Besides, as his correspondence and his repeated services to Virginians during the War indicate, he retained many of his early Virginia friends. Some of them were by 1859 influential Southern editors or politicians. Furthermore, on May 29, 1823, he married Julia Coalter, sixteen-year-old daughter of David Coalter, formerly of South Carolina, and sister-in-law of former Senator William C. Preston and Chancellor William Harper, of South Carolina. Even in the cotton South, then, Mr. Bates had important connections.

Mr. Bates was the youngest of twelve children and his father died when he was only a boy. He had older brothers who helped him through three years at Charlotte Hall Academy in Maryland and who would have enabled him to go on to Princeton had an accident not forced him to give up schooling altogether. His relative, James Pleasants, member of Congress and governor of Virginia, secured him an appointment as midshipman in the Navy, but his mother's Quaker principles apparently dissuaded him, though they did not prevent his serving as sergeant in a volunteer company of militia from February to October, 1813. In the meantime his father's oldest brother, Frederick, went west and became judge of Michigan Territory; then secretary and acting governor of Louisiana Territory, 1806–1812; secretary of Missouri Territory, 1812–1820; and governor of Missouri, 1824–1825.

In 1814, therefore, Edward Bates moved to Missouri, studied law, and in 1816 was admitted to the bar. Here he soon made a place for himself, served as prosecuting attorney before Missouri became a state, and then played an active part in the Constitutional Convention of 1820. In the new State he became attorney-general in 1820 and United States district attorney from 1824 to 1826. In 1827 he went to Congress as an Adams anti-Democrat for one term. But this was the period of Bentonian supremacy in Missouri and

Mr. Bates was defeated for reëlection. Then the new Whig Party nominated him for the United States Senate, but he was again defeated. From this time forward he assumed leadership in the Whig Party of Missouri, and was offered the secretaryship of War in the Fillmore Cabinet in 1850. This he declined. In fact, after service in the Missouri Senate from 1830 to 1834 and in the Missouri House of Representatives from 1834 to 1836, he retired from public office entirely except for a brief period as judge of the Land Court in St. Louis, from 1853 to 1856. After his retirement from Congress in 1829 he lived on a farm on Dardenne Prairie, in St. Charles County, near enough to St. Louis to continue his legal practice. In 1842 he moved back to the suburbs of the city. Mr. Bates always showed keen interest in trade on the Mississippi and in a rail connection with the Pacific Coast, and in 1847 he won national prominence by presiding over a Chicago convention for river and harbor improvement. In 1856 he presided over the Whig National Convention in Baltimore. In 1858 Harvard granted him an LL. D. Hence Mr. Bates was well known in 1859, and his life of retirement and the resulting freedom from embroilment in the heated quarrels of the day gave him a tremendous advantage over other leaders.

Mr. Bates's political views, too, made him a desirable candidate for the presidential nomination. He was Southern-bred, lived in a border state, understood the South, and yet vigorously opposed secession, allied himself with the " Free-Labor " Party in Missouri, and opposed both repeal of the Missouri Compromise and the admission of Kansas under the Lecompton Constitution. He disliked slavery. In the very year 1859 his sister Sarah, with his approval, freed slaves worth many thousands of dollars. He believed the Federal Government had the right to forbid slavery in the Territories, but he would have abided by the Missouri Compromise agreement. He regarded as *obiter dicta* all the pronouncements in the Dred Scott case save the decision that under Missouri law Scott could not be a citizen of the State, and hence could not sue in the courts. He did not favor Federal guaranties of civil rights for negroes. In all matters Bates was a moderate. A great admirer of both Jefferson and Clay, still a Whig without unfortunate Republican or Democratic antecedents, Bates could have won the support of moderates in both North and South. But he was not nominated. He was never an orthodox Republican; it was to conciliate the unionist element of the Border States that he was chosen for the Cabinet.

The diary speaks for Mr. Bates during the eight years it covers. But certain features of it are worthy of comment. It throws interesting new lights on our national history. It seems significant that after twelve months of constant speculation on the nominee of the Republican Party, Mr. Bates first mentioned Lincoln as a possibility only on April 26, 1860, just twenty days before the Convention. Moderate and Border-State man though he was, he gave indication even before his first interview with Lincoln that in the event of secession he would support coërcion by armed force to preserve the Union. And throughout his cabinet career he did urge vigorous prosecution of the war while men of more extereme views vacillated. On the other hand, his moderation, his orderly, legal mind, and his respect for constitutional principles led him repeatedly to oppose arbitrary uses of the war powers against civilian populations. Hence he combined severe criticism of the ineffectiveness of the military officers with characteristically vigorous protests over their infringement of the constitutional rights of civilians, and he once made the shrewd comment that somehow the officers who were the poorest fighters against the enemy were the bravest oppressors of civilians. Mr. Bates respected Lincoln and felt that he was usually right if he would only follow his own judgment, but he considered Lincoln weak and deplored his inability to stand out against the influence of men whom Mr. Bates distrusted. From the first he urged Lincoln to be President and to be Commander-in-Chief of the Army in fact as well as in name.

Interestingly enough, Gideon Welles is rarely mentioned; yet Mr. Bates agreed with him in many estimates of men, notably in his early dislike and suspicion of the Radical Republicans and in his distrust of Stanton and Seward. Mr. Bates resented, too, Mr. Seward's interference in the affairs of his department. He early lost confidence in McClellan, and he felt a keen distrust of Halleck. He opposed the creation of the State of West Virginia and the admission of Nevada. In the *Trent* Affair, his first impulse was to approve our action, and he set out to justify it on legal grounds. Mr. Bates throws out intimations of political influences in the Supreme Court, but his diary is disappointing in its failure to deal adequately with the history of the Court or of the Attorney-General's Office during the War.

On matters of larger policy, Mr. Bates showed considerable acumen. He perceived clearly that success in the War involved political as well as military considerations. He thoroughly understood the importance of Europe's attitude toward the War. And he saw from the beginning the significance of the Mississippi Valley. Before the War, he stressed its importance in making unionists in the Northwest; during the War, he urged upon the Government the importance of the Mississippi in military strategy. He and his friend Eads seem together to have persuaded the Government to acquire gunboats for naval warfare on the river. Mr. Eads himself gave Mr. Bates credit for the idea.

The diary is important, too, as a study of the workings of national and local politics. Mr. Bates carefully watched the use of government patronage. He found a place in his own office for one son, secured Lincoln's personal appointment of another son to West Point, and helped get a promotion for still another son in the Army, and a comfortable appointment in the Navy for the one who had been in his office. He took good care of his political friends, too. He also gave advice on appointments in other states. Yet he was scrupulously honest in his political dealings. When an operator in Wall Street sent him a check for $500 for a "private" opinion whether the 10.30 notes were receivable for customs duties. he returned the check and declined to express an opinion. And he did not tolerate dishonesty in political friends. In Missouri politics he belonged to the Conservative group which was attacked from one side by the Peace Democrats and secessionists and from the other by the Radical Republicans. After his resignation from office, he returned to St. Louis to make a valiant fight against the control of Missouri by the Radicals. The diary therefore provides a valuable study in state politics of early Reconstruction.

For the social historian, too, Mr. Bates's diary is useful. He was interested in the minutiæ of life. The weather, his garden, his servants, his financial dealings, the cost of a watch, his changes from summer to winter clothing, repairs on the outbuildings, all find a place in his diary.

One of the most interesting features of the diary is the breadth of reading and familiarity with works of literature and history that it reveals. Mr. Bates quotes most frequently from the *Bible* and Shakespeare. Many of his quotations are from sources unknown to the present editor. But those which Mr. Bates labeled or the editor was able to place show that he had read the following books: John S. Mill's *On Liberty* and *Considerations on Representative Government*, Samuel Pepys's *Diary*, Adam Smith's *Wealth of Nations*, Thomas Ewbank's *Inorganic Forces Ordained to Supersede Human Slavery*, Benton's *Abridged Debates*, *The Letters of Junius*, Carlyle's *Frederick the Great*, Horace Binney's *Inquiry into the Formation of Washington's Farewell Address*, *Official Opinions of the Attorneys-General*, Jefferson's *Notes on Virginia*, *The Letters of Marcus Tullius Cicero to Several of His Friends*, Lord Campbell's *Lives of Chief Justices*, Lord Campbell's *Lives of Lord Chancellors*, Lord Campbell's *Shakespeare's Legal Acquirements Considered*, Heeren's *Reflections on the Politics of Ancient Greece*, Lucan's *Pharsalia*, Mary L. Putnam's *A Tragedy of Errors*, John Evelyn's *Diary and Correspondence*, Francis Lieber's *Fragment* on *Washington and Napoleon*, Francis Lieber's *Reminiscences of an Intercourse with Mr. Niebuhr the Historian*, Aristotle's *Politics and Economics*, Thiers's

History of the French Revolution, Guizot's *Democracy in France*, Frances Burney D'Arblay's *Diary*, Enoch Wines's *Commentaries on the Laws of the Ancient Hebrews*, McPherson's *Political Manual for 1866*, and parts at least of the *Works of British Poets, Including Translations from the Greek and Roman Authors*. He knew the following well enough to quote from them: *The Bible*, Horace's *Sermones*, Dr. Johnson's *Vanity of Human Wishes*, Ben Jonson's *Every Man in His Humour*, Shakespeare's *Antony and Cleopatra, Hamlet, Henry V, Richard III, Henry VIII*, Sir John Harrington's *Epigrams*, Pope's translation of the *Iliad of Homer*, Pope's *Ode on Solitude*, Pope's *Essay on Man*, Young's *Night Thoughts*, James Thomson's *The Seasons*, and Robert Burns's poems. The books on this impressive list were read by a lawyer of the trans-Mississippi West in the first half of the Nineteenth Century—by a man who spent much of his time on a farm and made no pretensions to cultivation or formal education.

It remains only to identify the members of Mr. Bates's family mentioned in the diary. His wife, Julia, remains an obscure figure who apparently did not accompany him to Washington social functions, but went regularly to church. Little is revealed about her save her attendance on sick relatives and the fact that Mr. Bates regarded her as a model wife. Originally he had seventeen children. Only eight of them survived to enter the pages of the diary. The eldest, Barton, was a lawyer who lived on a farm on Dardenne Prairie in St. Charles County. He had studied law under Hamilton R. Gamble, who was his mother's brother-in-law and his father's law partner. When Gamble became governor he appointed Barton a judge of the Supreme Court. Barton was subsequently *elected* to the same office, but resigned for political reasons early in 1865. He became wealthy through lead-mining and railroad enterprises, was at one time president of the Old North Missouri Railroad, and was associated with Mr. Eads in the building of the Eads Bridge at St. Louis. During the period of the diary his father depended largely on him for both financial aid and general advice. Caroline Bates was Barton's wife. They had eight children. The eldest, Onward or "Onwy," lived with his grandfather in St. Louis after Mr. Bates's return from Washington. Cora and Hester stayed with Grandfather Bates while they attended school in the city. Sarah, Peggy, Tarlton, and Eads were some of Barton's other children.

Nancy was Mr. Bates's second child, but of her one learns little. Julian, the third, was a physician in Florissant, a suburb of St. Louis. He was graduated at the Medical School of the University of Pennsylvania in 1855 and during the War served as medical examiner of the First Enrollment District of Missouri and as surgeon and colonel in the Missouri militia. His wife was Sarah F. Woodson, daughter of Charles F. Woodson, of St. Charles County, a former Virginian. Edwa and Winona were Julian's daughters.

Fleming was the fourth child. He had a wife and child whose names are not revealed. Little is said of him, except that he grieved his father by serving in the Confederate Army throughout the War.

Richard, the fifth child, caused his father great unhappiness through his escapades. After Mr. Bates went to Washington "Dick" married Ellen Woodson and they had a son named Charles F[?]. Bates. During the first part of the Lincoln administration Dick served as chief clerk in the Attorney-General's Office. His habits made his father finally request his resignation. Then he was given a new trial, but he had not yet reformed, and so Mr. Eads arranged with the Navy Department to assign him to duties on shipboard that would be pleasant but would keep him at sea. Apparently after this Mr. Bates had no more trouble with him.

Matilda, the sixth child, like her sister, remains colorless as far as the diary is concerned. About the time of Mr. Bates's death she married Major Edward B. Eno.

John Coalter Bates, known as "Coalter," was a source of great pride to his father. He was graduated from Washington University in St. Louis. When only nineteen, he enlisted and fought at Antietam, Fredericksburg, Chancellorsville, and Gettysburg. He served on General Meade's staff from 1863 to 1865. He saw hard fighting and won rapid advancement. After the War he remained in the Army, served thirty years on the frontier, then fought in Cuba and the Philippines, and in 1906 became chief-of-staff and lieutenant-general.

The youngest child, Charles Woodson Bates or "Woody," was given an appointment to West Point. After remaining there through the War he failed in his examinations and entered a St. Louis bank.

Mr. Bates had a brother, Fleming, in Virginia, whose daughter, Mrs. Flementine Ball, and granddaughter, Eliza B. Hudnall, enter the diary. Dr. Bates of Wheeling had two daughters, Ella and Sarah J. Then there were Dr. Frederick Bates, of Missouri, and his wife, Lavinia, and their children. Edward Bates had two sisters who are mentioned several times: Sarah Bates, who died before Mr. Bates went to Washington and Mrs. Wharton, who died after his return. Mrs. Bates had been born a Coalter and had a brother John D. Coalter, who lived in Missouri and was in politics. She had another brother, Beverly, whose son, John Coalter, enters the diary. Mr. Bates's mother had been a Virginia Woodson, and numerous Woodsons lived in Missouri. But to untangle the Woodson and Coalter relationships would require a separate genealogy.

CHAPTER I

1859

April 20. Today was published in St Louis papers (copied from the New York Tribune) a recent letter of mine to the Whig Committee of New York, in answer to their call upon me for my views and opinions on the politics of the country, and the signs of the times.[1]

St. Louis, Feb. 24, 1859.

To Messrs. J. PHILIPS PHOENIX, WILLIS BLACKSTONE, H. M. BININGER, DAVID J. LILEY AND H. R. SMITH, Committee, New York.

SIRS: A short time ago I was favored with your note of the 7th inst., covering a resolution of the Committee, to the effect that it is inexpedient at this time further to discuss or agitate the Negro question, but rather to turn the attention of the people to other topics—" topics of general importance, such as our Foreign Relations, including the Extension of Territory; the building of Railroads for National purposes; the improvement of our Harbors, the navigation of our Rivers to facilitate Internal Commerce; the subject of Currency, and a Tariff of Duties, and other means of developing our own internal resources, our home wealth, and binding together by ties of national and fraternal feelings, the various parts and sections of our widely extended Republic."

Your letter, gentlemen, opens a very wide field, in asking for my " opinion upon the subject, and my views as to the signs of the times." Books have been written upon these matters, and speeches delivered by the thousand; and yet the argument seems as far from being exhausted as it was at the beginning; and I take it for certain that you do not expect or desire me to discuss at large, all or any of these interminable quarrels. That I have opinions upon all or most of them, is true—not the opinions of this or that party, ready to be abandoned or modified to suit this or that platform, but my own opinions—perhaps the more fixed and harder to be changed because deliberately formed in the retirement of private life, free from the exigencies of official responsibility and from the perturbations of party policy. They are *my* own opinions, right or wrong.

As to the Negro question—I have always thought, and often declared in speech and in print, that it is a pestilent question, the agitation of which has never done good to any party, section or class, and never can do good, unless it be accounted good to stir

---

[1] This present version of the letter is that of the *New York Tribune* of April 16, 1859.

up the angry passions of men, and exasperate the unreasoning jealousy of sections, and by those bad means foist some unfit men into office, and keep some fit men out. It is a sensitive question into whose dangerous vortex it is quite possible for good men to be drawn unawares. But when I see a man, at the South or the North, of mature age and some experience, persist in urging the question, after the sorrowful experience of the last few years, I can attribute his conduct to no higher motive than personal ambition or sectional prejudice.

As to the power of the General Government to protect the persons and properties, and advance the interests of the people, by laying taxes, raising armies and navies, building forts and arsenals, light houses, moles, and breakwaters, surveying the coasts and adjacent seas, improving rivers, lakes, and harbors, and making roads—I should be very sorry to doubt the existence of the power, or the duty to exercise it, whenever the constituted authorities have the means in their hands, and are convinced that its exercise is necessary to protect the country and advance the prosperity of the people.

In my own opinion, a government that has no power to protect the harbors of its country against winds and waves and human enemies, nor its rivers against snags, sands and rocks, nor to build roads for the transportation of its armies and its mails and the commerce of its people, is a poor, impotent government, and not at all such a government as our fathers thought they had made when they produced the Constitution which was greeted by intelligent men everywhere with admiration and gratitude as a government free enough for all the ends of legal liberty and strong enough for all the purposes of national and individual protection. A free people, if it be wise, will make a good constitution; but a constitution, however good in itself, did never make a free people. The people do not derive their rights from the government, but the government derives its powers from the people; and those powers are granted for the main, if not the only, purpose of protecting the rights of the people. Protection, then, if not the sole, is the chief end of government.

And it is for the governing power to judge, in every instance, what kind and what degree of protection is needful—whether a Navy to guard our commerce all around the world, or an Army to defend the country against armed invasion from without, or domestic insurrection from within; or a Tariff, to protect our home industry against the dangerous obtrusion of foreign labor and capital.

Of the existence of the power and duty of the Government to protect the People in their persons, their property, their industry and their locomotion, I have no doubt; but the time, the mode and the measure of protection, being always questions of policy and prudence, must of necessity be left to the wisdom and patriotism of those whose duty it is to make laws for the good government of the country. And with them I freely leave it, as the safest, and indeed the only, constitutional depository of the power.

As to our Foreign Policy generally, I have but little to say. I am not much of a progressive, and am content to leave it where Washington [Jefferson] placed it, upon that wise, virtuous, safe maxim—"Peace [. . .] with all nations; entangling alliance[s] with none." The greedy and indiscriminate appetite for foreign acquisition, which makes us covet our neighbor's lands, and devise cunning schemes to get them, has little of my sympathy. I view it as a sort of political gluttony, as dangerous to our body politic as gluttony is to the natural man—producing disease certainly, hastening death, probably. Those of our politicians who are afflicted with this morbid appetite are wont to cite the purchase of Louisiana and Florida, as giving countenance to their inordinate desires. But the cases are wholly unlike in almost every particular. Louisiana was indispensable to our full and safe enjoyment of an immense region which was already owned, and its acquisition gave us the unquestioned control of that noble system of Mississippi waters, which nature seems to have made to be one and indivisible, and rounded off the map of the nation into one uniform and compacted whole. Nothing remained to mar and disfigure our national plat, but Florida, and that was desirable, less for its intrinsic value, than because it would form a dangerous means of annoyance, in case of war with a Maritime Power, surrounded as it is, on three sides by the ocean, and touching three of our present States, with no barrier between. The population of Louisiana and Florida, when acquired, was very small compared with the largeness of the territory; and, lying in contact with the States, was easily and quickly absorbed into and assimilated with the mass of our people. Those countries were acquired, moreover, in the most peaceful and friendly manner, and for a satisfactory consideration.

Now, without any right or any necessity, it is hard to tell what we do not claim in all the continent south of us, and the adjacent islands. Cuba is to be the first fruit of our grasping enterprise, and that is to be gotten at all hazards, by peaceful purchase if we can, by war and conquest if we must.[2] But Cuba is only an outpost to the

[2] This was the substance of the Ostend Manifesto which Buchanan as Minister to Great Britain had joined Ministers John Y. Mason and Pierre Soulé in promulgating. As Secretary of State under President Polk, Buchanan had tried to buy Cuba. In his second, third, and fourth annual messages he urged Congress to coöperate with him in securing it by negotiation.

Empire of Islands and continental countries that are to follow. A leading Senator[3] has lately declared (in debate on the Thirty Million bill[4]) that we must not only have Cuba, but all the islands from Cape Florida to the Spanish Main, so as to surround the Gulf of Mexico and Caribbean Sea, and make them our "*mare clausum*," like the Mediterranean, in old times, when the Roman Emperor ruled both its shores, from the pillars of Hercules to the Hellespont.[5] This claim of *mare nostrum* implies, of course, that we must own the continent that bounds *our sea* on the west, as well as the string of islands that inclose it on the east—that is, Mexico, Central America, and all South America, so far south at least as the Orinoco.[6] In that wide compass of sea and land there are a good many native governments, and provinces belonging to the strongest maritime powers, and a narrow continental isthmus which we ourselves, as well as England and France, are wont to call the *highway of nations.* To fulfill the grand conception, and perfect our tropical empire, we must buy or conquer all these torrid countries, and their mongrel populations. As to buying them, it strikes me that we had better waite [sic] awhile, at least until the Government has ceased to borrow money to pay its current expenses. And as to conquering them, perhaps it would be prudent to pause and make some estimate of costs and contingencies, before we rush into war with all maritime Europe and half America.

I am not one of those who believe that the United States is not an independent and safe nation, because Cuba is not a part of it. On the contrary, I believe that we are quite capable of self-defense, even if the "Queen of the Antilles" were a province of England, France

[3] Robert Toombs of Georgia : Whig state legislator, 1837–1840, 1841–1844 ; states' rights Democratic congressman, 1845–1853 ; U. S. senator, 1853–1861. He was later a leader in the Georgia Secession Convention, and congressman, brigadier-general, and secretary of State under the Confederacy.

[4] January, 1859, *Senate Reports,* 35 Cong., 2 Sess., ser. no. 994, doc. no. 351. The bill purposed to appropriate $30,000,000 " to facilitate the acquisition of Cuba by negotiation." Senator Slidell (*infra,* Nov. 24, 1859, note 89) introduced it on January 10, 1859 (*Cong. Globe,* 35 Cong., 2 Sess., 277) ; it was reported favorably by the Committee on Foreign Relations of which he was chairman, on January 24, 1859 (*ibid.,* 35 Cong., 2 Sess., 538) ; it was debated at great length on January 24, February 9–10, February 15–17, February 21, and February 25 (*ibid.,* 35 Cong., 2 Sess., 538–544, 904–909, 934–940, 960–968, 1038, Appendix [155–169], 1058–1063, 1079–1087, 1179–1192, 1326–1363) ; but because of opposition, it was withdrawn on February 26 (*ibid.,* 35 Cong., 2 Sess., 1385–1387). At the next session, on December 8, 1859, Senator Slidell reintroduced this bill (*ibid.,* 36 Cong., 1 Sess., 53), had it referred to the Committee on Foreign Relations on December 21 (*ibid.,* 36 Cong., 1 Sess., 199), reported it out favorably to the Senate on May 30, 1860, but because of opposition did not push it (*ibid.,* 36 Cong., 1 Sess., 2456). He promised to call it up again at the next session, but when that time arrived was too busy seceding to bother about Cuba.

[5] On January 24, Toombs had said, "Cuba has fine ports, and with her acquisition, we can make first the Gulf of Mexico, and then the Caribbean Sea, a *mare clausum.* Probably younger men than you or I will live to see the day when no flag shall float there except by permission of the United States of America . . . that development, that progress throughout the tropics [is] the true, fixed unalterable policy of the nation." *Ibid.,* 35 Cong., 2 Sess., 543.

[6] I. e., as far as Venezuela.

or Russia; and surely, while it remains an appendage of a comparatively feeble nation, Cuba has much more cause to fear us than we have to fear Cuba. In fact, gentlemen, I cannot help doubting the honesty of the cowardly argument by which we are urged to rob poor old Spain of this last remnant of her Western empire, for fear that she might use it to rob us.

But suppose we could get, honestly and peaceably, the whole of the country—continental and insular—from the Rio Grande to the Orinoco, and from Trinidad to Cuba, and thus establish our *mare clausum*, and shut the gate of the world across the Isthmus, can we govern them wisely and well? For the last few years, in the attempt to govern our home Territories of Kansas and Utah, we have not very well maintained the dignity and justice of the nation, nor secured the peace and prosperity of the subject people.[7] Can we hope to do better with the various mixed races of Mexico, Central and South America, and the West India Islands? Some of those countries have been trying for fifty years to establish republican governments on our model, but in every instance have miserably failed; and yet, there was no obstacle to complete success but their own inaptitude.

For my part, I should be grieved to see my country become, like Rome, a conquering and dominant nation; for I think there are few or no examples in history, of Governments whose chief objects were glory and power, which did ever secure the happiness and prosperity of their own people. Such Governments may grow great and famous, and advance a few of their citizens to wealth and nobility; but the price of their grandeur is the personal independence and individual freedom of their people. Still less am I inclined to see absorbed into our system, " on an equal footing with the original States," the various and mixed races (amounting to I know not how many millions) which inhabit the continent and islands south of our present border. I am not willing to inoculate our body politic with the virus of their diseases, political and social—diseases which, with them, are chronic and hereditary, and with us could hardly fail to produce corruption in the head and weakness in the members.

Our own country, as it is, in position, form and size, is a wonder which proclaims a wisdom above the wit of man. Large enough for our posterity, for centuries to come: All in the temperate zone, and therefore capable of a homogeneous population, yet so diversified in climates and soils, as to produce everything that is necessary to the comfort and wealth of a great people: Bounded east and west by

---

[7] Bitterness over the slavery question had reached the point of armed conflict, raids, and murder in Kansas in 1855–1856, and Utah was at this time subject to frequent Indian raids. It was in 1859, too, that the Republicans tried to prohibit polygamy in Utah and the Democrats succeeded, probably with slavery in other territories in mind, in preventing Congressional legislation on the subject.

great oceans, and bisected in the middle by a mighty river, which drains and fructifies the continent, and binds together the most southern and northern portions of our land by a bond stronger than iron. Beside all this, it is new and growing—the strongest on the continent, with no neighbor whose power it fears, or of whose ambition it has cause to be jealous. Surely such a country is great enough and good enough for all the ends of honest ambition and virtuous power.

It seems to me that an efficient home-loving Government, moderate and economical in its administration, peaceful in its objects, and just to all nations, need have no fear of invasion at home, or serious aggression abroad. The nations of Europe have to stand continually in defense of their existence; but the conquest of our country by a foreign power is simply impossible, and no nation is so absurd as to entertain the thought. We may conquer ourselves by local strifes and sectional animosities; and when, by our folly and wickedness, we have accomplished that great calamity, there will be none to pity us for the consequences of so great a crime.

If our Government would devote all its energies to the promotion of peace and friendship with all foreign countries, the advancement of Commerce, the increase of Agriculture, the growth and stability of Manufactures, and the cheapening, quickening and securing the internal trade and travel of our country; in short, if it would devote itself in earnest to the establishment of a wise and steady policy of internal government, I think we should witness a growth and consolidation of wealth and comfort and power for good, which cannot be reasonably hoped for from a fluctuating policy, always watching for the turns of good fortune, or from a grasping ambition to seize new territories, which are hard to get and harder to govern.

The present position of the Administration is a sorrowful commentary upon the broad democracy of its professions. In theory, the people have the right and ability to do anything; in practice, we are verging rapidly to the One-Man power.

The President, the ostensible head of the National Democrats, is eagerly striving to concentrate power in his own hands, and thus to set aside both the People and their Representatives in the actual affairs of government. Having emptied the Treasury, which he found full, and living precariously upon borrowed money, he now demands of Congress to entrust to his unchecked discretion the War power, the Purse and the Sword. First, he asks Congress to authorize him, by statute, to use the Army to take *military* possession of the Northern Mexico, and hold it under his *protectorate*, and as a security for debts due to our citizens [8]—*civil* possession would not answer,

---

[8] Dec. 6, 1858, James D. Richardson, *Messages and Papers of the Presidents*, V, 514. See *infra*, Feb. 15, 1860.

for that might expose him, as in the case of Kansas, to be annoyed by a factious Congress and a rebellious Territorial Legislature.

Secondly: Not content with this, he demands the discretionary power to use the Army and Navy in the South, also in blockading the coast and marching his troops into the interior of Mexico and New Granada, to protect our citizens against all evil-doers along the transit routes of Tehuantepec and Panama.[9] And he and his supporters in Congress claim this enormous power upon the ground that, in this particular at least, he ought to be the equal of the greatest monarch of Europe. They forget that our fathers limited the power of the President by design, and for the reason that they had found out by sad experience that the monarchs of Europe were too strong for freedom.

Third: In strict pursuance of this doctrine, first publicly announced from Ostend,[10] he demands of Congress to hand over to him thirty millions of dollars to be used at his discretion, to facilitate his acquisition of Cuba.[11] Facilitate how? Perhaps it might be imprudent to tell.

Add to all this, the fact (as yet unexplained) that one of the largest naval armaments which ever sailed from our coast is now operating in South America, ostensibly against a poor little republic far up the Plate River,[12] to settle some little quarrel between the two Presidents.[13] If Congress had been polite enough to grant the President's demand of the sword and the purse against Mexico, Central America and Cuba, this navy, its duty done at the south, might be made, on its way home, to arrive in the Gulf very opportunely, to aid the " Commander-in-Chief " in the acquisition of some very valuable territory.

I allude to these facts with no malice against Mr. Buchanan, but as evidences of the dangerous change which is now obviously sought to be made in the practical working of the Government—the concentration of power in the hands of the President, and the dangerous policy, now almost established, of looking abroad for temporary glory and aggrandizement, instead of looking at home, for all the purposes of good government—peaceable, moderate, economical, protecting all interests alike, and by a fixed policy, calling into safe exercise all the talents and industry of our people, and thus steadily

[9] J. D. Richardson, *op. cit.*, V, 516-517.
[10] *Supra*, April 20, 1859, note 2.
[11] J. D. Richardson, *op. cit.*, V, 508-511.
[12] Rio de La Plata in South America.
[13] An expedition of some 19 ships, 200 guns, and 2.500 men which was sent against Paraguay because a vessel of that nation had fired upon the United States steamer *Water-Witch*. A mere show of force sufficed to secure both an apology and an indemnity on February 10, 1859. The President of Argentina was so interested and so pleased that he presented the commander with a sword.

advancing our country in everything which can make a nation great, happy, and permanent.

The rapid increase of the Public Expenditures (and that, too, under the management of statesmen professing to be peculiarly economical) is an alarming sign of corruption and decay.

That increase bears no fair proportion to the growth and expansion of the country, but looks rather like wanton waste or criminal negligence. The ordinary objects of great expense are not materially augmented—the Army and Navy remain on a low peace establishment—the military defenses are little, if at all, enlarged—the improvement of Harbors, Lakes and Rivers is abandoned, and the Pacific Railroad is not only not begun but its very location is scrambled for by angry sections, which succeed in nothing but mutual defeat. In short, the money to an enormous amount (I am told at the rate of $80,000,000 to $100,000,000 a year) is gone, and we have little or nothing to show for it. In profound peace with foreign nations, and surrounded with the proofs of National growth and individual prosperity, the Treasury, by less than two years of mismanagement, is made bankrupt, and the Government itself is living from hand to mouth, on bills of credit and borrowed money!

This humiliating state of things could hardly happen if men in power were both honest and wise. The Democratic economists in Congress confess that they have recklessly wasted the Public Revenue; they confess it by refusing to raise the Tariff to meet the present exigency, and by insisting that they can replenish the exhausted Treasury and support the Government, in credit and efficiency, by simply striking off their former extravagances.

An illustrious predecessor of the President is reported to have declared "that those who live on borrowed money ought to break." I do not concur in that harsh saying; yet I am clearly of opinion that the Government, in common prudence (to say nothing of pride and dignity), ought to reserve its credit for great transactions and unforeseen emergencies. In common times of peace, it ought always to have an established revenue, equal, at least, to its current expenses. And that revenue ought to be so levied as to foster and protect the Industry of the country employed in our most necessary and important manufactures.

Gentlemen, I cannot touch upon all the topics alluded to in your letter and resolution. I ought rather to beg your pardon for the prolixity of this answer. I speak for no party, because the only party I ever belonged to has ceased to exist as an organized and militant body.

And I speak for no man but myself.

I am fully aware that my opinions and views of public policy are of no importance to anybody but me, and there is good reason to fear that some of them are so antiquated and out of fashion as to make it very improbable that they will ever again be put to the test of actual practice.

Most respectfully,

EDWARD BATES.

The Republican publishes the letter to *gratify the curiosity of my numerous friends throughout the country*, but gives no opinion, neither praise nor censure.

The Evening News is rapturous in its applause, and glorifies me without measure or moderation.

The New York City papers eagerly published the letter, with few editorial comments, for the most part with moderate praise—I have seen only the Tribune (Greel[e]y's [14]) The Times (Raymond's [15]) the Express (Brooks' [16]) and the Herald (Bennett's [17]) [.]

I expected a sour reception from the Republican papers—Especially the Tribune and Times—on account of my openly opposing the further agitation of the Negro question. The Tribune,[18] tho' well pleased with the rest of the letter, is clearly not well pleased with that part, but makes a distinction in my favor, between the two kinds of opposition to aggitation [sic]—one (with which he charges Hiram Ketchum [19]) he characterises as subserviency to the ' Slave power ' and a tacit aid to their efforts to propagate and extend slavery. The other (which he supposes may be my position) a desire to stop the slavery aggitation [sic], with a view to more national questions, but with a readiness to resist the efforts of the Southern propagandists in their efforts to spread slavery where we do not find it.

---

[14] *Infra*, Feb. 2, 1860, note 47.

[15] *Infra*, Feb. 4, 1860, note 61.

[16] *Infra*, Sept. 20, 1860, note 12.

[17] James Gordon Bennett: journalist in Boston, New York, and Charleston ; then Washington correspondent ; next editor of the New York *Courier and Enquirer*, 1829–1832, and of the *Pennsylvanian*, 1832–1833 ; and finally editor-owner of the *New York Herald*, 1835–1867. He made the *Herald* one of the most enterprising and spectacular of papers and kept it independent. He had supported Taylor (Whig) in 1848, Pierce (Democrat) in 1852, Frémont (Republican) in 1856, and was to support Douglas against Lincoln in 1860 and Lincoln against McClellan in 1864, Johnson against the Radicals in 1865–1866 and the Radicals against Johnson in 1866–1867. At the outbreak of the Civil War, Bennett wished to let the Southern States go in peace, but when war came he supported it.

[18] For editorial comment see the *New York Tribune*, April 16, 1859.

[19] Chairman of the Whig General Committee of New York City. Bates originally sent his letter to Ketchum in February, but it disappeared and he had to recopy it out of his letter-book and resend it for publication. *Ibid.*, April 16, 1859. Ketchum represented moderate anti-Seward opinion in New York, was a delegate to the National Union Convention in Baltimore, but opposed the formation of a third party. He promised to support Mr. Bates if he were nominated by the Republicans.

The letter I think, is well written and effective. But some of my friends, I am sure, think me imprudent, in coming out so plainly upon the subjects treated of. I am not so timid, perhaps not so prudent as they—Upon the whole, the letter has been most favorably received in St Louis.

April 21. A bad, rainy day all day long. Yesterday afternoon, my young friend, Lieutenant J. E. B. Stuart,[20] came out, with his wife and child and spent the night with us. He starts today for Memphis, on his way to Va., having just come from Fort Reilly,[21] on leave for 6 months.

Mr. Wm. Glasgow Jr. gave me some plants w[hi]ch. he brought from the Hot Springs of Washetaw.

1. Native grape, resembling the Isabella, but thought to be better.
2. Native Muscadine grape.
3. Yeopan—Evergreen shrub producing red berries (supposed the same shrub used for Tea, near Norfolk[)].
4 Rattan—a slender aspiring, green vine.

The plants are very dry, and I fear will not grow[.] . . .[22]

Note—I was called on today by Mr. John Churchman (and his son) with a letter of introduction from A. H. H. Stuart.[23]

April 22d. (*Good friday*). Rainy and cold all day, and the Roads excessively muddy—

Tallies

2d. Pepys' Diary, 234. note. 1. 12. May 1665. [1854 ed., H. Colburn, London] gives an account, of the use of Tallies (or notched sticks) in keeping the accounts of the English Treasury. It seems that the use of Tallies was continued until some 25 or 30 years ago. They were negotiable, and sold in the market, like our Treasury notes—

See Smith's Wealth of Nations, Book 2. Ch : 11.

Apl 24. *Sunday*—Attended the Pine street Church to hear Mr. McPheeters[24] preach[.]

Today the first tulip of the season full blown.

---

[20] James E. B. Stuart of Virginia : graduate of West Point in 1854 ; Indian fighter : lieutenant in the U. S. Army until he resigned when Virginia seceded ; then major-general in the Confederate Army until he died of wounds in 1864.

[21] This should be Fort *Riley* which was near Junction City, Kansas.

[22] A marginal note telling where he set the plants.

[23] Alexander H. H. Stuart of Virginia : Whig congressman, 1841–1843 ; secretary of the Interior, 1850–1853 ; unionist until Virginia seceded ; leader in the reconciliation movement after the War ; debarred member-elect of Congress in 1865.

[24] Samuel B. McPheeters, though personally loyal under his chaplain's oath of allegiance, insisted that the church must not meddle in civil affairs or take sides in the Civil War. He was expelled from the State by the military authorities, then sustained by Lincoln who rescinded the order of expulsion and sent instructions that the military must not interfere with churches, and finally dismissed from his pastorate by the unionist portion of his own congregation.

Apl 27. Dined with F. P. Blair Jr [25]—the first [t]ime I was ever
in his house—invited specially with Judge Jno. C. Richardson [26]
and C Gibson,[27] to meet Mr. Schuyler Colfax [28] M.[ember of]
C.[ongress] of Indiana.

The object of Messrs. Blair and Colfax, no doubt, was to have a
confidential conference with me and a few of my known friends, so
as to approximate the terms upon which the Republican party might
adopt me as its candidate for the Presidency, and I and my friends
might co-act with them, in federal politics, upon honorable relations.

Both those gentlemen are influential leaders of their party, and
both declare that I am their first choice. They both say that Mr.
Seward [29] cannot get the nomination of his party, perhaps not because he is not the acknowledged head of the party and entitled
to the lead, but because the party is not quite strong enough to
triumph alone; and his nomination therefore would ensure defeat.[30]
Mr. Colfax is very anxious to consolidate the whole N.[orth] W.[est]
so as to ensure what he considers the main point for which, as he
understands it, his party contends—i. e—that the U. S. shall not
extend slavery into any country where they do not find it already
established.

< To that I have no objection >

Mr. C.[olfax] is also a very warm friend of Mr. Blair, and is
anxious to consolidate in Missouri, so as to put Mr. B.[lair] on a
good footing with a majority in the State.

And, working for that end, Mr. Blair is eager to form a combination within the State, upon the precise question of slavery or no
slavery in Missouri. This, undoubtedly, would be good policy for
Mr. Blair personally, because it would strengthen the local free soil
party (of which he is the acknowledged local head) with all the
forces that I and my friends could influence. But I doubt whether
it would be good policy for us to be come parties to such an organi-

[25] Francis P. Blair, Jr., of Missouri: an ardent Freesoiler, congressman, 1857–1859 and
1861–1862; major-general in the Civil War; U. S. senator, 1871–1873; supporter of Bates
for the Republican nomination for the Presidency in 1860; advocate of Johnsonian moderation in Reconstruction.

[26] A close personal friend of Bates; judge of the Supreme Court of Missouri; opponent
in 1860 of the sectionalism of both Lincoln and Breckinridge and advocate of Bell and
Everett.

[27] Charles Gibson: a Virginia-born Whig leader of Missouri who had studied law under
Bates; an ardent unionist in 1861; solicitor of the U. S. Court of Claims, 1861–1864; a
loyal Lincoln man until 1864 when he broke with the President, resigned in a public
letter of protest, and supported McClellan; later a Johnson Democrat. At this time he
was Bates's political manager.

[28] Republican member of the House of Representatives from Indiana, 1855–1869; speaker
of the House, 1863–1869; a Radical in Reconstruction politics; vice-president, 1869–1873.
At this time he was apparently working for Bates's nomination for the Presidency.

[29] *Infra*, March 5, 1861, note 26.

[30] Conservatives who feared extremism on slavery would not have voted for Seward, and
he had won the implacable hatred of the large Know-Nothing group, and of Greeley and
the *Tribune*. See *infra*, Aug. 19, 1859.

zation. Such a course supposes affirmative action, i. e. the passage of a law for the prospective abolition of slavery; and it can hardly be necessary to incur the labor and encounter the prejudice incident to that course *now*, when it is plain to be seen that, by the irresistable [*sic*] force of circumstances, without any statute to help on the work, slavery will soon cease to exist in Missouri, for all practical and important purposes. This latter view, I think ought to be constantly inculcated, and kept before the public mind, by the press—It ought to be habitually mixed up (as it properly belongs to the subjects) with all our views and arguments on public economy—[,] Manufactures, mining, Commerce, handicraft-arts, and grain and cattle farming. This line of policy would aid and accelerate the drain of slaves from the State, which is, even now, rapidly going on, to supply the growing demand in the South.

Mr. Colfax, concurring with a good many Republican papers, is much put out by the first paragraph of my N.[ew] Y.[ork] letter,[31] denouncing the agitation of the negro question. He seemed to think that it was a denunciation of the Rep[ublica]n. party, and would turn many against me.

I think otherwise; and that its effects will be good. It is chiefly the friends of Mr. Seward who make the objection, and they of course, would be astute in finding or making any plausible objection, to get a rival out of the way. If my letter had been universally acceptable to the Republicans, that fact alone might have destroyed my prospects in two frontier slave states, Md. and Mo., and so I would have no streng[t]h at all but the Republican party. As it is, all sensible Republicans know that it is the Southern democracy which was and is the first and chief and constant agitators [*sic*] of the question. And even now, such men as Blair and Colfax are fully satisfied of my true position, and the true meaning of the paragraph. And such papers as the Tribune[32] of N. Y. and the Advertiser[33] of Boston, tho' they might wish it otherwise, are content with it as it is. While the Baltimore papers (Clipper[34] and Patriot) warmly accept it. Being *true*, I of course stand by it, as I must stand by all truth—Moreover, in cool policy, I am satisfied that it is best as it is.

April 28. I have just recd. a late number of the "*Constitution*" (the Washington Union, with a new name[35] and a new Editor[36]— the old having sunk into imbecility and odium) in which I find that

[31] See *supra*, 1–9.
[32] *New York Tribune*, April 16, 1859.
[33] *Boston Daily Advertiser*, April 18, 1859.
[34] *Baltimore Clipper*, April 19, 1859.
[35] The *Constitution*, first issued April 13, 1859; it had previously been called the *Union*.
[36] George W. Bowman.

I and my N. York letter are honored with a long Editorial leader,[37] particularly dull and inconclusive.

The Nat:[ional] Intel[ligence]r. of Apl. 23d., by way of offset, gives a letter of Gov: Wise[38] to a friend[39] in Alabama, which it says. is far more sweeping than my letter is, in its denunciations of the Administration.

And truly Mr. Wise's letter is far more general and bitter in its condemnation than any writing that I have seen, since Buchanan's accession—I preserve the paper for future use.

I do not see how to reconcile that letter of Mr. Wise with his recent letter[40] pledging his support to Mr. Letcher,[41] for Govr. of Va. on condition that he supports the Administration[.]

April 29, Saturday—This is the anniversary of my arrival in St Louis, 45 years ago—Apl. 29, 1814. Then, I was a ruddy youth, of 20, now I am a swarthy old man of 65, with a grey beard, and a head beginning to grow bald. In that lapse of time, I have witnessed mighty changes in population, locomotion, commerce and the arts; and the change is still going on, with a growing impetus. And every year adds to the relative importance of the Central position of St Louis. Already, it is the focal point of the great Valley, and, in course of time, will become the seat of Empire in North America. I will soon sink into oblivion, but St Louis—the *village* in which I studied law—will become the seat of wealth and power—the ruling city of the continent.

" *Slavery, Ethnologically Considered* "

The New York Saturday Press of Feb 19. 1859, contains a curious and very interesting essay[42] read by *Thomas Ewbank* (Feb 8. 1859) before the New York Ethnological Society.

This paper is the most suggestive of any thing I have read for a long time—It suggests the causes of and the necessity for diversities of races of men—As savage and untaught Peoples cannot have that sort of powers which comes of *Knowledge*, art, *Science*, they can use little else than their own *animate forces;* whereas, all the great forces of Nature are *inanimate.*

The author surmises that the Earth could not produce food enough to sustain life in the multitude necessary to do the work by their bodily strength—*animate force*—that is now actually done by

---

[37] April 19, 1859.

[38] Henry A. Wise of Virginia: Democratic congressman, 1833–1844; governor, 1856–1860; opponent of secession until it became inevitable; brigadier-general in the Confederate Army.

[39] David Hubbard of Alabama: states' rights Democratic congressman, 1839–1841 and 1849–1851; Confederate congressman, 1861–1863.

[40] Henry A. Wise to a Democratic elector for one of the Senatorial districts of the State, March 21, 1859, *Daily National Intelligencer,* April 15, 1859.

[41] John Letcher of Virginia: Democratic congressman, 1851–1859; governor, 1860–1864; a leader in the Washington Peace Convention of 1861; opponent of secession until it came.

[42] Later published as *Inorganic Forces Ordained to Supersede Human Slavery,* William Everdell & Sons, N. Y., 1860.

machinery—*inanimate force*—the power of dead matter put in motion and kept at work, by mind, by knowledge.

He thinks that steam, and electricity and other motors yet to be found out, and their various applications by inventive art, will change the character of labor, and increase its amount incalculably—The slave, he thinks, will become an *overseer*—that is, instead of doing a little work himself, he will direct steam &c how to do a great deal.

. . .[43]

May 3d. tuesday— . . .

I regret to find that Thomas Hare, coachman, is disagreeable to the rest of the servants, in consequence of which he has given me warning, last sunday night.

Tom is intelligent, active and very expert in the management of horses and carriage; but I fear he is given to drink. He attributes his disagreement with the other servants to the difference of religion—They are all Roman Catholics, and he is an English Churchman.

I have spoken to Tom Farry to try and get me another man[.]

Dined with Mr. Lindell[44] today. As usual, he was very kind and respectful, and after dinner he insisted on taking me down town in his own carriage.

May 6. Paid (at the Mechanic's Bank) my note for $100—date Nov 1. 1854, due at *fifty four months*—endorsed by W. H. Barksdale, *Treasr.*—This is one of the notes given for my subscription of $1000, to the "*City University*." Mr. Charless[45] says it is the *last*—I hope so, but am not certain whether it is the 9th. or 10th. note.

God forgive me for the meanness of begrudging a voluntary subscription. The object is most worthy, and if it had been carried out on the plan and in the spirit understood at the time of subscribing, I should begrudge nothing in my power to give. But it has not been managed to my liking.[46]

May 8. (*Sunday*) It rained hard yesterday afternoon, which again interferes with the planting of seeds—The weather is warm, and for the first time this season, I doft my double-breasted cloth waistcoat and put on a thinner—black satin—

Noon—the air is sultry and masses of clouds lying about, portending rain—and the *Rain Crows* (Cookeoos) are croaking for another shower.

---

[43] An entry in red ink in which Bates secures a town lot for his son, Woodson, as a fee for past legal service.

[44] Peter Lindell: wealthy merchant, real estate operator, and hotel owner; founder of the first packet-boat line between St. Louis and Pittsburgh; incorporator of the Missouri Insurance Company.

[45] *Infra*, June 4, 1859, note 75.

[46] See *infra*, July 23, 1859.

John. C. Boone spent the night here, and returned to town about 10. oclock. He is about to buy a house and lot in Stoddard's addition, and settle there.

Sister Sarah [47] is very ill, and Julia [48] attends her continually, night and day, and is consequently, much worn down. I staid at home, not going to Church.

My letter [49] to the N. Y. Com[mitt]ee. (whig) has attracted great attention, and has been published throughout the Union, (except perhaps the extreme South, whose papers I rarely see.) The letter has attracted various criticisms in the Press: The Democrats, of course, condemn: The Americans, as far as I have seen approve— Many of the Republican papers approve, without reserve—Some of them however, and those influential, consider my denunciation of agitation a grave offence—a disqualifying error. concur[r]ing as they do in the rest.

In one assumption (and that erroneous) all seem to concur. The Press and private persons all assume that the letter is a *Candidate's* letter—a ' platform' and a ['] bid for the Presidency '! They forget that it is an answer to a *Whig* committee, which itself begun [sic] by denouncing the agitation.

[*Marginal Note.*] However men may agree or disagree with me, in the particular views expressed, the general tone of the letter appears, to be approved every where; and I am sure it has substantially increased my reputation for courage and firmness as a man, and perspicacity as a writer.

A great many papers are sent to me now, with comments on the letter—pro and con. And many private men write to me in terms very flattering to my vanity—Among them *Saml. P. Bates* [50] of Meadville Pa.—His beginning is frank and manly and induces a desire to cultivate him. I have answered his letter[.]

. . . [51]

May 18. Went with Julia to Florissant,[52] to vis[i]t Julian [53] and Sally.[54] Dined with them and returned in the evening. I never saw Sally so handsome—a good family reason for it—Julian is well and his professional prospects improving—They both seem very happy.

---

[47] Sarah Bates died on August 12, at the age of 86. See *supra,* " Introduction."

[48] Mrs. Bates. See *loc. cit.*

[49] *Supra,* 1–9.

[50] Lecturer on education ; formerly principal of the academy at Meadville : at this time superintendent of the Crawford County schools in Pennsylvania.

[51] Comments on the weather and on the state of his garden : the progress of his tulips, narcissus, snow drops, flags, pioneys [sic], snowballs, the Harrison or yellow rose, his grape vines, raspberries, blackberries. gooseberries. strawberries, Japanese potatoes.

[52] Florissant, a town of St. Louis County, sixteen miles northwest of the city of St. Louis. Here Dr. Julian Bates lived. Here, too, was the family burying-ground where Bates's mother and sister were interred.

[53] Next to the eldest of Mr. Bates's living sons—a physician in Florissant. See *supra,* " Introduction."

[54] Julian's wife, formerly Sarah Woodson.

Note. Julian got his buggy broke today, by leaving his horse standing, unhitched, while he visited a patient. The carriage, he says, is not badly hurt, but I fear the horse may be spoiled.

May 20. Note—Subscribed for the *National Intelligencer* For *Julian*, and pd. the bill for one year—$6.00 see receipt of Mr. James, the agent.

May 20—My letter to the New York Whig Com[mitt]ee., which has had such a run in the papers, and has been so variously criticised, gives occasion, every now and then, for tickling my vanity. A small instance occur[r]ed today, in the person of one *Mr. Harding* of Massts.,—father in law to Dr. Oliphant—The old gentleman is stone deaf, but seeing me cross the street from my office to the French restaurant, expressed a strong desire to be introduced to me—He wanted to tell his friends when he went home, that he had shakened [*sic*] the hand that *wrote that letter*—

Dr. O[liphant] (who has never spoken to me since the Montesquou trial [55]) followed me into the restaurant, and with much politeness and many apologies, requested me to go to his house (next door) and be introduced to Mr. H.[arding] saying that it would be a great gratification to the old gentleman—I went.
. . .[56]

May 21. Slavery in the District of Columbia.

It is strange to see how suddenly and totally men and parties do change their opinions upon even great constitutional questions, when they become *party questions*[.]

In *Benton's Abridged Debates.* Vol 9. p 415 (12 Feb: 1827) it appears that Mr. *Barney* [57] presented a petition of Citizens of Maryland, for the abolition of Slavery in the District,—and moved that it be printed &c.

Mr. McDuffie [58] opposed—He thought it impertement [*sic*] in citizens of *the States* to meddle in the matter &c: It belonged exclusively to the people of the District &c [.] He considered Slavery a deplorable evil, and when the People of the District petitioned to get rid of it, *he would be as ready as any man to grant their request* &c.

It was but a few years afterwards that leading partizans thought it necessary to change the doctrine, so clearly announced by Mr. McD.[uffie] in both particulars—1st. They now deny that the Ex-

---

[55] Gonsalve and Raymond de Montesquieu were two wealthy French youths tried for murders committed in cold blood in 1849 at Barnum's City Hotel. After two juries disagreed, the Governor pardoned Gonsalve, the gunman, on the ground of insanity, and Raymond because he had not participated in the shooting. The trial caused international excitement.

[56] Planting of Chinese sugar cane, water melons, lima beans, Yankee pumpkins.

[57] John Barney, Federalist congressman from Maryland, 1825–1829.

[58] George McDuffie of South Carolina: anti-Jackson Democratic congressman, 1821–1834; governor, 1834–1836; U. S. senator, 1842–1846.

istence of Slavery in the District ought to depend upon the wishes
of the people there—and 2d. They deny the Power of Congress to
abolish it.—

In the Territories

Formerly, nobody questioned the Power of Congress, but it was
considered a matter of expediency only; and consequently it was
disputed on grounds of policy only— Now, the Southern Democracy is in such a strait, that it is driven to the most revolting absurdities: But that is alway[s] so when men are resolved to maintain a
known wrong against a known right—They insist that the Constitution, *proprio vigore*, carries slavery into the Territories—According to this new light, the constitution (which most of that party
affect to consider only a *League between the States*) is the *local law*
in the Territories. Slavery being carried into the Territories *by the
constitution*, of Course Congress has no power to expel it, and cannot delegate the power to the Territorial Legislature, nor to the
People—and the people themselves have no such power—And so,
there is no power on Earth to abolish slavery in the Territories!!

The *argumentum ad absurdum* used to be thought a sufficient refutation—not so now. Junius [59] was half right in saying that
"When a man is determined to believe, the very absurdity of his
doctrine confirms his faith."

The constitution, I suppose, is the Law of the *States* which made
it and exist in Union by it; and is not law [*sic*] the Law of the Territories, which are subject acquests; And yet, according [to] these
learned Thebans, it carries slavery into the Territories, where it *is
not law*, but does not carry it into Pennsylvania and Massachusetts,
where it *is* law!

Those who hold that belief may well say—" *Credo quia impossible
est.*" [60]

May 24. To day, *Sarah Bates*, by one single deed, set free all her
remaining slaves—being 32 in number. The deed was proven in
Court, by John. S. McCune and Edward Bates, two of the subscribing witnesses—the witness being C. Woodson Bates. [61]

She has long wished to accomplish this end but was never quite
ready to do it till now.

In her late severe sickness, the though[t] of leaving her slaves
to be held as property and to serve strangers after he[r] death,
seemed to give her great distress. She talked of it painfully, sleeping
and waking.

[59] *Infra*, May 25, 1865, note 25.

[60] Bates does not seem to have quoted accurately. St. Augustine in his *Confessions* VI.
5. (7) said " Credo quia absurdum est," and Tertullian in *De Corne Christi* (Chap. V,
part II) said, " Certum est quia impossibile est." But then Bates seldom did quote *exactly.*

[61] Mr. Bates's youngest son. See *supra*, "Introduction."

Having executed the deed, and then fulfilled her long-cherished wish, she seemed relieved of a burden, and greatly cheered and lightened.

The negro[e]s are very good-looking generally, and are worth at least $20.000.

May 25. "A fool with a majority on his side, is the greatest tyrant in the world."—2. Carlisle's [*sic*] Fred[eric]k the Great, p 50[.]

May 27. The N. York Commercial advertiser of May 23d. contains a very complimentary notice of my letter to the Whig Committee,[62] and extracts the part of it against the rage for foreign acquisition—heading it, Bates *versus* Fillibusterism [*sic*]. Such a compliment from such a paper goes for something.

If my letter does no other good, I hope it will embolden some men, both North and South, to speak out boldly against the system of aggression and plunder, whose feelings are right, but have heretofore been too timid to denounce it. The truculent impudence of certain buccaneers in the South seems to have taken the start of public opinion, and silenced the opposition of the timid and the peaceful.

I see by the Nat:[ional] Intelligencer of May 24. that there is established in Baltimore (and the 1st. No. actually issued) a Weekly Periodical called " *The American Cavalier* " which professes to be— "A *Military* Journal, devoted to the extension of American Civilization."

The *Cavalier* declares that it will " place its feet upon [on] the broad platform of the [']*Monroe doctrine,*['] and will maintain that the Government of the U[nited] States is the only *legal* arbiter of the destiny of American nationalities." (!)

Sir Knight (the Editor of the Cavalier) stimulated by the prospect of universal expansion, talks grandiloquently thus—" This nation is the *Empire of the People,* and as such we shall advocate its extension until 1 [*sic*] every foot of land on the *continent* (wonder if he means to leave out the Islands?—Perhaps, as he is a *cavalier,* he'll go only where [he] can *ride*) owns only *our* flag as the National emblem, and that flag the ["] *Stars and stripes* ["]—Aye, we say, add star to star until our Republican constellation is a very *sun of light*[,] throwing its genial rays into into [*sic*] the humblest home of the poor man, in the most distant *part of the earth*[!]—<what! outside the " *Continent!* "> Let not the virgin soil of America be polluted by oppression—[;]<Can he mean to abolish slavery?> Let it not be the continued seat of war and bloodshed; <No more fighting then I hope> let the *great people* <and why not the little ones too>rise up as one

62 *Supra,* 1–9.

man and command peace and love to be enthroned as the presiding genii of this new world." [63]

There is a good deal more of that sort of nonsense—

"And then he pierc'd his bloody-boiling breast, with blameful—bloody blade!"

It is perhaps fortunate that such political charlatans do commonly disclose the dangerous absurdity of their projects, by the stupid folly of their language.

The paper, observe, is to be *military*—All this spread of ' American Civilization ' is to be done by *martial law*. Buchanan wants to take *military* possession of Mexico; and Douglas wants a *seabound* Republic!

The *Louisville Journal* of May 26—sent me by some one—contains a long article, written with ability (I *guess* by Judge Nicholas [64]) with a view to organize a general Opposition Party. He argues that the only way to beat the Democrats effectively is for the Republican party to abandon its separate organization, and unite its elements with the general opposition. He thinks that the *Abolitionists* proper, will not go with the *Republicans*, any how, and that the Republicans, altho' very strong, are not more numerous than the other elements of opposition; and that standing alone, they are, like the Democrats, *sectional*—But, fused with the other elements, and thus taking the character of the general opposition, the party would become essentially national, and would easily put down the sham Democracy.

I read in the papers that a Company is formally organized down South, to increase the *African labor* of the Country—i. e. import slaves—and that *DeBow* [65] is a head man of it.

This is said to be the result of the deliberations [66] of the " Southern Commercial Convention " [67] at its late session in Mississippi—Vicksburg.

---

[63] Mr. Bates has quoted inaccurately. The punctuation and capitalization are changed, and with the exception of " *legal* " and " *Empire of the People* " the italics are Mr. Bates's.

[64] Samuel S. Nicholas : judge of the Kentucky Court of Appeals. 1831–1837 ; author in 1857 of a series of essays on *Constitutional Law*.

[65] James D. B. De Bow : economist ; short-time editor of the *Southern Quarterly Review* published at Charleston, South Carolina ; editor of the *Commercial Review of the South and Southeast* (later *De Bow's Review*) which he founded in New Orleans in 1846 ; superintendent of the U. S. Census under President Pierce ; and a leader in the Southern Commercial Conventions.

[66] May 9–13, 1859. On May 10, L. W. Spratt of South Carolina, Isaac N. Davis of Mississippi, and John Humphreys of Mississippi introduced resolutions urging a reopening of the African slave-trade, and Humphreys, G. V. Moody of Mississippi, and J. D. B. De Bow of Louisiana made speeches supporting them. On May 12, the Convention voted 40–19 for repeal of all laws prohibiting the importation of African negroes. A committee on the " legality and expediency " of the slave-trade was appointed to report to a later convention.

[67] This was one of a series of " commercial conventions " of the 1850's in which Southerners sought to analyze their economic and commercial ills and find remedies that would enable them once more to overtake the North in economic development.

Are these men mad, that they organize in open defiance of the law, avowedly to carry on a felonious traf[f]ic, and for an object, tho' not distinctly avowed yet not concealed,—to dissolve the Union, by cutting off the *slave* states, or at least the *cotton* states?

Again—are these men fools? Do they flatter themselves with the foolish thought that we of the upper Mississippi will ever submit to have the mouth of *our River* held by a *foreign* power, whether friend or foe? Do they not know that that is a *fighting* question, and not fit to be *debated?* The people of the upper Miss[issip]pi. will make their commerce flow to the Gulf as freely as their waters. If friendly suasion fail, then war: If common warfare will not suffice, they will cut the dikes, at every high flood, and drown out the Delta! [68]

[*Marginal Note.*] June 4. I see by the papers, that since the adjournment of the *Southern convention*, there has been a great *anti-slave-trade* meeting held at Vicksburg—called to order by Foote [69] and presided over by Judge Sharkey [70]—which denounced all that the Convention had done about the slave trade.

June 4. Saturday—Men as old as I am, it is said, are apt to be croakers and to complain of the degeneracy and corruption of the times. Certainly I am deeply disgusted and sick at heart to witness the impudence with which vice and profligacy bare their brazen faces to public [view], glorying in their shame. Examples—

1. Carstang v Shaw

The case of Effie. C. Carstang v Henry Shaw,[71] for a breach of promise to marry, occupied the Court of Common Pleas for a week, ending last thursday afternoon—For the Pl[ain]t[i]ff: Wm. Holmes (ex Presbyterian Minister) Wright [72] & Shrive—For the

---

[68] The Northwest's need of a free outlet through the lower Mississippi to the sea had always played an important rôle in national history. The South thought that this factor would force the Northwest to follow it in secession. The editor, however, decided (in a detailed study made of Southern Illinois in 1860–1861) that railroad building of the 1850's had made at least that portion of the Northwest which lies east of the Mississippi equally dependent by 1861 upon rail connections with the Northwest, and that this importance of both outlets actually forced a strongly pro-Southern Southern Illinois to defend the Union, since preservation of the Union was the only way to maintain *both* the river and the rail outlets. Mr. Bates's comment throws interesting light upon this same influence of the Mississippi upon Missouri unionist sentiment.

[69] Henry S. Foote of Mississippi: Unionist U. S. senator, 1847–1852; governor of Mississippi, 1852–1854; opponent of states' rights and secession. He later moved to Memphis, Tennessee. As a member of the lower house of the Confederate Congress, he criticized Davis severely. When Lincoln's peace proposals were rejected, he resigned and was imprisoned by the Confederacy, but finally was allowed to remove to Union territory.

[70] William L. Sharkey of Mississippi: elective chief justice of the Court of Errors and Appeals, 1832–1850; president of the Southern Convention at Nashville in 1850; provisional governor of Mississippi under the Johnsonian restoration of 1865.

[71] A wealthy English-born St. Louis merchant of cutlery who created the Missouri Botanical Garden.

[72] Uriel Wright: spell-binding St. Louis criminal lawyer; state legislator; an ardent unionist until the capture of Camp Jackson (see *infra*, Nov. 25, 1865, note 74) aroused his indignation and led him to enlist in the Confederate Army.

Def[endan]t: Shepley[73] & Bates—It was a preposterous case I have no doubt a conspiracy to extort money from Mr. Shaw, who is very rich. Upon the evidence, it is my conscientious belief, that the verdict ought to have been for the defendant. Yet we were all astonished that a verdict was rendered, after but a few minutes['] deliberation, for the Plaintiff, with an assessment of damages, *$100,000*!!!

This atrocious verdict has excited, as it ought, the indignant denunciation of the public. We have moved for a new trial, and I do not doubt that Judge Reber[74] will take pleasure in cleansing his record from so foul a blot upon the administration of justice.

I preserve the names of the jurors who were so stupid or so wicked, or both, as to give that verdict. Here they are—<Valentine Crancer, George. W. Shadwick, Ferd: Kohler, George. H. Smith, Henry Schneider, J. L. Casperson, Charles Chenot, Leon Deno, Samuel Finch, Mauritz Sternbach, J. P. Young, Wm. N. McQueen.>

I knew not one of the jury personally—the last one, McQueen is a young Scotchman, and a merchant, and I had hoped better things of him[.]

This abominable verdict shocked the moral sense of the community, and made most men fear for the safety of property and character. But next morning it was eclipsed by a crime, far more horrible.

2. On friday morning, June 3d. *Joseph Charless*,[75] one of our most useful and best citizens, was brutally shot down in the street, as he was going to his place of business, by one *Joseph Thornton*, without provocation, without any apparent cause,[76] and without a moment's time for consideration. He was shot twice and each wound was mortal. I saw him some, 20 or 30 minutes after he was shot, lying on the floor in the store of Mr. Thompson (just at whose door, in *Market* Street, between 3d. and 4th. the crime was done). A few hours after he was removed to his own house, where he lingered in agony, until 7 or 8 oclock this morning, when he was relieved from his sufferings, and passed, I trust, to a better life.

It is a sad thing to me and to the whole city. I knew Mr. Charless, a boy in his father's house, forty five years ago, and have marked his course through the world ever since—A man of energy and enterprise, eminently successful in business. Of high character and unspotted reputation. For many years a professor of Christianity and now an elder in the Presbyterian church—The Pine Street

---

[73] John R. Shepley, law partner of Bates.

[74] Samuel Reber, judge of the Court of Common Pleas.

[75] Importer, manufacturer, jobber of drugs, president of the Mechanics' Bank, director of the Pacific Railroad Company, alderman, director of public schools, a founder of Washington University.

[76] Mr. Charless had once been compelled to testify against him in court.

Church, in charge of Revd. Mr. McPheeters. He leaves a wife, and one child, a daughter married to a gentleman of Louisiana.

As to the murderer, Thornton, he was seised immediately and put to jail. It was feared yesterday, so general and so high was the excitement, that he would be seised by the mob and torn to pieces; at night the Military was called out, but the night passed in tranquil[l]ity—Mr. C.[harless] still lived and the certainty of his speedy death was not yet known. Today there is a gloomy tranquil[l]ity *on the surface*, but judging from several indications, there is a deep settled feeling of revenge diffused among the people and a general distrust of the penal justice of the law—and, from all the signs, I think it more than probable that the poor wretch will meet his doom to night.

For him I have no pity, but I dread the consequences of such unlawful violence. Such lawless acts are dangerous precedents, and the wound[s] they inflict upon society are incurable. The nearest friends of the family, Mr. Drake [77] et al: I believe, use all their influence to calm the people, and prevent mob violence.

[*Marginal*] *Note.* . . . [Rain—then cool weather] Yesterday I wore my over coat—*Raglan*—all day, in the court house and walking the streets. And now, Sunday morning, we need and have a good fire in the furnace.

Carlisle [*sic*] tells us (Vol 2. p. 254.)[78] that prince Frederick in his restrained position and *penal* civil occupation at Cüstrin,[79] became—"a man politely impregnable to the intrusion of human curiosity; able to look cheerily into the very eyes of men and talk in a social way, face to face, and yet continue intrinsically invisible to them—"

Somebody has written about the ring of *Gyges*,[80] which, being turned in a particular direction, made the wearer invisible. But this power of social and moral *invisibility* in Prince Frederick, is far more efficient in controlling the conduct of men and the actual business of Society. Still, great as the power it gives, a most unhappy faculty, which cuts off its possessor from all personal sympathies, and holds his heart in cold isolation. An admirable quality no doubt, in a *born* ruler of men, who is high above the common sympathies of life, and too great to be comfortable. The Prince who like Frederick, has the faculty forced upon him in the hard

[77] Probably C. D. Drake; see *infra*, Feb. 12. 1863, note 13.

[78] *History of Frederick II of Prussia.*

[79] Frederick II was imprisoned at Cüstrin in close confinement and later forced to work in the auditor's office there, as part of his father's effort to break his will and turn him from literature and music to military pursuits.

[80] A king of Lydia in the Seventh Century, B. C., who according to classical tradition (Herodotus tells the story) was enabled to murder his predecessor and secure his throne and his queen through the powers of invisibility given him by this magic ring.

school of oppression and suspicion, is sure to be a tyrant, when he comes to power; and the private man who habitually acts out the policy of self-concealment, is equally sure to become a cold and selfish egot—

Shakespeare or Shakspere.

Col: Fuller, ex Editor of the New York Mirror, writing from London, gives account of his visit to the British Museum—In the "Autograph Room" where are collected the hand writings of thousands of notorious [sic] men—Kings and Queens, Statesmen, Warriors, Poets, orators, Artists—

There, among the rest, he saw a letter from the Great Dramatist, the name not spelt as we are wont to spell it, but written with his o[w]n hand—*Shakspere*—

June 8. International Law—*Naturalized Citizens*—Their rights as such, against the claims of their Native Country—

The Mo. Democrat of June 10 (and various papers a few days older [81]) contains a short letter [82] from Mr. Cass,[83] Secretary of State, in answer to one Le *Clerc* of Memphis Tenn:, a Frenchman born but naturalized here. Secretary Cass tells Mr. Le Clerc, in plain brief terms, that his *American Citizenship*, by *Naturalization*, will not exempt him from the claim of the French government for military service, if he should expose himself to the power of that Government, by visiting France.

This seems very strange to me. The right of expatriation is denied by many of the Governments of Europe; but our Government has always affirmed it. Our Constitution and statutes affirm the right and regulate the manner of using it. Under these laws, Mr. Le Clerc is or is not a citizen of the U. S—Here at home, *he is a citizen*, as perfectly and absolutely as any native born. If he choose to visit France, his native country, with a pas[s]port in his pocket, vouching for him as an American Citizen, is he less entitled to the protection of this country than a native born American citizen with a like pas[s]port in his pocket? Or does Mr. Cass mean to affirm that *any American Citizen*, found in France, is liable to be forced into the army, to fight the battles of France?

I do not know whether, in the practice of the State Dep[art]m[en]t., there is any distinction made in granting pas[s]ports, be-

---

[81] E. g., the *National Intelligencer* of July 21, 1859.

[82] It is copied into the diary. The original is in the archives of the State Department.

[83] Lewis Cass, of Michigan: governor, 1813–1831; secretary of War, 1831–1836; minister to France, 1836–1842; Democratic U. S. senator, 1845–1848, 1849–1857; secretary of State, 1857–1860. He was an imperialist, a strong nationalist, and a leading advocate of "squatter sovereignty" in the Territories. In December, 1860, he resigned from the Cabinet in protest against Buchanan's weak policy toward secession.

tween *native* and *naturalized* citizens—or whether the fact is mentioned at all.[84]

[*June 15*]

["Rights of Naturalized Citizens Abroad.

"Secretary Cass renders the following decision, in answer to a communication of a naturalized citizen who is desirous of visiting his native land:

"DEPARTMENT OF STATE,
"WASHINGTON, *May 17, 1859.*

"To Mr. Felix LeClerc, Memphis, Tenn.:

"SIR: Your letter of the 13th instant has been received. In reply, I have to state that it is understood that the French Government claims military service from all natives of France who may be found within its jurisdiction. *Your naturalization in this country will not exempt you from that claim if you should voluntarily repair thither.*

"I am, sir, your ob't ser't,

"LEWIS CASS."]

June 15. I read in the Nat[ional] Intel[ligence]r.[85] recd. to day, that this letter of Mr. Cass has called forth much comment, in so much that the Adm[inistratio]n. deems an explanation necessary, and so, it is announced that a full statement of the views of the Govt. will soon be made[.]

(See Forward, 3 pages for 2d. letter)[86]

(See Forward, 6 pages)[87]

June 15. Wednesday— . . .

June 15. Horse Railroad—To day they began to lay down the rails in Olive Street, along the square next East of Lucas Market. They expect to complete it, from 4th. St. to 17th. St: by the 4th. July.

June 15. This day I took up my note to *Peter Lindell*[88] for $1000 and interest at 6 pr. ct: for a little over 2 yrs. He refused to charge more than 6 pr. ct: and seemed quite willing for me to keep it as long as I pleased.

He holds another note of mine for $500.[89]

Fleming[90] and his wife and child came out, and are with us to-night.

Carlisle's [*sic*] Frederick the Great—vol 2. p 308[.]

---

[84] The same passport exactly was issued to both native-born and naturalized citizens. This paragraph is added in the margin.

[85] June 14, 1859.

[86] The parenthetical note was added later in red pencil. It refers to the entry of June 20.

[87] In black ink again. It refers to the entry of July 19.

[88] *Supra*, May 3, 1859, note 44.

[89] After Mr. Lindell's death his heirs embarrassed Mr. Bates by calling this note. See *infra*, Oct. 18, 1865.

[90] The third of Mr. Bates's living sons—later a Confederate officer. See *supra*, "Introduction."

Election of the Kings of Poland—Worth reading, for comparison with some of our own elections.[91]

June 16. Wrote a long letter to S. Colfax[92] of Inda. shewing plainly my views of the slavery question and the Dred Scott decision—Sent him also copious extracts of my letter to Gov Means[93] (of 1854) and a copy of my letter to Mr. Kennett,[94] of 1856. These are not *for the press*, but are not *secret* and may be shewn to his friends, at his discretion.

June 20. Monday Morning—Barton[95] has been with us two days, it being too wet to plough at home. . . .

Senator Green

The Weekly Mo. Rep:[ublican] of June 17 contains a set speech of Hon: James. S. Green,[96] on Politics, gotten up, no doubt, with a special eye to his future—another election—He cannot fully *defend* Buchanan's administration, yet supports it—He is against Douglas'[97] *popular Sovereignty*, yet supports *him*[98]—On one point of Territorial government however, he is clear, i. e—Congress ought to *intervene* to put down Polygamy and other crimes in Utah.

[*A clipping from the* National Intelligencer *of June 15, 1859, charging that the expedition sent to Paraguay under Captain Shubrick[99] was insufficiently provided with ammunition.*]

[*A long editorial from the* Missouri Daily Democrat *of June 29, 1859, denouncing Secretary Cass and President Buchanan for surrendering a right maintained by President Fillmore and Secretary Everett in the case of Mr. Francis Allibert,[1] the country of whose birth claimed his military service. The editorial is headed "Degra-*

---

[91] This Carlyle entry is in red pencil.

[92] *Supra*, April 27, 1859, note 28.

[93] John H. Means of South Carolina: governor, 1850–1852; a leading advocate of secession in 1850 and 1861; a colonel in the Confederate Army, killed in 1862.

[94] Luther M. Kennett: St. Louis merchant; vice-president of the Pacific Railroad Company; president of the Iron Mountain Railroad Company; mayor, 1850–1853; Know-Nothing congressman, 1855–1857, elected in opposition to Thomas H. Benton.

[95] Mr. Bates's eldest son. See *supra*, "Introduction."

[96] An anti-Douglas Democrat from Missouri: successor of Douglas as chairman of the Senate Committee on Territories; leader of the revolt against Benton in 1849; congressman, 1847–1851; U. S. senator, 1857–1861. His Confederate sympathies led to his arrest by Federal troops at the outbreak of the Civil War and to his expulsion from the Senate.

[97] Stephen A. Douglas of Illinois: Democratic congressman, 1843–1847; U. S. senator. 1847–1861; chairman of the Committee on Territories; nominee of the Northern Democrats for the Presidency in 1860.

[98] Douglas and Buchanan had recently split the Party in their quarrel over "popular sovereignty." Green was a clever politician indeed if he could support both at once.

[99] William B. Shubrick had entered the Navy in 1806, and had served in the War of 1812 and the Mexican War. For the naval expedition against Paraguay which he commanded see *supra*, April 20, 1859, note 13.

[1] Francis Allibert was a native of France who left in 1839 just as he was drawn as a conscript. He became a naturalized American in New Orleans in 1845. On his return to France in 1852, he was arrested, but upon protest of the United States was ultimately released.

ation and Disfranchisement of Naturalized Citizens by the National Democracy . . ."]

[*A reprint from the* New York Express *referring to this case.*]

Naturalized citizens—Sec.y. Cass—See *back* 3 pages—Forward 6 pages.[2]

[*A column from the Washington* Constitution *on " The Rights and Liabilities of Naturalized Citizens " in justification of Secretary Cass's position.*]

[*A newspaper copy of Senator Douglas's letter to Colonel John L. Peyton written August 2, 1859, about the LeClerc matter and the slave trade.*]

On this subject, of the effect of naturalization, see my two letters to Mr. Welling[3] of the Nat:[ional] Intel[ligence]r.—See current Letter Book.

June 23. . . .

Today attended some of the closing exercises of the students of Washington University.

Barton will leave us tomorrow morning. He has been down some days transacting business i. a. he has bought a carriage and pair of horses and a negro woman.

Fleming and wife and child are here tonight—Also Dick[4] and Dick Woodson[5]—

No news from Matilda[6] lately. She is on a visit to Louisiana and Han[n]ibal, having gone up with her cousin Julia Coalter.[7]

Note. Gave Coalter[8] a watch today—the first he has ever owned. Bo[ugh]t. of Crane & Jones, for $35.

June 24. (*Friday*) . . . [Cold, rainy weather.] Barton I suppose will not go today—nor Coalter, who rides his (B[arton]'s) saddle horse, while B.[arton] drives his new horses.

Right of Search.[9]

Carlisle's [*sic*] Frederick the Great, Vol 2. 524—Citing the Gentlemen's Magazine for 1739. p 103—A notable instance in which popular influence is brought to bear upon the English Ministry and Parliament. The object was to force England into war with Spain—for maritime ' outrages ' in the American seas. The

---

[2] The references are to June 15 and July 19.

[3] James C. Welling: literary editor of the *National Intelligencer* in Washington, 1850–1865; advocate of Bell and Everett in the election of 1860; loyal supporter of Lincoln during the War; assistant clerk of the Court of Claims under Bates. 1863–1865; later, president of St. John's College and then of Columbia University.

[4] Mr. Bates's fourth son. See *supra*, " Introduction."

[5] Son of a cousin of Mr. Bates.

[6] Mr. Bates's younger daughter. See *loc. cit.*

[7] A niece of Mrs. Bates who later married Mr. Davis of Pike County.

[8] John Coalter Bates, fifth of Mr. Bates's living sons, who served in the Army with distinction. 1861–1906. See *loc. cit.*

[9] In red pencil.

Spaniards claimed the *right of search* and, in some instances enforced it with cruel insolence—as in the case of the English Capt. Jenkins, who was boarded by a Spanish *garda costa* off the coast of Florida, his vessel rum[m]aged and plundered, and himself grossly abused— whipped, half-hanged, and one ear cut off—. This led to the Spanish war and the overthrow of Walpole's long administration. The ministry was against the war mitigated the outrages as far as possible, and insisted on peace. But public opinion prevailed against the power of the crown, removed the minister and made the war.

[A clipping from a Missouri newspaper giving "By telegraph from Washington" Senator Douglas's letter of June 22 stating the conditions upon which he would be willing to have his name presented to the Democratic National Convention as a candidate for President. They were: Adherence to the principles of the Compromise Measures of 1850, the Kansas-Nebraska Act of 1854, and the Cincinnati Platform of 1856, " as expounded by Mr. Buchanan in his letter accepting the nomination." He will not accept the nomination, if the platform thrusts into the party creed new issues such as a revival of the African Slave Trade or the doctrine that the Constitution of the United States either establishes or prohibits slavery in the Territories of the United States.]

As long ago as Nov:, 58, in private letters to Mr. Welling [10] of the Nat:[ional] Intel[ligence]r. and Mr. Ridgway of the Richmond Whig (besides in several newspaper articles previously) I assumed that Mr. D.[ouglas] was in position to dictate to his party; as the southern democrats needed him quite as much as he needed them. This letter is the *dictation*, and his party must obey him or dissolve itself.

Mr. D.[ouglas] however is no statesman. He is only a very cunning politician. He can never succeed before the whole people, without presenting some absorbing question to make them forget his antecedents [*sic*]. In order to keep in with present rulers and present popular whims, he has lent his name to extreme notions and fantastic propositions[.]

1. He is the author of the " Wilmot proviso " in the joint resolution, for the admission of Texas. 1845[.] Also in the Oregon territorial bill.

2. He introduced a bill to *create* the State of California and thrust it into the Union.

3. To pander to Prest: Pierce'[s] silly scruples, he proposed to improve harbors by local tonnage duties[.]

4. He holds that according to the Dred Scot[t] case, the Constitution carries slavery into the Territories. And yet he holds that

---

[10] *Supra*, June 20, 1859, note 3.

slavery being there by force of the constitution, still, *Congress*, must not protect it there. But, notwithstanding its constitutional exist-ance [*sic*] there, still, he holds that the *Territorial Legislature* can exclude it.

5. On Prest: Buchanan's demand of a grant of the war power—the right to use the army and navy to redress the wrongs of our people in Mexico and on the Isthmus—Mr. D.[ouglas] said in debate, that the Prest: ought not only to have the particular power now demanded from Congress, but every where and always.

Note. This last is referred to in the able speech of Senator Dixon [11] of Cont. on the 30.000.000 bill [12]—see Nat[ional] Intel:[ligencer] June 30. 1859.

6. Mr. D.[ouglas] being for a long time, chairman of the Com-[mitt]ee. on Territories and as such having the drawing of the Organic acts, habitually introduced clauses importing that the Con-stitution was *the law* of the Territories—and that the Territories themselves *are a part of the* U. S. (see specially the Nebraska act §'s 6 and 14.)

Moreover, (see same §6) power is granted to the legislature over " all rightful subjects of legislation consistent with the Constitution of the U. S. and the provisions of *this act*." *Other acts*, it seems, may be overridden at pleasure.

The § 14. declares that *the Constitution* and laws of the U. S. not locally inapplicable shall have the *same force in the Territory of N.[ebraska] as elsewhere* WITHIN THE U. S. Except, &c (the Mo. Compromise). But the proviso (Badger's [13]) declares that nothing herein contained shall be construed to revive or *put in force* any law or regulation [legislation] which may have existed prior to 20[6] Mar:[ch] 1820 either protecting[,] establishing, prohibiting or abolishing slavery.

Note.[14] In Harper's Monthly Magazine for *Sept. 1859*, Mr. Douglas comes out in an elaborate article upon Slavery in the Ter-ritories [15] which being reduced to its elements, is nothing more nor less than Mr. Cass' old notion of *Squatter Sovereignty. Note*

---

[11] James Dixon of Hartford, Connecticut : Whig congressman, 1845–1849 ; Republican U. S. senator, 1857–1869 ; strong supporter of Lincoln in the War and of Johnson in Reconstruction. This speech against the acquisition of Cuba on the ground that it was a scheme to further slave interests was one of his best efforts.

[12] *Supra,* April 20, 1859, note 4.

[13] George E. Badger of North Carolina : secretary of the Navy, 1841 ; Whig U. S. sen-ator, 1846–1855 ; opponent of the War with Mexico, of the Wilmot Proviso, of " squatter sovereignty," and of secession ; a pro-slavery nationalist who supported the Compromise of 1850 and the Kansas-Nebraska Act.

[14] Added later.

[15] Stephen A. Douglas, " The Dividing Line between Federal and Local Authority. Popular Sovereignty in the Territories," *Harper's New Monthly Magazine,* XIX (Sep-tember, 1859), 519–537.

again [16]—The Nat[iona]l. Intelligencer [17] has come out in a series of articles (editorial) not *professing* to answer Mr. D.[ouglas] but answering him effectually, both by argument and by historical references.

[*A reprint from the* London Photographic News *of a paragraph announcing the " Extraordinary Discovery" that sounds can be photographed.*]

When this is brought to pass, we shall realise the thought of the Poet—

> " Where Truth in person doth appear,
> Like words congeal'd in northern air[.] "

and this other thought—

> " He out of words could extract matter,
> And keep it in a glass, like water."

July 2d. Saturday—A very hot day. At night the greatest rain storm of the season—Note—our house is badly infested *with Fleas*[.]

. . .

July 4. A very bright day—cool and breesy. Dr. J. W. Wilson and family her[e], and some young friends[.]

July 5. . . .

For some days past, my sister [18] has been in a very precarious condition—not sick with any painful disease, but being frequently taken with a difficulty of breathing, as if the lungs were too weak to clear the throat. I think it is but the weakness of old age, the natural decay of the organs. I should not wonder at her going off any hour.

As to me, I feel, tho' in perfect bodily health, an indolence and indecision not common with me. The cause, I fear, is the mixing up of my name in Politics. I am suffering a serious injury, professionally and perhaps, socially, by the many suggestions, in various parts of the country, to take me up as the Opposition candidate for the Presidency. The idea is presented in so many ways and sometimes in a shape so plausible, as to force itself upon my attention and withdraw my thoughts from other topics more practical and more necessary to my interests. A large section of the Republican party, who think that Mr. Seward's nomination would ensure defeat, are anxious to take me up, thinking that I could carry the Whigs and Americans generally, and thus ensure the Northern States and have a strong party in the border slave states, consisting of Whigs and

---

[16] Added still later.
[17] Sept. 10, 13, 15, 17, and 20, 1859.
[18] Sarah Bates. *Supra*, May 8, 1859, note 47.

Americans. I must try to resist the temptation, and not allow my thoughts to be drawn off from the common channels of business and domestic cares. Ambition is a passion, at once strong and insidious, and is very apt to cheet [sic] a man out of his happiness and his true respectability of character.

July 9. Saturday—Sat (the 2d. time) to Mr. Cogswell [19] the painter, for a portrait. Mr. C.[ogswell] seems to be an excellent artist: His picture of Joseph Charless [20] is to the life.

Mr. Woodson's [21] daughters, Jennie and Nelly are here also Sally, Julian's wife—

This year, I have attended less than usual to the cultivation of the lot— The grapes have been a good deal neglected, not trained and pruned rightly. A great deal of the fruit has been destroyed by the rot, still, there is enough remaining for an ample family supply. Our supply of berries—*goose—rasp* and straw was scanty—Blackberries promising, not yet ripe.

I have a curiosity, in the shape of a *Japan* potato. A small piece was planted in April 1858, and grew feebly that year: Left in the ground last winter, It is now growing boldly, the vines (spiral like the hop,[)] runs [sic] on tall poles, and now I think, if stretched out straight, would be 20 feet long. It has a multitude of blooms, or rather buds, not expanded, on the upper part of the vine, and, on the lower part, at the foot stalk of the leaves, little round tubors [sic] or potato[e]s, now about the size of duck slot [sic]. . . .

I think the vine is as handsome as the Madeira vine, but not so odorous. The potato[e]s in the ground I cannot judge of till next fall.

July 14. . . .

Full moon last night—Good hope of rain for two days past—The Rain-Crows (or Cookoos) are croaking loudly this morning.

Jennie and Nelly Woodson still here—Kate Wilson came home with them last night[.]

We have workmen making sundry repairs about the house and outhouse—My contract is with George Full (a jobber) apparently a very respectable Englishman—a friend of Robt. Baker.

Note. Pd. Mr. Full, yesterday, $100, on a/c[.]

July 15. To day I paid Dr. [   ] Billingslea $5. for his medical attendance upon Lear (my mother's freed woman). He presented a

[19] William Cogswell of New York lived and painted, at various times, in New York City, Philadelphia, Chicago, St. Louis, and California. He did a Lincoln portrait and also the "President Grant and Family" of the National Gallery in Washington, and the portraits of Grant and of Chase in the Capitol.

[20] *Supra*, June 4, 1859, note 75.

[21] A cousin of Mr. Bates whose mother was a Woodson. The Woodsons lived on Dardenne Prairie (*infra*, July 30, 1859, note 61).

bill stating Lear as my servant. I refused to pay the bill as a debt due by me, or to make myself, in any way liable for such claims, as there are now near 40 free negro[e]s emancipated by my mother and sister, but handed him $5. in acknowledgment of his kindness to Lear.

The National Intelligencer of July 12, contains various articles worth memory[.]

1. Botts'[22] letter about the liability of naturalized citizens to compulsory military service—in condemnation of Sec.[retar]y. Cass' doctrine[.]

2 The " Mexican Question "[23] by *Geo*[*rge*] *L. Stevens*[.]

3. "*Mobilization* "[24]—as applied to the Prussian Army. Explanation of the term—taken from a French Military Journal[.] <The term I think is also used in France, and, in its generic sense, means only—the common meaning of the word—the putting of troops in condition to *move* or march—E. B.> " In Prussia, says the *Journal*, the obligation of military service is incumbent on all." . . .

" The military system of Prussia rests upon an organization which divides the forces of that monarchy into two distinct armies: the one the army of the line, or regular troops: the other the army of the reserve, or the militia, who are called the *landwehr*, and which consists of the same men who, having passed through the army of the line, are subject to *landwehr* duty, from their 26th. [25th.] to their 32d. year[.]

Besides the *landwehr*, which is divided into [a] first and [a] second levy, there is also the *Landsturm* or general levy, which comprises men between the ages of 40 and 50 years."

4th. A curious *snake story*, which seems well: avouched—A man was bitten by a rattlesnake, spots appeared on him like the spots on the snake, and when he died (which was in a few hours) there was found on his person, an exact likeness of the snake—true as a degeurrotipe [daguerreotype]—extending from the wound, on the hand, up to the shoulder, and down the body, to the groin.[25]

[*Marginal*] *Note*. Nov 20. 1859. A case fully as remerkable [*sic*][.]

A child of Dr. Nott of S. Carolina was killed by lightning last summer. A tree in the yard was struck at the same time, and upon

---

[22] John M. Botts of Virginia: Whig congressman, 1839–1843, 1847–1849; defeated Know-Nothing candidate for Congress in 1854; opponent of the " gag law " of 1836, of the annexation of Texas and the Mexican War, and of secession. On Virginia's withdrawal from the Union, he withdrew from public life, was imprisoned by the Confederacy but finally paroled, and later became a leading Conservative supporter of Johnsonian restoration policies.

[23] This appeared in the issue of July 11, not in that of July 12.

[24] This, too, appeared in the issue of July 11. And Mr. Bates has not quoted from it accurately.

[25] This, too, appeared in the issue of July 11, rather than that of July 12.

the body of the child was found a miniature degurretipe [daguerre-otype] picture of the tree, beautifully exact.

July 16. Paid George Full $217.20 for divers repairs about the House and outhouse—

July 17. Sunday—Went to church and heard Mr. *Davis* preach quite a fluent and flow[e]ry discourse, on the parable of *Dives* and *Lazarus*[.]

Mr. Davis is a young man (of poor, respectable Welsh parents here in St Louis) Educated for the ministry, chiefly by contributions of the churches here. At the instance of our Pastor, Mr. Anderson,[26] just before his recent departure *for Europe*, the session of our church (in my absence) invited Mr. Davis to take Mr. A.[nderson]'s place and occupy our pulpit during his absence. Last Sabbath Mr. *Cox*[27] preached and administered the Lord's supper, while Mr. Davis only gave out a hymn.

Now, it is ascertained that Mr. Davis is not *licenced to preach* the *Gospel*, and therefore, notwithstanding the invitation, has no more authority in the pulpit than any other *layman*.

I have spoken to Mr. Bishop[29] about it, who seems to concur with me in the opinion that the proceeding is irregular and against the discipline of the church—He says that at the time the Session passed the invitation, they thought that Mr. D.[avis] was a licentiate. But I do not know that Mr. Bishop concurs with me in believing that the precedent thus set is dangerous. It is dangerous in many ways, and among others, in lowering the official standard of our ministers. Whoever begins by disregarding or dispensing with the known law, for convenience' sake or in respect of persons, will be easily tempted, for the same reasons, to make new law, equally without authority. I fear the consequences.

[*Marginal Note.*] Saturday, July 23d. I mentioned the subject to Revd. Mr. Brook[e]s,[30] of 2d. church, who admits that the pro-ceeding is irregular and without law—but seemed to think that, *under the circumstances, and Mr. D.[avis] being a very clever young man*, no harm would come of it &c[.]

I answered that it was dangerous to depart from the known laws of the church— When we begin to depart, there is no rule for stop-

[26] Samuel A. P. Anderson, Virginia-bred Presbyterian clergyman, pastor since 1851 of the Central Presbyterian Church.
[27] Probably Samuel H. Cox, Presbyterian clergyman; at this time, president of Ingham University for women, at Le Roy, N. Y.
[28] See *infra*, July 25, 1859.
[29] Daniel H. Bishop. See *loc. cit.*
[30] James H. Brookes, eloquent " premillenialist " minister of the Second Presbyterian Church, 1858–1865 (?), and of the Compton Avenue Church, 1865–1897, editor of the St. Louis (Presbyterian) *Truth*, and author of several religious books.

ping the departure. *You* dispense with one law to day; *I* with another tomorrow. And both of us, having assumed the *dispensing* power, will soon assume the power to make new law, to suit our convenience.

July 18. Monday—Attended the funeral of James. H. Bacon (who died suddenly saturday night) at the Union Presbyterian church. My wife, and daughter Matilda attended the body to Bellefontaine Cemetery, but I did not, having business at the Office.

.　.　.

Several persons lately have died of sun stroke[.]

July 19. (tuesday) Attended the funeral of Mrs. Asa Wilgus from Christ's Church to Bellefontaine Cemetery.

Very hot and dusty, but a brisk breese.

See back 6. pages.—This evening I recd. the National Intelligencer of the 16th. July, which contains a long extract from a recent letter of Mr. Cass,[31] Sec.y. of State, to our Minister at Berlin,[32] about the liability of naturalized citizens to compulsory service in the army of their native country, if they go back *voluntarily.*

In this letter Mr. Cass abandons the ground taken in his letters to LeCle[r]c[33] (a frenchman at Memphis) and Hoffer[34] (a German at Cinc[inna]ti.). He now holds the equality in this respect, of native and naturalised Citizens; but does it in a confused and clumsy way, as if the change in his opinion had been wrought rather by fear of the consequences, than conviction of the right.

I was grieved to see the Nat:[ional] Intel:[ligencer] support Mr. Cass' first view, and now in its comments[35] on his last letter (which is open to the sharpest criticism) refusing to turn with Mr. C[ass].

I have prepared a long letter (Private) to Mr. Jas. C. Welling,[36] assistant editor of the Nat:[ional] Intel[ligence]r., giving my views on the subject and placing the question, I think, on impregnable grounds.

Note[37]—Mr. Welling answered me in a very friendly letter *of 5 sheets*—making a very good argument, I think *against our naturalization laws,* but (these laws being in force) no argument at all against our duty to protect the citizanes [*sic*] we have made.

---

[31] *Supra*, June 8, 1859, note 83.

[32] These instructions to the American Minister to Prussia Joseph A. Wright, July 8, 1859, may be found in the archives of the State Department.

[33] See *supra*, June 8, 1859.

[34] Secretary of State Cass to Mr. Hoffer of Cincinnati, June 14, 1859, in the archives of the State Department.

[35] July 16, 1859.

[36] *Supra*, June 20, 1859, note 3.

[37] Inserted later.

I have replied in the most friendly spirit, but, I think, clinching the argument on my side[.]

["KENTUCKY TO BE STRUCK FROM THE ROLL OF SOUTHERN STATES.— The Charleston *Mercury* says that 'if the recent meetings for the reception of Senator CRITTENDEN in Kentucky, are a reflex of the feelings and opinions of the people of that State, she may as well be stricken from the roll of Southern States.'

"Very well; let Kentucky be stricken from the roll of the Southern States, and let the rest of the slaveholding States that will not learn political lessons from the South Carolina Gamaliels, be stricken out too. But how much of the South will then be left?"]

July 23 (saturday). Revd. Mr. Nicholson (Methodist) now of Hamilton. O.[hio] late of Baltimore, came to my office, introduced by Mr. Keith, to talk about the Am[erica]n. Colonization Society, of which he is Gen[era]l. Agent.

He wants to get up a meeting, in hopes to revive a spirit in favor of the Society, now grown languid, almost to atrophy.

Late in the evening—too late for business, being detained at my office professionally—Attended a meeting of the Trustees of the *City University*, to meet Revd. Dr. Wines,[38] but did not see the Dr. as he had left before my arrival. It seems that a com[mitt]ee. had been appointed—Judge H. R. Gamble[39] and Revd. Dr. Mc-Pheeters[40]—to try to procure a President for the C.[ity] U[niversity]. They, it seems, had spoken to Dr. Wines and got him to come out and examine for himself.

I asked what was the present condition of the Institution—Mr. Gill said "We are out of debt[.]"—I suppose there is no endowment, and no income. Someone—perhaps Dr. W. M. McPheeters[41]—said it was the intention to open a subscription in all the Churches in the City concerned in the enterprise—Old School Presbyterian—with a view to get $2000 from each church, as a *temporary* endowment, so as to induce Dr. Wines to assume the control, and build up the University by his personal efforts.

The house itself (NE corner Pine and 16th.) is large and well built, but has no ground attached, only a little paved back yard. An excellent house for a preparatory Grammar School. But as the beginning of *an University*, a mere futility.

---

[38] See *infra*, July 25, 1859.

[39] Hamilton R. Gamble, of Missouri: old-time Whig; brother-in-law of Mrs. Bates; one-time law partner of Mr. Bates; judge of the Missouri Supreme Court. 1850–1854; author of a dissenting opinion in the Dred Scott case in the state court; a strong advocate of the Union in Missouri at the outbreak of the Civil War; Conservative Unionist war governor of Missouri from June, 1861, until his death in January, 1864.

[40] *Supra*, April 24, 1859, note 24.

[41] A prominent St. Louis physician, at this time surgeon of the U. S. Marine Hospital and an editor of the St. Louis *Medical and Surgical Journal*. North-Carolina-bred, he joined the Confederate Army as a surgeon when the Civil War came.

I have had no great hopes of the Institution ever since the managers determined to *stick it down* on a little lot in the thick of the City, to enable 'the boys' to walk conveniently from their fathers' houses to school! I told them, in public meeting, some two or three years ago, that by those means, they might possibly succeed in making a pretty good preparatory school for young boys (which was not the thing we proposed to make) but a *first class* University (which we did design to make) never.

The $1000 which I subscribed and paid towards the *University,* is the only voluntary contribution which I ever begrudged, and that only because it seems to me perverted from its object.

I dont[*sic*] expect to subscribe any more.

July 24. . . .

July 25, Monday—By invitation supped at Mr. Bishop's [42] in company with Revd. Dr. *Wines* [43] (a professor in Washington College Pa.) who visits St Louis preparatory to the organization of the *City University* (old school Presbyterian) it being intended to offer him the presidency. I like his appearance very well. He seems to be a plain, solid man, and he has a high reputation for learning.

There were present also Revd. Dr. McPheeters [44]—and Mr. Bishop's two neighbors [*sic*], Mr. Brown and Dr. Johnson—I never saw Dr. J[ohnson] before, tho' he tells me he has lived in the City 8 years—Also Mr. Davis, the young gentleman who preaches in *our* pulpit, *though not licenced to preach.* [48] Before, he came in, we—Drs. Wines and McPheeters, Mr. Bishop and I—were conversing on the subject, and all of us agreed that it was entirely irregular and against the laws of the church. Mr. Bishop said that the session invited Mr. Davis entirely at the instance of Dr. Anderson, and that that [*sic*] the Session presumed of course, that Mr. D.[avis] was licenced.

After Mr. D.[avis] came, the topic was renewed, and he, at first, seemed very confident that it was right—*we*, some of us, said it was irregular &c—He asked emphatically, who was to blame—I answered, the *Session,* for inviting a man to preach in our pulpit without *knowing* that he was licenced (I did not say, as perhaps I ought, *you*, for accepting the invitation and assuming the place of our pastor, *knowing* that you were not authorised to preach, by any church judicature[.])[.] He asked, are they to be blamed for

---

[42] See *supra*, July 17, 1859.

[43] Enoch C. Wines: for many years a teacher; then a Presbyterian minister; professor of ancient languages at Washington College, Pennsylvania. When the City University failed and was abandoned in 1861, he accepted the secretaryship of the New York Prison Association and became a penologist of note.

[44] *Supra*, April 24, 1859, note 24.

[45] See *supra*, July 17, 1859.

their ignorance? I answered, yes certainly—when knowledge is a
duty, ignorance is a crime—He acquiesced in that and remained
silent—I added only, I am afraid that the great personal merits of
Mr. Davis will make us submit to a great breach of our law.

After supper, a meeting of the trustees of the City University.
There was no preparation. Nobody was prepared with a plan.
Every thing was at odd ends, and no unity of opinion and views.
There was a " free conversation " with Dr. Wines, and a great many
suggestions, but no direct proposition. After a while, a resolution
was passed offering the presidency to Dr. Wines, at a salary of
$3000—and then I left—Dick driving me thro' the dark, home by
11. p. m[.]

July 26. Tuesday— . . .

Mr. Bullard of Boston, brother of the late Revd. Dr. Bullard,[46]
introduced by Dr. Jno. B. Johnson.[47]

July 27. A bright day, pleasantly cool—On going in to the office
[I] found on my desk, the card of Wm. G Bates [48] of Massts.—He
called to see me (with Capt: Bissell) telling Dick that he was a
couzen [sic] of my old friend I. C. Bates [49] of Northampton, and
that he wished to see me, partly on that account, and partly for my
politics[.]

. . .

Colfax. Recd. a letter today, from Mr. Colfax [50] who expresses
himself much pleased with my long letter, amended in its phraseology
in some particulars, as suggested by him; and he asks leave to shew
the letter to Mr. C. A Dana [51] of the Tribune. Of course, I have
no objection; my letter, tho' not written for publication, is not secret.

He also encloses, for my inspection, a letter from Mr. Dana to
him, by which I find that D.[ana] prefers Chase [52] to Seward—(but

[46] Artemas Bullard, agent of the Massachusetts Sunday-School Union, 1828–1834; Mississippi Valley agent of the American Board of Commissioners for Foreign Missions, 1834–1838; minister of the First Presbyterian Church in St. Louis from 1838 until killed in a railroad accident in 1855.

[47] A Massachusetts-trained physician of St. Louis, professor in the St. Louis Medical College (Washington University), a founder (1847) and vice-president (1850) of the National Medical Association.

[48] A lawyer of Westfield, Massachusetts; Whig state senator, 1841; member of Governor Briggs's Council, 1844–1845.

[49] Isaac C. Bates: anti-Jackson Democratic congressman, 1827–1835; Whig U. S. senator from Massachusetts from 1841 until his death in 1845.

[50] *Supra*, April 27, 1859, note 28.

[51] Charles A. Dana: assistant to Greeley on the *New York Tribune*, 1847–1862; special commissioner of the War Department, 1862–1863; assistant secretary of War, 1863–1865; later, editor of the *New York Sun*. He was an ardent war-time supporter of Lincoln, then a bitter enemy of Johnsonian restoration, but finally a Liberal Republican seeking reform of Grantism. In 1859 he was still in complete sympathy with Greeley.

[52] *Infra*, March 5, 1861, note 27. Chase, a perennial aspirant to the Presidency was really in 1859 a leading candidate for the Republican nomination, but lost it, partly because his own state was not united in his support and partly because he, like Seward, was too extreme on slavery to win moderate votes.

does not want either) as a candidate for the Presidency—and enquires, with apparent interest, about the present condition of "the Bates movement." Dana says—"If B.[ates] can be put forward as a representative of the emancipation cause in Missouri he will be the strongest candidate we can have. With any other man we shall have the Fillmore split over again[.]"

<*Note* this letter from D.[ana] to C.[olfax] is dated July 10[.]>

About the same time Colfax wrote to Gibson,[53] and sent him, among other things, a letter from Mr. Bowles,[54] editor of the Springfield Republican (Massts.) to him, C[olfax].[ ]Bowles, I believe, is in full concert with the Tribune of N. York, and Colfax, Defrese[55] and other party leaders in the North West, to bring me out as the candidate of the Republicans. They are all afraid of Seward—they have personal objections doubtless, but their main ground is their full conviction that with Mr. S.[eward] for their candidate defeat, is inevitable.[56] And they seem to think, that if S.[eward] is not nominated, his friends will take care that neither Bankes[57] nor Chase, nor any other Republican shall be. In that event, they think me the most available candidate—the only man in fact, who, getting the Republican vote, can also secure the general support of the Americans and Whigs. Some of them tell me that Mr. Weed[58] (who is understood to be Mr. Seward's "master of the horse" in N. Y.) goes for me, second.

Mr. Bowles says in his letter, that my N.[ew] Y.[ork] letter[59] "ought not to have been written." As a measure of policy, I differ from him widely.

1. It is satisfactory to the real economists every where[.]

2. It pleases the manufacturers, who need protection, especially in Pa.

3. It is agreeable to all the old whigs.

---

[53] *Supra,* April 27, 1859, note 27.

[54] Samuel Bowles—anti-slavery leader, strong supporter of Lincoln against the Radical Republicans, advocate of moderation toward the South—made his *Springfield Republican* one of the most powerful influences in the North.

[55] John D. Defrees of Indiana: lawyer and state legislator; first chairman of the Indiana Republican State Committee, 1856–1860; editor of the *Indianapolis State Journal.* He must, in the end, have supported Lincoln's candidacy, for Lincoln appointed him government printer in 1861.

[56] See *supra,* April 27, 1859, note 30.

[57] Nathaniel P. Banks of Massachusetts: Democratic congressman, 1853–1855; American Party congressman and speaker of the House, 1855–1857; Republican congressman, 1857, 1865–1873, 1875–1879, 1889–1891; governor of Massachusetts, 1858–1861; president of the Illinois Central Railroad, 1861; major-general of volunteers, who served in Maryland, in the Shenandoah, at Vicksburg, in Louisiana, and in Texas, 1861–1865. As a former Know-Nothing, he was more "available" in 1860 than Seward whom the Know-Nothings hated.

[58] Thurlow Weed: editor of the *Albany Evening Journal;* for years the most powerful political figure in New York politics; one of the early managers of the National Republican Party. At this time he was managing Seward's campaign for the Republican nomination.

[59] See *supra,* 1–9.

4. It is not offensive to the Americans at the South, very pleasing to those of the North.

5. It is rank poison to the proslavists of the South, and by resisting their propagandism—and hence, conciliatory to all their enemies.

6. The objection of Mr. Bowles, and other leading Republicans to my denunciation of slavery agitation, is, in my judgment, a positive advantage.

1. It keeps me separated from the Republican party, and yet not so far removed as to prevent their support: 2d. It allays the prejudices of Whigs and Americans farther south, who might not be willing to support any man who was fully identified with the Republican party. 3. It gives to the whole letter an air of courage and sincerity which may tend to beget a general feeling favorable to the writer, and especially among the multitude who are now disgusted with the frauds and misman[a]gement of all the parties[.]

["The Presidency in 1860." [60]

"In this week's issue we run up the name of Hon. EDWARD BATES, of Missouri, for President in 1860; subject to the decision of the Union Convention.

"It is useless for us to eulogise EDWARD BATES; he is too well and favorably known to the whole nation, for us to attempt to add anything to the lustre of his character. He is the man to lead on to victory the columns of the mighty 'Union Party,' that is daily gathering strength all over the country. With him at our head. we can break up, and disband the two pernicious and sectional parties, the Democratic and the Republican, whose strife and wrangling over mere abstractions, have brought us several times upon the very verge of civil war.

"EDWARD BATES, is an eminently conservative man, and if elevated to the high position of Chief Magistrate of the Nation, will administer the government upon those truly national principles which actuated the earlier Presidents.

"Should EDWARD BATES be nominated, we feel assured that the Union men of Missouri will exert themselves to secure his election, as patriots should do when their country is in danger."]

July 30, Saturday. . . .

Coalter and Woodson came home today, after a visit of several weeks to Dardenne prairie.[61] They came down in Barton's little wagon, bringing *Onward* [62] with them, and have promised to take him home in a few days. Caroline [63] sent us a number of good things for the table—Bacon, Lard, Meat[.]

---

[60] A clipping from the *Louisiana (Missouri) Journal* of July 25, 1859.

[61] A prairie in St. Charles County about thirty miles northwest of St. Louis on which the village of Dardenne grew up. Here lived Mr. Bates's eldest son, Barton, and also the Woodsons—his cousins—and many of his oldest friends. He himself, had lived on a farm on the prairie from 1828 until 1842.

[62] Mr. Bates's eldest grandchild, Barton's son. See *supra*, "Introduction."

[63] Mrs. Barton Bates.

Mr. Welling.[64]   This evening I recd. a long letter from J. C. Welling (actual editor of the Nat:[ional] Intel[ligence]r.) in answer to mine to him, on the, now, much mooted question of the status of our naturalized citizens, and their liability to compulsory military service, if, for any reason, they return voluntarily to their native country. He had taken ground with Sec.y. Cass' first letters,[65] and asserts,—and goes far to prove, by the letters of Sec.y.s Marcy[66] and Webster[67]—that the liability continues. I the contrary. But we concur entirely, in contempt for Mr. Cass, on account of his sudden change (with the whole Adm[inistratio]n.) through fear of popular opinion.

Cass. Poor Cass! He clings to office with the tenacity of a drowning man, and under the most humiliating circumstances. His character as a Statesman, as a Publicist, as a constitutional lawyer, dont [*sic*] weigh a feather in the scale against the honors and emoluments of Office: His personal consistency and self-respect are sacrificed without a scruple, to get or to retain a *place*, under any President, upon any doctrines, and with any associates in power.

[*A clipping from the* Missouri Republican *of July 30, 1859, quoting from the* New York Express *the facts that in Georgia all Whigs had received five out of six of the Democratic nominations for Congress.*]

Whigs lead the Democrats.

Aug: 6. C. F. Woodson[68] arrived this, Saturday, evening, to make me his long promised visit.

<*Note.* Mr. W.[oodson] returned home on the 10th.—evening train[.]>

[*Note.*] *Pears.* Mr. Woodson knit in several *buds* of the of the [*sic*] *Little June pear*, on the stock of the *big american*.

Health

Note. We are in a bad way about sickness. Though none of us is very ill, still we are badly at fault for lack of help—viz: *Sister*[69] is helpless—*Nancy*[70] barely able to creep about—*Johan[n]a* (the Cook) with a bad boil on heach [*sic*] hand—*John O'Neill*—sick in town (now convalescent) *Tom: Hare*, sick at home—And so William and the two boys have to do all the out work.

---

[64] *Supra,* June 20, 1859, note 3.

[65] *Supra,* June 8, 1859.

[66] William L. Marcy of New York, Democratic secretary of State under President Pierce, 1853–1857. For Marcy's views on naturalization see Secretary of State Marcy to Mr. Daniel in Italy, Nov. 10, 1855, and Marcy to Mr. Florence, Feb. 17, 1857, in the State Department archives. See also Francis Wharton, *A Digest of the International Law of the United States,* II, 386.

[67] No outstanding cases arose under Daniel Webster's secretaryship of State, 1850–1852.

[68] A cousin of Mr. Bates.

[69] Sarah Bates who died on August 12, 1859.

[70] Mr. Bates's elder daughter. See *supra,* "Introduction."

Johnny Kelly has engaged to come tomorrow evening, as a temporary supply.

Horse Railroads, in the City.

On Monday the 8th. Augt. I saw the car in operation for the first time, on *Market street* running to and fro, between 4th. and 16th. streets.

The Olive street track was used early in July, but there was some error in the rails which had to be taken up and reset—

On Morgan street also, they are advancing rapidly[.] And on 5th. street they are pushing forward the double track.

Augt. 10. (Wednesday). The Mo. Democrat of today, contains a leader on the late *Southern elections*—in Tenn: K.y. and Va. shewing a large gain of the op[p]osition, and concludes that " The result of the Southern elections leaves but two opposition candidates for the Presidency in the field, Edward Bates of Missouri and John Bell [71] of Tennessee[.]"

And adds a brief but high eulogy of both.

[*Note.*[72]] The same paper of Aug: 13. contains a strong leader headed—"African Colonization v African Immigration," in which the Editor labors to shew that, in the Presidential election, next year, the question will come up—will be forced by the South—of repealing the laws against the Slave Trade. He says that Stephens [73] of Ga., in his late speech at Augusta,[74] suggested, without directly proposing it, and that Davis [75] of Mi.[ssissippi], intends to introduce the measure of repeal at the next session of Congress. And he thinks that that will be sure to bring up the counter proposition to colonize our free blacks in Central America and other tropical countries. He thinks that several Senators, e. g. Doolittle,[76] Wade [77] &c, go heartily for this last.

---

[71] Whig congressman, 1827–1841; secretary of War, 1841; U. S. senator, 1847–1859; nationalist, moderate, opponent of the aggressive faction of the slavocracy. Bell had opposed the "gag rule" in 1836; he had favored compromise in 1850; he had opposed the Kansas-Nebraska bill and the admission of Kansas under the Lecompton Constitution.
[72] Added later.
[73] Alexander H. Stephens of Georgia: congressman, 1843–1859, 1873–1882; vice-president of the Confederacy. A Whig until 1852, then a Democrat, he was always a moderate. In the 1830's he had opposed nullification; he had favored the annexation of Texas, but had opposed the Mexican War. Now he was working for reconciliation of the sections. He opposed secession until it was accomplished. As Vice-President of the Confederacy he was the champion of states' rights and civil liberties.
[74] The speech, delivered July 2, 1859, is given in Henry Cleveland, *Alexander H. Stephens,* 637–651.
[75] Senator Jefferson Davis.
[76] James R. Doolittle of Wisconsin: Free-Soil Democratic leader in New York and then Wisconsin, 1844–1856; Republican U. S. senator, 1857–1869. During the Civil War he was a staunch supporter of Lincoln against the Radicals and in Reconstruction a Johnsonian Moderate. At this time he was an extreme advocate of states' rights on slavery within states but a vigorous opponent of any compromise with slavery in national territory.
[77] Benjamin F. Wade of Ohio: Republican U. S. senator, 1851–1869; opponent of the Kansas-Nebraska bill and the Lecompton Constitution; bitter denouncer of Lincoln for his moderation; leading Radical impeacher of Johnson. At this time he was a leader of the most extreme group in Congress.

Southern Elections. Slave trade

[*A clipping from the* Missouri Daily Democrat, *headed " The Southern Elections," which points out that though " the Opposition have failed to carry" Virginia, Kentucky, Tennessee, and North Carolina, " they have made considerable gains in all of them." The conclusion is that there exists through the South a general dissatisfaction with the extreme policies of the Democracy.*

"The result of the Southern election leaves but two Opposition candidatas [*sic*] for the Presidency in the field, Edward Bates of Missouri, and John Bell of Tennessee. There is no earthly doubt, that if either shall receive the nomination from the Republican Convention, he will be elected. We are free to confess that the Tennessee statesman has a most commendable record. He is, perhaps, the most consistent public man now living in the United States. He had the manhood to vote against the Kansas-Nebraska bill, and to oppose the entire territorial policy of which that measure was the initiation. Though the leader of the American party in Tennesee, he never joined the Order—never entered a lodge or took an oath—and this fact would not be without its force in a Presidential canvass. He has sacrificed his public career to his convictions—but though broken he has always refused to bend. Take him all in all, John Bell is a very distinguished man, and an honor to Tennessee.

"Edward Bates is a man of not inferior character and antecedents, and of superior abilities. He is, in addition, an earnest, though moderate, opponent of slavery, and accordingly approaches nearer to the Republican standard than his Tennessee compeer. Throughout the broad South these two men are the only men that can be named as possible candidates of the Opposition. Crittenden[18] is buried deeper than if he lay with the Titans beneath the mountains. His Douglas letter[19] last summer capped the climax of his disasters.

"We do not deny that there are other Southern men, such as John M. Botts[80] and Kenneth Raynor,[81] who are conspicuous in their opposition to the National Democracy, but we repeat that of the Southern Opposition only Bates or Bell can be elected to the Presidency. Missouri would vote for Bates, and Tennessee would doubtless vote for Bell, and either would receive a large vote in the central slave States. How many Southern States either would carry, is a matter of little moment, for the united free States will govern the result of the election."]

The great gain of the opposition in the recent elections in the South—i.e. N.[orth] C.[arolina] Tenn: K.y.——is making a decided

---

[18] John J. Crittenden of Kentucky: U. S. senator, 1817–1819, 1835–1841, 1842–1848, 1855–1861; attorney-general under Harrison, 1841, and under Fillmore, 1850–1853; governor of Kentucky, 1848–1850; congressman, 1861–1863. He believed in congressional non-intervention in the Territories, opposed both the Lecompton and Topeka constitutions for Kansas, supported the Constitutional Union Party in 1860, and led the movements for a compromise in 1861. He helped keep Kentucky from seceding and sponsored her position of neutrality in the first months of the War.

[19] A letter from J. J. Crittenden to T. Lyle Dickey, Aug. 1, 1858, in which in verifying a conversation of the preceding April, Crittenden praises Douglas's course in the Senate and then grants Dickey permission to print the letter publicly. It was used to help defeat Lincoln whom Crittenden did not wish to see in the Senate.

[80] *Supra*, July 15, 1859, note 22.

[81] Kenneth Raynor of North Carolina: member of the Constitutional Convention of 1835; state legislator; Whig congressman, 1839–1845; solicitor of the U. S. Treasury, 1877–1884. He opposed secession.

impression. The opposition is encouraged and the Democrats alarmed.

And now, the more recent success in Texas, in Houston's election for Govr., adds point to the feelings on both sides, and calls forth very pointed observations in the press.

The Charleston Mercury [August 13, 1859]—(I copy from the Mo. Rep[ublica]n. of Aug 20)—is pointed in its abuse of Genl. Houston, and open in its disclosures of the policy of the State rights party, as to reviving the slave trade—

It says of Houston—" His national aspirations and base treachery to his section and the slave institutions of the South had destroyed him, notwithstanding his great former services, his personal popularity[,] and his eloquence and adroitness in speaking. The old self-seeker fell, it was hoped[,] to rise no more in Texas."

And thus it seems that *former services*, great popularity, and eloquence and tact, all go for nothing, when they are not employed in support of the *Slave Institutions of the South*—He is a traitor who ought to fall never to rise again—He is " one of the greatest enemies to the South, and most unmitigated demagogues within our borders—a Southern free Soiler!"

The same article is clear also in favor of the reopening of the slave trade, but thinks the question was prematurely, and therefore imprudently raised by the party in Texas—

" The *State rights party* of Texas started an unnecessary and disastrous issue. They made the re opening of the slave trade the great question in the election, dividing their own party and driving off many. The speeches of the canvas[s] were filled chiefly with the subject. Houston saw his advantage " &c[.]

" The S[t]ate rights party of Texas have brought defeat upon themselves by making an unpracticable and mischievous issue. Let it be a lesson to be remembered. The people of the South should be informed on the subject, but to make it a matter of voting and a living issue, dividing our people, is a foolish and fatal move.["]

" Let the subject be considered calmly and thoroughly sifted *by discussion merely. When the South is in position to act on it*, it will be time enough to make it an issue. But until then, such a use of it is only fraught with evil. *In this instance*, it has paralized [*sic*] the State rights party of Texas, and raised to power one of the greatest enemies to the South, and most unmitigated demagogues within our borders—*A Southern Free soiler*[.] " [82]

---

[82] Samuel Houston (Indian fighter under Jackson. Democratic congressman from Tennessee, 1823–1827, governor of Tennessee, 1827–1829, revolutionist and victorious general in Texas, president of the Republic of Texas, 1836–1838 and 1841–1844, U. S. senator, 1846–1859) had just been elected governor of Texas on a Free-Soil ticket. He held this office until he was deposed in 1861 for refusal to take the oath of allegiance to the Confederacy.

Then, there are such things as *Southern Freesoilers*—and one of them, it seems, is far from being alone—he has friends and accomplices enough to make him Governor of the extreme Southern State—Sam Houston, guilty of " *base treachery to his section* "[,] "one of the greatest enemies to the South and most unmitigated demagogue[s]." "A Southern freesoiler," is actually elected Governor of Texas !! *Quære.* is Texas treacherous to its section—a free soil State?

August 12. Sarah Bates (my eldest sister) died last night—½ past 12 oclock—. She expired without pain or suffering, by the me[re] decay of nature. She was in her 86th. year—would have completed it, if [s]he had lived to the 26th. of Nov: next.

[*August 13.*] On Saturday the 13th. we buried her in the family burying ground at Florissant,[83] adjoining the grave of our mother on the north side.

Augt. 19. thursday—This afternoon took Mrs: Bates and our friend (old) Mrs. McPheeters, of Raleigh N.[orth] C.[arolina] to see Mr. and Mrs. Isaac Read, at (Upper) Alton—Went up by boat, and returned next day, in the same way. Had a very pleasant trip, which I think was gratifying to our Alton friends.

. . .

Note—Woody sick with some fever—Tom Hare is well, and John O'Neill nearly so.[84]

[*A clipping from the* Missouri Democrat *of August 20, 1859, giving a " Circular of the Republican National Committee " issued at a meeting in Albany a few days before. It states the purposes of forming the Republican Party, lists the abuses of the Buchanan Administration, and then urges consultation and coöperation of the Opposition under the Republican banner.*]

The Mo. Democrat of Aug 20. contains a circular address of the *Republican National Committee*[.]

It is brief, calm and well-written. It declares that " The Republican party had its origin in the obvious necessity for *resistance to the aggressions of the slave power* and maintaining for the states respectively their reserved rights and sovereignties." It is at once indignant and contemptuous toward the administration of Buchanan. Otherwise, its [*sic*] moderate and practicable in tone[.]

The Mo. Rep:[ublican] of 20 Aug. contains a leader from the " States "[85] (Douglas') assuming, as a certainty, that Seward will be nominated by the Republicans, and insisting that the Democrats

---

[83] *Supra*, May 18, 1859. note 52.

[84] See *supra*, Aug. 6, 1859.

[85] " The ' Irrepressible Conflict,' " Washington *States*, Aug. 15, 1859.

can beat *him*. It is the obvious policy of the Democrats of all stripes, to hold out that idea, knowing that Mr. S.[eward] cant [*sic*] get a vote outside of the Rep[ublica]n. party and may lose a good many within it.[86]

In that particular their strategy suits me well: The Republican leaders (many of them) are sagacious men, and cannot help seeing the reason why the Democrats insist upon having Seward for their adversary—they think they can surely beat him, but if Bell or I were nominated, they fear the result might be different[.]

Aug: 24. Wednesday—Went up to pay our long-promised visit to our friends in Dardenne Prairie [87]—Julia took Nancy and me in her carriage. Julia was taken sick with dysentery and remained housed at Barton's—Nancy was also very unwell. I visited round a little, but staid longest at Mount Airy.

. . .

[*August 31.*] On the 31. (wednesday) Julia being pretty well restored, we returned home, leaving Nancy at Mt. Airy, and bringing along with us our little grandson, Tarlton.[88]

Sept: 2d. Woody and William go up to Dardenne, in the Boys' carriage, taking up the maid servant, Mary Smith, to wait on Nancy. The chief object of the boys however, is to take their sport in shooting squirrels, which now abound around the prairie.

. . .

Sept. 4. (Sunday). This is my birthday—I am 66.

My cold, taken yesterday is increasing.[;] the morning is cool and cloudy and I find much relief in putting on wollens [*sic*]. I am not well enough to go to church, as I wished to do, having been absent, in St Charles C.[ount]y. last sunday. But for this cold, my general health is as good as it has been for many years.

Some one has sent me the *Constitution* [89] referred to in the Democrat and I find it vulgarly abusive, in a style quite unworthy the organ of the Governm[en]t. and unprovoked by my letter. It suits *me* well however, and shews both the weakness and the fears of the party. While it abuses me rudely, it is violent in its abuse also of the whole Republican and American parties—All right:

I have seen it asserted in print, that Mr. Buchanan himself writes Editorials for the "Constitution," and a well-informed friend, who is a good judge of style, thinks he wrote the piece in question.

---

[86] See *supra*, April 27, 1859.

[87] *Supra*, July 30, 1859, note 61.

[88] A grandson of Mr. Bates—Barton's son.

[89] Washington *Constitution*, Sept. 1, 1859.

[*Mr. Bates inserted the paragraph from the* Missouri Democrat:

"The *Constitution* criticises the recent letter of Edward Bates, of Missouri, to J. Clemens and others, committee &c., apologising for not being present at this grand jubilee of the Opposition in Tennessee. The *Constitution* regrets to see so flagitious a document so full of slanderous misstatements and willful misrepresentations, printed over the signature of a man like Mr. Bates."]

[*A Clipping from the* St. Louis Evening News:

"Edward Bates

"The Lexington *Express*, in its last issue, makes the following declaration:

"For President of the United States, our first choice is, as announced on the 18th of February last, the Hon. EDWARD BATES, of St. Louis, but we could and would just as cordially support the Hon,[.] JOHN J. CRITTENDEN,[90] or Hon. EDWARD EVERETT.[91] There are dozens of others that we could mention who would be fully entitled to our warmest support; but we prefer MR. BATES' because he is a part of the West, a section of country quite overlooked by the Nationals, in their determination to dissever the Union upon an abstract question that they have kept in full blaze for a great number of years; because he has not been identified with the legislation of the country; because he is a statesman in the broadest and fullest sense, a conscientious christian gentleman who could in no way be contaminated by the corruptions of our national capital. We prefer Mr. B. also because he would favor the building of the great Pacific Railroad over the Central of Missouri route, the best, we think, that can be selected, taking into view the route to be traversed, and the centre of population, trade, &c."]

The "Putnam Republican Banner" of Greencastle I[ndian]a. Aug 31, also nominates me[.]

Also, the *St. Joseph* (Mo.) *Free Democrat* (lately edited by Mr. Grant, now by *Messrs. Boynton* and [   ])   An able article urging the union of all the elements of opposition, closes with a strong recommendation of me, and praise far beyond my desert.

New Jersey   The Nat:[ional] In[telligence]r. of Sep 1. contains the resolutions of a Democratic State Convention.[82] The Resolutions are better drawn than we commonly find in *democratic literature;* and the propositions worth remembering, in future discussions—They support *squatter Sovereignty, on principle;* meaning Douglas.

Sept. 8. James. G. McPheeters stopped me on the street to tell an anecdote [*sic*], which he says gave cause to great amusement. Last sunday he attended a great Sunday school meeting, up town. The Superintendant [*sic*] put a number of miscellaneous questions, to

---

90 *Supra*, Aug. 10, 1859, note 78.

91 Unitarian clergyman; professor of Greek at Harvard, 1815–1826; congressman, 1825–1835; governor of Massachusetts, 1836–1840; minister to Great Britain, 1841–1845; president of Harvard, 1846–1849; secretary of State, 1852–1853; U. S. senator, 1853–1854. He opposed agitation of the slavery issue and plead for compromise until Sumter was fired upon. Then he became the great orator of the Union cause.

92 They appear in the issue of August 31, not in that of September 1.

test the general knowledge of the Scholars—Well children, said he, can you tell me who is President of the U.[nited] States? Yes, yes—said a half a dozen young voices—Buchanan! Right, but would it not be more polite to say *Mr.* Buchanan? Yes, *Mr.* Buchan[an], said the boys.

Then, in order to test the boldness of the children, and as a foundation for some intended remarks against precipitate judgments of the future—said he—" Now children, can you tell me who will be the next President?" There was a dead pause for a few seconds, when a bright faced little boy on a back seat, cried out—" Yes sir, I can tell you,—Mr. Bates—Pa says he ought to be, and I reckon the People will do right."

And then there was a general shout for the little politician, who had so much faith in his father's judgment and the people's virtue.

Sunday; Sept. 20. . . .

Our young friend, Charles Watkins, seems to be sinking rapidly with consumption. His parents being written to at Petersburg Va., have come out to take him home *to die.* I called to see them yesterday at Dr. J. W. Wilson's—Julia called also. They seem greatly comforted to find that their son is treated here with so much respect and friendship. They will leave for Va. on monday.

[*Marginal Note.*] Oct: 12. Andrew Venable tells us that he has just heard that Charles Watkins died, a few days since, at his father's house, near Petersburg Va.

Caroline and her two youngest children have been with us for some time (Onward *lives* with us and goes to school with our boys, at the Washington University) and Pamele Hatcher. Barton went up last tuesday, expecting to return saturday or monday—yesterday or tomorrow. He will probably bring down with him Charlotte Hatcher or our Nannie and her maid servant, Mary Smith—We look for them tomorrow.

The trial of Thornton for the murder of Joseph Charless[93] is set for tomorrow—It was set for last monday, but postponed on account of the sickness of Def[endan]t's counsel, Mr. Kribben.[94]

I am retained to aid the prosecution (Mr. Manro [*sic*] Circ[ui]t Atty), by the friends of the family, the Messrs. Blow,[95] the brothers in law, and M. Le Boujouoir, the son in law. Mr. Maro [*sic*] tells me there will be no trouble in proving the *corpus delicti,* and we can for[e]see no defense but a pretence of insanity[.]

There will probably be much difficulty in getting a jury.

---

[93] *Supra,* June 4, 1859.

[94] *Infra,* Dec. 23, 1859, note 61.

[95] Henry T. Blow: manufacturer, merchant, and mine-owner; early Free-Soiler; state senator, 1854-1858; delegate to the Chicago Convention which nominated Lincoln; strong union man who helped to prevent Missouri's seceding; minister to Venezuela, 1861-1862; Republican congressman, 1863-1867.

Wednesday, Sept. 21. The trial of Jos: W. Thornton for the murder of Joseph Charless, begun on monday, was concluded this day, at 3. p. m. by his full conviction[.]

Wednesday, Sept. 21. Today, at the Boatmen's S.[avings] I.[nstitution] discounted my note *for $1000*—at 90 days. to pay my note of 1000$ being one of the notes given to Louis Brand, for Julian's house and lot in Florissant.

. . .

Yesterday, Barton, with his wife and two younger children, Palm: Hatcher, and a servant girl, went to Lucius' on a visit and have not returned[.]

There are with us tonight—Jenney and Julia Woodson,[96] Kate Wilson—Andrew Venable and Dick Woodson[.]

The Agricultural and Mechanical Fair of St. Louis County commenced on Monday the 26th. of September. The Exhibition is in great variety and excellence. Almost every thing said to be an improvement on last year; and the crowd immense. . . .

Our house has has [*sic*] been crowded with company all the week—Barton, wife, 3 children and servant—Lucius, wife and child—3 Miss Hatchers—2. Miss Woodsons—and Lenny [?] Woods—

Mr. Browning [97] of Quincy came home with me from the Fair wednesday and spent the night. Mr. Gibson [98] met us here by appointment and we had much political discourse. He is hopeful and zealous, but thinks I ought to come out in a written declaration of principles, such as I avowed in my letters to him and to Mr. Colfax [99] Both Mr. Gibson and I think that the time has not come for it, nor has any striking circumstance occurred to call for a public declaration[.]

Sept. 28. Death of Biddy Lay, or Laihy.—

Beautiful little Biddy, daughter of Mary, the washer woman, died very suddenly on the *28th. of Sept* (wednesday)[.] On the 26th. she was stung on the foot by a *wasp*, which gave great pain and excitement, which was soon subdued by proper remedies, and the child seemed almost well. She had a little fever until the morning of the 28th. Then Dr. Wilson was sent for and prescribed some slight remedies, and went away, thinking the child in no danger. About noon she was taken with convulsions and died in an hour and a half.

---

[96] Daughters of Mr. Bates's cousin at Dardenne.

[97] Orville H. Browning of Illinois: Conservative Republican U. S. senator, 1861–1863; opponent of the Emancipation Proclamation; supporter of Johnson against the Radicals; secretary of the Interior, 1866–1869. At this time, though a close friend of Lincoln, he was trying to win Illinois to the nomination of Bates for President. In the Republican Convention he worked to win support for Bates as first and Lincoln as second choice.

[98] *Supra*, April 27, 1859, note 27.

[99] See *supra*, June 16 and July 27, 1859.

Julia attended to her personally, with all possible care. She was the pet and favorite of us all, and prized by every one of the family. She was buried, thursday 29th., in the Rockspring grave yard. Julia and I and Matilda attended the burial, with our servants and a few of Mary's friends from town. To my surprise, there was no Priest. Yet in one particular the service was solemn—When the grave was filled and the mound smoothed off, all (myself and family included) without a word being spoken, knealt in silence, on the wet grass, around the grave, for a few moments, and then rose and slowly walked away.

It was a touching scene to me, for I loved little Biddy well. She was a playmate of my grand children, and looked up to me as a friend and protector.

Octo 6. . . .

Octo 8. . . .

Saturday evening I went out to Florissant,[1] to Julian's where my wife has been for more than a week (with Mrs. Woodson [2]) attending Sarah [3] and her sick child[.]

The child was expected to die every hour, but lingers on astonishingly, shewing a wonderful tenacity of life. I returned home sunday evening, and now (monday night) we do not hear of the child's death.

Julian is in better health and spirits than he was when I was out there, a week ago. He seems to be getting into practice, having several calls while I was at his house.

Note. One little sign of his improvement in health and hope is that he playfully paid me one years [*sic*] rent of the house and lot where he lives, I having given him a lease, for 5 yrs., he paying the taxes and the nominal rent of $1. pr. an:[num.]

Getting home sunday night, I found my old friend Revd. John Watt, at our house. He has come down from Glasgow I suppose, to attend the Synod of our Church, which will sit in St Louis next wednesday.

Edmund Randolph [4] (a candidate for Att[orne]y. Gen[era]l. of California and I suppose the same to whom *Walker* [5] granted the transit route in Nicaragua) made a speech in San Francisco, Aug: 5. 1859—a pamphlet of 14 closely printed pages. It smacks of filli-

---

[1] *Supra*, May 18, 1859, note 52.

[2] Wife of Mr. Bates's cousin—Julian Bates's mother-in-law.

[3] Sarah Woodson Bates, Julian's wife.

[4] Son of Peyton and grandson of Edmund Randolph of Virginia. He went to California in '49 and helped organize the State and was connected with the Walker filibustering expedition to Nicaragua.

[5] William Walker, New Orleans and California journalist who led several filibustering expeditions: one to Mexico in 1853–1854, two to Nicaragua, in 1855–1857 and in 1857; and two to Honduras, in 1858, and in 1860. He was finally shot for treason in Honduras in 1860.

busterism [*sic*], and is discursive yet eloquent, and above all, is bitter and implacable against Buchan[an] and his administration—see it—

Mr. Eldred sent me the pamphlet.

Oct: 12. Wednesday. Dr. James Pollard called on me, at my office (accompanied by Mr. Minor) and presented me a letter of introduction from his uncle Wm. C. Rives.[6] Dr. P.[ollard] comes to settle in St Louis.

Senator Broderick[7] of California has been killed in a duel by Judge Terry.[8] The papers contain full accounts of the fact, the cause and the probable consequences. The Mo. Democrat of yesterday, contains a detailed nar[r]ative of the fight, the death, the funeral, and the correspondence.

Col: Baker[9] delivered the funeral oration *over the dead body.* And it was his masterpiece, brief, terse, suggestive, politic. He alleges a conspiracy to *kill off* Broderick out of the way, and that he was killed by contrivance and trick: That the personal quarrel was a mere pretense, the murder being a part of the political programme of the *Lecompton Lecompton* [*sic*] *Democrats.* He does but suggest these things; but the newspapers echo every thought, and enlarge and multiply every charge, in bitter and exag[g]erated details. This catastrophe will, very probably, destroy all the advantages gained by the *Lecomptonites* in the late election—so mote it be.

Jeff[erso]n. Davis—

The Nat[iona]l. Intel[ligence]r.[10] of Oct: 4. contains the speech of Col Davis before the Democratic Convention of Mississippi, at Jackson, July 6. 1859.

It may be useful for reference hereafter—Such men as he, smart, it may be, but impulsive, rash, imprudent, are always assuming untenable positions and advancing indefensible propositions, and thus bringing their party into trouble[.]

Oct: 13. Thursday. Last night my son Julian's child died and today was buried in the family graveyard. Julian came in to make

6 Virginia Democrat; congressman, 1823–1829; U. S. senator, 1832–1834, 1836–1839, 1841–1845; minister to France, 1829–1832, 1849–1853; member of the Peace Convention in Washington in 1861; member of the Confederate Congress.

7 David C. Broderick: Tammany politician who removed to California in '49; Democratic "boss" of California; U. S. senator, 1857–1859. As senator, Broderick vigorously attacked political corruption in both California and Washington, and opposed the pro-slavery policies of Buchanan.

8 David S. Terry, chief justice of California and leader of the pro-slavery party, who challenged Broderick to a duel and killed him.

9 Edward D. Baker: Whig and then Republican congressman from Illinois, 1845–1846, 1849–1851; Republican leader in Democratic California, 1852–1860; U. S. senator from Oregon, 1860–1861. He was an important factor in winning California for Lincoln, and his great oratorical powers were used effectively for the Union, in Congress and out, until he was killed in battle in 1861. The Broderick funeral oration was remembered as his most notable speech.

10 The speech begins in the issue of October 3 and is concluded in that of October 4.

preparations for the burial this afternoon—Matilda, Fleming and his wife and R. G. Woodson [11] went out in two hired carriages.

They returned (all except Fleming's family) and got home about 7 oclock p. m. in a hard rain.

Julia has been in attendance on the sick babe for two weeks, and no doubt, is worn down with watching. Instead of two weeks, her absence seems to me like two months.

To day I saw C. Gibson, [12] just returned from the Lexington Whig meeting. It passed off very well—Passed a string of resolutions (rather high flown in language, but right in sentiment and doctrine) denouncing Democracy, proposing a general union of *the opposition* and calling a convention of *all the opposition*, to meet at Jefferson City, Dec: 28. 1859.

They nominate me as their first choice for the Presidency.

This is a good beginning and if followed out in the same spirit, by the State opposition convention, may lead to great results in other States.

[*A clipping which reprints from the* Philadelphia American *"A Card from J. R. Giddings"* [13] *denying the charge that he was connected with the John Brown raid, but at the same time blaming Southern despotism for giving provocation for the Brown attack.*]

Oct: 25. The Harper's Ferry insurrection.

The papers are teeming with accounts of the late out-break at Harper's Ferry. It seems that Capt. John Brown—" old Brown "— " Ossawattomie Brown " of Kansas notoriety, has astonished the Country by the opening scene of his wild and mad project to abolish slavery by a general servile insurrection.

With only 17 or 18 *white* men, and 5 or 6 free negro[e]s, to aid him, he took possession of the armory and other public works at Harper's [Ferry] and had full possession of the town. This was all done by a *coup de main* in the night[.]

Troops, regular and volunteers, were soon brought to bear upon him, and after the killing of several citizens and soldiers, and of the most of Brown's men white and black (including his two sons) the old man, and two or three of his men were taken.

Brown himself, tho' badly wounded in the head, by sabre cuts, and in the body, by a bayonet through the kidneys, is said to have exhibited, in a very marked manner, a calm self-possession, and a cool, quiet courage, very rarely seen. He must be a madman—to say nothing of the wickedness of the design, the wild extravagance and

---

[11] A son of Colonel C. F. Woodson, a cousin of Mr. Bates.
[12] *Supra*, April 27, 1859, note 27.
[13] *Infra*, May 19, 1860, note 14.

utter futility of his plan, prove it. And his cool intrepidity and, apparently, conscious rectitude do but confirm it.

At last accounts, he was undergoing examination before the preliminary Court.

[*Marginal Note.*] There was found among Brown's papers, a plan of a Provisional Governmen[t] of the *U S*, of which it seems, he was the chief.

For the moment, the Country, especially Virginia, is mad with excitemen[t]. And, as might have been expected, the Democracy is turning every stone to make party capital out of it. Very probably, they will overdo the thing and produce a reaction.

Oct: 26. R. M. Field[14] brot' to my office and introduced to me, his college mate, *Judge Saml. Miller*, of Rochester N. Y. He is retired from business—being rich, I suppose—and has been travelling thro' the Southern states, Cuba &c[.] He seems to be a warm politician, a whig, I suppose, as he claims special friendship with Govr. Hunt[15]—He has served in the N. Y. Senate, and has been a Judge.

Says he is *personally* very friendly with Mr. Douglas, who is a relative of his wife.

Also, there was introduced to me today, Mr. *Henry Livingston*, editor of the *Alta California.*

I had an hours [*sic*] talk with him and find him a pleasant, intelligent man. Judge Miller (who casually met him in my office) says he knew him in his youth, that his father is a worthy citizen of Rochester, now fallen poor.

[*Three clippings from the* St. Louis Evening News: *1. " Gov. Wise*[16] *and Old Brown"*[17] *quoting at length from a Richmond speech in which Governor Wise characterized Brown; 2. "Pierce for President" predicting that the Pierce men will lie low until Douglas, Wise, Hunter,*[18] *and Breckinridge*[19] *have defeated each*

---

[14] Roswell M. Field: St. Louis lawyer who initiated and tried the Dred Scott case in the Circuit Court; a staunch unionist who helped prevent Missouri's secession; an authority on land-title disputes arising out of the conflicting claims under Spanish, French, and congressional grants prior to the organization of the State.

[15] Washington Hunt: Whig governor of New York, 1850–1852; congressman, 1843–1849; supporter of the Compromise of 1850; chairman of the Whig National Convention in 1856; chairman of the Constitutional Union Convention which nominated Bell and Everett in 1860; McClellan Democrat in 1864; delegate to Johnson's National Union Convention in 1866.

[16] *Supra,* April 28, 1859, note 38.

[17] *Supra,* Oct. 25, 1859.

[18] Robert M. T. Hunter of Virginia: Democratic congressman, 1837–1861; Confederate secretary of State, 1861–1862; then Confederate senator, 1862–1865; representative of the Confederacy at the Hampton Roads Conference with Lincoln and Seward in 1865. He was a leading advocate of states' rights and a strong candidate for the nomination for the Presidency in the Democratic Convention at Charleston in 1860. He remained in the Senate in 1861 until Virginia seceded.

[19] John C. Breckinridge of Kentucky: Democratic congressman, 1851–1855; vice-president of the U. S., 1857–1861; U. S. senator, 1861; candidate of the Southern

other and will then try to secure Pierce's nomination as a dark horse; 3. "Gov. Wise Ahead" pointing out how fortunate the John Brown raid was for Governor Wise's aspirations for the nomination for President.]

Oct 28. Friday—Met in the street and introduced by Mr. F. P. Blair[,] [20] Mr. Berlingame [21] of Massts. and Capt C[G]oliver. Had a few minutes['] pleasant discourse, and Mr. Blair promised to bring them to my house.

The Nat:[ional] Intel[ligence]r. of Oct 25 contains Att.y. Genl. Black's [22] answer to and criticism of Mr. Douglas' unlucky article on Squatter Sovereignty, as published in Harper.[23]

Also, a valuable letter from its London correspondent (Pishey Thompson). This letter contains, i.a. the following[:]

1. A good view of the affairs of Italy, and Europe generally.

2 Repair of Railways in England requires, *annually*, 20.000 tons of iron—26.000.000 wooden sleepers—to get which sleepers, 300.000 trees—which trees require for their growth, 5000 acres of land[.]

3 Dr. Davy [24] of Dublin, it seems, has detected *arsenic* in several kinds of vegitables [*sic*], as turnips and cabbage the arsenic is taken up by the vegitables [*sic*] from certain kinds of artificial manures, such as *Superphosphate.*

4. That Bunyan did not write the "Pilgrim's Progress," but copied it from an old work of the 15th. century, written by one G. de Geideville—See back, last vol: date December: 8. 1857. St Louis Ev. g. News Oct 31. 1859

Democracy for the Presidency in 1860; opponent of congressional action on slavery in the Territories. When the War came he believed in the abstract right of secession but opposed it in practice, and yet also opposed coërcion of states to keep them in the Union. He tried to secure adoption of the Crittenden Compromise, but finally joined the Confederate Army, became brigadier-general, fought in Kentucky in 1861–1862, at Shiloh, Vicksburg, Baton Rouge, and Port Hudson in 1862, at Jackson, Chickamauga, and Missionary Ridge in 1863, and in southwest Virginia, at Cold Harbor, in the Shenandoah, and in Early's raid on Washington in 1864. In February, 1865, he was made Confederate secretary of War.

[20] *Supra*, April 27, 1859, note 25.

[21] Anson Burlingame of Massachusetts: state legislator; Know-Nothing and then Republican minister to China, 1861–1867; Chinese ambassador to negotiate with foreign powers, 1867–1870.

[22] Jeremiah S. Black of Pennsylvania: eccentric attorney-general under Buchanan; secretary of State during Buchanan's last three months; severe critic of Lincoln's use of the war powers. At this time he was conducting Buchanan's political campaign against Douglas. It was Black who advised Buchanan that the states could not secede but that the President could not use force to prevent their seceding.

[23] See *supra*, June 24, 1859, note 15.

[24] Edmund Davy, British chemist, professor of the Royal Dublin Society, who did notable work in applying chemistry to agriculture.

"Hon. Edward Bates."

"'No Southern man stands fairer at the North than Mr. BATES, but it will be idle for his friends to attempt to secure his nomination or endorsement by the Republican Party unless he makes some more tangible declaration of sympathy with the leading principles for which it battles, than he has yet done.' <Dubuque Daily Times.[>]

"'Judge BATES may be an Emancipationist or Free Soiler as stated, and it is not to be denied, that the fact of the many statements to that effect, published in the Republican papers, never having been denied in any authoritative way, is sufficient to raise a presumption of their truth.'—<St. Joseph Daily West.[>]

"'Jordan is a hard road to travel.' Were Mr. BATES to 'define his position,' would it not be universally regarded as a 'bid for office['] ; and yet if he prefers not to obtrude his opinions upon the public on the eve of a Presidential election, until he is in some authoritative way asked for them, his dignified silence is misconstrued to his disadvantage by parties on both sides of Mason and Dixon's line.

"Fortunately, Mr. BATES has been the leading man in Missouri for a great many years past, and his stable, old-fashioned, conservative principles are too well known in every precinct and hamlet in the State to admit of the slightest doubt. For him to attempt to explain, qualify, or negative all that is said and written about him, would absorb his whole time, and would require him to abandon professional engagements, on which he is dependent for the support of himself and family. Such a course has never been demanded, even of avowed Presidential candidates, and certainly ought not to be required of a private though eminent gentleman, whose life-long liberality has left him dependent on his personal exertions for support, and who is quietly pursuing the 'even tenor of his way,' amid all the 'noise and confusion' now making in the political world.

"The ultra Republican journals, (for instance, The New York *Courier & Enquirer*, advocate of Senator SEWARD,) oppose Mr. BATES on the ground that he was opposed to FREMONT, the Republican nominee in 1856. and threw all his influence in favor of MILLARD FILLMORE. It is not likely that the Whigs and Americans of Missouri Will find cause of objection to Mr. BATES in this fact.

"If Mr. BATES should ever be a candidate for the Presidency, it will be time enough to know whether he has made any radical changes in his political faith. As he is not given to vascillation[sic], and has never been known as a warm-hearted, faithful and Union-loving man, his friends and supporters in the country would know, without the help of a pre-arranged catechism, that he would make a safe and acceptable President, both for the North and the South."

Nov 2d. Wednesday. Some months ago Dr. Oliphant introduced me to his father-in law, Mr. *Harding* of Hingham, Massts. at the special request of Mr. H.[arding] who, it seems, was very desirous "to shake hands with me." The old gentleman was very deaf and we could not converse—To day the Dr. introduced, on the street, young Mr. H.[arding] the son, who is here on a visit with his bride.

A few days ago, I casually met Mr. F. P. Blair in the street in
company with *Mr. Burlinghame* [25] of Massts. and his friend Capt
Goliver. Mr. Blair promised to bring them to my house to spend
an evening, but failed. To day, hearing, from Mr. Chester Harding,
that Messrs. B[urlingame] and G.[oliver] were about to start for
the East this afternoon, I called at the Planters' House and left my
card, they being out.

They called on me, and I had a short talk with Mr. B[urlingame].
He seemed warm and zealous for me—He said *we* (meaning the
Rep[ublican]s: of N.[ew] E.[ngland]) adopt fully the policy of
Colfax [26]—we are not for running an ultra man. He says that
Banks [27] is for me *first*, and that *Dana* [28] of the Tribune, is warmly
my friend.

His time was so short that we had little opportunity to inter-
change opinions and explanations—He read my *last* letter to Colfax
and declared it quite sufficient for him. [29]

Note. A few days ago, R. M. Field introduced his friend *Judge
Saml. Miller* of Rochester N. Y.

And Mr. Sam Knox [30] introduced his friend Mr. Kellog[g] [31] of
Pittsfield Mass:—late Speaker of the H[ouse] of R[epresentatives].

Last night Mr. McCune brot over (and sat an hour with me) his
two friends, Revd. Mr. Peabody, and Mr. *Sanbourn*, principal of
"The Mary Institute" (the Female branch of Washington
University[)].

Mr. S.[anbourn] is a New Hampshire man, and has served some
years in the Legislature there. Says in Politics, he is an Old
Webster Whig, and nothing else: that he has sometimes written for
the [   ] an old whig paper there—and is urged to do it
again—with an intimation that he intended to continue his writing,
as occasion may serve—

He expressed a strong wish to read some of my newspaper essays,
which he had heard of, and I promised to hunt up some for him—
Those about the Territories in particular—

I have recently received friendly letters from several editorial
gentlemen, whose caution, it seems to me is verging upon the extreme,
urging the impolicy of premature action, in bringing out candidates

[25] *Supra*, Oct. 28, 1859, note 21.
[26] See *supra*, April 27, 1859.
[27] *Supra*, July 27, 1859, note 57.
[28] *Supra*, July 27, 1859, note 51.
[29] See *supra*, June 16 and July 27, 1859.
[30] St. Louis Republican lawyer who later (1862) opposed Francis P. Blair, Jr. (*supra*,
April 27, 1859, note 25) for Congress, and, though Blair was declared elected, then
succeeded in getting Blair unseated and in securing his seat from June 10, 1864 to
March 3, 1865.
[31] Ensign H. Kellogg, lawyer and manufacturer, long a member and sometime speaker
of the lower house of the Legislature.

for the Presidency. Mr. Welling [32] of the Nat[iona]l. Intel[ligence]r. (an undoubted friend) and Mr. *James E. Harvey*, who, I suppose, is Editor of the "*North American* and U. S. Gazette" of Phila[delphia]. They both think it premature to have any state or local nomination of an *opposition* candidate, until the *Republican* party (the strongest element of opposition) has spoken.

I do not fully concur in that opinion. True, if the Republican party have the magnanimity to take a candidate outside of their own ranks, it is but simple justice to concede to them the free choice of the man; and every local nomination ought to be hypothetical only, and subject to the *Republican* right of choice. But time is short now, and it is very important, even now, before men are too deeply committed to other courses, to harmonize and unite all the elements of opposition, in the doubtful states like this, by ra[i]sing a standard around which all of them can rally, and thus give courage and confidence to the timid and the doubting.

" EDWARD BATES' VIEWS ON SLAVERY "

Nov: 8. Tuesday—The St Louis *Evening News* of this day, has a long Editorial, with the above heading.

After stating the impropriety of Mr. B[ates]'s volunteering his views unasked for, that he, as yet is no candidate, and that untill [*sic*] he is made such, his views on slavery will probably be no better known to the public than they are now—The News proceeds to state what it understands to be Mr. B[ates]'s views. In the main, the News is right, tho' some passages of the article, would need to be somewhat altered in phraseology, before I could give my full sanction.

I had not the slightest intimation of the article until I saw it in print.—

Nov 9. The Democrat of today copies the News' article, and calls it *authoritative*. In the afternoon Mr. Mitchell [33] (Editor of the News) called at my office to Explain, and said that he had gone to the Democrat office and informed them of their mistake—that he had no authority, and had not spoken to me on the subject of the article, and that I knew nothing about it <which is strictly true[.]> That he wrote the article upon his general knowledge of my public course and expressed opinions.

The News, no doubt, would be glad to get the reputation abroad of being *my organ*, or at least of being on confidential terms with me. That reputation would give it a currency which it cannot get by its

---

[32] *Supra*, June 20, 1859, note 3.

[33] A. S. Mitchell, editor of the *St. Louis Evening News*, a conservative unionist. In 1861 he went to New York to become one of the editors of the *Times*.

own force. But Mr. Mitchell, with all his zeal and good feelings, has not the discretion to entitle him to implicit trust.

Nov 9. The Revd. Mr. Peabody called at my office and introduced his friend *George G. Fogg* [34] Editor of the *Independent Democrat*, Concord. N.[ew] H[ampshire].

Had a short conversation. Mr. F.[ogg] tho' editing the Democrat, seems very decided against the Democracy, and especially *Mr. Pierce*, against whom, no doubt, his feelings are sharpened by local controversy.

Mr. F.[ogg] is a young looking man, but probably older than he looks, for Mr. P.[eabody] tells me that he was active and strong in putting down Isaac Hill,[35] many years ago.

Speaking of Mr. Pierce—I see that his name is not unfrequently mentioned of late, as a possible candidate for the Presidency, before the Democratic Convention. His local, home paper disclaims it flatly, but that is a small sign. And I notice that *Roger A. Pryor*,[36] lately elected to Congress from Va., to fill the vacancy of Wm. O. Goode [37] dec[ease]d., declares Mr. Pierce his *first* choice, *confessing* that, in a certain contingency, he would go for Mr. Douglas.

This Mr. Pryor is the same who, sometime, edited the Richmond "*South*," and, when Douglas opposed the administration on the Lecompton question denounced him as an inbred vulgarian, who had gotten a little outside polish, by being allowed for a time, to associate with Southern gentlemen—But, a short time after, edited the *Douglas organ* at Washington, "The States[.]" [38]

<*Nov 21.* It is intimated now, that, in divers quarters, feelers are thrown out, to ascertain the possibility of setting up Mr. Buchanan for a second term! Verily, the party is at a low ebb when it is driven to that extremity.>

Nov 11. Friday Night. . . .

This day was appointed for the Execution of Jos: W. Thornton, the murderer of Joseph Charless. There was a considerable crowd in the street near the jail, and I saw some men on house tops, as if to look over in the yard. I suppose he was hanged, having heard nothing to the contrary.

[34] A Free-Soil and Republican leader in New Hampshire who supported Lincoln in the Convention of 1860 and, as a reward, was made minister to Switzerland. 1861–1865. His *Independent Democrat* was one of the most influential papers in New Hampshire.

[35] Editor of the (Concord) *New Hampshire Patriot*, 1808–1829. 1840–1847; state legislator, 1820–1822, 1826, 1827; second comptroller of the U. S. Treasury, 1829–1830, until rejected by the Senate; Democratic U. S. senator, 1831–1836; governor, 1836–1839; U. S. subtreasurer at Boston, 1840–1841.

[36] An extreme states' rights Virginian; agitator for secession; Democratic congressman from 1859 until Virginia seceded; brigadier-general in the Confederate Army.

[37] State legislator, intermittently from 1822 to 1852; member of the Virginia Constitutional Convention, 1829, 1830; Democratic congressman, 1841–1843, 1853–1859.

[38] Published in Washington; after November 9, called the *States and Union*.

Note. A short time ago, John C. Hamilton [39] of N. Y. sent me a copy of Mr. Binney's late work [40] upon the question of the authorship of Washington's Farewell Address, and tod[a]y I received a letter from him (dated Nov 7) commending the work of Mr. Binney, as a masterly criticism, containing *all* that Washington's friends could desire, and *almost all* that he (Mr. H.[amilton]) could desire for his father's fame.

He speaks of Binney, Pettigru [41] (of Charleston) and me, as men of *central* minds (?)—Says that Mr. Pettigru will prepare a notice of the work for newspaper publication in the *South*, and requests me to do it in the *West*.

I am inclined to comply with his request, but have not yet had time to peruse Mr. Binney's work. I learn (from newspaper notices) that the able and judicious criticism of Mr. Binney has settled the the [sic] controversy, well and honorably to all parties.

Mr. Hamilton, I think, had been hars[h]ly dealt by, on account of his claiming, in his " Life of Hamilton," the authorship, for his father.

I am glad, especially on account of the wounded feelings of Mr. Hamilton, that the question is now settled to the satisfaction of all.

I will write to Mr. H.[amilton] in a few days.

Nov: 12. Saturday. . . .

The Nat[iona]l. Intelligencer of the 10th. contains some curious particulars of the " Trial of the Harper's Ferry Insurrectionists[.] "

On the 7th. Nov: (Capt: Cook [42] being lately arrested and brot in since the discharge of the Grand Jury which indicted the other prisoners) " the. G.[rand] Jury was sworn and immediately proceeded to their room, to consider of the case of Captain Cook." And, in *about two hours* presented a bill agst Cook—

" On the [re]assembling of the Court *in the afternoon*," *C. B. Harding pros[ecutin]g. att[orne]y:* [43] stated that [as] there were

---

[39] Fourth son of Alexander Hamilton. He wrote a *Life* of his father, and edited his writings.

[40] *An Inquiry into the Formation of Washington's Farewell Address.* Horace Binney was a Philadelphia lawyer of national reputation who at this time had retired to write and correspond prodigiously.

[41] James L. Petigru had seldom held public office because his views were not popular in South Carolina, but he was the recognized head of the bar and was given the task of codifying the laws of the State. He had been a leading opponent of nullification in Jackson's day and now, though an old man, vigorously attacked secession and was one of the leading unionists of the South.

[42] John E. Cook, a young lawyer from Connecticut, brother-in-law of Governor A. P. Willard of Indiana, had been a leader in the radical Free-State Party in Kansas. He joined the Brown conspirators at Topeka in November, 1857, spent the winter of 1857–1858 drilling with others of Brown's friends at Springdale, Iowa, and was one of the leaders at Harper's Ferry.

[43] Harding, being regular prosecuting attorney, was junior counsel for the State in these cases.

a number of witness[es] in the case of Cook who would not be in the case of Stevens [44]—he would, if agreeable to counsel on the other side, move to take up the case of Cook first.[45]

Thos. C. Green [46] (Cook's counsel) objected—he had not yet even read the Indictment &c[.]

The Court then proceeded with the case of A. D. Stevens (who was brought in and laid on a mattress, ([*sic*] being greatly emaciated by his wounds)[.]

"After a considerable number of the Jury men had been obtained, Mr. Hunter [47] [a]rose and stated that he had just received a despatch which would probably dispense [interfere] with the further proceedings in [the] empanelling [of] a jury[.] He then read the following telegraphic despatch from Gov Wise—To And: Hunter.

["]Richmond[,] Nov[.] 7, 1859.

["]Dear Sir:

["]I think you had better try Cook, and *hand Stevens over* to the Federal authorities[.]

Respectfully[,]

H[.] A. Wise [48]

["]Mr. Hunter stated that he had been in correspondence several days with Gov Wise, and had in his possession a number of facts [important to the development of this case] which were unknown to the public, and would[,] for the present, remain so. He had[,] since his last letter to the Governor, come into the possession of other facts[,] which pointed to Stevens as the *most available* party to be *handed over* to the Federal authority, as he felt assured that enough *would be ascertained* to result in bringing before the Federal bar, *a number* of the *prominent Abolition Fanatics* of [in] the *North*."

"Mr. Harding<the regular prosecuting att.y.>objected to the proceedings and insisted that the case should be proceeded with. *He was not in league with Gov*[ernor]*: Wise* or any body else. *He was not feed* by any one "&c[.]

" Mr. Sennott [49] <Stevens' counsel> remarked that he had not consulted with his client, and[,] as the jury had partly been chosen, he

---

[44] Aaron D. Stevens, a veteran Free-State fighter in Kansas under the name of " Colonel Whipple," had joined Brown's forces at Topeka in 1857 and had been drill-master of the group at Springdale, Iowa, during the winter of 1857–1858.

[45] The quotation ends here. Throughout these pages, the quotations are inaccurate. Where possible, variations from the original have been indicated. The italics throughout are Mr. Bates's, not the *National Intelligencer's.*

[46] Ex-mayor of Charlestown, assigned by the Court as counsel for all of the prisoners. Brown later released him when his own counsel arrived.

[47] Andrew Hunter, lawyer of Charlestown, Virginia, appointed by Governor Wise as chief prosecutor of John Brown and his fellow-conspirators.

[48] *Supra,* April 28, 1859, note 38.

[49] George Sennott, a young Democratic lawyer of Boston who volunteered his services as defense counsel.

wd. not consent that the State should *hand over* the prisoner[s] to the Government, for what purpose was known to Gov[ernor]: Wise, and had been foreshadowed by the remarks of Mr. Hunter. If time had been allowed him, the trouble had in the empanelling of the [a] jury wd. have been dispensed with."

"Mr. Hunter remarked that he wd. then proceed immediately with the case of Stevens, and *hand over* [hand the prisoner,] Harrison who was [has] not yet [been] indicted[,] [to the Federal Court.]— It was immaterial to him whether *Stevens would prefer a trial or not*.["]

Mr. Sennott asked a moment's delay, and after a conference, announced that Stevens " accepted the offer of th[e] State, to *hand him over* to to [*sic*] the Federal authorities["]—and he was *handed over* to the Marshal<who, I suppose *just happened* to be there[.]>

Mr. Harding (the prosecuting att.y.) "desired the clerk to enter his earnest protest against the whole proceedings. He considered the proceedings wrong[,] and wished it so shown on the docket[.]"

Judge Parker[50] to the Clerk—"*Do no such thing. I* wish no *such protest* entered on the docket of this Court."

The prisoner was *handed over* and the Jury discharged.

Cook, being indicted on the 7th. was put upon trial in the morning of the 8th.—

He made "a full confession, [. . .] relating *every thing* connected with the insurrection," which Mr. Hunter, in open Court, read to the Jury.

And yet the paper says—" He seems to be in fine spirits, and is not without hope of a verdict in his favor." How so, after a *full confession?* Is it because he is attended by his two b[r]others in law, Gov. Willard[51] and Mr. Crowley?

We'll see to what good uses Democratic policy can turn the Insurrection; and Cook's case may serve as a key to unlock the mystery. If the others (who, *Mr. Hunter* thinks, are connected in some way, with " prominent abolition fanatics of the *North* ") be all condemned, and Cook be allowed to escape, by acquittal, pardon or commutation, people will be apt to conclude that it is a convenient and safe thing, even for traitors and murderers and negro-insurrectionists to be near of kin to a *Democratic* Governor in the *West*[.]

Note.[52] Cook was hanged on the 16th. Nov: but was very near escaping the [noose] over night—He and Coppie[53] got out of the

---

[50] Richard Parker of Winchester, Virginia : Democratic congressman, 1849–1851 ; judge of the Circuit Court, 1851–1869. He apparently tried to conduct a fair trial and did show calmness in time of excitement.

[51] Ashbel P. Willard, brother-in-law of Capt. Cook and Democratic governor of Indiana, 1857–1860.

[52] Inserted later.

[53] Edwin Coppoc, a Quaker of Springdale, Iowa, had joined the John Brown band during the winter of 1857–1858 while they were drilling in Springdale.

jail, by picking a hole thro' the wall, and were not discovered until they had mounted [the] *yard* wall and were ready to jump down outside, when a sentinel outside saw Cook and fired upon him[.]

[*A newspaper article headed " Republicanism of Jefferson " gives extracts from letters of Jefferson to Robert R. Livingston, December 14, 1800, Jefferson to William Short, October 3, 1806, [1801?] and Jefferson to John Dickinson, December 19, 1801, with the comment:*

"What Mr, [*sic*] Jefferson says above of Federalism '*retiring into the judiciary as its stronghold*,' and '*from that battery beating down all the works of Republicanism*,' could not more forcibly describe the present position and aims of modern Democracy, which relies wholly on the Judiciary to uphold all its flagrant usurpations, and all its outrages upon the interests of free labor and free institutions."]

I suppose these letters may be found now in Jefferson's (posthumous) Published Works.[54]

I never agreed with Mr. Jefferson and the pretended Democrats who claim to be his desciples [*sic*], in their fear and jealousy of the judiciary. Perhaps they had a keener insight than I have, into the *political* tendencies of the Courts. In fact I am, by education and long habit, a "court man." I have a great respect and reverence for the bench, but always on the assumption that the men who occupy the bench are *Judges* and not party *Politicians*—That they are fully impressed with the sacred character of their functions, and anxious to discharge their whole duty by *adjudging and determining* the *causes brought before them;* and never make a pretext of the *cause* to go beyond the record and soil their ermine by trying to settle political questions between rival parties.

See forward Nov 26[.] [55]

When they thus tarnish their character and pervert their functions, they deserve all the censures with which Jefferson could visit them.

So also, I respect the Clergy and venerate their sacred functions. But when they turn politicians, and preach partyism in the pulpit, I denounce them more than I would other men, in proportion as their calling is higher and their conduct ought to be purer.

In Jefferson's time, it was suspected that the Court leaned to the Federalists, and *therefore* it was condemned: Now, it is seen that the Court leans to the Southern Democracy, and *therefore* it is praised.

Both were wrong—It was not censured *then* because it decided *wrong*, nor praised now because it decides *right*. But both censured and praised alternately, for its supposed *party bias.*

---

[54] They are found in the *Writings of Thomas Jefferson* (H. A. Washington. ed., 1854), IV. 337 ; IV. 413 ; IV. 424.

[55] Added in the margin.

Nov 17. 1859. [A clipping from the Missouri Republican *of November 17, 1859, which quotes from the* Washington State's *praise of Hon. James A. Pearce* [56] *who, because of "the recent glorious victory of the Democrats in Maryland," was sure of reëlection to the United States Senate.* [57]*]*

The "*States*" Mr. Douglas' organ, is so eager to win adherents in all quarters, that it over steps the bounds of modesty and prudence, in making its meretricious advances to all available politicians whose old party connexions have become, by any cause, relaxed.

In Fillmore's time, Mr. Pearce was a good Whig and a very respectable Senator. But, like many other pretty good men, he lacked the courage to stand up for the right, against a truculent ruling party. He *caved* [*sic*] in Pierce's time, and, as I think against his judgment and conscience, supported the Kansas-Nebraska bill, that fruitful source of all the evils that have followed, from the various misgovernment of Kansas down to Brown's rebellion.

I think Mr. P[earce]'s conscience hurt him for deserting the Whig cause, but it was not quite enough hardened to let him openly become a "*democrat*"[.]

Perhaps now, the flattery of the Douglas Democracy may win him over entirely, especially if they can give him a quid pro quo, in the shape of a seat in the Senate. In 1856, he denied being a Democrat, and refused, when urgently invited, to take part in a Democratic meeting—His neighbor, Judge Chambers,[58] told me so, at the Baltimore Whig convention—But times change &c[.]

[Another clipping from the Missouri Republican *of November 17, quotes from the* Richmond Enquirer *a truculent article—probably an editorial—about the State's putting its house in order and bringing to justice offenders of every social grade, especially those Northern men who, it claimed, were the instigators of the John Brown raid.* [59]*]*

When Va. finds occasion, under the Constitution, to demand from any other State, the surrender of a *fugitive* from her justice, I cannot, for the life of me, understand what *the South* has to do with it. The Enquirer has become very Democratic: In his opinion, the demand and refusal of a fugitive from Justice is no longer a question of *law,* for the consideration of the Tribunals, judicial and executive,

[56] Whig congressman, 1835–1839, 1841–1843; U. S. senator, 1843–1862. He remained a Whig as long as possible, but in 1860 was reëlected to the Senate as a Democrat.

[57] For the original article see the Washington *States and Union,* Nov. 12, 1859. The name of this was changed with the issue of November 9 from the *States* to the *States and Union.*

[58] Ezekiel F. Chambers: Whig U. S. senator, 1826–1834; judge of the Court of Appeals, 1834–1851; a strong states' rights leader who sympathized with the secessionists but urged caution and compromise upon Marylanders.

[59] " To a ' Small Slaveholder,' " *Richmond Enquirer,* Nov. 8, 1859.

of the particular states concerned, but a question of *politics*, " for the *People* of Virginia and the *South* to consider."

" The Executive of Virginia *will vindicate her honor* "—Of course, or it is a poor shabby Executive.

But, it seems that the *Southern* States (not the *other* States, nor the *neighboring* States, but *the* Southern states, all of them) are expected to rally to Va. " when she orders her house to be set in order." Poor Old Virginia! She can no longer set her own house in order—The *Southern States* must do it for her!

" How are the mighty fallen! " When I was a Virginian we all thought that the noble old Commonwealth was quite able to order her own affairs, without asking the protection of Missouri and Arkansas and Florida!

" But the end is not yet." Why, what remains to be done but to hang the convicts? Does Gov: Wise's organ want to offset the treason of Brown and Cook by another treason of its own? Does Gov Wise want his rival, Mr. Seward, convicted of treason, and hanged out of the way? And if that cannot be, does he want to make his own meditated treason *safe*, by rallying the *Southern* States to his protection?

The Mo. Rep[ublican] of Nov 17. Extracts two pretty long leaders from the " *New York Commercial* " and the " *New York Evening Post* "[60]—the former headed " Mr. Bates speaking by Proxy " and the latter "A Southern Statesman on Slavery."

Both the papers are Republican, and both the articles are commendatory—They will work favorably in the North, perhaps injuriously, to some extent, in the South.

They were written in consequence of the late article in the Evening News professing to define my principles and views upon slavery, and they assume (erroneously) that I wrote, substantially at least, if not literally, the News' article.[61] They evidently do not intend that attribution as a censure, because they speak of the article as able, terse and brave.

[*A clipping from the* Missouri Democrat, *of November 17, 1859, headed "MR. BATES AND THE REPUBLICAN" tells of the Republican's assertion that Mr. Bates did not authorize the statement of his political opinion published originally in the* Evening News.[62] *The* Democrat *announces that the* Republican *is not in Mr. Bates's confidence, and therefore cannot know anything about his political opinions, quotes the assertion of the* News *that its summary*

---

[60] Nov. 12, 1859.
[61] See *supra*, Nov. 8, 1859.
[62] Nov. 8, 1859.

was based solely on Mr. Bates's public record and private conversations, and then adds:

> "As far as we are concerned in this matter, *we state by authority and as an absolute fact, that Mr. Bates does endorse every word and sentiment contained in that statement.*"]

Every body seems disposed to speak in emphatic and extreme language.

Now it is true the News' article is, in substance and effect, a true expression of my views, but not in *every word and sentiment*, as the Democrat says. And this much I have said, to all who talked to me on the subject—i. a. Mr. Blair.[63] And that I suppose is what is meant by "we state by authority" for I have given *authority* in no other way. I have always thought and often said that slavery is an evil, social, moral and political, but I have never said that it was inconsistent with Christianity.

Nov. 21. Monday. . . .

Our friend Lieut: J. E. B. Stuart,[64] with his wife, child and 2 servants (free negro women) have [*sic*] been with us for several days—On return to Mr. S[tuart]'s post, Fort Reilly,[64a] after leave of absence for some months. My young friend is prosperous. Besides a very good professional standing, he has lately invented a "Sabre attatchment [*sic*]" to fasten the sabre to the belt and detach it with ease and speed. The Govt., he tells me has paid him $5000 for the use of his patent—

He tells me a good deal about "Old Brown." He was at his capture—and has his dirk.

" The Evening News'["] article—E Bates and slavery [65]—

Papers and letters come thronging in upon me from all quarters N.[orth] and E[ast]—as far south as Baltimore, highly approving &—

Among others—The *Baltimore Patriot*—The (Phila.[delphia]) *North American and U. S. Gazette* [66]—the N. Y. Times [67] and the Tribune [68]—and sundry papers in the states of Ohio, Inda. and Ills:—Also, the Springfield (Mass:) Rep[ublica]n. and the N. Y. Century.[69]

---

[63] Francis P. Blair, Jr. ; *supra*, April 27, 1859, note 25.

[64] *Supra*, April 21, 1859, note 20.

[64a] See *supra*, April 21, 1859.

[65] See *supra*, Nov. 8, 1859.

[66] "Mr. Bates' Views of Slavery," *Philadelphia North American and United States Gazette*, Nov. 12, 1859.

[67] "The Presidential Question," *New York Times*, Nov. 14, 1859.

[68] "Edward Bates," *New York Daily Tribune*, Nov. 14, 1859.

[69] A weekly published in New York from Nov. 19, 1859 to May 4, 1861. This number referred to by Mr. Bates was the very first issue, dated November 19.

And private letters from various gentlemen e. g. Genl. Paxton of Pa. Mr. Randall of Worcester Massts., Mrs. Slade of Ohio—Mr. Hanna [70] of Inda.—&c[.]

These all are very flattering to my vanity; and lead me to believe that (without some great change before next spring) my nomination for the presidency, is more probable than that of any other man. But I will not set my heart upon it, so as to be painfully disappointed in case of failure. If I fail of the nomination, I cannot but be cheered with the knowledge that I have already been more honored than any other mere private man.

A new war with Mexico! The Mo. Repub:[lican] of to day contains a message from Washington stating that in consequence of brigand *Cartevens'* massacre and burning at Brownsvill[e], Texas, many troops have been ordered thither, and that the *Government has resolved* to take possession of *the Northern States of Mexico*!!

The Government has resolved—not to chastise the bandits, but to *take possession* of States—how many not said[.]

N. B. Next day comes the news that Brownsville is *not* sacked— The people's throats are *not* cut, and so, the President has countermanded the order for the march of troops! They cannot quite make a case of it, to electioneer upon, and therefore, they must still stick to Brown's rebellion, untill [*sic*] some more popular project can be started.

GASTON of *N.*[*orth*] *C*[*arolina*]. *His opinion on Slavery.*

The *Century* (Weekly of Nov: 19. 1859.) contains an elaborate article, signed S. W, in answer to a previous article in the same paper, signed "*Provincialist*[.] "

In the course of his article S. W. quotes a passage from an address of Judge Gaston [71] to the Students of the university (having already quoted freely from *Jefferson's* Notes on Va.) as follows—

"On you[,] too[,] will devolve the duty which has been too long neglected[, . . .] of exterpating [*sic*] [providing for . . . the ultimate extirpation of] the worst evil that afflicts the southern part of our confederacy. Full well do you know to what I refer;[,] for on this subject there is[,] with [all of] us[,] a morbid sensitiveness

---

[70] Robert Hanna of Indianapolis: member of the Indiana Constitutional Convention in 1816; registrar of the land office, 1820–1830; Whig U. S. senator, 1831–1832; state legislator, 1832, 1833, 1836–1839, 1842–1846.

[71] William Gaston: outstanding liberal; great orator; chief justice of the North Carolina Supreme Court; worker for religious liberty; opponent of slavery whose cruelties his decisions did much to mitigate. This particular address was published as *Mr. Gaston's Address Delivered before the Philanthropic and Dialectic Societies at Chapel-Hill, on the 20th of June, 1832.* Mr. Bates's quotation from it is not very accurate.

which gives warning of even [even of] an approach to it. Disguise
the truth as we may, and throw the blame where we will, it is slavery
which[,] more than any other cause, keeps us back in the career
of improvement. It stifles industry and represses enterprise;[——]
it is fatal to economy and providence;[——] it discourages skill,
[——] impairs our strength as a community, and poisons morals at
the fountain head."

November 23. [A clipping from the Lexington Express *gives a
list of delegates from Lafayette County to the Jefferson City Convention to be held December 28, 1859. It urges a full meeting so
that Loco-focoism [72] may be utterly crushed in Missouri.]*

[A clipping from the St. Louis News *of November 23, 1859, reports
the action of the Grand Jury at Norfolk, Virginia, which had found a
true bill on an indictment against one S. Danenburg, a merchant of
the city, for seditious language, because he declared that John
Brown was a good man, fighting in a good cause, and that owners
had no right of property in their slaves.]*

We are informed in holy writ, that men must answer *for every
idle word they speak.* But I had thought that the good old Commonwealth had such a holy horror of *Adams'* sedition laws, that
in its statute book there could hardly be found a law to warrant
the solemn indictment of a man for such silly talk. But I see
now plainer than ever, that the Slave states live in constant dread;
and fear will make wise men foolish, and kind men cruel.

[A clipping from the Evening News *of November 23, which gives
an account of the interview between Governor Wise and John Brown
and his companions at Charlestown, Virginia, and tells of the offer
of South Carolina to send military aid to Virginia to keep order
on the day of execution.]*

Gov Wise [73] is still bent on making the most of Brown and his
rebellion, in the way of politics. For there does not seem to be
any thing in the law or the justice of the case, to require *the Governor* to go several hundred miles, from Richmond to Charlestown,
to talk with the condemned and tell them how certainly he will hang
them all! Wise Governor! And as brave as WISE!

But poor old Virginia needs no longer fear old Brown and his
sons. The great and gallant South Carolina will protect her!
"Any amount" of military aid is ready for her defence! By the

---

[72] Originally the equal rights doctrines of a radical wing of the New York Democrats
who were especially opposed to monopolies. The term was used at this time to indicate
a general tendency to radicalism within the Democratic Party.
[73] *Supra*, April 28, 1859, note 38.

way, I did not know before, that the Gov of S.[outh] C.[arolina] had the right to raise troops at his discretion and send them where he pleased.

I'm glad however that the Va. Governor declines the offer, for I have no doubt that if needed at the hanging, he could get Prest: Buchanan to send him another dozen marines![74]

Can it be true that Virginia is sunk so low that she cannot, in peace and safety, hang 3 or 4 convicted felons, without the aid of foreign troops—domestic either!

These politicians I fear, are running their political tricks into contemptible weakness.

Thursday. Nov 24—It rained all day, and I staid at home[.]

[*A clipping announcing that the Republicans were not completely victorious in the New York state elections, but that Democrats were chosen for three offices through the support of the Americans, who held the balance of power.*]

It would seem from this, that the Americans[75] hold the balance of power.

If that be true then the Republicans of N. Y. will not nominate Mr. Seward,[76] for the Americans will never be brought to his support. And then Mr. S[eward]'s friends will take care that no other man within that party shall be nominated. They may admit that *their party* is not strong enough to carry the day, but will never submit to have their leader made secondary *within* the party.

Note.[77] The National Intelligencer of Nov: 29th. contains an admirable sermon,[78] delivered, on the 24th. Nov: in Trinity Church, Washing[ton] City, by the Revd. C. M. Butler.[79] D. D. Rec[t]or of that Church—Text. "What nation is there that hath statutes and judgments so righteous as all this law?" Deut:4.8.

<Sunday. Dec: 4. Detained at home by bad roads and weather, caused this sermon to be read in the family—read by Dick—>

---

[74] Buchanan had sent a company of marines under Colonel Robert E. Lee to help suppress the insurrection. At the execution, 1500 Virginia troops stood guard to prevent a rescue.

[75] The American Party or Know-Nothings.

[76] See *supra*, April 27 and Aug. 19, 1859.

[77] Added later.

[78] The sermon appeared in the issue of November 28, not that of November 29.

[79] Clement M. Butler, Episcopal clergyman, was rector of Trinity Church, Washington, D. C., from 1849 until 1861.

Thanksgiving Day.

["A REMONSTRANCF [sic]—By D. Dun Brown.

"Respectfully addressed to his Excellency, Gov. Bob (Robt. M.) Stewart.

<*"* For the Missouri Democrat.>

"Dear Governor Bob! though, by pardons, you rob
　　Our State and State's Prison, of much service due,
Is that any reason, this 'Thanksgiving' season,
　　You should rob *us and cheat us* of Holidays, too?

"What! *you*—a live Yankee!—not to let us say 'Thankee,'
　　One day in the year, o'er our turkies and pies—
Not to speak of the *drinking!*—Why, of what are you thinking,
　　Our Gov'nor—*not* WISE, but quite *other*-wise!

"Well! allow me to say, there will yet come a day
　　Of THANKSGIVING, *you'll* neither 'appoint' nor 'confirm'—
When all o'er the State, *sober* people elate,
　　Will join in 'Thank God!'—THE LAST DAY OF YOUR TERM!"]

The Governors of most of the States (26) had appointed *Nov: 24*
as a day of thanksgiving and prayer. Govr. Stewart[80] of Mo.
declined to appoint a day! Cause not know[n]. And the Mo.
Rep:[ublican] thinks it perfectly right to refuse to thank God on
the day appointed in most of the "Abolition States" !! [81]

　　　　"If there was nothing to forbid it,
　　　　'Tis impious because they did it."

Why not have another sundy. and another Gospel?
English views of the Harpers [sic] Ferry affair.
[*Reprints of a long article from the* London Times, *of November
5, 1859, and of a shorter article from the* London News, *November
2, 1859, discussing the events at Harper's Ferry.*]
　　The extreme sensitiveness of the Slaveholding States and the
passionate hurry and trepidation in which they act in regard to
the negro question, in all its forms, are unhappy proofs of their
consciousness of continued danger. Fear is a mean passion in itself,
and produces a brood of other mean passions—suspicion, revenge,
cruelty. A man always under the influence of fear, can hardly rise
to the dignity of justice, or yield to the force of truth. "The first
law of Nature"—the *higher law* of self-preservation—is always

---

[80] Robert M. Stewart, a pro-slavery Democrat, for many years state senator, had
defeated James S. Rollins, the Whig candidate, in 1857 by 47,975 to 47,641 votes. As
governor from 1857 to 1861, he fought the anti-slavery movement, but he supported the
Union when war came.
　[81] "Thanksgiving," *Missouri Republican*, Nov. 22, 1859.

present to his mind and exciting his baser passions, to guard against
the dreaded danger by all the means in his power, whether wise
or foolish, just or unjust, humane or cruel.

This state of feeling is perhaps, natural to all communities in which
slavery largely abounds; and that perhaps is the strongest argument
against the existence of slavery at all.

A government whose fundamental principle is the legal equality
of all its citizens, ought to confine itself to regions where the *citizens*
can do all the labors of life, and ought not to accept as a gift,
any country whose productive labor must, of necessity, be done by
slaves.

Buchanan The Constitution.

Nov 26. The Nat[iona]l. Intel[ligence]r. of Nov 22, contains a
Powerful Leader, headed " *Questions and Answers.*" in reply to the
" *Constitution.*" [82] It is full of politico-historical references, on the
negro question—The Territories—The Dred Scott case—Douglas—
Black [83]—Brown [84] of Missi.—Reverdy Johnson [85]—and especially
Prest: Buchanan. As to reverential submission to the *political* de-
cisions of the Supreme Court, by the other Departments of the
Government, a citation is made of a very pointed speech of *Senator*
Buchanan, in the 27th. Congress, in debate on the Bill to incorpo-
rate a Banke [*sic*] of the U. S. wherein he declared that he " would
never consent to place the liberties of the people in the hands of
any [86] judicial tribunal " and that the S.[upreme] C.[ourt] (during
Marshall's time) " had inclined towards the highest assertion of
Federal Power."

<Citing Ap[pen]d[i]x. to Cong[ressiona]l. Globe, 1. Sess: of 27
Cong: p 161.>

see back to Nov 12

Again, to shew that Mr. Buchanan was the persistent supporter
of the Mo. Compromise, and for extending it to the Pacific, citing
his letter to Mr. Yanc[e]y [87] of date May 18. 1848. Wherein he

---

[82] " The National Intelligencer and Senator Brown," Washington *Constitution*, Nov.
19, 1859.

[83] *Supra*, Oct. 28, 1859, note 22.

[84] Albert G. Brown, Democratic governor of Mississippi, 1844–1848; congressman,
1839–1841, 1847–1853; U. S. senator, 1854–1861; Confederate senator, 1862–1865. He
had supported the Mexican War, but had opposed the Wilmot Proviso, the Compromise
of 1850 and the Topeka Constitution for Kansas. In 1860 he was talked of for the
Democratic nomination for President. In November, 1860, he opposed calling a secession
convention in Mississippi but supported secession when the convention met.

[85] One of the great lawyers of the nation; Whig U. S. senator from Maryland, 1845–
1849; attorney-general in Taylor's Cabinet, 1849–1850; Democratic senator, 1863–1868;
minister to Great Britain, 1868–1869; a great moderate; staunch unionist who opposed
secession and took active part in the Washington Peace Convention of 1861; supporter
of the Government but opponent of its arbitrary measures during the War. He voted
for the Thirteenth Amendment, but supported Johnson after the War.

[86] The italics are Mr. Bates's.

[87] *Infra*, Nov. 29, 1859, note 94.

declares it " the best if not the only mode of finally and satisfactorily adjusting this vexed and dangerous question."—and adds that " he could not abandon the position which he had thus *deliberately and conscientiously taken*, and assume *any other* that *could be* presented." [88]

<*Note*. Mr. Buchanan also wrote a letter of the same sort, to Senator Slidell,[89] tho' I cant [*sic*] now remember the date—E. B.>

It is amazing to see, in what rapid succession, the Democracy and it's *great* leaders take first one and then the other side, always enforcing their fickle opinions with intolerant violence, and claiming for *both sides* in succession, that no man can deny their " great principle " without being either a traitor or a fool.

Nov: 29. [A clipping from the St. Louis News, *of November 9, 1859, headed "A Southern Ultraist." It quotes from a letter written by Ex-Governor Adams* [90] *of South Carolina declining an invitation to a dinner for Senator Chesnut.*[91] *Adams thinks " the leaders " are too much under the influence of " ' blandishments at Washington ' to be able to do justice to the South." He is distinctly in favor of a Southern Confederacy—" Why, then, waste our breath in deprecating the impracticability of a slave code, which nobody in the South wants or ever advocated? " The question of reopening the slave trade would " only distract those* who love the Union better than Slavery." " *The advocates of this measure," he says, " will promptly unite with its opponents whenever the latter say they are ready for dissolution."*]

This Gov: Adams, I think, is the same *National Democrat* and *lover of the Union*, who, when in office, two or three years ago, recommended to the Legislature to pass a law to exempt one or more negro[e]s for each owner from liability for debt! This was done for the avowed purpose of diffusing the slave interest more widely through the body of the people, so as to have as many as possible interested in *the institution*, when the question becomes (as it soon

---

[88] The italics this time are the *Intelligencer's* or Buchanan's, but are not accurately reproduced.

[89] John Slidell of Louisiana: Democratic congressman, 1843–1845; U. S. senator, 1853–1861; Confederate commissioner to England and France, 1861–1865, whose capture at sea created the "*Trent* Affair." He had been offered a cabinet position under Buchanan, and was a close adviser of the President, and a leader of the extreme states' rights and secessionist Democrats.

[90] James H. Adams, governor of South Carolina, 1855–1857: a leading advocate of nullification and states' rights in 1832, and as early as 1851, an advocate of secession. Toward the end of his governorship he had proposed a reopening of the African slave-trade. This and his extremism on secession cost him defeat for the U. S. Senate in 1858, but he played a leading rôle in the secession convention of 1860.

[91] James Chesnut: wealthy planter: Democratic U. S. senator, 1858–1860; General Beauregard's aide who conveyed to Major Anderson the evacuation order that began the Civil War; brigadier-general in the Confederate Army. In the Senate in 1859 he was making powerful speeches in support of slavery and was agitating secession.

will become) not a question *between States*—slave and free—but *within the States*, between slaveholders and non slave holders.

Gov Adams then foresaw that, ere long, it would come to that, and was trying, by that device, to interest a larger body of the people in slavery, and so make it popular. <[*Marginal Note.*] I notice lately, that in some parts of *Virginia*, attempts are making to accomplish the same end—Petitions are in circulation among the people, for a law to exempt one slave for every head of a family.> But this provision against the coming struggle *within* the State, is too slow to meet the exigency of the pending contest among the States, and so Gov Adams comes out openly for Dissolution! Evil times have come upon us too soon, when men of standing openly avow a meditated treason, for national destruction!

But the means by which the treason is to be made effectual, is as foolish as the end designed is wicked. A Southern confederation! A simple impossibility!—S. Carolina, to be sure, might afford to blow and bluster for a while, in her central security, if the frontier slave states, Maryland, Virginia Kentucky and Missouri, will agree to be her body guard. But the Mississippi Valley is one and indivisible. The lower states, if so foolishly inclined, would always stand at the mercy of the upper States whose people and whose commerce will command the natural passage to the ocean, as irresistably [*sic*] as their mighty waters do.[92] And all sensible men down south, know that as well as we do here. Such ranters as Adams and Shorter,[93] and Yanc[e]y [94] and Brown [95] and Davis,[96] may talk like Captain Bobadil,[97] but they will act like him too.

Nov 30. To night a meeting is to be held of *the Opposition* to appoint Delegates to the convention to be held at Jefferson City, on the 28. Decr. primarily to nominate State Officers, but (as I am given to understand) chiefly to nominate me for the Presidency.

Here in St Louis, I think there will be entire harmony and concert of action among all classes of the opposition—Whigs, Americans, Republicans. If the same harmony can be secured in the other counties, the State will be safe for the elections next year, both State and Federal.

The Republicans in Mo. will go with us frankly and in good faith. It is their obvious interest to do so, for it will greatly strengthen

---

[92] See *supra,* May 27, 1859.

[93] John G. Shorter: judge of the Circuit Court of Alabama, 1852–1861; Confederate congressman, 1861; governor, 1861–1863; an ardent secessionist even as early as 1859.

[94] William L. Yancey of Alabama: Democratic congressman, 1844–1846; Confederate commissioner to England in 1861; Confederate senator, 1862–1863; one of the earliest and most extreme of the secessionists. A year and a half before this the North had been aroused by the publication of his "Scarlet Letter" to James Slaughter which disclosed his efforts to organize resistence to Federal authority.

[95] Governor Joseph E. Brown of Georgia. *Infra,* Dec. 2, 1859, note 8.

[96] Senator Jefferson Davis.

[97] A military braggart of the first order in Ben Jonson's *Every Man in His Humour.*

them here at home, and ensure to them an influence in the national councils of their party greater than the influence of twice their number any where else.

Note.[98] The Republicans hold a separate convention at Jefferson, on the same 28th. of Decr., to appoint delegates to *their* National convention.

December 1. [*A clipping from the* Missouri Democrat *of December 1, 1859, telling of "The Opposition Convention" in St. Louis on November 30 to choose delegates to the Opposition Convention to be held on December 28, at Jefferson City. Edward Bates was put forward by this meeting as its candidate for the Presidency.*]

Dec. 1. Note.[99] The meeting was held, not very large but most respectable and influential in its composition and harmonious in action. I[t] appointed a numerous Delegation to the Jefferson City Convention, to be held on the 28th. And declared its preferance [*sic*] for me as *President.* Jas S. Rollins as Governor [1] and Dr. Morris [2] as Lieut: Governor[.]

December. 1. Wednesday....

Lavinia Meredith and Julia Coalter are here, these two days past, on a visit to our girls[.]

The Evening News' exposition of my views of Slavery [3] has a wonderful run. It is published every where as an "Important Political Document" and every where, in the free States, it is greeted with applause; and I have not seen it harshly spoken of any[where], though I do not get many Southern papers.

A great many papers are sent me from the free states with high compliments—To day I recd. two—The Berks and Schoulkill [*sic*] Journal of Reading Pa.—and the True Democrat, of Joliet Ills: Also, the *Delaware County Republican* of Chester, Pa. is personally complimentary, and likes all the article, except the part about the Fugitive Slave law—I had already recd. several of the more influential papers of Phil[adelph]a. N[ew] York and Boston, speaking of me in terms far beyond my merits.

I think now, that the probabilities of my nomination are strengthening every day. In the present state of public feeling, the Republican party (even if they desired it, which I think they do not) will hardly venture to nominate Mr. Seward.[4] And I have many

---

[98] Added later.
[99] Written into the margin with red ink.
[1] He ran for Congress instead, on the Bell-Everett ticket, and was elected, serving from 1861 to 1865. Rollins was originally a Whig. He was a slave-holder who opposed slavery in the Territories—a unionist who supported Lincoln and the War but opposed many of the *extreme* measures in prosecuting the War.
[2] State Senator Walter B. Morris.
[3] See *supra*, Nov. 8, 1859.
[4] See *supra*, April 27 and Aug. 19, 1859.

and strong assurances, that I stand second—first in the N.[orth] W.[est] and in some states in [the] N.[orth] E.[ast] and 2d. in N. Y. and Pa. In the latter (Pa.) Mr. Cameron,[5] for local reasons, stands first, but he has no strength elsewhere.

Decr. 2. . . .

The Principal Resolutions of the *Opposition* meeting held night before last (which were adopted *unanimously* by *Republicans, Americans Free Democrats* and *Whigs*) are the following—

1. "That the Honorable Edward Bates well deserves the reputation he enjoys for statesmanship patriotism and purity of life. That his stable and conservative character is the surest guaranty that, if elected President, his administration will restore tranquility to the Country, and economy, justice and dignity to the Government. And therefore, we nominate him for the Presidency and pledge him the enthusiastic support of the united opposition of this city and County."

2. "That while the elements of the opposition in this City and County may differ among themselves on some questions, yet we declare ourselves thoroughly united in uncompromising hostility to the corruption, extravagance and misrule of the so called National Democracy[.] That we will waive all differences of opinion existing amongst ourselves in the support of Edward Bates for the Presidency, in order to restore the Government to its primitive purity, and to obtain for the Great West its just influence in the National Councils."

3. "That the great and leading object of the Opposition of this City and County, at this time, is the expulsion of the National Democratic Party from the control of the Federal and State Governments, which they have prostituted to the basest ends, engendering sectionalism, debauching public virtue, and lavishing the public money for electioneering and partizan purposes."

[*Marginal Note.*] The meeting also passed resolutions recommending Mr. Rollins for Governor and Dr. Morris for Lieut Governor.[6] And appointed a numerous Delegation (de mediatate lingua) to attend the Jefferson convention.

[*Two clippings from the* Missouri Republican *of December 2, 1859, give:*

1. The Secession Resolutions passed by the Legislature of South Carolina, December 1, 1859.

2. A letter of Jno. J. Holliday protesting against having been named a delegate by the St. Louis Opposition meeting in which he says:

---

[5] *Infra,* March 5, 1861, note 29.
[6] *Supra,* Dec. 1, 1859, notes 1 and 2.

" I was originally an Old Line Whig, more recently a Native American,
but *never was, am not, and hope and believe I never will be*, a Black
Republican, or be caught affiliating with them in any way, manner or
shape. I wish it then to be distinctly understood that I am an Anti
Black Republican, now and for ever."]

I dont [*sic*] know this Mr. Holliday, but guess that he has not a
very definite idea of his own political status. He was once, it seems,
a *whig*, but that perhaps was so long ago that he has forgotten all
the good old principles of that party. He was "more recently" a
Native American; but does not inform us what he is now. He is
positive about one thing only—he will neve[r] be a Black Republican,
or be *caught* affiliating with them in *any way, manner* or *shape*. No
matter how they may moderate their tone; no matter what good
measures or good men they may support, nor what bad measures and
men they may oppose, he never will affiliate with them!

What will he do then and where will he go? Most likely he will
"be caught affiliating with" Gov McWillie [7] of Mis[sis]sippi., and
Gov: Brown [8] of Ga. and the S.[outh] Carolina Legislature, in a
treasonable attempt to destroy the Nation and build on its ruins a
Confederacy of *the Slaveholding States!* He is quite too virtuous
and patriotic to coäct with *black* Republicans, for any object, however good, because they are opposed to the planting of slavery where
they did not find it; but I fear, will not be found too virtuous to
affiliate with the Democracy of Texas (and other slave holding
States) in their eager efforts to reopen the African Slave trade!!

Dec. 3 Saturday—At the invitation of R. M. Field,[9] dined at
Barnum's [10] to meet his friend, *Col: Dean* of Madison Wisn: (and
Mr. Alexr. Kayser) Mr. Dean is a Massts. man, some years in the
N. W., and married Miss Morrison, a niece of Mrs. Kayser.

I did not find Mr. D.[ean] a very attractive or communicative
man, tho' he told me an ugly story about Gov Floyd [11] borrowing

---

[7] William McWillie: South Carolina lawyer and legislator who became a Mississippi
planter in 1845; Democratic congressman, 1849–1851; governor of Mississippi, 1858–1860.
He was early an agitator for secession.

[8] Joseph E. Brown: back-country Democratic governor of Georgia, 1857–1865; an
ardent pro-slavery secessionist. His states' rights principles were so strong that he
continued to oppose the Confederate as he had opposed the Federal infringement of them.
In 1866 he urged submission to Radical reconstruction, but in 1871 he led in restoring
Democratic control and became U. S. senator from 1880 to 1891.

[9] *Supra*, Oct. 26, 1859, note 14.

[10] Barnum's City Hotel at Third and Vine Streets.

[11] John B. Floyd of Virginia: Democratic governor, 1849–1852; secretary of War,
1857–1861. He was an old-school Jeffersonian who believed strongly in states' rights
but opposed secession until after he left the Cabinet on December 29, 1861 over
Buchanan's refusal to withdraw Major Anderson from Fort Sumter. In 1861 he was
accused of having concentrated government arms in the South and of fraud in the use
of Indian trust bonds. See *infra*, May 8, 1862, note 30. As secretary of War and as
a Confederate officer he shared with Joseph E. Johnston Jefferson Davis's dislike.

public money from his (F[loyd]'s) brother, who was Territorial Secretary there—which money is still unpaid.

"Let us beware (and the warning extends a great deal further than to the matter in hand) of making a good cause rediculous [*sic*] by our manner of supporting it, of assuming that exaggerations on one side can only be redressed by exaggerations as great, upon the Oother [*sic*]." French, English, Past and Present p 84.

Sometimes however—

> "Wounds by wider wounds are heald
> And poisons by themselves expell'd[.]"

Dec 5. Mr. Meredith—To day a good looking young man called on me in the office, stating that his name was *Meredith*, settled here as a lawyer, that he had written a book about Justices of the Peace, and was about to have it published at Cincinnati (and shewed me a letter from a publishing house there) that he was out of money, and was trying to raise some by borrowing small sums from different members of the bar—and wished, desired $5. on loan. I lent him the money, now wholly free from doubt that all was not right. But I'd rather lose a little any time, than send away empty, a worthy young man who might be in actual need.

I never heard of him before.

Dec 6 Tuesday. Genl. T. M. Ewing of Lexington, called with Mr. Gibson,[12] to see me. I find that a notion has gotten out among the *opposition* members of [the] Assembly that may defeat the *opposition* Convention altogether—It seems that some of them think that they are too good to *sit in Convention* with *Black* republicans! They may find themselves in a hopeless minority, too weak to control one single electoral vote, if the *Black* republicans should happen to think themselves too good to *vote* with whigs and Know nothings!

Wednesday, Dec 7. . . .

To day, at the special request of the great painter, *Chester Harding*,[13] I agreed to sit for a picture, and had my first sitting about noon.

Squatter Sovereignty [14]

The National Intelligencer of Dec 3d. contains two very strong articles, signed, the one, *A Kentucky Lawyer* (Judge S. S. Nicholas [15]?) the other *C. M.* [G. M.] of New York. (Christo: Morgan [16]?)

---

[12] *Supra*, April 27, 1859, note 27.

[13] A portrait painter of considerable reputation who lived in Western New York. Philadelphia, Pittsburgh, Paris, Kentucky, and St. Louis, studied in England. and did portraits of many prominent men from James Madison to General Sherman. His "John Randolph" is in the Corcoran Gallery in Washington.

[14] The heading was added later in red pencil.

[15] *Supra*, May 27, 1859, note 64.

[16] This could not have been Christopher Morgan as the initials in the *Daily National Intelligencer* were actually G. M.

Both about Squatter Sovereignty and the Dred Scott case. The first is a happy answer to Mr. R. Johnson,[17] and goes far to prove that Johnson himself *annuls* the Dred Scott decision in its essential point, while his whole argument rests upon that decision, in all other particulars.

The 2d. states three propositions—*1*. Congress has power over slavery in the Territories, to admit or exclude[.]   (Right). *2* Congress failing to act, then the *Ter*[*ritoria*]*l. Legislature* has the full power—their laws being valid until expressly repealed by Congress[.]   (That must depend on the organic law. There can be no such Legislature until created by Congress, and no legislative powers but such as Congress grants[.])   *3* " In all cases the convention to form a State constitution, may provide therein for the admission or exclusion of slavery, *such a provision being inoperative until expressly approved by Congress.*"[18] <The first clause is a simple truism, for a *State* would be a contemptible affectation of sovereignty, if it could not put what it pleased into its constitution. The 2d. clause is a rank heresy—There is no such thing as a *Territorial* Convention to make a *State* constitution. It is of the essence of an *American State*, that it creates itself and makes its own constitution; and therefore, the *State* must pre-exist, and then make its constitution. And when made, I deny that Congress has any power to alter or abolish it, or even to pass judgment upon it. If the clause about slavery needs the approval of Congress, why not the whole instrument? The idea is at war with the sovereignty and indepen[den]ce of a State—In fact, it is *no state*, if its constitution can be dictated by Congress.[>]

A very different set of ideas prevailed when the Mo. *State* Convention (of which I was one of the youngest members) formed our *State* constitution. The first thing we did, was to form *the State*, and the next was to form a *Constitution to govern the State*—see the preamble [19]—

[*Marginal Note.*]   I drafted that preamble and offered it as a substitute for a long and involved writing prepared by Judge John Rice Jones.[20] The terms were well considered and the words thoughtfully chosen to convey the true meaning.

We did not doubt our power to make *a State and a Constitution*, and we did both, without waiting for any approval of Congress,

---

[17] *Supra*, Nov. 24, 1859, note 85.

[18] The italics are Mr. Bates's.

[19] This preamble says " We the people of Missouri, inhabiting the limits hereinafter designated . . . do mutually agree to form and establish a free and independent republic, by the name of the ' State of Missouri,' . . ."

[20] The first English lawyer in Indiana Territory, 1787–1808; early settler (1808) in Missouri; law partner at Potosi of Moses Austin, the founder of Texas; president of the Legislative Council of the Territory; influential member of the Constitutional Convention of 1820; judge of the Missouri Supreme Court, 1821–1824.

and put them—the State *and the* Constitution—into instant operation. And I myself was a sworn officer (Att.y. Genl.) of that *State*,
under that *Constitution* for a year, nearly, before the State was admitted into the Union. Congress indeed, refused, for a time, to
admit us into the Union, but it did not presume to "approve" or
pass judgment upon *our* Constitution, and did not pretend to set
up and enforce its former Territorial Government here, nor to
meddle, in any manner, with *our State* or the orderly operation of
our constitutional government.

All these recent notions about Territories are newfangled inventions, hatched in the feverish brains of factious partizans[.]

Dec: 8. This is thanksgiving day, as appointed by *Gov Stewart* [21]
of *Mo.* (who refused to appoint the 24 Nov: which had been appointed by 26 other States, because, as was surmised, all the Yankees
and abolitionists thanked God that day! And he did not choose to
be caught in such company, tho' born among them[.])

I went in town with the intent of attending the 2d. church and
hearing Mr. Brookes [22] preach, but was prevented. My old friend
"Squire" Tom Sappington called to see me, and knowing that it
was a holiday, and hence supposing that I had nothing to do, sat
on all the forenoon, telling me a great many anechdotes [*sic*] of the
early time. Among other things, he told me that the first *waggon*
load of potato[e]s ever taken into St Louis for sale was in the fall
of 1807—that the waggon was driven by his brother *Jack*, and the
potato[e]s were sold for half a dollar a bushel. At that time, his
father was settled on *Gravois*, very near where he now lives.

Last night Gov Foote [23] (now of Memphis) delivered a Lecture
at the M. L. Hall, having for a subject "The Patriot President[.]"

I did not hear the lecture and was disappointed in not seeing Mr.
Foote. I called at Barnum's [24] for the purpose, but he had left, early
in the morning.

Dec 9. Richard C. Vaughan,[25] of Lexington, called to see me,
bringing with [h]im three young gentlemen—Mr. Crittenden [26]

---

[21] See *supra*, Nov. 24, 1859, note 80.

[22] *Supra*, July 17, 1859, note 30.

[23] *Supra*, May 27, 1859, note 69.

[24] Barnum's City Hotel at Third and Vine Streets.

[25] A friend of Mr. Bates from Lexington, Missouri; general in the state militia; backer
of Mr. Bates for the Presidency in 1860; delegate to the Missouri Conservative Union
Convention in 1866; father of John M. Vaughan whom Mr. Bates appointed clerk in the
Attorney-General's Office.

[26] Thomas T. Crittenden was a son of Henry who was a younger brother of John J.
Crittenden, U. S. senator and Kentucky unionist. Thomas had been graduated from
Center College in 1855, had studied law under his uncle, John J., and had moved to
Missouri in 1857. He was a Conservative Democrat, a unionist who served in the Fed-
eral Army, a congressman, 1873–1875, 1877–1879, and governor of Missouri, 1881–1885.

(brother of Maj: C.[rittenden] [27] who went with Lopez [28] to Cuba and was shot at Havanna [*sic*]). Mr. *Neill*, a frank, bold young man, son of old Major Neill of Fayette, a staunch old fogy whig like myself. And *Mr. Beard*, a fine looking young lawyer, who has been settled for some time at Lexington, but [is] now on his way to Memphis, having accepted an eligible offer of partnership there— He is a son of Revd. Dr. Beard,[29] Prest. of the College at Lebanon Tenn:

Mr. Vaughan tells me that Mr. Beard was perfectly charmed with my conversation about Territories and new States, and was very anxious to come and have a further talk.

Dec 10. Saturday—Mr. Vaughan and Mr. Beard came to the office, but I missed them, being engaged elsewhere—Mr. Harding [30] is progressing rapidly with my picture.

[*A clipping with the caption " Opposition Meeting in Iron Co." which tells of a meeting on December 10, organized to send delegates to the Opposition Convention scheduled to assemble at Jefferson City on December 28. The Iron County meeting instructed its delegates to support* "JAMES ROLLINS [31] *for Governor and* EDWARD BATES *for President."*] [32]

Dec 12. Monday—Mr. Vaughan, I am sorry to find, has left town without my seeing him again. Nor did he get the package which I had prepared for his little son, my namesake—

Mr. Gibson [33] has not yet returned from Jefferson City, and I have not yet heard how he gets along with the malcontents of the Legislature.

Decr. 17. Saturday night. Mr. Gibson has not yet returned from Jefferson City, and I hear nothing on the subject of our proposed opposition convention. I fear there may be some serious obstacles in the way, tending to mar our harmony. But, if some ultra South Americans prove to be refractory, better get clear of them now than be encumbered with them next year.

---

[27] William L. Crittenden of Kentucky: West Point graduate in 1845; first lieutenant in the Mexican War who resigned his commission in 1851 to go as a filibuster to Cuba where he was shot by a Spanish firing squad.

[28] Narcisco Lopez, wealthy Venezuelan, later a Spanish army officer in Cuba. He organized three filibustering expeditions to Cuba from the United States (1849, 1850, 1851) on the last of which he was captured and executed.

[29] Richard Beard, circuit-riding Presbyterian clergyman and school teacher; president of Cumberland College at Princeton, Kentucky, 1843–1854; first professor and head of the department of theology of Cumberland University at Lebanon, Tennessee, 1854–1880.

[30] See *supra*, Dec. 7, 1859.

[31] *Supra*, Dec. 1, 1859, note 1.

[32] This clipping is pasted onto the front cover of the diary.

[33] *Supra*, April 27, 1859, note 27.

Judge Leonard [34] tells me that he has written to Senator Wilson (Gen: Robt.) [35] warning him of the folly and the dangers of a split.

Judge Wood (Wm. T.) [36] is zealous. I'm glad he is going to the convention, as he is very popular in the western Counties.

James. G. McPheeters is hearty in the cause, and is going up. He is in correspondence with Gov: Graham [37] of N.[orth] C.[arolina] with the view of secur[ing org]anization of the opposition in that state.

The news papers and my written correspondence indicate increasing brightness in my prospects; and the fierce quarrels in Congress about the speakership,[38] do but increase the desire of conservative men, to see a change of administration. <[*Marginal Note.*] The Democrats in the H[ouse] of. R.[epresentatives] are rabid in their denunciations of the Republicans, and their threats to dissolve the Union. I am satisfied that all those apparent bursts of passion are part of the programme, regularly " plotted and set down " for action, as the most likely way to sustain the sinking party.> I have just recd. a letter from *Winter Davis* [39] of Md., who is the leading *South American* in the House: He is serious and sad about the bad spirit prevailing in Congress and the Southern Democracy in the country, but he is firm and hopeful of better things. He thinks there is a good likelihood of a concentration of *all* the opposition on me, for the Presidency—He thinks my *present* position right and fortunate, and my *known* opinion and associations more acceptable than those of any other man. Consequently, he urges the prudence of retecence

---

[34] Abiel Leonard: lawyer of Old Franklin, 1819–1863; judge of the Supreme Court of Missouri, 1855–1858.

[35] Brigadier-general in the Mormon War, 1837; Whig lawyer and state legislator; U. S. senator, 1862–1863; a staunch unionist during the War; vice-president of the Convention of 1861 which kept Missouri in the Union.

[36] As the Whig candidate he had once defeated David R. Atchison for a seat in the Legislature from Western Missouri. He served as judge of the Circuit Court from 1854 to 1856 when he moved to St. Louis. During the War he led in the efforts of the Pine Street Church to prevent the military from interfering with their minister, Dr. McPheeters. See *supra*, April 24, 1859, note 24.

[37] William A. Graham: Whig U. S. senator, 1840–1843; governor of North Carolina, 1845–1849; secretary of the Navy, 1850–1853; Confederate senator, 1864–1865; supporter of Johnson in Reconstruction. He was an outstanding moderate, at this time vigorously opposing secession as unjustified in theory and suicidal in practice. He was strongly urged for nomination by the Constitutional Union Party for President in 1860. When his State seceded, he went with it, but in the Confederate Senate he voted for peace without independence.

[38] Acrimonious and defiant speeches in a House seething with excitement continued, from December 5 until Pennington of New Jersey was finally chosen speaker on February 1 on the forty-fourth ballot.

[39] Henry Winter Davis of Baltimore: congressman, 1855–1861, 1863–1865; first a Whig, then a Know-Nothing. He had helped break the deadlock in the House in 1859–1860 by changing his vote to the Republican candidate. Then his conservatism prevented his turning Republican and he helped organize the Bell-Everett party in Maryland in 1859–1860. He opposed secession but attacked Lincoln for abuse of the war powers. Ultimately he went completely over to the Radical Republicans and in 1864 attacked Lincoln violently from within his party for a too moderate Southern restoration policy.

[*sic*], and deprecates, as dangerous, all attempts to define my position more plainly—write no more public letters—let well enough alone.

And I receive many other similar letters, from various states.

Genl. NOEL[L],[40] one of our new M.[embers of] C[ongres]s made his debut the other day in the angry debate about the Speaker. I am glad to hear that he sustained himself very well in a fierce col[l]oquy with a fiery disunion democrat of the South.[41] He denied the right of secession, and denies the possibility of a dissolution of the Union by any other means than a bloody revolution.

I am glad to find that Noel[l], tho' he did turn Democrat to get a seat in Congress, s[t]ill retains a portion of his good, old whig principles[.]

Reverdy Johnson[42] of Md. I have lately read Mr. Johnson's pamphlet of 48 pages, upon *Popular Sovereignty* in the Territories,[43] and I confess to a feeling of mortification in finding that a man of his reputation as a lawyer, could write such a book.

Mr. Johnson is, no doubt, an excellent *Common* lawyer: A good manager of causes—and in suits *inter partes*, a case-gaining man; but he is certainly no constitutional lawyer, no statesman. Instead of discussing the question in a logical and lawyer-like way, he treats the subject in a narrow personal spirit, making himself the mere partizan of Mr. Douglas in his quarrel with Mr. Buchanan, and using the occasion to snub and belittle his successor in Office, Att.y. Genl. Black,[44] towards whom he seems to entertain no higher feelings than derision and contempt.

Mr. J.[ohnson] is a new convert to democracy, and as he is known to have a very high opinion of his own ability and learning, it is thought by some that he he [*sic*] wrote this pamphlet with a view to his own advancement. If Douglas could be made President, and he, Mr. J.[ohnson] his great champion on his favorite principle of Squatter sovereignty, his chance would be very good for high office, e. g. Sec.y. of State, or even chief Justice, if Taney[45] would only die out of the way, as is very likely in a few years.

As it is, I think that Buchanan and Douglas, Black and Johnson have nearly consumed each other in the using.

[*Marginal Note.*] Mr. Johnson denies that the Dred Scott case determines that the Constitution takes slavery into the Territories,

---

[40] John W. Noell: lawyer of Perryville, Missouri; clerk of the Circuit Court, 1841–1850; state legislator, 1850–1854; Democratic congressman, 1859–1863.

[41] W. Porcher Miles of South Carolina: mayor of Charleston, 1855–1857; Democratic congressman, 1857–1860; Confederate congressman, 1861–1864; colonel on the staff of General Beauregard.

[42] *Supra*, Nov. 26, 1859, note 85.

[43] *Douglas' Doctrine of Popular Sovereignty in the Territories; Its Counterpart.*

[44] *Supra*, Oct. 28, 1859, note 22.

[45] *Infra*, Nov. 27, 1861, note 72.

and calls Prest: Buchanan "*a dullard*" for saying that it does—
While the Pres[iden]t: and Vice Prest: and all the Southern
Democracy hold that it does—and make that supposed absurdity the
Palladium of their political faith—

[*A long editorial from the* St. Louis Evening News *of December
17, 1859, in opposition to the* "*Free Negro Law*" *which had just
passed the Missouri Senate. The* News *gives the major provisions
of the bill:*

> "It prohibits any Slaveholder from rewarding his faithful Slave for
> long years of devoted service by giving him his freedom, unless he enter
> into a bond of $2,000 to remove the emancipated Slave from the State
> forever. It provides that every Free Negro or Mulatto, over the age of
> eighteen years, now living in the State, shall leave it before the first
> Monday in September, 1860, on pain of being sold at public auction into
> Slavery for life. All Free Negroes and Mulattoes under eighteen years
> of age, shall be bound as apprentices till they are twenty-one years of
> age. twelve months after the expiration of which, they shall leave the
> State, or be sold into Slavery. Any Free Negro or Mulatto who shall
> come into the State, after the first Monday in September, 1861, and
> remain twenty-four hours, shall be sold into Slavery."]

Dec: 19. Monday. Mr. Gibson [46] has returned from Jefferson
City, where he has been for a week or more, trying to keep down a
threatened difficulty among the American and Whig members of the
Legislature, who objected to unite in the opposition Convention, [47]
with the Republicans. He had to use, no doubt, some boldness and
decision, to bring the most dissatisfied to reasonable terms; and has
succeeded, as men of his tact and courage are apt to do, in making
a very good compromise: It is agreed to postpone the meeting of
the convention, from the 28th. of Decr. to the 22d. of February, and,
in the mean time, Mr. G.[ibson] insisted, as a condition of postponement, that they should commit themselves in writing to what they
all declared orally—my nomination for the Presidency. They did
it, with some hesitation and reluctance on the part of several but all
of them did it, except three. The paper was drawn up by Mr.
Gibson and is as strong as I could desire it.

Note[.] Mr. Letcher [48] of Saline, tells Mr. Gibson that he,
L.[etcher] will procure the signatures of the other *three[.]*

Mr. G.[ibson] thinks it good policy to delay the publication of the
nomination, until about the time of the adjournment of the Assembly—about new year.

The paper was not presented to Drs. Sitton [49] and Morris [50] (and
other Rep[ublican]s: in the Assembly, if there be any) because it

---

[46] *Supra*, April 27, 1859, note 27.

[47] See *supra*, Nov. 30, 1859.

[48] William H. Letcher of Saline, organizer of the Bates movement in 1860 and of the
Missouri Conservative Union Convention of 1866 in support of Johnson.

[49] James O. Sitton, member of the Missouri House of Representatives.

[50] State Senator Walter B. Morris.

was thought best that they should speak separately in their own convention.

This nomination is a great point gained, and (especially if followed up by a similar movement in Maryland) will go far towards ensuring my adoption by the Republican Convention. And the voice which proclaims that adoption, will, I think, sound the knell of the National Democracy, as now organized.

[*Marginal Note.*] Dec: 30. Frank Blair,[51] who is just from Washington, tells me that the 'Opposition' at Washington is growing impatient for Mo. to speak out. He says that Winter Davis[52] told him that as soon as the Mo. opposition should come out openly for me, Maryland would follow suit.

Dec: 22. thursday. . . .

Beautiful ice on Lake Lindell, and fine weather to put it up. It is from 5 to 7 inches thick. Our Icehouse is nearly filled—½ a day more will complete the job, and then we will have an excellent job[.]

Mr. Harding[53] has a[l]most completed a picture of me. *He* is well pleased with it, and says that it will do justice both to me and to himself. In one respect it differs from all former pictures of me. The beard is different, growing now all over the face except the upper lip, and the hair upon the cheeks being much darker than the rest, gives, I think, a different cast to the whole countenance.

The *New Territory* of *Jefferson.* (Pike's Peak.) Some one has sent me a Newspaper entitled

" Rocky Mountain News "

" Vol: 1.["] "Auraria and Denver, *Jefferson*, Thursday Nov. 10. 1859—No. 25[.]"

Until this No. the paper was headed *Kansas. T.*[*erritory*] now Jefferson. T[erritory].

It seems that the People in that region (which is within the lines of Kansas Territory, as established by the famous K[ansas] and N.[ebraska] act) have, by their own free will, and have [*sic*] elected a governor and a Legislature. The legislature has convened, and the Governor has sent them a regular message—This paper contains the message—Note: The paper sent to me was accompanied by the printed rules of the Legislature.

For any thing I know to the contrary, it may be proper enough to establish a Territory there; but I fear that these examples of a Squatter Sovereigty will lead to bloodshed, as they have already led to much virulent wrangling. The Demagogues of Democracy have well nigh destroyed the power of the U.[nited] States over

51 *Supra*, April 27, 1859, note 25.
52 *Supra*, Dec. 17, 1859, note 39.
53 *Supra*, Dec. 7, 1859, note 13.

the Territories, by asserting powers in the people of the Territories, which cannot be exercised, and exciting hopes which cannot be gratified.

The Government established professes to be only *Provisional.* And the message of the Governor—*R. W. Steele*,[54] is a modest and conservative paper, which might well serve as a model to some of our self-sufficient State governors[.]

—I see the name of *Eli Carter*, as a Councilman: wonder if he is my old acquaintance at Warrenton.

Dec: 23. I was called on to day by Mr. *Thos: W. Swe[e]ney*, of the house of *Morris. L. Hallowell & Co.*[55] 333, Market Street Phil[adelphi]a., who introduced himself, saying that he was anxious to see me face to face, and talk a little before he returned home. His senior, Mr. Hallowell,[56] he says is a quaker and a great friend of mine, thinking, now that Clay is gone, that I am the only man to take his place.[57]

Mr. S.[weeney] seems to be a warm politician. He has been travelling in the South for some months, and to to [*sic*] my surprise, says that many persons there—old whigs, chiefly, talk of me with great favor. He professes to think my prospects in Pa. better than any other man's. I do not think that his opinion is much to be relied upon, for it is plain that, on political subjects, his zeal is greater than his knowledge.

Says that he knows Mr. Glover[58] well (calls him *Sam*) and that G and R[59] are the attornies of his house.

Tells me that he is the man who was published at Atlanta Ga., as an *abolitionist.* But that afterward, the Paper retracted in print, and the man who gave the information, in writing.

[*An editorial from the* Missouri Democrat *of December 23, 1859, printing a letter from John M. Krum*[60] *to Christopher Kribben*[61] *in opposition to the* "Act concerning slaves, free negroes and mulat-

---

[54] Robert W. Steele, after living in Ohio, 1820–1845, in Iowa, 1845–1855, in Nebraska, 1855–1859, had in April of this year moved to Denver—then in Kansas Territory—where he conducted mining operations. After a few months' residence he helped organize "Jefferson Territory" without the sanction of Kansas or Congress and was its governor for two years until Congress gave it legality as Colorado Territory.

[55] A well-known firm of importers and jobbers of silks.

[56] A wealthy merchant who was a director of the Bank of the United States and of the Pennsylvania Railroad. His large silk trade with the South made him particularly eager for the preservation not only of the Union, but also of good relations with the South.

[57] Henry Clay, who had died in 1852, had always been Mr. Bates's political exemplar.

[58] Samuel T. Glover; active supporter of Bates for the Republican nomination in 1860; anti-slavery Conservative; a unionist who did much to prevent Missouri's secession.

[59] Glover and Richardson, law firm. For Richardson see *supra*, April 27, 1859, note 26.

[60] *Infra*, Jan. 9, 1860, note 14.

[61] St. Louis lawyer, old-line Democratic politician, supporter of Douglas.

toes " [62] *then pending before the Missouri House of Representatives. The* Democrat *agrees in opposition to the Bill but ridicules Judge Krum, a Democrat, for opposing it.*]

. . .

Dec: 25. Sunday. . . . Went to church, and heard Mr. Farris [63] preach a solid, *dull* sermon.

Decr. 26. Monday. A mild, pleasant day. Dined at home, having for pleasant company, some of our friends—Richardson,[64] Glover,[65] Broadhead,[66] Brackenridge [67] (these my own special friends, personal and political) and several younger persons, of both sexes. Spent a very pleasant day.

Decr. 27. Mr. [   ] Goodrich [68]—the famous Peter Parley—called on me at the office (I having left my card at his lodgings some days ago[)]. I find him a very pleasant and sociable man, and I was much pleased with him.

I told him that we were plain people who never gave entertainments, but that my family would be pleased if he would go out with me some evening and spend the night with us privately. He seemed much pleased, and accepted the invitation with alacrity—I'll take him out soon.

Decr. 29. thursday. . . .

On the next page is the nomination of Edward Bates for the Presidency, by the *Whig* and *American* members of the Missouri Legislature. Most of them, I flatter myself, did it with a hearty good will; but some few, I suspect, did it reluctantly, and rather than meet the consequences of a refusal.

My friend C. Gibson, on full consultation with the leading members, prepared the instrument not just as he would, but adapting it to the hopes and fears of individuals.[69] And I doubt whether any other man could have gotten all the signatures.

[63] *Supra,* Dec. 17, 1859.
[63] Robert P. Farris, Presbyterian minister who was the first editor, 1866–1895, of the (Old School) *Missouri Presbyterian.*
[64] *Supra,* April 27, 1859, note 26.
[65] *Supra,* Dec. 23, 1859, note 58.
[66] James O. Broadhead: St. Louis lawyer; state legislator, 1846–1847, 1850–1853; ardent unionist; U. S. district attorney, 1861; lieutenant-colonel in the Union Army; provost marshal, 1861–1863; special counsel for the Government in the "Whiskey Ring" cases, 1876; Democratic congressman, 1883–1885; minister to Switzerland, 1893–1897.
[67] Samuel M. Breckinridge: St. Louis lawyer; judge of the Circuit Court, 1859–1863; a staunch unionist in 1861 whose anti-secessionist speeches helped to keep Missouri in the Union.
[68] Samuel G. Goodrich of New York City, formerly of Hartford and of Boston, editor of the *Token* (an American giftbook annual), and, under the pen name "Peter Parley," author and editor of juvenile books and periodicals.
[69] See *supra,* Dec. 19, 1859.

Copy

Nomination of E Bates for the Presidency, by the *opposition* members of the Mo. Legislature.

December [   ] 1859.[70]

The undersigned members of the Legislature of Missouri express our preference for Edward Bates as the most suitable and conservative Candidate for the Presidency.

Mr. Bates has not been in public life for thirty years. He has declined the highest offices in the gift of the President. He seeks no office, and has no partizans to reward. During the entire existence of the Whig party, he was among its most active and able members, and for a long series of years, upheld its "stainless banner," at times almost "solitary and alone," against overwhelming majorities in this state. He has connected himself with none of the parties that have sprung into existence since its dissolution, but as an "Old Line Whig" has constantly employed his energies and talents in opposing the heresies corruptions and extravagance of National (?) Democracy. He is a Virginian by birth and education and a Missourian by adoption. He recognizes no circumstances under which the Union is to be dissolved. His locality is central and his principles are national. He is eminent in his advocacy of a Pacific Railroad, and on any route rather than none, believing the American people can build it wherever they please and he favors a judicious system of internal improvements in the state and nation. He is a western man and the west is entitled by rotation to the President. Whatever may be his opinions upon questions which National (?) Democracy has reduced to mere abstractions we know he is unalterably opposed to the agitation and agitators of Slavery North and South. His private life is unsullied, and his public record unassailable. If elected President, his administration "would restore peace to the country and purity to the Government:" and we solemnly believe a crisis has arrived in the affairs of the Nation, that threatens the perpetuity of our institutions, and that all patriotic citizens should make great concessions in order to avert the danger.

While we may differ with him on some questions, which under any other circumstances we would not waive, we believe he is on the whole the most available and proper man in the nation as the great

---

[70] The heading including the date is written by Mr. Bates in red ink. What follows including the signatures is copied by someone who wrote a readable hand.

Conservative candidate of 1860. And we present him to the people as such.

N. W. Watkins [71]	Thos. W. Cunningham
Robt. Wilson [72]	Thos. S. McGaugh
Genl. Jas S. Rains	Marcus Boyd
O. Guitar	Geo. W. Hampton
James Harris [73]	Jas. W. Owens
G. T. Woodson [74]	Wm. Newland
James A. Pritchard	Mortimer McIlhany
J. B. Harris	Wm. H. Letcher [75]
Thomas J. C. Fagg	I. H. McIlvaine
Saml. F. Taylor	Isaac H. Wood
Saml. Maguire	P.[B.(?)]A. Hill
John Scott	Aikman Welch
O. B. Smith	John. F. Gooch

[*A cutting from the* Missouri Democrat *of December 29, 1859, showing that in the assignment of membership on committees in the United States Senate, the chairmanships of all of the important committees, viz., Foreign Affairs, Commerce, Post Offices, Territories, Naval Affairs, Judiciary and District of Columbia had all been given to the South.*]

This *sectional* organization of the Committees of the Senate is a proof so open and shameless, of the local and partizan character of the of the [*sic*] Southern Democracy, that hereafter, any pretence of nationality on their part, must be recognized at once, as false and hypocritical.

The wonder is, considering the daily conduct of their chief leaders in Congress and at home, that they have so long had the cool impudence to call themselves *national* men and supporters of the constitution. But they assert falsehoods so often and so long that, at last, they seem to believe their own wild inventions—e. g. they appear quite sincere in the preposterous belief that they themselves, are more wise, more just, more brave than other people! While the world laughs in their faces, at the absurd assumption.

[*Pasted upon the same sheet without comment is a list of the Committees of the House of Representatives, published in February, 1860.*]

Decr: 31, Saturday night, this last of the year. The weather is very cold. The ice now upon [the] ground, and in many parts of the streets of St Louis, fell, as hail and sleet, on the 2d. day of Decem-

---

[71] *Infra*, March 1, 1860, note 15.
[72] *Supra*, Dec. 17, 1859, note 35.
[73] *Infra*, May 9, 1860, note 3.
[74] A cousin of Mr. Bates.
[75] *Supra*, Dec. 19, 1859, note 48.

ber. There has been more cold weather in this present month than I have sometimes seen here in a whole winter.

A truly hard season this; for, added to the unusually cold weather, the crops are not large, the wild *mast* is next to nothing, and the money market very stringent; and very many persons are thrown out of employment.

[*A clipping from the* Missouri Daily Democrat *reprinting an article from the* Scientific American *which reproduces a disquisition in blank verse from the* Detroit Tribune *on fresh air and ventilation.*]*

[*A portrait of Garibaldi.*]

["Are all Foreigners Abolitionists!"]

[" We find the following choice morcel in the south side Democrat of April 27, 1852, Roger A. Pryor [76] being the editor.

"There must be a last battle between slavery and abolition. The struggle will end only with the destruction of one or the other of the two hostile parties.—Shall the South postpone the last decisive conflict until defeat is inevitable?—The strength of the enemy is hourly increasing. Every ship load of emigrants discharged in the streets of New York, augments the forces of the abolition, and every decennial count of the population of the country marks the rapid decline of the South."]*

"Irrepressible conflict." Horrid doctrine in *Mr. Seward;* all right in *Mr. Pryor.* Mr. P.[ryor] now an M. C. and once editor of Mr. Douglas' organ "The *States*," [77] now professes to be ashamed of Douglas, and declares that he will not support him, unless it be to defeat *Seward* or some other *black* Republican.[78]

[*A clipping headed* "*Where the Shoe Pinches.*" *telling of the difficulty experienced by old Whigs in becoming Democrats.*]*

[*A clipping giving the names and birth-dates of the* "*Royal Family of England.*"]*

[*A clipping headed* "*To the Public*" *giving Bank President Ferdinand Meyer's version of a dispute over bank reorganization between Mr. Meyer and State Legislator James W. Owens.*]*

---

* A clipping pasted into the front cover of the diary.

[76] *Supra*, Nov. 9, 1859, note 36.

[77] Published in Washington; after November 9, called the *States and Union.*

[78] This note was added on the cover of the diary when the clipping was pasted—sometime after early December, 1859, for Pryor did not become a member of Congress until then.

CHAPTER II

1860

[*January 1*,] *Sunday*—New Year's day. Bright and beautiful but very cold. . . .

We had communion in our church to day: Four of five new members were admitted—among them Mrs. Rippey, the young widow of a son of Matthew Rippey[.]

When service was over, Dr. Anderson [1] detained me a little, to introduce me to his old teacher, Mr. Reed, [2] now *Professor* Reed of a college in Madison, Wisconsin[.]

[*A newspaper reprint of a letter written by Ex-President Millard Fillmore on December 16, 1859, to a " New York Union Meeting " in which he defends the Compromise of 1850 but brands the repeal of the Missouri Compromise in 1854 as " unjustifiable." He says:*

"Whatever might have been the motive, few acts have ever been so barren of good and so fruitful of evil. . . . The lamentable tragedy at Harper's Ferry is clearly traceable to this unfortunate controversy about slavery in Kansas, . . . I would say to my brethren of the South: Be not alarmed, for there are few, very few, at the North who would justify in any manner an attack upon the institutions of the South, which are guaranteed by the Constitution. . . . And I would say to my brethren of the North: Respect the rights of the South; assure them by your acts that you regard them as friends and brethren. And I would conjure all in the name of all that is sacred, to let this agitation cease with the causes which have produced it."]

Most true

. . .

Jan 2d. Monday, A bright fine day, tho' cold. I paid a few calls during the day—i. a. Mrs. Hugh Campbell. [3]

[*January*] *7th. Saturday.* The weather continued very cold till last afternoon, when the thaw began. . . .

---

[1] *Supra,* July 17, 1859, note 26.

[2] Daniel Read, formerly professor of political economy and constitutional law and also vice-president at Ohio University; then professor of ancient languages at Indiana University, 1843–1855; now (1855–1868) professor of mental philosophy, logic, rhetoric, and English literature at the University of Wisconsin; and later, president of the University of Missouri, 1863–1876.

[3] Hugh Campbell was an Irish-born merchant, first in North Carolina, then in Virginia, later in Philadelphia, 1833–1859, and finally in St. Louis, 1859–1879. During the War he served with Joseph Holt (*infra*, Feb. 2, 1860, note 49) and Judge Davis (*infra*, Feb. 26, 1863, note 43) on a commission which Lincoln set up to adjust claims brought against the military in the West.

The ice, which incumbered [*sic*] many parts of the road and streets ever since the 2d. of Decr., is rappidly [*sic*] passing off. The ways are sloppy every where and in some parts of the roads, the mud is already deep.

S. G. Goodrich, (Peter Parley) [4] gratified us by spending the last night with us. His presence was a real treat to the children, and he seemed to enjoy himself finely.

He made me a beautiful present—his new work—the *Animal Kingdom*, in 2 volumes splendidly bound in Russia leather, and enriched with a multitude of prints.

Note. Mr. G.[oodrich] is a good deal of a politician withal, and knows the *status* of most men at the north. Judge Loring [5] of the Court of Claims, is his brother in law, and he says is in an irksome condition at Washington, being very much petted by the Southrons for his firm conduct in the famous case of Burns,[6] the fugitive slave, while in reality his own views differ very widely from theirs.

He tells me also that Senator Wilson [7] of Massts. raised himself from humble station, having started as shoe maker in a country town, in Massts.

[*A formal note of January 5 from S. G. Goodrich is pasted into the diary.*]

Note Mr. Harding,[8] the painter, confirms this. Wilson, he says is really a superior man—far above Sumner [9] in all but scholarship. Mr. Goodrich and Judge Loring married sisters—named Boot[t].

[*A long communication printed in the* Missouri Democrat *of January 7, 1860, which points out that the reason the North cannot*

---

[4] *Supra*, Dec. 27, 1859, note 68.

[5] Edward G. Loring, United States commissioner and judge of the Probate Court. Massachusetts sought punishment for Loring after the Burns trial. He had been appointed lecturer in the Law School at Harvard, but the overseers now refused to confirm that appointment. The Legislature sought his removal as probate judge, but the governor refused. In 1858 on a renewal of this request of the Legislature, Governor Banks did remove him. Buchanan then gave him the justiceship of the U. S. Court of Claims in Washington which he held until 1877. He was opposed to slavery, but felt he must enforce the law in the Burns case.

[6] Anthony Burns was an escaped Virginia slave returned to his master after a trial in Boston, in spite of a huge mass meeting in Fanueil Hall addressed by Wendell Phillips and Theodore Parker and despite an attempt at rescue by a mob led by Minister Thomas W. Higginson. Burns was later ransomed from slavery by Boston subscriptions.

[7] Henry Wilson: ardent anti-slavery man who withdrew from the Whig Party in 1848 because it refused to adopt an anti-slavery plank; editor of the *Boston Republican*, 1848–1851; Free-Soil and later Republican senator, 1855–1873; vice-president of the United States, 1873–1875. He had been challenged to a duel by Preston Brooks for denouncing Brooks's assault on Sumner, and in March, 1859, he had won fame through a widely circulated defense of free labor in reply to Senator Hammond of South Carolina.

[8] Harding was originally a Massachusetts man. *Supra*, Dec. 7, 1859, note 13.

[9] Charles Sumner of Massachusetts: Free-Soil and then Republican senator, 1851–1874; a founder of the Free-Soil Party; chairman of the Senate Committee on Foreign Relations, 1861–1871.

*allow slavery to be taken into the Territories is the fact that, as the
advocates of slavery are always pointing out, slavery is "inconsistent
with the liberty of the press, the liberty of speech, religious freedom,
schools, and the diffusion of knowledge, common humanity, the
rights of property, and the right of the majority to govern, according
to the Constitution and the laws."]*

[*A clipping recommending Edward Bates of Missouri for President in 1860 and Simon P. Cameron of Pennsylvania for Vice-President.*]

Jany. 9. Monday. The thaw still continues. . . .

As preparations are being made for the nomination of presidential candidates, men are waxing warm and assuming their positions. The *Baltimore Patriot* (chief organ of the Opposition in Maryland) of the 4 and 5 of Jan.y. comes to me today, with my name at the head of the columns, and a somewhat grandiloquent proclamation of my *many virtues and abilities.*

I have also recd. a letter from Mr. Ridgeway Editor of the Richmond Whig, from which I draw good hopes of the support of the Opposition in Virginia.

My nomination for the Presidency, which at first struck me with mere wonder, has become familiar, and now I begin to think my prospects very fair. Circumstances seem to be remarkably concurrent in my favor, and there is now great probability that the Opposition of all classes will unite upon me: And that will be equivalent to election.

The Democracy is rent into factions and distracted, and even those factions have no reliable leaders. They agree in nothing but in waging the sectional war of South against North. On the Tariff, Internal Improvements and foreign policy—on the Public Lands, the Pacific R. R. and the questions of ordinary government, they differ widely. Here in St Louis they had an Eighth of Jan.y. meeting and angrily split asunder (and held separate meetings) in the interest respectively of Buchanan and Douglas. It is a little strange that the new converts from Whiggery—Churchill,[10] Bogy,[11]

---

[10] Samuel B. Churchill: St. Louis lawyer and editor of the *Bulletin*, a Whig journal; Democratic state senator, 1858–1861. He sympathized with the South but stopped short of secession. He opposed Lincoln's coërcive measures, sought to prevent war and bring a peaceful compromise, and had to leave the State when the supporters of Lincoln gained control.

[11] Lewis V. Bogy: St. Louis lawyer; organizer and president of the St. Louis and Iron Mountain Railway; later U. S. commissioner of Indian Affairs, 1867–1868; Democratic senator, 1873–1877.

Cook [12] Hogan [13] and [   ] are staunch for Buchanan, while the old liners—J. M. Krum,[14] C. F. Jackson,[15] A. J. P. Garesché,[16] Kribben &c go for Douglas.

Can it be reserved for me to defeat and put down that corrupt and dangerous party, the Democracy? Truly, if I can do my country that much good, I will rejoice in the belief that I have not lived in vain.

[*Marginal Note.*] On the tenth of Jan.y. I recd. a letter from W. G. Snethen, Edr. of the Balt[imor]e. Patriot, wherein he seems to expect a communication with me, more frequent and full than my prudence can at once accede to. I infer from his letter that the Md. opposition came out so quickly, to get the start of the opposition union Convention which Mr. S.[nethen] and some others begin to suspect is but a cheap way to sell out to the Democrats.

Jan: 11. . . .

I staid at home today, partly on a/c of the ice, but chiefly to prepare an answer for Chs: Wiggins to send to California, ads Eldridge [17] and Laurecel. If I have any important work to do now, home is the only place to do it, for in town I am prevented by the great numbers who call on me to talk politics.

Besides, I am not a little annoyed by the applications of Painters and other artists (some of them excellent men and skillful artists) to "*sit*" for pictures, busts, &c. *Harding*,[18] and *Cogswell* [19] have both just finished my pictures—Harding's ½, Cogswell's full length—standing. Each artist is fully satisfied with his effort, and both pictures are I believe, approved by visitors. Cogswell thinks that *his* is better than his own picture of Mr. Charless—and that is saying a great deal, for *his Charless* is excellent.

---

[12] Probably William M. Cooke, lawyer and judge, vigorous opponent of Benton, and later of F. P. Blair. He was strongly pro-slavery. When the Civil War came he joined the Confederate Army and served in the Confederate Congress.

[13] John Hogan: Irish-born Methodist minister; wholesale grocer; Illinois Whig politician who had moved to St. Louis; Democratic postmaster of St. Louis, 1857–1861; congressman, 1865–1867; then again a minister. At this time he was a strong supporter of Buchanan against Douglas.

[14] John M. Krum: St. Louis lawyer; judge; mayor; and ardent Douglas Democrat who turned Republican and supported Lincoln when the Civil War broke out.

[15] Claiborne F. Jackson: state legislator, 1846–1858; state bank commissioner, 1858–1860; governor of Missouri, 1861; an ardent pro-slavery man; upholder of "popular sovereignty." In 1849 he wrote the "Jackson Resolutions" which declared for the right of Southerners to take slaves into the Territories. In 1861 he called a secession convention and tried to take Missouri into the Confederacy, but was driven from the state governorship instead.

[16] Alexander J. P. Garesche: St. Louis lawyer; lifelong Democrat who opposed secession but believed that the South had a right to maintain slavery.

[17] Probably Shalor W. Eldridge: hotel-owner in Kansas City and Lawrence, Kansas; free-state leader of Kansas; member of the National Committee of the Friends of Kansas. He brought several parties of northern immigrants safely to Kansas.

[18] *Supra*, Dec. 7, 1859, note 13.

[19] *Supra*, July 9, 1859, note 19.

I have promised to sit for *Conant*,[20] but, for the present, have not time.

[*Note*.]   Jan 19   <Both Harding's and Cogswell's are now on exhibition in the City, and I hear that the public pronounces decidedly in favor of Cogswell's, both as a likeness and as a work of art.

Mr. Brownlow, the sculptor, has undertaken to make a bust of me in stone (at the instance of friends of mine, who have subscribed to bear the expense).   Mr. Brownlow, to aid his work, has caused Photographs to be taken (by Browne) in several aspects— The profile (I never saw *my* profile before) pleases me better than any likeness of myself I ever saw.>

Jan. 13.   Mr. Stokes[21] of Tenn in debate in the H[ouse] of R[epresentatives] shews very clearly that it was the fault of the Democrats that the House remained unorganized, for want of a speaker (see Nat: Intelr. Jany 10.).[22]   He was often interrupted by democratic members, by question.   At last, he turned upon them by questions of his own, and drew from several of them, the open and shameless declaration of their factious and disorderly temper— That they would not vote with Republicans, in any contingency— that they would desert their own candidate, Mr. Bocock,[23] if Republicans voted for him ! !

Here are some of these virtuous, wise and *National* statesmen— Singleton[24] of Missi.   Rust[25] of Aks:—Vallandingham[26] [*sic*] of O.[hio] Wright[27] of Tenn: (under the pretence of instruction of

---

[20] Alban J. Conant of Chelsea, Vermont, and Troy, New York, who moved to St. Louis in 1857; artist; archeologist; and curator of the State University.   During the Civil War he did portraits of Lincoln, Stanton, and other leaders.

[21] William B. Stokes: Whig congressman, 1859–1861; major-general in the Union Army; Republican congressman, 1866–1871.

[22] This appears in the issue of January 9, not in that of January 10.

[23] Thomas S. Bocock of Virginia: Democratic congressman, 1847–1861; skilled parliamentarian; speaker of the Confederate House of Representatives, 1862.   He supported the Kansas-Nebraska bill and the Lecompton Constitution for Kansas.   In the long contest over the speakership of the House in 1859–1860, he was the Democratic candidate for that office.

[24] Otho R. Singleton: Democratic congressman, 1853–1855, 1857–1861, 1875–1887; Confederate congressman, 1861–1865.

[25] Albert Rust: Democratic congressman, 1855–1857, 1859–1861; brigadier-general in the Confederate Army.

[26] Clement L. Vallandigham: Democratic congressman, 1858–1863.   He was so extreme a states' rights Democrat that he not only defended the Southern position during the pre-war period, but was uncompromising in his opposition to war for coërcion of the South.   He also opposed emancipation by national enactment and Lincoln's arbitrary use of the war powers which he regarded as a violation of the constitutional rights of states and individuals.   He was finally arrested for treason by General Burnside (*infra*, Nov. 29, 1861, note 97) in 1863, convicted by a court martial, and then, on the intercession of President Lincoln, banished to the South.

[27] John V. Wright: Democratic congressman, 1855–1861; colonel in the Confederate Army; Confederate congressman.

the Tenn Legislature—Does the simpleton suppose that the State Legislatures have power to instruct Rep[resentative]s: in Congress?) and Avery [28]—

It is plain that these factionists are in a fit of impotent rage, which disqualifies them from acting upon judgment, and makes them the willing slaves of their adversaries. They set up a candidate for Speaker, pretending that he is the most fit man of their party, and yet they allow their bitterest enemies to drive them from his support, by voting for him! Yet these men prate about principle and honor!

Mr. Douglas—The papers inform us that Mr. D.[ouglas] is so far convalescent as to take his seat occasionally in the Senate. A few days ago he took occasion to declare that he firmly adhered to his doctrine of slavery in the Territories (i. e—that it may be abolished by Territorial power)[29] and that he would not accept a nomination of the Charleston Convention,[30] on any contrary platform[.]

His position is very critical. Probably, he will not be nominated; but, failing in that, if he were only a man of principle and courage, he might still command his fortune, so far at least as to preserve his local preëminence. But I think he lacks those qualities, and will sink despised, as one who " went up like a flaming rocket, and came down like a smutty stick." And I do not see that the Democratic leaders of the *South* are in a much better condition. They, like him, have attempted to build a great house upon a false foundation. Beginning with a great lie, they have made Truth their enemy; and truth is a hard enemy to beat, and when beaten in a particular contest, "won[']t stay whipped[.]"

Revd. Mr. Watt has been with us some days[.]

[*The* Missouri Statesman *of January 13, 1860, under the heading* " The Free Negro Bill " *prints several adverse opinions of Tennessee legal authorities on the constitutionality of that State's proposed bill, with the hope that members of the Missouri House of Representatives will read them carefully before approving their own similar bill.*]

Jan. 15. sunday.

Jarvis Island and *Baker's* Island in the Pacific[.] The N.[ew] Y.[ork] Observer of Jany. 12—page 14. has an item under the head *Westward Enterprise*, in which it is said that a ship sailed from Honolulu for those Islands, having on board *Gov.* Wilder's wife of Jarvis I.[sland] and Chs. H. Judd Esqr. (*Gov* of Baker's I.[sland]) and his bride, (formerly Miss E. C. Cutts of Portsmouth N.[ew] H.[ampshire.])

---

[28] William T. Avery of Tennessee: Democratic congressman, 1857–1861; lieutenant-colonel in the Confederate Army.

[29] His Freeport Doctrine.

[30] The Democratic National Convention of 1860.

The article says that *these lone islands of the Pacific are now part and parcel of the American Republic.*

That is news to me. I never heard of those *parts of the Republic* before[.] [31]

[*January 19.*] [*A clipping from the* St. Louis Press *of January 19, 1859, announcing that Governor Stewart* [32] *has not yet signed the* " *Free Negro Bill,*" [33] *and hoping that he will not sign it.*]

Jan 23—Monday—. . .

Barton came down friday, bringing us a waggon [*sic*] load of various good things in the eating line.

Fleming, wife, child and servant, will leave us to day: they go in town to Dr. J. W. Wilson's, and expect to go up to St Charles Co. tomorrow—to remain, at " Solitude " I know not how long.

Jan.y. 27. This afternoon, I was calle[d] on, at my office, by a gentleman who introduced himself, as *Mr. Hall* [34] of Auburn, N. Y— said he had a letter of introduction to me from Mr. Seward, but, being separated from his trunk in travelling, could not now produce the letter. His conversation I thought was constrained and *un*communicative, which made me a little doubtful whether or no he was trying to *pump* me. That doubt perhaps produced a corresponding reserve on my part. He professes to be a warm friend of Mr. Seward, who, he says is really a conservative man, and not an ultra, as he is charged withal. He explained how Gov Seward came to recommend to the Legislature of N. Y. his school policy (which gave rise to the charge made by the K[now-]N[othing]s, that he was *bidding for the Irish vote*[)] [35]—He got it from old Dr. Nott,[36] his former teacher—

---

[31] Jarvis Island was discovered in 1835 by Michael Baker, an American. In 1858 Captain Davis of the U. S. S. *St. Mary's* took formal possession of the island for the United States. But in 1889 the English ship *Cormorant* took possession in the name of Her Majesty, and today Jarvis Island appears on many maps as British. The title is uncertain. The same Michael Baker discovered Baker Island in 1832. Britain is said to have leased this island to the Pacific Islands Company. The title is still uncertain between the United States and Britain. Both islands are valuable only for guano. There is no record of our ever sending officials to them. On March 2, 1861, Secretary of State Black did issue a certificate assigning Baker's right in both islands to the American Guano Company. If anyone at all went to the islands in January, 1860, it must have been an agent of the Guano Company.

[32] *Supra*, Nov. 24, 1859, note 80.

[33] See *supra*, Dec. 17, 1859.

[34] Benjamin F. Hall had studied law under Mr. Seward and had then become his partner. He served as a Whig legislator, as mayor of Auburn, and as chief justice of Colorado Territory, 1861–1863. Under President Fillmore he had compiled and indexed the opinions of the attorneys-general.

[35] As governor, Seward had urged and secured, in 1842, the passage of a school law which created a public Board of Education in New York City and gave state funds to it instead of to the (Protestant) Public School Society which had previously conducted excellent schools with state funds. The Catholics had demanded this and Seward had complied: his friends said, as an act of justice to Catholics who were large tax-payers; his enemies said, because it would win him the increasingly powerful Catholic vote.

[36] Eliphalet Nott: Congregational clergyman; president of Union College at Schenectady, New York, 1804–1866.

Also, as to his *Higher law* speech [37] in the Senate—he got that from Prest Taylor.

Mr. H.[all] promised to call again, and, on better acquaintance I may form a higher opinion of him[.]

Dined today, with my wife, at Dr. J. W. Wilsons [*sic*], and saw there Mrs. Read of Alton, and her young son Henry—also her son Frederick of Kenawha—also a Miss Read—sister to Mrs. Abbott of Alton—a large, unhandsome woman.

Jan 28 (Saturday). Dined with Mr. and Mrs. Eads.[38] at Barnum's [39] and met there casually, Judge Williams [40] of Kansas formerly of Iowa.

H. R. Gamble,[41] father and son, arrived today from Norristown Pa. on a hasty visit—

Mrs. Isaac Read (and son Henry) of Alton, and Miss Read late of Lynchburg Va. came with my family (from Dr. Wilson's) to spend the night with us.

[*A clipping from the* Baltimore Patriot *lists itself and the* Cumberland Telegraph *and* Elkton Whig *as the Maryland newspapers which have already come out in favor of Bates for President. Then it asks:*

"Who comes next? Let us see whether old Maryland, by the universal voice of her Opposition press, will not say to Missouri, where her BATES Convention meets in February, 'All hail, EDWARD BATES, the next President of the United States!'"]

This looks promising for Maryland, and Colfax [42] writes me that Gov: Hicks [43] (of Md.) is openly on my side and that the Opposition of the Md. Legislature will soon give me their endorsement.

[*Note.*]   Feb 2.   Farther north and east, my prospects grow brighter every day—Letters inform me that all parts of the Oppo-

---

[37] A speech in the Senate on March 11, 1850, during the debate on the compromise measures, in which Seward argued that the Constitution limited Congress's power in the Territories and devoted the public "domain to union, to justice, to defence, to welfare, and to liberty," but that in any case "there is a higher law than the constitution" which is inconsistent with slavery. *Cong. Globe*, 31 Cong., 1 Sess., Appendix, 260–269.

[38] James B. Eads, inventor and engineer; at this time merely the inventor of a diving bell, but later internationally known as a builder of gunboats during the Civil War, as the constructor of the Eads Bridge at St. Louis, and as an authority on hydraulic engineering.

[39] Barnum's City Hotel at Third and Vine Streets.

[40] Joseph Williams: formerly justice of the Supreme Court of the Territory of Iowa, 1838–1846; chief justice of the Supreme Court of the State of Iowa, 1846–1848; at this time judge of the U. S. District Court in Kansas.

[41] *Supra*, July 23, 1859, note 39. In 1854 he had retired from public life in Missouri and moved to Norristown, near Philadelphia. But he returned in 1861, to help meet the crisis of civil war.

[42] *Supra*, April 27, 1859, note 28.

[43] Thomas H. Hicks: Know-Nothing governor of Maryland, 1858–1862. He became leader of the conservative element of Maryland as secession threatened. He was himself a slave-holder and disliked abolitionists, but he vigorously opposed secession, and, though he objected to military interference in Maryland by the Federal Government, he kept the State in the Union, and later became a Republican U. S. senator, 1862–1865.

sition are going for me, and that there is a general impression of my success.

. . .

Jan: 31. tuesday—Yesterday was a beautiful day—warm—At night, a distinct ring around the moon (in 2d. ¼) a sure sign of bad weather. Julia and I spent an hour at Mr. McCune's—met Dr. Post,[44] wife and daughter[.]

This morning, cold and raw with a brisk wind from the north, with a *spitting* of snow. This baulks Julia's intended visit to Florissant [45] today.

. . .

Feb. 2. thursday, Julia went to Florissant and brot. Sally [46] home with her in the evening. . . .

[*A clipping prints (1) a letter of December 2, 1859, to Horace Greeley [47] from Postmaster Glass [48] of Lynchburg, Virginia, saying that, because of its incendiary character, his postoffice will not deliver copies of the* New York Tribune; *and (2) Greeley's peppery rejoinder.*]

This slip I cut from the N.[orth] W.[est] Times of Jany 25th. published at *Viroqua Badax County* Wis:

It is amazing to see the insolent boldness of usurpation and the blind, servile submission of party zeal. The P.[ost] M.[aster] Gen[era]l.[49] has already authorised his deputies scattered through the Country, to judge whether the mail matter coming to their offices is fit or unfit to be circulated; and to that end, to commit *a felony* (as defined by the post office law) by breaking packages and examining their contents. And this little post master Glass does but act out the spirit of his master, when he undertakes to decide that a

---

[44] Truman M. Post: minister of the First Trinitarian Congregational Church of St. Louis, 1851–1882; professor of ancient and modern history at Washington University; lecturer and trustee of the Chicago Theological Seminary.

[45] *Supra,* May 18, 1859, note 52.

[46] Sarah Woodson Bates, Julian's wife.

[47] Horace Greeley was editor of the *New York Tribune,* 1841–1872, and one of the most uncompromising opponents of slavery. When the crisis came, he opposed the Crittenden Compromise because he preferred disunion to extension of slavery. He believed that if a majority of Southerners so desired they should be allowed to secede. Yet when the War came he supported it vigorously and attacked Lincoln for not earlier declaring for emancipation. From 1863 to 1865 Greeley sought to secure peace with the South. In Reconstruction he urged general amnesty for Southern whites and full equality for negroes.

[48] Robert H. Glass, states' rights editor of the strongly Democratic *Lynchburg Republican,* a major in the Confederate Army. He was father of the present (1932) U. S. senator, Carter Glass.

[49] Joseph Holt: Kentucky lawyer who became postmaster-general in March, 1859, and secretary of War in December, 1860. He was at this time a Democrat, but on the outbreak of civil war, denounced secession, vigorously supported Lincoln, and became judge-advocate general of the Army, and, later, fanatical prosecutor of Lincoln's assassins and opponent of Johnsonian moderation.

public journal, in all its numbers, present and future, is incendiary
and must be suppressed. Its circulation is forbidden by the *laws of
the land*, he says; and lest the *laws* should fail to uphold his partizan
tyranny, he asserts that it is forbidden also, by *a proper regard for
the safety of society*. He is the judge it would seem not only of *the
laws of the* LAND, but also of the " higher law " of *Salus Populi!!*

Will he suppress, as incendiary Senator Mason's speech,[50] advising
treason in case the wrong man should be chosen President?

[*Note.*[51]]   And see [the] Nat:[ional] Intel[ligence]r. of Feby 7—
correspondence[52] of Mr. Vallandingham[53] [*sic*] of Ohio with the
P.[ost] M.[aster] Genl.[54] about the suppression of a religious
paper[55]—published at Dayton, O.[hio] (by the P.[ost] M.[aster]
at Luney's creek Hardy C.[ount]y. Va.)

This little paper[56] has (on the under side of the slip) a Presidential ticket such as I have not seen elsewhere Viz—For President
Wm. H. Seward—For V.[ice] P.[resident] Edward Bates.

Feby 4. Saturday. Today, in the morning, sat to *Conant*[57] for
my picture (for Barton). *Note.* Mr. C.[onant] says (and that is the
highest praise I could extort) that *Cogswell's*[58] picture of me " is
really a good portrait." *Harding's*[59] he thinks a dead failure.
Browne's photograph[60] of me (the side face) he thinks one of the
best photographs he ever saw and an admirable likeness.

At Mr. Johnson's room, at the Library, saw Mr. [   ] Raymond,[61] of the N.[ew] Y.[ork] Times, and had and [an] hour's talk.
Doubtless a most intelligent man, but he seemed reserved, and rather
wat[c]hing me than displaying himself. *I* talked freely and I suppose he thought imprudently. But knowing his political Status,
I talked so on purpose. Seeming to be very open and bold, I took
care to say nothing that I had not said and published often before.

---

[50] James M. Mason of Virginia : Democratic congressman, 1837–1839 ; U. S. senator,
1847–1861 ; Confederate commissioner to Great Britain and France whose capture at sea
created the " *Trent* Affair." At this time he was a leader of the pro-slavery states'
rights party, agitating for Virginian secession. The speech referred to was made on
the floor of the Senate, December 14, 1859. *Cong. Globe.* 36 Cong., 1 Sess. 149.

[51] Added later.

[52] It appears in the issue of February 6, not in that of February 7.

[53] *Supra*, Jan. 13, 1860, note 26.

[54] Joseph Holt. But the correspondence was with Horatio King, first assistant postmaster-general.

[55] The *Religious Telescope*, the Reverend John Lawrence, editor.

[56] Probably the *North West Times* cited above.

[57] *Supra*, Jan. 11, 1860, note 20.

[58] *Supra*, July 9, 1859, note 19.

[59] *Supra*, Dec. 7, 1859, note 13.

[60] *Supra*, Jan. 11, 1860.

[61] Henry J. Raymond : founder and editor of the *Times* ; Republican congressman, 1865–
1867 ; an organizer of the Republican Party. In 1858 he declared for Douglas, but in
1860 was urging Seward's nomination. When Lincoln was chosen, Raymond supported
him.

Mr. R.[aymond] is here on an [en]gagement to lecture, and will leave on monday.

Mr. *J. H. Van Alen*[62] of N. Y. calls to see me[,] introduced by Colfax.[63] Says he came out with no business but to see *me* and the Mississippi Valley—He is a regular descendent of the old Dutch settlers, and belongs, I infer, to a wealthy family—Is an ardent Rep[ublica]n. and says he is a straight old whig, as his father was before him, and still is. He does not seem to me a deep politician— of good feelings I should judge, but impetuous—Too impulsive to be safe. Rich I suppose and willing to spend freely for the cause.

I suppose he is really on a tour of observation for the information of deeper men at the east.

I dined at the Planters,[64] with him, Raymond and Gibson[65]— Also, I read to him my two letters[66] to Mr. Colfax—

[*A long editorial from the* Missouri Republican *of February 4, 1860, headed " Next Presidential Election," urges the nomination of Mr. Douglas and pleads with the politicians to cease their intrigues against him, but agrees to support anybody who can defeat a " Black Republican."*]

This leader of the Mo. Rep:[ublican] is very significant. There is a good deal of skilful duplicity in it. It goes more openly for Mr. Douglas than ever heretofore, and I think, with a good deal of tact, threatens the South with D[ouglas]'s power. It denounces southern demagogues and leaves the way wide open to oppose the Charleston[67] nominee, if it be any other than Douglas. It admits that heretofore, *u*national and disunion sentiments prevailed in the Southern Democracy, by asserting that " a [. . .] feeling that the Union is [still] *worth preserving*, is springing up <a new thing just beginning> in Kentucky[,] Tennessee[,] Texas[,] Virginia and Alabama." But nothing is said of this new-born patriotism in Mississippi, Georgia and the Carolinas.

The locality of Mr. D.[ouglas] is made a strong argument—" He comes [. . .] from the right quarter [. . .], a central *State*— . . . The central States *have a right to claim* [,] *at this time*, a President from their section of the Union."

---

[62] James H. Van Alen, a New Yorker of means who dabbled in politics. He not only visited Missouri for political purposes, but attended the Pennsylvania Convention of 1860, and made several political trips to Washington during the War. He and Bates became friends and Bates helped secure him a brigadier-generalship in 1862 which he resigned in 1863.

[63] *Supra*, April 27, 1859, note 28.

[64] The old Planters' House, scene of a momentous conference between Southern sympathizers and Federal officers on June 11, 1861.

[65] *Supra*, April 27, 1859, note 27.

[66] See *supra*, June 16 and July 27, 1859.

[67] The Democratic National Convention was to meet at Charleston, South Carolina.

It insists upon having Mr. Seward only, as the Republican Nominee, and urges upon the *Rep[ublican]s*: the necessity to make a nomination to suit the Democrats!

It gives to the Democrats a great deal of good advice, and some pretty stern orders, and yet avows that—" *We* do not belong to that party! "

" Touching the question of Slavery[,] as presented by southern ultra politicians[,] it is not of *sufficient dignity* to authorise any division of the Democratic party." [68]

And yet it is a *Constitutional* question, whether the Constitution does or does not carry slavery into the Territories.

Heretofore the Mo. Rep[ublican] has persistently claimed that Slavery would be the only question in the next presidential election.

The papers inform us now that *Prest Buchanan* is preparing a message in favor of a Pacific R R,[69] or rather *two* Pacific Railroads. Both Pierce and Buchanan pretended to be in favor of the road, but have done literally nothing towards the accomplishment of the object.

Under the pretence of surveying routes, they have sent out on exploring trips, some worthy votaries of the p[h]ysical sciences, who, I believe, have been very industrious, for we have as the result of their labor, 8 or 10 quarto volumes about the size of a family bible. They contain very little about the road, but are filled up mainly with a mass of learning on the great national subjects of *Geology, Ornithology* and *ichthyology*, and many beautiful pictures of rocks, beasts, birds and fishes!

These men pretend to have constitutional scruples about making a railroad through our own country, but have none at all about establishing roads through Central America and Mexico, and keeping up armies to protect and defend them—Witness—i. a. the late treaty with Juarez,[70] the pretended President of Mexico.

Thomas Allen's [71] (Poetical) address—Candidate for Govr. Feb 10. 1860[.]   Very Silly[.]

[*A long newspaper article headed " Gubernatorial Question."*]

---

[68] The italics and some of the capitalization, punctuation, and spelling in all of these passages are Mr. Bates's.

[69] For years agitation for a Pacific railroad and the rivalries of various western cities over the eastern terminus of such a road had loomed large in politics. St. Louis was a leading contestant, and so was Chicago with Douglas as its advocate. Southern cities, too, had claims on the terminus. There were even proposals to build the railroad through Mexico or Panama.

[70] Benito P. Juárez, Liberal leader of Mexico. Through being head of the Supreme Court, he had become President of Mexico in 1858 when revolution unseated President Camonfort. In 1861 he was legally elected in his own right.

[71] New York lawyer; editor of the Washington *Madisonian*, 1837–1842; government printer, 1837–1842; St. Louis railroad promoter, builder, and president, 1848–1881; Missouri state senator, 1850–1854; Democratic congressman, 1881–1882.

(*Feb 15.*)   The *Juares* treaty [72] we are now told, is pending before the Senate, and that the President and his party are using all means and appliances to bring over enough Senators ($\frac{2}{3}$) to ratify the treaty. I am a little doubtful about some of the Republican Senators: They may lack the moral courage to stand out against all the appliances that may be brought to bear upon them. No doubt, the Adm[inistratio]n., and especially the extreme Democracy, will leave no efforts untried, in the way of coaxing, bullying and bribing.

This wretched treaty, is, I hope, the last effort to carry out that part of the Cincinnati Platform [73] which requires the Adm[inistratio]n. to establish our dominion over the Gulf of Mexico and the Carribean [*sic*] Sea. If it fail in the Senate, as it ought, well and good: But if it be ratified, by a servile Senate, I hope the House will refuse the appropriations necessary to carry it out. [74]

Feby 17. . . .

Last saturday afternoon I took out, in my buggy, Rev: Dr. Wines [75] to Florissant, [76] and staid at Julian's till monday morning. There is quite an effort making to begin to build up a Protestant Church there—

In sunday morning a Sunday School was organized, (Julian taking an active part) then, in the forenoon, Dr. Wines preached an excellent discourse, and afternoon Mr. *James*, an Englishman and Baptist, preached a fair sermon:

I authorised Julian to say that, if they organized a Sunday School, I would send them a $5. library—

Note, sent the Library wednesday, with three hymn books (packed in the same box, but in a separate package, addressed to *Mrs. Dr. Wherry*, who gave me $1.50, to pay for them)[.]

Today Mr. [   ] *Usher* [77] of Terre Haute, called to see me, at the office, and talked politics an hour or more. He is a fine looking man, under 40—talks like a moderate Republican, says he was an old whig, and seems to be a good " Bates man[.] "

---

[72] Officially known as the McLane-Ocampo Treaty. In it we agreed to pay $4,000,000, one-half of which was to be used to offset claims of Americans against Mexico. Mexico gave us three perpetual rights-of-way with ports of entry at each end, and the privilege of transporting troops over them. The United States was to be permitted to protect these routes. Mexico agreed to religious freedom and exemption from forced loans for Americans in Mexico. Tariff reciprocity was established. There was mutual guarantee of protection of the nationals of the two countries, and each government bound itself to seek the aid of the other in securing such protection. The two countries were to act jointly in suppressing discord near the frontier. See *supra*, April 20, 1859, note 8.

[73] The 1856 platform of the Democratic Party drawn up in convention at Cincinnati.

[74] The Treaty was occasionally debated between January 4 and May 31, but the discussion took place in secret executive session and no record is preserved. The Treaty was rejected on May 31 by a sectional vote of 18 to 27.

[75] *Supra*, July 25, 1859, note 43.

[76] *Supra*, May 18, 1859, note 52.

[77] John P. Usher: Indiana lawyer; attorney-general of Indiana, 1861-1862; assistant secretary of the Interior, 1862-1863; secretary of the Interior, 1863-1865.

He was introduced, in fact, by Mr. H. N. Hart, but said that Mr. Baker (Sec.y. of the Chamber of Commerce) was to have brought him up, but was too busy.

Same day, Mr. Broadhead [78] brot to my office and introduced Mr. Reed (Editor of the Louisiana paper) who tells me that all is right now in Pike, since the late meeting to appoint delegates to the Jefferson City Convention (to be held on the 29th. Feb[).]

Mr. R[eed] seems a modest and sensible young man.

Feb 22. I spent this day almost entirely in the inspection of the public Schools. Being urgently invited by *Mr. Divoll*, the Superintendent, I went around with him and several of the directors, and visited the three great new School houses—called respectively, " the Washing[ton] "—" the Clay "—" the Everett "—*Each one* of them fournishing [sic] good accom[m]odation for over 600 pupils.

During the last year, the Board has accomplished a noble work. It has erected (at an expense of over $100,000) nine new School Houses, including the three great ones above mentioned, and is now actually teaching 9000 children! The teachers as a whole body, are believed to be unsurpassed, in all the nation: The physical accom[m]odations both for teachers and pupils, are admirable in general arrangement and in detail: And, in the methods of instruction, all the best improvements of the age are adopted and carefully carried out.

The Corporation—" The Board of President and Directors of the St Louis Public Schools "—is now an accomplished success—I[t] educates 9000 children—besides the High School and the Normal School, both of which are eminently prosperous—I[t] is amply endowed, and its increasing revenues will enable it hereafter, to expand its range of instruction, until it can teach every thing that befits a gentleman or gentlewoman to know. Already it is, in my judgment, far the greatest Institution in this rising City, and the greatest public benefactor.

Ira Divoll, the Superintendant [sic], seems to be the life and soul of the institution to whom, in large measure, its present success and bright prospects, are due. He seems to me to be the very man, qualified in every particular. In praising Mr. D.[ivoll] I must not forget the solid good qualities of his predecssor, Mr. Tice, who, tho' less brilliant and active than Mr. D.[ivoll] and perhaps less well informed, was nevertheless a valuable and useful officer.

After spending most of the day in visiting the schools, at night I attended a great meeting at the High School, where there were excellent musical exercises by the pupils, followed [by] speeches by Mr. Divoll, Dr. Eliot,[79] Mr. Bates, and Professor Tower.

---

[78] *Supra*, Dec. 26, 1859, note 66.

[79] William G. Eliot, founder and minister of the Church of the Messiah (Congregational Unitarian) in St. Louis, 1835–1870, and chancellor of Washington University.

The whole passed off satisfactorily.

I spent the night at Judge Richardson's.[80]   The first that I have slept in town for about two years.

[" Our Platform·" [81]

" 1. The Union—it SHALL be preserved.

" 2. A Railroad to the Pacific, by the Government.

" 3. A Tariff for Revenue and Protection.

" 4. A Bank of the United States.

" 5. The Improvement of Rivers and Harbors.

" 6. A *rope* for *all* [82] Traitors and Insurrectionists.

" 7. *Tar and Feathers* for all Abolitionists.

" 8. *Rotten Eggs* for the Secessionists.

" 9. The *gibbet and cat o' nine tails,* for Nullifiers.

" 10. The finger [83] of scorn for all editors who publish incendiary articles.

" 11. The election of men of good sense to Congress.

" 12. The appointment, by the President, of a *Fool Killer,* who shall reside in Washington City.—Waverly Visitor "]

1. 2. 3–5—Good, without amendment or addition[.]

4. Good, *per se*, in principle—Doubtful in the concrete.

6. A rope for each one! that's extravagant. 'T would raise the price of hemp too high.

7. Needless—only forbid Cuffie [84] to be a politician, and the Abolitionists will sink out of sight.

8. Not to pelt with—but cooked into nog, and they forced to drink it, a sure remedy for secession.

9. No, no, that's not the way—Only turn them under in politics, and they, and not the laws, will be nullified.

10. Good, as far as it goes, but not enough. Refuse to buy or read their books and papers, and forbid Congress-men to advertise them in the Capitol, by resolutions and speeches, as Clark [85] did the Helper book.[86]

11. In the abstract good: In the concrete, doubtful. Should not every representative " reflect the true image of his constituents? "

---

[80] *Supra,* April 27, 1859, note 26.

[81] A clipping pasted into the diary.

[82] " All " was underscored by Mr. Bates on the clipping.

[83] The newspaper uses the symbol of a hand with a finger pointing.

[84] Originally a proper name brought from Africa, but now used as a contemptuous generic term for Negro.

[85] John B. Clark, of Missouri: a pro-slavery Democratic congressman from 1857 until in which he, a North Carolinian, sought to show that the South was falling behind the North industrially, eonmically, and socially because slave labor could not keep pace resolution was offered on December 5, 1859, *Cong. Globe,* 36 Cong., 1 Sess., 3; the speech was made on December 5 and 6, *ibid.,* 3–4, 15–18.

[86] Hinton Rowan Helper's *Impending Crisis of the South: How to Meet It* (N. Y., 1857) in which he, a North Carolinian, sought to show that the South was falling behind the North industrially, economically, and socially because slave labor could not keep pace with free labor. The book was based upon economic, not humanitarian, arguments and Helper was not interested in the negro. But the *Impending Crisis* became effective anti-slavery propaganda and infuriated the South.

And, in this pure Democracy, have not the men of no sense or bad sense, as good a right to be represented as the men of good sense? Fie! Mr. Visitor! you are undemocratic!

12. No, never—too dangerous—It might make an interregnum in all branches of the Government.

The Weekly Republic of Feby 18 and Nat:[ional] Inte[lligence]r. Feb 16 contains—

1. Correspondence of Gov: Gist [87] of S.[outh] C.[arolina] and Gov Hicks [88] of Md. about the S.[outh] C.[arolina] proposition for a Convention of the *Slaveholding States*,[89] in which Govr. Gist denies that the object is *Disunion*—That Fib of G.[ist] is, like hipocracy [*sic*], the homage which vice pays to virtue.

2 Proceedings of the *K.[now] N.[othing]* members of the Loua. Legislature, in which the majority—17 to 7—go over bodily to the Democrats, and blindly pledge themselves to support the Charleston nominee,[90]—whoever he may be.

3. Speech of Mr. Ferry [91] M.[ember of] C.[ongress] of Conn[ecticu]t. on Slavery &c[.]

4. Speech of F P Blair Jr.[92] at N. Y.

[*A clipping from the* [Missouri Republ]ican *reporting resolutions adopted at a Democratic meeting in Cass County.*]

These Cass Co.[unty] Democrats are full of zeal, and deserve praise for their *obstinate* valor: They are humane and generous also, in that they still admire and sustain Buchanan, in spite of the contempt of the world, poured upon him[.]

Feb 25. Gibson [93] and other friends have returned from the *Indiana* Rep[ublica]n. Convention, and report favorably. A large majority of the delegates appointed to the Chicago Convention,[94] is made up of "Bates men"—20 to 6 or 22 to 4. *H.y. S. Lane* [95] for Govr.— a zealous man and powerful on the stump[.]

---

[87] William H. Gist used all of his power as governor (1858–1860) to bring about secession. In his messages to the Legislature he stressed the inevitability of secession. On October 5, 1860, he wrote confidentially to all Southern governors except Houston of Texas announcing South Carolina's probable secession and asking coöperation. He kept the South Carolina Legislature in special session to call the secession convention as soon as Lincoln was elected.

[88] *Supra*, Jan. 28, 1860, note 43.

[89] After the John Brown attack at Harper's Ferry, South Carolina had passed resolutions, on December 22, 1859, urging the slave-holding states to meet and take measures for united action. *Reports and Resolutions of the General Assembly of South Carolina* (1859), 578–579.

[90] I. e., the Democratic nominee for President.

[91] Orris S. Ferry: Republican congressman, 1859–1861; brigadier-general in the Union Army; U. S. senator, 1867–1875. In the election of this year (1860) he lost his seat to a Democrat.

[92] *Supra*, April 27, 1859, note 25.

[93] *Supra*, April 27, 1859, note 27.

[94] The Republican National Convention of 1860.

[95] Leader of the Republican Party in Indiana, formerly a Whig congressman, 1840–1843, and chairman of the Republican Convention of 1856. Lane was elected governor but served only four days and then resigned to become U. S. senator, 1861–1867. He helped turn the 1860 nomination to Lincoln.

In Ohio, the Delegates are appointed by Districts, and, as far as heard from the prospects are good. In Hamilton County (Cunti.) 3 out of 4 of the Delegates are known Bates men. And Mr. Corwin [96] is appointed a delegate from his district.

Senator, *James A Pearce*,[97] of Maryland—

He, I believe, has many good qualities in him, but they seem not to be mixed in due proportion. He loves truth and justice and would act them out, *if convenient* and *consistent with his personal success*: And he loves official rank and party influence and would like to enjoy them along with conscious rectitude, *if he could*. But he seems to lack courage and will: He halts between opinions not fully resolved which to sacrifice—his ambition to truth and justice, or truth and justice to his ambition.

Most likely he will fall, as men commonly do who try to sit on two stools at once. His re-election to the Senate is now pending in the Md. Legislature, and, in reference to that fact, he has lately come out with a letter, declaring that he joined the Democrats in *1855*. and will be true to them in their present difficulty—He will support the Charleston [i. e. Democratic] nominee, *whoever he may be* and *on whatever platform*.

In *1854*, he joined the Democrats in supporting the Kansas bill, yet he says in the published letter, that he joined in 1855. Still, in 1856 he denied his democracy—A democratic meeting was held in his town, ·and a comm[itt]ee. appointed to wait upon him and request him to come and make a speech—He declined—telling them that they were mistaken, that he was not a Democrat.

This was told me by Ex Senator *Chambers*[98] (a neighbor and personal friend of Mr. P.[earce]) at the Baltimore Whig Convention in Sept. 1856.

Now, that he has fully identified himself with the waning Democracy, sinking under the weight of its increased sins, they may safely venture to break the implied promise of reward, and refuse to re-elect him to the Senate. Indeed, it is intimated that his rival, Stewart,[99] an old democrat's friends [that the friends of his rival, Stewart, an old Democrat,] will never go over to Pearce, but [will] concentrate rather upon one Mr. Long.[1]

---

[96] Thomas Corwin: Whig congressman, 1831–1840; governor of Ohio, 1840–1842; U. S. senator, 1845–1850; secretary of the Treasury, 1850–1853. At this time he was a congressman again, 1859–1861,—a Republican, but a reluctant one, who dodged the real issue by advocating abolition of slavery in the *Territories* and then supporting the right of each new *state* to decide the question for itself. Lincoln appointed him minister to Mexico, 1861–1864.

[97] *Supra*, Nov. 17, 1859, note 56.

[98] *Supra*, Nov. 17, 1859, note 58.

[99] James A. Stewart: lawyer of Cambridge, Maryland; Democratic congressman, 1855–1861.

[1] Edward H. C. Long: state senator in 1860; former Whig congressman, 1845–1847. He was defeated for the senatorship in 1860 by Senator Pearce.

I never regret to see these half breed Whigs beaten—they have some virtues left, but just enough to cheat with, by varnishing over their newly-adopted Democratic vices.

Feb 26th. Warm weather for some days.
The first *Crocus* of the season, bloomed in the open garden—

Feb 28th. Frogs singing for the first time, this evening[.]
Feb 28. To day (and yesterday) the weather is warm, for the season, murky and drizzly. The mud is very bad, and the roads dangerously out of order.

Yesterday the Gen[era]l. Assembly convened, in special session, at Jefferson, under the Governor's[2] proclamation, and much anxiety is felt as to what they will do to aid the Railroads, and whether they will do any thing to reform the Banks. I expect little good from them, as they seem wholly absorbed in their partizan schemes, and partyism now, especially the Democratic, has become little better than a series of deceptions and frauds.

[*Marginal Note.*] That Maryland House of Delegates is a fair representative of Democratic ignorance and impudence. By resolution, they questioned Gov: Hicks[3] to ascertain whether or no he had congratulated Speaker Pennington[4] upon his election; and he answered them as they deserved, and sent them off with a flea in their ear—

[*A clipping shows the Governor's answer to them:*

"I cannot admit the right of the House of Delegates to make any such inquiry of me; and the respect which, in my opinion, ought to be observed by each Department of the Government towards every other, precludes me from returning any answer to such a message, other than the acknowledgment of its receipt."]

Tomorrow the Opposition Convention[5] will sit at Jefferson, and I expect will be numerously attended. I doubt not, it will nominate me for the Presidency, yet I wish it was over, for it contains a good deal of combustible material, which it may be hard to keep down so as to prevent an explosion.

Among the whigs and Americans[6] in the interior, there is a degree of timidity quite surprising. Some of them even go the length of saying that the[y] are anxious to support me, but cant [*sic*] do it if the 'Black' Republicans support me[.]   <Washington Adams

---

[2] Robert M. Stewart's. *Supra*, Nov. 24, 1859, note 80.

[3] *Supra*, Jan. 28, 1860, note 43.

[4] William Pennington, formerly governor of New Jersey (1837–1843), now a Whig congressman (1859–1861) just elected speaker of the House of Representatives as a compromise candidate after a two months' deadlock. He was defeated for reëlection as a Republican in November of this year.

[5] Originally planned for Dec. 28, 1859. See *supra*, Dec. 17, 1859, and *infra*, March 1, 1860.

[6] The American Party or Know-Nothings.

and such like>—that is, they are *for* me if I have no chance of election, but against me if I have any chance! "Call you that backing of your friends? A plague upon such backing." I'd rather have them open enemies.

There was a strong *opposition* meeting at Carondalet—Bernhard Poeping presiding—endorsing me fully—See Mo. Dem[ocrat] of today.

The Mo. Dem[ocra]t. of today is full of interesting matter—

1. The able speech of H. Winter Davis[7] in Congress, in answer to the shameful resolution of the Maryland House of Delegates,[8] denouncing him for his vote for Speaker Pennington.

2. *Editorial* on the "Opposition Convention" (to sit tomorrow) strong, bold, judicious and conciliatory.

3. *Editorial*, "*A new plank* in the National Democratic platform"—the adoption, by the Senate, of Jeff: Davis' resolution[9]—substantially requiring a slave code for the Territories—

<I thought, from all the outward shewings, that the Charleston Convention[10] would be forced to nominate Douglas, in spite of the hot opposition of several Southern leaders; but if they insist upon "the Slave Code," he cant [*sic*] be nominated—and if nominated on that platform, his defeat is inevitable. If *the South* insist upon that plank, it is a strong sign that the more desperate southern leaders are still bent upon their old treason of a *southern Confederation*. If they make that platform and put upon it an out and out southern candidate, then I shall believe that it is not done with the hope of electing a President, but for the purpose of uniting the South more closely, with the view of breakin[g] up the Union and forming a Southern confederation!

A futile treason, impossible of consum[m]ation, as vain and impotent as it is wicked.[>]

The signs indicating my nomination are growing, in number and strength every day. Several State conventions (as Indiana and Connecticut) have appointed "Bates" Delegates to the Chicago Convention.[11] The People and the Press too, have taken the thing in hand. Many town and County meetings, in all the northern half of the Union, have declared for me; and a vast number of Newspapers, from Massachusetts to Oregon, have placed my name at the head of their columns. <[*Marginal Note.*] Among others, the *Delaware* Journal has my name up.>

But, knowing the fickleness of popular favor, and on what small things great events depend, I shall take care not so to set my heart

[7] *Supra*, Dec. 17, 1859, note 39.
[8] *Journal of the Proceedings of the Senate of Maryland*, January Session, 1860, p. 249.
[9] Feb. 2, 1860, *Cong. Globe*, 36 Cong., 1 Sess., 658.
[10] The Democratic National Convention of 1860.
[11] The Republican National Convention of 1860.

upon the glittering bauble, as to be mortified or made at all unhappy by a failure.

March 1. The *Opposition Convention*, which sat at Jefferson City yesterday, accomplished its work harmoniously and well. Composed as it was, of Whigs, Americans, Republicans—pro slavery and anti slavery men, I apprehended some jarring and discord, and was rejoiced to find that they accomplished their object, harmoniously and unanimously—

I was nominated enthusiastically, and the declaration of principals [*sic*] (stronger on some points than I thought could be safely offered) was passed without a dissenting voice.

The declaration embraced Protective tariff—Internal improvements, Pacific Railroad, a Free Homestead—and denounced the "Heresies" of the Democracy on slavery in the Territories—The Convention then adjourned.

At night there was a ratification meeting, in which stirring speeches were made by J. C. Richardson,[12] U. Wright,[13] Gen Gardenhine [?] W. H. Letcher of Saline, Mr. Anderson[14] of Pike and Col C. S. Clarkson of St Louis Co.[unty] and perhaps others[.] (Judge Richardson presided.[)]

Next day there was a volunteer meeting of part of the members of the Convention, (in which Genl Watkins[15] presided) which after endorsing the nomination, took some measures towards the appointment of deligates [*sic*] to the proposed "National Union Convention"—so far as to raise a Com[mitt]ee. with power to appt. Delegates.

There was a great crowd at Jefferson, the Legislature having just reassembled. I hear that the Democracy was greatly surpised at the result: They expected a convention composed of such heterogenious [*sic*] materials would quarrel, explode and break up in a row; and when it had accomplished its purpose and adjourned harmoniously and full of zeal, they began to fear that a "United Op[p]osition" was not a thing impossible.

I think that convention will exert a powerful influence within the State, and may have a strong bearing upon the action of parties elsewhere.

Note—This is the first State Convention in which all the parties in opposition—Republicans, Free[-Soil] Democrats, Americans and Whigs—all united in one body and acted harmoniously for the attainment of one object. It is at once the sign and the means of

[12] *Supra,* April 27, 1859, note 26.
[13] *Supra,* June 4, 1859, note 72.
[14] *Infra,* June 22, 1860, note 63.
[15] Nathaniel W. Watkins, state legislator, member of the State Convention of 1861 until he joined the Confederate (Missouri) State Guards.

harmonious action on a larger scale. And we may reasonably hope that it will go far [toward] abating and finally removing the mutual prejudices which set us so fiercly and unreasonably against each// other[.]

[*A clipping from the* Missouri Democrat *of March 3, 1860, gives the resolutions adopted by the Pennsylvania Democratic Convention.*]

March 5. To day, I was called upon by Mr. Bates of Massachusetts, a cousin of Isaac C. Bates:[16] He was introduced by Capt Bissell—

Also, Mr..Tuck [17] of New Hampshire, ex-M.[ember of] C.[ongress] introduced by Mr. Nathl. Holmes. And had a good deal of conversation with both.

Mr. B.[ates] is, I think, an old whig, and Mr. T.[uck] an old Democrat, who went off on the free soil question, and is now a zealous Republican.

They both (tho' doubtless differing among themselves) profess to be good "Bates men" and talk emphatically, about "the cause."

Got a long letter today from *T. J. Coffey* [18] of Indiana Pa. He was a member of the late Pa. Convention of the "People's Party" [19] and is a Delegate to the Chicago Convention. He is buoyant and seems confident of my nomination, although the Delegation is under instruction to vote for Senator Cameron. That, he thinks, is a mere compliment, which will be fulfilled by casting one vote—And then, I, being the first choice of nearly half of the Delegates (of Pa.) and the second choice of all, will be sure of the united support of all of that delegation. And that, considering the favorable signs in other States, he thinks will make my nomination sure.

Also, Mr. Gibson [20] shewed me a letter to him of Mr. Van Allen,[21] of N. Y.—who attended the Pa. Convention—He is in high spirits, and says that after the convention, Cameron "backed down" and agrees that the vote of Pa. may be cast for me in the convention,

16 *Supra,* July 27, 1859, note 49.

17 Amos Tuck: Independent congressman, 1847–1853; Moderate Republican in 1860; member of the Peace Convention in Washington in 1861; naval officer of the port of Boston, 1861–1865.

18 Titian J. Coffey had come out from Pennsylvania to study law in Edward Bates's office in St. Louis. He had been one of the organizers of the Republican Party in Pennsylvania and was at this time working there for Bates's nomination. Bates rewarded him with the assistant attorney-generalship, and he wrote some of the important legal opinions rendered by Bates during the War.

19 "The People's Party" was organized in Pennsylvania to include all of the Opposition to the Buchanan Democracy—Republicans, Americans, Whigs, and Anti-Lecompton Democrats. The bitterness existing in Pennsylvania, especially between Republicans and Americans, made coöperation under any of the national party names impossible, but in the "People's Party" they could all join. The "People's" Convention of 1860 sent the Pennsylvania delegates to the Republican National Convention.

20 *Supra,* April 27, 1859, note 27.

21 *Supra,* Feb. 4, 1860, note 62.

on the single condition that he may have the honor of transferring it, by *magnanimously declining in my favor.*

To day, and heretofore, conversed with Mr. [   ] *Benjamin*, who is or is to be, editor of the St Joe "West." The paper, tho' against me heretofore, is now to hoist my flag. Mr. B.[enjamin] is quite a young man, and I have some misgivings about him.

March 10. The *Baltimore Patriot* of March 6, in a very positive leader, declares that the Democratic programme for the Presidential election, is definitively settled, by a caucus of M.[embers of] C[ongres]s. That Breckenridge[22] [*sic*] and Seymour[23] are the men, and that they will be forced upon the Charleston Convention, by a combination of Democratic powers not to be withstood.

That will be a very weak ticket, and may be easily beaten if the Chicago Convention[24] should make a conservative nomination. There is room to fear that, if the Democrats make that nomination, the ultra wing of the Republicans may insist upon setting up one of their extreme men. That would lead to a third ticket, and probably throw the election into the House[.]

March 10. The *Nat[iona]l. Intelligencer* of the 6th. contains the proceedings in full of the Opposition Conventions of *N. Carolina* and *Missouri.* The former recommends Wm. A. Graham[25] as 1st. choice and Washington Hunt[26] 2d. choice, for the Presidency, and appoints Delegates to the National Union Convention[.] The latter nominates E. Bates *independently* and without reference to any other convention. And both denounce the Democracy[.]

March 10. Today the *Republican Convention* sits in St Louis, to appoint Delegates to the Chicago Convention. It is understood that they will nominate me, and probably call for a distinct statement of my views upon the various questions touching slavery in the Territories, and perhaps some other points.

Mar 13. They did just as was expected—passed a string of resolutions—Recommended me to the Chicago Convention, and appointed delegates.

I am given to understand that tomorrow I may expect to receive a letter from the Delegates, calling on me for a precise statement of my position on the main points concerning slavery in the Territories, and perhaps some others.

---

[22] *Supra,* Oct. 26, 1859, note 19.

[23] Horatio Seymour, governor of New York, 1853–1855, 1863–1865, who advocated letting the people of the Territories decide the slavery question and believed they would decide it against slavery. He tried to avert war by a compromise, but when that failed supported Lincoln. Throughout the War, however, he defended individuals' and states' rights against arbitrary war measures, and insisted that the defense of the Union and not abolition of slavery should be kept the object of the War.

[24] The Republican National Convention.

[25] *Supra,* Dec. 17, 1859, note 37.

[26] *Supra,* Oct. 26, 1859, note 15.

March 13. Yesterday morning Mr. [   ] Gray of New York, called to see me (bearing a strong letter from F. P. Blair jr [27][.] I met him coming out to my house, as I went in. We went to my office and had an hour's talk on the politics of the day. He says that he came out on purpose to see me—That [he] is a warm friend of Mr. Seward, personally and politically, yet, under the circumstances, thinks that Mr. S.[eward] if nominated, might fail of election,[28] and therefore goes for my nomination.

I regret that he was obliged to depart so soon (in the afternoon) as I wished to know him better, and yet was bound to leave him, and go into Court to attend to a case.

I hear since, thro' Mr. Dick,[29] that he was well pleased with his interview with me[.]

Today called to see me (introduced by Capt. Eads [30]) Mr. *John M. Richardson* of Springfield, Greene Co.[unty] Mo. a leader of the Rep[ublica]n. party in this State—a member of the Convention which sat her[e] on the 10th. and now a Delegate to the Chicago Convention.

I read to him several of my letters, to Colfax [31] &c. and he seemed well satisfied, and warm for my nomination[.]

[*March 17*] [*A clipping from the* National Intelligencer *of March 17, 1860, protesting against the intrusions of whites upon Indian lands.*]

[*A clipping from the* National Intelligencer *of March 17, 1860, headed " Indefinitely Postponed." It quotes from the* New Orleans Bulletin *of March 10 an editorial deprecating sectional agitation and announcing that joint resolutions upon the subject of federal relations, offered in the Louisiana Senate, have been indefinitely postponed. The article from the* Bulletin *says:*

> " Postponement of the resolutions ' is consistent and proper; for upon what grounds can we call upon the North and West to frown down sectionalism, to place their heels upon agitation, if, at the same time, we give it countenance and support? How can we call upon our brethren to do that which we ourselves refuse to perform? . . . What is patriotic and praiseworthy in Maine must be so also in Louisiana. This the common sense of the masses must perceive, and Southern Legislatures generally, in giving the go-by to the invitation of South Carolina to meet in a great political Convention, have done nothing more than reflect a sound public sentiment—' "]

The So: Carolina Resolutions to destroy the Union [32] meet with but little sympathy. S.[outh] C.[arolina] I think, stands alone in

[27] *Supra*, April 27, 1859, note 25.

[28] *Supra*, April 27, 1859, note 30.

[29] *Infra*, Dec. 24, 1863, note 3.

[30] *Supra*, Jan. 28, 1860, note 38.

[31] *Supra*, June 16 and July 27, 1859.

[32] See *supra*, Feb. 22, 1860, note 89. The underscoring was done later in red pencil.

the real wish to dissolve the Union. Every where else in the South, the *threat* seems to be only a political trick, used in *terrorem*, to frighten timid people into the support of favorite southern measures.

In So: C[arolin]a: I do believe the leaders are silly enough to be in earnest, and self-conceited enough to imagine that other people may mistake their wicked folly for wisdom and honor.

The legislatures of only two S[t]ates (Mis[sis]sippi and Alabama) have answered favorably to S.[outh] C[arolina]'s call to treason. Louisiana lately refused. Va. very mildly and politely declined—The Gen[era]l. Assembly did barely *not accept* the proposition; but it did not (as Washington enjoins in the Farewell address) " frown indignantly " [33] upon the attempt. And the Democrats, I hear in their convention, were for accepting the invitation[.]

Here in Mo. Gov Stewart [34] did not even lay the S.[outh] C.[arolina] resolutions before the Gen[era]l. Assembly, knowing that, whatever other faults the Gen[era]l. Assembly may have, it would " frown indignantly " upon all such attempts.

The Herald St Louis March 18. 1860 " Squatter Sovereignty " Many authorities

[*A whole column of quotations from leading men in support of popular sovereignty headed by one from Stephen A. Douglas and one from Senator James S. Green [35] in a letter of December 10, 1849, to J. M. Minor. Senator Green says, " Congress can make no rule or regulation respecting SLAVES or horses, or other private property . . . but only respecting the property belonging to the United States."*]

Yet Congress forbade whisky, by the act of 34, in Jackson's time[.]

[*A clipping from the* National Intelligencer *of March 24, 1860, commenting upon a letter from Edward Bates which it printed in the same issue. The editorial says:*

" Mr. Bates expresses himself with a frankness due to his high personal character, . . . Those—perhaps now not a great many—who have known this estimable gentleman as long as ourselves, and especially those who had an opportunity of marking his standing in Congress, where he was the peer of . . . leading men of that brilliant era, will not be surprised at the ability which pervades his present letter or the honest straight-forwardness of its avowals. These avowals, we suspect, will hardly conciliate the favor of uncompromising partisans on either side of the sectional issue, or the Territorial question, but for that reason they may combine the approbation of moderate men, who are willing to concede something of the *summum jus*, for the sake of harmony and a beneficient administration of the Government."] [36]

---

[33] Washington urged his countrymen to frown indignantly " upon the first dawning of every attempt to alienate any portion of our country from the rest, or to enfeeble the sacred ties which now link together the various parts."

[34] *Supra*, Nov. 24, 1859, note 80.

[35] *Supra*, June 20, 1859, note 96.

[36] This last clipping and comment are folded into a separate sheet of paper.

[*The letter was written on March 17, 1860, in response to seven direct questions put by a committee* [37] *of the Missouri Republican Convention which decided to support Mr. Bates for the Presidency.*]

SIRS: B. Gratz Brown,[38] Esq., as President of the Missouri State Convention, which sat in St. Louis on the 10th of this month, has officially made known to me the proceedings of that body, and by them I am enabled to know some of you as delegates to the Chicago Convention, representing the Republican party of Missouri.

. . .

. . . I have held no political office, and sought none for more than twenty-five years.

Under these circumstances, I confess the gratification which I feel in receiving the recent manifestations of the respect and confidence of my fellow-citizens. First, the Opposition members of the Missouri Legislature declared their preference for me as a candidate. Then followed my nomination by a Convention composed of all the elements of the Opposition in this State. And now, the Republicans of Missouri, in their separate Convention just held in St. Louis, have reaffirmed the nomination, and proposed, by their delegates, to present me to the National Convention, soon to be held at Chicago, as a candidate for the first office in the nation.

These various demonstrations in my own State are doubly gratifying to me, because they afford the strongest proof that my name has been put forward only in a spirit of harmony and peace, and with a hope of preventing all division and controversy among those who, for their own safety and the public good, ought to be united in their action.

. . .

Now, gentlemen, I proceed to answer your questions, briefly indeed, but fully, plainly, and with all possible frankness; and I do this the more willingly because I have received from individuals many letters—too many to be separately answered—and have seen in many public journals articles making urgent calls upon me for such a statement of my views.

1. *Slavery—Its Extension in the Territories.*

On this subject, in the States and in the Territories, I have no new opinions—no opinions formed in relation to the present array of parties. I am coeval with the Missouri question of 1819-'20, hav-

[37] The committee consisted of Peter L. Foy (*infra*, May 31, 1860, note 37), Henry T. Blow (*supra*, Sept. 20, 1859, note 95), F. A. Dick (*infra*, Dec. 24, 1863, note 2), Stephen Hoyt, G. W. Fishback (*infra*, March 31, 1865, note 48), Charles L. Bernays (*infra*, Sept. 20, 1860. note 39), Jno. M. Richardson, O. D. Filley (*infra*, Dec. 24, 1863, note 1), William McKee, Barton Able (*infra*, May 3, 1860, note 90), and J. B. Sitton (*supra*, Dec. 19, 1859, note 49).

[38] *Infra*, Feb. 15, 1864. note 44.

ing begun my political life in the midst of that struggle. At that time my position required me to seek all the means of knowledge within my reach, and to study the principles involved with all the powers of my mind, and I arrived at conclusions then which no subsequent events have induced me to change.

The existence of negro slavery in our country had its beginning in the early time of the colony, and was imposed by the mother country against the will of most of the colonists. At the time of the Revolution, and long after, it was commonly regarded as an evil, temporary in its nature, and likely to disappear in the course of time; yet, while it continued, a misfortune to the country, socially and politically. Thus was I taught by those who made our Government, and neither the new light of modern civilization nor the discovery of a new system of constitutional law and social philosophy has enabled me to detect the error of their teaching.

Slavery is a social relation, a domestic institution. Within the States it exists by the local law, and the Federal Government has no control over it there. The Territories, whether acquired by conquest or peaceable purchase, are subject and subordinate, not sovereign like the States. The nation is supreme over them, and the National Government has the power to permit or forbid slavery within them.

Entertaining these views I am opposed to the extension of slavery, and, in my opinion, the spirit and the policy of the Government ought to be against its extension.

2. *Does the Constitution carry slavery into the Territories?*

I answer no. The Constitution of the United States does not carry slavery into the Territories. With much more show of reason may it be said that it carries slavery into all the States. But it does not carry slavery any where; it only acts upon it where it finds it established by the local law. In connection with this point I am asked to state my views of the Dred Scott case, and what was really determined by the Supreme Court in that case. It is my opinion, carefully considered, that the court determined one single point of law only; that is, that Scott, the plaintiff, being a negro of African descent, not necessarily a slave, could not be a citizen of Missouri, and therefore could not sue in the Federal Court; and that for this reason, and this alone, the Circuit Court had no jurisdiction of the cause and no power to give judgment between the parties. The only jurisdiction which the Supreme Court had of the cause was for the purpose of correcting the error of the Circuit Court in assuming the power to decide upon the merits of the case. This power the

Supreme Court did exercise by setting aside the judgment of the Circuit Court upon the merits, and by dismissing the suit without any judgment for or against either party. This is all that the Supreme Court did, and all that it had lawful power to do. I consider it a great public misfortune that several of the learned Judges should have thought that their duty required them to discuss and give opinions upon various questions outside of the case, as the case was actually disposed of by the court. All such opinions are extra-judicial and of no authority. But, besides this, it appears to me that several of the questions so discussed by the Judges are political questions, and therefore beyond the cognizance of the judiciary, and proper only to be considered and disposed of by the political departments. If I am right in this, and it seems to me plain, the precedent is most unfortunate, because it may lead to a dangerous conflict of authority among the co-ordinate branches of the Government.

3. *As to the Colonization of the Free Blacks.*

For many years I have been connected with the American Colonization Society, of which the rising young State of Liberia is the first fruit. I consider the object both humane and wise, beneficent alike to the free blacks who emigrate and to the whites whom they leave behind. But Africa is distant, and presents so many obstacles to rapid settlement that we cannot indulge the hope of draining off in that direction the growing numbers of our free black population. The tropical regions of America, I think, offer a far better prospect both for us and for them.

4. *As to any inequality of rights among American citizens.*

I recognise no distinctions among American citizens but such as are expressly laid down in the Constitution; and I hold that our Government is bound to protect all the citizens in the enjoyment of all their rights every where, and against all assailants; and as to all these rights, there is no difference between citizens born and citizens made such by law.

5. *Am I in favor of the construction of a railroad from the Valley of the Mississippi to the Pacific ocean, under the auspices of the General Government?*

Yes, strongly. I not only believe such a road of vast importance as the means of increasing the population, wealth, and power of this great valley, but necessary as the means of national defence and of preserving the integrity of the Union.

6. *Am I in favor of the measure called the Homestead bill?*

Yes. I am for guarding the public lands as well as possible from the danger of becoming the subject of common trade and speculation; for keeping them for the actual use of the people; and for granting tracts of suitable size to those who will actually inhabit and improve them.

7. *Am I in favor of the immediate admission of Kansas under the Wyondotte Constitution?*

I think that Kansas ought to be admitted without delay, leaving her, like all the other States, the sole judge of her own Constitution.

Thus, gentlemen, I believe I have answered all your inquiries, in a plain, intelligible manner, and I hope to your satisfaction. I have not attempted to support my answers by argument, for that could not be done in a short letter; and, restraining myself from going into general politics, I have confined my remarks to the particular subjects upon which you requested me to write.

Your obliged fellow-citizen,

EDWARD BATES.

March 28. . . .

Note. I saw young Williams (son of Willis L) in the street to day. Hearing of his wild career I did never expect to see him again. *Politics—My late letter to the Rep[ublican]s of Mo.*[39]—

The Mo. Democrat of today has many extracts from other papers, commenting upon the letter in a manner very flattering to my vanity. Most of the papers quoted are in the west and N.[orth] W.[est] but not all—The Baltimore Patriot is full and jubilant, and my old friends of the National Intelligencer [40] go as far in their complimentary kindness as my self-love could ask.

My letters too from various states, recd. today are equally satisfactory—1. F A. Ryan of Appleton Wis: 2. S Colfax [41] at Washington—3. Truman Smith [42]— "old *Truman*" of Conn: (now practising law in N. Y. tho' still *living* in Conn:[)]

April 2. The newspapers bring me today President Buchanan's most remarkable Message to the H[ouse] of R.[epresentatives] dated March 23d., recd. and discussed 29th. and referred to the judiciary Com[mitte]e.[43] The Prest. protests agst. the examination (by

[39] *Supra*, 111–114.
[40] March 24. 1860.
[41] *Supra*, April 27, 1859, note 28.
[42] Formerly Whig congressman. 1839–1843. 1845–1849; U. S. senator, 1849–1854; now a New York lawyer living in Stanford. Lincoln made him judge of the Court of Arbitration under the Treaty of 1862 with Great Britain.
[43] The message was dated March 28. See J. D. Richardson, *Messages and Papers of the Presidents*, V, 614–619.

Cavode's Com[mitt]ee.[44]) about his connection with the use of money in the Pa. elections. He does not deny the power of impeachment, but he objects to the examination (mainly) on two grounds—1. There are no distinct charges made against him, but vague generalities only surmised—2. The charges should be exhibited and the enquiry made, before the *Judiciary Com[mitt]ee.* (as was done in Judge Peak's [Peck's] case [45]) and not a Special Com[mitt]ee. like Cavode's [*sic*]—where his accuser he says is made his judge[.]

It is a passionate, weak, drivelling Message, false in doctrine, and done in very bad taste—

It assumes, preposterously, that there can be no investigation by the House, into suspected abuses, until there are specific charges against particular individuals. Whereas the common practice, and almost of necessity, is to institute the enquiry for the very purpose of finding out whether it is or is not proper to make specific charges. Formerly (as long ago as the impeachment of Judge Chase [46]) the House was familiarly called "the *Grand Inquest of the Nation.*" As such the House itself is not a *trier* but an *accuser*—In cases of impeachment it is emphatically so; and the Committee is only an agency, used by the House, for its better information[.]

But the President commits a strange blunder in assuming to dictate to the House, by what Committee it must make its enquiry.

And it is a blunder equally grave to assume that the House can institute the enquiry only for the purpose of impeachment. Surely, if the enquiry should disclose a wrongful use of money, patronage or other influences, injurious to the purity of elections, that would be a good foundation for legislation, to prevent such abuses in future.

It strikes me that the President commits a very grave mistake in assuming that he has any Legislative functions—He says, with all gravity, that *the People* have "conferred upon him *a large measure of legislative discretion*"—Again, he says—"*In his legislative capacity*, he might, *in common* with the Senate and the House, insti-

[44] John Covode: mill-owner; state legislator; anti-Masonic Whig congressman, 1855–1857; Republican congressman, 1857–1863, 1867–1871; member of the Congressional Committee for the campaign of 1860. The Covode Committee was set up on his motion to investigate alleged attempts of President Buchanan to bribe and coërce congressmen into voting for the Lecompton Constitution. A majority report condemned the President; a minority report exonerated him. Congress took no action. The investigation had probably been instituted largely to provide campaign material for the Republicans.

[45] James H. Peck, judge of the U. S. District Court of Missouri, was impeached for imprisoning an attorney and suspending him from practice for writing a newspaper review of Peck's decision in a land case; he was acquitted.

[46] Samuel Chase, Maryland lawyer and judge, Revolutionary leader, war profiteer, opponent of ratification of the Constitution, later arch-Federalist justice of the U. S. Supreme Court, 1796–1811, was impeached by the House but acquitted by the Senate on charges of an intemperate charge to a Baltimore grand jury and gross unfairness in the conduct of the trials of Fries for treason and of Callender for sedition.

tute enquirry [*sic*], to ascertain any facts which ought to influence his judgment, in approving any bill."!!

He thinks he has this power *in common* (i. e. like, in the same manner and to the same extent) with the Senate and the House—)[*sic*] [47] He can depute committees, take testimony, and compel the presence of persons and papers, imprison the refractory &c.

In my judgment, it is a gross error to mistake the *veto* for *a legislative power—It* may indeed prevent legislation sometimes, but never can make a line of law.

Prest. Buchanan is unfortunate in the use of phrases: He talks in this message about the approaching time when he shall *voluntarily retire* from the public service, as if he were going out of his own mere motion, and not by the expiration of his right to remain. This, I suppose is a mere error in composition, like the statement in one of his annual messages, that it became necessary to send "*an eminent citizen of Pennsylvania*," as minister to China. [48]

This assumption of immunity by the Prest. is but another evidence of the loose and unprincipled practices of the Government, and shews that these practices are fast obliterating the lines of demarkation between the coördinate branches of government.

Even now, the Senate is making a direct incroachment [*sic*] upon the jurisdiction of both the House of Rep[resentative]s: and the President. *Senator Green* [49] of Mo. has introduced a resolution, [50] declaring that [William Medill], [51] Comptroller of the Treasury has been guilty of gross misdemeanor, and is not fit to be continued in office!

This seems to me a direct invasion of the President's power to remove—And an attempt to supersede the House's power to impeach: And an open pre-judgment of the Senate's own power to try impeachments.

In fact, it is a bold attempt to destroy the balance of power among the coördinate branches, and upset the constitutional organization of the Government.

[*Marginal*] *Note.* This protest-message of the President was referred to the Judiciary Committee, and a report [52] made thereon, by Mr. Hickman [53] of Pa. The report, though a full answer and

[47] This parenthesis was inserted apparently without reason.

[48] President Buchanan called him "a distinguished" not "an eminent" citizen. "First Annual Message," Dec. 8, 1857, J. D. Richardson, *op. cit.*, V, 446. The minister was William B. Reed, professor of American history at the University of Pennsylvania.

[49] *Supra*, June 20, 1859, note 96.

[50] April 3, 1860, *Cong. Globe*, 36 Cong., 1 Sess., 1502.

[51] Democratic congressman, 1839–1843; assistant postmaster-general, 1845; commissioner of Indian Affairs, 1845–1850; lieutenant-governor, 1852–1853; governor of Ohio, 1853–1855; now first comptroller of the U. S. Treasury, 1857–1861.

[52] April 9, 1860, *House Committee Reports*, 36 Cong., 1 Sess., ser. no. 1069, doc. no. 394.

[53] John Hickman: Democratic congressman, 1855–1861; Republican congressman, 1861–1863. At this time, though in Congress as a Douglas Democrat, he was seeking the Republican nomination for the Vice-Presidency.

refutation of the message, is not written, I think, with the force and beauty befitting an occasion so important[.]

Mr. Houston [54] (of Ala.) and Mr. Taylor [55] (of Loua.)—minority of the Com[mitte]e.—made a contrary statement, trying to sustain the President—See Daily Mo. Rep.[ublican] Apl. 14.

April 7. My letter to the Mo. Republicans [56]—

A good many papers in the interest of the *Third Party* movement, in Kentucky and Tennessee and in this State, have come out strongly against my letter—that part of it at least, which goes against the extension of Slavery into the Territories—

All seem to take their cue from the Louisville Journal, and, wonderful to tell, accuse me of reopening the agitation of the Slavery question!

Last summer, the Louisville Journal and its like, were violent agitators on the slavery side of the question. They "*out niggered*" the Southern pro slavery Democrats—Now they charge me with *Aggitation* [*sic*], for simply declaring an opinion in answer to direct questions, fairly put to me.

The "Missouri Statesman" (W. F. Switzler [57]) yielding to K.y. influences, has been led blindfold into this unwise move (I'll shew its *un*wisdom in another place.)

See particularly the "Statesman" of March 30 and April 6— both Editorial and adopted.

The charge that I reopen the *agitation* of the slavery question is a mere pretence. The real objection to the letter is that it resists *pro slavery agitation*—by denying that slavery is a good thing; by denying that the constitution carries slavery into the Territories; and by affirming that good policy is against its extension.

These are the real, but concealed grounds of objection. But even these would not have produced the *irruption* against me but for the manoeuvers of the " Gen[era]l Com[mitt]ee. of the Nat[iona]l. Union Party." There are some excellent men on that Com[mitt]ee, but they are dupes—the tactitions [*sic*] on the Com[mitt]ee. have planned the whole thing to elect the democratic nominee, and thus far, have worked the scheme with some skill—They may perhaps accomplish that end in Mo. but I think they are too weak to succeed

---

[54] George S. Houston: chairman of the Judiciary Committee; congressman, 1841–1849, 1851–1861; governor of Alabama, 1874–1878; U. S. senator, 1879; a Douglas Democrat who opposed secession until it was accomplished, and then supported the Confederacy.

[55] Miles Taylor: New Orleans lawyer; sugar planter; Democratic congressman, 1855–1861.

[56] See *Supra*, 111–114.

[57] William F. Switzler, editor of the *Missouri Statesman* of Columbia, Missouri, 1843–1885, nominated Everett for the Vice-Presidency in the Baltimore Convention of 1860. Though he opposed Lincoln, he remained a unionist when the War came. But in 1864 and thereafter he supported the Democrats.

any where else. The idea of a *third party* has already the prestige of imbecility, and, excluding me and my friends, will I think, die out of mere inanition. There was very little favor towards me in K.y. and Tenn: from the start—on the contrary a jealousy—Blanton Duncan's letter to me was a trap to catch me, and carry out the formed design to get me out of the way—I surmise that the object of his letter was to get me pledged to "the New Party," by offering before hand to accept its nomination, when he and his immediate associates had no idea of nominating me, thus killing me off with the Republicans. My answer defeated that aspect of the plan, by declining to accept or reject any nomination *before it was offered.* But perhaps in avoiding *Silla* I ran upon *Caribdis* [sic], by declaring that I would be "no party to any plan for the running a *third ticket* without any hope of success in the Electoral colleges" as that would only operate as a diversion in favor of the Democrats.

And I do not doubt that that answer of mine to Mr. Duncan is the cause (or rather the occasion) of the simultaneous abandonment of me by a good many papers in K.y., Tenn: and Mo.

I have reason to think that the immediate supporters of Messrs. Crittenden [58] and Bell, respectively, were resolved, from the beginning of the move, that One of them and not *I*, should be placed at the head of *the opposition*, and that rather than see me there, they would effectually—perhaps formally—join the Democrats.

It is very doubtful with me whether the Balt[imor]e. convention [59] will ever organize *under the programme* of the Gen[era]l. Com-[mitt]ee., so as to make a nomination according to its requirements— Each *State Convention* to nominate *two*, and the Gen[era]l. Convention to choose from those so nominated, only—. But if they do nominate, no one need be surprised if they adopt the Democratic nominee of Charleston—mark that—If they nominate me, (which is most unlikely) it will be because they are convinced that they are not a national party; in fact, not a party at all, and because they are also convinced that I will get the Chicago nomination,[60] and be elected without their help.

[*April 8.*] I have just now (Apl. 8. afternoon) recd. a letter from *Hiram Ketchum*,[61] long and more communicative than usual (yet still somewhat reserved). He approves of my letter—will exert himself for my nomination at Balt[imor]e.[62]—is against the idea of a *3d. party*—cant [sic] get along without the concurrence of Chicago [63]—and *I* the only man that Balt[imor]e. could nominate who

[58] *Supra*, Aug. 10, 1859, note 78.
[59] The National Constitutional Union Convention met at Baltimore, May 7, 1860.
[60] I. e., the Republican nomination.
[61] *Supra*, April 20, 1859, note 19.
[62] At the National Union Party Convention.
[63] The Republican National Convention at Chicago.

would stand any chance at Chicago—Cant [*sic*] go for Douglas, in any event—but intimates the possibility of his supporting a Democrat, if Baltimore and Chicago fail to agree, and Charleston [64] name an acceptable man.

Mr. K.[etchum] also encloses to me, a letter which he had just recd. from *Mr. Walker* Sec.y. of the 'Nat[iona]l. Union Com-[mitt]ee. ['] at Washington, dated March 30. The letter is studiously dark and carefully avoids any direct expression of fact or opinion—The party is rising—good news from all quarters—"The People are obviously looking to it *with interest* "—If they act patriotically, " have no doubt *it will determine the result* of the coming contest in such a way as shall be for the best interest of the country." Impossible to forecast who who [*sic*] will be the nominees—" *Every thing* will depend upon what shall then have been done at *Charleston;* and upon what it will then be manifest will be done at Chicago."

Altho' this letter is dark and doubtful, yet one thing is plain enough to me—i. e—It is the *Secretary's* opinion that the New Party will not make any independent nomination of its own, but will choose between Charleston and Chicago.

[*Marginal*] Note—I see in the N.[ew] Y.[ork] Tribune [65] a letter from Washington, importing that Mr. Bell is in the City, and that a plan is on foot to arrange with the Rep[ublica]ns., for *Baltiomore* [*sic*] to nominate *McLean* [66] and Bell, and for *Chicago* to adopt them—That scheme wont [*sic*] take, tho' the letter says Mr. Bell approves it.

The naked truth is, that the idea of forming a new party now, and under existing circumstances is simply absurd. The gentlemen concerned in the movement—and some of them are good men and wise— must make up their minds, and that quickly, to do one of three things—support the Democratic nominee, or the Republican nominee, or themselves sink into political nonentity.

April 9. Monday. Yesterday afternoon I attended the funeral of Mad[am]e. Labbadie,[67] *nee Gratiot*, widow of Sylvester Labbadie dec[ease]d. at the house of her brother-in-law, P[ier]re. Chouteau Jr.[68] Thus has passed away another of the old inhabitants; and

---

[64] I. e., the Democratic National Convention.

[65] April 5, 1860.

[66] John McLean of Ohio: congressman, 1813–1816; postmaster-general, 1823–1829; justice of the U. S. Supreme Court; 1829–1861. He had won fame through his dissenting opinion in the Dred Scott case, and had been a strong candidate for the Free-Soil presidential nomination in 1848 and for the Republican nomination in 1856.

[67] Mme. Labad[d?]ie was born Victoire Gratiot. See footnote 71. Her husband was son of a fur-trader and himself one of the oldest settlers.

[68] A St. Louis fur-trader who at one time controlled most of the trade of the upper Mississippi and Missouri valleys. He was part owner of the Iron Mountain iron mines and of the St. Louis rolling mills and was one of the incorporators in 1850 of the Ohio and Mississippi Railroad. He was one of the great ante-bellum financiers of the country— worth several millions. His father was Jean Pierre Chouteau a leading fur-trader who came to St. Louis in 1764.

now very few remain of all that I found here on my first arrival in St Louis, in 1814. I saw at the funeral Mr. and Mrs. Von Phul [69] and Mrs. Hunt, and I believe these are all that I saw there of the *old inhabitants.* Mr. Chouteau I did not see: His grandson, Ben Sandford tells me that he is hopelessly blind. A few years ago I attended the funeral of my excellent friend Mrs. Cabanné, [70] and now that Mrs. Labbadie is dead, there remain but two daughters of that large and most amiable family, the Gratiots [71]—viz Mrs. P[ier]re. Chouteau and Mrs. De Mun. [72]

This is the dryest spring I ever knew—Vegitation [*sic*] is suffering. The weather has been very warm for some days—Today we began to use ice on the table—Also, I substituted cotton for wollen [*sic*] socks, and a single breasted satin waistcoat for a double-breasted velvet.

[*A clipping which quotes from the* Nashville News *an article headed " Doctrine of Secession—Historical Reminiscence," dealing with Josiah Quincy* [73] *and his " secession " speech in the House on January 14, 1811.*]

This clip is a point of political history, useful, in a double sense, as shewing when and by whom the false doctrine of secession was first openly broached in Congress, and as shewing how, in the course of events, extreme partizans are apt to change sides with each other.

Mr. Quincy was a northern man and an extreme Federalist, and Mr. Poindexter [74] a southern man and an extreme Republican[.]

Apl 10—. . . .

Judge Gamble [75] came out with me, and spent the night. His daughter May came out with Julia in the forenoon, to stay some days.

---

[69] Henry Von Phul, merchant and owner of river-boats, was one of the wealthiest men of the State. He had settled in St. Louis in 1811. Mrs. Von Phul had been Rosalie, daughter of Dr. Saugrain who had migrated to St. Louis in 1800.

[70] Mrs. John P. Cabanné, formerly Julie Gratiot. See footnote 71. Her husband, a rich Frenchman who settled in St. Louis in 1806, was one of the city's leading fur-traders and merchants.

[71] Charles Gratiot, the founder of the family, was a French Huguenot who came to St. Louis as a merchant in 1777 via Lausanne, Switzerland, and Charleston, South Carolina. He had nine children, all leading citizens in their own right, and when he died, one of Missouri's most respected citizens, he left a huge fortune.

[72] Mrs. Jules De Mun, formerly Isabelle Gratiot. Her husband, the son of a French nobleman and Santo Domingo sugar-planter, was himself a fur-trader and merchant who moved to Missouri about 1804.

[73] Josiah Quincy: a New Englander of the purest strain; Federalist congressman, 1805–1813; Boston lawyer and state legislator, 1813–1829; president of Harvard College, 1829–1845. For sixty years he was an ardent and uncompromising opponent of slavery. He fought the annexation of Louisiana in 1803 and the admission of the State of Louisiana in 1811, and belonged to a group of New Englanders who played with the idea of dissolution of the Union because they were overruled in these other matters.

[74] George Poindexter of Mississippi: congressional delegate, 1807–1813; congressman, 1817–1819; governor, 1819–1821; U. S. senator, 1830–1835; a pro-slavery leader. In a great debate in Congress in 1811, it was Quincy who threatened secession, and the Southerner who defended the Union.

[75] *Supra,* July 23, 1859, note 39.

April 17. It is a curious fact that this day is the first time that I ever received *Rent*, for real estate put out on lease. My agent Charles Stepnay, paid me $25. which he had just collected from John Calvert, tenant of one of my lots in Carondalet, being the first half year's *gale*[.]

[*A clipping from an unidentified newspaper, with the heading "A Speaker's Warrant, equivalent to a Habeas Corpus," giving the decision of a New York Court that Congress could "summons" as witnesses "parties in the hands of a State or county officer," and compel their attendance.*]

In high party times, questions of this sort are apt to be determined on political rather than legal grounds. Courts, like individuals, become astute in finding reasons to support the action of men on their own side.

Very lately, one Sanborn,[76] of Massts. being in contempt of the U. S. Senate, for refusing to attend as a witness, before the Harper's Ferry Com[mitte]e. was arrested on attachment. The arrest was covertly and harshly made, and the prisoner *hand cuffed.*

He was brot. by Hab:[eas] Corp:[us] before the S.[upreme] C.[ourt] of Massts. and discharged, on the ground, as declared by C.[hief] J.[ustice] Shaw,[77] that the Senate's Sergeant at Arms cannot act in Massts. *by deputy*—there being no provision for the appointment of deputies.[78]

[*A clipping from the* New York Times *headed "The Political Relations of the States and Races to be Determined by the Census of 1860," which shows the hopeless minority into which the once powerful South has sunk in the Nation.*]

"At this rate of growth, in another ten years the Mississippi Valley will out-vote all other sections of the Union; and since the Northwest grows double as fast as the Southwest, it will be safe to say that in another generation the north half of the Mississippi Valley, . . . *will have the majority of votes in the House of Representatives.* . . . after 1860, there will be little room for a balance of power. Whatever is the clear, defined opinion of the free States will become the dominant policy of the Union. But if any one is apprehensive of such a result, let him remember that a party *in* power is far more conservative than one out. To render radicalism powerless, let it be put *in* power[.] "][79]

April 22d.—Sunday afternoon. A most bright and beautiful day— . . . Some of the earlier trees, such as maple, box elder &c

---

[76] Franklin B. Sanborn, teacher, writer, reformer, friend of Emerson and Alcott. As secretary of the Massachusetts State Kansas Committee he encouraged John Brown in Kansas, then tried to dissuade him from the Harper's Ferry plan, but finally aided him in it.

[77] Lemuel Shaw, chief justice of Massachusetts, 1830–1861.

[78] *Sanborn* v. *Carleton*, April, 1860, 81 *Mass. Reports* 399–403.

[79] Cf. Hinton R. Helper, *The Impending Crisis of the South: How to Meet It*, New York, 1857.

are in full leaf—almost. The Elms have been *shedding seed* for some time, and the Oaks are in full tassel. As to flowers—Hyacinths, Johnquils[*sic*], and that class generally, are gone. Tulips are in prime, 300 were counted open in the garden this morning. . . .

Dr. Calhoun of St Charles, preached at our church this forenoon, a good, solid, well-delivered discourse upon Matt: 9:12—"The whole need not a physician, but they that are sick."

Rice, our poor old terrier dog is dead. He was found dead near the stable this morning, killed probably by *Scagrag* or some other large dog, in a fit of jealous anger, as I observed them following the young slut Queen, last night.

The boys buried him in the garden, at the foot of the Cypress tree, on the south side.

Dr. Wilson (B. F.) came out with me and staid the night of the 24th. Apl.

April 26. Visitors called to see me—1. *Mr. Pettyjohn*, Editor of the [   ] *Centralia*—says there is a good feeling for me in *Egypt*, but first (on a point of State pride,) they must support Lincoln.[80]

2. Dr. *J. Hayes Shields*—late of Chester Co.[unty] Pa. introduced by letter of *John Hickman*[81] M.[ember of] C[ongress]. Dr. S.[hields] is quite a young man and seems a very warm politician—Anti-Lecompton. I suppose=to Republican by fall[.]

[*An editorial from the* Missouri Republican *of April 26, 1860, reporting the threats of certain Southern members of the Democratic Convention in session at Charleston that should Mr. Douglas be nominated or should the platform fail to include certain of their extreme demands, they will secede from the Convention. The* Republican *minimizes the importance of such threats and believes that the only hope the South has of avoiding a "Black Republican" president and protecting their own institutions is in supporting " the regular Democratic ticket."*]

Apl 27. The National Intelligencer of April 21./60 contains the testimony of Ex *Govr. Ro. J. Walker*[82] given before the '*Cavode*' [*sic*] Investigation Com[mitt]ee.[83] of the H[ouse] of R.[epresentatives] in relation to the frauds and villainies of the Kansas government.

---

[80] After twelve months of entries about the coming nomination this—just twenty days before the Convention—is the first mention of Lincoln as a possible nominee.

[81] *Supra*, April 2, 1860, note 53.

[82] Pennsylvania-bred Democratic U. S. senator from Mississippi, 1835–1845; secretary of the Treasury, 1845–1849; governor of Kansas in 1858 until he resigned rather than be used by Buchanan in forcing a slave constitution upon Kansas. His testimony helped defeat the Lecompton Constitution in Congress. He was a strong unionist and remained so when his State seceded.

[83] *Supra*, April 2, 1860, note 44.

The documents accompanying the testimony are—

1. Gov. Walker's Explanatory letter to the Nat:[ional] Intel [ligencer].

2. W[alker]'s letter to Prest: Buchanan—dated—Lecompton (K.[ansas] T.[erritory]) June 28. 1857—

3. Prest: Buchanan's letter to Gov Walker, in answer dated Washington, July 12. 1857.

The curtain is beginning to rise upon the complicated rascalities of the Kansas affair. The Presidents [*sic*] share in it is now pretty well known—His bold assumptions at first—his prevarications and underhand tricks afterwards; and finally, his imbecility, and the hopeless impotence with which he became an unresisting tool in the hands of the unscrupulous members of his cabinet.[84]

Some day I may take the trouble to dissect these letters of Buchanan and Walker, and shew the folly and knavery of their details. I do wonder that a man of Walker's reputed sense and known shrewdness should write such nonsense—e. g. the Nebraska-Kansas bill directed *how* the State constitution should be made, and if made otherwis[e], it is *nul*[*l*] *and void*!!

[*Marginal*] *Note*—This letter of Walker discloses the all-governing policy of the Democrats, for the last ten years or more—the acquisition of Southern territory, to be made into Slave states. It closes in a rhapsody thus—"Cuba! Cuba! (and if possible, Porto Rico also) and then your administration will go out in a blaze of glory!"[85]

April 30. Mary Lay (servant) At her request, the balance due her for service, is this day paid to *Fleming Bates*. He has now given me his note for $251.46, at one day after date, bearing 10 pr. ct interest from date till paid—It is agreed that when payment is wanted, he shall have 30 day's [*sic*] notice[.]

The note is to me, as trustee for Mary Lay, and the reason it is so done, is to keep the money out of the reach of her drunken spendthrift husband.

[*May 2.*] [*A letter of Thomas Corwin*[86] *accompanying a speech which Mr. Bates had requested is pasted into the diary.*]

May 3. At home today, confined by a severe cold on the lungs, without any known cause: Came home sick yesternoon.

---

[84] Perhaps Buchanan in all of this was merely consistent in pursuing the *laissez-faire* policy which he believed wise.

[85] Southerners wanted new slave territory. Buchanan's attempts to acquire new possessions seem, however, to have arisen not from a desire to help Southerners extend slavery, but from a hope that an imperialist program might divert interest from the heated sectional dispute.

[86] *Supra*, Feb. 25, 1860, note 96.

Held quite an audience at the office yesterday. Besides several town *friends*—Gibson,[86a] McPherson,[87] Dick,[88] Eads,[89] Able[90]—there were two gentlemen fresh from California, Messrs. *Bell*[91] and *Staples*, on their way, as Delegates to the Republican Convention at Chicago. They were prudently reserved as to how they would cast their votes in Convention, saying that coming from the other side of the continent, prudence required them to seek all means of knowledge before full committal. Yet they seemed very friendly and well-disposed towards me.

Mr. Staples seemed surprised—I thought pleased—when I told him that I had just recd. a letter from Oregon (S. Francis) informing [me] that the State Rep[ublica]n. Com[mitte]e. had instructed for me[.]

May 3. Yesterday, the last news from the Democratic Convention at Charleston was that the Delegates of 5 or 6 states had withdrawn, in dudgeon, because the Convention would not agree to a *Slave Code* for the Territories; and that two or three other States—i. e—Georgia and Virginia—had taken time to consider whether or no they would withdraw also.

To day (not having yet seen any papers) I hear that the Convention has broken up *in a Row*.

If this be so, the whole subject of the election is at sea, without chart or compass, and all calculations will be no better than guessing—

I *guess* that there will be at least two Democratic candidates, nominated by their respective cliques.

I *guess* that great efforts will be made to turn the Baltimore National Union Convention into a " Democratic Aid Society " (as Snethen has already called it) and not without some serious fears of success.

And I *guess* that the more radical Republicans may be emboldened to put up an extreme man at Chicago.[92]

[86a] *Supra*, April 27, 1859, note 27.

[87] A Conservative Republican politician; delegate to the National Union Convention at Baltimore in 1864; personal friend of Mr. Bates.

[88] *Infra*, Dec. 24, 1863, note 3.

[89] *Supra*, Jan. 28, 1860, note 38.

[90] Barton Able, formerly captain of boats in the Mississippi and Missouri River trade, 1847–1858; now a commission merchant in St. Louis; a Free-Soil Democrat, who, as a legislator in 1856, had voted for emancipation in Missouri; now a delegate to the Republican Convention in Chicago.

[91] Dr. Samuel B. Bell, lawyer and then Presbyterian minister of New York who went as a missionary to California in 1852. He served in the state legislature and was president of the first Republican state convention.

[92] In comparison with Mr. Bates, Lincoln was this " extreme man," and there is no doubt that his chances were improved and Bates's injured by Democratic disagreement in Charleston.

As far as my prospects are concerned, I should have been pleased to see the Charleston Convention make a nomination, and put up their strongest men.

May 4. The Mo. Democrat of today contains an old letter of mine <the greater part of it, copied from the N. Y. Tribune> to Mr. Stone of Western New York. The letter is dated Sept. 6. 1848 and is in answer to one from Mr. S[tone], who—as a member of the Buffalo Convention,[93] which nominated Van Buren[94] and Adams,[95] propounded questions to me—viz[.]

1. Has Congress power to prohibit slavery in the Territories?—
2. Having the power, is it right to use it?
3. Would I object to be named as V.[ice] President?

I ansd.—to the 1st.—Yes—certainly—

to the 2d.—a matter of expediency only—

to the 3—Yes, I would object, on many grounds giving some of them.

I had forgotten this letter entirely, and it comes to light now, I think, very opportunely. At least it will shew that my lately published opinions upon slavery and the Territories were not newly adopted to curry favor with the Rep[ublican]s: but were formed and expressed long before the Republican party came into existance [*sic*].

[*A clipping from the* Baltimore Patriot *quoting the views of Judge McLean*[96] *as similar to those of Mr. Bates. In a letter of July 28, 1848, Mr. McLean had written:* "*Without the sanction of law, slavery can no more exist in a Territory than a man can breathe without air.*"]

There was another letter of Judge McLean, about that time, addressed to Judge Hornblower[97] of N. J. which stated, if I remember aright, that Congress had the power to *exclude*, but not the power to *permit*, slavery in the Territories.

See *Evansville Weekly Journal*, of May 3./60 where the letter is re-produced, but is not exactly such as I supposed.

May 9. Within the last few days, I have received calls from several California Delegates to the Chicago National Convention

[93] The National Free-Soil Convention of 1848.

[94] Martin Van Buren was the candidate of a Utica convention of Barnburners, the radical wing of New York Democracy, who had withdrawn from both the state and national Democratic conventions.

[95] Charles Francis Adams had joined with Charles Sumner in calling a convention of Anti-Slavery Whigs at Worcester to protest the nomination of Zachary Taylor. See *infra,* Feb. 26, 1861, note 22.

[96] *Supra,* April 8, 1860, note 66.

[97] Joseph C. Hornblower: chief justice of the Supreme Court of New Jersey, 1832–1846; quondam professor of law at the College of New Jersey; vice-chairman of the Republican National Convention in 1856; author of a famous decision that denied the power of Congress to enact a fugitive slave act.

(Rep[ublica]n.) viz—Sam Bell,[95] [   ] Staples, [   ] Lane [   ]
Cheeseman, and Judge Hinkley. They were very polite and pleasant. They may go, in Convention, for Mr. Seward, but if not, they
may be counted among my friends.

Note—Mr. Staples, told me that Col Fremont [99] (with whom he
[is] very friendly) had authorised him to withdraw his name, if
proposed in Convention—saying that he would not run against any
man (acceptable on general grounds) who was zealous and thorough,
like himself, on the Pacific R. R. question.

May 9. This day assembles at Baltimore, the Convention of the
National Union Party.

In the afternoon, I got a telegram from *Sol Smith*[1]: Stating that
he was the *only* member of the Mo. Delegation *in my favor*, and
asking advice, whether under the circumstances, my name should be
put up at all. I did *not* answer, for several reasons, but chiefly
becaus[e], till that moment, I did not know that Mo. had any delegation there; nor do I now know when, where or by whom they were
appointed. The appointment has never been published in our
papers—Late in the evening, I learn by public telegraph, that Col:
Switzler[2] and Maj: Harris[3] are also Delegated.

May 10. With my wife, this afternoon, visited Mr. Eads'[4] family,
at Compton Hill, and there met Mr. Elwood of N York (state) a
Delegate to the Chicago Convention. He says that his Delegation
is, of course, unanimous for Mr. Seward, but will not obstinately
press him, if they find that he cannot be elected, or even that his
election is doubtful[.]

I told him that Col Fremont would not be run, to conflict with a
probable man on this side pledged to the Pacific R. R.[5]

I must see him again—

—*Note*—Did see him next day. He called at my office, in company
with Mr. Eads and Dr. Cogswell,[6] a Massachusetts Delegate to the
Chicago Convention.

[95] *Supra*, May 3, 1860, note 91.
[99] John C. Frémont : son-in-law of Senator Benton of Missouri ; an explorer and mine-owner who was implicated in the Bear Flag revolt in California in 1846 ; Free-Soil U. S. senator from California, 1850–1851 ; unsuccessful first Republican candidate for the Presidency in 1856. During the War his indiscretions as major-general in Missouri caused Lincoln trouble, and when Lincoln removed him he became the storm center of abuse of Lincoln and of intrigue to prevent Lincoln's reëlection in 1864.
[1] Solomon F. Smith : a former traveling stage-comedian ; since 1853 a St. Louis lawyer. In 1861 as a member of the Missouri Convention he was to play an important rôle in keeping the State in the Union.
[2] *Supra*, April 7, 1860, note 57.
[3] James Harris of Boone County, Missouri : U. S. deputy surveyor ; county surveyor ; Whig legislator ; judge of the County Court.
[4] *Supra*, Jan. 28, 1860, note 38.
[5] See *supra*, Feb. 4, 1860, note 69 ; May 9, 1860.
[6] George Cogswell : surgeon : bank president ; an organizer of the Republican Party in Massachusetts ; member of the Governor's Executive Council, 1858–1859 ; a collector of internal revenue from 1862 until anti-Johnson activities led to his removal in 1866.

May 10. The *National Union Convention* at Baltimore was presided over by Governor Washington Hunt [7] of N. Y. and its proceedings were conducted with great caution and apparent harmony. There was very little speaking and no attempt to construct a *platform*, or declare any line of policy. It does not even plainly appear whether or not the Convention considered itself as forming and inaugurating a *new party*, dissolving old party ties, and disbanding the Whigs and Americans there represented.

All, I believe, which the Convention did was to nominate Mr. Bell of Tennessee for President and Mr. Everett [8] of Massachusetts for Vice President, and appoint the necessary committees.

Unless something more than that were done it were better that the Convention had never been held. The nominees are worthy and excellent men, but without any organized party to sustain them, and without any strong hold upon the affections and the zeal of the people, it seems to me that there is hardly a possibility of their accomplishing any real good.

If they have really formed a *new party*, it is absolutely necessary to have a *platform* or declaration of principles—To say only that they go for the Constitution and the enforcement of the laws, is only what every other party says. Some times, when parties are broken, as now, *a man* arises whose bold character and strong *will* make him a *platform* of himself, and he creates a party of his own—Such was Jackson, under *his* circumstances; but such is not Mr. Bell (tho' intrinsically a better man than Jackson) in the present crisis.

Since the nomination I have seen but few papers, and none containing any enthusiastic response. In fact, there was no zeal *in the Convention*, and none among the people *in its favor*. I think it will wilt down into nothing—not strong enough even to make a dangerous diversion. Should I be nominated at Chicago, I think the N.[ational] U.[nion] party will not prevent my getting the vote of the state. But should any other man be nominated there, then the new party may give Mo. to the Democratic candidate. And that is about all the effect it will have in Missouri, unless indeed, the Democrats should fail to re-unite at Baltimore, and should foolishly run two tickets. In that event Mr. Bell may get a very respectable vote.

[*Marginal Note.*] The Nat:[ional] Intel[ligence]r. of May 15, introducing a letter from Baltimore, says—" *The late Baltimore Convention* " [9] " It may truly be said that, in point of respectability, the recent *Whig Convention* [10] at Baltimore was never surpassed— we will not say [never] equalled—by any political assemblage ever before convened in our Country."

---

[7] *Supra*, Oct. 26, 1859, note 15.
[8] *Supra*, Sept. 4, 1859, note 91.
[9] The title of the article.
[10] The italics are Mr. Bates's.

This is the only instance in which I have known it called a *Whig* Convention: It does not call itself so, but profess[es] to make a *new party*.

[*A clipping from the* Missouri Democrat *headed* "*EXTRA. National Republican Convention. GREAT EXCITEMENT. Contest between Lincoln and Seward. Result of the First and Second Ballots. LINCOLN NOMINATED ON THE THIRD BALLOT*," *gives an account of the Chicago nomination.*] [11]

May 19. The Chicago Republican Convention is over. That party, will henceforth, subside into weakness and then break into pieces, its fragments seeking, each its own safety, in new affiliations and other organizations.

By mere accident I think, certainly unexpected by me, my name was made to loom up before the country, until my nomination by that convention was thought very probable. A large portion of the most moderate and prudent men of that party was anxious for my nomination, wishing to strengthen their party by giving to it more of a national character, and thus secure the alliance of the remnants of the Whig and American parties. This they thought they could do by selecting me—a known Whig who had never been united with either the Amer[ica]ns. of [or] Repub[lica]n. party. But their views were not acceptable to the Convention. A large majority thought very differently, and so, my political life has closed—personally. I have no future—I may hereafter <as I have done for the last 30 years> occasionally make a speech or write an essay, but I shall not engage so deeply in any political question as to be seriously disturbed by the result.

The convention sat on the 16th., 17th. and 18th. of May for the selection of candidates for President and Vice Prest. There were Delegates (I believe) from more than 20 States—including the slave states—Md. Va. K.y. Mo. and Texas. There was an immense crowd: Some estimate it as high as 20.000, making a very formidable outside pressure—among them, many of my Mo. friends[.]

At the beginning it was generally thought that the contest would be between Mr. Seward and me, and that the Convention would take the one or the other, as it might determine the question whether the party should act independently upon its own internal strength, both as regards numbers locality and moral support, or modify its platform and mollify its tone, in order to win a broader foundation and gather new strength, both numerical and moral, from outside—i. e. the Whig and American opposition. The shew in favor of other candidates was understood to be complimentary only, to the respec-

[11] This clipping is pasted onto the fly-leaf at the front of the diary.

tive local favorites. But all calculations based upon these views were, as the event proves, signally erroneous.

For some cause, as yet unknown to me, Mr. Seward's popularity in the North west disappeared, as by magic, and a morbid fear of him took its place. In all that region except Michigan, he was dropped, and opposed indeed, with a sort of spasmodic terror. This is strange to me—for surely, if the party felt strong enough to go alone, Mr. S.[eward] appeared to me its legitimate leader and true exponent. And I thought <perhaps in my silly egotism> that if they waived Mr. S.[eward] there would be almost a political necessity to fall back upon me. But not so the convention. Its objection to Mr. S.[eward] seems to have been personal and not political nor prudential. And this I think plainly appears both from the platform and the candidates placed upon it—

1. *The Platform*—It is a great departure from the few mild, plain truths embodied in the call for the convention. It is exclusive and defiant, not attracting but repelling assistance from without. To please the Germans unreasonably, it galls (not to say insults) the Americans and all the Republicans who came in through the American party—such as Gov Banks,[12] Mr. Colfax,[13] and the like. It lugs in the lofty generalities of the Declaration of Independence, for no practical object that I can see, but needlessly exposing the party to the specious charge of favoring negro equality—and this only to gratify a handful of extreme abolitionists, led on by Mr. Giddings.[14] And it affirms, untruly, that the normal state of every Territory is Freedom—this is not true of Louisiana and Florida.

I do not however, lay a great stress upon the platform. I never had much respect for Party Platforms— They are commonly suggested by the extreme men of the party, under the pressure and duress of circumstances, and adopted from necessity rather than choice, by the more solid and reliable men of the party. And in fact, are hardly ever intended to be literally carried out—*never* among *Democrats*.

2. *The Candidates*—Mr. Lincoln personally, is unexceptionable, but politically, is as fully committed as Mr. Seward is, to the extremest doctrines of the Republican party. He is quite as *far north* as Mr. Seward is. And as to the V.[ice] P[resident]—Mr. Hamlin[15]

---

[12] *Supra*, July 27, 1859, note 57.

[13] *Supra*, April 27, 1859, note 28.

[14] Joshua R. Giddings, of Ohio, Whig congressman, 1838–1859,—a relentless foe of slavery—played an active part in the Chicago Convention.

[15] Hannibal Hamlin of Maine: Democratic congressman, 1843–1847; U. S. senator, 1848–1857; Republican governor, 1857; now again U. S. senator, 1857–1861; vice-president, 1861–1865.

is not the right person : He has no general popularity, hardly a general reputation; and his geography is wrong. His nomination can add no strength to the ticket, however fit he may be as an individual, and however popular in Maine. It was a great blunder to overlook P[ennsylvani]a. in selecting the V.[ice] P[resident]—Cameron or Read,[16] in common prudence, ought to have been chosen.

[*Marginal Note.*] A few days after this was written, Mr. Goodrich [17] a delegate from Massts. to C[hica]go. Convention, called to see me (said he came down on purpose) and told me how that happened. To soothe the wounded pride of N. Y. on losing Seward, the V.[ice] P.[residency] was offered her. She declined to *step down*. Pa. was then consulted—She suggested Cameron : The North said no, he's a slippery fellow, a political gambler—*Reeder* [18] (Ex. Gov: [of] K.[ansas] T.[erritory]) was there and made some faint show *for himself*. Then, Preston King,[19] or some of his friends, suggested Hamlin, and it took without opposition—King and Hamlin he says are like Siames[e] Twins.

[*Marginal*] *Note*—Read of Pa. seems not to have been thought of. If it had been the real wish of the Party to nationalize itself, it surely would have determined otherwise; but, as matters stand, it will be hard to defend the Platform and the men upon it, from the charge of sectionalism—Some indeed already accuse the Convention of ostentatiously proclaiming its sectionalism, by striking out, on a formal vote, the word *National*, from the name of the Party.

Some of my friends who attended the Convention assure me that the nomination of Mr. Lincoln took every body by surprise: That it was brought about by accident or trick, by which my pledged friends had to vote against me. As thus—great deference was expected to be paid to the wishes of the doubtful states—Pa. Inda. Ills: and Mo.—a meeting was called of those states. Mo. was excluded, as not within the category of *doubtful*, supposing that here we had not even a chance—Ills: was instructed for L.[incoln] (understood to be only complimentary) although the leading men in the delegation were

[16] John M. Read: Philadelphia lawyer; state legislator, 1822–1823; U. S. district attorney, 1937–1844; U. S. solicitor-general; Pennsylvania attorney-general; organizer of the state Republican Party; justice of the Supreme Court of Pennsylvania, 1860–1874.

[17] John Z. Goodrich of Stockbridge, Massachusetts: lawyer; manufacturer; Whig congressman, 1851–1855; member of the Peace Convention which tried to prevent war in 1861.

[18] Andrew H. Reeder, of Easton, Pennsylvania. In 1854 he was appointed first governor of Kansas. He had tried to deal justly with free-state and slave-state men in Kansas, but when he appealed t- President Pierce against the Border Ruffians, he was dismissed. Then he turned Republican and became a leader of the Anti-Slavery Party in Kansas.

[19] Democratic congressman from New York. 1843–1847, 1841–1853; now Republican U. S. senator, 1857–1863; chairman in this campaign of the National Republican Committee; loyal supporter of Lincoln during the War and of Johnson in Reconstruction.

known to be in my favor—Browning,[20] Phil[l]ips[21] &c Inda.—tho'
pledged to me at its state convention, went over to Mr. L.[incoln]
without a struggle. And Penn: being nearly evenly balanced, of
course sided with the doubtful western States—That determined
the result.[22] The thing was well planned and boldly executed. A
few Germans—Schutz[23] of Wics: and Koerner[24] of Ills, with their
truculent boldness, scared the timid men of Inda. into submission.
Koerner went before the Inda. Delegation and assured them that if
Bates were nominated the *Germans* would bolt!—<I hear that, some
hours afterwards, when the mischief was done, he told a friend of
mine that if Bates were nominated, he'd take the stump for him.[>]

I think they will soon be convinced, if they are not already, that
they have committed a fatal blunder—They have denationalized
their Party; weakened it in the free states, and destroyed its hopeful
beginnings in the border slave states.

Here in Mo. they have utterly destroyed their friends, who have
made so gallant a fight, against all odds, and have postponed indefinitely the making of Mo. a free State.

But after all, what better can be done than support Lincoln?
Personally unexceptionable; his integrity unimpeached; his talents
known and acknowledged; and his industry and moral courage fully
proven. Politically, (aside from the negro question) all his antecedents are right—square up to the old Whig standard. And as to
the negro question (which ought not to overrid[e] and subordinate
all others) his doctrines, as laid down *for use*, are, in my judgment,
substantially right. The objections are only to certain ill-considered
phrases used by him in the excitement of political debate, from
which enemies may draw unfavorable inferences, and which friends
may easily explain away.

---

[20] *Supra*, Sept. 21, 1859, note 97.

[21] David L. Phillips: formerly a Baptist minister, now a journalist and politician; anti-Nebraska Democratic editor of the *Jonesboro Gazette*, 1854–1856; an organizer of the Republican Party of Illinois in 1856; unsuccessful candidate for Congress in 1858. He supported Lincoln in the 1860 Convention, and was rewarded by appointment as U. S. marshal of the Southern District of Illinois in 1861 and in 1865.

[22] Pennsylvania's delegation, the day before the nomination, voted informally 60 for Lincoln and 45 for Bates, as their second choice. Bates could not know what the historian now knows, that Pennsylvania was secured to Lincoln rather than Bates by the promise of Lincoln's manager, David Davis, that Cameron should have a cabinet position, and that Indiana deserted Bates for Lincoln because of a similar promise to Caleb Smith.

[23] Carl Schurz: German revolutionist; American reformer; immigrant to Philadelphia in 1852; now (1855–1861) a Wisconsin lawyer who campaigned vigorously in German for the Republicans; minister to Spain, 1861; brigadier-general of volunteers, 1862–1865. After the War he became a correspondent of the *New York Tribune*, editor of the *Detroit Post*, and the (St. Louis) *Westliche Post*, and finally Republican U. S. senator from Missouri, 1869–1875, and secretary of the Interior, 1877–1881.

[24] Gustave Koerner: German revolutionist who came to Illinois as a refugee in 1833; justice of the Illinois Supreme Court, 1845–1849; an original Democrat whose anti-slavery views made him a Republican; a Lincoln manager in 1858 and 1860; minister to Spain, 1862–1864.

[*Marginal Note.*] Today Mr. Shepley[25] introduced to me Mr. Poor,[26] of Portland, Maine—a young man of gigantic proportions, jolly temper and free and easy conversation—Seems well posted up in passing politics.

May 31. A few days ago, O. H. Browning,[27] of Quincy, (who was one of the Ills: Delegates to Chicago, and very much my political friend) called to see me (having written me an urgent letter, which reached me the same day he called) to consult me on the subject of Mr. Lincoln's nomination, and get me to take an active part [in] support of it, by taking the stump in Illinois. He said that he came not only on his own account, but urged by some of the leading Republicans of Illinois and several Delegates from New England, who had met at Springfiel[d], after the adjournment of the Convention. He said that those gentlemen were very anxious on the subject, and that both he and they were of opinion that a word for [from] me now, in favor of Lincoln might be very influential with the Whigs and Americans in the doubtful states, especially Illinois, Indiana and Penna.

At the same time, Mr. Goodrich[28] of Massts., called to urge the same thing. Mr. G.[oodrich] sd. that he and his colleagues went to Chicago as friends of Mr. Seward, but expected to *have to* vote for me. That Mr. Lincoln's nomination was unexpected to them, and forced upon them by the sudden course of the doubtful states.

I at once declined to take the stump, but intimated that I would write a letter in support of Mr. L.[incoln] which I thought better than any speech[e]s I could deliver. Afterwards I consulted with a few special friends—Gibson,[29] Broadhead,[30] Richardson[31] and Glover[32]—who all agreed that my position required me to support Mr. Lincoln, and that as to the manner of doing it, I should consult my own prudence. Thereupon I resolved to write a letter to Mr. Browning for publication. I have written to Mr. Browning a private note informing him of my determination. And Judge Richardson has written to Mr. Lincoln informing him of the fact.

I learn now that Messrs. Akers[33] and Ewing,[34] who made publication renouncing me, in consequence of my letter to the Republican

[25] John R. Shepley, law partner of Bates.
[26] John A. Poor: editor of the *State of Maine*; lawyer; state legislator; railroad promoter.
[27] *Supra*, Sept. 21, 1859, note 97.
[28] *Supra*, May 19, 1860, note 17.
[29] *Supra*, April 27, 1859, note 27.
[30] *Supra*, Dec. 26, 1859, note 66.
[31] *Supra*, April 27, 1859, note 26.
[32] *Supra*, Dec. 23, 1859, note 58.
[33] Thomas P. Akers: lawyer; Methodist minister; professor in the Masonic College at Lexington, Missouri; Know-Nothing congressman, 1856–1857.
[34] Ephraim B. Ewing: secretary of State of Missouri, 1848–1852; state attorney-general, 1856–1859; now elective judge of the Supreme Court. He was not reëlected in 1860.

delegates of this state,[35] and Mr. Switzler[36] of the Mo. Statesman, who hauled down my flag from the head of the column, for the same reason, are beginning already to repent their rashness, and to wish they had their letters and their editorial leaders back again. They begin to fear that their third party movement will be a dead failure, and that having alienated my friends, their chance for offices is very small.

Gibson told me that Switzler had written to Foy[37] of the Democrat, to make interest for Akers to be run for Governor, and that Foy sternly refused, saying that after Akers' course (in deserting Bates) he was *spotted* by the Rep[ublica]ns.—and so was Genl. Wilson[38]—and could not get their support for any thing.

Note. June 2d. In conversation with *Stephen Hoyt* this day, he told me that he saw Col: Switzler's letter to Foy, and that [it] was as I had heard.

He also told me that Genl. Wilson was in the City yesterday taking counsel and deliberating whether or no he will accept the nomination for Governor lately tendered to him by the general committee of the " Constitutional Union Party." There was to have been a convention of that party held at Jefferson City last thursday, which I understand, entirely failed; and the Committee therefore, had to assume the power to nominate, rather than let the whole organization sink into nonentity. Genl. Wilson has played his *role* with less tact and less courage than I thought belonged to him. Now, I think, he has no prospect of election, as Govr., and his course in the last few months, has certainly not raised his reputation, as a politician or a man.

Quære—Have, those gentlemen up the Country, in espousing the *new party*, abandoned their old party associations—Are they no longer *Whigs* and *Americans* respectively, or do they belong to two parties at once?

June 2. [Severe hailstorm.] . . .

June 3. . . .

[*A clipping from the* Buffalo Commercial Advertiser *of June 1, 1860, denying the statement that Ex-President Fillmore intends to support the Chicago nominations. He considers the Republican*

---

[35] *Supra,* 111–114.
[36] *Supra,* April 7, 1860, note 57.
[37] Peter L. Foy, Republican leader of St. Louis, editor of the moderate Republican *Missouri Democrat,* backer of Mr. Bates for the Republican nomination in 1860, postmaster of St. Louis from 1861 until March 31, 1867. In 1865 the Radicals tried to secure his removal, but Postmaster-General Dennison sustained him as Mr. Bates's personal appointee.
[38] *Supra,* Dec. 17, 1859, note 35.

*Party " dangerous " because " sectional," and " if he has any prefer-
ences," they are probably " directly for Bell and Everett."*]

The annexed clip came to me under the frank of Mr. Fillmore,[39]
and I wonder that it was not accompanied by a word of explanation—There seems to be a lack of spirit and decision about Mr.
F.[illmore] which I regret to see. If he has absolutely retired from
public life and refuses to take any part in current politics, why
not say so?—Why leave his own " home organ " to speak so doubt-
ingly[?]—" *If he have any preference* " it is for Bell and Everett [40]—
If he really wish Bell and Everett to be supported, why not support
them by his open declaration in their favor, rather than take this
shilly shally course to " damn with faint praise," the men of his
choice.

This timid and equivocal course displeases me, it is not up to the
old standard of Mr. F[illmore]'s frank and manly character.

June 5. Barton's wife with her three youngest children (the
other two being here already) came down on a visit to us—Charlotte and Nettie Hatcher (and Bel[l]e Branch) are also here.

June 6. C. F. Woodson, arrived to day. He came down with a
view to join me in a visit to Pilot Knob. Unluckily, Mr. McCune,
who was to go with us, is absent in Pike County.

[*A clipping from the* Baltimore Patriot *of June 7, 1860, which
quotes the opinion of the* Richmond Whig *that the ticket of the Constitutional Union Party is* " as sound, as conservative, as national, as
perfectly safe for the South, as any ticket can possibly be."]

And so, it seems that the Richmond Whig thinks it is commending Mr. Bell to the favor of the nation and brightening his prospects for the Presidency, by affirming that he regards *slavery* as [a]
blessing both to the *master* and the *slave—A blessing to* the *South,*
to the *Union* and to the *World!*

And Everett too—It is with equal pride and pleasure that the
Richmond Whig recognizes his sound position in regard to the
black blessing.

In this view of the matter it is no longer hard to understand how
it is that so many men are ready and anxious to sacrifice every thing
else to the power and interests of slavery—seeing that it is a blessing
to every body, at home and abroad—to the master and the slave—a
blessing every where and always—at home and abroad—to the South,
to the Union and to the World! A Universal blessing this slavery

---

[39] As President, Millard Fillmore had sponsored the Compromise measures of 1850
because he felt that the Union was more important than any specific settlement of the
slavery problem. This same desire to silence slavery agitation had led him to run for
the Presidency in 1856 on the Know-Nothing ticket. It led him now to oppose Lincoln,
in 1864 to support McClellan, and in Reconstruction to defend Johnson.

[40] *Supra*, May 9 and 10, 1860.

is, and therefore, of course, no man can be wise or good who does not desire to see it upheld, propagated, spread every where, and conferred on every body!

The Richmond Whig, entertaining this view of *soundness*, vouches for the *soundness* of Messrs. Bell and Everett! [41]—Does he not slander them?

[*Another clipping from the* Baltimore Patriot *reprinting another editorial in which the* Richmond Whig *urges the Democratic bolters then assembled in Convention in Richmond to nominate Bell and Everett.*]

A few days afterwards, the *Richmond Whig* contained another article (copied also into the Baltimore Patriot) flattering and coaxing the Southern bolters from the Charleston Convention, who were just about to meet in Richmond,[42] and urging them to adopt *Bell*, who is vouched for—and some citations made to prove it—as thoroughly proslavery, so much so as to satisfy the veriest fireeater of the South.

<I doubt whether Mo. Whigs and Americans will stand up to the *Union Party* on such terms, or continue to support Mr. Bell, when they know him to be fully identified with the disunionists, Yanc[e]y,[43] Rhett,[44] Shorter[45] & Co.>

[*A clipping from an unnamed paper reprints an item in the* Anzeiger *of June 15, 1860, which points out that the Republicans are withdrawing from the Missouri Opposition. As evidence it prints the letter of Barton Bates and Arnold Krekel[46] declining the nominations for the Legislature recently tendered them because of "the change in the aspect of political affairs."*]

June 16. I am afraid that B.[arton] Bates and A. Krakel [Krekel] have been a little precipitate in their withdrawal. I wish they had held on a little while longer, at least until after the publication of my Lincoln letter, and after the Baltimore Democratic Convention. For the "Union Party" I think, must wilt down. If there be but *one* Democratic candidate, it has no possible chance; and if there be *two*—Douglas and a fire-eater—most of the Southern *Union men* (so miscalled) will have to affiliate with the extreme Southern Democrats, and perhaps be absorbed by them.

---

[41] *Loc. cit.*

[42] The seceders from the Democratic National Convention at Charleston met in Richmond on June 11 and nominated Breckinridge.

[43] *Supra,* Nov. 29, 1859, note 94.

[44] Robert B. Rhett of South Carolina: Democratic congressman, 1837–1849; U. S. senator, 1851–1852; Confederate congressman, 1861. He was one of the earliest advocates of secession and resigned from public office because his State would not secede in 1852. In 1860 he reassumed leadership in the withdrawal of the Southern states.

[45] *Supra,* Nov. 29, 1859, note 93.

[46] Arnold Krekel, Prussian-born lawyer of St. Charles, president of the Radical Missouri State Convention of 1865.

[*A clipping from the* Baltimore Patriot *of June 18, 1860, which reprints an editorial from the* Richmond Whig *urging the Baltimore Convention to adopt Bell and Everett as candidates.*[47]]

The Richm[on]d Whig is eager to get into a majority, however composed. Down to the time of Brown's rebellion,[48] it was eager to unite with the Republicans—"the blackest of the black" to beat the Democrats. Now he[49] coaxes and begs both factions of the Democrats, both at Richmond and Baltimore, to *adopt Bell and Everett!!*

I am afraid the poor man drinks, for he used to have some sense.

[*Another clipping from the* Baltimore Patriot *gives its own editorial opinion that Mr. Bell's views on slavery, as shown by his record, make him a safe candidate for the Democrats of the South.*]

June 16. Yesterday, I mailed to Mr. O. H. Browning[50] of Quincy, Illss: my promised letter in favor of the nomination of Mr. Lincoln for the Presidency. And today, I handed a copy to Mr. P. H. Foy,[51] Editor of the Mo. Democrat, to be published in his paper, but *not before next tuesday;* thinking it but right to allow to the person to whom the letter is addressed a day or two the start.

What influence this letter may exert upon the Whigs and Americans in the doubtful states, I cannot, as yet, conjecture—My friends in Illinois, I am sure, overrate my influence with those classes. We shall see.

[*Marginal*] Note. Foy told me to day, that not a paper in Indiana which supported Fillmore in /56, has come out for Bell and the new party[.] [52]

But here in Mo. I am confident that it will take the spirit out of the "Constitutional party," and leave it a dead letter. Certainly I owe that party nothing, and have no personal spite against it; but it is too plain to be overlooked, that some of its presses and aspiring politicians have played the fool egregiously: Trying to play a double game—"to hold with the hare and run with the hounds"—they pretend utterly to ignore the negro question, and yet they begin by denouncing me for my opinions on that question. That is unjust to me and unwise, as the means of attaining their end.

Mr. Rollins,[53] now a candidate for Congress, is in rather a sorry pickle. Going even beyond my op[in]ions about slavery and the Republican party,—with plenty of letters out to prove it—he shrinks from the support of my letter to the Mo. Delegates, and tries to deny his own status. He is anxious to get in his outstanding letters. He

[47] *Supra*, May 9 and 10, 1860.
[48] See *supra*, Oct. 25 and Nov. 12, 1859.
[49] Ridgeway, editor of the *Whig.* See *supra*, June 24, 1859 and Jan. 9, 1860.
[50] *Supra*, Sept. 21, 1859, note 97.
[51] *Supra*, May 31, 1860, note 37.
[52] *Supra*, May 9 and 10, 1860.
[53] *Supra*, Dec. 1, 1859, note 1.

was in St Louis 2 or 3 days ago, but did not call *on me*. Glover [54] says that he came down to try to get back a strong letter which he wrote Broadhead [55] last winter. I hope he did not get it. But if he did, no matter—there are plenty more like it. This very day my friend Rd. C. Vaughan [56] (who spent last night with me) told me that he had Mr. R[ollins]'s letters to the same effect.

I dont [*sic*] intend to take any active part in the August election, unless provoked to it. But if those gentlemen, especially Messrs. Switzler [57] and Rollins persist in making me the standard by which they measure the degrees of political heterodoxy, I will take care that, in claiming the benefits of that line of conduct, they shall bear the burden also.

[*Marginal Note.*] June 22. Today, Mr. Glover [58] handed me a letter from Browning [59] to him (written at Springfield, Ills: 19th. June) praising my letter in the highest—quite too florid I think, for a man of Browning's gravity.

[*Later Marginal Note.*] Since then I have recd. a letter from Browning of the same sort, and one from Colfax.[60]

[*A clipping from the* Missouri Republican *of June 18, 1860, accusing the " Black Republicans " of gross election frauds—buying seats in Congress, and the like.*]

[*A clipping from the* St. Louis Evening News *of June 19, 1860, telling of the settlement of a contested election for the House of Representatives.*]

June 22. I clip this piece of impudent ribaldry from the Mo. Repub[lica]n. of June 18. I used to wonder that men were not ashamed to make such reckless and desperate statements without any proof; but now that I see every day, such renegade Whigs as the Mo. Rep[ublica]n. defending and denying the crimes of the Democratic party, in definance [*sic*] of the clearest proof, I cease to wonder at the mendacious blackguardism poured out upon such men as Davis,[61] to say nothing of the others named in this dirty piece.

It seems that *every* Democrat in the House voted *for* Barrett,[62] *the Democrat*—and so *every one of them* voted *against* Anderson [63]

[54] *Supra*, Dec. 23, 1859, note 58.
[55] *Supra*, Dec. 26, 1859, note 66.
[56] *Supra*, Dec. 9, 1859, note 25.
[57] *Supra*, April 7, 1860, note 57.
[58] *Supra*, Dec. 23, 1859, note 58.
[59] *Supra*, Sept. 21, 1859, note 97.
[60] *Supra*, April 27, 1859, note 28.
[61] H. Winter Davis. *Supra*, Dec. 17, 1859, note 39.
[62] John R. Barret: St. Louis lawyer; Democratic congressman from March 4, 1859 to June 8, 1860, when Francis P. Blair, Jr., who had contested his election, was seated in his stead. Blair then resigned and Barret was chosen by the Legislature in the election here discussed to complete his own unexpired term. He was defeated for reëlection in the popular vote of 1860.
[63] George W. Anderson: lawyer of Louisiana, Missouri; a former Know-Nothing; member of the Missouri House of Representatives, 1859–1860; a Lincoln elector in 1860; Radical congressman, 1865–1869.

the American. But the virtuous Rep[ublica]n. has no word of censure for *them*—It is all right for *Democrats* to vote men in and out of Congress on *party grounds:* But it is a terrible crime for Republicans and Know Nothings to do the same thing!

Poor Paschall![64] I fear he has caught the moral mange from his Democratic Associates.

Mr. Rollins[65] is pursuing a strange course in his canvas[s]. He comes out strongly pro-slavery, and is anxious to free himself from all complicity with my letter to the Mo. Delegates[.][66]

I have written to him about it, pointedly[.]

[*Note.*][67] Coming home after an absence of 6 weeks, I learn that Mr. Rollins came down to St Louis to see me—That [he] had earnest conversations with some of my friends i. a—Barton, and that he made explanations which they received as satisfactory.

June 29. Renewed my note at the " State *Savings* Institution "—Note for $2000 date June 29—at 90 days—due Sept. 29—Charles Gibson[68] indorser—I paid discount=$41.77—

Preparing to start (on Monday July 2d.) to So: Carolina, taking wife to visit her sisters[69]—and her niece, Julia F. Coalter.[70]

I take for travelling money $500—in gold 200 and three bills of the Boatmens S.[avings] I.[nstitution] for 100 each—and some change in my pocket=say [　　　]

[*The following clipping from the* Charleston Courier *of July 14, 1860, is here pasted into the note-book without comment, but with ample blank space around it, as though Mr. Bates felt moved to write some comment, and meant to do so later:*

" *What is He Doing?*—EDWARD BATES passed through Atlanta on the 5th inst., whereupon the *Locomotive* reports:

" ' This old Black Republican passed through here yesterday. He took the Georgia train. He looks very venerable, having tolerably white whiskers. His eyes have a nervous and restless appearance. We felt such an utter contempt for him that his presence was painful to us. We do not like to see the fanatic tribe polluting our soil. We hope he may never come to Atlanta again, if he can make it convenient to go round the place. That the State of Missouri should suffer so foul an apostate to remain in her borders is an everlasting stain upon her escutcheon.' "]

---

[64] Nathaniel Paschall: editor of the formerly Whig *Missouri Republican* of St. Louis which had now turned Democratic and was bitterly opposing the Republicans and Know-Nothings.

[65] *Supra*, Dec. 1, 1859, note 1.

[66] *Supra*, 111–114.

[67] Added some time in August.

[68] *Supra*, April 27, 1859, note 27.

[69] Mrs. Bates was born in South Carolina, daughter of David Coalter, who came to Missouri in 1818. One of her sisters was Mrs. Hamilton R. Gamble of Missouri (*supra*, July 23, 1859, note 39), but she had three sisters still in South Carolina: the wife of U. S. Senator W. C. Preston; the wife of Chancellor Harper, the distinguished jurist; and the wife of Dr. Means, a physician.

[70] Daughter of a brother of Mrs. Bates who had remained in South Carolina.

[*A clipping on "The Origin of 'Pent-Up Utica'" and its author.*]

[*A clipping reprinting from the* Quincy (Illinois) Herald *a long letter of W. A. Richardson*[71] *denying that he would vote for Lincoln in preference to Breckinridge,*[72] *and declaring that he will support no one save Douglas.*]

[*A clipping from the* Missouri Statesman *of August 17, 1860 accuses the Breckinridge Democrats of Missouri and Governor Jackson*[73] *of a bargain whereby their two wings of the Party were to support Jackson for governor as a pro-Douglas candidate and then after the election were to send Green*[74] *to the United States Senate as a Breckinridge man and call a state convention to instruct the Missouri electors to vote for Breckinridge rather than Douglas. The Statesman reprints from the* St. Louis Daily Bulletin *of August 14 a letter from Trusten Polk*[75] *and James S. Green calling such a convention of Breckinridge men and accusing the Douglas Democrats of the State of splitting the Party through their failure to coöperate.*]

Aug. 26—sunday. Our pastor being still absent, we (I, wife, Nancy and Coalter) attended the Union, in the fore noon, and heard Mr. Porter deliver a very solid, good sermon. There was a very interesting incident after [the] sermon—the admission, baptism and communion with, a young man named *Joseph. Y. Puryear.* It seems, according to a brief statement made by the minister, that Puryear is a native of New Mexico, a son of a respectable family of fortune and position. Born and bred in the church of Rome, he knew nothing about any other untill [*sic*] sent to school at New York. There he had a young friend who brought to his knowledge the Bible and Catechism, as used by protestants, which he studied carefully and became satisfied that "that was the right way." Returning home to N.[ew] M.[exico] his parents and family were much distressed and made him very uncomfortable, in so much that he left home and friends (in fact ran away) and went to sea, as a common sailor, still keeping up his protestant reading and association for several years. At last his parents urged him to come home, promising that if still a protestant, he should not be annoyed on that account.

Now, on his way home, to fortify himself against difficulty and temp[t]ation, he desired to join himself in full communion, with a Protestant Church, and so, he was this day, received into the Union Church, was baptised by Mr. Porter and partook of the Lord's Supper, with the officers of the Church[.]

[71] William A. Richardson of Illinois: state legislator, 1836–1842, 1844–1846; major in the Mexican War; Democratic congressman, 1847–1856, 1861–1863; U. S. senator, 1863–1865.

[72] *Supra,* Oct. 26, 1859, note 19.

[73] *Supra,* Jan. 9, 1860, note 15.

[74] *Supra,* June 20, 1859, note 96.

[75] *Infra,* Sept. 6, 1860, note 91.

Who knows but that he may be "a chosen vessel" to carry the gospel truth to the Gentiles of New Mexico!

Tuesday Sept. 4. This is my birth day. I am 67. I invited my friends, Broadhead,[76] Richardson[77] and Glover,[78] to dine with me today, Broadhead and Glover were both engaged, so that I only had the pleasure of Mr. Richardson's company.

This day made a new arrangement for professional business. Have dissolved with R. G. Woodson and intend to practise alone.

While R. G. Woodson and my son Richard have formed a partnership—

I will continue to occupy my old office, and they will take a new one, more in the thick [of] the town.

Tho' separate, we will help each other as far as we can.

The National Intelligencer of *August 23d.* contains several articles worthy to be noted.——

Party Politics—and herein

1. A letter of *Wm. W. Boyce*[79] M.[ember of] C.[ongress] of S.[outh] C.[arolina] in answer to D. L. Provence and W. S. Lyles, proposing resistence by force (which is treason) in case of Lincoln's election.

2. A letter of *B. F. Perry*,[80] of Greenville S.[outh] C.[arolina] protesting against the treason.

3. Proceedings of Breckenridge Democratic Convention, held at Charlottesville Va.[81]

Note. They made an ineffectual attempt to harmonize with the Douglas men, then in convention at Staunton[82]—The *Dugs* repulsed their advances rather scornfully—They distinctly repudiated the Pacific RR plank in the Douglas platform[.] [83]

4. Speech of *Senator Johnson* of Tennessee, on Prest: Buchanan's veto of the Homestead Bill.[84]

---

[76] *Supra,* Dec. 26, 1859, note 66.

[77] *Supra,* April 27, 1859, note 26.

[78] *Supra,* Dec. 23, 1859, note 58.

[79] Democratic congressman, 1853–1860; strong advocate of states' rights and secession; Confederate congressman, 1861–1864.

[80] Benjamin F. Perry: state legislator; editor of the unionist *Southern Patriot*; delegate to the nullification conventions of 1832 and 1833 and to the Democratic Convention at Charleston in 1860; a staunch unionist and opponent of secession from 1830 to 1860 and in the Convention of 1860. When the State voted secession, he went with it. In 1865 he won a reputation for fair-mindedness as provisional governor of South Carolina under Johnson.

[81] A Virginia convention which met on Aug. 16, 1860.

[82] Another Virginia convention which also met on Aug. 16, 1860.

[83] A resolution in regard to railroads was not acted upon "but it was agreed in the committee on resolutions that they would not endorse the resolution of the National Convention in regard to the construction of internal improvements by Congress."

[84] Delivered in the Senate, June 23, 1860. *Cong. Globe,* 36 Cong., 1 Sess., 3267–3270. The speech appears in the *Intelligencer* on August 22 not on August 23 with the other items.

As to Mr. Boyce, he is a poor helpless creature.   His letter was written under duress, yielded in sheer cowardice.

I spent some weeks with my wife's friends, living in his District, Fairfield S.[outh] C[arolina], and heard of the efforts made to commit him, and of his extreme reticence on the matter.   But Maj: Lyles and his friend Provence (two real salamanders) failing to bring him out by any private means, published their call in a newspaper.   Then he could not help himself; and as things are seldom well done which are done upon compulsion, his letter is a most contemptible failure— in fact, in principle and in logic—Beginning with the downright falsehood, that the great principle of the Republicans is *negro equality*, we need not wonder at any of the absurdities into which his premises lead him.

But I do wonder that those political maniacs are not afraid to teach their negro[e]s so constantly, how to justify insurrection against lawful authority, and bloody rebellion, and change those crimes into duties of virtue and honor.

[*Note.*]   Nov: Mr. Boyce has since made a speech, at Columbia, *openly* urging immediate secession.   Thereupon, the Nat[iona]l. Intel[ligence]r. republishes Mr. Boyce's pointed letter against against [*sic*] secession, (in 1851)—— making him contradict and answer himself, just as it had already made C. J. Faulkner [85] of Va. and Howell Cobb [86] of Ga. contradict and answer themselves.

As another proof that this rebellious spirit in the South is a new invention, I would refer to Judge O'Nealls [87] [*sic*] " [Biographical Sketches of the] Bench and Bar of South Carolina " vol 2.   In vit: McDuffie[.] [88]

Judge O'Neall says that McDuffie's graduation speech at South Carolina College was in laudation of the U.[nited] S.[tates] Constitution, and its expected perpetuity, and contrasts it with some of his after speeches, so hostile to the Constitution.

It is matter of especial wonder that the *Salamanders* should be so foolish as to continue to expose themselves to ridicule and contempt, by continuing those threats of treason.   They still say (and

---

[85] Charles J. Faulkner: Democratic congressman, 1851–1859; minister to France, 1859–1861; assistant adjutant-general in the Confederate Army.   In 1832–1833 he had urged the gradual abolition of slavery, and had condemned South Carolinian nullification.   In 1861 he so vigorously supported secession that he was arrested when he landed in this country upon his return from France.

[86] Democratic congressman, 1843–1851, 1855–1857; speaker of the House, 1849–1851; and governor of Georgia, 1851–1853; now secretary of the Treasury, 1857–1860; later chairman of the Confederate Convention, 1861, and major-general in the Confederate Army.   Cobb had opposed Calhoun's efforts in 1849–1850 to create a Southern *bloc*, had favored the Compromise of 1850, had sought to prevent any new agitation of the slavery question, and had been a great Southern unionist leader; but upon Lincoln's election he came out vigorously for secession.

[87] John B. O'Neall was made judge of the South Carolina Court of Appeals in 1828, and ultimately became chief justice of the State.

[88] *Supra*, May 21, 1859, note 58.

some of the "Union" men are mean enough to join in the cry) that
Lincoln's election would endanger the Union—

How? Who is going to rebel, and commit treason for that cause?
Not the Republicans, surely: Not the "Union Party," for they
profess a special devotion to the Union: Not the Douglas Democrats,
for Mr. Douglas in his late Norfolk speech,[89] denounces such resistance as simple treason, and affirms the duty of any President to put
down such traitors. And so there are no traitors found to do the
mischief but a handful of bullying *Brackenridge Democrats*—Here,
in St Louis County, some 275, and in the whole S[t]ate only about
11.000! And this contemptible squad of an impotent faction are,
it seems, to make such men as Washington Hunt[90] *pretend* to be
afraid of Lincoln's election!

Sep 6. The Mo. Rep:[ublican] of this day contains Gov Polk's[91]
great Breckenridge speech[.][92]

The National Intelligencer of Sept. 6th. contains a leader headed
"*A Friendly remonstrance*,"[93] in relation to the charge against the
Breckenridge Democrats of the South, as hostile to the Union. That
article contains quotations from a late speech of *Senator Hunter*[94] of
Va., made in the Breckenridge convention at Charlottesville[.][95]

The first quotation admits the existence of a disunion party at the
south—says he—" Unless we can show (to)[96] States, *already uneasy
and discontented as to their position in the Union*, that there
is a party within the Government, disposed to do them justice, which
is either strong enough now, or likely soon to become strong enough,
to wield the power and influence of *this* government, for their defence
and protection, *is it probable that we can* retain them in the
confederacy!"[97]

Again—Mr. Hunter distinctly admits that the notions of the
Southern Democracy about slavery—what they now call *great principles—constitutional rights*—are all new inventions, started within
the last few years—

Says he—" When I [first] entered the Federal Councils, which was
at the commencement of Mr. Van Buren's administration, the moral
and political status of the slavery question was very different

---

[89] August 25, 1860. See the *Norfolk Argus*, Aug. 27, 1860.
[90] *Supra*, Oct. 26, 1859, note 15.
[91] Trusten Polk of St. Louis: pro-slavery Democratic governor of Missouri, 1857; U. S.
senator, 1857–1862; and Judge-advocate general in the Confederate Army.
[92] Made to the citizens of Pettis County, Missouri.
[93] It appears in the issue of September 5 instead of that of September 6.
[94] *Supra*, Oct. 26, 1859, note 18.
[95] See *supra*, Sept. 4, 1860.
[96] Mr. Bates should have used brackets instead of parentheses.
[97] In this and the following quotation there are several inaccuracies of capitalization
and punctuation, and all but the first and third italics are Mr. Bates's and not the
Intelligencer's.

from what it now is. Then, the Southern men themselves, with but few exceptions, admitted *slavery to be a moral evil*, and palliated and excused it upon the plea of necessity. Then, there were few men of *any party*, to be found in the non-slaveholding states who did not maintain both the constitutionality and the expediency of the anti-slavery resolution, now generally known as the Wilmot proviso. Had *any man* at that day, ventured the prediction that the Missouri restriction would ever be repealed, he would have been deemed *a visionary and theorist of the wildest sort!*"

The same paper also contains a leader headed "Utopian Politics" [98] shewing the fallacy of the *Charleston Mercury*, in its wild and fanatical comments upon Mr. Douglas' Norfolk speech [99] (repeated at Raleigh [1]) to the effect that Mr. Lincoln's election, like that of any other man lawfully elected, must be submitted to, and the laws enforced. The article shews very plainly, the wicked absurdity of the *Mercury's* views.

Sept 10. Monday—Bought Julian's horse *Jack*, for $100—pd.—I will have to return Barton's horse, Sam Breckenridge, which he sent down to me in exchange for my mare, Eva, which I sent up to him, sometime ago. *Sam*: I hear is a fine horse on the farm, but un-practised in shafts, and judging from the boys' report of his quali-ties, I'm rather afraid to drive him about town.

. . .

(see forward. Dec 20)

[*A clipping from the* Tri-weekly St. Louis Evening News *of September 11, 1860, headed "Southern Feeling," quotes an unsigned letter from New Orleans dated September 4, strongly in favor of disunion. The correspondent declares:*

"There never was such a chance for any portion of the earth to become as prosperous and rich as the South would, by a separation from the nightmare of the Union." Europe, for commercial reasons, would have to side with the South. Lincoln's election is to be desired, because "that alone will arouse the people to a true sense of their position." "There are *now ten secessionists* to every one that existed four months ago."]

Disunion! Treason!

I am astonished, less at the wickedness than the brazen impudence of this avowal. This paper, The *Evening News*, is I believe, the leading "*Union*" organ in this City and State, and the editor, Mr. *A. S. Mitchell*,[2] I always considered until now, really a Union man,

[98] This *does* appear in the *Intelligencer* of September 6, 1860.

[99] See *supra*, Sept. 4, 1860, note 89.

[1] September 4, 1860. See the *North Carolina Standard*, Sept. 5, 1860.

[2] *Supra*, Nov. 9, 1859, note 33.

and not a traitor. But now, he makes occasion to obtrude his threatened treason upon the public. He lugs in this monstrous letter (of a nameless scribbler) as if only to get a chance ostentatiously to endorse it—and he does *endorse every syllable of it*—its wicked principles, its false facts and its stupid arguments.

The country is coming *rapidly* and *inevitably* to the result of separation by the negro line!—and that will be a *glorious consummation*, if the South will only be *unanimous* in favor of the treason!!

Thank God, there is no likelihood that the *South* will ever be *unanimous* in favor of such folly and wickedness.

[*A clipping from the* New York Tribune *of September 13, 1860, reporting a meeting of the Worcester County Anti-Slavery Society at which Lincoln was roundly abused for his pro-slavery views and a resolution was passed declaring the Union* " *a gigantic conspiracy against justice and God, a covenant with death, and an agreement with hell.*"]

There seems to be striking coincidence of opinion between the Ev.[enin]g. News and the Antislavery Society. The one thinks the "Union" a *nightmare;* the other thinks it a covenant with death and an agreement with Hell!

And these two classes of men unite in denouncing the whole Republican party, as *sectional*, and dangerous to the *Union!!*

The same No. of the News contains the letter of the Hon. *H.y. W. Hilliard*[3] of Alabam[a] to Exprest Fillmore, He professes great devotion to the Union &c, and great horror of the Republicans—insists that they are about to *trample down the constitution &c* calls them " a party which ignoring every other question, rallies its followers to a crusade against slavery."

How can Mr. H.[illiard] being an honest man, say that the Rep[ublica]ns. *ignore every other question?* He must know the untruth of the statement.

But Mr. H.[illiard] with all his lofty patriotism and devotion to the Union, is himself a partizan versitile [*sic*], unsteady, unreliable, and lives in a State whose leading men are very prone to denounce and revile the Union. He has been a Whig, a K.[now] N.[othing] a Buchanan Democrat (as this letter shows), declares now that " Mr. Breckenridge[4] [*sic*] is the exponent of my views; he stands upon a platform which I approve "—but, politic[al]ly, goes for Bell.

Mr. H.[illiard] has " boxed the political compas[s] " except the single point of Republicanism—I suppose it is true that he is no

---

[3] A Montgomery lawyer; quondam university professor; Whig congressman, 1845–1851; supporter of Fillmore and the Know-Nothings in 1856 and of Bell and Everett in 1860; brigadier-general in the Confederate Army; after the War a Republican. He opposed secession until it was accomplished.

[4] *Supra*, Oct. 26, 1859, note 19.

Republican, *black* or *red*, but only a very respectable aristocrat, whose ambition makes him covet notoriety, and whose principles hang so loosely about him, that in his eager pursuit of distinction, he has exhibited himself, in rapid succession, for and against every other party.

He is too flitting and versitile [*sic*] to be a leader of any party, and nobody minds what he says. This letter of his is a *volunteer*, not called out by any person nor by any adequate circumstances, but is a mere display of his own prurient egotism. Rightly understood, it means only this—"Attention the Nation! I, Henry. W. Hilliard of Alabama am alive and kicking, and mean to save the Union!!"

Thank ye, most patriotic Mr. Henry. *Whirlegig* [*sic*] *Hilliard!*

September 19. Money matters. My debts, in the aggregates, amount to $4.500. Of which there will fall due in a few days two notes, amounting together to $3200.

To meet those liabilities (and some contingencies) I have borrowed the means from the Boatmen's Savings Institution—[(]my friend Charles Gibson [5] making the arrangement for me) for that end—Gave my note, with C. Gibson endorser, $4000—Date Sep 19. 1860, at six months after date.

Note—Sept. 24. Took up my note at the Union Bank (being my last note given to *Louis R Brand*, for house and lot in Florissant [6]— Principal—$1000—2 yrs. in[teres]t. 200.83=$1200.83 Due 25th. but pd. to day for convenience.

Sept. 20. My last *political* letter—as I think.

The Republican Com[mitt]ee. of Keokuk having invited me to attend a mass convention of the People of Iowa, Illinois and Missouri, at Keokuk, to be held on the 10th. of October, I this day sent my answer (which is dated, Sept. 15) to the Com[mitt]ee., J W Rankin [7] and others.

I declined to attend the meeting, on the ground that I really cannot afford it, but must stay at home and go to work.

This letter, I think, is the best written and most effectual of all my letters that have been published in this political campaign. It will probably give offense to some members of the *Constitutional Union party*, but I hope it will tend to confirm the doubtful friends of Lincoln, and strengthen some of the timid. I treat the new party with less respect than it thinks itself entitled to, and denounce its

---

[5] *Supra*, April 27, 1859, note 27.

[6] *Supra*, May 18, 1859, note 52.

[7] John W. Rankin: a lawyer of Keokuk, Iowa; former district judge; now a state senator; a supporter of Cameron in the Republican Convention until it was obvious that Cameron could not be nominated, when he voted for Lincoln.

fusion with the Democrats, north and south, as " factious and dangerous," and predict that the members will be absorbed and lost in the different wings of the Democracy.

[*Marginal*] *Note.* My letter was published in the Democrat, St Louis, Oct 1.—badly printed from a hasty copy (made by Geo: Maguire) The paragraphs are sadly broken, punctuation worse, and some verbal errors. Oct: 2 the Anzeiger[8] publishes a copy in German translated by Dr. Berneys,[9] who gives me an equivocal compliment, by calling it a " wonderful " letter.

Some one sent me the N[ew] York Evening Express of Sep 15, containing—i. a. 'Union' *fusion* speeches of *Hiram Ketchum*[10] of N. Y. and *Uriel Wright*[11] of St Louis, and a very silly editorial about *saving the nation*, Southern rebellion &c. Mr. Brookes[12] evidently feels whipped, and, like an oaf of a boy detected in some clumsy trick, he frets and scolds, and deals in impotent threats which only show his consciousness that his tricks are discovered, his plans defeated, and that, henceforth he is impotent, even for mischief.

I think Mr. Wright must have been cought [*sic*] unawares, or he never could have made so poor a speech. Probably he was called on unexpectedly and (as it was arranged for him to speak a few days later) was afraid of consuming the material prepared for that expected occasion; and so, was disconcerted, and made a miscellaneous sort of a speech, far below his common grade.

Sept. 21. John. C. Richardson[13] (late Judge of the Supreme Court) died last night, after an illness of not quite a week. A man of talents, honor, truth. A sound lawyer and most worthy gentleman. Kind, amiable, social, and he could hardly have been otherwise, for the best affections of the heart were constantly cultivated, by the sweetest and most endearing associations of domestic life. Frank, sincere and generous, he won the regard of all his associates, and few men have been so fortunate in securing the great blessing of this life—the warm affection of wife, children and friends.

---

[8] The *Anzeiger des Westens* published at St. Louis by Dr. Boernstein; edited by Dr. Bernays.

[9] Charles L. Bernays of St. Louis, a well-to-do German immigrant who had become editor of the *Anzeiger*. He was later (1861) appointed consul to Zurich as a reward for his political aid to Lincoln.

[10] *Supra*, April 20, 1859, note 19.

[11] *Supra*, June 4, 1859, note 72.

[12] James Brooks, formerly a lawyer, newspaper correspondent, and state legislator, of Portland, Maine, had founded the *New York Express* and was its editor from 1836 to 1873. He was a Whig congressman, 1849–1853; then a Know-Nothing; now a Democratic congressman, 1863–1866, 1867–1873; opponent of Lincoln's war policies; supporter of Johnson in Reconstruction. At this time he was voicing commercial New York's desire to avoid war at any cost—even by letting the South secede unhindered.

[13] *Supra*, April 27, 1859, note 26.

[*September 22.*] On the 22d., Saturday, I presided in the Bar meeting which passed propositions, far better than common—prepared by Mr. Drake.[14]

In the afternoon attended the funeral, as one of the bearers—at the house, at the Baptist Church—6th. St and Locust—and thence to the grave at Bellefontaine.

[*September 26.*] [*An editorial clipped from the* Missouri Republican *of September 26, 1860, recalling that the Green* [15]-*Hughes* [16]-*Polk* [17] *State Democratic Convention at Jefferson City refused to pass a resolution authorizing the "Breckinridge Electors" to vote for anyone whose election might defeat Lincoln. The* Republican *charges that the purpose of their refusal was really to prevent the election of Bell or Douglas who might save the Union, and to ensure the election of Lincoln in order to provoke secession and the destruction of the Union—their real object.*]

[*September*] *26th.*—Last night, the Prince of Wales,[18] and *suite* reached St Louis and stopped [at] *Barnum's,*[19] where lodgings had been prepared for them. They were plainly but cordially received at landing, (having come down from Alton by boat), and every thing, I hear, was conducted decently and in order—more so than was expected, considering the large and promiscuous crowd.

I did not make the acquaintance with all of the Prince's company, but some of them I found to be high samples of intelligence, and good breeding. I was particularly pleased with the Earl of St Germanes.[20] His son, Mr. Eliot, is a pleasant young man[.] Dr. Ac[k]land, is frank, sensible, and I suppose learned. Capt. Grey [21] (a son of Sir Geo: Grey [22] and nephew, I believe, of Earl Grey) a pleasant off hand man—he is, as L[or]d. St Germans told me, a Captain of Guards, and one of the Queen's equiaries [*sic*]. The young L[or]d. Hinchenbrooke (the junior title <I think> of Earl Sandwich <Montague> [)]) seems to be a dull youth, ill-favored and with a stammering voice. The Duke of Newcastle [23] is

14 *Infra.* Feb. 12, 1863, note 13.

15 *Supra,* June 20, 1859, note 96.

16 Charles J. Hughes of Kingston, Missouri: state legislator, 1844–1850, 1856–1858; sympathizer with the South who for declining to take the "test oath" was disbarred, 1863–1865; many years a judge at Richmond in Ray County.

17 *Supra,* Sept. 6, 1860, note 91.

18 Albert Edward, later King Edward VII.

19 Barnum's City Hotel at Third and Vine Streets.

20 Edward G. Eliot, third Earl of St. Germans: long a member of Parliament; envoy to Spain; quondam lord-lieutenant of Ireland; now lord steward of the household and confidential adviser to Queen Victoria on family matters, 1857–1866.

21 George Henry Grey.

22 Long member of Parliament and cabinet minister; at this time chancellor of the Duchy of Lancaster in Lord Palmerston's Cabinet.

23 Henry P. F. P. Clinton, fifth Duke of Newcastle: long a member of Parliament and cabinet minister; minister of War during the Crimean War; now secretary of State for the Colonies, 1859–1864.

a thickset course looking [*sic*] man, with huge red whiskers and beard, barely touched with gray. I had very little conversation with him, and cannot speak of his mind.

Genl. Bruce is a slender good looking man, perhaps 45 or 50, polite and affable.

Lord Lyons [24]—present British Minister resident at Washington— is no doubt, a man of superior sense—I have heard so—but he seemed to me unattractive and cold, with a countenance disturbed and uneasy, and an expression very like a suppressed sneer. I think there must have been no good feeling between him and the Duke of Newcastle— Perhaps some dispute about precedence. At home, the Duke is far his superior in rank, both as holding a higher title and older no- bility; besides, he is special guardian of the Prince in his travels. But, on the other hand Lord Lyons is *here*, the special representative of the Queen, and as such, may claim a local superiority over all other British subjects.

Two of L[or]d. L[yons]'s *attachés* were along—one a handsome smooth-faced youth, whose name I have forgot, the other a han[d]- some man, under 30, with a full brown beard and a merry eye, and seems quite *au fait*, and well able to take care of himself in any American crowd. i. e. Mr. Worne [Warre].

The Prince and suite attended the Fair to day. <I was one se- lected to go with them, and, with Col Rob: Campbell,[25] rode out and in, in the same carriage with L[or]d. St Germains> They seemed highly pleased with the exhibition, and especially with the order and decorum of the immense crowd (estimated by some, at 60.000) drawn by curiosity, to see the Prince and his nobles. L[or]d. St Germains said to me that he never saw a large, promiscuous crowd so well-dressed and well-behaved.

Nat[iona]l. Intelligencer of Sept. 27—contains a correspondence between *Amos Kendall* [26] and ex Speaker *Orr* [27]—worth reading— about secession and enforcement of law[.] [28]

Also " Everett [29] thirty years ago[.] " [30]

---

[24] Richard B. P. Lyons, in the diplomatic service since 1839, was minister to the United States from 1858 to 1865 and managed the difficult relations of the Civil War with extraordinary tact.

[25] A former trapper and fur-trader; since 1835 a St. Louis merchant, hotel-proprietor. and bank president—one of the best known capitalists of the region.

[26] A Kentucky newspaper editor; political manager for Jackson; fourth auditor of the Treasury, 1829–1835; postmaster-general, 1835–1840. In 1860 he was writing articles against secession.

[27] James L. Orr of South Carolina: Democratic congressman, 1849–1859; speaker of the House, 1857–1859; tireless opponent of agitation of the slavery question. In 1851 and again in 1860 he sought to prevent secession—though he admitted the right. But when his State withdrew, he went with it. After the War he was a Johnson Conservative, and later a Republican.

[28] It appears in the issue of September 26, not in that of September 27.

[29] *Supra*, Sept. 4, 1859, note 91.

[30] This does appear in the *Intelligencer* of September 27.

See Mo. Statesman, Sep 28[.][31]

It seems that, at the late Democratic *Breckenridge* convention held at Jefferson City,[32] *C. F. Jackson*,[33] lately elected Govr. of Mo. as a *Douglas man*, openly declared for *Breckenridge* [34] [*sic*] and proclaimed his unalterable support of the *Jackson Resolutions* [35] so *miscalled*. *Tempora mutantur* &c[.]

It really does begin to look as if Douglas would *not* get a single electoral vote.

Oct 2. Note. Govr. Jackson's position seems to be doubtful. The Douglas men in St Louis at a late meeting, [appointed] a committee to interrogate Gov Jackson. Also denounced Senators Green [36] and Polk,[37] and State senator Churchill[.] [38]

Note[.] As soon as the Gov. elect heard from the Com[mitt]ee, he took the stump, and declared that Brackenridge's doctrine was right, but that it was his duty duty [*sic*] to sup[p]ort Mr. Douglas, *because he was the regular nominee.*

Oct 6. saturday.[39] . . . Upon the whole, this has been a strange year: The Spring opened very early, so as to give an early start to vegitation [*sic*]—followed by cool dry weather. The spring flowers, roses Tulips &c, I noticed were unusually short-lived, beaming in beauty only a few days. All kinds of fruit—peaches, apples, pears, are ripe several weeks earlier than common.

So in the natural world—so also, in the political, all things are anomalous. Here in America, old parties are broken up and all the elements in chaotic confusion. The Union Party and both wings of the Democracy, each feeling its own weakness, are all trying to *fuse* against Lincoln—But the more they try the more they drive off their best men, to act with the Republicans—Meredith [40] of Penna., and Thos: Ewing [41] of Ohio, have lately come out openly for Lincoln—And now *J. O. Broadhead* [42] of St Louis (my special friend) has

---

[31] A marginal note.

[32] A state convention which met on September 20, 1860.

[33] *Supra*, Jan. 9, 1860, note 15.

[34] *Supra*, Oct. 26, 1859, note 19.

[35] Resolutions which Jackson introduced in the Missouri Legislature in 1849 upholding the Southerners' right to take slaves into the Territory. In becoming a "Douglas man" he had supposedly given up this position for the theory of "popular sovereignty."

[36] *Supra*, June 20, 1859, note 96.

[37] *Supra*, Sept. 6, 1860, note 91.

[38] *Supra*, Jan. 9, 1860, note 10.

[39] Originally dated October 5, written over into October 6.

[40] William M. Meredith: Philadelphia lawyer; secretary of the Treasury, 1849–1850; member of the Peace Convention of 1861; attorney-general of Pennsylvania, 1861–1867; counsel for the U. S. in the Geneva Arbitration of 1870. For years he had been a powerful Whig politician, and he still controlled a large following in Pennsylvania.

[41] Whig U. S. senator, 1831–1837, 1850–1851; secretary of the Treasury, 1841; secretary of the Interior, 1849–1850; delegate to the Washington Peace Convention of 1861; political adviser of both Lincoln and Johnson.

[42] *Supra*, Dec. 26, 1859, note 66.

distinctly declared himself on the same side. His letter to that effect, appears in the *Mo. Democrat* of today (Oct: 5)[.]

In Europe, the course of *reformatory* Revolution is onward in a most remarkable manner. Garibal[d]i,[43] having revolutionized Sicily in a few weeks, crossed to the continent and, as if by magic has conquered the whole kingdom and entered Naples in triumph, the whole people and most of the Army and Navy joining him. The King[44] fled to Gaëta,[45] and that is all that remains to him—and that is a frail and temporary defence.

The Liberator's troops have also entered the Pope's[46] dominions, routed his Holiness' army under Genl. La Moricier[47] (who has fled) and has the remnant of the army of the Pope—30 or 40.000 strong—beseiged, with hardly a hope of escape—if indeed, the soldiers wish to escape.

Garibaldi's avowed object is to consolidate all Italy into one Kingdom, under Victor Emanuel,[48] and wherever he conquers, he proclaims "Victor Emanuel, *King of Italy!*" There seems to be now no obstacle to the immediate accomplishment of the design, except only Austria's claim and possession of Venitia [*sic*]. And I suppose that cannot long hold out[.][49]

Garibaldi is the wisest revolutioner that has appeared in Europe. He does not, like his predecessors, aim to *destroy* all former governments, and build up, anew, in their stead—" La Repoublique, *Democratic et sociale.*"—That is anarchy, and is sure to run into despotism. He labors to *reform*, enlarge, stren[g]then, guard—to build up a nation of the first rank, to be governed, not by impulsive Democracy, but by a reasonably free constitutional monarchy. And all the signs are in favor of his perfect success.

Europe has gotten over its Democratic furor, and now, we may look for real reforms and durable institutions.

The Troops of Garibaldi have entered the Papal States, conquering as they march. Already they have gained a victory over the papal army under La mircier, who saved himself by flight to

---

[43] Giuseppe Garibaldi, Italian patriot, after several unsuccessful attempts at revolution, was now completing a successful march from Sicily to Naples, during which he and his " red shirts " had freed all of Southern Italy from Bourbon rule and had united it to Northern Italy under Victor Emmanuel. Garibaldi had seized Naples itself on September 7 and on November 7 Victor Emmanuel made his formal entry.

[44] Francis II, last Bourbon King of the Two Sicilies.

[45] A fortified seaport northwest of Naples which finally surrendered to Garibaldi on February 13, 1861.

[46] Pius IX's.

[47] C. L. L. Juchault de Lamoricière: French general; political leader in the Revolution of 1848; opponent of Louis Napoleon's overthrow of the Republic in 1851; exile, 1852–1857; commander of the Papal armies in 1860.

[48] Victor Emmanuel II of Sardinia in 1848; Victor Emmanuel I of Italy in 1861.

[49] Venetia was ceded to Italy in 1866 after the Austro-Prussian War of that year, but the Pope held Rome until 1870.

Ancona.[50] It is not supposed that Garibaldi's troops will attempt to enter Rome, as the "eternal City" is protected by a French garrison, and it would not do to make an enemy of the French Emperor.[51] He is thought to be favorable to consolidation of Italy and the making of it a first-class power, albeit, a little jealous of the rapid aggrandizement of King Victor. Besides, he is necessary to the cause, as he is the chief, if not the only power, who can peacefully keep Austria from meddling in the Italian revolution.

The last news is, that King Victor has gone to Naples, to take personal possession of the Kingdom, and that Ancona, after a long siege, has surrendered to Garibaldi's forces Genl. La Moriciere and his army being prisoners of war.

Oct: 7. Sunday. This was communion day in our Church, and Dr. Anderson [52] preached a good discourse from—"the whole need not a physician, but they that be sick" and "I came not to call the righteous, but sinners to repentence[*sic*]."

. . .

Monday the 8th.— . . . Julia has determined (as I cant [*sic*] go with her) to take Levinia Meredith and go on a visit to Dardenne.[53] They will start tomorrow morning.

Octo 12 (Friday) . . . this morning, friday, there was a killing frost—Robt. Baker told me that he saw ice more than ½ inch thick. He says that knowing that his sweet potato vines must be frozen, he rose early and mowed off the frozen tops, which he says, being mown before the thaw begins, will prevent the *potato*[*e*]s from being frosted. . . .

Julia, who (with Lavinia Meredith went up last Saturday, to visit our friends in Dardenne prairie, is expected home tomorrow—or, at farthest, Monday—and will probably bring with her, little Tarlton.

The Nat[iona]l. Intelligencer of Oct 9. contains a very strong leader, headed "Sound Democracy"[.] It is in defence of *Mr. Everett* [54] against the charge of abolitionism, and it shews by various quotations of the speeches of conspicuous democrats, and their public acts, the falsehood and the inconsistency of the Democrats on the subject of slavery. It is a wonder that those Democrats are not ashamed of their gross tergiversations[.] see also Nat.[ional] Intel.[ligencer] of Oct [   ] quoting the speeches of Gov Wise [55]

---

[50] A seaport on the Adriatic coast of Italy northeast of Rome.
[51] As long as the French troops remained, the Pope retained Rome; but, as soon as domestic difficulties forced Napoleon III to withdraw his garrison in 1870, Rome fell and was added to the Kingdom of Italy.
[52] *Supra*, July 17, 1859, note 26.
[53] *Supra*, July 30, 1859, note 61.
[54] *Supra*, Sept. 4, 1859, note 91.
[55] At Norfolk, Sept. 27, 1860, quoted in the *National Intelligencer*, Oct. 12, 1860. See *supra*, April 28, 1859, note 38.

and Senator Hunter,[56] and a long extract from a speech of Mr. Faulkner [57] in 1832—This last is stronger anti-slavery than any thing that Seward or Greel[e]y [58] ever uttered.

Oct 13. Saturday—I have been engaged in the Land Court pretty much all this week—Wednesday and thursday in trying the eject-ment of Waugh v Blumenthal for a lot in Carondalet (in which we recovered ½) and friday and saturday in trying Lindell [59] v Hannegan (Sully) not completed—argument for monday.

Note—Wife came home from Dardenne,[60] (having been gone a week) bringin[g] little Tarlton.

During the last few days we have been receiving returns of the elections of Indiana, Ohio and Pennsylvania.[61] All three of those states, heretofore thought doubtful, have gone by safe majorities, for the Republicans; and now the election of Lincoln is as certain as any future, human event.

That fact changes materially all the aspects of the future, and ought to lead every reflecting man to serious contemplation.

1. The Democratic party, as organized and managed since Polk's accession to the Presidency, in 1845, is *destroyed* by Lincoln's elec-tion: The northern and southern wings can never re-unite, as the southern wing never was *democratic* i. e. never went for a really *popular* government.

2 The Republican party, made up chiefly of old Whigs, and pro-fessing, in the main, Whig policies, will soon absorb all the Whigs who have not already fully identified themselves with one or the other of the Democratic factions, and will also absorb the greater part of the northern Democrats. If the Rep[ublica]ns. be but moderately wise—liberal in its patronage—refusing to *annex* south-ern Territory—prudently protecting home industry—moderately but persistently improving the highways and depots of commerce among the states—and preserving peace and friendship with foreign na-tions—it will (by that name or another, suggested by its new ele-ments) become the permanent, governing party.[62]

3. My own position and course will require the most careful con-sideration. Every body expects Mr. Lincoln to offer me one of the Departments, and every body seems to expect that I will accept it, as a matter of course; and yet, if offered, I will certainly decline it,

---

[56] At the Charlottesville Convention (see *supra*, Sept. 6, 1860) on Aug. 16, 1860, quoted in the *Intelligencer*, Oct. 9, 1860. See *supra*, Oct. 26, 1859, note 18.

[57] In the Virginia House of Delegates, quoted in the *Intelligencer*, Oct. 13, 1860. See *supra*, Sept. 4, 1860, note 85.

[58] *Supra*, Feb. 2, 1860, note 47.

[59] *Supra*, May 3, 1859, note 44.

[60] *Supra*, July 30, 1859, note 61.

[61] These states held their state and congressional elections in October.

[62] It was apparently this probability rather than fear of what Lincoln would do to their slaves, that induced Southerners long accustomed to rule to secede.

if I can do so without violating a plain duty: If the President can fill the place designed for me, with the right sort of man from the right section, so as as [*sic*] [to] generalize his administration and make it seem to be (as in fact, it will be) national, then I will certainly refuse.

My pecuniary circumstances (barely competent) and my settled domestic habits make it very undesirable for me to be in high office with low pay—It subjects a man to great temptations to live above his income, and thus become dishonest; and if he have the courage to live economically, it subjects his family to ridicule. I earnestly desire to find a way of escape from the necessity of taking any conspicuous office, for the reasons suggested. But there is another reason touching personal ambition, equally strong. I have not now to learn (for I know it already, by experience) that a man m[a]y win quite as much reputation by refusing as by holding office. My position is anomalous. A national reputation has been forced upon me, without my having any official influence or conspicuous position. In another view, I am peculiarly circumstanced: It has several times happened to me, that when honors that I did not desire were urged upon me, I was unable to get nominally inferior places, which I would have preferred. Now, if I must be forced into public life, I would rather have a seat in the Senate than any office in the gift of Prince or People—But that is beyond my reach. In the Senate, I could render far more efficient service, to both the Country and the administration, than in either of the Executive Departments; and, at the same time, could be much more at my ease, acting in a sphere more congenial to my tastes and habits. But, as a seat in the Senate is not attainable, I can only hope (in case of Lincoln's election) that circumstances may arise to allow me to decline office, consistently with my position and my honor.

　Oct. 15 monday— ...

[*A paragraph from the* New York Tribune *of October 13, 1860, showing how completely Washington Hunt* [63] *has changed his mind. Speaking at Albany in July, 1860, he denounced Breckinridge* [64] *as a purely Southern candidate, whose election would be* " *the most unfortunate result of all.*" *Yet now in October he is advocating an electoral ticket seven of whose members are Breckinridge men.*]

　Govr. Hunt is a man for whom I have felt great respect and regard, for some years, and now I am really sorry to find him caught in such pitiful plight. I knew before that N. Y. politicians generally, were considered slippery and not " fit to tie to in a storm." But I really thought that Washington Hunt, was rather an exception to the rule,

---

[63] *Supra*, Oct. 26, 1859, note 15.
[64] *Supra*, Oct. 26, 1859, note 19.

and was disposed to trust him very far. My faith was a little shaken last Spring, when Professor Davi[e]s[65] (of Columbia College) told me how adroitly Hunt, Duer,[66] Brooks[67] (and perhaps himself) had managed the N. Y. State Convention at Troy, preparatory to the "Union" Convention at Baltimore, which nominated Mr. Bell. I knew then, that somebody was to be cheated, for I knew that Brooks was in favor of Houston[68]—or pretended to be, in order to sell out at a better price, to some other aspirant—but of course I could not foresee what form the fraud would finally take.

I am *certain* that the clique never was, in good faith, for Bell, and I am equally confident that they did not intend, at first, to have any coalition with the two factions of the democracy but having left the safe harbor of *Whig* policy and being out on a voyage of discovery, hoping to find some individual profit for themselves, they have drifted into their present forlorn position, which makes them, at once wretched and rediculous [*sic*].

[*October 21.*]   On Friday night (Oct: 19) Mr. Douglas made a speech at the West front of the Court House, to an immense crowd— several of my sons[69] being there—It was, I understand, only a warming over of his *standing* speech on squatter Sovereignty, with some slight additional ingredients, to suit the local market e. g—that he occupied *old Whig* ground!

Saturday, he went up to Jefferson City, to make a speech, and returned at night.

Note, I hear that Mr. Crittenden[70] is in town—Perhaps at Mr. Cabel[l]'s[71] or Mr. Hunton's. I must call and see him.

Oct 22d.   Dined, at Mr. Hunton's, with *Mr. Crittenden*[.]

He looks older and feebler than I ever knew him, tho' he is well preserved for a man of his age—say 73 to 76—He seems much alarmed at the state of politics in the South, believing that there really will be an attempt to break up the Union.

---

[65] Charles Davies: West Point graduate of 1815; professor of mathematics and philosophy at West Point, 1816–1837; professor of mathematics at Trinity College, Hartford, 1839–1841; paymaster and treasurer of the Military Academy at West Point, 1841–1846; professor of mathematics and philosophy at the University of New York, 1848–1849; and now professor of mathematics at Columbia College, 1857–1865.

[66] W. Denning Duer, son of President William A. Duer of Columbia College and grandson of Colonel William Duer, Revolutionary statesman and assistant secretary of the Treasury under Washington. Because Lincoln was eager to conciliate the Conservative Republicans and commercial interests of New York, Secretary Chase offered Duer the post of assistant treasurer.

[67] *Supra*, Sept. 20, 1860, note 12.

[68] George S. Houston of Alabama. *Supra*, April 2, 1860, note 54.

[69] Bates had seventeen children, of whom six sons were living at this time.

[70] John J. Crittenden. *Supra*, Aug. 10, 1859, note 78.

[71] Edward C. Cabell, formerly a Virginia lawyer and then a Whig congressman from Florida, 1845–1846, 1847–1853, who had moved to St. Louis in 1859. In the War he served in the Confederate Army.

[*Marginal Note.*]   Mr. C.[rittenden] urged me to use my influence to get Mr. Lincoln to make a soothing address [71a] (which I declined) and I have recd. sundry letters on the same subject—from Wyndham Robertson [72] of Rich[mon]d. and others.

He was very complimentary to me, declaring that he would give all the money he had or could raise, to make me President.

I am more than ever satisfied that Mr. C.[rittenden] was duped into the prominent part he was made to act in this third party movement.   Designing men used his abilities and his good name, to set up their political lottery, knowing that *he* could not draw a prize.

<*Note.* Oct: 27. Mr. C.[rittenden] is advertised to speak at St Louis, Monday 29th. Oct[.]>

Note.[73]   he did make the speech, and a poor, *shilly-shally* speech it was.   There was nothing positive about it except his denunciation of the Republican party, as sectional, &c[.]

Oct 24.   My old friend Mrs. Dr. Simpson [74] died today, and I am called to take part in the funeral, as I am in the funerals of all the *old inhabitants.*   I have known Mrs. Simpson ever since *May* 1814.

Oct 28 (sunday) . . . The general drought continues. . . . Our cisterns have failed.   We began to *haul* water three days ago.

We used the last of our ice on the 26th. Oct: having had a better supply than common, and used it without stint, all the hot weather.

Nov 1.   Wednesday— . . .

Nov 7.   Yesterday the Presidential election went off in peace and qu[i]etness.   Lincoln foremost, Douglas next, Bell next, *cum longo intervallo*—and Breckenridge [75] [*sic*] far behind—with under 600 votes in St Louis.

The Rep[ublica]n. candidates—Voulaire and Vastine—for Circ[ui]t. Att[orne]y and assistant C[ircui]t. Att.[orne]y. elected by handsome majorities.

To day the telegraph informs us that Penna. and N. York have gone largely for Lincoln—so that his election is considered sure.

[71a] Lincoln refused to do this or to make any public statement, because "I could say nothing which I have not already said, and which is in print, and open for the inspection of all.   To press a repetition of this upon those who have listened, is useless; to press it upon those who have refused to listen, and still refuse. . . . would have an appearance of sycophancy and timidity which would excite the contempt of good men and encourage bad ones to clamor the more loudly."

[72] Governor of Virginia, 1836–1837; now Virginia legislator, 1858–1865; a states' rights unionist who opposed both secession and coërcion of states, but went with his State when it did secede.

[73] Added after October 29.

[74] Wife of Robert Simpson, physician, former alderman and postmaster, and treasurer of the Boatmen's Savings Institution.

[75] *Supra*, Oct. 26, 1859, note 19.

To day I was visited at my office by a number of gentlemen—among the rest was Mr. *Todd* of Platte C[ount]y. Mo. (proprietor of a female seminary) who was introduced, at his special request, by Judge Meeker: Mr. Todd is a near relative of Mrs. Lincoln and is on his way to Springfield to visit the Lincolns. I had a pretty long talk with him, and read him part of my letter to Wyndham Robertson [76] of Rich[mon]d. Va. He seemed much pleased at the interview.

[*A newspaper clipping giving a letter from Charles F. Vanderford of St. Louis, " Corresponding Secretary, Union Guard " to Mr. Jno. A. Inglis [77] of Cheraw, South Carolina, asking about the true state of public opinion in South Carolina. Mr. Vanderford declares of Missourians: " There are those who would not deny the justice of secession, however they might deplore it."*]

" *Union men* " Disunionists!

" There are those who would not deny the *Justice* of secession, however the[y] might deplore it. Such are some of the *best men* in this community!"

It begins to be apparent that a good many of these *Union men*, par excellence, whose special vocation it is to save the nation, are apologists for disunion, and see no *injustice* in it. Here is a trusted officer of the *body guard* of the Union, conceding the *justice* of the adversary cause, and consequently, the injustice of his own—thus betraying the cause which he pretends to support.

In the same spirit of insincerity and timidity, the same party, at the North, from Massts. to Pa., bargained and fused with Democrats and Disunionists, of every stripe, to beat the Rep[ublica]ns., *per fasant repas*, and yet had the assurance, here in Mo. to urge Republicans to vote their ticket. Poor *Union Party!* It must, inevitably sink, because it has no distinct object, no principle and no courage. I am sorry that so many really clever and useful men will have to sink with it.

Nov 15. S. T. Glover [78] tells me today that Senator Jas. S. Green [79] has the positive promise of Prest: Buchanan, to give him (in case of his defeat in the new election of senator, coming on this winter) the vacancy place of the later [*sic*] Peter. V. Daniel,[80] as an associate Justice of the Supreme Court of the U.[nited] States!!

---

[76] *Supra,* Oct. 22, 1860, note 72.

[77] Judge of the Supreme Court of Appeals of South Carolina and chancellor of the State. He was soon to be president of the state convention whose ordinance of secession he drafted.

[78] *Supra,* Dec. 23, 1859, note 58.

[79] *Supra,* June 20, 1859, note 96. He *was* defeated but did not get the justiceship.

[80] Before he became justice of the Supreme Court, Daniel had served as Virginia privy councillor, 1812–1835, and U. S. district judge, 1836–1841.

Only think of it! The Democrats, in filling high offices, pay not the slightest attention to adaptiveness—to the qualifications suitable to the place. Mr. Green has but little learning of any sort, and almost no law. Naturally, a *smart man*, with no scholastic education, he started in life too young to be a *lawyer*, and then plunged into politics without the slightest preparation, ignorant alike of the Science of government generally, and of our own political history.

I think Mr. Glover said that Mr. G.[reen] *himself*, told him that he was sure of the Judgeship, if he lost the Senatorial election.

[*November*] *18th. Sunday*—I did not go to church today, the carriages being full without me.

. . .

Julian's wife (with Louisa Hall) still here on a visit. Julian himself was down 2 or 3 day[s] last week[.]

Yesterday I received the long contested Patent [?] for the Hunot claim and handed it over to Mr. Lindell.[31]

Wednesday night. Nov 22. . . .

The news from *the South*, as to secession, does not improve. The leaders of the movement, in Alabama, Georgia, and especially S. Carolina, are more urgent than ever, taking every means to get their followers pledged to extreme measures, and to draw in and commit the timid and the doubtful, without allowing time to look to the consequences and reflect upon the bottomless pit that lies before them.

Still I think that (except with a few demented fanatics) it is all brag and bluster, hoping thus to make a better compromise with the timid patriotism of their opponents. In playing this dangerous game, they may go farther than they now intend, and actually commit their states to open rebellion and civil war. If they *will* push it to that dread extremity, the Government, having been as mild and forbearing as possible, up to that point, will no doubt, find it wise policy to make the war as sharp and prompt as possible, in order to shorten it, and prevent its running into social and servile war,[32] and chronic anarchy, such as prevails in Mexico.[33]

The letters and telegrams from *the South*, bear plain evidence of of exagiration[*sic*], and make a false shewing of the unanimity of the people, in support of the traitorous design. A very little time will show.

---

[31] *Supra*, Oct. 13, 1860; May 3, 1859, note 44.

[32] Here is an assumption as a matter of course that the South will be kept in the Union by force, made by a border state man before any communication with Lincoln. It gives early indication of the uncompromising position Mr. Bates later urged upon President Lincoln.

[33] The last clause, from " and chronic " on, was crowded in later.

If we must have civil war, perhaps it is better now, than at a future day.

Cyrus Edwards,[84] of Alton Ills: (whom I had not seen for 30 years) called at my office to see me today, and we had a good long talk. He is a member of the Ills: legislature, for Madison County, having yielded to urgent entreaty to quit his long privicy [*sic*] and lend the force of his private reputation to turn the scale in that hitherto Democratic County. In order to [secure] a Rep[ublica]n. majority, and consequently ensure Trumbull's[85] re-election to the Senate, it was deemed very important to call out such retired men as Mr. Edwards to carry Madison and Sangamon Counties. It was done effectually, and the victory is complete—Illinois is republicanized in all its departments.

I gave Mr. E.[dwards] a copy of my Keokuk letter.[86]

Yesterday, [the] 21, *Johanna Townshend* handed me $120 to be handed to Fleming Bates, to be held by him on the same terms on which he holds her other money for which she has his note—I gave my receipt to her and today I handed him the money and took a like receipt from him[.]

Note. Fleming has paid me for Barton the tuition fees for *Onward*[87] which I had advanced to the Washington University = $80— he paid to Julia sometime ago $20—and to me, to day $60,[.]

Nov 24. I hear today, that Bernard Pratte,[88] last night, shot a bu[r]glar, in the act of breaking into his house. It is said the thief cannot survive[.]

Sunday, Nov[ember] 25. . . .

Montgomery's Rebellion. The notorious Capt. Montgomery,[89] it seems, is again in the saddle, in southern Kansas, with a following of 150 desperados (which he brags that he can increase at pleasure, to 300) scouring the Country, taking what he pleases, arresting and trying whom he pleases, and now and then shooting or hanging those who are particularly obnoxious.

---

[84] Early settler in Illinois; lawyer; many years a state legislator; promoter of education in the State; president of the Board of Trustees of Shurtleff College.

[85] Lyman Trumbull: justice of the Illinois Supreme Court, 1848–1853; U. S. senator, 1855–1873; chairman of the important Judiciary Committee in the Senate. Originally a Democrat, he deserted his party because of the slavery issue and, as a Republican, helped secure Lincoln's nomination in 1860. Later he voted for Johnson's acquittal and then rejoined the Democratic Party.

[86] See *supra*, Sept. 20, 1860.

[87] Ten-year-old grandson of Mr. Bates—Barton's son.

[88] A wealthy merchant; quondam fur-trader; sometime mayor; state legislator.

[89] James Montgomery, a leader of the anti-slavery forces in Kansas, had driven back a party of Missourians under a deputy-marshal in 1857. When in 1858 some Missourians had killed a free-state Kansan, he had pursued them and killed five in revenge. Then the U. S. cavalry had been sent to punish him, but he had defeated the cavalry. In the Civil War he served in the Union Army.

Government troops are ordered agst him, from Fort Leavenworth, and Genl. Harney [90] has gone up in haste, to take command in person.

Gov Stewart [91] has ordered a portion of the Militia of Mo., to protect the S.[outh] W.[est] frontier, and the Brigade of Genl. D. M. Frost,[92] of this county, is to march this morning, going, by rail, with all speed, as far as the P.[acific] R. R.[93] will carry them (to Syracuse) and thence continue, on foot, to the frontier.

Genl. F[rost]'s brigade consists, mainly, of the uniformed volunteer companies of St Louis, made up chiefly of young men accustomed to the quiet comfortable life of counting rooms, offices and workshops. A hasty campaign in this bitter weather, I fear, will go very hard with them. On their account, I am more afraid of Jack Frost and rough fare, than of Capt Montgomery. Montgomery's men are said to be desperate outlaws, enured to guerrilla life, well mounted, perfectly armed with the best modern weapons, and accustomed to live at free quarters. Their object is not to fight regu[l]ar battles, but to maraud and plunder: and being strong enough to repel small parties, there is small likelihood of a general battle, and hardly any of a general capture of the insurgents.

Sergeant Major Byrne [94] told me last evening that of the troops to march from Leavenworth, there was but a single squadron of horse— abt. 100. These will be hardly able to subdue Montgomery's 150 ruffians, and of course he will not fight them when supported by the infantry and militia.

Nov 28. Wednesday. This morning, the Banks in St Louis (except the Exchange Bk) suspended specie payment. This course was thought to be rendered necessary by the financial difficulties, spreading from N. Y. every where[.] There are real pecuniary causes for these difficulties, but the crisis was precipitated and aggravated by the present political disturbances. Whatever may be the ultimate result, the suspention [*sic*] will be a great present relief, by enabling the banks to accom[m]odate trade, and thus, get the produce of the country to market.

[90] William S. Harney, a brigadier-general who had seen service in Florida, in Mexico, on the frontier, and in Oregon, was now in command of the Department of the West with headquarters at St. Louis. When the War came, he helped prevent Missouri's secession.

[91] *Supra*, Nov. 24, 1859, note 80.

[92] Daniel M. Frost, West Point graduate who had seen service in Mexico, in Oregon, and on the frontier, but had resigned in 1853 to become a lumber merchant and fur-trader in St. Louis. As state senator he secured the enactment of a new militia law and then became brigadier-general under it. In this capacity he led the expedition above mentioned and later commanded at Camp Jackson on the outbreak of civil war until Federal troops forced his surrender. Then he entered the Confederate Army.

[93] The Pacific Railroad—chartered by the Missouri Legislature in 1849, was completed to Kansas City in 1865. It was sold to the Missouri Pacific in 1876.

[94] Probably Charles C. Byrne of Missouri who in 1864 was promoted to the rank of captain of volunteers. He served as commissary in the Subsistence Department.

Nov 29. Thursday. This is *Thanksgiving* day (here, and in most of the States—Tho' Gov Jos: S. [E.] Brown [95] of Ga. has proclaimed a day (yesterday) of *Fasting* and *humiliation*—I think they need both—*fasting* may reduce their animal spirits and make them less rampant and aggressive—and *humiliation* seems to be specially needful to abate the *selfconceit* of the G[e]orgians, and bring them down to the level of other men.[)]

I stay at home. Wife is gone to church, to hear Mr. Post [96] D. D. preach.

Col: G. H. Crossman [97] U. S. A—just from Utah (and his son Frederick—clerk of Shapleigh & Day [98]) called [to] see me, and sat an hour or so—He talks very plainly abt the adm[inistratio]n., especially Sec.y. Floyd,[99] who exiled him to Utah—and says the army generally favored a change, there was so much corruption and tyranny in the adm[inistratio]n. of the Army.

He told me—i. a. that before he was sent out to Utah, and while he was commis[s]ary here, Sanger came to him with an order from Secy Floyd to furnish ho[r]ses to a large amount, and *all the corn* (no quantity mentioned) that might be needed by the army in Utah, at *98* cents pr. bushel. He was then buying freely at *53*, and expressed his surprise &c[.] Sanger then said that that price was to be given *for the corn*, because it was known that he must lose money on the horses, which he was to furnish at $159 a head !

No wonder that Sec.y. Floyd wanted Col: Crossman out of the way.

Today, Coalter takes *Tarlton* home in my buggy and will return monday, as the school adjourns over [   ].

American Characteristics (English view)

It was once smartly said of us, by that caustic critic, Revd. *Sydney Smith*, the Americans are remarkable for two apparently opposite qualities, viz—*animal courage* and *moral cowardice*. But the Reverend and acute joker is fairly beaten by the following terse and graphic phrase, taken from " *The London Saturday Review.*"—"The American People have principles of *barking* entirely distinct from their principles of *biting*."

This London article has some striking views tending to shew that, without the union of the S[outhern] and N[orthern] states, Slavery not only could not be extended, but its existence in the S.[outhern] States would be put to hazard.—Supposing the Southern confederation established—"it is [surely] clear that every question now pending between themselves and the North, would become at once

---

[95] *Supra,* Dec. 2, 1859, note 8.
[96] *Supra,* Jan. 31, 1860, note 44.
[97] George H. Crosman of Massachusetts, West Point graduate of 1823, had served in the Quartermaster's Department of the Army since 1830.
[98] A hardware house of St. Louis owned by Augustus F. Shapleigh and Thomas D. Day.
[99] *Supra,* Dec. 3, 1859, note 11.

an *international question.* Every point now at issue in the domestic forum of Congress, would come under the cognizance of the general society of nations. . . . It is plain[, however,] that every attempt of the southern States to expand beyond the territory absolutely secured to them would be resisted, not simply by their Northern neighbors, but by the whole strength of European civilization. The more reckless spirits of the South are pushing on their quarrel in the belief that, if they were once disembarrassed of the Union, they could rend province after province from Mexico and fill each successive acquisition with their slaves. *But Europe would have a word in the matter*—It is simply the incorporation of the North with the South which prevents European Statesmen from treating the annexations of the U. S. as avowed extensions of the area of Slavery." [1]

These few suggestions lead to a train of argument that ought to convince the most skeptical. But " none are so blind as those who *will not* see."

(for Prest.)

Vote of Ills:		*Vote of Va.*	
For Lincoln	171. 106	Bell	74. 681
" Douglas	158. 254	Breckenridge [*sic*]	74. 323
" Bell	4. 851	Douglas	16. 375
" Breckenridge [*sic*]	2. 292	Lincoln	1. 929
" Smith	35		
			167. 308
	336.538		

And thus it appears that the vote of Illinois is more than double that of Virginia—i. e. 169.230 more[.]

It is also true, (tho' I have not the table before me) that Mo. votes stronger than Va., and has now a larger white population than any other slave state.

Decr. 8. Presidential vote of Virginia—(Nat:[ional] Intel.[ligencer] Dec 6/60) *Richmond, Decr. 5.* " The Electors met here today, for the purpose of casting the vote of the State. On assembling, the *six* Breckenridge [*sic*] electors *declined to take part*, on the ground that, though by the *technicalities of the law,* the[y] might be entitled to vote, they *were not in fact, elected.* The *nine* Bell Electors then filled the vacancies, and cast the vote of the State for Bell and Everett. There is to be a complimentary banquet given to *them* (who?) to[-]night." [2]

---

[1] "A Slave-Holding Republic," *Saturday Review of Politics, Literature, Science, and Art,* IX (Nov. 17, 1860), 610–611. The italics are Mr. Bates's. The punctuation and capitalization are not accurately reproduced.
[2] The italics are Mr. Bates's not the *Intelligencer's,* and the punctuation and capitalization again are not accurate.

This is very strange to me; and if not a usurpation of power, is at the least a dangerous precedent. These *six* gentlemen undertake to annul the certificate of the returning officer (the Governor), to judge and overrule his act, and substitute their own opinion of *right* and *equity* for what they are pleased to term ["] the *technicalities of the law*."!

If this precedent should be recognized and followed, it may turn out to be a fruitful source of corruption, fraud and treachery. Perhaps these six electors thought that as there was no chance to *elect Brackenridge* [*sic*], *their* office was a useless thing, their own *personal* affair, which they might make free to subordinate to their feelings of gentlemanly delicacy! If the[y] could have elected Mr. Breckenridge [*sic*], probably they would have voted according *to law*, and said nothing about *technicalities*.

[*Marginal Note.*] I see that the Mo. Dem[ocra]t. and other papers praise them for their *magnanimity*—Cheap magnanimity that, which costs nothing, and bestows nothing useful.

Madison on Secession.

[*A clipping giving three letters from James Madison to Nicholas P. Trist, dated May 29, December 23, and January 20, 1832.*] [3]
These letters from Mr. Madison [4] to Mr. Trist [5] (never published before) came out lately, in the N.[ew] Y.[ork] " World," and I clip them now from the Baltimore Patriot of Decr. 4.

[*A clipping from the* National Intelligencer *of December 4, 1860, which reprints from the* Charleston Mercury *of November 30 "A Call to Army and Navy Officers* " " *who are now engaged in the military service of the Government of the United States, to renounce at once the sword and the rations of the vulgar oppressor.*"]

The presses and the politicians of *the South*—extreme I mean— seem to me absolutely demented. South Carolina, in preposterous egotism, is determined to rush headlong out of the Union, *all alone*, nothing doubting that, by her *specific gravity*, she can drag down into the pit, after her, the *Cotton States* at least, if not all the *South*. And now, about to set up for herself, she is calling by the *Mercury* <Mercury, you know, among the Greeks, was the God not only of Orators, but of thieves and liars also> upon all South Carolinians

---

[3] See the *Writings of James Madison* (G. Hunt, ed.). IX, 480–482, 489–492. The last letter not only was not printed in a collection of Mr. Bates's time, but is not even in the Hunt edition of Madison's *Writings* or in the Madison Papers in the Library of Congress.

[4] Madison was living in retirement at Montpelier. In this correspondence with Trist he sought to reconcile his position in the Virginia Resolution of 1798 with his strongly national opposition to South Carolina nullification in 1832.

[5] Nicholas P. Trist, lawyer of Charlottesville, Virginia, who had married Jefferson's granddaughter, was private secretary to President Jackson. He later won fame as the negotiator of the Treaty of Guadalupe Hidalgo with Mexico in 1848.

who are *officers* in the Army and Navy, *to desert* and turn their arms against the Nation which educated and honored [them], and to which they have sworn allegiance!

"S.[outh] C.[arolina,"]—it seems, ["]wants *her* soldiers around her now," "and will take care of them all!["]—Poor little S.[outh] C[arolina]! She has a total white population of about 277.000, and of that number not more than 40.000 can be capable of bearing arms. She is poor, her planters generally in debt, and her people generally, doomed to " force a churlish soil for scanty bread." How can she maintain armies and navies? Yet it seems, she is not only to maintain her own State troops, but vast numbers of volunteers from other States. Unless S.[outh] C.[arolina] can, like Napoleon. I, make War pay its own costs, I think she is in a fair way to be bankrupt[.]

[*Two clippings pasted on the same page print and comment upon Major Philip Harry Lee's letter of November 26, tendering Governor Gist* of South Carolina the services of the Twenty-second Regiment of Maryland Volunteer Light Horse. Major Lee's language is sulphurous.*]

Note. The Balt[imor]e. Am[erica]n. also says there is no such Regiment and no such man as Maj: Lee.

[*A clipping headed " Secession of New-York City " which reprints from the* New York Express *an article announcing that "Nev-York City will soon emancipate itself from the Northern Confederacy Republican policy is bringing about, and become the free entrepot of all North America."*]

Dec: 8. Here is another instance of the of the [*sic*] principle and courage of these *soi desans* [*sic*] *Union* men. They not only vote with southern disunionists, and encourage the seceding States, but they are for dismembering the States themselves. The City of N[ew] York, it seems, is to set up for herself!! The entertainment of such anarchic notions ought to be a sufficient warning to all men of sober sense, against the incalculable mischief, of any division at all.

Dec. 11. Tuesday. I am confined at home to day (as I have been several days lately) by a severe cold which I have had for some time, and which is renewed from time to time with the changes of the weather. . . .

Note. We have *bought* but little firewood this fall. By Mr. Lindell's [7] express permission, we are cutting the trees along our eastern line of fence (which seriously interfered with the crops) so as to leave an open space for a road. This supply, with what we get from the Pasture—cutting out, as we do, to improve the grass and beautify

Supra, Feb. 22, 1860, note 87.
Supra, May 3, 1859, note 44.

the grove—will furnish nearly, if not quite, a full supply for the winter.

[*A clipping printing three short items: (1) the announcement of the election of a Conservative, who opposes secession, as United States senator from Arkansas; (2) an extract from Thomas R. R. Cobb's* [8] *speech counseling secession; (3) a reprint from the* Augusta Chronicle *worrying whether the new government will be monarchical or republican.*]

Decr. 16. Sunday—Got home this morning to breakfast (having arrived in town too late last night to come out) on my return from a hasty visit to Springfield, to see Mr. Lincoln, for the first time since his election.

Last thursday I recd. a message from Mr. Lincoln to the effect that he would come down the next day to St Louis, to see and consult me, about some points connected with the formation of his Cabinet. I thought I saw an unfitness in *his coming to me*, and that I *ought to go to him*, as soon as his wish to see me was known. Accordingly, I had him telegraphed that I would wait on him saturday.

Went up friday night. Saturday morning called on him at his room in the Capitol, and had a free conversation—till interrupted by a crowd of visiters—and then, at his suggestion, and for greater privacy, it was arranged that we should meet again at my room, at 3 p. m.

I found him free in his communications and candid in his manner. He assured me that from the time of his nomination, his determination was, in case of success, to invite me into the Cabinet—and. in fact, was so complimentary as to say that my participation in the administration, he considered necessary to its complete success.

He did not attempt to disguise the difficulties in the way of forming a Cabinet, so as at once to be satisfactory to himself, acceptable to his party, and not specially offensive to the more conservative of his party adversaries. He is troubled about Mr. Seward; feeling that he is under moral, or at least party, duress, to tender to Mr. S.[eward] the *first* place in the Cabinet. *By position* he seems to be entitled to it, and if refused, that would excite bad feeling, and lead to a dangerous if not fatal rupture of the party.[9] And the actual appointment of Mr. S.[eward] to be secretary of State would be dangerous in two ways—1. It would exasperate the feelings of the

---

[8] Georgia lawyer; state supreme court reporter; author of a digest of Georgia laws; member of the Montgomery Convention which established the Confederacy. He was a noted slavery controversialist, an eloquent advocate of secession, and by speeches like this played a leading rôle in Georgia's withdrawal from the Union.

[9] Bates and Nicolay (*infra*, Dec. 16, 1860, note 11) do not exactly agree in their accounts of Lincoln's attitude toward Seward in this interview. Welles's account of Seward's appointment supports Bates. (Gideon Welles, *Diary*, II, 388–389.)

South, and make conciliation impossible, because they consider Mr. S.[eward] the embodiment of all that they hold odious in the Republican party—and 2. That it would alarm and dissatisfy that large section of the Party which opposed Mr. S[eward]'s nomination, and now think that they have reason to fear that, if armed with the powers of that high place, he would treat them as enemies. Either the one or the other of these would tend greatly to weaken the Administration.

<these particular arguments, as set down, are my own, but they were all glanced at in the conversation.[>]

He said that if this difficulty were out of the way, he would at once offer me the *State Department*—but, failing that, he would offer me the Att.y. generalship, and urge my acceptance.

He did not state, and I did not choose to press him to state, who would probably fill the other Departments, or any of them. Inde[e]d, I suppose he does not yet know—so much depends on Mr. Seward's position, and upon the daily-changing phases of political affairs.

He assured me however, that I am the only man that he desired in the Cabinet, to whom he has yet spoken a [or] written a word, about their own appointments[.]

I told Mr. L.[incoln] with all frankness, that if peace and order prevailed in the country, and the Government could now be carried on quietly, I would decline a place in the Cabinet, as I did in 1850— and for the same reasons. But *now*, I am not at liberty to consult my own interests and wishes, and must subordinate them to my convictions of public duty, and to the necessity in which I find myself, to sustain my own personal character, by acting out, in good faith, the principles to which I stand pledged. And that, therefore, and as matter of duty, I accepted his invitation, and in that view, would take either office in which he might think I would be most useful. That as a matter personal to myself, and in regard to my private affairs, the Att.y. Genl.'s place is most desirable.

He replied that he never intended to offer me either of the Departments deemed laborious, as involving a great many details of admininstrative business—That, in short, I must be either Sec.y. of State or Att.y. Genl.

I suggested that my visit to Springfield could hardly escape the vigilance of the press and probably the truth would leak out—He said he didn't care if it did, for his mind his mind [*sic*] was fully made up as to me. And further, if I thought, after consultation with friends, that it would be best to let his offer be known, and would write him so, he would stop conjectures, by letting it be known as a fact—but not the particular office.

[*Marginal Note.*]   On the 18th. Decr: I wrote Mr. L.[incoln] that friends here thought it advisable that the fact of my connection with the adm[inistratio]n. should be made public.   On the 20th. I recd. a note from him, dra[f]ting a publication to the effect that he had offered and I had accepted a place in the Cabinet, but what particular place not yet determined.[10]

Feeling under necessity to offer the *State* Dept. to Mr. S.[eward] and having some reason (hope at least) to beli[e]ve that he wd. decline it, he is anxious to *know* the fact; and I must try the best methods I can to ascertain it for him, without committing him.[11]

---

[10] *Complete Works of Abraham Lincoln* (J. G. Nicolay and J. Hay, eds.), I, 660.

[11] John Nicolay, Lincoln's private secretary (*infra*, Feb. 28, 1862, note 18), describes this same interview between Lincoln and Bates:

"*Springfield, December 15, 1860.*—When I went to breakfast this morning I found the name of Mr. Bates on the hotel register. He soon after came into the diningroom and seated himself at the head of the table near which I was sitting, and where I had ample opportunity to study his appearance. He is not of impressive exterior. His hair is gray, his beard quite white, and his face shows all the marks of age quite strongly.

"He came to Mr. Lincoln's room at about 9 A. M., entering with very profuse civilities and apologies for having come before Mr. Lincoln's hour. (He had not yet come from home.) He said that when Mr. Blair informed him that Mr. Lincoln designed visiting him, he had at once replied that he would not think of permitting that to be done, but that it was his duty to wait upon the President-elect, etc. etc. (His flow of words in conversation is very genial and easy, seeming at first to verge upon extreme politeness, but soon becoming very attractive. Afterwards, in serious conversation with Mr. Lincoln Mr. Bates became quite earnest and spoke his thoughts in clear concise language, indicating a very comprehensive and definite intellectual grasp of ideas and a great facility in their expression.) Leaving him in the room with the morning paper to look at, I went to notify Mr. Lincoln of his presence, who soon returned with me.

"Their meeting (they had an acquaintance of eight years' standing) was very cordial; and the ordinary conversation being over, Mr. Lincoln entered at once upon the important subject matter of the interview.

"Without further prelude Mr. Lincoln went on to tell him that he had desired this interview to say to him that since the day of the Chicago nomination it had been his purpose, in case of success, unless something should meantime occur which would make it necessary to change his decision, to tender him (Bates) one of the places in the Cabinet. Nothing having ocurred to make a change of purpose necessary (he had waited thus long to be enabled to act with caution, and in view of all the circumstances of the case) he now offered him the appointment.

"He said in doing this, he did not desire to burden him with one of the drudgery offices. Some of Mr. Bates's friends had asked for him the State Department. He could not now offer him this, which was usually considered the first place in the Cabinet, for the reason that he should offer that place to Mr. Seward, in view of his ability, his integrity, and his commanding influence and fitness for the place. He did this as a matter of duty to the party and to Mr. Seward's many and strong friends, while at the same time it accorded perfectly with his own personal inclinations,—notwithstanding some opposition on the part of sincere and warm friends.

"He had not communicated with Mr. Seward, and did not know whether he would accept the appointment, as there had been some doubts expressed about his doing so. He would probably know in a few days. He therefore could not now offer him (Bates) the State Department, but would offer him what he supposed would be most congenial, and for which he was certainly in every way qualified—the Attorney Generalship.

"Mr. Bates replied by saying that until a very few days ago he had received no word or hint even, that any of his friends had made any such application in his behalf. He expressed himself highly gratified at the confidence which Mr. Lincoln manifested in him by the offer just made. He alluded to the fact that ten years ago he had declined a similar offer made by Mr. Fillmore. Were the country in the same condition in which it was then—were things going along in quiet and smoothness—no inducement would tempt him to assume the duties of such a position. But the case was different. The country was in trouble and danger, and he felt it his duty to sacrifice his personal

Note. Mr. L.[incoln] read me a letter that he had just recd. from Mr. Gilmer [12] M.[ember of] C.[ongress] of N Carolina, urging him to make some declarations &c and a draft of his ans[we]r., which ought to be satisfactory, declining to publish any thing, but referring to his speeches—to particular passages—the pages of the printed debates[.] [13]

Mr. Gilmer is evidently acting in good faith, the rather as he got Mr. Corwin [14] to enclose his letter.

Dec 19. I read in a news paper to day, about the *S. Carolina* dissolution convention, which met on monday, Dec 17, at Columbia[.] Yesterday—18. Dec—it adjourned *to Charleston*, because the small pox *raged* in Columbia—*two* new cases having occurred *since last thursday*—½ a case a day! Very brave for revolutionists!

Note [15]—Suppose the small pox should begin to *rage* in *Charleston* at the *rate of a ½ a case a day*, then it may become proper, *under the quarantine laws*, to remove the Custom House to *Sullivan's Island*—There is law for that, and the Convention sets an apt example[.]

The small pox was hardly the *true reason* for moving the Convention to Charleston. The leaders were becoming alarmed for the result of their desperate experiment, and wanted the outside pressure, which is much stronger at Charleston than Columbia.

[*A clipping giving statistics from the "Annual Report of the Commissioner of the General Land Office."*]

Dec 20. Genl. Coalter [16] tells me today, that the news by Telegraph is, that the [South Carolina] Convention has postponed action for *ten days.* Now, on the brink of the gulf, they are waking

---

inclinations, and, if he could, to contribute his labor and influence to the restoration of peace in, and the preservation of, his country.

" Mr. Lincoln expressed himself highly gratified at his determination.

" Much further conversation was had both during the morning and in the afternoon when Mr. Lincoln called on him again at the hotel. Their views were very frankly and fully exchanged.

" Mr. Bates's conversation shows him to be inflexibly opposed to secession and strongly in favor of maintaining the Government by force if necessary. He forcibly illustrates his temper by saying that he is a man of peace and will defer fighting as long as possible; but that if forced to do so against his will, he has made it a rule *never to fire blank cartridges."*

This passage is taken from the MS. Notes of John Nicolay in the possession of his daughter, Miss Helen Nicolay, who supplied this copy.

[12] John A. Gilmer; Whig state senator, 1846–1856; now Know-Nothing congressman, 1857–1861; Know-Nothing candidate for the speakership in 1859; a Confederate congressman. He deplored agitation on slavery, opposed the admission of Kansas under the Lecompton Constitution, and vigorously fought secession and worked for compromise. Lincoln offered him a cabinet position, but after trying to get Lincoln to restate his position concerning the South, he declined, and went with his State into secession.

[13] Dec. 15, 1860, *Complete Works of Abraham Lincoln*, I, 658.

[14] *Supra*, Feb. 25, 1860, note 96.

[15] Added later.

[16] John D. Coalter, brother of Mrs. Bates and long a member of the Missouri Legislature.

to the necessity of considering some details, settling some preliminaries, before taking the plunge. Until now the leaders, intent only upon *committing* the the [sic] people, and *precipitating* revolution, refused to allow any thing to be considered, but the naked fact of *secession*, lest the difficulty of arrangin[g] the details, and the ghastly consequences, when looked right in the face, cow the people into "submission."

I think [it] is now evident that the leaders had no detailed plan, but a vague determination to break the bonds of the Union and rush into anarchy, hoping <being misled by their grotesque egotism> to drag after them, the Cotton States at least if not the whole South; and then, take their chance to patch up a new Confederation, or, better still, erect a Cotton Kingdom!!

They begin to pause and consider. The border States—speaking through the press—denounce their arrogant dictation—and even in the Senate, Govr. Johnson,[17] of Tenn: denounces them with equal emphasis. They begin to see that they cannot *drag* after them, the other slave states—and if the others did go out with her, she could no more govern the new confederation than the old one. Poor demoralized S. Carolina! This is the last expiring struggle of her pride. She is doomed to impotence and poverty. Her best men will leave her.

She has not, I fear, got the good sense and courage to stop in her mad career. That course would condemn to obloquy and exclusion, all her present leaders, and they would rather ruin the Country than submit to that degradation. Therefore, I suppose she will take the plunge.

[*A clipping which reprints from the* Charleston Courier *a report of the proceedings of a meeting of the South Carolina Historical Society during which the Corresponding Secretary stated that the records of the South Carolina Constitutional Convention of 1790 had been deliberately burned by official order so that posterity should never know the amount of opposition and lack of unanimity in the Convention.*]

The People of S.[outh] C.[arolina] however widely they may differ in fact, have a politic desire to present an undivided front to outsiders, and to appear before the world as all of one mind. This feature of their character (the desire to keep up *appearances* whatever the *facts* may be) is not shewn for the first time, in their *present* revolutionary struggle. As long ago as 1790, the Convention which formed their constitution, deliberately *burned its records*, to conceal from posterity the the differencies [sic] of opinion which existed among them.

See the annexed newspaper clip.

---

[17] Andrew Johnson, governor of Tennessee from 1853 to 1857, but now U. S. senator.

[*A clipping giving the Manifesto of a caucus of Southerners in Congress dated December 13, 1860, in which they say that the unreasonableness of the Republicans has extinguished all hope of relief within the Union, and that the only thing left for the South is to withdraw from the Union as speedily as possible.*]

[*A clipping from the* St. Louis Evening News *reprinting a long editorial of the* Richmond Whig *which insists that all possible means within the Union, including a convention of Southern States, must be tried before the South hastily secedes, and that then, if an adjustment cannot be found, the South must demand a division of the vast properties of the Nation which belong to it as well as to the North.*]

[*A clipping reprinting a letter of Governor Wise* [18] *of Virginia in which he urges Southerners to fight for their rights within the Union since it is the Northerners who are violating and the Southerners who are defending rights guaranteed by the Constitution.*]

[*A clipping giving the electoral and popular votes of the several states for President in 1860.*]

[*A clipping giving the population of cities under the 1860 census and commenting upon their relative sizes.*]

Decr. 21.—This winter solstice is true to its character. . . . Nat[iona]l. Intel[ligence]r. Dec 22. 1860[.]

["HENRY CLAY ON THE SOUTHERN CONFEDERACY IN 1850.

"If this Union shall become separated, (said Mr. CLAY,) new Unions, new Confederacies will arise; and with respect to this, [—] if there be any—I hope there is no one in the Senate [—] before whose imagination is flitting the idea of a great Southern Confederacy to take possession of the Belize and the mouth of the Mississippi—I say in my place, never, [!] *never*, [!] NEVER [!] will we who occupy the broad waters of the Mississippi and its upper tributaries consent that any foreign flag shall float at the Belize or upon the turrets of the Cres[c]ent City. [—] Never! [—] NEVER! "] [19]

I knew, of course, that Mr. Clay [20] held the opinion that the Mississippi River was not politically (any more than physically) divis[i]ble. But I did not know that he had publicly declared it in the Senate, and in terms so terse and emphatic. I am glad to find such great authority for an opinion to which I am so fully pledged. [21]

[*A clipping from the* St. Louis Evening News *of December 31, 1860, which discusses the calling of a Missouri State Convention and a convention at Baltimore of all the Border Slave States with dele-*

---

[18] *Supra*, April 28, 1859, note 38.

[19] A speech on the Compromise bill on July 22, 1850. *Cong. Globe*, 31 Cong., 1 Sess., Appendix, 1413. He had made a similar pronouncement in a speech on Feb. 6, 1850. *Ibid.*, Appendix, 127.

[20] Bates had been a follower and great admirer of Clay.

[21] See *supra*, May 27, 1859.

gates appointed by the governors as the only means by which temperate action and the preservation of the Union may be ensured.]

"The madness of the hour" seems to have perverted the judgment of men usually sober. If there be two ways to do a thing they choose the wrong rather than the right, the unlawful rather than the lawful. The calling of a convention of the People is an *extraordinary* act, not provided for in the constitution. It is not among the granted powers of the Genl. Assembly—nor the Governor nor the Judiciary. It is omitted in the constitution *by design.* [When] Such convention is called *the People* [*the Assembly*] assumes to speak and act for *the People*, in their sovereign capacity. And so, there is no limit to its power[.]

As to a convention of the border states—that is an open breach of the constitution of the U. S. which forbids every contract or agreement between the s[t]ates[.]

Note. The State of Mississippi by its convention in 1851, denied the right of secession, and charged the legislature with *usurpation*, in assuming the power to call the convention.

[*A clipping which prints a national anthem by F. Widdows called* "*The Constitution*" *urging the preservation of the Union.*]

[*A clipping giving a letter of "A Republican" of New Bedford, Massachusetts, suggesting a cabinet for Mr. Lincoln in which Edward Bates would be Secretary of the Interior; John McLean,*[22] *Secretary of State; Simon Cameron,*[23] *Secretary of the Treasury; Sam Houston,*[24] *Secretary of War; Moses H. Grinnell,*[25] *Secretary of the Navy; John M. Botts,*[26] *Postmaster-General; and Edward Stanley,*[27] *Attorney-General.*]

Dec 30. sunday. Attended our own church in the forenoon and heard an excellent discourse, by Dr. Anderson.[28]

In the afternoon (in obedience to a telegraphic summons) went to Springfield, to see Mr. Lincoln.

Arrived at Springfield at 8.30 p. m.

After Supper met Mr. L.[incoln] at Genl. Cameron's room, and had a sort of general conversation for some two hours[.]

[22] *Supra,* April 8, 1860, note 66.

[23] *Infra,* March 5, 1861, note 29.

[24] *Supra,* Aug. 10, 1859, note 82.

[25] A wealthy New York merchant and foreign shipper, who was especially interested in rebuilding the American merchant marine; president of the Chamber of Commerce, 1843–1848; bank president; Whig congressman, 1839–1841; member of the Union Defense Committee during the War; collector of the Port of New York, 1869–1870; naval officer of customs, 1870–1871.

[26] *Supra,* July 15, 1859, note 22.

[27] Edward Stanly: North Carolina lawyer; Whig congressman, 1837–1843, 1849–1853; North Carolina state legislator, 1844–1846, 1848–1849; state attorney-general, 1847; San Francisco lawyer and Republican politician, 1853–1872.

[28] *Supra,* July 17, 1859, note 26.

After Mr. L.[incoln] retired, I remained in company with Mr. Cameron and a Mr. Sanderson [29] of Phil[adelphi]a. (who tells me that he was a member of the *Whig* convention of Balt[imor]e. of 1856.) I did not find out what brought Senator Cameron to Springfield. It is generally surmised however, that he is a strong candidate of [for] Sec.y. of the Treasury.[30] I found him pleasant enough in conversation, but rather reticent about politics and parties. There was nothing private or confidential between us, and I suppose he did not wish me to know the object of his visit—our meeting there was accidental.

Monday [December] 31. Had two long conversations with Mr. L[incoln] in the forenoon and afternoon, in the course of which he shewed me a number of letters from eminent Republicans at the East, and I was surprised to find that some of those [came from men] whom I had thought the most ultra—Among the letters were several from Mr. Seward. He goes as far as any one I have yet seen, in liberality in the filling of the Cabinet. He recommends that two or three Bell men be taken, and gives the names of some that would be acceptable to him viz Scott [31] of Va., Graham,[32] Gilmer [33] (and another, whose name I have forgotten) and one in Tenn: perhaps Nelson [34]—

I knew that Mr. L.[incoln] felt himself under a sort of necessity to offer Mr. Seward the State Department, and suppose that he did it in the hope that Mr. S[eward] wd. decline. But Mr. S.[eward] in a brief note says that after consultation with and advice of friends, he accepts. I [think] this is unfortunate, and [that it] will complicate Mr. L[incoln]'s difficulties. Not that Mr. Seward personally, is not, eminently qualified for the place, in talents, Knowledge, experience and urbanity of manners; but, at the South, whether justly or unjustly, there is a bitter prejudice against him; they consider him the embodiment of all they deem odious in the Republican party. And at the North and in the N.[orth] W.[est]

---

[29] John P. Sanderson, lawyer, editor, author; political friend of Cameron who appointed him to the chief clerkship of the War Department in 1861 which he later relinquished to become a lieutenant in the Army in 1863.

[30] Cf. Welles's explanation of this trip of Cameron's to Springfield. Gideon Welles, *Diary*, II, 389-390.

[31] Winfield Scott enlisted under the influence of the war spirit of 1812, and by 1814 was a brigadier-general. In 1841 he became commander-in-chief of the Army; he led the American forces in the Mexican War. In the Civil War, though a Virginian, he remained loyal and served as commander-in-chief until it became evident to Lincoln that his age incapacitated him for effective command. Lincoln tactfully manoeuvered his resignation on November 1, 1861. See *infra*, Oct. 18, 1861 ; Nov. 1, 1861.

[32] William A. Graham of North Carolina. *Supra*, Dec. 17, 1859, note 37.

[33] John A. Gilmer was offered a cabinet position but declined. *Supra*, Dec. 16, 1860, note 12.

[34] Thomas A. R. Nelson, Unionist congressman, 1859-1861, who remained loyal to the Union when his State voted secession, but was imprisoned by the Confederates when on his way to Washington to attend Congress.

there is a powerful fraction of the Rep[ublica]n. party that fears and almost hates him—especially in N. Y.[35]

I left Springfield at 6. in the evening, got to my office, in the City before midnight, and home to breakfast *Jany 1. 1861.*

NOTE. Seeing Mr. L[incoln]'s difficulties in filling his cabinet, I told him, most candidly, that I was ready to relieve him, as far as possible –that I had not agreed to take office, except as a *painful duty,* and that if he could fill the places without me, it would be a relief rather than a disappointment. He answered promptly—" No I cant [*sic*] do better than that—that State cant [*sic*] be pulled up."

---

[35] *Supra,* April 27, 1859, note 30; Jan. 27, 1860.

CHAPTER III

1861

Professor McCoy   See his letter of Jan 15/61.   [*A picture of a sculptured likeness of Professor McCoy.*]

[*A clipping from the* Daily Express *of January 24, 1861, headed "Tickets for the Convention" urging Missouri Union men not to elect to the Convention men who are only half-heartedly for the Union, but only men who are willing to declare themselves unequivocally for the Union under all circumstances.*]

Constitutional Union Ticket Mo. rep[ublica]n.   *Feb 5. 1861.* also The Citizens'—or straight Union Ticket (which was elected by 5000 majority[)]

[*A clipping giving the "Constitutional Ticket" and the "Declaration of Principles Unanimously Adopted by the Bell and Democratic Conventions" and some editorial comment of the* Republican *thereon.*]

From Louisville Journal of Feb—11th.

[*A clipping reporting that, when he tried to make a secessionist speech, Blanton Duncan was shouted down in Nashville, Tennessee, by a crowd who adjourned to another hall to hold a Union meeting.*]

St Louis Convention election Feb 1861.   Citizen's Ticket and address[.]

[*Two broadsides headed "To the Citizens of St. Louis County" printed between American flags. The address is a plea for the Union, drawn up "by order of the Executive Committee of the Citizens' Union Meeting" of St. Louis County and signed by J. C. Campbell, L. G. Picot,*[1] *C. Gibson,*[2] *and A. S. Mitchell.*[3] *All Union men of St. Louis are urged to vote on February 18 for the Constitutional Union Ticket in the election of delegates to the Convention.*]

Feb 18.   Borrowed from the Boatmen's Savings Institution $8000— and gave my note for the am[oun]t. payable in *one year*—with *Barton Bates* and *Charles Gibson* endorsers.

---

[1] Louis G. Picot, St. Louis lawyer, an expert on land titles. His large properties were seized during the War on the charge that he sympathized with the South, but were later restored.

[2] *Supra,* April 27, 1859, note 27.

[3] *Supra,* Nov. 9, 1859, note 33.

[*A broadside dated St. Louis, February 18, 1861:*

**"To the BELL MEN OF ST. LOUIS
THERE IS TREACHERY"**
In the Election to-day.

"While the BLACK REPUBLICANS Have been pretending to support the ' UNCONDITIONAL UNION TICKET,' the Anzeiger clique have given instructions that Judge GAMBLE's name should be stricken from the ticket, and it is being done in all the German Wards in the City. The intention is to beat Gamble at all hazards. Will you permit this act of treachery to be consummated? It is yet in your power to rebuke this insolence, and to elect the whole ' CONSTITUTIONAL TICKET,' upon which Judge Gamble's name appears."]

This was a scurvy trick. Gamble was keep't [kept on] *their* ticket, only to get the strength of his name : He belonged to, and was elected upon the The [*sic*] *Citizen's* ticket[.]

[*Two broadsides or ballots (probably they were used for both purposes) giving the " Constitutional Union Ticket for State Convention." The nominees listed are: John D. Coalter,*[4] *Luther M. Kennett,*[5] *D. A. January, Hamilton R. Gamble,*[6] *Henry S. Turner, Albert Todd,*[7] *Dr. George Penn, Wm. T. Wood,*[8] *Lewis V. Bogy,*[9] *N. J. Eaton, John W. Wills, Uriel Wright,*[10] *P. B. Garesche, Henry Overstolz, Charles S. Clarkson. At the top is a soldier-boy waving a flag with " Union for the Union" emblazoned upon it.*]

[*A broadside or ballot giving the " Citizens' Union Ticket for the State Convention." The candidates listed thereon are: Sam. M. Breckinridge,*[11] *John How, Dr. M. L. Linton,*[12] *Hudson E. Bridge, Thomas T. Gantt,*[13] *Hamilton R. Gamble,*[14] *John F. Long, Uriel Wright,*[15] *Ferdinand Meyer, Henry Hitchcock, Robert Holmes, James O. Broadhead,*[16] *Sol. Smith,*[17] *Isidor Bush, and John H. Shackelford. This broadside carries a likeness of Washington surrounded by flags over the quotation " ' Discountenance whatever may* suggest *even the* suspicion *that this Union can,* in any event, *be abandoned.'—Washington's Farewell Address.*"]

This ticket elected by an average vote of abt 5000.

[4] *Supra,* Dec. 20, 1860, note 16.
[5] *Supra,* June 16, 1859, note 94.
[6] *Supra,* July 23, 1859, note 39.
[7] *Infra,* Jan. 1, 1866, note 7.
[8] *Supra,* Dec. 17, 1859, note 36.
[9] *Supra,* Jan. 9, 1860, note 11.
[10] *Supra,* June 4, 1859, note 72.
[11] *Supra,* Dec. 26, 1859, note 67.
[12] *Infra,* April 25, 1865, note 89.
[13] *Infra,* Feb. 5, 1864, note 3.
[14] *Supra,* July 23, 1859, note 39.
[15] *Supra,* June 4, 1859, note 72.
[16] *Supra,* Dec. 26, 1859, note 66.
[17] *Supra,* May 9, 1860, note 1.

Feb 19. Paid my note held at the Boatmen's S.[avings] I.[nstitution] $4000 (tho' not due till March 22.)   C Gibson being the endorser—the note taken up and cancelled[.]

Feb 19. Also, paid my note to *Peter Ferguson* for $1000—and interest 41.44—=[   ]

And now, I have no *cash* notes out, but one to Peter Lindell [18] for $500, which he says m[a]y remain as long as I please.

There is indeed, another note held by Robert. B. Frayser,[19] which is not to be *paid* but accounted for, as part of my share of my sister Sarah's Estate (of which he is adm[inistrato]r.[)]

And so I am ready to go to Washington and leave myself and family with a good supply for present uses[.]

Feb.y. On the 26th. at 4. p. m. left St Louis for Washington on Prest. Lincoln's invitation to take a place in his administration, accompanied by my son Richard—and joined, on the car, by J. F. St James of St Genevieve, (a fine, sprightly young creole who made a bold canvas[s] last fall, on the Republican side). Had a pleasant run, arriving at Washington in 50 hours, that is, at 6 oclock on Thursday the 28th. of February, and took rooms which had been reserved for me at the National Hotel, by the friendly foresight of Mr. Moses Kelly, Chief Clerk of the Interior Department.

Immediately after my arrival, I was called to a dinner (at my hotel—the National) given by Mr. Spa[u]lding,[20] M.[ember of] C.[ongress] of Buffalo N. Y. at which I met Messrs. Lincoln, Hamlin,[21] Seward, Chase, C. F. Adams,[22] Welles,[23] and several other dignitaries[.]

Friday and saturday, overrun by a swarming crowd—Had a private talk with Mr. Seward, and think we will agree pretty well—I object only to the urgency with which he invited me to take up my quarters at his house, as his guest until I can make permanent arrangements.

[*A clipping giving the electoral and popular vote of 1860 by states.*]

---

[18] *Supra*, May 3, 1859, note 44.

[19] Son-in-law of Mr. Bates's sister, Mrs. Wharton.

[20] Elbridge Spaulding: Buffalo lawyer and banker; currency expert; Whig congressman, 1849–1851; Union congressman, 1859–1863; member of the Congressional Executive Committee which helped manage Lincoln's campaign.

[21] *Supra*, May 19, 1860, note 15.

[22] A Democrat who turned Whig because of his views on slavery and then turned rebel against Whiggery for the same reason; Free-Soil candidate for the Vice-Presidency in 1848; congressman, 1859–1861; supporter of Seward for the 1860 nomination; campaigner in the Northwest for Lincoln; conciliator in Congress, 1860–1861. He was in Washington to confer with Seward on his duties as minister to the Court of St. James's. This, his only meeting with Lincoln, left him a permanently unfavorable impression of that President.

[23] *Infra*, March 5, 1861, note 30.

March 3. Sunday. I believe I offended several persons by refusing to converse with them about their office seeking—I determined to begin life in the City, by declining to work on the sabbath.

Being invited by Mr. Jos: C. G. Kennedy,[24] (Super[intende]nt. of the Census Bureau) I went with him to Dr. Gurley's[25] church and heard a good sermon, and then dined with Mr. K[ennedy]. This is the Church I expect to join— O.[ld] S.[chool] Presbyterian.

Mar: 4. Monday. The inauguration of President Lincoln took place in peace and without an accident—the day was fine, the crowd immense, and perfect order prevailed every where[.]

Mar 5. Nomination and confirmation of heads of Departments— that is, State, Wm. H. Seward;[26] Treasury, S. P. Chase;[27] Interior, Caleb. B. Smith;[28] War, Simon Cameron;[29] Navy, Gideon Welles;[30] P.[ost] M.[aster] Genl., Montgomery Blair;[31] Atty. Genl. Edward Bates[.]

March 6th. Wednesday. I was inducted into office, the oath being administered to me, by Judge Nelson[32] of the Supreme Court, at the State Department.

---

[24] Lawyer and statistician, originally of Meadville, Pennsylvania; secretary of the Census Board, 1849; then first superintendent of the new Census Bureau. He compiled the Census of 1850 and worked on the Census of 1860 from 1859 until the funds were exhausted in 1863.

[25] Phineas D. Gurley, Old School Presbyterian minister of the Fifth Street Church in Washington, 1854–1859; minister of the New York Avenue Church formed by the union of the Fifth Street and Second Presbyterian churches; at this time chaplain of the Senate; Lincoln's minister during the War.

[26] Governor of New York, 1838–1842; Whig and then Republican U. S. Senator, 1849–1861; secretary of State, 1861–1869; leader of the extreme anti-slavery Republicans of the East.

[27] Free-Soil U. S. senator from Ohio, 1849–1855 and 1861; governor of Ohio, 1855–1859; secretary of the Treasury, 1861–1864; chief justice of the Supreme Court, 1864–1873; a persistent advocate of negro suffrage, and perennial aspirant to the Presidency.

[28] Indiana lawyer and editor; Whig congressman, 1843–1849; member of the Peace Convention of 1861. It was David Davis's promise of this cabinet post for Smith that had secured Indiana's support and helped turn the nomination to Lincoln in 1860. Smith now opposed all compromise with the South.

[29] Wealthy Pennsylvania business man and shrewd political manipulator; Democratic U. S. senator, 1845–1849; Republican U. S. senator, 1857–1861 and 1867–1877; secretary of War, 1861–1862; minister to Russia, 1862. He was at this time building the effective party machine which he was to control for years to come, and was able to muster enough support for his own nomination to force Lincoln's managers to promise him the secretaryship of War in exchange for convention votes for Lincoln. He was so unfortunate as secretary of War that Lincoln had to appoint him minister to Russia to be rid of him.

[30] Quondam editor of the *Hartford Times*; Connecticut state legislator; postmaster under Jackson and Van Buren; chief of a Navy Department bureau, 1846–1849; secretary of the Navy, 1861–1869; an organizer of the Republican Party in Connecticut; head of his State's delegation to the 1860 convention. In the Cabinet Welles and Bates agreed in distrusting Seward and Stanton and in protecting Lincoln against Radical intrigue.

[31] Originally a Kentucky lawyer who had moved to St. Louis and become a protégé of Senator Benton; U. S. district attorney, 1839–1841; mayor of St. Louis; judge; resident of Maryland after 1853; counsel for Dred Scott; chairman of the Republican Convention in Maryland in 1860; delegate to the National Republican Convention; conciliator of sections in 1861 and again in Reconstruction. The Radicals finally forced him out of the Cabinet in 1864, but he continued to support Lincoln and Johnson and to advise them unofficially.

[32] Samuel Nelson: New York circuit judge, 1823–1831; justice of the New York Supreme Court, 1831–1845; justice of the U. S. Supreme Court, 1845–1872. He had voted with the slave majority in the Dred Scott case, and later opposed the invasion of civil rights under the "war powers."

My predecessor, Edwin. M. Stanton,[33] gave me every facility and
aid in the office—took me to the Supreme Court and presented me
there—and offers all assistance for the future.

At night—Prest. Lincoln's *first Cabinet Council*—intended, I
suppose to be formal and introductory only—in fact, uninteresting.

Mar 8. Friday night—Prest. Lincolns [*sic*] first reception a
motley crowd and terrible squeeze[.]

Mar 9. Saturday night. A Cabinet Council upon the State of
the Country. I was astonished to be informed that Fort Sumter,
in Charleston harbor *must* be evacuated,[34] and that General Scott,[35]
Genl. Totten[36] and Major Anderson[37] concur in opinion, that, as
the place has but 28 days [*sic*] provision, it must be relieved, if at
all, in that time; and that it will take a force of 20,000 men at least,
and a bloody battle, to relieve it![38]

<[*Note added after March 16.*] For several days after this, con-
sultations were held as to the feasibility of relieving Fort Sumter,
at which were present, explaining and aiding, Gen Scott, Gen Totten, Com[m]odore Stringham,[39] and Mr. Fox[40] who seems to be *au
fait* in both nautical and military matters. The *army* officers and
navy officers differ widely about the degree of danger to rapid moving vessels passing under the fire of land batteries—The *army* officers think destruction almost inevitable, where the *navy* officers think
the danger but slight. The one believes that Sumter cannot be
relieved—not even provisioned—without an army of 20.000 men and
a bloody battle: The other (the naval) believes that with light,

---

[33] *Infra*, Jan. 13, 1862, note 27.

[34] Fort Sumter was built on a shoal entirely surrounded by water. It commanded the
entrance to Charleston Harbor, but was not completed when the War came. Major
Anderson had moved all of his troops to Sumter on December 26 because, though unfin-
ished, it was more defensible than the forts on the mainland.

[35] *Supra*, Dec. 31, 1860, note 31.

[36] Joseph G. Totten: West Point graduate of 1805 who had served in the War of 1812
and the Mexican War; since 1838 chief engineer of the Army in which capacity he had
supervised the building of most of our forts. Scott wished Totten to succeed him as
commander-in-chief in 1861, but Totten felt himself too old.

[37] Robert Anderson, in command of the Union garrison in Fort Sumter, was a West
Point graduate of 1825 who had seen service in the Black Hawk, Florida, and Mexican
Wars. He was a Kentuckian of Virginia descent but of unquestioned loyalty, and though
he believed dissolution of the Union was inevitable and personally wished to avoid bloodshed, he faithfully carried out Lincoln's orders even when it meant armed conflict in
what he considered the hopeless cause of trying to hold Sumter.

[38] Cf. Gideon Welles, *Diary*, I, 3–6.

[39] Silas H. Stringham, who had served in the Navy since 1809 [1810?] was made flag
officer of the Atlantic Squadron in 1861. See *infra*, Nov. 13, 1861, note 35.

[40] Gustavus V. Fox, Annapolis graduate of 1841, had served in the Mexican War but
had resigned in 1856. Through the influence of Montgomery Blair, his wife's brother-in-
law, he was summoned in February by General Scott to plan the relief of Sumter, but
Buchanan vetoed the plan. Lincoln put him in charge of the expedition which arrived
April 12, in time to see the bombardment but too late to aid. He served as assistant
secretary of the Navy throughout the War.

rapid vessels, they can cross *the bar* at high tide of a dark night, run the enemy's forts (Moultrie [41] and Cummings' Point [42]) and reach Sumter with little risk. They say that the greatest danger will be in landing at Sumter, upon which point there may be a concentrated fire. They do not doubt that the place *can* be and *ought* to be relieved. Mr. Fox is anxious to risk his life in leading the relief, and Com[m]odore Stringham seems equally confident of success.

The naval men have convinced me fully that the thing can be done, and yet, as the doing of it would be almost certain to *begin the war*, and as Charleston is of little importance, as compared with the chief points in the Gulf, I am willing to yield to the *military* cou[n]sel. and evacuate Fort Sumter, at the same time stren[g]thening the Forts in the Gulf, so as to *look down* opposition, and guarding the coast, with all our naval power, if need be, so as to close any port at pleasure[.]

And to this effect, I gave the President my written opinion, on the 16th. of March[.>]

March 16. The President of the United States has required my opinion, in writing, upon the following question

"As[s]uming it to be possible to now provision Fort Sumter, under all the circumstances, is it wise to attempt it?"

This is not a question of lawful right nor physical power, but of prudence and patriotism only. The right is in my mind unquestionable, and I have no doubt at all that the Government has the power and means, not only to provision the fort, but also, if the exigency required, to man it, with its war complement of 650 men, so as to make it impregnable to any local force that could be brought against it. Assuming all this we come back to the question "Under all the circumstances is it wise *now* to provision the fort?["]

The wisdom of the act must be tested by the value of the object to be gained, and by the hazard to be encountered in the enterprise. The object to be gained by the supply of provision, is not to strengthen the fortress, so as to command the harbor and enforce the laws, but only to prolong the labors and privations of the brave little garrison that has so long held it, with patient courage. The posses-

---

[41] Fort Moultrie stood four miles from Charleston on the south shore of Sullivan's Island, connected with the mainland northeast of Sumter. It stood on a sand-pit and its walls were so low that on the sea side sand had drifted up to the top of them "so that cows could actually scale the ramparts." When South Carolina seceded Anderson's troops had been in Moultrie, but on his own initiative, in the absence of orders from Washington, Anderson had spiked his guns, had evacuated indefensible Moultrie, and had moved to Sumter on December 26. On December 27, South Carolina troops had entered Moultrie.

[42] Cummings Point was the partially fortified northern end of Morris Island just south of Moultrie and also connected with the mainland. Moultrie and Cummings Point occupied the two capes at the entrance to Charleston Harbor and Sumter lay between them.

sion of the fort as we now hold it, does not enable us to collect the revenue or enforce the laws of commerce and navigation. It may indeed involve a point of honor or a point of pride, but I do not see any great national interest involved in the bare fact of holding the fort, as we now hold it—and to hold it at all we must supply it with provisions. And it seems to me that we may in humanity and patriotism, safely waive the point of pride, in the consciousness that we have the power and lack nothing but the will, to hold Fort Sumter in such condition as to command the harbor of Charleston, cut off all its commerce, and even lay the City in ashes.

The hazards to be met are many and obvious. If the attempt be made in rapid boats light enough to pass the bar in safety, still they must pass under the fire of Fort Moultrie and the batteries on Morris Island.[43] They might possibly escape that danger, but they cannot hope to escape the armed guard boats which ply all night from the Fort to the outer edge of the bar[.] These armed guard boats would be sure to take or destroy our unarmed tugs, unless repelled by force, either from our ships outside the bar, or from Fort Sumter within; and that is war. True, war already exists by the act of South Carolina; but this Government has thus far, magnanimously forborne to retort the outrage. And I am willing to forbear yet longer, in the hope of a peaceful solution of our present difficulties. I am most unwilling to strike—I will not say the first blow, for South Carolina has already struck that [44]—but I am unwilling "*under all the circumstances*" at this moment to do any act which may have the semblance, before the world of beginning a civil war, the terrible consequences of which would, I think, find no parallel in modern times. For I am convinced that flagrant Civil war in the Southern States would soon become a social war, and that could hardly fail to bring on a servile war, the horrors of which need not be dwelt upon. To avoid these evils I would make great sacrifices, and fort Sumter is one; but if war be forced upon us by causeless and pertinacious rebellion, I am for resisting it with all the might of the nation.

I am persuaded moreover, that, in several of the misguided States of the South, a large portion of the people are really lovers of the Union, and anxious to be safely back, under the protection of its flag. A reaction has already begun, and, if encouraged by wise, moderate and firm measures on the part of this government, I persuade myself that the nation will be restored to its integrity without the effusion of blood.

---

[43] At Cummings Point. See *supra*, March 9, 1861, notes 34, 41, 42.

[44] The South Carolinian battery on Morris Island had fired on the steamer *Star of the West* on January 9, 1861, when she was trying to land reënforcements at Sumter and had forced her to return to New York without landing her troops.

For these reasons, I am willing to evacuate fort Sumter, rather than be an active party in the beginning of civil war. The port of Charleston is comparatively, a small thing. If the present difficulties should continue and grow, I am convinced that the real struggle will be at the Mis[sis]sippi for it is not politically possible for any foreign power to hold the mouth of that river, against the people of the middle and upper vall[e]y.[45]

If fort Sumter must be evacuated, then it is my decided opinion that the more Southern forts Pickens,[46] Key West &c should, with out delay, be put in condition of easy defense against all assailants; and that the whole coast, from South Carolina to Texas, should be as well guarded as the power of the navy will enable us.

Upon the whole, I do not think it *wise now* to attempt to provision Fort Sumter.

[*March 29.*] On the 29th. of March, in Cabinet Council on these subjects, I suggested that, in the desultory conversations by which we had usually conducted o[u]r consultations, it was hard to arrive at definite conclusions, and therefore I proposed that the President should state his questions, and require our opinions *seriatim.* This being agreed to, I immediately wrote and read the following memorandum—

" It is my decided opinion that Fort Pickens and Key West ought to be re inforced and supplied so as to *look down* opposition, at all hazards—And this, whether fort Sumter be or be not evacuated."

" It is also my opinion that there ought to be a *naval* force kept upon the Southern coast, sufficient to *command it*, and, if need be *actually close* any port that, practically, ought to be closed, whatever other Station is left unoccupied."

" It is also my opinion that there ought to be immediately established, a line of light, fast-running vessels, to pass, as rapidly as possible, between N. Y. or Norfolk at the North, and Key West or other point in the gulf at the South."

"As to fort Sumter, I think the time is come when it ought to be either evacuated or relieved."

The President was pleased with this mode of proceeding, and requested the other ministers to do the like—which was done—Mr. Seward gave his advice for the immediate evacuation of fort Sumter.[47]

April 8. Monday. To preserve continuity on this important subject, I skip over several days—

---

[45] See *supra*, May 27, 1859.
[46] On the tip of Santa Rosa Island commanding the entrance to Pensacola Harbor in Florida. Pickens was successfully reënforced in April and was held by Union forces throughout the War.
[47] Cf. G. Welles, *Diary,* I, 9.

This Adm[inistratio]n. has kept its own counsel pretty well, yet, its general purpose to preserve its authority as far as possible, in the South, seems to be known by the press, though its particular means are still only guessed at. For some days, the public is much excited with rumors of military expeditions to various points, tho' most of the guesses point rather to the Gulf than to Charleston.

In fact, at this moment, the matter stands thus—An expedition to *provision* fort Sumter, well appointed, consisting of light-draft, rapid steamers (drawing only 5 or 6 feet, so as to pass Charleston bar) commanded by Mr. Fox,[48] leaves N. York to day or tomorrow, and will reach Charleston on the 11th., or 12th. at farthest. If Maj: Anderson [49] hold out till then, one of two things will happen— either the fort will be well provisioned, the Southrons forbearing to assail the boats, or a fierce contest will ensue, the result of which cannot be foreseen—The fort may be demolished or the City burned—In either case there will be much slaughter.

The President has sent a private messenger to Govr. Pickens,[50] notifying him that *provisions* only, and not men, arms or am[m]unition, will be landed, and that no attempt will be made to reinforce the fort, unless the provisions or the fort be fired upon.[51]

From the first, I have insisted that it was a capital error to allow batteries to be built around fort Sumter—the erection of those batteries being an *assault*, equal to the throwing of shells. In answer to my direct question today, the Sec.y. of War (Genl. Cameron) told me that the erection of batteries to assail fort Pickens wd. not be allowed—if attempted the Fort would prevent it with shot and shell.

A large naval force is ordered to the southern coast, and, in 3 or 4 days, either there will be some sharp fighting, or the prestige of the Government will be quietly reëstablished[.]

To day, Mr. A. Roane, for long, first clerk in the A.[ttorney] G[eneral]'s office, resigned and went south, he being, in reality, a secessionist, I appointed my son, *Richard Bates*, to fill the vacancy, and fixed the salary at $1600—the same that Mr. Roane received.

Until now, Richard held a special and contingent clerkship, created under the California land claim act, and his salary payable out

---

[48] *Supra*, March 9, 1861, note 40.

[49] *Supra*, March 9, 1861, note 37.

[50] Francis W. Pickens: Democratic congressman, 1834–1843; minister to Russia, 1858–1860; now governor of South Carolina, 1860–1863; a leading states' rights man and nullifier in 1832–1833; delegate to the Nashville Convention of 1850 which considered secession. It was he who ordered the firing on the *Star of the West* (*supra*, March 16, 1861, note 44) and now demanded Anderson's surrender of Sumter.

[51] On April 1 Seward had given Justice Campbell a written memorandum which said: "The President may desire to supply Sumter, but will not do so without giving notice to Governor Pickens." It was this promise which Lincoln now fulfilled. This notification led the Confederacy to demand immediate evacuation and then to order its guns to fire upon Sumter before the provisions arrived.

of the contingent fund. He is now the regular *first* clerk of the office.

Titian. J. Coffey [52] of Pa. [was] appointed my Assistant on the [   ] of April, and immediately began his duties[.]

Apl. 12./61. C.[abinet] C.[ouncil] [53]

S.ec.y. [of] State. Proposes to send Geo: Ashmun [54] to Canada as a special (secret) agent &c to keep political feelings right—at $10 a day and expen[se]s. *Agreed*[.]

Secy of War, produces letter from Sam Houston [55]—declining the help of U. S. troops, to the commanding officer U. S. [A.] in Texas.—till orders from Washington.

Prest: said he had a conference with the Mayor of this City—Advises the resu[m]ption of work on the west wing of Treasury building—to keep the people of Washington in good humor [56]—Agreed[.]

Capt. Talbot [57]—just from Charleston made his report—

Mr. Goodrich [58]—made report of his message to Gov Pickens [59]—notice of intention to provision Fort Sumter.

Apl: 15nth. Memo:[randum] of E Bates in Cabinet[.]

Now that we are at open war, it is my opinion.

1 That the mails ought to be stopped in the revolted states, forthwith.[60]

2 That the Southern ports, at least from Charleston to New Orleans, ought to be closed at once.[61]

3 That the mouth of the Mississippi ought to be effectually guarded, so as to prevent all ingress and egress.

4 That the approach to New Orleans, by Lake Ponchartra[i]n ought to be at our entire command.[62]

---

[52] *Supra,* March 5, 1860, note 18.

[53] This whole entry is scribbled onto a loose sheet which is pasted into the diary.

[54] Massachusetts lawyer; Whig congressman, 1845–1851; director of the Union Pacific Railroad; chairman of the Republican National Convention which nominated Lincoln.

[55] *Supra,* Aug. 10, 1859, note 82.

[56] The central portion of the Treasury Building was built in 1836 after a fire had destroyed the old structure, but the west wing was begun only in 1855. Work had been suspended until Lincoln resumed it in 1861.

[57] Theodore Talbot who, with R. S. Chew of the State Department, was sent by President Lincoln on April 6 to Charleston. Talbot took instructions to Major Anderson which he was to deliver, if permitted, but permission was refused.

[58] According to other accounts it was R. S. Chew, not Goodrich, who took the message to Governor Pickens announcing that Sumter would be provisioned.

[59] *Supra,* April 8, 1861, note 50.

[60] They *were* stopped by a general order of the Post Office Department of May 27, 1861. See Postmaster-General Blair to the Speaker of the House of Representatives, July 12, 1861, *Cong. Globe,* 37 Cong., 1 Sess., 115.

[61] Lincoln proclaimed a blockade from South Carolina to Texas on April 19, 1860. J. D. Richardson, *Messages and Papers of the Presidents,* VI, 14–15. He extended it to North Carolina and Virginia on April 27, 1861. *Ibid.,* VI, 15.

[62] Farragut captured the New Orleans forts on April 28, 1862, and Butler occupied the city on May 1.

5 That the Mississippi river at the mouth of the Ohio, ought to be commanded by the Government so as to control the navigation and trade at that centre.   And [63] to that end, we must have a floating force, sufficient to command the river and its banks.[64]

6 That the safety of St. Louis ought to be ensured.[65]

7 The Seat of Government, of Course must be protected, cost what it may.[66]

8 We must maintain full command of the Chesapeake Bay—as that locks up Virginia and Maryland and half of North Carolina—and to that end, we must maintain Fort Munroe [sic].[67]

9 Harpers ferrry [sic] and Gosport ought to be protected, if possible.[68]

Note: Of course I am for "enforcing the laws" with no object but to reinstate the authority of the Government and restore the integrity of the nation.   And with that object in view I think it would be wise and humane, on our part so to conduct the war as to give the least occasion for social and servile war, in the extreme Southern States, and to disturb as little as possible the accustomed occupations of the people.

The plan of practically closing the ports of the insurgent States and cutting off all their Sea-ward * commerce seems to me the easiest cheapest and most humane method of re[s]training those States and destroying their Confederation.   Their people are high spirited and ready enough to fight, but impatient of control and unable to bear the steady and persistent pres[s]ure which we can easily impose and which they have no means to resist.   They are an anomalous people—the only agricultural people that I know of, who cannot live upon the products of their own labor, and have no means of their own to take those products to market.

Cotton and Sugar, their only staples must be exported and sold, in order to procure the very necessaries of life.   They *must sell* or

---

[63] This last sentence was inserted later.

[64] By the middle of May General B. M. Prentiss was already at Cairo with a small force, and in September Grant, with headquarters at Cairo, took command of the region about the mouth of the Ohio.

[65] Frémont took command in St. Louis in July and was succeeded by David Hunter in November, 1860, and later by Halleck.

[66] Communication with the North was completely severed on April 21 and Washington was unprotected.   But by April 27 there were 10,000 troops in the city.   Protection of Washington was to play an important rôle in all eastern campaigns of the War.

[67] Fortress Monroe was defended by Colonel Justin Dimick and 300 men who turned some of their guns landward and held the fort until General Butler arrived on May 22, 1861, with sufficient strength to hold it throughout the War.

[68] On April 20 the Gosport (Norfolk) Navy Yard was partially destroyed and then abandoned the next day by the Union forces.   On April 18, the commander at Harper's Ferry demolished the arsenal, burned the armory, and abandoned that town.   It remained a strategic point and subsequent military events proved how wise it would have been to hold it.

* "Sea-ward" was written in later.

sink into poverty and ruin; and if their ports be closed, they *must* send their products northward, to the ports of the States yet faithful. In that way their products will find their way into the markets of the world, and they will be compelled to receive their foreign supplies, through the same channels. And thus *our* duties (somewhat deminished [*sic*], it may be) will still be paid, and the people of the loyal states will get the profits of the trade. While they getting no revenue from duties, must resort to direct taxation, and that to an extent their people cannot long endure.

This plan it seems to me if strictly and persistently enforced, while it would not necessarily lead to the shedding of a drop of blood, would nevertheless, be very *coersive* [*sic*] and very promising of success. At all events it is the most feasible project for the accomplishment of our main end, that has occurred to my mind.

Others may think it wiser and better to adopt a line of action more bold and warlike, and to enforce the laws at the point of the bayonet, in the field. If that opinion prevail then I have a suggestion to make, as to the point of attack which seems to me, at once the most vulnerable and the most important.

On this hypothesis it is my opinion that the Government ought to take and hold with strong hand, the City of New Orleans, And that, I believe can be done without much fighting, provided the plan be judiciously matured and the preparations be made with intelligence, secresy [*sic*] and celerity.

I suggest *some of the means* not presuming to cover all the details of a design so complicated and so beyond the range of my habitual thoughts. And

1 The Naval force on the Gulf ought to be stronger than necessary for a mere blockading squadron and the enemy might be made to understand it so. And there ought to be on board the Squadron some of our best artillery, to cooperate with the force to descend the river.

2 There is, up the river, a class of men, the hardiest on the continent—the boatmen now for the most part not well employed, and likely to see worse times, as soon as the trade of New Orleans is stopped or crippled, by our squadrons in the Gulf. These men are hardy and bold, and will be ripe for such a brilliant enterprise.

I know several gentlemen who know these men perfectly and can exercise a great influence over them. I think that 8 or 10.000 of these men could be promptly engaged, by using the proper agencies. These, being equipped and concentrated at Cairo, might with such other means as may be thought needful, run to New Orleans, in four days, or less and there cooperating with the fleet, might very probably take the City without a serious struggle[.]

The success of such a scheme might make it proper to use some freedom in stopping the mails and Telegraphs for a few days.

I do not propose this plan, for I greatly prefer to accomplish the end by blockade. But if regular war be inaugurated in the valley of the Mississippi, we must command the mouth of the river, and ought to command also the mouth of the Ohio. This last would protect and control the commerce and navigation of nearly ten millions of our people[.] [69]

Respectfully submitted

Note 2. In order to ensure constant employment to the insurgent troops our cruisers could frequently look in upon the enemies [sic] forts, if only to see that they are well manned and guarded, and now and then make a shew of force off the most exposed points of enemy coast.

[*Two clippings, one giving a map of the fortifications in Charleston Harbor, the other a map of those in Pensacola Harbor.*]

Ap 23rd. E Bates' mem:[orandum] in Cabinet Counsel [sic]. The People of Maryland and Virginia are in a ferment, a furore, regardless of law and common sense.

In Maryland there is not even a pretence of *state* authority, for their overt acts of treason.

In Virginia it is a mere pretence, for, by their own law, **the act** of the Convention was to have no effect until ratified by the People.[70]

Yet both in Maryland and Virginia, they are in open arms against us, and by violence and terror they have silenced every friend of the Government.

They think and in fact find it perfectly safe to defy the Government, And why? Because we hurt nobody; we frighten nobody; and do our utmost to offend nobody. *They* cut off *our* mails; *we* furnish theirs gratis. *They* block our communications, *We* are careful to preserve theirs—*They* assail and obstruct our troops in their lawful and honest march to the defense of this Capitol [sic] while *we* as yet have done nothing to resist or retort the outrage.[71]

They every day are winding their toils around us, while *we* make no bold effort to cut the cord that is soon to bind us in pitiable impotence[.]

---

[69] It is interesting to note that while others were expecting a speedy victory by a march on Richmond, Bates was this early persuaded of the importance of the slower method of blockade and that he saw what military leaders did not comprehend until much later—the significance of the West and the Mississippi in military strategy. See also *supra,* May 27, 1859.

[70] The Virginia State Convention had met on February 13, 1861, but since unionists were in a majority, it did not vote to secede until April 17, after Lincoln's call for men, and then, only on condition that secession should not be effective unless ratified by popular referendum. Ultimately a majority of voters did approve, but the vote was not taken until several weeks after state officials had by executive action made secession irrevocable.

[71] On April 19 a mob in Baltimore attacked a Massachusetts regiment on its way to Washington as it passed through the city, and a riot ensued. Then the Baltimoreans destroyed the railroad bridges and telegraph wires. When the soldiers proceeded by boat to Annapolis, they found the tracks torn up there, too.

They warm up their friends and allies, by bold daring, and by the prestige of continued success—While we freeze the spirits of our friends every where, by our inaction and the gloomy prestage [*sic*] of defeat.

They are active and aggressive every where from the Patapsco [72] to the Mississippi; while we are aggressive no where, and active only in slow preparations for the defence of this City. Of course this City must be defended, but I am persuaded that some of its best means of defence may be found in active aggressive measures elsewhere.

But I am asked, under present embarrassing circumstances, what can we do?

I answer

1. We *can*, with our present means, close up Hampton Roads, and Elizabeth River, and thus cut off the water communication from the Bay to Richmond and Norfolk and Petersburg, and between Norfolk and the two other cities.

2. We *can* obstruct the Railroad from Portsmouth, to the South and Southwest (and repeat the operation as often as need be)—and that will retard, if not prevent the enemies' supplies from that direction, and destroy the trade of that section.

3. We *can* do the same to the Alexandria Railroad.

4. Baltimore having wantonly cut off her main line of R. R. to the North, we can easily cut her off from the rest. And I see nothing to hinder us from closing the mouth of the Patapsco.

5. We *can* command the Mississippi at its great centre—the mouth of the Ohio and the surrounding region. That point ought to be securely occupied, at whatever cost. Because, as a means of preserving the integrity of the nation it is second to none on the continent.[73]

6. We *can* stop the mails in the insurgent states.[74]

These things we *can* do, and in my judgment, ought to do—and that quickly—Assuming that the mouth of the Mississippi is effectually blockaded.

As a counsellor of the President, I do not presumptuously set myself up as a commander. I give my opinions only; and whatever other counsels prevail, still, to the utmost of my ability, and with all my little influence, I will support the Government to the very end—But I desire it to be remembered that in my opinion affirmative and progressive measures are absolutely necessary to our safety.

---

[72] A Maryland river which enters Chesapeake Bay about thirteen miles below Baltimore.
[73] *Supra*, April 15, 1861, note 64.
[74] See *supra*, April 15, 1861, note 60.

Note. Fort Monroe commands the channel of Hampton Roads—
i. e. the mouth of James River—And being well manned, it can
sink any vessel that attempts to *run* the passage.

Opposite Fort Monroe, at the distance of one mile and a quarter,
across the channel of Hampton Roads, stands *Castle Calhoun*, in
the water, on the flat or shoal called *Rip raps*[.] This castle I
believe was never finished (tho' heavy guns were mounted in it many
years ago.). It is very strong, prepared for the heaviest ordnance,
and *case-mated*.

I do not know whether or not there are guns in it now, but there
is no garrison. I do not profess to understand much about fortifications, but I fear that it may fall into the hands of the enemy, and
be made the efficient means (in aid of a beseiging [*sic*] land force)
to reduce Fort Monroe.

Ought it not, at once, to be either garrisoned or destroyed?

I attach great importance to our possession of that point, in force.
It will be a great safeguard to this Capital, and to the whole bay,
and a strong curb upon Virginia and N. Carolina.

April 29. 1861. Cabinet Council

I propose that the employés of all the Departments—from the
head Secretary to the lowest messenger, be required to take, anew,
the oath of allegiance—agreed.

I propose—

1. Fort Monroe being streng[t]hened, to *close* Hampton Roads—so
as to prevent any outlet from Richmond and Norfolk—

2. To station an armed vessel, (or if we have none at hand) to
establish a battery, so as to cut off all communication, by water
between Richmond and Norfolk.

3. To reinforce Gosport [75] with a force to look down *local* opposition—and to spare men for detachments along the line of [the] R. R.
towards the S.[outh] and S.[outh] W.[est]—<these three points
talked over but nothing concluded>

Genl. Scott comes and says two or three steamboats belonging to
the R. R. and P. O. line to Acquia Creek,[76] sent for by the owners
for the purpose as he believes, of bringing troops up, to attack the
city and proposes that we take them—(They were taken and armed
with one heavy gun and howitzers.)

Harper[']s Ferry [77]—There ought to be at least 15,00 men there,
with orders not only to repel force, but to pursue and take or destroy
the assailing force.

---

[75] Abandoned April 20–21.
[76] In that day, one often took a boat to Aquia Creek below Alexandria to get a train
to the South. See *infra*, Oct. 22, 1861, note 13.
[77] Abandoned April 18.

Fort Monroe, It ought to be so strengthened as to offer no temptation to assail it from without.[78]

Secy. Welles—says that the subordinate officers of the steamer Merrimack [79]—Robb et al—have resigned and refused to do duty, steam being up—

Lieut Aulick [80] introduced—was sent down to take the Merrimack to Philad[elphi]a.—yesterday ready—no men to spare—Commodore McCauley,[81] offered to lend me 30 men and—the com[modo]re. said he thought we should need the ship to help defend the yard—He is old &c.—he said to me take the ship—I sent down to examine the sunken *wrecks*—report—a passage—I asked for and got two howitzers to keep off tugs &c.

Capt Robb came and said the comm[odo]re. had changed his mind wanted to keep the ship for defence [82]—Capt Sinclair and other officers tried to dissuade me.[83]

July 5.   My Son John Coalter Bates, having received the appointment of first Lieutenant in the Eleventh (new) Regiment of Infantry, left us this day, under orders to report at the head quarters of his Reg[imen]t. at Fort Independence, Boston harbor.

This is an era in his life, for it is the first time he ever left home—even when attending College, he still lived at Home.

July 8.   This day George. T. Woodson,[84] having been appointed a captain in the 13th. (new) Reg[imen]t. of Infantry, left us under orders to report at his Regimental head quarters, at Chicago[.]

[*A clipping from the* Philadelphia Daily Evening Bulletin *of August 21, 1861, giving a long obituary notice of Colonel Paxton.*[85]]

August 27. Mexico Memorandum read by Edward Bates (A[ttorney] G[eneral]) in Cabinet Council. August 27. 1861. in support of his objections to the proposition to open negotiations with

---

[78] See *supra,* April 15, 1861, note 67.

[79] There were several old-class ships in the Norfolk Navy Yard, but the *Merrimac* though "wholly dismantled" was "the most valuable vessel at the yard," and later, in Confederate hands, newly armored, was to prove a powerful weapon.

[80] John H. Aulick of Virginia had served in the Navy since 1809, and was retired shortly after this. Welles (*Diary,* I, 41–47) says that it was Commander James Alden who was to take the *Merrimac* to Philadelphia, but this portion of Welles's *Diary* was written after 1869 and Bates's account is probably more reliable.

[81] Charles S. McCauley, the officer in command of the Norfolk Navy Yard had fought in the War of 1812, but was now too old for effective service. He was retired in December, 1861, not in time to prevent his destroying the property at Norfolk and evacuating on April 21, instead of holding the Yard. Welles said he was "faithful but feeble and incompetent for the crisis."

[82] The Norfolk Navy Yard fell into Confederate hands April 21, 1861. It might have been held, save for politics in Washington and the ineptitude of McCauley and Aulick.

[83] These last three paragraphs are a paraphrase of Welles's remarks. Cf. G. Welles, *Diary,* I, 42–54.

[84] Son of a cousin of Mr. Bates.

[85] Joseph Paxton, wealthy Quaker, Pennsylvania iron manufacturer, organizer of the Reading Railroad, and influential Whig protectionist.

President Juarez,[86] for a treaty, to guarantee the payment of interest on the Mexican debt for five years, and take security upon the public lands, mining right &c.

In view of Mr. Corwin's [87] last two letters to Mr: Seward, it is now apparent that the Genl: Government of Mexico is little more than a name, and is utterly unable to preserve order and protect quiet people:

That the country is overrun by armed bands of robbers made [up] of the fragments of the late contending armies of Miremon [88] and Juarez:

That, in fact, the country has reached the point of anarchy: That the customs Duties being pledged to pay the interest on the foreign debt, the Treasury has almost no sources of supply, and is, in fact, bankrupt: [89]

That, in this State of things, after the Government of Juarez (the liberal party, so called) has dragged out a doubtful existence, for a few months, with no pecuniary means but those precariously supplied by forced loans and other irregular expedients, the shadow of a Congress (Which is all that remains to Mexico of a constitutional Government) has, it seems, passed a law forbid[d]ing all payments on account of the public debt, for two years.[90]

This, I suppose, is understood, as a withdrawal of the pledge of customs duties to pay the interest and reduce the principal of Debts due to British and French subjects. And therefore, the British and French ministers protest against the measure, and threaten to haul down their flags and leave the country—in other words they threaten to appeal to their respective sovereigns to protect the interests of their subjects, by force of arms.

Under these circumstances, an appeal is made to our Government, through our excellent minister there, Mr. Corwin; to come to the rescue of Mexico and endeavor to help her through the present crisis, by guarante[e]ing the payment of interest upon Mexico's foreign debt—amounting, as is now said to only $62.000.000 <But I have reason to think that the amount is much nearer $150.000.000> for five years.

---

[86] *Supra*, Feb. 4, 1860, note 70.

[87] *Supra*, Feb. 25, 1860, note 96.

[88] Miguel Miramón, leader of Mexican revolts, 1856–1858, became President of Mexico in February, 1859, as the candidate of the reactionist party. He spent his whole period of office trying to subdue the revolt of the Liberals under Juárez, but was finally overpowered and driven from the country in December, 1860.

[89] In a convention of 1842 with Great Britain and subsequently in similar agreements with Spain and France, Mexico had promised to set aside a specified portion of the customs duties at Tampico and Vera Cruz to meet her obligations to those nations.

[90] It was this law, passed July 17, 1861, which gave the excuse for the Anglo-Franco-Spanish joint intervention in Mexico.

And to secure ourselves against loss, we are to take a mortgage upon the public lands and mining interest in the northern states of Mexico—and perhaps an absolute title to lower Calafornia [91] [*sic*].

And this is urged upon us, not upon the ground that we ought to take advantage of the poverty and helplessness of Mexico, to dismember that distracted nation, for our own aggrandizement—but for fear that England and France will do it if we do not! [92] And this precautionary fear is supposed to be a sufficient reason to induce this country to brave all the dangers, certain and contingent, which may grow out of a measure so important—a step, which taken, cannot be easily retraced.

I cannot approve of this proposition. And this for many reasons.

1. If we were in peace and prosperity, as for many years past, I would think it highly impolitic to constitute ourselves the volunteer guardians of the crippled and insane nations round about us, upon any supposed grounds of national philanthropy.

2 But we are not in peace and prosperity; we are in no condition to assume the guardianship of poor distracted Mexico; we are ourselves torn by civil dissensions; wasted by civil war: and tasked to our utmost capacity, to preserve the integrity of our own nation. Congress would not have voted half a million of men and five hundred million of dollars, if they had not believed that the war we are now waging with our own countrymen is far more dangerous to our institutions and more terrible in its progress, than a foreign war, with all maratime [*sic*] Europe.

We may indeed prove our boldness under such adverse circumstances, by volunteering to thrust ourselves between united France and Britain and their interest or their ambition. But I am not brave enough to do it—I would do anything which the exigencies of the times might demand to resist their encroachments upon our home interests. And their assaults upon our National honor. Already they are jealous of our growing power, and are watching occasions to give us a crippling blow. And I would not give them that occasion by departing from the wise maxim of Washington [Jefferson]—" Peace with all nations: entangling alliances with none."

6 [93] But, gloss it as we may, the world will understand that we are actuated in this entierprise [*sic*] not by any love or pity for Mexico, as a nation, but by our old passion for indiscriminate acquisi-

---

[91] Under instructions from Seward, Corwin negotiated a treaty with Mexico in which we guaranteed payment of three per cent on Mexico's indebtedness for a period of five years, and Mexico mortgaged to us all the public lands and mineral rights of Lower California, Chihuahua, Sonora, and Sinaloa, which we were to take over on foreclosure if at the end of six years Mexico did not repay us with six per cent interest.

[92] France did later make the attempt. Our own civil trouble led us to handle this whole series of threats of European interference without once invoking the Monroe Doctrine.

[93] There are apparently omissions here of numbers 3, 4, 5.

tion, which cheats us into the belief that every accession of land or people is a gain; that is not my opinion. I See no good likely to result to our country from the full success of the enterprise—When we have paid five years [*sic*] interest on the Mexican debt—ten millions or more—and have secured the absalute [*sic*] title to the mortgaged property, the Mexican nation will have been dismembered, and we shall have gained a loss—we shall have stre[t]ched ourselves out into weakness: have gotten a longer and less convenient frontire [*sic*]; and have made a new and Stronger motive for further acquisition. All this, I think, will do our country no good, but serve to prove that our morbid appetite for annexation is still insatiate, even in the extremity of our present distress.

7 But can we do it in peace and safety? Even if we can persuade our own people, in this time of fear and calamity, to bear cheerfully the additional burden, how are we to get along with Great Britain and France? Even now they are strongly tempted to favor the insurgents, and are only waiting for a decent pretext, to make a tolerable justification, before Christendom, for taking open part against us.

When we begin by dismembering Mexico, what is to restrain them from following our example? And if they choose to do it, we certainly, have no power to prevent them; and I am not aware of any right of ours, to complain, even, of the act: nor do I see that it could injure us. And as to the people of Mexico themselves, I think it probable that, worried out by two generations of civil war, which has reduced them to poverty and anarchy, they would gladly accept protection and peace from any hand that is strong enough to give it to them.

I do not participate in the fears of those who profess great apprehensions of the occupation of Mexico, by any European power. If England, France or Spain held Mexico to day, I would have no more fears from that quarter than I have now from Canada. Indeed, it might be a great advantage to this country to have a stronger and more stable Government in Mexico. A moderate degree of lateral pressure might serve to keep our sections more compactly together, while there would be little danger from the dependent country, for it is always true that a home government (other things being equal) is stronger than a province ruled by a distant nation. The fear, I think, is not that Mexico ruled by a foreign power, would be a formidable enemy: but that the possession of Mexico by a European power, would forestall our design to annex it.

8 I have no desire to acquire another acre of Mexican land (I have no objection to Lower Calafornia [*sic*], for that, by ob[v]ious facts, is different from the rest of Mexico): and I have a decided repugnance to the absorption of the mongrel people of Mexico (some

7 or 8 millions) who, I think, are wholly unfit to be our equals,—friends and fellow citizens.

9 I have sometimes thought that it would be desirable for us to get the control of a region of country, somewhere in or near Central America say from Yucatan to Venezuela—to serve as a place of refuge for the free negroes of this country: but I have never made a point of it, and [94] do not now.

10. It has been suggested that we ought to make haste to get control of the contiguous parts of Mexico, in order to forestall the Confederate States, in case they achieve their independence.—That is not a supposable case, for it is a civil and political impossibility that the C. S. A. can permanently hold the lower Mississip[p]i against the people of the middle and upper valleys of that river. That river is one and indivisible, and *one* power will control it from Pittsburg and St. Paul to New Orleans, whether that power be republican or imperial. The *Government* may be changed, but the river cannot be divided.[95]

11 I apprehend that Prest. Juarez, who is but the chief of a party, knows the instability of his position and could be driven to make such a treaty as is now proposed, by sheer necessity only, and without any hope of permanent relief, by that means, but only a transient respite from impending ruin.

I believe it is historically true that no Mexican President has long maintained his power, after breaking the constitution by alienating a part of his Country. And I believe that if the plan were consum-[m]ated, Prest. Juarez would soon find himself deposed from his nominal seat of power. And who then will fulfil our treaty?

12 If it be possible to make such a treaty, and have it confirmed by the Senate (which I greatly doubt) I believe it woul[d] be a very unpopular measure at home. <[*Marginal*] *Note* The treaty, nevertheless was made, I being studiously kept studiously [*sic*], in ignorance of it. In fact I supposed that project was abandoned until the tre. [*sic*] treaty was presented to the Senate, and rejected a[l]most unanimously—only 3 or 4, voting for it.[96]> Formerly, when the ruling sp[i]rits of the present rebellion, were the prominent politiceans [*sic*] of the nation, acquisition at the South was the controlling policy. And that fact is a reason (in addition to many others) why the north may be expected to oppose such a treaty, as strongly as it opposed Mr. Buchanan's project for a Protectorate over Mexico.[97]

---

[94] "Nor" is crossed out and "and" substituted in blue pencil.

[95] Here again is Mr. Bates's confidence in the unifying effect of the Mississippi River. See *supra*, May 27, 1859, note 68.

[96] See *supra*, Aug. 27, 1861, note 91.

[97] The McLane-Ocampo Treaty of 1859 ; see *supra*, Feb. 15, 1860.

The attempt I fear will divide the North, by reviving the party names and party issues, and will give to the lurking enemies of the Union, at once the occasion and the means to draw a distinction which we cannot endure, and separate, before the people, the cause of the Adm[inistratio]n. from the cause of the country.

13 I am afraid that the bare fact of such a proposition as this, may alienate from us a large and influential class of the best people in Europe, whose sympathy and moral support we now enjoy—I mean the middle class of manufacturers and cultivators, of which class Mr. Bright,[98] of the British house of Commons, is a fair exponent. And that class is strong enough to check even the ministers of the crown, and modify their international action.[99]

14 The measure, as I understand it, proposes to submit the matter to the decision of England and France—that is, they are to be asked to waive all stringent measures to enforce their debts against Mexico, and to accept our promise to pay the interest for five years, and of course, to ratify our mortgage upon a large portion of the assets of Mexico.[1]

I think there is small likelihood that Great Britain and France will agree to that. All they can get by it is the payment of five years [sic] interest, but the sum total of the principal remains unpaid, while a large portion of property which constituted their Security, is absorbed by us and placed beyond their reach. As a mere mercantile transaction, I think the proposition is almost certain to be rejected.

Still, the mere proposition on our part, must disclose to the world our design upon Mexico,—to dismember it at least, if not to absorb it altogether. And if that does not deprive us of the sympathy of all christendom, I know not what will.

France and England will know, right well, how to deal with such facts. They may answer us that they do not desire our aid in securing and collecting their debts. Having gotten our secret and put us in the wrong, they may, if they choose, pick a quarrel out of the transaction and go to actual war upon it, in preference to the more doubtful question of the Blockade. And the least evil which I should fear, under the circumstances, would be their acknowledgement of the Confederate States.

---

[98] John Bright: manufacturer; reformer; member of Parliament since 1843; advocate of free trade and of the Reform Bill of 1867. He was a strong opponent of slavery, a great admirer of Lincoln and a close friend of Sumner, and one of the most powerful friends the North had in England.

[99] The opposition of Mr. Bright and his friends and many of the mill operatives to slavery made them strongly support the Northern cause, and their influence *was* important in preventing the Government's recognition of the Confederacy.

[1] In the Twentieth Century we *have* actually taken it upon ourselves to see that certain Caribbean nations remain solvent and pay their debts to European nations whose forceful collection of them our Caribbean policy discourages.

I am oppressed with the subject, and alarmed at the prospect. And if the proposition be pressed into action, I dread its consequences, far more than I do any evils which sprung [*sic*], or are likely to spring from the unfortunate battle of Bull Run.[2]

Genl. M. C. Meigs'[3] pass to leave St Louis! Granted by Maj: McKinstrey[4] Provost Martial [*sic*] 1861[.]

[*In the envelope upon which this note is written is the pass itself.*]

<*Sept 30, 1861*>[5] The public spirit is beginning to quail under the depressing influence of our prolonged inaction. Our people are weary of being kept always and every where upon the defensive. The ardent spirit of our young men is checked and mortified because no scope is given to their enterprising boldness. We absolutely need some dashing expeditions—some victories, great or small, to stimulate the zeal of the Country, and, as I think, to keep up the credit of the Government.

I hear, on pretty good authority, that the enemy is so posted at several points along the Potomac, as to command, at pleasure, the navigation of that river.

Why is this allowed? Is it from sheer weakness on our part? It compromises our safety at home, and degrades our honor abroad. It isolates the Capital by closing its only outlet to the ocean, and thus makes the impression upon both parties to the contest, and especially upon foreigners, that we are both weak and timid.

Are we to encounter no risk? Can war be conducted without any danger? I care not how cautious our commanders may be in securing certain important points (such as this city) which must, on no account, be put to hazard. But some gallant enterprizes are necessary to establish the prestige of the army and thus increase its positive strength. And I have no doubt that a few such enterprizes— even at the hazard of some Regiments—some Brigades—would contribute largely to the general result, and accelerate our final success.[6]

It were easy to indicate several inviting theatres for such enterprises; and our army, both officers and men are eager for such active service.

I do trust that the naval expedition to the southern coast, will not be delayed much longer.

---

[2] The rout of the Federal forces on July 21, 1861.

[3] *Infra*, Dec. 31, 1861, note 68.

[4] Justus McKinstry, West Point graduate of 1838, had served in Mexico and in California. In 1861 he was on the staff of General Frémont in St. Louis. After Frémont's removal he was arrested, imprisoned, and ultimately dismissed from the Army in 1863. Then he became a stock-broker and Frémont's confidential political agent.

[5] This whole entry was written on a double and a single letter sheet and inserted into the diary, with the date added later in pencil.

[6] Bates, like Lincoln, had an early comprehension of the political side of military strategy.

The whole coast, from Hat[t]eras to Fernandina,[7] with the exception of some 2 or 3 points, lies absolutely, at our mercy. We should scour that coast—look into every bay and river—thread the passages among the islands, and make every planter along the coast feel that he is in our power.

The well-armed, light-draft, quick-moving steamers (of which we must by this time have a good supply) will be able to perform all this good service; while the larger ships can carry whatever troops may be needed to garrison the few places which we may desire to take and hold, and to make incursions into the country, when desirable, and at the same time may dominate the open sea.

I am credibly informed that along the coast—on the islands and on the main—between Charleston and Fernandina, there are from 3 to 4 millions dollars worth of Sea Island Cotton, now in course of harvest. To say nothing of the Rice plantations, which abound on the coast of Georgia—all this cotton is easily within our reach. There are very few white people along that coast, but large plantations and many negro[e]s. The cotton already picked and ginned, is merchandize [sic], ready to our hand—and as to that still in the fields, there are plenty of negro[e]s there to pick and gin it for our use—and, with a little management by way of increased bonus for over work—they will do it quicker for us than for their masters.

I suppose it would not be hard for us to seise one or more of the Cotton Ports; and, in that case, we could easily get out enough cotton to make a full supply for home consumption, and some for Europe.

A fair success in such an enterprise would, I think be attended by immediate and great results[.]

1. It would, at least harras [sic] and alarm the enemy, weakening his resources, while it necessitates increased and more extensive action on his part.

2. It would call back, for home defence, a large number of troops, now engaged at distant points, in aggressive operations against us.

3. It would revive the spirit of the north, already beginning to droop under the depressing influence of our non action. That spirit will rise high, as soon as we shew that we have taken the affirmative, and mean henceforth to *do* something, and we have heretofore *suffered* all things.

4. It Will restore and strengthen the public credit[.]

5 It will satisfy foreign nations that we are in earnest, and willing and able to win success—and then, we will have little trouble about *Blockade*[.] [8]

---

[7] I. e., from North Carolina to the northern boundary of Florida.

[8] Bates, again like Lincoln, realized fully the importance of victories to the securing of European confidence in Northern success and hence to the prevention of aid for the South.

Oct 1. 1861. Cabinet Meeting

It is now evident, that the Adm[inistratio]n. has no system—no unity—no accountability—no subordination. Men are appointed, and not trusted—interfered with by side agencies, and so, relieved from all responsibility. Of course therefore, things run all wrong— Our generals have no information of the number or position of the enemy.

Adjutant General Thomas [9] says that the Generals *do not* make reports of their troops, as they ought. He, Genl. T.[homas], does *not* know what troops are here around Washington ! !

Knows nothing about the troops in Mo.—Genl. Fremont [10] *does not* report.

There is to be a meeting of heads of Bureaux and I advised (all that I said) "*trust* the heads, and hold them responsible—when you assign a duty to them, require them to do it, and don't interfere with them—if they fail, dismiss, or otherwise punish them, and that sum[m]arily[.] "

Talking about getting information and cutting Railroads, the Prest. proposed that "Judge Bates' man should be sent for"— Therefore nem con, I telegraphed J. E. D. Cozens to come on and bring two men that he can trust.

—*note* afterwards J. E. D. Cozens came and brought Andw. Hamilton—we arranged that he should go back to St Louis and thence return working his way through all *Secessia*—The last I heard of H.[amilton] he was near Knoxville, Tenn.

Friday Oct 18. Cabinet Meeting

Several commissions to Col[onel]s et al: issued by Genl. Fremont, putting them in actual service from a day certain but subject to the approval of the President.

After some talk—loose—it was I believe, referred to [the] Sec. of War, to settle them—the officers to be examined by *the board*, and if found right, [   ]
Genl. Scott—

It seemed at last agreed that Gen Scott by reason of his age and infirmities, can *command* no longer.

The Prest. then read to us a draft of a letter to Gen S.[cott] (delicately and handsomely written) importing that Gen S.[cott]

---

[9] Lorenzo Thomas: West Point graduate of 1823 who had served in Florida and Mexico; assistant adjutant-general in Washington, 1840–1846, 1848–1853; then chief-of-staff to General Scott, 1853–1861; now adjutant-general of the Army, 1861–1868; secretary of War *ad interim* in 1868 under Johnson.

[10] John C. Frémont was at this time a major-general in charge of the Department of the West with his headquarters at St. Louis. See *supra, May 9, 1860, note 99.*

had expressed a wish to be retired, under the act, and only with-[h]eld it at the Prest.'s request; that he would no longer object—

That he would still, sometimes, need his advice—not so often as to burden him—and was disposed to deal generously by the Genl.'s military family—

Note—Mr. Seward left early, and before Gen Scott was mentioned[.]

Tuesday Oct 22.   Cabinet Council

Present all.   Capt Cravens [11] U. S. N. commanding Flotilla in the Potomac, reports great progress made by the rebels with their batteries along the river—stretching from Matthias' point [12] up—at intervals, for more than 25 miles, and having at the different places, at least 40 heavy guns—so as, in fact to command the river.   Two of his vessels are between their strongest batteries, and opposite Acquia Creek. [13]

The Capt says—judging by the camp fires—that the enemy is increasing his force below, near the batteries, every day—Each night there are more and more fires, and less in the region of Occoquan. [14] He thinks they are preparing to pass over into Maryland.

If that be so, they are growing desperate in their present position; and if we let them cross it is our folly and crime.   The fact that we allow them to obstruct the river is our deep disgrace.

There was some discussion about the battle near Leesburg [15] yesterday and last night—a most unsatisfactory affair.

Baker's [16] brigade was driven back with great loss.   Baker and several other high officers were killed—the total loss not known but supposed from 2 to 300.   McClellan [17] was to go up in person.

[11] Thomas T. Craven had served in the Navy since 1822—in 1850–55 and 1858–1860 as commandant of midshipmen at Annapolis.   He was stationed on the Potomac in 1861, under Farragut on the Mississippi, 1862–1863, and in European waters after 1863.

[12] Spelled "Mathias."   A village thirty miles below Washington.

[13] A river-port at the outlet of a deep tidal channel about fifty-five miles below Washington.   It was the terminus of a railroad from Richmond.

[14] A village about six miles up the Occoquan River from where it flows into the Potomac not far below Mount Vernon.

[15] The Battle of Ball's Bluff where the Union force was disastronsly defeated when General Stone, under misinformation about the enemy, actually crossed the Potomac into Virginia instead of making a feint of doing so.

[16] *Supra*, Oct. 12, 1859, note 9.   He had raised a regiment of volunteers and, though still senator, had led a brigade at Leesburg.

[17] George B. McClellan, West Point graduate of 1846, served in Mexico, on the Pacific Coast, and in Europe, but resigned in 1857 to become chief engineer and later vice-president of the Illinois Central Railroad.   When the War came, he was given command of the Department of the Ohio with the rank of major-general.   After the Battle of Bull Run he commanded the Army of the Potomac until political considerations and his constitutional unwillingness to attack led Lincoln to remove him in November, 1862.   He became the candidate of the combined opposition to Lincoln in 1864 and ran for the Presidency as a man who could secure both peace and union—Lincoln seemed to have sacrificed both—but he ran on a platform that seemed to urge peace even at the cost of union, and was defeated.

<I hear tonight that a large part of our force has passed the river—both Banks [18] and Stone [19] are on the Va. side and I do and [*sic*] not doubt that the most strenuous efforts will be made to press the enemy, for our Generals are I think by this time, (besides other motives) heartily ashamed of inaction and inefficiency—the weather is very bad for active operations, by reason of constant rain last night and today, still I expect hard fighting.>

Another subject in C.[abinet] C.[ouncil] was the vexed question of the recall of Genl. Fremont. The report of Adj't. Genl. Thomas,[20] made by direction of the Sec of War put it, I thought, beyond all question that the removal must be made and instantly— The President seemed to think so, and said it was now clear that Fremont was not fit ~~to~~ for the command—that Hunter [21] was better— Still, at the very pinch, the Sec of State, came again, as twice before, to the rescue—and urged delay—" not today, put it off a little "— The idea (gotten by Mr. Chase from Dr. Eliot [22]) seemed to be that the Army was devoted to Fremont and had full confidence in him! while the evidence to the contrary is overwhelming—Hunter and Curtis [23] openly declared it—as stated in Adjutant Genl. Thomas' report, and as far as I know, none actively support him, but his own pet officers and contractors—Yet strange! both Cameron and Chase gave in and timidly yielded to delay; and the President still hangs in painful and mortyfying [*sic*] doubt. His suffering is evidently great, and if it were not connected with a subject so momentous, would be ludicrous.

I spoke as heretofore, plainly, urging the Prest. to avoid the timorous and vacillating course that could but degrade the Adm[inistratio]n. and make it weak and helpless—to assume the powers of his place and speak in the language of command. Not to send an order clogged with conditions and provisos—send a positive order or none at all. To leave him there now would be worse than prompt removal—for you have degraded him before the world and thereby un-

---

[18] See *supra*, July 27, 1859, note 57. At this time Banks was serving as major-general of volunteers in the Department of the Shenandoah.

[19] Charles P. Stone, graduate of West Point in 1845, had served in the Mexican War and on the Pacific Coast until he resigned in 1856. At the outbreak of the War he was put in command of the District of Columbia. His disaster at Ball's Bluff led him to ask a Court of Inquiry, but McClellan exonerated him and the matter was dropped until he was suddenly arrested in February, 1862. See *infra*, Nov. 1, 1861, note 28.

[20] *Supra*, Oct. 1, 1861, note 9.

[21] David Hunter, graduate of West Point in 1822, had served in Mexico and on the frontier, had commanded the main column at Bull Run, and was now serving as major-general of volunteers in Missouri under Frémont whom he succeeded on November 2.

[22] *Supra*, Feb. 22, 1860, note 79.

[23] Samuel R. Curtis: West Point graduate of 1831; civil engineer in the West; lawyer of Keokuk, Iowa, 1855–1861; Republican congressman, 1857–1861; member of the Peace Convention of 1861; at this time brigadier-general in the Department of the West. He commanded the Department of the Missouri, 1862–1863, the Department of Kansas, 1864–1865, the Department of the Northwest, 1865.

fitted him for the command, if otherwise capable—You have countermanded his orders,[24] repudiated his contracts and denounced his
contractors, suspended his officers and stopped the progress of his
fortifications—If under these circumstances we still keep him in
command, the public will attribute the fact to a motive no higher
than our fears. For me—I think too well of the soldiers and the
people, to be afraid of any Major General in the Army. I protested
against having *my* State sacrificed on such motives and in such a
cause.

Still I fear he will be allowed to hang on until he drops in very
rottenness. And if we persist in this sort of impotent indecision,
we are very likely to share his fate—and, worse than all, *deserve it.*

November 1—A memorable day. C.[abinet] C.[ouncil] called at
the unusual hour of 9. a. m. to consider of Gen Scott's letter to Sec:
[of] War, declaring his wish, by reason of age and increased ill
health, to retire from active military duty, under the recent act of
Congress.[25]

The order was drawn up by the President himself (the retirement of the general being his absolute right, under the act) and was
done chastely and in excellent taste.[26]

—In the afternoon the Prest: and all the heads of D[e]p[art-
men]ts. waited upon Genl. Scott at his quarters and had a very
touching interview. The Prest. made a neat and feeling address,
and the Genl. briefly replied, from the depths of his heart—I told
the Genl. (what was told me by Revd. Dr. Halsey [27] of Norristown
Pa.) that there were many religious associations, formed for the very
purpose of daily praying for his health and happiness; and he seemed
deeply moved.

At the suggestion of Mr. Seward, it seemed to be hastily agreed
(tho' I never consented) that Genl. Stone should be deprived of his
command for imputed misconduct in the matter of the battle of
Balls [*sic*] bluff (Leesburg) in which Baker rashly threw away his
life.[28] <*note*, at an other [cabinet council] some time after, Stone
fully vindicated him self before the P[r]est: in council>

---

[24] Lincoln, after first giving Frémont a chance to recall it himself, had countermanded
his order of emancipation of the slaves and confiscation of the property of all Missourians
who took up arms against the United States. Lincoln also forbade him to carry out his
order to shoot as traitors, after a trial by court martial, all Missourians found with
arms in their hands.

[25] "An Act Providing for the Better Organization of the Military Establishment," Aug.
3, 1861 (*Statutes at Large . . . of the United States*, XII, chap. XLII, sec. 15, p. 289),
provided that any officer who had served forty consecutive years might be retired with
pay upon application to the President.

[26] See J. D. Richardson, *Messages and Papers of the Presidents*, VI, 40.

[27] Luther Halsey, former professor of theology at Western Theological Seminary in
Alleghany, Pennsylvania, at the Seminary in Auburn, New York, and at Union Theological
Seminary in New York City, now living in retirement at Norristown.

[28] *Supra*, Oct. 22, 1861. On January 28, 1862, Secretary of War Stanton gave an order
for Stone's arrest on unfounded conspiracy charges made by a Committee of Congress.
Stone was imprisoned in Fort Lafayette for six months.

It was agreed that Genl. McClellan [29] should succeed Scott. Still the President doubted as to the manner of it, not being certain that there is any such Officer as " General in chief "—I said " the *General in chief*—or *chief General*—is only *your lieutenant.* You are constitutional " Commander in chief," and may make any general you please, your second, or lieutenant, to command under you."

It was so done[.]

Thos. Sherman

Nov 13. The News is fully confirmed of the success of Com[modor]e. DuPont [30] and Genl. W. T. Sherman [31] <T. W. S.? Rd. B>,[32] in the expedition to Beaufort S.[outh] C[arolina]. The Forts at Port Royal [33]—*Bouregard* <N & H>[34] [*Beauregard*] and *Walker*—were shelled by the fleet, in grand Stile [*sic*]. The enemy fled " like quick-silver " leaving flags, arms, papers &c. The success was perfect—My friend Capt Jno. Rogers, was the first to land and plant our flag on Fort Walker (the main fort)[.]

Profiting by Com[modor]e. Stringham's blunder [35] (in coming home after he had taken Hatteras) [DuPont] and [Sherman] will push their victory[.]

Sherman has some 15000 good troops for land service, and no doubt will use them with all vigor—He has every incentive, patriotism, ambition, hope, fear—all conspire to make him anxious to extend and magnify his success.

The victory, if properly followed up, and especially, if repeated at other points, will send a chill to the heart of all the southern coast.

[29] *Supra,* Oct. 22, 1861, note 17.

[30] Samuel F. Du Pont, grandson of Jefferson's friend Du Pont de Nemours, had served in the Navy since 1815, had controlled the Gulf of California during the Mexican War, and was, at the outbreak of the Civil War, superintendent of the Philadelphia Navy Yard. His victory at Port Royal was followed by a disastrous defeat at Charleston in April, 1863, which led him to resign his command.

[31] This should be Thomas W. Sherman, brigadier-general, a West Point graduate of 1836 who had served in Mexico and on the frontier. At the outbreak of the Civil War, he was stationed in Maryland and helped open the communications through Baltimore to the North. He had been occupied from July to October capturing and holding Bull's Bay, South Carolina, and Fernandina, Florida, as bases for the blockading Union fleet. Now, from October to March, 1862, he was engaged in attacking and then holding Port Royal and Beaufort.

[32] The bracketed suggestion that this should be T. W. instead of W. T. Sherman was apparently initialed by Richard Bates, Mr. Bates's fourth son, who was first clerk in the Attorney-General's Office.

[33] Port Royal was the name of (1) the island upon which Beaufort was situated. (2) a village near Beaufort, and (3) the Sound which gives access to Beaufort. Fort Walker guarded the entrance to Port Royal Sound on the South and Fort Beauregard guarded it on the North.

[34] This seems to be in the same penciled writing as the " Rd. B." above, and probably indicates that both notes were added after Nicolay and Hay's *Lincoln* appeared.

[35] On August 29, Commodore Stringham, coöperating with General B. F. Butler, had captured Fort Hatteras and Fort Clark off the coast of North Carolina to the great joy of the North. But he had later been so criticized for not following up his victory that, at his own request, he was relieved of his command. See *supra,* March 9, 1861, note 39.

The spirit of the north, begin[n]ing to flag, for lack of some success, will be re-animated, and the finances cannot fail to feel the invigorating impulse.

[*Marginal Note.*] *Nov 15.* Sec: Chase hasten[e]d to N. Y. to take the tide at the flood,[36] and telegraphs back that prospects are very good—credit rising.

Affairs look better in Mo. Maj Genl. Halleck [37] has gone to take command at St Louis—a new Dept. is created West and South of Mo., with Maj Genl. Hunter [38] to command[.] Genl. Halleck visited me the night before he started, and I had with him a very gratifying conversation. He is imputed to have high military ability—I found him a frank straightforward man. He urged me to write to him and give the names of men with whom he can confer, and to write to *my friends* to call upon him.

(Note, I have written to Barton,[39] Broadhead [40] and Glover.[41])

He seems disposed to act in cordial coöperation with my friends, including the Governor.[42]

Mr. Gibson [43] is the accredited agent here of Govr. Gamble, and the Departments are yielding to his and my solicitations to forward the needful supplies[.]

Nov 16. The news is fully confirmed, to the effect that James. M. Mason [44] and John Slidell,[45] Envoys of the C.[onfederate] S.[tates] to Great Britain and France, respectively, have been captured. The[y] slipped out from Charleston in a small armed vessel—reached Havanna [*sic*] in safety. Whence they got on board the British Mail-steamer *Trent*. On passage from S[H]avanna [*sic*] to England, Capt Wilkes,[46] in the U. S. Steamer San Jacinto, overhauled the Trent (perhaps waylaid her) in the Bahama passage, and took from her the two ministers and their secretaries—McFarland [47]

---

[36] To sell government bonds.

[37] Henry W. Halleck, West Point graduate of 1839; an officer in the engineering service until 1854 when he resigned to practice law and engage in mining and railroading in California. Halleck commanded the Department of the Missouri from November, 1861, until March, 1862, and the Department of the Mississippi, which included that of the Missouri from March until July, 1862. He then served as general-in-chief in administrative work in Washington until 1864 and as chief-of-staff until the end of the War.

[38] *Supra,* Oct. 22, 1861, note 21.

[39] Mr. Bates's eldest son.

[40] *Supra,* Dec. 26, 1859, note 66.

[41] *Supra,* Dec. 23, 1859, note 58.

[42] Hamilton R. Gamble. *Supra,* July 23, 1859, note 39.

[43] *Supra,* April 27, 1859, note 27.

[44] *Supra,* Feb. 2, 1860, note 50.

[45] *Supra,* Nov. 26, 1859, note 89.

[46] Charles Wilkes: South American explorer who had been in the Navy since 1818. After the *Trent* incident he was made commodore and given command first of the James River Flotilla and then of the West Indian Squadron, but he was tried by court martial, convicted in April, 1864, and condemned to a severe reprimand and three years' suspension.

[47] E. J. Mcfarland of Virginia, Confederate secretary of Legation in London.

(of Va., I believe) and Eustis[48] of La. <Their papers also were seised and will probably give us useful and curious information.>[49]

The San Jacinto brot. them in to Hampton roads, and sent them to New York.

While the fact gives great and general satisfaction, some timid persons are alarmed, lest Great Britain should take offence at the violation of her Flag. There is no danger on that score. The law of Nations is clear upon the point, and I have no doubt that, with a little time for examination, I could find it so settled by English authorities. I cant [sic], at the moment, refer to cases,[50] but I feel sure that the principle has been more than once, acted upon by Lord Stowel[l].[51] Not only was it lawful to seise the men, but, I think, the ship itself was subject to confiscation.

[Marginal Note.] Nov 18. The Nat[iona]l. Int[elligence]r. of today contains a good editorial on this subject[.]

Col Van Alen[52] was at my house, and we talked over a good deel [sic] of army matters—i. a—he stated that Genl. McClellan had no intention to fight a great battle soon. That McC.[lellan] understands that ⅓ of the Manassas army will be entitled to discharge in Jan.y. or Feb.y. and he thinks that ⅔ of that ⅓ will refuse to re-enlist, and then he will have an easy victory.

This does but confirm my old opinion (which I told McDowell[53] six weeks ago) that there could be no general battle between the two grand armies.[54]

Nov 19. At night visited by Mr. Barrett[55] of the Pension Bureau, and Genls. Cullum[56] and P St. Geo: Cooke.[57] Cullum seems to be

---

[48] George Eustis, Jr., of New Orleans: Know-Nothing congressman, 1855–1859; secretary of the Confederate mission in Paris.

[49] A marginal addition.

[50] The cases would have been those in which England claimed the right of search and seizure and we denied it in wars where England was a belligerent and the United States a neutral.

[51] William Scott, Baron Stowell, was a great international lawyer, who, as judge of the British High Court of Admiralty from 1798 to 1827, rendered many important decisions which helped write England's views into international law. He was not only judge in the *Tiger* case (*infra*, Nov. 30, 1861) but in the to us vitally important *Polly* case (1800) and *Essex* case (1805).

[52] *Supra*, Feb. 4, 1860, note 62.

[53] Irwin McDowell, graduate of West Point in 1838, had served in Mexico and as adjutant-general in the War Department. He was in command of the undrilled troops at the first Battle of Bull Run. After repeated defeats under McClellan, he was retired in 1862.

[54] This prediction proved surprisingly true until late in the War.

[55] Joseph H. Barrett: lawyer; Vermont state legislator, 1851–1853; secretary of the Vermont Senate, 1853–1855; editor of the *Cincinnati Gazette*, 1857–1861; Ohio delegate to the Republican Convention of 1860; U. S. commissioner of Pensions. 1861–1868.

[56] George W. Cullum: West Point graduate of 1833; officer in the Engineering Corps. 1833–1861; aide to Scott in 1861; chief-of-staff to Halleck, 1861–1864; superintendent at West Point, 1864–1866.

[57] A West Point graduate of 1827 who had served in the Mexican War and on the frontier ever since. Though a Virginian with a son and son-in-law in the Confederate Army, he remained loyal to the Union, and served, largely in administrative work, throughout the War. Since he was made brigadier-general in the regular Army as of November 12, 1861, Bates's efforts must have been successful.

a good man and *learned* in his profession, but dull. Cooke is mortified at being overstaughed [*sic*]—He is offered Brig: Genl. of Vol[unteer]s., but that is not enough and I am helping him all I can, to a place in the Regulars next after Mansfield[.][58]

Nov. 20. I was invited to a party last night, by Col: J. W. Forney,[59] to meet Mr. Prentis[60] (of the Louisville Journal); but cd. not attend by reason of a visit of Genl. Cullum,[61] who, on the eve of departure for Mo., desired a conference with me, on Mo. affairs. He goes out I understand, as chief of Staff for Genl. Halleck.[62]

I suspected when I recd. Col Forney's invitation that the object was not so much to shew personal respect to Mr. Prentice as to discover the biasses [*sic*] of certain high officers, and set certain political triggers. I'm glad that circumstances prevented my attendance, as now, I can look on and judge as an outsider.

Coffey[63] was there, a keen observer. Secys Smith and Cameron— Tom Clay[64] and other Kentuckians.

In the course of the evening, Cameron came out openly (as he did in C.[abinet] C.[ouncil] last friday) in favor of arming and organizing *negro soldiers* in the south. Smith opposed it vehemently (as he and I had done in C.[abinet] C.[ouncil])

[*Note.*] Since that time, I hear that some prying letter writer communicated the whole affair to the N. Y. papers (the Times) and so, the matter took open air.

[*November 27.*] And now (Nov 27) Count Gurouski[65] tells me that Prentice[66] has come out, in bitter denunciation of Cameron—in shape of a Washington correspondent of the Louisville Journal. The Count assumes, very reasonably, that Prentis is the author.

[*Marginal Note.*] Since then, I learn that Prentice disclaims the authorship of the letter, and says that Cameron was misunderstood.

---

[58] Joseph K. F. Mansfield: graduate of West Point in 1822; officer in the Engineering Corps; inspector-general of the Army; brigadier-general in the regular Army, now in command of Camp Hamilton in Virginia.

[59] John W. Forney: editor of the *Philadelphia Press* and the *Washington Chronicle;* Democratic clerk of the House, 1851–1857; Republican clerk of the House, 1860–1861; secretary of the Senate, 1861–1868. After twenty years as a loyal Buchanan Democrat, Forney split with Buchanan in 1857 over the patronage and became a Douglas Democrat. In 1860 he was a Lincoln Republican, later a Johnson Republican, then an anti-Johnson Radical, and finally a Democrat again.

[60] George D. Prentice had become editor of the Whig *Louisville Journal* in 1831. During the War he steadily supported the Union but criticized Lincoln's use of governmental power.

[61] *Supra,* Nov. 19, 1861, note 56.

[62] *Supra,* Nov. 13, 1861, note 37.

[63] *Supra,* March 5, 1860, note 18.

[64] Thomas H. Clay: son of Henry Clay, uncompromising unionist; supporter of Bell and Everett in 1860; opponent in the Legislature of Kentucky in 1861 of that State's "neutrality" policy. In 1862, he was appointed minister to Nicaragua.

[65] Adam, Count Gurowski, Polish revolutionist and author who had lived in the United States since 1849; translator in the State Department.

[66] *Supra,* Nov. 20, 1861, note 60.

Note, in this connexion—The other day, Mr. Blair joked Cameron with a newspaper quotation (real or supposititious [*sic*]) to the effect that he (C.[ameron]) had fairly elbowed Fremont [67] out of his place, and himself quietly taken his seat in [the] stern-sheets of the Abolition boat!

Nov 27. No news yet from Pensecola [*sic*], beyond the first rumor that our forces were bombarding the rebel forts.[68]

From *Mo.*—a telegram from Gov Gamble [69] confirms the report [that] Genl. Price [70] has turned and is moving north towards the centre of the State. This movement is, I think not prompted by Price himself, as a separate enterprise agst. Mo., but is part of the genl. plan of the enemy. As long ago as last March, I told the Cabinet that the real struggle must be in the valley of the Mississippi.[71] And now, that it is apparent that the rebel army of the Potomac can do nothing but hold the Capitol [*sic*] in siege, and that the enemy cannot defend the seaboard, it is the obvious policy of the enemy to [strengthen] the defence of the Mississippi, and to that end, they must fortify the river, and for that purpose they must have time to remove men and artillery, and therefore it is wise in him to keep us fully occupied in Mo. and Kentucky.

That is clearly the policy of the enemy. And as clearly it is our policy to assume the aggressive, and, at almost any hazard, to cut his communications, and prevent as far as possible, the removal of heavy guns from the East to the west—from Va. and the coast to the Missi[ssippi].

Today I spent chiefly in business preliminary to the coming session of the S.[upreme] C.[ourt] called at the clerk's office, ex[amine]d. the docket, the C[our]t. room, my own closet, and recd. many kind suggestions from Mr. Carroll,[72] the clerk, about the details of business. Called on C.[hief] J.[ustice] Taney,[73] and had a conversation

---

[67] Frémont had tried to free slaves and confiscate Confederate property by a military order revoked by Lincoln. *Supra*, Oct. 22, 1861, note 24.

[68] On November 22 Fort Pickens and the men-of-war *Niagara* and *Richmond* began a two days' bombardment of Fort McRee and other Confederate fortifications. On January 1, 1862, there was another artillery exchange. But it was not until May 9, 1862, that the Confederates burned and evacuated the forts and the Navy Yard at Pensacola.

[69] *Supra*, July 23, 1859, note 39.

[70] Sterling Price: Democratic congressman, 1845–1846; brigadier-general of volunteers in the Mexican War; governor of Missouri, 1853–1857; major-general of Missouri Confederate militia under Confederate Governor Jackson (*supra*, Jan. 9, 1860, note 15). He had been driven out of St. Louis by General Lyon, but later defeated and killed Lyon in one engagement, and captured 3,000 Missourians in another, before he was forced to flee. And his raids, or threats of them, continued to harass Missouri.

[71] *Supra*, March 16, April 15, Aug. 27, 1861; also May 27, 1859.

[72] William T. Carroll, a grand-nephew of Charles Carroll of Carrollton, was clerk of the Supreme Court from 1827 to 1862.

[73] Roger B. Taney: eminent Maryland lawyer; attorney-general of Maryland, 1827–1831; attorney-general of the U. S., 1831–1833; secretary of the Treasury, 1833–1834; chief justice of the U. S. Supreme Court, 1835–1864. He wrote the decision in the famous Dred Scott case of 1857 and tried in vain to restrain the arbitrary governmental infringements of personal liberty during the Civil War.

much more pleasant than I expected. Called also on Judge Wayne [74] and had an agreeable talk. I infer from the remarks of both the judges that, probably, but little business will be done, and that not in as strict order as is usual.

At night, Count *Gurouski* called to see me, and talked, as usual, very freely—quite as bitter and censorious as ever. Just now, he seems to have a special spite against the *diplomatic corps*—all of them *except* Baron Gerolt of Prussia, and Mr. Tassara of Spain— He says all of them except Gerolt, were in a furious flutter about the capture of Slidell and Mason [75]—declaring that it was an outrage and that England would be roused to the war-point, &c. that Gerolt quietly said—pish! the thing is right in itself, and if it were not, England wd. no[t] go to war for it—

The Count gave me a short biographical [sketch] of most of the ministers—e g

1. *L[or]d. Lyons,*[76] son of the Admiral who won the peerage. Of a respectable but humble family—L[or]d. L.[yons] he says, has an uncle who is a farmer near Chicago.

2. *Mr. Mercier*[77] (of France) only plainly respectable. Born in Baltimore, where his father was French consul[.]

3. Mr. *Tassara*[78] of Spain—really a great man—a wonderful genius—of respectable but not noble origin—at first a news-paper writer—then a distinguished member of the Cortes, and secretary thereof (the 2d. office in its gift) [.]

4. Mr. Stoekel [79] (of Russia) nobody in Russian society, though personally worthy. As a minister, admitted of course to court, but not recd. at all in the aristocratic society of Petersburg. His wife is American—A Yankee—a very clever lady[.]

5. *Count Piper,*[80] of Sweden, the only genuine aristocrat, of ancient and high descent. He is the lineal descendant of the famous Count *Piper*, Minister of State of king Charles XII [81]—a man of no great talents, but of high and honorable principles[.]

6. *Baron Gerolt* [82] of Prussia. A very amiable and learned gentleman. Of noble connexion, but not himself noble, until the

[74] James M. Wayne: judge of the Superior Court of Georgia, 1824–1829; Democratic congressman, 1829–1835; now justice of the U. S. Supreme Court, 1835–1867.

[75] *Supra*, Nov. 16, 1861.

[76] Envoy Extraordinary and Minister Plenipotentiary from Great Britain, 1858–1865. *Supra*, Sept. 26, 1860, note 24.

[77] Henri Mercier, Envoy Extraordinary and Minister Plenipotentiary, 1860–1863.

[78] Gabriel Garcia y Tassara, Envoy Extraordinary and Minister Plenipotentiary, 1857–1867.

[79] Edward de Stoeckl, Envoy Extraordinary and Minister Plenipotentiary, 1854–1868. He it was who negotiated the sale of Alaska.

[80] Edward, Count Piper, Minister Resident of Sweden, 1861–1864, and Chargé d'Affaires of Denmark, 1863.

[81] Sweden's soldier-king who ruled from 1697 to 1718.

[82] Envoy Extraordinary and Minister Plenipotentiary, 1843[?]–1871.

last few years, when he was made a baron, by the influence of Humboldt,[83] who was his friend and patron.

Gerolt was well-learned in mineralogy and mining, and (upon Humboldt's recommendation) served some years in Mexico, as director of silver mines for an English company. He is skilled in various sciences, and is the only foreign diplomat who maintains close relations with American savan[t]s.

7. Chivalier [sic] *Bertenatti*,[84] of Italy. Of no high connexions. Educated for the priesthood, but not ordained. For sometime a journalist. A man of fair talents, but not at all distinguished by the gifts of nature or fortune, except that he is minister of the rising state of Italy.

[*Marginal*] *Note.* In this same conversation the Count said that it was well enough to give Capt Wilkes [85] the credit of originality and boldness in seising Mason and Slidell, but, in fact, the Secy. of State sent orders to the consul at Havanna [sic], to notify Wilkes and tell him what to do.[86]

Nov 28 Thursday, Thanksgiving day. The offices closed. Contrary to expectation, I did almost no work, and took no exercise. Heard Dr. Smith preach a pretty good, matter o' fact sermon—in which, by the way, he said that Sec.y. Chase, in ans[we]r. to the N. Y. bankers, said there was a prospect of a speedy settlement of our political troubles, and that the Balt[imor]e. Sun, albeit unused to give good news, had a telegram to the same effect—This surprises me and I dont [sic] believe it.[87]

Nov 29. C.[abinet] C[ouncil]. The Prest: read a part of his message,[88] for criticism. An excellent argument on the relative bearings of labor and capital; shewing very clearly, the fallicy [sic] of those who hold that *Capital* is *patron* and labor *client*. On the contrary, he shews that labor is the *parent* of Capital, which is only the surplus of labor beyond the consumption of the laborer—That they exist together in the same hand, in a majority of cases in this country—That is, the man who starts in life a hireling, on

---

[83] Alexander, Baron von Humboldt, wealthy German naturalist, traveler, diplomat, author, who was a close friend of the King of Prussia.

[84] The Chevalier Joseph Bertinatti, Minister Resident, 1861–1867.

[85] *Supra*, Nov. 16, 1861, note 46.

[86] The State Department has no record of such an instruction from Seward. On the contrary, Seward wrote confidentially to Charles F. Adams in Great Britain on November 27: "The act was done by Commander Wilkes without instructions, and even without the knowledge of the Government." John B. Moore, *A Digest of International Law*, VII, 768.

[87] The editor was unable to find any such telegram in the *Baltimore Sun.*

[88] "First Annual Message," Dec. 3, 1861, J. D. Richardson, *Messages and Papers of the Presidents*, VI, 44–58.

the farm or in the shop, saving his wages, soon becomes a *landlord* or a *boss*, thus turning his own surplus labor into capital, and wielding it himself—so that he is, in his o[w]n person, both labor and capital.

<It seems to me that the Economists do but embarras[s] themselves with the misuse of words—Labor, in fact *is* Capital—as much so as the money that buys it—it is the original self-existent thing, while capital is but its fruit.>

Of course all this has its bearing upon the slavery question. And in referering [*sic*] to my letter of 1852. to Gov Means [89] of S.[outh] C.[arolina] I find that I have partly treated of the subject long ago[.]

A message from Com[modor]e. DuPont [90] to the Sec of Navy shews that the rebels, in panic at the bombardment at Port Royal,[91] had evacuated Tybee Island [92] with its strong forts, and retired to Fort Pulaski,[93] which is at our mercy, in good shell range, being on[ly] 600 y[ar]ds.—and had sunk vessels in the river to destroy the navigation—and that the people of Savanna[h] are fleeing incontinently, with such property as they can safely carry off[.]

<Note—9. p. m. I hear outside, that Savanna[h] has voluntarily surrendered[.] [94]>

Com:[modore] DuPont further says that our smaller vessels have gone up the various rivers to and around Beaufort [95]—The Country is utterly abandoned by the whites, and disorder reigns supreme. The fugitive masters sometimes return in the night and try to drive off their slaves, using extreme violence &c[.]

Cotton in great quantities lies about, in barns &c and uncovered— not ginned, and of course, not packed—in fact they have no bagging and bale rope—

The cotton is being gathered by the army as fast as possible, to be sen[t] north, but whether to be ginned before or after sent, I do not know.

I urged in C.[abinet] C.[ouncil] the signs of disruption of the rebel grand army—to move its heavy material and men as fast as can be *secretly* done, well knowing that they cannot resist us upon the coast, and that the main struggle must be (as I foretold from the beginning,

---

[89] *Supra*, June 16, 1859, note 93.

[90] *Supra*, Nov. 13, 1861, note 30.

[91] *Supra*, Nov. 13, 1861, note 33.

[92] The large island which forms the southern side of the entrance to the Savannah River in Georgia.

[93] A fort on Cockspur Island which commands the entrance to the Savannah River.

[94] Savannah did not surrender until December 20, 1864. But Fort Pulaski was evacuated after bombardment on April 10–12, 1862, and the Federal forces were able completely to close Savannah to trade after February, 1862.

[95] See *supra*, Nov. 13, 1861.

it would be) in the valley of the Miss[issipp]i.[96]   I was listened to *this time* with profound attention[.]

Byrnside's [97] amphibious expedition—strange to say is not yet ready—and stranger still, its destination is not known, even to the President—whether to co[o]perate in the removal of the enemy's blockade of the Potomac, or some new descent upon the southern coast.

At last, it is given out that Gen Butler's [98] expedition will go to Ship Island, in the Gulf.   That was not the original destination. But he cannot be sent north of Florida, for Sherman [99] is there, and he being a Maj: Genl., ranks Sherman[.] [1]

See Banker's Magazine [XVI, 401–406], for December.   (sent me by J. Smith Homans) an essay upon—Govt. Tresy. notes and Bank paper.—

Nov 30.   Mr. *Hodge* [2] furnishes me with a case bearing strongly, as he thinks, upon the case of *Slidel[l]* and *Mason.* [3]

The American ship *Tiger*, Capt. Clark, of Phil[adelphi]a. Pratt & [   ] owners.

The Tiger sailed from Phil[adelphi]a. in ballast (in 1808), for France, to bring home goods purchased before the embargo—She was seised on the outward passage by a British cruiser, and condemned before Sir Wm. Scott [4]—because she had on board a despatch from the French Minister (France and Great Britain being then at war)[.]

The way Mr. Hodge knows it is this—The owners, after condemnation of the vessel, had a correspondence with the Secy of the

---

[96] See *supra*, Nov. 27, 1861.

[97] Ambrose E. Burnside of Rhode Island, West Point graduate of 1847, who had served in Mexico and on the frontier, but had resigned in 1853 to manufacture the breech-loading rifle which he had invented.   His Rhode Island regiment was one of the first to arrive to defend Washington.   Now he was at Annapolis, a brigadier-general of volunteers, organizing a coastal expedition, which did not sail until January, 1862, but then was successful in capturing the North Carolina forts and fleet.

[98] Benjamin F. Butler, Massachusetts Democratic politician who had supported Breckinridge for President, but had turned strongly unionist when secession came.   He had got himself elected brigadier-general of militia and led almost the first troops to arrive in Washington which he reached by landing at Annapolis and rebuilding the railroad to Washington.   He commanded in Baltimore, at Fortress Monroe, and in the land attack on Fort Hatteras (*supra*, Nov. 13, 1861, note 35).   On this present expedition he took command of New Orleans on May 1, 1862.

[99] *Supra*, Nov. 13, 1861, note 31.

[1] Butler remained a problem, and often an embarrassment, throughout the War.   He was a "political general" of higher rank than most regular soldiers and had neither military capacity nor human discretion, and yet, as a prominent Democrat fighting for the Union, could not be displaced or disciplined.   And he had a particular penchant for bitter controversy and personal publicity.

[2] There was no "Hodge" in either the Department of the Treasury or the State Department.   He may have meant A. H. Dodge, clerk of the third class in the State Department.

[3] *Supra*, Nov. 16, 1861.

[4] *Supra*, Nov. 16, 1861, note 51.

Treasury,[5] to cancel their bonds (under the embargo law) and for that purpose sent a copy of the record of condemnation.[6]

Perhaps these papers were destroyed by the burning of the Treasury building, but if so no doubt the correspondence may be found among the papers of Pratt & Co., owners of the Tiger.

*Official power over the mails—*Opinion of Atty Genl. Cushing[.][7]

Decr. 6. The Nat[ional] Intelligencer of today, contains a leader headed "A Question of law" and after stating the action of P.[ost] M.[aster] Genl. Blair in excluding from the mails certain news papers in favor of disunion, refers at large [to] the proceedings in the latter part of Mr. Pierce's adm[inistratio]n. (1856.) in which Jeff Davis[8] was conspicuous. In many places in the South, news-papers which they called incendiary were suppressed, and the question being brought, by the then P.[ost] M.[aster] G.[eneral] James Campbell,[9] before Atty. Genl. Cushing, he gave an elaborate opinion,[10] strongly affirming the right and duty to *suppress* the bad documents—and of course making each deputy p.[ost]m.[aster] the judge!

He was hailed in the south as a "very Daniel" and, however wrong the opinion the south and *the party* are stopped.

[*Two newspaper clippings[11] containing communications from William H. Seward relating to "Contrabands." The first is dated December 4, 1861, and addressed to General George B. McClellan; the second is dated January 25, 1862, and addressed to Ward H. Lamon.[12]*]

The Nat[ional] Intel:[ligencer][13] contains also a very curious *order* from Mr. Seward Sec of State "To Major General Geo: B.

---

[5] Albert Gallatin, great Swiss-born secretary of the Treasury, 1801–1814.

[6] The Embargo practically forbade shipment of any goods out of the United States. Any ship which had legitimate business not in violation of this Act could sail after first satisfying the customs officers as to the cargo and then giving bonds—to two or three times the value of the ship—for its return. When a ship was sunk or captured these bonds could only be redeemed by proof of that fact.

[7] Caleb Cushing of Massachusetts: Whig congressman, 1835–1843; envoy to China, 1843–1845; judge of the Supreme Court of Massachusetts, 1852–1853; attorney-general of the U. S., 1853–1857. In 1841 he became a Democrat and chairmaned the Democratic Convention of 1860. He was pro-Southern in his sympathies, hated abolitionists, and in January predicted dissolution of the Union. But when the War came, he turned Republican and aided Lincoln with both legal advice and political help.

[8] Davis was said to have instigated the request of Campbell for an opinion.

[9] Catholic Democratic leader of Philadelphia who turned his support to Franklin Pierce in spite of Pierce's anti-Catholic leanings and, as a reward, was made postmaster-general, 1853–1857.

[10] March 2, 1857, *Official Opinions of the Attorneys-General of the United States,* VIII, 489–502.

[11] From the *National Intelligencer,* Dec. 6, 1861, and Jan. 31, 1862.

[12] A close personal friend and former law-partner of Lincoln's who had accompanied Lincoln from Springfield to Washington and in March had been sent to Charleston with S. A. Hurlbut, as the personal freind of the President, to ascertain the facts about rumored Union sentiment in South Carolina. He served as marshal of the District of Columbia from 1861 to 1865.

[13] "Contrabands in the District," on Dec. 6, 1861.

McClellan " about negro[e]s escaping from *Va.* into this District. <Date Dec 4.[>]

This is a strange document, and I cannot well determine whether its errors and ambiguities result from careless haste or cautious casuistry. But certainly, I never did see, in so short a document, so many points of doubt and difficulty, or so little clearness of thought or precision of language.

1. The order being highly penal and requiring prompt execution, by the *immediate* arrest of the offender, ought to be very plain—but it is not, for 2. It applies to all persons *held to service.* Not negro-slaves only, but also apprentices, boatmen, soldiers—all who are bound to service, without respect to color—3 Held to service by the laws of *Virginia*: not Maryland, nor any other State—4 And *actually employed* in *hostile service* agst. the U. S—not peaceful service, such as making bread, powder or tobacco—4 [*sic*] Escape *from the lines of the Enemy's forces*—(not from their master's plantation &c)—5. And are *received* within the lines of *the* army of the Potomac. *Received*, by whom? Escaping into, and received within, are two very different things. The one implies only the act of the fugitive, the other implies a *receiver* as well as the fugitive received— 6 THIS DEPARTMENT *understands* &c. Now, I do not understand how the *State* Dept. can so understand the subject as to feel it a duty to give *any* order to the Genl. in chief—

7. SUCH PERSONS—i. e. not negro[e]s, nor slaves generally, but persons claimed to be held to service *under the laws of Va.* only, and *actually employed* in *in* [*sic*] *hostile service,* agst. the U. S. and who have escaped *from the lines of the enemy's forces,* and are *received* within the lines of *the* army (our army, I suppose) of the Potomac— *afterwards* coming into the *City of Washington* (not Georgetown, nor the rest of the District of Columbia) are *liable* (by law of course) to be arrested &c, upon the *presumption arising from color,* that they are fugitives from labor. Now, under the laws of Va. and Md., the presum[p]tion arising from color is not that black people are *such persons* as are above described, but only that they are *slaves*—not that they are fugitives from another state, in the sense of the " fugitive slave law," nor *fugitives* at all.

8 *Such hostile employment* (not the *escape* and *reception* as aforesaid) is a full answer to all further claim to service &c.

9. " Persons thus employed and escaping " *are received into the military protection* of the U. S.—Who receives them? When? And at what precise *punctum temporis,* as Govr. Wise [14] would say?

10. And their arrest, as *fugitives from service,* should be *immediately* followed by a *military* arrest of the parties making the seisure.

[14] *Supra,* April 28, 1859, note 38.

<As the arrest is to be *military*, and as the order is addressed to the Genl. in Chief, I had supposed that the proper person to give the command was the Secretary of *War*.

I remark generally that the *order* seems to me very imperfect in not providing any means for ascertaining whether or no, the persons arrested are really *such persons* as are particularly described in the body of the order.[>]

11. " Copies of this communication will be sent to the Mayor of the City of Washington and to the Marshal of the District of Columbia "—Not to the Mayor of Georgetown nor to the Levy Court of of [*sic*] the District. And hence (and see no 7, *supra*) the inference is plain that the order is restricted in its operation to the City of Washington proper.

Dec 6. Friday—Met A. S. Mitchell [15] now of the N.[ew] Y. [ork] Times, by chance, in the porch of the Prest's house—barely shook hands—He seemed shy and reserved, remembering no doubt, his foolish article agst. Gamble,[16] and my sharp answer to Mr. Raymond [17]—

<[*Note.*] Dec. 10—Mr. M.[itchell] has not called upon me, and I have not seen him since> [*Marginal Note.*] Afterwards, by accident, I met Mr. M.[itchell] in Mr. Gibson's [18] office, when a few words passed in genl. conversation, evidently embar[r]assed on his side.

A supposed intrigue against me.

Dec 10. Recd. a letter to day from W P Johnson [19] of St Louis (who is he?) warning me of an intrigue to put me down and to fill all the high places in and connected with Mo. The writer attributes the scheme to what he calls the " Blair clique." I think he must be mistaken, for, tho' it might not be hard to " drive me from the Cabinet," it would be hard to carry out the details of the plan. But, " fore-warned, fore-armed "—

Note. The Mo. Democrat of Dec 6 (copied into the *News* of same date[)], contains suggestions of the same sort, indicating that the thing is talked of in Mo.—(see clip from the News)[.] This article in the Democrat is evidently a *feeler*. The Democrat speaks of my *withdrawal*, but suggests its improbability. Some of the N.[ew] Y.[ork] papers—e. g. the Herald—speak out more plainly. I am not at all concerned about it. If there be really such a plot, ten to one,

---

[15] *Supra,* Nov. 9, 1859, note 33.
[16] The Governor of Missouri. *Supra,* July 23, 1859, note 39.
[17] *Supra,* Feb. 4, 1860, note 61.
[18] *Supra,* April 27, 1859, note 27.
[19] Waldo P. Johnson: Missouri lawyer; judge; legislator; member of the Washington Peace Convention of 1861; Democratic U. S. senator, from March 17, 1861, until his expulsion. He was at this time an officer of the Confederate Missouri infantry and later became a Confederate senator.

those who dig the pit will *fall* into it, without my taking the trouble to *push* them in.

Note. Jan.y. 10. 1862. The thing above spoken of, if there be such a thing, will come to a head very soon; for today the senate expelled Messrs. Polk [20] and Johnson, Mo. Senators, and Gov Gamble [21] will have to fill their places. I hear from Mr. Gibson,[22] that the Govr. thinks he cannot possibly appoint Col Blair [23]—that it wd. ruin him at home. <[*Marginal Note.*] I hear now, that Col Blair " is out of the ring." The term of the office by the Gov's appointment, is short at best and precarious, with no certainty that the legislature wd. renew it—and perhaps he has had a hint that the Govr. wd. not appt. him.> And I think he cant [*sic*] safely appoint Genl. Coalter [24]—it wd. injure him both at home and abroad. Possibly he may find it best to appoint Glover [25] or Stephenson [26] or—B. Bates,[27] or Judge Sam: Breckenridge[.][28]

[*A clipping which prints Seward's letter of December 16, 1861, in reply to a Republican Club of Philadelphia which wishes to urge his candidacy for the Presidency in 1864. Seward unequivocally declares his loyalty to Lincoln and silences further talk of himself.*]

Dec 17. The first use of Artillery, in the battle-field.[29]

I had forgotten, if I ever read before, that, " On the battle-field of Crecy, in 1346, artillery thundered, for the first time in history."

I have just read it in a sermon of the Revd. Dr. Roswell. D. Hitchcock,[30]—preached in N.[ew] Y.[ork] Octr. 20. 1861. (See Rebellion Record—Spirit of the Pulpit)[.]

Dec 21 . . .

I went out today, first time for four days, being confined with [a] dull head ache and vertigo.

Went with the Prest., on his invitation to see the erection of a pontoon bridge at the Eastern Branch,[31] above the bridge. It was quickly and beautifully done. We passed over it in the Prest's

---

[20] *Supra,* Sept. 6, 1860, note 91.

[21] *Supra,* July 23, 1859, note 39.

[22] *Supra,* April 27, 1859, note 27.

[23] *Supra,* April 27, 1859, note 25.

[24] *Supra,* Dec. 20, 1860, note 16.

[25] *Supra,* Dec. 23, 1859, note 58.

[26] John D. Stevenson: state legislator for many years; once president of the state Senate; active worker for the Union at the outbreak of the War; now colonel of the Seventh Missouri Regiment, which he had raised.

[27] Mr. Bates's eldest son.

[28] *Supra,* Dec. 26, 1859, note 67.

[29] This whole entry, except the parenthetical reference at the end, is written in red ink.

[30] Congregational minister and educator; professor of church history at Union Theological Seminary in New York City, 1855–1880.

[31] The Anacostia River, which flows into the Potomac just below Washington, is called the Eastern Branch of the Potomac.

1861] THE DIARY OF EDWARD BATES 213

carriage (the Prest. and Messrs. Colfax[32] of Inda. and Dubois[33] of Ills: and I) and afterwards a battery of 12 lb: field artillery— and some horsemen at the gallop. The Bridge swayed very little, even under the artillery.

Note. Col Alexander, the commander, said this was the first time he had ever known artillery cross over a *pontoon* bridge, *in America*.

At the same time and place saw a man "walk the water" with each foot in a little water-tight canoe. He carried in his hand a slender paddle, as a help, apparently, both to preserve his erect position and incre[a]se his motion[.]

1861 Dec. 25. C.[abinet] C.[ouncil] at 10. a. m. to considder [*sic*] the relations with England, on Lord Lyons'[34] demand of the surrender of Mason and Slidell.[35] A long and interesting session lasting till. 2 p. m.

The instructions of the British Minister to L[or]d. Lyons were read. They are sufficiently perem[p]tory, and without being very specific as to the precise elements of the wrong done, the "affront" to the British flag, the point on which the British confidently claim that the law of Nations was broken by us, is that Capt Wilkes[36] did not bring in the *Trent*, the Steamer for adjudication, so that the matter might be judged by a prize court, and not by the Capt, on his quarter deck.

Then was read a draft of answer by the Secretary of State—

But before treating of that, I wish to note down several matters of interest that occur[r]ed in the session, tending to explain and give color to various parts of the transaction[.]

1 Genl Cameron said that his Assistant Mr. Scott[37] had rec'd a letter from Mr. Smith[38] (our agent in England for bringing soldiers['] clothes) to the effect—i. a. that Mr. Smith had rec'd information from respectable sources in London, that Commander Williams, the British mail agent on board the *Trent*, had declared that the whole matter, and measures of the capture had been arranged at Havanna [*sic*], by the Com[missio]n[er]s., Slidell and Mason themselves, and our Capt Wilkes' [*sic*] [.]

[32] *Supra*, April 27, 1859, note 28.
[33] Jesse K. Dubois had been in the Legislature with Lincoln and had been nominated and elected by the Republicans for the auditorship of Public Accounts in Illinois in 1856, and in 1860 on the recommendation of Lincoln.
[34] *Supra*, Sept. 26, 1860, note 24.
[35] See *supra*, Nov. 16, 1861.
[36] *Supra*, Nov. 16, 1861, note 46.
[37] Thomas A. Scott, general superintendent, 1858–1859, vice-president, 1859–1861, 1862–1874, and later president, 1874–1880, of the Pennsylvania Railroad. Governor Curtin had put him in charge of the equipment and transportation of state troops. Cameron appointed him assistant secretary of War on August 1, 1861, and, until he resigned in June, 1862, he handled the transportation problems of the War Department.
[38] Probably Hugh Smith of Kentucky, American consul in Dundee, Scotland.

This might seem incredible, if it stood alone, but that something of the sort was variously reported and believed, in well informed circles in England, is a fact, shown by other corroborative facts. For during the session, Senator Sumner [39] (who as chairman of the Com[mitt]ee. of Foreign relations) was invited in, to read some letters which he had just rec'd from England—from the two celebrated M. Ps *John Bright* [40] and *R[ichar]d* Cobden [41]—One of those letters—*Bright['s]* I think—states, as news of the day, that at Havanna [sic], Slidell and Mason *dined with Capt Wilkes on board his ship* San Jacinto and then and there arranged for the capture, just as it was, in fact, done! (If this be so Capt Wilkes will have to be Dealt with, some other day.)

I must doubt the truth of this statement in as much as it seriously implicates Capt Wilkes[.]

[*Note.*] Jan 1st. 1862[.] A gentleman—a visiter at my house—whoes [sic] name I have forgotten in the multitude of calls—told me that *Capt Wilkes* was receiving to day, at the Madison House and was complaining bitterly of the surrender of Mason and Slidell, as a craven yielding and an abandonment of all the good he had done by there [sic] capture[.]

But, on the part of M[ason] and S.[lidell] the policy is obvious and they could bring on a rupture between us and England—actual war or even a threatening quarrel—they would gain by a single stroke more than they could hope to accomplish by years of negotiation.

These letters tend to show that in England there is about one feeling—all against us—about the capture. The passions of Mr. Bull are thoroughly aroused about his dignity and the honor of his flag.

The opposition (L[or]d. Derby [42] &c.[)] relied upon it, as a fit occasion, to force a ministerial crisis, and the adm[inistratio]n. (L[or]d. Palme[r]ston,[43] Russell [44] &c) were, or *had to be*, quite as warm in assuming to be the special guardians of the national honor! So the whole nation is of one mind and *must* have satisfaction[.]

[39] *Supra,* Jan. 7, 1860, note 9.

[40] *Supra,* Aug. 27, 1861, note 98.

[41] Manufacturer, economist, reformer ; member of Parliament since 1841 ; proponent of free trade and parliamentary reform ; close friend of Charles Sumner. Though a leading pacifist, he supported the North in the Civil War because it represented opposition to slavery.

[42] Edward G. G. S. Stanley, Earl of Derby, member of Parliament since 1822, periodically a cabinet member since 1833, prime minister in 1852, 1858–1859, 1866–1868, was leader of the Conservatives who were eager to use this incident to recognize the South.

[43] Henry J. Temple, Viscount Palmerston (Whig, member of Parliament since 1807, intermittently a cabinet member since 1827, prime minister, 1855–1858, 1859–1865) would have liked an excuse to aid Southern independence, but did nevertheless maintain neutrality. Failure to give satisfaction in this crisis might well have given England the excuse her ruling class wanted to make war upon us.

[44] Lord John Russell, Whig member of Parliament since 1813, frequently in the Cabinet, prime minister, 1846–1852, 1865, now foreign secretary, helped prevent Britain from siding with the South.

2 The French government fully agrees with England that the seisure of S[lidell] and M.[ason], *as made* (i. e. without bringing in the Trent, for adjudication) was a breech [*sic*] of the laws of nations. And this appears by the instructions sent to Mr. Mercier,[45] the minister here, who has furnished Mr. Seward with a copy.

Partly by the letter of instructions, but ma[i]nly by letters from our own minister, Mr. Dayton,[46] and divers private letters, it appears that France is in a very bad condition in regard to trade and finance, oweing [*sic*] in a large measure as the French suppose, to our blockade (which besides the cotton trade cuts off the whole commerce of Boardeaux [*sic*] in wines, fruits and silks with Norleans, Mobiel [*sic*] and Charleston[)]—In short, if England can pick a quarrel with us, on the pretense of this seisure, France will join with England in forceibly [*sic*] opening the blockade and consequently, acknowledgeing [*sic*] the C.[onfederate] S.[tates] of A[merica] and that is war, And we cannot afford such a war.

The first and immediate effect would be, to withdraw all our forces, land and naval from the southern coast—The suspension of all our revenue from customs. The distruction [*sic*] of our foreign commerce. The probable capture of our sea ports—and ills innumerable—The scene would be reversed! The southern coast would be open and the northern blockaded.

In such an event, it would be small satisfaction to us to believe, as I do, that it would be sure to light up the torch of war allover [*sic*] Europe, the effects of which upon christendom I am not wise enough to foresee.

In such a crisis, with such a civil war upon our hands, we cannat [*sic*] hope for success in a super added war with England, backed by the assent and countenance of France. We must evade it— with as little damage to our own honor and pride as possible. Still we must avoid it *now* and for the plain reason that *now* we are not able to meet it. Three months hence if we do half our duty upon the sea coast and upon the Miss—issippi, the case may be very different. And happily for us it is that [in] yielding to the necessity of the case we do but reaffirm our old principles and carry out into practice the tr[a]ditional policy of the country, as is clearly shown by Mr. Seward in quotations from Mr. Sect. of State, Madisons [*sic*] instructions to our minister to England, Monroe, in 1804[.] [47]

45 *Supra*, Nov. 27, 1861, note 77.

46 William L. Dayton of New Jersey: Whig U. S. senator, 1842–1851; Republican candidate for the Vice-Presidency in 1856; attorney-general of New Jersey, 1857–1861; now minister to France, 1861–1864, where he was working hard to prevent French aid to the Confederates.

47 While Madison was secretary of State, it was England who was searching our ships and seizing men, goods, and ships, and the United States who was insisting upon the immunity of neutral vessels. In the seizure of Mason and Slidell our positions were reversed.

<*Note.* One of the letters read at the meeting was a letter from Thurlow Weed,[48] at Paris, to Mr. Seward whereby it appears that Mr. Weed wrote the famous letter[49] of Genl Scott which lately appeared in our papers—At least Mr. Weed says that he is just going with a draft of the letter, to wait upon the Genl and get his approval and name to it>—So the world wags—

> ["]The squire killed the boar,
> And the knight had the gloire."

Mr. Seward's draft of letter to Lord Lyons[50] was submitted by him and examined and criticised by us with (apparently, perfe[c]t candor and frankness;) all of us were impressed with the magnitude of the subject and believed that upon our decision depended the dearest interest, probably the existance [*sic*], of the nation.

I (waiving the question of legal right—upon which all Europe is against us, and also many of our own best jurist[s] [51][)] urged the necessity of the case: that to go to war with England now, is to abandon all hope of suppressing the rebellion: as we have not the possession of the land nor any support of the people of the South. The maratine [*sic*] superiority of Britain would sweep us from all the southern waters! our trade would be utterly ruined and our treasury bankrupt—In short, that we *must not* have war with England.

There was great reluctance on the part of some of the members of the cabinet—and even the President himself—to acknowledge these obvious truths: but all yielded to the necessity, and unanimously concur[r]ed in Mr. Sewards [*sic*] letter to L[or]d. Lyons, after some verbal and formal amendments. The main fear I believe, was the displeasure of our own people—lest they should accuse us of timidly truckling to the power of England[.]

I know not how it happened, but a rumor is currant [*sic*] and pretty extensively believed, that I had much more to do with bringing about the arrangement than the facts would warrant! For instance—as soon as Mr. Sewards [*sic*] letter was published, came Baron Gerolt,[52] Prussian minister, with his congratulations upon the result, and in, terms almost direct, imputed to me the main views

---

[48] *Supra,* July 27, 1859, note 58.

[49] A long letter on the *Trent* Affair, written in Paris, December 2, which appeared in the London papers on December 5. It is printed in the *National Intelligencer* of December 20.

[50] *Supra,* Sept. 26, 1860, note 24. For the letter referred to see the *Works of William H. Seward* (Geo. E. Baker, ed., 1884), V, 295–309.

[51] See John B. Moore, *A Digest of International Law,* VII, 768–779, for opinion on this case. Seward himself wrote, "If I decide this case in favor of my own Government, I must disavow its most cherished principles, and reverse and forever abandon its most essential policy." But in spite of this sober final judgment of Mr. Seward, when news of the capture first came, many of the best American jurists joined Mr. Bates in applauding it and justifying it. See C. F. Adams, "The Trent Affair," *Am. Hist. Rev.,* XVII (April 1912), 540–562.

[52] *Supra,* Nov. 27, 1861, note 82.

and arguments of Mr. Sewards [*sic*] letter—for which, by the way, he had no better warrant than some similarity of thought expressed by me in previous conversations with him—And since then, the Bremen minister, Mr. Schleiden,[53] has talked to me in the same way. Both of them expressed great satisfaction at what they called the honorable settlement of the affair, and said that was the general feeling of the foreign ministers.

Some representatives of the press also, have gotten the erroneous idea of my supposed influence in the matter. They say that I had difficulty in bringing over two or three members. Coffey[54] tells me this. He heard a prominent *letter writer* talking in that way to Gov Curtin[55] of Pa. Of course I make no attempt to correct or explain these things the attempt would make the matter worse, and would be a bad precedent.

1861   Dec 28.   Britton. A. Hill[56] of St Louis (his authority is not much to be relied upon) says that Genl. Fremont is an *opium eater*— that his behavior and manner, his staring and contortions prove it— moreover that he detected the odor upon his breath.

Note—I never repeat *as a fact*, what I hear from Mr. Hill.

Dec 31.   Ever since last date, the weather has been mild and beautiful. . . .

I do wonder at the slowness of our military movements. Byrn-side's expedition has not yet sailed.[57] He says he is ready, he says he *is* ready *and yet he does not go*—And the Naval men say that they are ready, and yet they do not go—

And just so with Butler's expedition[58]—*It does not go.* Meanwhile, all this charming weather is lost, and I fear that, at last, they will start just in time to catch the storms of winter.

I hear that a *Reg*[*imen*]*t. of Caval*[*r*]*y* has been sent to Sherman, in S. Carolina.[59]

[*Marginal Note.*]   Jan.y. 4 [1862]. I hear today, that Gen Sherman has taken a point on the Charleston and Savanna[h] R. R. near to Charleston[.]

We are expecting daily important news from the West. A great battle is imminent, near Bowling Green K.y. between the insurgents

---

[53] Rudolph Schleiden, Minister Resident of Bremen, 1854–1862.

[54] *Supra*, March 5, 1860, note 18.

[55] Andrew G. Curtin of Pennsylvania: former Whig politician who had helped turn the Republican nomination to Lincoln; governor of Pennsylvania, 1861–1867; one of Lincoln's most effective supporters in the prosecution of the War; minister to Russia, 1869–1872; Democratic congressman, 1881–1887.

[56] A New Yorker who had moved to Missouri in 1841; St. Louis lawyer; from 1863 to 1865 a partner in Washington of Thomas Ewing (*supra,* Oct. 6, 1860, note 41) and O. H. Browning (*supra*, Sept. 21, 1859, note 97) in Supreme Court practice.

[57] See *supra*, Nov. 29, 1861.

[58] See *loc. cit.*

[59] See *supra*, Nov. 13, 1861.

under A. S. Johns[t]on [60] and Buckner [61] and our army under Buell.[62] If Halleck [63] can only cooperate, and simultaneously, move upon Columbus, we may [stand] to win advantages decisive of the war. But I fear that their arrangements are not as perfect as they ought to be.

There is an evident lack of system and concentrated intelligence—Of course, I did not expect exact system and method in so large an army raised so suddenly, but surely, many of the deficiencies ought before now, to have been corrected.

For months past (and lately more pressingly) I have urged upon the President to have some military organization about his own person—appoint suitable *aid*[e]*s*—2—3—or 4—to write and carry his orders, to collect information, to keep the needful papers and records always at hand, and to do his bidding generally, in all Military and Naval affairs. I insisted that, being "Commander in chief" by law, he *must* command—especially in such a war as this. The Nation requires it, and History will hold him responsible.

In this connexion, it is lementable [*sic*] that Gen McClellan—the *General in chief*, so called—is, and for some time has been incapacitated by a severe spell of illness (and Genl. Marcy,[64] his chief of Staff—and father in law, is sick also[)]. It now appears that the Genl. in chief has been very reticent—kept his plans absolutely to himself, so that the strange and dangerous fact exists, that the Sec of War and the Prest. are ignorant of the condition of the army and its intended operations!

I see no reason for having a *Genl.* in chief at all. It was well enough to call the veteran *Lieut.* Gen. Scott so, when we had no enemies in the [*sic*] *in the field*, and no army but a little nucleus of 15.000 men. But now that we have several mighty armies and active operations spreading over half a continent, there seems to me

[60] Albert S. Johnston, West Point graduate of 1826 who had served in the U. S. Army, 1826–1834, in the Texas Army, 1836–1837, in the Mexican War, and again in the U. S. Army from 1849 until he resigned when Texas seceded. He served with distinction in high command in the Confederate Army until he was killed in battle on April 6, 1862. At this time he was commanding in Kentucky.

[61] Simon B. Buckner of Kentucky, West Point graduate of 1844, had served in the Army in Mexico and on the frontier, but had resigned in 1855. He had organized an effective Kentucky militia in 1860–1861 and commanded Kentucky's troops during the period of her neutrality. He tried to keep both Confederate and Union forces out of Kentucky, but when this failed he threw in his lot with the Confederates, became a brigadier-general, and at this time was fighting under Johnston.

[62] Don Carlos Buell of Indiana: West Point graduate of 1841 who had served in Mexico; officer in the Army, 1841–1861; brigadier-general of volunteers in 1861. He had been sent by McClellan to command the Army of the Ohio and to organize the Union forces in Kentucky. He marched on Bowling Green on February 6, 1862, and drove the Confederates temporarily back into Tennessee.

[63] *Supra*, Nov. 13, 1861, note 37.

[64] Randolph B. Marcy, West Point graduate of 1832 who had served in Mexico, on the frontier, and in Florida. He was McClellan's chief-of-staff until McClellan was displaced and then he was sent to the West on inspection duty.

no good sense in confiding to *one* general the command of the whole; and especially, as we have no general who has any experience in the handling of large armies—not one of them ever commanded 10.000 under fire, or has any personal knowledge of the complicated movements of a great army.

If I were President, I *would* command *in chief*—not *in detail*, certainly—and I *would* know what army I had, and what the high generals (my Lieutenants) were doing with that army.[65]

As to the Slidell and Mason affair, see my notes, elsewhere, at large.[66]

Dec 31. Since last date the weather has been and is remarkably fine. Mr. Eads[67] has been here, bringing his wife, Miss Genevieve and little Mattie—He has returned, by way of N.[ew] Y.[ork] to St Louis (leaving Genevieve with us, untill [*sic*] his return again in a few weeks)[.] He was sadly disappointed about gitting [*sic*] money, and went away in no good humor with Q.[uarter] M.[aster] G[eneral] Meigs.[68] I hope it will be all right soon.

I think he has made a very favorable impression upon the Navy Dept, especially with Mr. Fox,[69] asst. Sect: He will probably contract for the building of 4 of the 20 *iron ships* ordered for the Navy, at $500.000 a piece—perhaps a little more.[70]

Mr. Gibson[71] shewed me to day a letter from Gov Gamble[72] in very low spirits—Genl Halleck[73] rules out the malitia [*sic*]. The goods sent from here—those clothes and blanketts [*sic*]—expressly for Gambles malitia [*sic*] are taken and transfer[r]ed to other troops, this is too bad.

<[*Note.*] Jany 3 Mr. Gibson read me another letter from Gov Gamble in much better spirits. He thinks, in the main that Halleck is doing very well[.>]

Genl McClellan and his chief of staff, Genl Marcey [*sic*], are both very sick—Said to be typhoid fever—and this is making much difficulty.

---

[65] For an interesting study of this problem of the assumption of supreme military command by Lincoln see Sir Frederick Maurice's *Robert E. Lee, the Soldier*, 73–75, 223–224, and his *Statesmen and Soldiers of the Civil War*, 59–117.

[66] *Supra*, Nov. 16, Nov. 27, Dec. 25, 1861.

[67] *Supra*, Jan. 28, 1860, note 38.

[68] Montgomery C. Meigs: West Point graduate of 1836; officer in the Artillery and Engineering Corps ever since; commander of the expedition to Fort Pickens which had saved that fort; quartermaster-general with the rank of brigadier-general, 1861–1882.

[69] *Supra*, March 9, 1861, note 40.

[70] He did actually contract for seven armor-plated gunboats of 600 tons each to be finished in sixty-five days. He and Mr. Bates had suggested these gunboats for the Mississippi, and, before the War ended, he had built fourteen armored gunboats, seven "tin-clad" transports, and four heavy mortar boats, and had added several new ordnance inventions of his own to them.

[71] *Supra*, April 27, 1859, note 27.

[72] *Supra*, July 23, 1859, note 39.

[73] *Supra*, Nov. 13, 1861, note 37.

The Genl: it seems, is very reticent. Nobody knows his plans. The Sec of war and the President himself are kept in ignorance of the actual condition of the army and the intended movements of the General—if indeed they intend to move at all—In fact the whole administration is lamentably deficient in the lack of unity and co-action[.]   There is no quarrell [*sic*] among us, but an absalute [*sic*] want of community of intelligence, purpose and action.

In truth, it is not *an* administration but the separate and disjointed action of seven independent officers, each one ignorant of what his colle[a]gues are doing.

To day in council, Mr. Chase stated the condition of things in sorrowful plainness; and then, as usual, we had a " bald, disjointed chat " about it, coming to no conclusion.

It seemed as if all military operations were to stop, just because Genl McClellan is sick! Some proposed that there should be a council of war composed of Maj: Genls, in order that somebody besides the Genl in chief, may know something about the army; and be able to take command in case Genl McC[lellan] should die or continue sick.

I differed, and told the President that *he* was commander in chief, and that it was not his *privilege* but his *duty* to command; and *that* implied the necessity to *know* the true condition of things.

That if I was in his place, I *would know*; and if things were not done to my liking, I would order them otherwise. That I believed he could get along easier and much better by the free use of his power, than by this injurious deference to his subordinates[.]

I said, the Sec of War is but the Adjutant Genl. and the Sec of the Navy the Admiral of the commander in chief, and through them, he ought to know all that is necessary to be known about the army and Navy. And I urged upon him (as often heretofore) the propriety of detailing at least two active and skillful officers to act as his aid[e]s, to write and carry his orders, collect his information. keep his military books and papers, and do his bidding generally in military affairs.

But I fear that I spoke in vain. The Prest. is an excellent man, and, in the main wise; but he lacks *will* and *purpose*, and, I greatly fear he, has not *the power to command*.

CHAPTER IV

1862

Jan 1. Wednesday. A bright, warm day—All the world was out. At 11. a. m. I went (with Nancy, Matilda and Dick—wife did not go nor Miss Eads,[1] who is staying with us on a visit) *Sec: reg:* to wait upon the Prest. and lady—Saw all the Foreign Ministers, *en costume*—a gawdy show—The Judges of [the] S.[upreme] C.[ourt] also[.] Of course, we left just before 12, as the military and naval officers were marching in—another gawdy show—worth seeing *for once.* Coming out, at noon, found eager crowds at the gates, which were guarded by the police force.

I hear that when the gates were opened there was a rush of many thousands, overwhelming the poor fatigued President.

From 1 to 5 there was a constant stream of *callers*—from Judges of [the] S.[upreme] C[ourt], Senators and foreign ministers, down to privates—on all the heads of Depts.—less perhaps, it [at] my house than any—There was no disorder—tho' 2 policemen were needlessly sent to guard each house.

In fear of the repetition of former disorders, it was prudently resolved to give no refreshments. And so the day was very quietly and *respectably* spent.

Jan 2. In S.[upreme] C.[ourt] I was afraid of being forced into the trial of the School cases[2]—Glasgow et al v Hortiz,[3] and 5 others—being unprepared, having no printed brief (all the time expecting Field[4] to send me on a brief) but I was relieved, the court gave me a week to file a brief. And I can do it with good hope of success.

Jan 3 Friday. At night, visited by Truman Smith[5] and Professor Davies.[6] Mr. Smith is very dissatiesfied [*sic*]—"What pri-

---

[1] Daughter of James B. Eads of St. Louis. *Supra,* Jan. 28, 1860, note 38.

[2] Cases involving land appropriated for school purposes in Missouri. Mr. Bates had been judge of the Land Court in St. Louis, 1853–1856, had been instrumental in securing the legislation which confirmed the title of valuable lands for school purposes, had defended these titles as a lawyer, and was an expert on land law.

[3] See 1 Black 595–603. A case appealed from the Supreme Court of Missouri in which Glasgow *et al.* claimed land under a federal survey and Hortiz claimed the same land under an Act of Congress of 1812 granting clear title to all land occupied by inhabitants of Missouri before 1803. Bates argued the case for Glasgow *et al.* to uphold the Federal survey, but he lost the case, and the earlier title of Hortiz under the Act of 1812 was declared valid.

[4] Roswell M. Field: *supra,* Oct. 26, 1859, note 14.

[5] *Supra,* March 28, 1860, note 42.

[6] *Supra,* Oct. 15, 1860, note 65.

vate griefs he has, alas! I know not."—He thinks all the appointments are studiously wrong, that Mr. Lincoln is an imbecile and can
do no good, and he expects no good to be done by any body!

The Professor came on full of the idea that there would be created
another Asst. Sec. of War—and that he wd. suit the place exactly,
if the *military* part of the duty were assigned to him. He would
not let me forget—often repeating his proofs—how able a man he
is in *military science*, and how familiar he is with all the merits, positive and relative, of our officers, having taught nearly all of them—
mathematics—Doubtless Mr. Davies is a first-rate *mathematician*,
and knows Laplace [7] and Legendre [8] very well—and, upon the whole,
I like to see a man on good terms with himself.

I told him of my proposition that the President should appoint
aid[e]s, and he bit at the bait " as fierce as a rock fish," not doubting
that he is the fittest man in America, to be *chief of the President's
staff.*

Jany 4 Saturday. I do like Roscoe Conkling [9] of N.[ew]
Y.[ork]—A smart man—well cultivated, young, handsome, polite,
and withal a *good listener.*

He thinks Judge Davis [10] of N. Y. is figuring to get a new federal
judg[e]ship made *in the City* [of] N. Y. *for himself,* and that he is
trying to operate thro' Senator Harris,[11] by fulsome flattery, and
holding him up for the presidency &c[.]

Mr. C.[onkling] wants another *District* in the *Country,* not another
judge in the *City,* and is positive that the N. Y. delegation will oppose
the *Judge* but support the *District.*

Jan 5 Sunday. Went with Isaac Newton [12] and Mr. Hubbard of
Ohio, to Mr. Calvert's [13]—M.[ember of] C.[ongress] of Md. near
Bladensburg—dined there very pleasantly. Visited the agricultural
College and got acquainted with Prest. Onderdonck—and professor

---

[7] Pierre S., Marquis de Laplace, 1749–1827, great French mathematician.

[8] Adrien M. Legendre, 1752–1833, also a famous French mathematician.

[9] A young Republican congressman from New York, 1859–1863, 1865–1867; U. S.
senator from 1867 until he resigned in 1881 as a protest over Garfield's refusal to allow
him to dictate New York appointments; a Radical during Reconstruction; Republican boss
of New York State.

[10] Noah Davis: New York lawyer; now justice of the state Supreme Court, 1857–1868;
later a Republican congressman, 1869–1870; U. S. attorney, 1870–1872; and again judge
of the New York Supreme Court, 1872–1887. It was he who sentenced " Boss " Tweed to
prison in 1873.

[11] Ira Harris of Albany: justice of the New York Supreme Court, 1847–1859; Republican
U. S. senator, 1861–1867; friend of Sumner; but a supporter of Lincoln against the
Radicals.

[12] Isaac Newton, was a Pennsylvania Friend who served as commissioner of Agriculture
throughout Lincoln's administration. He frequently called to chat with Mr. Bates, and
always came stocked with an amazing amount of " secret " political gossip.

[13] Charles B. Calvert: Maryland planter; vice-president of the U. S. Agricultural
Society; founder of the Maryland Agricultural College; early advocate of a U. S.
Department of Agriculture; Whig unionist congressman, 1861–1863.

Glover,[14] a learned and very skillful entomologist. Mr. G.[lover] is a peculiar man, striking and instructive[.] I hope to know him better.

Mr. Calvert is a pleasant gentleman[.] Has a fine place somewhat out of repair. Extensive greenhouses admirably kept. One thing struck me—a large iron cannon mounted about 100 yds. in front of the door. On enquiry, I found it one of the first big guns brought over by his ancestor Charles Calvert,[15] Lord Baltimore, who settled Maryland.

Jan 10. Went to court expecting to argue my school cases,[16] and ready to do it, but Mr. Hill[17] complained of being unwell and so it was passed—the C.[hief] J.[ustice][18] saying that he wd. not *call it* again, but that we might argue it wheneve[r] we pleased so as not to displace another case[.]

Jan 10. Friday. Disappointed in the S.[upreme] C.[ourt] by the postponement of the School cases, I hastened to C.[abinet] C.[ouncil] where we had a free consultation, which disclosed great negligence, ignorance and lack of preparation and forethought. Nothing is *ready*. McClellan is still sick, and nobody knows his plans, if he have any (which with me is very doubtful). The expeditions for the South do not go [19]—nobody knows why not—The boats and bomb-rafts at Cairo are not ready [20]—not manned—Indeed we do not *know* that the mortars have reached there—Strange enough, the boats are under the *War* Dept., and yet are commanded by *naval* officers. Of course, they are neglected—no one knows any thing about them.

I advised the Prest. to restore all the floating force to the command of the *Navy* Dept. with orders to coöperate with the army, just as the Navy on the sea coast does.

Again, I urged upon the Prest. to take and act out the powers of his place, to command the commanders—and especially to *order* regular, periodical reports, shewing the exact state of the army, every where. And to that end—

I renewed formally, and asked that it be made a question before the Cabinet,—my proposition, often made heretofore—that the Pres-

[14] Townend Glover: wealthy Rio-de-Janeiro-born, English-bred artist and scientist who came to America in 1836; first official entomologist of the U. S. Government, 1854–1878; professor at the newly established Maryland Agricultural College.

[15] The third Lord Baltimore, son of Cecilius Calvert, was governor of Maryland, 1661–1675, Lord Proprietor, 1675–1689.

[16] *Supra*, Jan. 2, 1862, note 2.

[17] *Supra*, Dec. 28, 1861, note 56.

[18] Roger B. Taney: *supra*, Nov. 27, 1861, note 73.

[19] Butler's and Burnside's. See *supra*, Dec. 31, 1861.

[20] They were being collected for the attack on Fort Henry which took place in early February.

ident as " Comm[an]der in Chief of the Army and Navy " do organize a *Staff* of his own, and assume to be in fact, what he is in law, the *Chief Commander.* His aid[e]s could save him a world of trouble and anxiety—collect and report to him all needed information, and keep him constantly informed, at a moment's warning—keep his military and naval books and papers—conduct his military correspondence,—and do his bidding generally "in all the works of war[.] "

It is objected (by both the Prest. and Sec of War) not that the thing is wrong or undesirable in itself but that the *Generals* wd. get angry—quarrel &c!! I answer—Of course the Genls—especially the Chief[21]—would object—. they wish to give but not receive orders—If I were Prest, and I found them restive under the command of a *superior*, they should soon have no *inferiors* to command. All of them have been lately made of comparatively raw material, taken from the lower grates [*sic*] of the army officers or from civil life. The very best of them—McClellan, McDowell,[22] Halleck[23] &c until very lately, never commanded more than a battallion [*sic*]. They have no experience in the handling of large bodies of men, and are no more to be trusted in that respect, than other men of good sense, lately their equals in rank and position. If therefore, they presume to quarrel with the orders of *their superior*—their constitutional commander—for that very reason, they ought to be dismissed, and I would do, it in full confidence that I could fill their places with quite as good men, chosen as *they* were chosen, from the lower grades of officers, from the ranks of the army, or from civil life.

There can be no lawful, just or honest cause of dissatisfaction because the President assumes, in practise, the legitimate duties of his place—His *powers* are all *duties*—He has no *privileges*, no powers granted to him for his own sake, and he has no more right to refuse to exercise his constitutional powers than he has to assume powers not granted. He (like us, his official inferiors) cannot evade his responsibilities. He must shew to the nation and to posterity, how he has discharged the duties of his Stewardship, in this great crisis. And if he will only trust his own good judgment more, and defer less, to the opinions of his subordinates, I have no doubt that the affairs of the war and the aspect of the whole country, will be quickly and greatly changed for the better.

I think it unjust to to [*sic*] those Genls. to impute to them such unsoldierly conduct. Very probably, they would object and grumble in advance, in the hope of deterring the President from that course, <for no man takes pleasure in having his own conduct closely and

---

21 George B. McClellan.

22 *Supra,* Nov. 16, 1861, note 53.

23 *Supra,* Nov. 13, 1861, note 37.

constantly scrutinized; >[24] but the resolve, once taken, would work its own moral and peaceful triumph. For those generals are, undoubtedly, men of sense, prudence and patriotism, and, for their own, as well as their country's good, would obey their official superior, as cheerfully and heartily as they expect their inferiors to obey them. If, however, contrary to professional duty, to the moral sense of right, and to sound logic, they should act otherwise, that fact would be proof positive of unfitness to command, and, for that cause, they ought to be instantly removed.

If a Major Genl. may be allowed to complain because the President has about him a *staff*—the means and m[a]chinery of knowledge and of action—why may not a Brigadier complain that his Major Genl. is so accom[m]odated? The idea seems to me absurd. The very thought is insubordinate, and smacks of mutiny.

My proposition assumes that the President is, in fact as well as theory, commander *in chief* (not in detail) of the army and navy; and that he is bound to exercise the powers of that high post, as *legal duties*. And that he cannot perform those duties intelligently and efficiently, by his own unassisted, personal powers—He must have aid[e]s, by whatever names you call them; for they are as necessary to the proper exercise of those official functions, as the bodily senses are to the proper perception and action of the individual man. If it be the duty of the President, as I do not doubt that it is, to command, it would seem to follow, of necessity, that he must have, constantly at hand and under his personal orders, the usual means and machinery for the performance of that duty, with knowledge and with effect.

In at least one important sense, I consider the Departments of War and Navy as constituting the *Staff* of the *Commander in chief*, and it does seem to me highly important that he should have, always near him, intelligent and confidential persons, to facilitate his intercourse with that multitudinous staff.

If it be *not* the President's *duty* to command, then it is *not* his *right*, and prudence would seem to require him to renounce all control of the affairs of war, and cast all the responsibility upon those who are entrusted with the actual command—But this he cannot do, because the constitution forbids it, in declaring that he " *shall be* Commander in chief."

I see not the slightest use for A *General in chief* of the army. When we had peace with all the world, and a little nucleous [*sic*] of an army, of about 15.000 men, and had the veteran Lieut. General Scott as our first officer, perhaps it was well enough to give *him* that honorary title. But now, that we have a war spreading over half a continent, and have many armies, reaching, in the aggregate to over 600.000 men, it is simply impossible for any one general, usefully and well, to command all those armies. The army of the Potomac alone is quite enough for any one man to command in detail, and more than almost any one can do, with assurance of good success.

The President being a Civil Magistrate and not a military chief, and being the lawful commander in chief of the army, needs, more than any well-trained general can need, in his intercourse with and his control of the army, the assistance of skillful and active aid[e]s, always near his person. And I indulge the hope that he will find it right to appoint and organize just such and so many as his exigencies may seem to require; and I say all this in the confident belief, that his own reputation, now and hereafter, and the present and permanent good of the Country, do require such an organization.[25]

Jan. 13. To night, I was taken by surprise in hearing that Mr. Cameron sec. of War, has resigned, and goes to Russia, in lieu of Cash: M. Clay [26]—and that Edwin M. Stanton [27] is to take his place. This was a street rumor in the afternoon. At night, I was told by Senator Harris,[28] that the nominations had been actually made. Strange—not a hint of all this was heard last friday, at C.[abinet] C.[ouncil] and stranger still, I have not been sent for by the Prest. nor spoken to by any member. The thing, I learn, was much considered saturday and sunday—Hay [29] told the ladies at Eames' [30] jocosely, that the Cabinet had been sitting *en permanence*—and Mr. E[ames] himself informed me that Mr. Seward had been with the Prest: the whole of Sunday forenoon.

[*Marginal Note.*] Upon reflection, it is not strange—When the question is of the retaining or dismissing a member of the *cabinet*, the Prest. could not well lay the matter before the *cabinet*—he must do that himself.

[25] See *supra*, Dec. 31, 1861. note 64.

[26] Cassius M. Clay, Kentucky abolitionist, editor, politician, had supported Lincoln in 1860 and expected to become secretary of War, but was appointed minister to Russia instead, 1861–1862, 1863–1869. He was now returning with a brigadier-generalship to make room for Cameron to be eased out of the Cabinet, but, when he got here, he refused to fight until the Government abolished slavery in the seceded states, and so the next year when Cameron tired of the post, he returned to Russia.

[27] Able Pittsburgh lawyer who practiced frequently before the U. S. Supreme Court; anti-slavery Democrat who believed in protection of slavery in the South where it legally existed; Free-Soiler in 1848; attorney-general in Buchanan's Cabinet, 1860–1861, where he vigorously opposed the plan to abandon Fort Sumter; bitter critic of Lincoln in 1860–1861; secretary of War, 1862–1868; professed supporter of Lincoln; treacherous enemy of Johnson. Bates shares Welles's distrust of Stanton even under Lincoln.

[28] *Supra*, Jan. 4, 1862, note 11.

[29] John M. Hay: poet; journalist; private secretary to the President; later, ambassador to Great Britain, 1897–1898; secretary of State, 1898–1905; historian of Lincoln.

[30] Charles Eames: International lawyer; commissioner to Hawaii, 1849; editor of the *Nashville Union*, in 1850, and the *Washington Union*, 1850–1854; minister resident to Venezuela, 1854–1857; at this time (1861–1867) counsel for the Navy Department and the captors in prize cases and for the Treasury Department in cotton cases.

There is a rumor in town, that Burnside [31] has landed to attack Norfolk (proven afterwards, as I expected at the time, false)[.]

Jan 24. Friday night—Barton Bates arrived on a visit—He is now a Judge of the Sup[rem]e. Court of Mo. under the provisional Govt.—

[*February 2.*] He still (Feb: 2.) remains with us and I hope will continue some days longer, and the rather because the weather has been very wet and muddy ever since he came.

Feb 2 Sunday morning . . .

I am sick of a bad cold, and cannot venture out today to church— I dare not get my feet wet or cold.

My good friend Colfax [32] breakfasted with us this morning. I think his manner is changed for the worse—he seems figitty [*sic*] and nervous, will not dwell upon a subject, but flits from theme to theme, as if afraid to rest under the moral microscope long enough to be examined.

Congress—There is a feverish excitement in both Houses: In the senate there were strong indications of opposition to the adm[inistratio]n. and Mr. *Hale* [33] led off very plainly in that direction, but recoiled, as to oppose the adm[inistratio]n. *now* is to oppose the *War* and the nation. But, as the steam is up, it must find a vent, and so is let off against individuals—Cameron is driven out, and exiled to Russia, and now they are battering away upon Welles, and many think that he must yield to the storm. I will not decide that injustice was done to Cameron— I do not judge his case. But I think that Welles gets hard measure for his faults. He is not strong or quick, but I believe him an honest and faithful man.

Out of doors, there is a formidable clique organized against Mr. Seward, who, fearing his adroitness, work very privily against him. Their object (at least *friend* Newton [34] thinks so) is to compel his retirement and put senator Harris [35] in his place. It is said that some of them have approached Mrs. Lincoln and not without success, making her believe that Mr. Seward is laboring with persistent effort, to override the Prest. and make himself the chief man of the adm[inistratio]n. They do tell me that she is made

[31] *Supra*, Nov. 29, 1861, note 97.

[32] *Supra*, April 27, 1859, note 28.

[33] John P. Hale of New Hampshire: U. S. attorney, 1834–1841; Democratic congressman, 1843–1845; Free-Soil candidate for the Presidency, 1852; anti-slavery U. S. senator, 1847–1853, 1855–1865; minister to Spain, 1865–1869. Hale was at this time not only an extremist opponent of Lincoln, but as chairman of the Committee on Naval Affairs was a leading factor in the corruption and "debauched system of personal and party favoritism" with which Welles found it so difficult to cope.

[34] *Supra*, Jan. 5, 1862, note 12.

[35] *Supra*, Jan. 4, 1862, note 11.

fully to believe *that*, but I have not seen any action of hers, in consequence.

Mr. Smith of the Interior does not escape. I hear that there is a strong combination against him—I hear of no charge in particular, only some alleged abuse of patronage and lack of vim. *Note.* He is very anxious to be translated to the Supreme bench.

I carefully keep myself clear of all these cliques and combinations. The new Sec.y. of War is a man of mind and action. He is well recd. by all, except that some of the army officers think that he is too peremptory—He'll cure them of that pretty soon—for he will assuredly, speak to them *in orders.*

I hear of no combined opposition against either Chase or Bates. [*A clipping giving* "*Committees of the Rebel Congress*" *and* "*The Rebel Cabinet.*"]

Feb 3. Certainly friend Newton [36] does hear more gossip than any one I know. He tells me "lots of news "—i. a. he says the combinations against Mr. Seward are stronger and hotter than ever, determined to thrust him out—their present programme (very wild)—is Stanton to be translated to State Dept.—*Holt* [37] to War office—*Bankes* [38] [to] Navy in place of Welles—But nobody yet found to take the Interior from Mr. Smith. <this ignores Harris [39] altogeher>

All this is very idle talk and only shews that there is a feeling of restless discontent. That feeling *will* continue until the army takes measures active, aggressive and successful. If we fail to do something effectual in the next 30 days, the adm[inistratio]n. will be shaken to pieces—the Cabinet will be re-modelled, and several of its members must retire. But the scene will be changed and confidence restored, if the Prest's orders be carried out—that is, if on or before the 22d. Feb: the armies, simultaneously, assume the aggressive upon the Potomac; upon the Miss[issipp]i. and in Tennee; upon N. Orleans; and upon Eastern Va. And especially if the independent expeditions of Sherman [40] and Burnside [41] and Butler,[42] and Hunter [43] (or Lane [44]) fully coöperate.

---

[36] *Supra,* Jan. 5, 1862, note 12.
[37] *Supra,* Feb. 2, 1860, note 49.
[38] *Supra,* July 27, 1859, note 57.
[39] *Supra,* Jan. 4, 1862, note 11.
[40] Thomas W. Sherman, *supra,* Nov. 13, 1861, note 31.
[41] See *supra,* Nov. 29, 1861.
[42] See *loc. cit.*
[43] See *supra,* Oct. 22, 1861, note 21.
[44] James H. Lane ; colonel in the Mexican War ; Democratic congressman from Indiana, 1853–1855 ; anti-slavery leader in Kansas, 1855–1861 ; Republican U. S. Senator from Kansas, 1861–1866 ; at this time brigadier-general of volunteers under General Halleck in Missouri where he led the Kansas brigade until his commission was cancelled on March 21, 1862.

In that case, it is impossible that we should *fail* every where; and if we succeed in half the instances, the rebellion will be effectually crippled[.]

Note. Col Van Alen [45] told me saturday night that it was reported that the Joint Com[mitt]ee. of Congress had demanded [46] of the Sec of War to remove Genl. Stone [47] from command (which wd. let *Gorman* [48] in). That he had a talk about it with McClellan, who said " They want a victim " to which the Col answered—" Yes—and when they have once tasted blood, got one victim, no one can tell who will be the next victim ! " Thereupon, the Genl. colored up, and the conversation ceased.

The thing struck me painfully, not that I understand the merits of Gen Stone's case, or undertake to accuse or acquit him, but I feared the establishment of a precedent for congressional interference with the command of the army, which might lead to the terrible results seen in France, in the days of the revolution.

I wrote a *confidential* note to Mr. Stanton to put him on his guard against hastily complying with the demand (sent by Dick)[.]

Feb 5   Wednesday. . . .

The Prest. is in trouble about granting a *reprieve* for Gordon—the pirate—the first conviction under the law making the African slave trade piracy [49]—I, being confined at home, sick, he wrote a note for my *legal opinion* whether he could grant a reprieve without entirely remitting the death penalty ! Of course I answered that there was no doubt about the *power*.

I told the Prest.—verbally, that I did not see any good reason for interfering at all unless he meant to pardon or commute—that there were men watching opportunities against him, and that by interfering at all he might give them a handle.

He sd. he had no intention to *pardon* Gordon but was willing to give him a short respite, and that yesterday at C.[abinet] C.[ouncil] all the members present, (tho' not asked *as a cabinet*) agreed to it— And said he'd consider it a little more.

---

[45] *Supra,* Feb. 4, 1860, note 62.

[46] The Joint Committee denied making any recommendation in regard to Stone, but it did hold an investigation and did send Stanton a report of the " conflicting " testimony taken about Stone, much of it damaging to the General, and a few days later, on February 8, Stone was arrested. The Joint Committee on the Conduct of the War, *Report* (*Senate Reports,* 37 Cong., 3 Sess., doc. no. 108, ser. no. 1153), II, 18.

[47] *Supra,* Oct. 22, 1861, note 19; Nov. 1, 1861, note 28.

[48] Willis A. Gorman ; colonel in the Mexican War ; Democratic congressman, 1849–1853 ; territorial governor of Minnesota, 1853–1857 ; now brigadier-general of volunteers under McClellan in the Army of the Potomac, later transferred to Arkansas.

[49] The law was enacted May 15, 1820. *Public Statutes at Large of the U. S.,* III, chap. CXIII, 600–601.

I also reminded him that the exact opposite of *Capt.* Gordon's case is coming up in the case of the Revd. [   ] Gordon [50] of Ohio, convicted of some offence agst. the fugitive slave law.

[*Marginal*] *Note.* The Prest granted Capt. Gordon a reprieve for two weeks.[51]

Feb. 5. Almost every day there are new instances of the hasty and blundering manner in which the Secy of State carries out his supposed powers about prisoners, and legal proceedings. And this can hardly fail to lead to serious embarras[s]ments.

To day I recd. a letter from the Asst. Dist Atty.[52] at Phila.[delphia], saying that the *Marshal* [53] had recd. a letter from the *Secy: of State* directing *him* to *transfer* all the prisoners held for piracy—several of whom are indicted and one, at least, convicted—to Fort Lafayette![54] That he—Asst. D.[istrict] Att[orne]y—in order to have the thing *regularly* done, had caused the men to be brot. up, on hab:[eas] Corp:[us] and, *with their assent*, the order of court made for their transfer!

And then he asks instructions whether he shd. deliver to the prisoners their private papers, and enter *nolle prosequi*, in all the cases.

I took the letter to the Prest. and told [him] that that was my first information altho' the marshal and att[orne]y were, by express statu[t]e, under my direction—that the proceeding was loose and irregular and could not fail to lead to embarras[s]ment—

The Prest. desired to keep the letter until he cd. send for Mr. Seward and consult about it.[55]

Feb 11. Barton left us early this morning, after a visit of two weeks—He will stop a few hours, to see Coalter, at Perryville, and then go on to Phila.[delphia] and wait to see Mr. Eads [56]—perhaps will go on with Eads to N. Y. and so home.

Feb 14. Friday. Having been confined by a bad cold &c for some days, today I attended the S.[upreme] C.[ourt] for a short

---

[50] George Gordon, president of Iberia College, Ohio, was convicted before Judge Wilson of the U. S. District Court of Northern Ohio for resisting the U. S. Marshal when he was attempting to capture a fugitive slave some two years before this. Gordon was sentenced to six months' imprisonment and payment of a fine of three hundred dollars and costs.

[51] Feb. 4, 1862. *Complete Works of Abraham Lincoln* (Nicolay and Hay, eds.), II, 121–122.

[52] J. Hubley Ashton, assistant U. S. district attorney of Eastern Pennsylvania until April, 1864, when Mr. Bates made him assistant attorney-general.

[53] William Millward.

[54] Near the middle of "the Narrows" entrance to New York Harbor.

[55] See *infra*, Feb. 25, 1862.

[56] *Supra*, Jan. 28, 1860, note 38.

time—Met Mr. Bartlett [57] of Boston and Mr. Lord [58] (Dan[ie]l.) both of whom are anxious to bring on the prize cases [59]—*Note*[.] Mr. Lord dined with me, and was very pleasant—Mr. Eads also here—

Went from Court direct to C.[abinet] C[ouncil]. Stanton there, quite restored to health.

The sec: of War read the official report of *the Burnside* expedition.[60]   The Genl. says that the success at Roanoke Island [61] was complete,[;] the fight lasted near two days. 4 forts (40. guns) taken, near or quite 3000 prisoners, and over 3000 stands of small arms. A few of the enemy, when driven to the north point of the island, escaped to the main[land] by swimming—30 or 40—

Genl. Wise [62] sick, taken to Norfolk before the fight, his son, Capt. O. J. Wise, killed.   The total killed and wounded of the enemy, not yet known.

Our killed 30 or 40—wounded abt 200.

The Naval force, under Com[modor]e. Goldsborough,[63] acted as usual, very well, bombarding the forts on the island thus putting them in condition to be stormed by the land troops.

As soon as the island was taken the Com[modor]e. despatched Commander Rowan [64] in pursuit of the enemys [*sic*] gun boats, which fled to Pasquotank river [65] (Elizabeth) [66] [.] He sank or captured all the boats except one small one which took refuge in a creek too narrow and shoal to be followed. Capt. R.[owan] also

[57] Sidney Bartlett, a Boston lawyer who frequently argued cases before the United States Supreme Court.

[58] Prominent Connecticut-bred lawyer who practiced in New York City from 1817 until 1868.

[59] A series of cases concerning the *Amy Warwick*, the *Crenshaw*, the *Hiawatha*, and the *Brilliante*, captured while running the blockade of Southern ports proclaimed by Lincoln in May, 1861. The owners appealed from the awards of the lower courts which had adjudged the ships lawful prizes. The Supreme Court by a 5–4 decision upheld the award. The four dissenters denied that the blockade was valid until Congress had officially declared war on July 13, 1861, and therefore denied that these ships taken before that date were lawful prizes. 2 Black 635–699.

[60] See *supra*, Nov. 29, 1861. For the report see Brig.-Gen. A. E. Burnside to Brig.-Gen. Lorenzo Thomas, Feb. 14, 1862, *War of the Rebellion*, ser. 1, IX, 75–81.

[61] An island off the coast of North Carolina in the channel connecting Albemarle Sound and Pamlico Sound and separated from the mainland by Croatan Sound. It was captured February 7–8.

[62] Henry A. Wise: *supra*, April 28, 1859, note 38.

[63] Louis M. Goldsborough, in the Navy since 1812, was put in command of the Atlantic Blockading Squadron in September, 1861. In February, 1862, he led the attack on North Carolina, and in May and June commanded the fleet in the James River, coöperating with McClellan. Criticism of his inaction in the James led him to retire.

[64] Stephen C. Rowan, who had served in the Navy since 1826 and fought in the Mexican War, provided naval protection for Washington during the first days of the Civil War, then fought under Stringham at Hatteras (*supra*, Nov. 13, 1861, note 35), and was now with the North Carolina expedition.

[65] A river of North Carolina which rises in the Dismal Swamp and flows southeastward into Albemarle Sound.

[66] Elizabeth City, on the Pasquotank River.

destroyed the enemy's battery at Cobb's point, and the People of Elizabeth burnt their own town. <[*Marginal Note.*] No—not the people—It was Henningsen's [67] ruffians—the same buccaneer Hennensen [*sic*] who was with Walker [68] in Nicaragua. Pity he was not hanged with his leader.> I was greatly surprised at one thing— Mr. Stanton suggested that *Frank Blair* [69] be appointed a Brigadier and trusted with the command of the Expedition down the Mississippi *from Cairo* to N.[ew] O.[rleans]! [70] Evidently, he has been strongly plied from outside, or he never wd. have thought of it—The President met it *in limine* saying that was the greatest business of all, and needed the highest general in that region. <[*Marginal Note.*] He added that it was generally thought that a man was better qualified to do a thing because he had learned how; and that in this case it was Mr. Blair's misfortune not to have learned.> It is very instructive to consider how much is won in this world, by bold and impudent pretention! The Messrs. Blair gain a great deal by claiming *all*—

[*Marginal Note.*] Feb: 25—It pains me to observe of late that Mr. Blair,[71] P.[ost] M.[aster] G.[eneral] concurs with me in nothing. With or without a reason, he takes the other side. I have the advantage of him—when he offers a good thing, I agree to it.

It must be that Fort Donelson (on the Cumberland) was attacked today, and tomorrow, I think we will here [*sic*] of a great victory or a sad defeat.[72]

Feb 17. At last we have reliable information that fort Donnelson [*sic*] has surrendered to Genl. Grant—a very large armament— 15.000 men[,] several Generals—Pillow,[73] A. S. Johns[t]on,[74] and perhaps some others—Floyd,[75] they say, stole off in the night, with 5000 men—Particulars not yet.[76]

---

[67] Charles F. Henningsen: Scandinavian immigrant to England; then a Carlist captain of lancers in Spain; a revolutionary soldier first in the Caucasus and then in Hungary; finally Kossuth's private secretary on his tour of America in 1851. He remained here, married a Georgia heiress, became a filibuster in Nicaragua in 1856–1857, and then served as a colonel in the Confederate Army in 1861–1862.

[68] *Supra*, Oct. 8, 1859, note 5.

[69] *Supra*, April 27, 1859, note 25.

[70] New Orleans was finally occupied on May 1 by a force that arrived by sea, but the Mississippi was not opened from Cairo to New Orleans until the fall of Vicksburg and Port Hudson, July 4–8, 1863, and then it was a greater soldier than Blair—U. S. Grant—who led the expedition.

[71] Montgomery Blair: *supra*, March 5, 1861, note 31.

[72] Fort Donelson, about sixty-three miles from Nashville, was attacked by General Grant and Commodore Foote on February 14 and was surrendered on February 16.

[73] Gideon J. Pillow: Tennessee lawyer; wealthy planter; major-general in the Mexican War; opponent of secession until it came; now brigadier-general in the Confederate Army. Because of this defeat at Donelson, Pillow was relieved of his command.

[74] *Supra*, Dec. 31, 1861, note 60.

[75] *Supra*, Dec. 3, 1859, note 11.

[76] A. S. Johnston did not fight at Donelson. Floyd turned over his command to Pillow who surrendered it to Buckner, and Floyd and Pillow fled and escaped capture.

Com[modor]e. Foote[77] did wonders, with the iron gun boats—
He recd. 2 wounds, but nothing very serious. The boats did excellent service, under the heavy guns of 3 forts, for an hour and ¼—
Two of them however, were disabled—The first shot from the
'Carondalet' dismounted the enemy's giant gun—180 pounder—and
the "St Louis" was struck by 64 heavy shot, which glanced off like
hail stones on the roof of a house.[78]

The news is that a large part of Price's[79] army in Mo. and the
greater part of his baggage train, are captured,[80] by our Genl.
Curtis.[81] It is also said (but not confirmed) that Com[modor]e.
DuPont[82] has taken Savannah Ga.[83]

Feb 18. The Prest.'s 2d. son, Willie, has lingered on for a week or
10 day[s], and is now thought to be *in extremis*[.] The Prest. is
nearly worn out, with grief and watching.—

Gordon the slaver

Two weeks ago, I warned the Prest. against granting a respit[e]
to Nath[anie]l. Gordon, under sentence of death, for *Piracy* (slave
trade).[84]

It is the first conviction under the act, and nothing shewn to impeach the legality or justice of the conviction. I was convinced
(and told the Prest: so) that the reprieve wd. be taken as an implied
promise of pardon or commutation, however strongly he might
asseverate to the contrary[.]

And now, my prediction is verified. Mrs. White (wife of Judge
White of N. Y.) with the mother and wife of Gordon, are here urging both the Prest. and me to commute the sentence to imprisonment
for life.

My ground of objection is that the Prest. has no right to stop the
course of law, except on grounds of excuse or mitigation found in the
case itself—and not to arrest the execution of the statute merely
because he thinks the law wrong or too severe. That would be to set

---

[77] Andrew H. Foote, in the Navy since 1822, had helped suppress the slave-trade on the African coast and through his writings had aroused sentiment at home against it. When the War broke out he was superintendent of the Brooklyn Navy Yard. In 1862 he commanded the Upper Mississippi Squadron at Forts Henry and Donelson and Island Number 10.

[78] These were two of the especially armored gunboats suggested and built by James B. Eads of St. Louis. See *supra*, Dec. 31, 1861, note 70; Jan. 28, 1860, note 38.

[79] *Supra*, Nov. 27, 1861, note 70.

[80] Price fled before Curtis into Arkansas. But on February 18 Curtis crossed into Arkansas in pursuit and on March 6-8 disastrously defeated Price and a greatly superior force at Pea Ridge.

[81] *Supra*, Oct. 22, 1861, note 23.

[82] *Supra*, Nov. 13, 1861, note 30.

[83] Savannah did not surrender until December 20, 1864. Fort Pulaski which com-
manded the entrance to Savannah was, however, completely cut off at this time and, on April 12, surrendered.

[84] See *supra*, Feb. 5, 1862.

himself above Congress, to assume the *dispensing power*, and to commit the very offense which lost one king of the House of Stuart his head, and another his crown.[85]

Note. The original application for pardon, upon which the Prest. granted the respit[e], was not shewn to me.

Note also. Gordon's counsel moved the Supreme Court, for a *prohibition*, and also for a *Certiorari*, which motion was overruled yesterday the 17th. Feb:

Feb 19. Recd. from the Prest. a package—letter from Judge Dean[86] and some other Doc[ument]s—urging the commutation of Gordon's sentence. I ansd. him hastily, but decidedly—advising him to decline to interpose any farther, to stop the course of law, in the case of Nathaniel Gordon.

[*Marginal Note.*]　Gordon was hanged at the appointed time[.]

Feb. 19. Wednesday. Last night Isaac Newton[87] called, as he often does, to see me, and gave me some startling and painful information. He says that Mr. Julian[88] (M.[ember of] C.[ongress] of Inda.) told him the night before that C. B. Smith (Sec.y. [of the] Interior) was in danger of being *indicted for bribery*—i. e. taking money for appointment to offices in his Dept: and that he will be indicted, unless he speedily, make arrangements with the parties who think themselves aggrieved. One charge is that he took $400 from a person appointed to a 2d. class clerkship—salary $1400 per an[num]:

I cannot believe this of Mr. Smith, and wont [*sic*] believe it without proof. If there be any truth in the story, I incline to think that it must be the work of some vile understrapper of an *office broker*, who screws money out of the needy applicant, under the pretense that he uses it to bribe the Secretary.

I have reason to believe that that sort of swindling has been practiced in connection with the business of my own office—Mr. Hosmer, clerk of the Penetentiary [*sic*] in this Dist: brought me an application for a pardon and desired me to exami[n]e the papers myself. I said I will send them to the Pardon clerk—He sd. he did not wish that, he was afraid to leave the papers with Cooper.[89] Why? He ansd., it is said that it *takes money* to get a favorable report from Mr. Cooper—Who says it? He heard it

[85] One of the "arbitrary" acts for which Charles I lost his head in 1649 and James II his throne in 1688 was the "dispensing" (a legal power of the Crown) with the operation of laws of Parliament which these kings did not like.

[86] Gilbert Dean: Democratic congressman, 1851–1854; justice of the New York Supreme Court, 1854–1855; lawyer in New York City, 1856–1870.

[87] *Supra,* Jan. 5, 1862, note 12.

[88] George W. Julian: Free-Soil and then Republican congressman, 1849–1851, 1861–1871; a Radical who supported extreme war measures and urged early and complete emancipation; extremist in Reconstruction; impeacher of President Johnson; untiring opponent of corruption, monopoly, and plunder of the public domain.

[89] John M. Cooper of Pennsylvania.

among the convicts—a *lawyer* in this Dist: said so—I ansd. any honest man who says so will be willing to swear to it, and I dont [*sic*] believe there is a lawyer in the District who will swear to the charge. I said further, if the charge is made and sustained by probable proof, I will help to put the clerk in to the penitentiary, but until such proof is brought, I will consider the charge a vile slander, made for the purpose of swindling the prisoners and their friends out of money, under the false pretence of bribing officers[.]

Feb 20. Thursday. This day, at 5. p. m. the Prest's son Wm. Wallace Lincoln died. A fine boy of 11 yrs., too much idolized by his parents.

Feb 21. A C.[abinet] C.[ouncil] at the State Dept.—the Prest absent. i. a. it was agreed to send Gen: Scott, as special minister to Mexico, to meet the British, French and Spanish rep[resentative]s: and try to mediate their affairs with Mexico. [90]

The capture of Fort Donelson [91] and Buckner's [92] army of 15.000 men has infused new life and vigor into our movements. Tho' Pillow and Floyd, with 5000 men, stole away in the night [93] by steam-boats, up to Clarksville, that [they] found that place intenable [*sic*], and retreated towards Nashville.

I think Nashville must fall into our hands. There is nothing in the river to hinder our boats, and a strong column of Buell's [94] army is pressing on in that direction—and we hear that the people of Nashville are bitterly opposed to the enemy making a stand there, so as to have a battle at their town.

Note. John Bell's rolling mill, just below Clarksville, which has been working largely for the enemy, was burnt by our troops.

From Mo. we hear that Genl. Curtis has driven out Price's army, following it into Arkansas and making large captures of men and property.[95] And that Lt. Gov Hall [96] (Gov Gamble [97] being absent) is reorganizing the civil Government all over the State. And that Genl. Halleck [98] is reassuring the people, by proclaiming [that] the military will act, no[t] against, but in aid of the civil power.

Feb. 22. Saturday. The ceremonies (under joint resolution) at the H[ouse] of R[epresentatives], were imposing. The Farewell

---

[90] Scott was not sent to Mexico.

[91] *Supra*, Feb. 14, 1862, note 72; Feb. 17, 1862.

[92] *Supra*, Dec. 31, 1861, note 61.

[93] *Supra*, Feb. 17, 1862.

[94] *Supra*, Dec. 31, 1861, note 62.

[95] *Supra*, Feb. 17, 1862.

[96] Willard P. Hall of St. Joseph: author of the laws of New Mexico Territory; Democratic congressman, 1847–1853; opponent of secession; unionist member of the Missouri Convention of 1861; lieutenant-governor, 1861–1864; governor, 1864–1865.

[97] *Supra*, July 23, 1859, note 39.

[98] *Supra*, Nov. 13, 1861, note 37.

address was read by Mr. Forney,[99] Secy. of the Senate. There was a great crowd, besides M.[embers of] C[ongres]s—the heads of Depts. Judges of the S.[upreme] C.[ourt] (the Ch:[ief] J.[ustice] absent) and the foreign ministers, and many of the high officers of [the] army and navy. At night, I dined with a pleasant party, at Baron Gerolt's [1]—The dinner was really given to Eads [2] and Gibson.[3] The weather very bad and I sick.

Wife spent the day nursing little Taddy Lincoln.

Feb 23d. Sunday—I staid at home, being unwell.

[February] 24 monday. Late last night, Mr. Newton [4] came in to tell me that the Prest had just recd. a telegram to the effect that Columbus was evacuated.[5] This morning the story is contradicted by another telegram. And now Gen McDowell [6] tells me that Com[modor]e. Foote [7] has made a reconnoisance [*sic*] in one of his boats, and finds a very strong fort there. Still, McDowell says that our affairs look bright and well—No certain news today from Nashville [8] or Savanna[h].[9]

I am anxious about Norfolk. The rumor is that we are about to attack Craney Island [10]—may be so, but I think if the attack is made at all, it will be a feint, to draw attention while we assail Suffolk.[11] Possibly it may be good policy to risk something in assailing Norfolk before the Merrimack is ready to make a desperate effort to escape.   ·

This afternoon, tho' very unwell, attended the funeral of Willie Lincoln—*Note.* The Depts. closed today on a/c of the funeral.

The morning was gusty, with several rain storms—cleared off in the afternoon, with very high wind. *Note.* Stepping out of my own door to speak to Klopfer,[12] with my loose gown on, I was laterally, blown away! Seised by the gust, I had to run before it, for fear of falling, till I caught hold of the boxing of a tree—then came my servant Tom [13] and helped me in.

---

[99] *Supra*, Nov. 20, 1861, note 59.

[1] *Supra*, Nov. 27, 1861, note 82.

[2] *Supra*, Jan. 28, 1860, note 38.

[3] *Supra*, April 27, 1859, note 27.

[4] See *supra*, Jan. 5, 1862, note 12.

[5] Columbus, Kentucky, was a Confederate stronghold and railroad terminus on the Mississippi, twelve miles below Cairo. The capture of Fort Henry on February 6 and of Fort Donelson on February 16 forced the evacuation of Columbus.

[6] *Supra*, Nov. 16, 1861, note 53.

[7] *Supra*, Feb. 17, 1862, note 77.

[8] Nashville fell February 26, 1862.

[9] *Supra*, Feb. 17, 1862, note 83.

[10] Near the mouth of the James River.

[11] A town about eighteen miles southwest of Norfolk on the Nansemond River. It controlled Norfolk's rail connections with the Confederacy.

[12] Henry A. Klopfer, head messenger in the Attorney-General's Office.

[13] Tom Hare who had come from Missouri with Mr. Bates.

Feb 25 Tuesday. C.[abinet] C[ouncil]. Quite a debate about the question of *parolling* [*sic*] prisoners—Genl. Wool [14] had been in conference with Genl. (Howell) Cobb [15] for an agreement to Exchange prisoners—and had authority also to agree *prospectively*, to *parol*[e] all prisoners *in excess* of exchange—Cobb insisted that *we* should send the parolled [*sic*] prisoners, at *our expense*, and deliver them at the *frontier* of the C. S. A.—Wool refused and so the negotiation was broken off, and Wool sent here for orders.

Mr. Seward and Mr. Blair thought that we were bound in honor to stand by the proposition, once made, to discharge future prisoners on parol[e], and Mr. Stanton seemed inclined the same way.

I insisted that we were under no obligation of honor, justice or even delicacy—that the proposition was wrong in itself and ought never to have been made, and that the negotiation being broken off by the absurd claim of Cobb, we ought not to renew it. Exchange prisoners actually taken, to be sure, but there is no propriety in binding ourselves before hand, to discharge future prisoners we may take, in excess of our men in the hands of the enemy. *We* expect to take many, and hope that *they* will take but *few*. *We* may have urgent occasion to keep some particular prisoners for future judgment. And when we have prisoners that we do not want to keep, we may, indulging a politic generosity, discharge them on our own terms.

Mr. Chase took the same grounds, substantially—Messrs. Welles and Smith assented, but said nothing in particular—and the Prest evidently concurred with us, having no faith that they wd. keep their parol[e].

Mr. Seward then yielded, and Mr. Stanton prepared an order to Genl. Wool accordingly.

Of late, Mr. Seward's deportment has been reserved and suspicious towards me. When he consults me at all, it seems as if it were done, rather with a desire to catch me in a difficulty, than to enlighten himself.

Lately, without my knowledge, he sent an order to the *Marshal* of the E.[astern] Dist of Pa. at Phil[adelphi]a., to remove the prisoners indicted of piracy (and one of them, Smith, convicted), being Southern privateers,—from *judicial* custody in *Phil*[*adelphi*]*a.* to the political prison at Fort Lafayette, N. Y.[16]

The first I heard of it was a letter from Mr. Ashton Asst Dist Atty informing me that upon the Ma[r]shal receiving the order, he, Ashton, caused the prisoners to be brot. up on Hab:[eas] Corp:[us]

14 John E. Wool had served in the Army since 1812 and had fought in the War of 1812, the War with Mexico, and Indian wars. He now commanded the Department of Virginia, but in 1863 he was retired because of advanced age.

15 *Supra*, Sept. 4, 1860, note 86.

16 See *supra*, Feb. 5, 1862.

and the Court—first asking them whether they were willing to be
transferred, and receiving an affirmative answer—ordered them to be
transferred! Mr. A.[shton] then asked my instructions whether
he should deliver to certain of the prisoners, their papers which
had been taken from them, and whether he should enter a nol: pros:
against them all.

I laid that letter before the President, stating that the proceeding
was very irregular, and that I declined to meddle in it, till better
informed. He sd. that he was sure Mr. S.[eward] did not intend
to impinge upon the duties of my office—that he wd. speak to him
&c.

For some time, the subject was not mentioned—hardly thought
of—on a/c of sickness and death in the Prest's family. But today,
after C.[abinet] C.[ouncil] I mentioned Mr. A[shton]'s letter to the
Prest, and expressed a wish to get it back, to be ansd. and filed, if he
was done with it. "Why,["] said he, ["]has not Mr. Seward talked
with you about it? He said, in the frankest manner possible, that
he would." I ansd. "No, he has never at any time, spoken to me
on the subject."

I thought the Prest. seemed surp[r]ised and mortified.

Feb 28. Friday. Sec: Chase, in C.[abinet] C.[ouncil] broached
the subject of licence to trade in seceded Territory, under the act of
Congress, and it seemed agreed that Chase's plan was good—beginning in the interior to see how the plan will work, before trying [it]
on the seaboard.

N. B. I left with the Prest. a note requesting to know whether
Woody [17] can or cannot go to West Point, because if not, I must send
him to school.

(*Note.* Some days afterwards, Mr. Nicolay,[18] the Prest's private
Sec.y. came to my office and said that the Prest. had to make an appointment of a *Cadet* for me, and asked the precise name—and got
[it], so, I feel pretty sure that Woodey will soon be apptd.)

Mar 3. I have just seen it stated in a paper to day that at the
organization of the new Congress of the C.[onfederate] S.[tates
of] A.[merica] *Thomas C. Johnson*, late of St Louis Mo., was run for
Clerk of the H[ouse] of R.[epresentatives] and beaten.

Bocock [19] of Va. was elected Speaker and *Hunter* [20] of Va. Prest:
pro: tem, of the Senate.

[17] Charles Woodson Bates, Mr. Bates's youngest child. See *supra*, "Introduction."
[18] John G. Nicolay: German-born publisher and editor of the (Pike County, Illinois)
Free Press; assistant to the Illinois secretary of State, 1856–1860; close friend of
Lincoln; private secretary to the President, 1861–1865; U. S. consul at Paris, 1865–1869;
editor of the *Chicago Republican;* marshal of the U. S. Supreme Court, 1872–1887;
historian of Lincoln.
[19] *Supra*, Jan. 13, 1860, note 23.
[20] *Supra*, Oct. 26, 1859, note 18.

Mar 7. In Supreme Court. The state of N. Y. has undertaken to tax the *Stocks* of the U. S. and the State Judiciary has affirmed the right. The case is now here, in the name of The People &c ex rel: B[an]k of the Commonwealth v The Tax Com[mis]s[ione]rs.[21] and I, at the request of the Relator and of the Secy of the Treasury, asked and obtained leave—to intervene.

March 11. tuesday, C.[abinet] C.[ouncil]. Sec.y. Stanton made a report (the very first thing we have had like a report) of the army, shewing great ignorance, negligence and lack of order and subordination—and reckless extravagance.

This report gives our first appro[a]ch to a knowledge of the number of men in govt employ—almost 700.000!!

The money part of the business has been shamefully managed—Requisitions come, for his signature, from the Q.[uarter] M.[aster] G[eneral]'s office—He signs, not doubting that the Q[uarter] M.[aster] G.[eneral] [22] can explain, but, on enquiry, finds that he too knows nothing about it.

The Secy. protested that he will not bear the responsibility, except his general share with the other members of the adm[inistratio]n.

That Genl. McClellan, assuming to be " General in Chief " has caused all reports to be made *to him,* and he reports nothing—and if he have any plans, keeps them to himself. I think Stanton believes, as I do, that McC.[lellan] has no plans but is fumbling and plunging in confusion and darkness.

I made a short speech, assuming my share of responsibility, which I said was little, considering the nature of my office, and, as heretofore urging the Prest. to take his constitutional position, and command the commanders—to have no " General in Chief "—or if he wd. have one, not allow him to be also a genl. *in detail* i. e. not command any particular army.[23]

The upshot was that McC.[lellan] being in the field, commanding the army of the Potomac, is relieved from being " Genl. in Chief " and all gens. commanding armies, [are ordered] to report directly to the Secy. of War.

Mar: 13. Several days ago McC.[lellan] took the field, with a mighty host, in Va. resolved to play the mischief with the great rebel army at Manassas.[24] He advanced cautiously " with fainting

[21] *The People of New York on the Relation of the Bank of the Commonwealth* v. *the Commissioners of Taxes for the City and County of New York.* 2 Black 620–635. The Supreme Court ruled that a state could not tax stocks or bonds of the United States even when held by a bank.

[22] Montgomery C. Meigs: *supra,* Dec. 31, 1861, note 68.

[23] See *supra,* Dec. 31, 1861, note 65; Jan. 10, 1862.

[24] The scene of two serious Union defeats: one on July 21, 1861, under McDowell (*supra,* Nov. 16, 1861, note 53); one on August 30, 1862, under Pope (*infra,* March 15, 1862, note 33).

steps and slow " from one deserted entrenchment to another—All was silent and desolate, with, here and there the smouldering ashes of burnt hay stacks and corn cribs—In short the enemy was gone, bag and baggage, big guns and all!

The adverse Genl. behaved impolitely: He did not send his card to Genl. Mc.[Clellan] P. P. C.[25] He did not even give public notice (as we commonly do) of his intended movement. It was very un-civil to treat our genl. so. If he had not relied upon the courtesy of the enemy to give him fair notice to quit, he certainly (with 200,-000 men at his back) would have taken some steps to find out the place and purpose of the enemy.

Upon the whole it seems as if our genl. went with his finger in his mouth, on a fool[']s errand, and that he has won a fool's reward.

> " For no man, sure, e'er left his house,
>   And saddled Ball with thoughts so wild,
>   To bring a midwife to his spouse,
>   Before he knew she was with child[.] "

But after all, the movement of the Grand Army of the Potomac was not wholly without results. It did actually capture one rebel captain and five privates—*Note*. This important fact I learn by a letter from McDowell to Chase.

[*Marginal Note.*] *Mar: 14.* Had a private talk with Secy. Chase. I reproached him kindly, for not backing me in urging the Prest. to use the authority of his place. He sd. the P.[resident] wd. do nothing till he had *a Sec: of War* that he had been working for 2. mos: to bring in *Stanton*, and when it was brot. about, his (C[hase]'s) hand was hardly seen in it.

Mar 15. McC.[lellan] contd. It was a great misfortune to Genl. McClellan[26] that he was made " Genl. in chief." If left in com-mand of a small army, probably he wd. have done good service and won an honorable name. Now, he is cast down, all the more notice-ably by the contrast with his late elevation. And scheming ultras at the north are now working to force the Prest. to deprive him of all comm[an]d. But, unless his imprudent friends betray him, he will be sustained, in his deminished [*sic*] position. I was opposed to his general control, and blamed him openly for several faults of omission and commission—for calling such a vast army here and

---

[25] A common abbreviation of the day for *pour prendre congé.*

[26] *Supra,* Oct. 22, 1861, note 17. By War Order No. 3 on March 11, 1862 (*Complete Works of Abraham Lincoln,* II, 137), Lincoln relieved McClellan from the position of general-in-chief, created three departments, and put Halleck in command of the Depart-ment of the Mississippi, Frémont in command of the Mountain Department, and McClellan in command of the Department of the Potomac to fight on against Richmond with no authority over the other departments.

making no use of it, but simply to guard this point—for permitting the blockade of the Potomac—for failing to protect the Potomac Canal and the Baltimore and Ohio R. R.

Mr. Stedman,[27] my Pardon clerk, is a warm friend [of] his—Some days ago he asked leave of absence, to go over and record "the forth coming battle." I told him he might go, but there would *be no battle*. He went and returned, deeply mortified; and today called on me and asked a conversation about the Genl. His purpose plainly was to deprecate my further opposition and, if might be, to excite my sympathy—He said that he had had a long talk with the Genl. but declared that he did not speak by his authority—I understood it—I assured him that I was neither the partizan nor the enemy of the Genl.—That as I had openly condemned certain things in him, I wd, as openly defend him against unjust assaults—But that he must remember that my influence in military affairs, is next to nothing.

Called on the Prest. and had a private talk. Warned him that extreme men in Congress were lying in wait agst. him, anxious to catch him in some error—and striving to *make precedents* against him, especially in regard to both the appointing and removing power—e. g. Ma[r]shal Laman's case,[28] and the pressure brought, to bear for the entire prostration of McClellan &c[.]

I warned him to stand firm on his present *rock* (as to the slavery question) and not yield an inch either to the fierce rush of the northern abolitionists or the timid doubters of the border slave states. I told him that nothing valuable was ever won, by timid submission—"You have taken your positions cautiously (said I), now maintain them bravely, and I will will [*sic*] sink or swim with you."

He answered me very kindly and frankly &c[.]

Mar 15. Coalter's Reg[imen]t [29]—11th. In[fan]t.[r]y., having marched over to Fairfax, and finding no enemy, was ordered to return to Alexandria today, and, as understood, is under marching orders down south, as part of McDowell's army—Destined, as I suppose, agst Norfolk and Richmond. McDowell [30]—I did not men-

---

[27] Edmund C. Stedman: poet; editor of the *Norwich Tribune* and *Winsted Herald* in Connecticut, 1852–1855; correspondent for the *New York World*, 1860–1862; now pardon clerk in the Department of Justice, 1863–1864. After 1864, he supported himself as a broker on the New York Stock Exchange while he wrote poetry.

[28] *Supra*, Dec. 6, 1861, note 12. On January 14, Senator Grimes attacked Lamon in a speech; on January 23, Senator Hale introduced and the Senate adopted a resolution of censure of Lamon for excluding senators from free access to the District jail; and on February 14, Hale demanded to know whether this resolution had been presented to Lincoln, and was informed that it had.

[29] His son, John Coalter Bates was a first lieutenant in the Army of the Potomac. See *supra*, July 5, 1861.

[30] *Supra*, Nov. 16, 1861, note 53.

tion in the proper place—was lately made a Maj: Genl. and put in command of Eastern Va.

. . .

Mar 15. Went to the Prest's to get the last news.

The telegrams from Halleck,[31] Foote[32] and Pope[33] are very satisfactory. Pope being in force at Mount Pleasant,[34] and Foote just starting down from Cairo with his Flotilla, the rebels precipitately evacuated New Madrid (Ft. Pillow.)[35] crossing the river as best they could, carrying, as Pope says, *their bodies*, lea[ving e]very thing behind—arms, artillery, transportation, immense stores of all sorts, the tents left standing. The booty must be very great for N.[ew] M.[adrid] was a depot for the adjacent posts. Genl. Schuyler Hamilton[36] is in command at N.[ew] M[adrid].

Foote left Cairo, at 7. a. m. yesterday, and now unless the enemy can stop him at *Randolph* (Chic[k]asaw Bluffs)[37] I know of no dangerous obstacle between him and N.[ew] O[rleans].

The enemy is really in a strait—If he move his iron boats up stream, to meet Foote, then he leaves the lower river open to Farragut[38] and Porter[39]—and [if] he send them down to meet the gulf force, then the coast is clear for Foote, and so, N.[ew] O.[rleans] must fall, an easy conquest.[40]

Mar 16. Sunday. In the forenoon, went over (with Dick) to and beyond Alexandria, in search of Coalters [*sic*] Reg[imen]t.

[31] *Supra,* Nov. 13, 1861, note 37.

[32] *Supra,* Feb. 17, 1862, note 77.

[33] John Pope, West Point graduate of 1842, who had served in Mexico and on exploring expeditions in the West, was summoned before a court martial in February, 1861, for a strong speech he had made against secession and Buchanan's weakness in failing to oppose it. Lincoln made him brigadier-general of volunteers and sent him to Missouri where he won fame at New Madrid and Island Number 10. After a disastrous defeat at the Second Battle of Bull Run, he was transferred to the Department of the Northwest.

[34] *Point* Pleasant was a village twelve miles below New Madrid. Pope occupied it on March 6.

[35] The fort at New Madrid was Fort Thompson, not Fort Pillow. The Confederates evacuated New Madrid and retired to Island Number 10, without a fight, on March 14.

[36] A West Point graduate of 1841 who served in the Mexican War, then resigned to manage a California mine, and reëntered the Army as a volunteer private. He soon became aide to General Scott and then assistant chief-of-staff under his brother-in-law, General Halleck. He won distinction at both Island Number 10 and New Madrid.

[37] Randolph was a village on Chickasaw Bluffs about thirty miles north of Memphis, Tennessee. Fort Pillow which commanded the river from the bluffs north of Memphis fell to a Union force on June 5, 1862.

[38] David G. Farragut: veteran of the War of 1812; resident of Norfolk at the outbreak of the Civil War until his loyalty to the Union forced him to move his family north; commander of the expedition to New Orleans, 1862; rear-admiral in 1862; captor of Mobile in 1863; admiral in 1866.

[39] David D. Porter: son and grandson of American naval officers; veteran of West Indies sailing and the Mexican Navy; officer in the U. S. Navy since 1829; savior of Fort Pickens to the Union, 1861; a commander in the New Orleans expedition of 1862; captor of Vicksburg in 1863, and of Fort Fisher which commanded Wilmington, North Carolina, in 1865.

[40] The New Orleans forts and fleet fell before the attacks of Farragut and Porter on April 18-28, 1862; the city was occupied May 1.

11th. Inf.y. Regt.—found them 3 or 4 miles out, on the Fairfax road.
Through the hard rains of saturday, many thousands of our troops
marched, from the various posts around, upon Alex[andri]a. and the
neighborhood.

The country is stripped of its timber and I saw many reg[imen]ts
—horse, foot and artillery—bavouacked [*sic*] in the muddy open
fields, without tents, and apparently, poorly supplied with food—we
took some small supply of food to Coalter's mess—found them cheerful and well, and anxious for marching orders down south.

There are many transports lying in the river, and I suppose
McDowell's[41] *corps d'armee* will soon be in the region of Norfolk.

√ *Mar 17.*   Attend S.[upreme] C.[ourt] to day. *Ch:[ief] J.[ustice]*
Taney is this day 86 years old—He delivered one or two opinions,
and seemed as alert as usual.

Note.   At the time of the adjournment of the S.[upreme] C.[ourt]
Monday 24. March, C.[hief] J.[ustice] Taney requested, the judges,
severally, to call to see him at his house before they le[f]t the city.
H[e] took an affectionate leave of each one, and told several of them,
especially Nelson,[42] that he did not expect to see them again.   That he
had a pre sentiment that he should die very soon.   Nelson dont [*sic*]
think he will live many weeks.[43]

Of course, there is a good deal of speculation about his successor,
but I have heard no man named, as likely to get the place[.]

Note.   The Nat[iona]l. Intelligencer contains, to day,[44] a letter of
Yulee[45] to one Finigan,[46] found lately at Fernandina [Florida,]
dated Jany [7]/61, disclosing the form of the conspiracy of senators
and others, to dissolve the union—and the resolutions passed by the
conspirators, in caucus, in Jany 1861[.]

That treacherous jew, *Yulee*, has, for months back, been trying
to " ly [*sic*] low and keep dark[.] "   But this letter, if it be genuine,
spoils his disguise.   It was found at Fernandina when our troops
took the place lately.

The same paper contains Gen'l. McClellans [*sic*] address to the
army, at Fairfax.

Also a touching a/c of how poor John Letcher,[47] Gov of Va., gits
[*sic*] it on both sides[.]

[41] *Supra*, Nov. 16, 1861, note 53.

[42] *Supra*, March 6, 1861, note 32.

[43] He did live until October 12, 1864, and retained his place on the bench until his death.

[44] Still March 17.

[45] David L. Yulee né David Levy: Hebrew born at St. Thomas in the West Indies;
lawyer in St. Augustine, Florida; delegate to Congress, 1841–1845; U. S. senator, 1845–
1851, 1855–1861; Confederate congressman, 1861–1865.

[46] Joseph Finegan, a leader of secession in Florida; Confederate brigadier-general in
command of the Department of Middle and East Florida.

[47] *Supra*, April 28, 1859, note 41.

Note. When over the river, sunday, I predicted, in conversation with some young officers, that leading officers of the rebels, who had any fortune, would soon be found slipping off to foreign countries. Thereupon Lieut. Gray of the 11th. Inf[an]try. regls. (son of Capt. Tom Gray, late of St Louis) said that Jeff Davis had a beautiful place *right opposite* Bourdeau[*sic*], France, which he purchased 6 mos: ago [48]—I did not ask his means of knowledge.

Mar: 22. At night I called upon Judge Swayne [49] expecting to salute him and stay a few minutes. The judge seemed very cordial and kept me till near midnight—

He told me i. a. that Judge Black [50] told him that there [are] persons authorised by the Confederate leaders to propose terms of accom[m]odation. On a doubt being suggested by S.[wayne] B.[lack] said with emphasis, " I *know* it—I *know it*—and they would be glad of any [terms] they would gladly accept any terms [*sic*] that would ensure their safety ["]—i. e. personal security agst: future consequences.

Mar: 26. To day, at my office—and tonight at my house, again had long talk, with Judge S.[wayne] about the filling of the va[ca]nt seats on the Sup[rem]e. bench. He thinks that a very strenuous effort is making to get C. B. Smith [51] appointed, and that the effort is almost crowned with success—That there is a bill pending to gerrymander the Circuits to suit—so as to give Smith a circuit without interferring [*sic*] with Browning [52]—nobody it [I] think objects to Browning—He is a proper man [53]—

Note[.] I have warned the Prest to be on his guard.

March 30. Sunday. Yesterday was bad weather . . . The rain still continues—11. a. m—

There has been a great movement of troops the last two days, either for embarkation down the river, or for the Va. side, to supply the places of those lately gone south.

[*A clipping from the* Missouri Democrat *of March 26, 1862, headed* " *Uriel Wright & Co. Gone to the Rebel Army—Startling Rumor.*"]

I read this morning in the Mo. Dem[ocra]t. of St Louis, a strange paragraph abt *Uriel Wright,*[54] to the effect that he, his son Jo and

[48] This was groundless rumor.

[49] Noah H. Swayne: a Virginian whose dislike of slavery sent him to Ohio; U. S. district attorney, 1831–1841; counsel for fugitive slaves; early convert to Republicanism; justice of the U. S. Supreme Court, 1862–1881.

[50] *Supra*, Oct. 28, 1859, note 22.

[51] The Secretary of the Interior; *supra*, March 5, 1861, note 28.

[52] *Supra*, Sept. 21, 1859, note 97.

[53] Neither Smith nor Browning was ever appointed.

[54] *Supra*, June 4, 1859, note 72. He had been a strong Union man until the capture of Camp Jackson (May 10, 1861), which he considered unjust, led him to join the Confederate Army.

other friends had fled to the rebel army. The a/c went on to state that after W.[right] and friends had been seen near Fenton, near Franklin station, the body of a man had been found in the woods, hanging, dead, upon a tree—and that it had been identified as U.[riel] Wright—The story is contradicted in the same article, to the extent at least at least [*sic*] of W[right]'s death—It is said that W[right]'s party is safe.

Apl. 2d. Wednesday night called on the Prest for leave of absence to take Woody[55] to Newburg[h].

Also to intercede to have Van Alen[56] made a Brigadier[.] (note[.] he was nominated next day[.])

Also, to ask the Prest to *give me* two Va. boys (prisoners of war at Camp Douglas Ills—taken at Fort Donelson) John Morris Jr and John. H. Pleasants [Jr.,] of Goochland Co. Va.[57]—

The Prest. gave them to me at once, by an autograph order, for them to be disposed of as I should prescribe—I sent the order immediately, with a letter to the officer in command of Camp Douglas, and another to the two young men.

Apl. 4. Friday night. At the Metropolitan Hotel N.[ew] Y[ork].

Yesterday, at 6. a. m. left Washington to take Woody to Dr. Sprole, at Newburg, for instruction preparatory to his entering, as a cadet, at West point. Got here last night, went up this morning, arriving at Newburg[h] at 9.30—remained several hours, and returned here at 5.

Dr. S.[prole] introduced me to several gentlemen—Dr. Deo—Mr. Harwell—Mr. George, Judge Taylor—and Mr. St John whom I had known before[—]also Revd. Mr. [   ]

Yesterday, in the cars, between Balt[imor]e. and Phila.[delphia] met C. K. Garrison,[58] who talked very freely on various subjects—i. a. he defended Genl. Stone[59] very warmly—Talking of Senator Baker,[60] he denounced him bitterly, as a liar and thief utterly destitute of principle, told of several of his rascalities in California, and declared that since he came on as senator he proposed this bargain—that he, Baker, being very intimate with the Prest and several members of the cabinet, would constantly keep him, Garrison, advised of the

[55] His youngest son whom Lincoln had appointed to West Point.

[56] *Supra*, Feb. 4, 1860, note 62.

[57] Both were sons of boyhood Virginia friends of Mr. Bates. Mrs. Bates was related to the Pleasants family. For young Pleasant's father see *infra*, April 17, 1862, note 2.

[58] Cornelius K. Garrison: general manager of the Upper Canada (public works) Company, 1828–1833; St. Louis operator of passenger and freight service on the Mississippi, 1833–1849; banker in Panama, 1849–1853; manager of the Nicaragua Steamship Company; banker and reform mayor of San Francisco, 1853–1859; now foreign shipping and railroad magnate of New York City, 1859–1885.

[59] *Supra*, Oct. 22, 1861, note 19; Nov. 1, 1861, note 28.

[60] *Supra*, Oct. 12, 1859, note 9.

secret measures and purposes of the Govt. if Garrison would furnish him with a good house in Washington, and $10.000 a year to live
upon, B.[aker] affirming that G.[arrison] cd. make any amt of
money in speculations based upon the knowledge so acquired.
G.[arrison] say[s] he refused the offer, but that B.[aker] persisted,
and referred it, in direct terms to his, G[arrison]'s confidential
business agent!

Note—the tale looks incredible—yet I think Baker was not a whit
too honest to make such a proposition—and I incline to think that
G.[arrison] would not have declined it, if he thought there was much
money in it.

Dr. Sprole has a wife and two daug[h]ters (very pleasant people I
think) a son a lieutenant in the army, and another a boy.

The Dr. said his course with Woody would be to prepare him as
well as he can upon the first six months['] course at the Point.

I made no special agreement but handed him $50. to begin with.

Apl. 6[5] Saturday. I [saw] very few persons that I knew in
N.[ew] Y[ork]—recd. a few cards—sent notes to Judge Betts [61] and
Dr. Lieber [62]—The morning gusty and dusty—then it rained till I
left at 4. p. m for Phila[delphia].--[Sunday, April 6.] Lodged at
the continental hotel—staid over the sabbath—Heard Dr. Barnes
preach a (rather cloudy) sermon on election, predestination, free
will &c[.]

[*April 6.*] Went to see Geo. A. Coffey, [63] after church, but missed
him—saw Mrs. T. J. Coffey[.] [64]

Dined with Mr. Hazelhurst and family, at the *table d'hote*.

[*Later April 6.*] I go home early in the morning.

[*Monday, April 7.*] Finding that no train wd. leave early on
monday, I took the 11 oclock train sunday night and go[t] home
before 7 in the morning—all well.

Apl 8. Tuesday. In C.[abinet] C.[ouncil] Official telegrams arrived while we were in session, that Island No. 10 had surrendered,
and the forts on the main[land] had been hastily evacuated.

[61] Samuel R. Betts: Democratic congressman, 1815–1817; New York circuit judge,
1823–1826; U. S. district judge, 1826–1867; authority on maritime law.

[62] Francis Lieber: economist, political scientist, prolific writer; German revolutionist
who, when forced to leave Germany, migrated to America in 1827; editor of the
Encyclopaedia Americana, 1829–1833; professor of history and political economy at the
University of South Carolina, 1835–1856, and at Columbia College, 1856–1872. In South
Carolina before the Civil War he had warned against secession. During the War his
advice was often sought by Federal Government officials.

[63] Philadelphia lawyer; abolitionist; organizer of the state Republican Party; delegate
to the Chicago Convention of 1860; U. S. district attorney for Eastern Pennsylvania.
1861–1864.

[64] *Supra*, March 5, 1860, note 18.

The two gun boats that so boldly ran the gauntlet of all the forts and got below them, enabled Genl. Pope [65] to cross the river from New Madrid, in face of the enemy, and and [sic] so be r[e]ady to assail the forts in [the] rear. Hence the hasty evacuation, before Pope could surround and bag them.

We are in hourly expectation of news from Grant and Bouregard [66] [sic]—also from Burnside [67] and from Hunter [68] on the southern coast—and especially from Farrigut [sic] and Butler near N. Orleans.[69]

Sec.y. Smith told me today that the N. Y. World [70] had published an atrocious libel on him—that he designed to prosecute with all vigor, and had retained Everts [71] [sic] for that purpose—He said that he had traced the thing up and found that Stedman [72] had carried to the Telegraph office a written despatch (with another man's name to it) identical with the libel. He asked me on whose recommendation I had appointed S[tedman]. I told him Van Alen's [73]—and I promised him that I wd. investigate the matter and do what was right—dismiss the clerk if I found him in fault[.]

Stedman explains the affair in entire consistence with his innocence, and says he will explain it personally, to Mr. Smith.

Apl. 9. Stedman tells me this morning, that he had a long explanation with Mr. Smith, he thinks satisfactory—in which he distinctly said to Mr. S.[mith] that he wd. vacate his place instantly, if Mr. S.[mith] desired it. Judging from what Mr. Smith said to me as well as to Stedman, I am sure that his object was, less to injure Stedman than to get information out of him to implicate others.

Apl. 9. Last night we had the rumor, and today the certain news of the most terrible battle of the war, fought near Pittsburg Landing

---

[65] *Supra,* March 15, 1862, note 33.

[66] Pierre G. T. Beauregard of Louisiana: West Point graduate of 1838; Mexican War veteran; officer of the engineering corps, 1838–1861; Confederate general who gave the order to fire on Sumter in 1861; second in command under Joseph E. Johnston in Virginia, 1861; A. S. Johnston's second in command at Shiloh where he took command when Johnston was killed; defender of Charleston, 1862–1864; opponent of Butler on the James, 1864, and Sherman in Georgia, 1864–1865.

[67] *Supra,* Nov. 29, 1861, note 97. He was busy attacking and capturing Beaufort and Fort Macon, south of Pamlico Sound, while Goldsborough took all that was left of the Confederate North Carolina fleet.

[68] *Supra,* Oct. 22, 1861, note 21. He had just succeeded Gen. T. W. Sherman at Port Royal in South Carolina and was in command of the Department of the South.

[69] *Supra,* March 15, 1862, note 40. Farragut and Butler were preparing for the attack on New Orleans.

[70] "Trouble in the Department of the Interior," April 2, 1862.

[71] William M. Evarts: noted lawyer; U. S. district attorney in New York, 1849–1853; chairman of the New York delegation to the Republican Convention of 1860; U. S. attorney-general, 1868–1869; secretary of State, 1877–1881; Republican U. S. senator, 1885–1891; counsel for Johnson in the impeachment proceedings in 1868, for President Hays before the Electoral Commission in 1877, and for the U. S. before the Geneva Arbitration Tribunal on the *Alabama* Claims in 1872.

[72] *Supra,* March 15, 1862, note 27.

[73] *Supra,* Feb. 4, 1860, note 62.

on the Tennessee—Genl. Grant commanding on our side, and Bouregard [74] and A. S. Johns[t]on [75] on the side of the Rebels—The fight
lasted two days—sunday and monday—[the] 6th. and 7th. of Apl.—
and was desperate and pertinacious on both sides. The first day,
the enemy had the advantage—drove us in towards the river and
occupied more than half our camp—both armies (the battle ceasing
for the night) slept on their arms in rain and mud, in the open field.
During the night, a large re-enforcement of Buell's [76] army came up,
and in the morning the battle was renewed and lasted all day—It
was not until 5. p. m. that the enemy gave way—Soon the retreat
became a rout, the enemy fleeing in great disorder, Buell's cavalry
pursuing even to Corinth.[77]

We have lost a great many valuable officers, and doubtless the
enemy has suffered as much or more. It seems to be certain that
their Genl. A. S. Johns[t]on [78] is killed and it is confidently said
that Bouregard [79] [sic] is, if not killed, put *hors du combat*, by having
an arm shot off.

Apl. 9. This great victory, following to [so] rapidly the capture
of Island No. 10, with all its armaments and munitions, must break
the heart of the rebellion. And, followed up, with speed and energy,
as doubtless it will be, will I hope, speedily lead to a general submission of the people in the revolted states. Still, the remnants of
the defeated armies, composed of men, now feeling that they are
outcasts and desperados, will, I fear, plunder and devastate large
portions of the southern country.

Genl. Halleck [80] as soon as he got news of the battle left St Louis,
in all haste, for the seat of war, and, with Pope's [81] and Buell's
armies, added to Grant's, will, no doubt, be able to extinguish the
rebel army in the Southwest. And this especially, if the Flotilla
promptly go down the river, sweeping away all obstructions.

After all this, N. Orleans will, I hope, will [sic] surrender, without a useless waste of blood.

Poor McClellan! [82] I really fear that he will fizzle down into
acknowledged impotence. He has an army now of more than 100.000,

[74] *Supra,* April 8, 1862, note 66.

[75] *Supra,* Dec. 31, 1861, note 60.

[76] *Supra,* Dec. 31, 1861. note 62. Buell's arrival turned a probable defeat into a great victory.

[77] Corinth was a strategically important Mississippi town at the junction of the Mobile and Ohio and the Memphis and Charleston railways, not far from Pittsburg Landing on the Tennessee River. It was evacuated on May 29-30, 1862,—finally abandoned without a battle.

[78] He *was* killed in this battle, April 6, 1862.

[79] This was a mistaken rumor.

[80] *Supra,* Nov. 13, 1861, note 37.

[81] *Supra,* March 15, 1862, note 33. Pope had taken New Madrid on March 14, and on April 7 had occupied Island Number 10 from which Foote's gunboats had driven the enemy. He was now ordered to join Halleck.

[82] On April 5, McClellan had landed at Yorktown to begin his "Peninsular Campaign."

in Eastern Va. and still he asks for more! because the enemy batteries
are stronger than he expected—I hear that the sec of War answered
him—"You were sent on purpose to take strong batteries." He has
a large force of cavalry for which he has no use and great difficulty
in getting supplies, in the narrow peninsulas (between James and
York rivers) in which he has chosen to act.

Of course, he can and *must* take both Richmond and Norfolk, but
I think he has committed a blunder, fatal to his reputation, in attempting to conquer those cities by approaching Rich[mon]d.
through that narrow peninsula. The enemy forces there do but
harmlessly hold their position so long as we command the water and
operate elsewhere. Whereas, if, at great cost of blood and money,
we take fort after fort, we drive them up to Richmond, or to their
army about Gordonsville,[83] we leave them a free passage south and
west.

If Gen McClellan wd. only (leaving ½ his army to hold the enemy
in check on James and York rivers) would [*sic*] send the other half
on the South side of James River, block Norfolk and ma[r]ch upon
Richmond, via Petersburg, the least defencible [*sic*] side,[84] Richmond
would be easily taken with all i[t]s men and munition, and the
hostile forces in the two peninsulas would be bagged and helpless,
and they and Norfolk would inevitably drop into our hand, without
the necessary use of fire or sword. But—"Quem Deus vult perdere,
prius dementat." [85]

I do believe that the Genl. has such a morbid ambition of originality that he will adopt no plan of action suggested by another—
He must himself *invent* as well as execute every scheme of operations. And yet it seems to me that he has but small inventive
faculty—Hence his inevitable failure.

Apl. 11. (McClellan contd.) I hear today that the enemy is
very strong in front of McC[lellan]—say 100.000—with many powerful batteries, and now by continued rains, the roads are impassible.
There is great ground to fear that we will be foiled if not defeated.
Now is the time—the enemy having drawn so many of his forces
into the peninsula—to cross James river, block or take Norfolk,
and march upon Richmond[.]

Last night I heard from Mr. Eames [86] that there is a current rumor
that Mr. Seward is going to *Corinth*,[87] and that his object is to propose terms of settlement with the rebels! I denied it, as absurd.

[83] A town southwest of Fredericksburg, between Orange and Charlottsville.

[84] I. e., the southern side. Petersburg is twenty-two miles due south from Richmond.

[85] "Quem Deus perdere volt . . . "—a late Latin translation of a lost line of Greek
tragedy.

[86] *Supra*, Jan. 13, 1862, note 30.

[87] The actual seat of the War in the West: *supra*, April 9, 1862, note 77.

But this morning the papers announce that Mr. S.[eward] is *gone to Corinth!*—the purpose not disclosed.

After mid day I hear another story, that Mr. S.[eward] is not gone West, but joins the excursion in the Revenue Cutter this afternoon and will probably go down to Old Point.

It was all a false report—He did not go[.]

At the War office today.

Apl. 14. C.[abinet] C.[ouncil] called specially today, to consider of a proposition to establish a *military govt.* over the *sea islands!!* [88] It seems that it is an abolition contrivance, to begin the establishment of a negro country along that coast. After a little conversation, Stanton, in a few words, shewed it up, and it was agreed to leave the whole matter to the War Dept.

Today, John Morris Jr. and Jno. H. Pleasants, the two young prisoners of war, given to me by the Prest., arrived here.[89] They came to Baltimore under Col Mulligan's [90] safe conduct, but were not allowed to pass down to Fortress Monroe, on their way home. So, they came here to see me, hoping still to get through. I mentioned their case to the Prest. He desired to see them—I took them to his presence, and had a short interview—kind and pleasant. The Prest. told them that he was glad to see them, as *friends of his friend Mr. Bates.*

I then called on Sec.y. Stanton, who said he wd. do any thing to oblige me, but that *at this moment,* he could not give passes to cross our lines. As they must be detained awhile, I invited them to come and stay privately at my house. They are here.

[*Note.*] In the afternoon of the 15th. they went to Balt[imor]e. being invited to stay at Dr. Thomas'—Dr. John Hanson Thomas [91] married the sister of that Mr. Gordon who married the daughter of Hampden Pleasants,[92] and hence the friendly relations. Note. Dr. T.[homas] is *sesesh* [*sic*], and has lately returned, on parole, from Ft. Warren.[93]

Apl. 14. Until now, Julian holds his house and lot in Florissant,[94] by lease only, but now that Coalter is provided for in the army and Woody is about to enter as a West Point Cadet, we (wife and I) determined to convey him the full title.

---

[88] The islands along the coast of South Carolina.

[89] *Supra,* April 2, 1862.

[90] James A. Mulligan: former editor of the Catholic (Chicago) *Western Tablet;* clerk in the Department of the Interior, 1857–1861; now colonel of the Twenty-Third Illinois Regiment, in command of Camp Douglas in Chicago.

[91] Thomas was sent to the Maryland Legislature by a special election in Baltimore on April 24, 1861, in which only one ticket—all secessionists—was put up. On September 12, 1861, he was arrested and, for a time, confined in Fort McHenry.

[92] The Pleasants family were Virginia relatives of Mrs. Bates.

[93] On George's Island in Boston Harbor.

[94] *Supra,* May 18, 1859, note 52.

Accordingly, we send him the deed, dated *April 11. 1862*. Matilda will take it. She is going out on a visit, with Mr. Gibson's[95] family, expecting to join them tomorrow night, in Baltimore[.]

Apl. 15. Matilda left, by the evening train for Baltimore, to join Mr. Gibson's family en route to St Louis—Mr. Gibson and Dick in co.[mpany]—(also, *my prisoners*, Morris and Pleasants as far as Baltimore)[.]

Matilda took but little money, only some $20 for pocket money. Gibson meant to take her to Mo. and back again, as his guest and at his expense, but I refused, and it was agreed that at his return, he wd. state the amt. and I should pay it then.

I shall send a check to Barton on the Boatmen's[96] for money to supply all her wants. (sent Apl 16.) for my bal:[ance], *in blank, to be filled by him when ascertained*, on the Boatmen's[.]

Apl. 17. Thursday. The Nat[iona]l. Intel[ligence]r. to day, contains a long editorial, headed " Political Interpolation " treating of some important constitutional questions—advancing, substantially, my old doctrine that there is no such thing as a Cabinet. It is justly sharp upon the careless and abusive use of the power to arrest &c[.]

The article begins by referring to the case of Genl. Stone,[97] and Senator McDougall's speech[98] thereon. In the course of the article, the editor quotes Sec.y. Seward's letter to L[or]d. Lyons[99] for the presumption that the acts of the heads of Depts. act [are] by authority of the Prest. <that is true, in so far as the act is appropriate to the office> and my letter to Marshal McDowell[1] of Kansas (23d. July, 61) to shew that the Prest must execute *all* the laws, and not a part only[.]

It cites MacCauley [Thomas B. Macaulay] at large to shew that in England, the *Cabinet* was not *made* but *grew*.

<see my letter to Jno. H. Pleasants,[2] in 1841>

Apl. 21. Monday night—Immense quantities of rain . . .

This, not only retards the armies in their movements, but must cause much sickness[.]

---

[95] *Supra*, April 27, 1859, note 27.

[96] The Boatmen's Savings Institution of St. Louis.

[97] *Supra*, Oct. 22, 1861, note 19 ; Nov. 1, 1861, note 28.

[98] James A. McDougall : attorney-general of Illinois, 1842–1846, of California, 1850–1851 ; Democratic congressman from California, 1853–1855 ; U. S. senator, 1861–1867 ; a " War Democrat " who supported Lincoln during the War and Johnson in Reconstruction. For this speech see April 15, 1862, *Cong. Globe*, 37 Cong., 2 Sess., 1662–1666.

[99] *Supra*, Sept. 26, 1860, note 24.

[1] James L. McDowell ; free-state leader of Leavenworth ; legislator ; mayor ; U. S. marshal, 1861–1864 ; major-general of militia charged with protecting Kansas against Confederate raids from Missouri.

[2] A boyhood friend of Edward Bates in Goochland County, Virginia ; founder and editor of the *Richmond Whig*, 1824–1841, and of the *Washington Independent*, 1841–1846. He was killed in a duel with Thomas Richie, Jr., of the *Richmond Enquirer* who had published a statement that Pleasants was about to found an abolitionist paper.

Today a letter came from Coalter to his mother. He is now in comfortable camp, in close proximity to the enemy—2½ miles from Yorktown and 1. mile from the nearest hostile battery—He is now in command of a Company (E. 11th. Inf[an]t.[r]y.) tho' only Lieut[enant] Com.[mand]er. and thinks himself fortunate in getting a Captain's command at the moment when hard fighting is expected.

Recently several actions have been brought against ministers, for seizure of persons and property i. a., agst Sec.y. Welles for refusing to give up money seised from certain gamblers, who had won it from one Galleher[?], a paymaster in the Navy—and agst ex Sec.y. Cameron for arresting Pierce Butler[3] and sending [him] to Ft. Lafayette[.] [4]

The circumstance created much talk and some excitement in the Cabinet. The Prest was a good deal stirred up, last friday, and talked about arresting the attornies. I suggested the propriety of getting congress to pass an act to regulate such actions—and Mr. Seward proposed that I should draw a bill—I have done so and shewed it to the Prest to Messrs. Chase, Blair and the Prest. [sic.] It is now in the hands of Mr. Seward, for criticism and suggestion[.]

note 22d. Apl. dellivered [sic] the draft to Senator Wade,[5] at Mr. Seward's suggestion[.]

Apl. 22. Judge Black[6] dined with me today. Talked very freely about the latter weeks of Buchanan's adm[inistratio]n. Cobb,[7] Floyd,[8] Thompson[9] &c[.] Thinks "Jake Thompson" as *honest* a man as he ever knew—Was very slow to believe in F[loyd]'s rascality but had finally to come to it.

Prest. B.[uchanan] said he would rather suffer death by torture than suffer S.[outh] C.[arolina] to take the Forts in Charleston harbor—and ordered them to be supplied—Floyd *pretended* to agree to it, but did not do it.

Trescott[10] (Asst. Secy of state) gave information that Floyd had promised the Carolinians that it should no[t] be done. B.[uchanan]

[3] Pierce Butler—son of Dr. James Mease of Philadelphia ; grandson of Pierce Butler, framer of the Constitution and U. S. senator (1789–1796, 1803–1804) from South Carolina—had taken his mother's family name. He was best known as the very wealthy divorced husband of Fanny Kemble, the actress. Though he lived in Philadelphia, he had large plantations in Georgia and was thoroughly Southern in his sympathies. In the spring of 1861 he made a trip to Georgia, and, on his return in August, was imprisoned for treason on the charge of arranging shipments of arms to the Confederacy.

[4] Near the middle of " the Narrows " entrance to New York Harbor.

[5] *Supra*, Aug. 10, 1859, note 77.

[6] *Supra*, Oct. 28, 1859, note 22.

[7] *Supra*, Sept. 4, 1860, note 86.

[8] *Supra*, Dec. 3, 1859, note 11.

[9] Jacob Thompson of Mississippi : Democratic congressman, 1839–1851 ; secretary of the Interior, 1857–1861 ; governor of Mississippi, 1862–1864 ; inspector-general of the Confederate Army, 1864 ; confidential agent in Canada, 1864–1865.

[10] William H. Trescot of Charleston, South Carolina : secretary of Legation in London, 1852–1860 ; assistant secretary of State, 1860–1861 ; member of the South Carolina Legislature ; officer in the Confederate Army ; holder of various minor diplomatic posts, 1876–1889.

insisted, F.[loyd] flew into arage [*sic*] and spoke violently and went out in a huff. The Prest then asked Black to go and tell F.[loyd] that he *must resign*. He, Black, refused—Then some other, Toucey,[11] bore the message, and F.[loyd] *resigned* giving for reason, that he could, no longer, *consistently with his honor*, serve with such an adm[inistratio]n.! Mr. Black agreed with me that old Buck ought to have kicked him out—Black call[e]d it "*spitting in the Prest's face and then resigning*[.] " Still the Prest. did not strengthen the Forts, and sunk [*sic*] so low as to assign the reason that he had given the Carolinians reason to think that he wd. not,[12] and because he feared that war wd. come *in his time*, if he did—

At night at Senator Wade's[13] met i. a. Mr. Gurley[14] of Ohio, who is proud of a speech he made some time ago denouncing Genl. McClellan's tardiness. The speech, it seems, has been printed both in England and France, and (as Mr. G[urley] thinks) had great influence in preventing the Govts. both of England and France from acknowledging the C.[onfederate] S.[tates of] A[merica].

Mr. G.[urley] is very open in denouncing Genl. McClellan, believes him a traitor and that he will continue to have his own army beaten, if possible—Says that just before his appointment to command he declared, in presence of his Physician (Dr. [   ]—the famous Homeopath) that the South was right and he wd. never fight against it—that the Southern Democracy had always governed the country and ought to govern it[.] Gu[r]ley evidently believe[s] him a *traitor*[.]

[*Note.*] Apl 29. <Since then, I am better acquainted with G.[urley] and talked freely. He talks with imprudent freedom, but I think honest indignation—Wade is more guarded in his talk, but evidently approves G[urley]'s opinions. I cannot concur in believing McC.[lellan] a traitor. With more charity I conclude that he is only a foolish egot. Within the last few days I have written to Barton Bates and Gen Van Alen,[15] not using those hard words, but to that purpose[.]>

Apl 28. Today the news comes that we have taken N. Orleans, but not authentic and without particulars[.][16]

---

[11] Isaac Toucey of Hartford, Connecticut; Democratic congressman, 1835–1839; governor of Connecticut, 1847; U. S. attorney-general, 1848–1849; U. S. senator, 1852–1857; secretary of the Navy under Buchanan, 1857–1861.

[12] On December 8 and 10, 1860, Buchanan had had two interviews with McQueen, Miles, and Bonham, representatives of South Carolina, in which they had assured him that Sumter would not be fired upon so long as Buchanan did not alter the *status quo*. The President apparently promised nothing, but none the less regarded this interview as creating a tacit understanding between him and the South Carolinians.

[13] *Supra*, Aug. 10, 1859, note 77.

[14] John A. Gurley: Universalist minister, 1835–1838; editor of the *Cincinnati Star and Sentinel* later called the *Star in the West*, 1838–1854; now a Republican congressman, 1859–1863, who was defeated for reëlection in 1862.

[15] *Supra*, Feb. 4, 1860, note 62.

[16] The Union fleet entered the Mississippi, ran the forts, and destroyed the Confederate fleet. On April 28 the last of the forts surrendered. On May 1 General Butler's troops occupied the city.

<Since then, the fact has been fully confirmed, and many particulars given, but not fully relied on, as the a/cs all come through rebel channels—There was no fighting. Genl. Lovel[l] [17] retreated with his army, taking what valuables he could and destroying much property[.]>

From the Balto: Sun April 10. 1862.

["PARDON DECLINED.—The pardon which President Lincoln has given to the Rev. Geo. Gordon,[18] now in the county jail at Cleveland, Ohio, states that Gordon was legally convicted of violating the fugitive slave law, but that, owing to his piety, learning and reverend calling, and the fact that he is sufficiently punished, he is unconditionally pardoned. The Cleveland Gazette says that when the document was handed to Gordon, he objected to the passage stating that he was 'legally convicted,' and declared that, if the point is pressed, he will positively decline the pardon. His purpose is said to be to use his own case in testing the constitutionality of the fugitive slave act."]

May, 1862. When the matter was brot. to my notice by a friend of the convict, and I was asked to recal[l] the pardon, or "do something in the business," I ansd. that the case was no longer in my office: That if Mr. Gordon had such a prurient desire for martyrdom, he must really, do the burning himself, for the President wd. not singe another hair of his whiskers: and that, I presumed, the keeper of the prison would turn him out, on view of the Prest.'s warrant of pardon; or at least require him to pay for his board and lodging, if he would insist upon remaining in the prison, as an *unpardoned convict.* I think that the Revd. G.[eorge] G.[ordon] must have evaporated, for I never heard of him since.

[signed] *E. B.* [19]

May 6. tuesday. Since last date, some great events have happened—and are now pressing to a conclusion. Gen McClellan (having chosen, as I think, very unwisely, to march upon Richmond through the peninsula) has done well in that mistaken course. Investing Yorktown, he made his works so perfect and his approaches so sure, as [to] force the enemy to evacuate and retreat without fighting. It is said (Gen Van Alen [20] telegraphs me so) that Davis came in person to Yorktown, and upon inspection of our works, and by advice of all his Generals except McGruder,[21] ordered evacuation.

---

[17] Mansfield Lovell, West Point graduate of 1842, had resigned in 1854 to enter business in New York City. When the War came, he went south, and now as a Confederate major-general, commanded at New Orleans. He succeeded in evacuating his troops and supplies and in retiring to Vicksburg.

[18] *Supra,* Feb. 5, 1862, note 50.

[19] Both clipping and comment are upon a sheet of paper pasted into the diary.

[20] *Supra,* Feb. 4, 1860, note 62.

[21] John B. Magruder, West Point graduate of 1830, had served in Mexico and on the Atlantic Coast. When Virginia seceded, he entered the Confederate Army, was commissioned a brigadier-general, fought on the Peninsula in 1861–1862, and commanded the District of Texas, 1862–1864.

Probably this order was given on thursday May 2d., and that the backward movement of troops and necessary munition, commenced immediately. But on saturday the 4th. and the night preceding, the town and forts were abandoned, leaving behind an immense quantity of heavy ordnance, ammunition and other stores generally. The enemy was hotly pursued thro' rain and mud, divers skirmishing occurred with his strong rear-guard—I expect ere now, our pursuing column is past Williamsburg.

Franklin's[22] division passed up York river, preceded by gunboats, hoping to take West Point ahead of the retreating rebels and thus cut them off from the R. R. thence to Richmond. I expect severe fighting there for, of course, the enemy would strain every nerve to save that point, as their safest, if not only available retreat.

Before leaving York, the enemy prepared and concealed divers torpedo[e]s and shells so as to be exploded unaware by our men. Several of our men were, in that way killed and wounded. This is not mere rumor, but Gen McClellan states it in a public despatch, and he adds that he will cause search to be made for those cruel and cowardly means of murder and have them removed *by the prisoners* taken from the enemy! in order that the enemy may reap the fruits of his own cowardly treachery. I hope he will put the prisoners of the highest rank foremost in this dangerous duty.

I know not on what authority, but in fact, these devilish devices for useless and cowardly murder are attributed to the *deserter* Maury—I long to see that fellow get his deserts.

The President has gone down to the seat of war, accompanied by Secs. Chase and Stanton—left last night, at 6. p. m.

No news of importance to day—

Note. At noon, went to the Smithsonian to attend a meeting of the " Establishment "[;][23] meeting postponed on a/c of the Prest's absence.

. . .

May 7. Wednesday night—attended a brilliant party at Secy Welles'—nothing particular. Had a good deal of conversation with Count Piper[24] (swedish Minister [)] and Baron (?) Hultzeman.[25] Austrian Minister.

---

[22] William B. Franklin, West Point graduate of 1843, had served in Mexico, on the frontier, and in Washington as engineer in charge of constructing the dome of the Capitol and the addition to the Treasury building. He was made brigadier-general of volunteers in May, 1861, served at Bull Run, in the Peninsular Campaign, and at Fredericksburg, but then for incompetency in the field was removed to a command in Louisiana and later to one in Texas.

[23] The "establishment," created by act of Congress as the governing body of the Smithsonian Institution, consisted of the President, the Vice-President, the Chief Justice, and the members of the Cabinet.

[24] *Supra*, Nov. 27, 1861, note 80.

[25] Chevalier Hülsemann, Austrian Chargé d'Affaires, 1841–1855; Minister Resident, 1855–1863.

May 8. thursday. The Prest. was expected last night, but has not yet returned—2½ p. m.—perhaps he anxiously awaits further results of McClellan's pursuit of the enemy.

Sec.y. Welles shewed me, an hour ago, a long dispatch from Williamsburg, shewing renewed success of Genl. McClellan—Johns[t]on's [26] army, in a very distressed and demoralized condition, has escaped across the Chiccahominy,[27] [*sic*] leaving behind th[e]ir sick and wounded and even the prisoners taken from us, (who were found in attendance upon their wounded enemies! left without food physic or phys[ic]ians![)] The enemy is almost starving. Some prisoners taken by us said that, for 48 hours they had nothing to eat but a little hard bread in their haversacks—several of them fainted from exhaustion[.]

We have more than 20.000 men at West point, nearer Richmond than the enemy is, and in condition to intercept him.

Peremptory orders are given to Goldsborough [28] to clear out James river with his fleet—let the Merrimack come out of Elizabeth river or stay in as she pleases. That's right. I urged it upon Welles sometime ago.

J. O. Broadhead [29] is here ([as] for some days past) staying at our house. He came as agent of the various Banks in St Louis, holding Floyd's acceptances.[30]

<The question being now before me by an unsatisfactory reference by the Sec.y. of war[.]>

Mr. B.[roadhead] declares his purpose to resign his office, as quite insufficient in the amt of pay.

May 9. Friday. No C.[abinet] C.[ouncil] today, The Prest. and Secs Chase and Stanton being still absent, at the seat of war, in E.[astern] Va.

---

[26] Joseph E. Johnston, graduate of West Point in 1829, had served in the Black Hawk, Seminole, and Mexican Wars, and on the frontier, and was quartermaster-general of the Army, 1860–1861, but resigned his commission to enter the Confederate Army when Virginia seceded. Though he was appointed brigadier-general, an old distrust or jealousy of Jefferson Davis for him, prevented his being assigned the rôles his ability seems to have warranted. He served in Virginia from 1861 to 1863, and then was sent in March, 1863, to oppose Grant in Mississippi and in Tennessee and Sherman in Tennessee, Georgia, and the Carolinas, 1863–1865.

[27] The Chickahominy River rises about sixteen miles northwest of Richmond and flows into the James River about sixty-two miles below Richmond.

[28] *Supra*, Feb. 14, 1862, note 63.

[29] *Supra*, Dec. 26, 1859, note 66.

[30] *Supra*, Dec. 3, 1859, note 11. When Russell, Majors & Waddell, to whom Floyd as secretary of War had given large contracts, became embarrassed after the panic of 1857, Floyd issued acceptances (which they had cashed) of their drafts in anticipation of future earnings. Then in 1860 Bailey, a clerk in the Department of the Interior, gave the firm $870,000 of Indian trust bonds in exchange for the worthless acceptances in order to save Floyd's credit. In all, the steal amounted to about $7,000,000. See *House Reports*, 36 Cong., 2 Sess., vol. II, doc. no. 78, ser. no. 1105; "The Floyd Acceptances," 7 Wallace 666–685.

I hear today that our Iron Gunboats, Monitor, Galena and others, went up James River yesterday, in command of Com[modor]e. John Ro[d]gers[.] [31]

Note—Came into the office this morning Mr. Dart (Anson) in regard to whose claims we lately gave an opinion to the Secy of the Interior, and says that there is an error in the opinion, in that it is based upon an act of Congress that has bee[n], 15 years, repealed[.] (Coffey [32] says it is not repealed[.])

I told him that I had to give so many opinions, that I did not doubt that I would commit some blunders, and wd. be glad to have them pointed out in time to correct them—but that it must be done in writing. He still insisted, pulled out a package of papers and said the Sec: [of the] Interior had sent him to shew them and explain to me, and perhaps I wd. change the opinion. I replied that I wd. not discus[s] my opinions orally, and would not reexamine, except upon written suggestions specifying the errors. In fact; I refused to talk any longer on the subject—and he went away, his reluctance to put his objections in writing leaving upon my mind the strong suspicion that he was trying to put a trick upon me.

May 11. Sunday. We have taken a pew (No. 61) in Dr. Smith's church—4th. Presbyterian N.[ew] S.[chool]—9th. St.—Tho' not very able, a very good preacher—he is so simple, earnest and sincere[.]

Last night heard a rumor, which today seems confirmed, that the rebels have evacuated Norfolk, having destroyed all public property, sinking the Merrimack &c.

Just as I expected—We had an overwhelming force, and might as well have taken Norfolk, with all that was in it, men and armament.

<Just here, Dick came in, fresh from the reading of the telegram, and says the enemy evacuated quietly, destroying nothing but the Merrimack[.]> From this I infer that the rebel commander at Norfolk, in view of our recent victories in the Mississippi and the almost certain capture of Richmond in a few days, gives up the cause as hopeless. <not so. They destroyed the Navy Yard by fire—I have since seen it.> [33]

At night I heard from Mr. Ames [34] (who seems to have it directly from Mr. Welles) that Com[modor]e. Goldsborough's [35] fleet under

---

[31] Rodgers had served in the Navy since 1828. When the War broke out he was ordered to supervise the construction of ironclads. Now, in 1862, he was commanding the expedition of gunboats into the James River where he temporarily silenced the Confederate batteries, but was forced to withdraw for lack of ammunition.

[32] *Supra*, March 5, 1860, note 18.

[33] The parenthetical correction was added later.

[34] Probably Congressman Oakes Ames, or one of his brothers, Oliver or Horatio, all of them wealthy Massachusetts manufacturers and war profiteers who were frequently in Washington milking the Government through highly favorable contracts (see e. g., Gideon Welles, *Diary*, III, 447–448) and who later won wealth and infamy through organizing the Crédit Mobilier steals.

[35] *Supra*, Feb. 14, 1862, note 63.

orders and actually on its way up James River, was stopped by peremptory order from the President! They say that this was done by the influence of the *secy of war*, and for the reason that the Navy already had too large a share of the glory of putting down the rebellion!

[*Marginal Note.*] May 12. I find by conversation with the Prest. who has just come home, that there is not a word of truth in it. The very contrary is the fact.

The retreating enemy on the narrow neck between James River and Chickahomminy [*sic*], has McClellan in rear and Franklin[36] in front, with his left flank upon James River, by which he gets his supplies from Richmond. Hard pressed, he may cross, in whole or in part, south of James River, and *escape*—In that case, there will be a painful responsibility on somebody—who?

We also have news of another terrible fight of the gunboats near Fort Pillow[37]—The enemy, with *8* boats came out from under the guns of Pillow and attacked our fleet of *6* boats. The battle lasted 1½ hour. We blew up 2 of the enemy boats and sank 1. and then the other 5 retired under the guns of Pillow, supposed to be badly damaged. Our boat, the Cincinnati, roughly handled, but capable of quick repair.

[*A printed invitation from the Young Men's Republican Union of New York dated May 12, 1862, inviting Bates to attend a reception in honor of "Parson" W. G. Brownlow of Tennessee and quoting with approval the acceptance letter of Brownlow in which he had said: "I am for the Union, though every other institution in the country perish! I am for sustaining this Union, if it shall require ' coercion,' or ' sabjugation [sic],' or, what is more, the annihilation of the rebel population of the land!"*]

May 13, tuesday—By the invitation of the Secy of the Navy, I joined a party, to make a tour of inspection of East Va.—The party consisted of Mr. Welles, wife and niece, Mr. Seward, his son, Mr. Fred;[38] and wife, myself, Dr. Whelan, Medical Director of the Navy, and wife, Mr. Goldsborough, attending Mrs. and Miss G[oldsborough] (wife and daughter of the admiral) Capt Dahlgren[39] and

---

[36] *Supra*, May 6, 1862, note 22.

[37] A Confederate fort on the Chickasaw Bluffs north of Memphis, Tennessee, at a bend in the Mississippi a little north of the mouth of the Big Hatchie River. It was occupied by Union soldiers on June 5, 1862.

[38] Frederick W. Seward, son of the secretary of State, and himself assistant secretary of State, 1861–1869, 1877–1881.

[39] John A. B. Dahlgren; officer in the Navy since 1826; organizer and head of the Ordnance Department of the Washington Navy Yard, 1847–1861; commander of the Navy Yard, 1861–1862; commander of the South Atlantic Blockading Fleet, 1862–1865.

daughter, Eva—Mr. Faxon,[40] Chief Clerk of the Navy, and several boys—Dahlgren, Faxon, Welles and Whelan[.]

Had a very pleasant time—Went up York and Pamonkey Rivers to McClellan's headquarters, at *Cumberland*—Up James river to Jamestown—visited Fortress Monroes [*sic*], the ruins of Gosport Navy Yard and Norfolk [41]—Walked through some of the streets of Norfolk, and found things very sad and sorrowful—Doors and windows closed, and the people, as far as I saw them, looked sulky and dogged.

Saw the wrecks of the Cumberland the Congress, and the Merrimack [42]—*Note*[.] Admiral Goldsborough [43] gave me a stick of white oak, large enough to be turned into a heavy cane, sawn from a beam of the *Merrimack*[.]

[*Note.*] Returned home, comfortable, monday morning May 19 and found all well[.]

While at Cumberland, saw the *Comte de Paris* [44] and *Duc de Chartres* [45] (aid[e]s to McClellan) and had a conversation of some length, with the *Prince de Joinville* [46]—He sought the interview, and was very frank in discourse. I was much pleased with him, for, in fact, he talked as much like a statesman as any one of my associates.

The young princes—Paris and Chartres—are, I hear, diligent in the study and practice of war, having probably, a politic forethought that they may one day be called to fight for the Throne of France.

I also saw Coalter, looking his very best, and hopefull [*sic*] of active service and professional distinction.

Returned to Washington, all well, Monday, May 19th.

June 2. Monday. This day my youngest son, Charles Woodson Bates (17 yrs old) entered the Military Academy at West point—

[40] William Faxon: an editor of the *Hartford Courant;* chief clerk of the Navy Department, 1861–1866; assistant secretary of the Navy, 1866–1869.

[41] The Gosport (Norfolk) Navy Yard was destroyed and then evacuated by the Union forces on April 20–21, 1861 (*supra*, April 15, 1861, note 68; April 29, 1861, notes 79 and 82), and then by the Confederates on May 10, 1862 (*supra*, May 11, 1862).

[42] The *Cumberland* and the *Congress* were wooden sailing frigates of the Union Navy destroyed on March 8, 1862, by the Confederate ironclad *Virginia* (formerly the *Merrimac*) which the Confederates had raised at the abandoned Norfolk Navy Yard and rebuilt as an ironclad. When the Confederates abandoned Norfolk on May 10, 1862, they sank the *Merrimac.*

[43] *Supra*, Feb. 14, 1862, note 63.

[44] Louis Philippe, Comte de Paris, son of Ferdinand, Duc d'Orleans, and grandson of King Louis Philippe, was the Orleans claimant to the French throne—in exile from 1848 to Napoleon's fall in 1870 and again from 1886 until his death. He was gaining military training by service on McClellan's staff. He fought at Yorktown, Williamsburg, and Gaines Mill in 1862.

[45] Robert, Duc de Chartres, the younger brother of the Comte de Paris, was also on McClellan's staff.

[46] François, Prince de Joinville, the third son of King Louis Philippe and uncle of the Comte de Paris and the Duc de Chartres, had brought his nephews and his own son to America to offer their services to the Union Army.

being attended there by Revd. Dr. Sprole, who deposited $80 to his credit—The Superintendant [sic] telling him that that was enough.

Note. On the 4th. of April I took Woody to Revd. Dr. Wm. T. Sprole, at Newburgh, N. Y. to prepare a little before his entry at "the Point." The Dr. Wood [sic] not fix any amt. of pay—I left with him $50—Lately I sent him $100—of which he deposited 80, for Woody.

June 4. Stedman [47] tells me today that, last night, a disgraceful scene occurred at Willard's: [48]

It seems that Senator Chandler [49] of Michn. was in the crowded lobby, drunk (a bad habit that has lately crept upon him) and abused Gen: McClellan roundly, finally calling him liar and coward! Whereupon Genl. *Sturgis*,[50] who happened to be in the crowd, came up and said—"Sir, I dont [sic] know who you are, nor care, but hearing you talk in this abusive way, against an absent man, I make free to tell you that it is you who are the liar and the coward!—And I am responsible for all I say." Thereupon Mr. C[handler] quietly departed.

In the last 10 days military events of the greatest moment have occurred, in rapid succession—1. Bouregard [51] [sic] has evacuated Corinth [52] without any serious fight—In fact giving Halleck [53] the slip, tho' I believe we have cut the Mobile R. R. south of him.

2. Jackson [54] surprised and captured our post at Front Royal,[55] taking about 1000 of our men, retaking Strasburg, Middletown, Winchester and Martinsburg, and driving Banks [56] across the Potomac, at Williamsport!

---

[47] *Supra,* March 15, 1862, note 27.

[48] Willard's Hotel on Pennsylvania Avenue.

[49] Zachariah Chandler: an organizer of the Republican Party in Michigan; Republican national committeeman since 1857; U. S. senator, 1857–1875; fanatical anti-slavery man; vigorous opponent of Lincolnian moderation; denouncer of McClellan; leading jingoist; bitter enemy of Johnson and the South. Cf. the above with Gideon Welles's comment in his MS. Diary, Dec. 5, 1866.

[50] Samuel D. Sturgis: West Point graduate of 1846 who had served in Mexico and on the frontier; commander at Fort Smith, Arkansas, in 1861 where he saved the Government property when his officers joined the Confederacy; brigadier-general of volunteers in Missouri and then Tennessee; commander of the Department of Kansas; now head of the defenses of Washington.

[51] *Supra,* April 8, 1862, note 66.

[52] *Supra,* April 9, 1862, note 77.

[53] *Supra,* Nov. 13, 1861, note 37.

[54] Thomas J. ("Stonewall") Jackson, West Point graduate of 1846 who served in Mexico, on Long Island, and in Florida, until 1851; teacher of natural and experimental philosophy and artillery tactics at the Virginia Military Institute; commander of the Confederate troops in the Shenandoah Valley from which he made forays into Union territory; one of the greatest generals—some think the *greatest*—of the War; the Federal Government's terror and Lee's ablest helper until he died of wounds received at Chancellorsville in May, 1863.

[55] A town in the Shenandoah Valley, twenty miles south of Winchester. On May 23, Confederate General Ewell attacked Colonel Kenly and took most of his 1,000 Union soldiers prisoners.

[56] *Supra,* July 27, 1859, note 57.

Our troops—Fremont on the west—McDowell [57] (with Shields,[58] Ord [59] &c) on the East—And Banks (with Sigel [60] now added) on the North—tried to hem him in and prevent his escape up the valley of the Shewnendoah [*sic*]. But by last a/cs, he was too sharp for them—passed Fremont, who did no more than skirmish with his rearguard.

It is shamefully true that the enemy's officers are vastly superior to ours in boldness, enterprise and skill, while our troops almost constantly beat theirs, with any thing like equal numbers and a fair field. If our Genls. now allow Jackson to escape, they ought to lose the public confidence, for obvious lack of enterprise and action.

3. McClellan has had a very hard battle in front of Richmond. Last saturday, the enemy, in the midst of a great rain, fell upon Genl. Casey's [61] division (separated by the flood in the Chiccahominy [*sic*], from its support) and cut it up terribly, something after the manner of the battle of Pittsburg landing. Night coming on, gave a respite, and by morning help came up—Sumner [62] and others—and drove back the enemy, with great slaughter, leaving 1200 of the foe dead upon the field, of whom more than 100 died by the bayonet—thus shewing the closeness and fierceness of the fight. Our loss tho' less, was very great.

Casey's division lost 8 guns, which cd. not be taken off in the retreat, the horses being killed.

Strange, we hear nothing from McClellan for 3 days. I fear that the heavy rain, all last night and today, may swell the Chiccahominy [*sic*], so as to separate his troops and expose them to great danger.

When I lately saw McClellan, I told him that if the enemy [were allowed] to cross the Chiccahominy [*sic*] in safety, Richmond would

[57] *Supra*, Nov. 16, 1861, note 53.

[58] James Shields: Irish immigrant to America in 1826; lawyer in Kaskaskia, Illinois; judge of the Illinois Supreme Court, 1843–1845; major-general in the Mexican War; governor of Oregon Territory, 1848–1849; Democratic U. S. senator from Illinois, 1849–1855, from Minnesota, 1858–1859, from Missouri in 1879; Union brigadier-general in Virginia, 1861–1863.

[59] Edward O. C. Ord: West Point graduate of 1839 who had esrved in the Seminole War and on the Pacific Coast; brigadier-general of volunteers in the Army of the Potomac, 1861; major-general in 1862, who was soon sent to serve under Halleck and Grant in the West.

[60] Franz Sigel: German revolutionist who migrated to America in 1852; school teacher, 1852–1861; officer at the capture of Camp Jackson in Missouri in 1861; brigadier-general of volunteers in Missouri and Arkansas against Price (*supra*, Nov. 27, 1861, note 70); now major-general in Virginia.

[61] Silas Casey: West Point graduate of 1826, who had served on the frontier, in Mexico, and on the Pacific Coast; brigadier-general of volunteers in 1861; commander of a division in the Army of the Potomac until August, 1862; and thenceforth defender of Washington; author of Casey's *Infantry Tactics*.

[62] Edwin V. Sumner: officer who had served in the Army since 1819—in the Black Hawk and Mexican Wars and on the frontier; commander of the Department of the Pacific, 1861; officer in the Army of the Potomac on the Peninsula, at Antietam, and at Fredericksburg. He was appointed commander of the Department of the Missouri in 1863, but died en route to St. Louis.

be evacuated, without any hard fighting. But, now, since Bouregard [*sic*] has been forced to abandon Corinth, without any other safe place to make a stand, Johnston [63] and Lee will be forced to stand at Richmond, and fight their last great battle there—For to retreat from Rich[mon]d. now is to demoralize their army and give up their cause—They can never raise another great army.

[*July 3, 1862.*] [*A note written on a long yellow envelope containing a ragged paper.*]

Here is one proof of the lazy carelessness with which very important business is often transacted in the Departments at Washington.

[*A much scratched, interlined, and ragged paper marked " Private Resolution No. 2." The Resolution concerns the claim of Marshall O. Roberts* [64] *for the loss of the steamer* Star of the West. *Stanton had refused to act upon the claim because before he became Secretary of War, he had been consulted as counsel in the case. Congress therefore authorized the Attorney-General to act in his stead, and ordered that any money he directed should be paid from the Treasury in payment of the claim.*]

[*A note on the reverse side of the Resolution:*]

Here is a striking instance of the loose way in which very important business is done in the Departments at Washington. This ragged document is the " Exempli[fi]cation " of a Resolution of Congress, sent from the State Department to the Atty Genl., and upon which *I* actually awarded $175.000, against the U.[nited] States, which was promptly paid.

[*signed*]   Edwd. Bates[.]

[*In addition, the paper had upon its back a note by the Chief Clerk of the State Department, W. Hunter,* [65] *to the effect that the content of the paper " as marked and corrected " was a true copy of the original resolution on file at the Department of State.*]

Emigration of Free Blacks.

Sept 25. The President having submitted to all the Heads of Departments, the question of the propriety of seeking to make treaties with the American Governments within the tropics, and the

---

[63] *Supra*, May 8, 1862, note 26.

[64] Wealthy New York merchant; owner of the first luxuriously equipped Hudson River boats; railroad promoter; holder of contracts to supply the U. S. Navy with whale-oil and to transport mail via Panama to California; owner of the *America*, which carried 1,000 reënforcements to Fortress Monroe in 1861, and of the *Star of the West*, which was damaged when the Confederates fired upon it while it was trying to land reënforcements at Fort Sumter on January 9, 1861.

[65] William Hunter: son of U. S. Senator William Hunter of Rhode Island; translator in the State Department, 1829–1833; clerk in the Diplomatic Bureau, 1833–1852; chief clerk, 1852–1866; second assistant secretary of State, 1866–1886.

gap from 6/5/62 - 9/29/62

European Powers which have Colonies within the tropics, with the view to obtain safe and convenient places of refuge for the free colored population of this Country—as well those who are already free, as those who may become free, by the operations of the war— I have thought it best to present, in writing, a brief synopsis of my views.

First. I am clearly of opinion that it is wise and humane to form such treaties with all of those Powers, or as many of them as will agree to our terms. The more the better, both for the Government and the individual emigrants, because it enlarges the range of choice, and the inducements and opportunities for both.

Second. I think that such treaties ought to be single, confined to that one object, so as to avoid, if possible, all other debateable questions, and all disturbing elements. And I think it would be desirable, to have inserted a clause (if that may be) to preserve the treaty from abrogation, in case of a future war.

Third. Such treaties ought, of course, to be mutually beneficial to the contracting parties—i. e. to the foreign Governments, by offering a supply of population and labor, such as they desire; and to us, by mitigating our embar[r]assment on account of that same population—drawing off at once, a portion of that population, and enlarging and multiplying the channels of trade and friendly intercourse, so as greatly to accelerate that drainage in the future.

But besides that, and to secure that end, such treaties ought, carefully, to provide for the just and humane treatment of the emigrants—e. g. ensuring an honest livelihood by their own industry, either in the voluntary service of others, or upon their own land, or both; and guaranteeing to them " their liberty, property and the religion which they profess."

Fourth. We ought, I think, to open as many channels, and offer as many inducements, for the egress of that population, as possible, to the end of satisfying the judgment, and gratifying the wishes, and even the whims, of the various classes of emigrants, and of all the diversities of our own people, who are disposed, in any manner, to advance the great enterprise.

Fifth. Simple emigration is free; for I do not know of any *foreign* State whose laws prohibit men, only because they are negro[e]s, from coming in, acquiring a domicil[e] among the people, owning property, and establishing a civil and social status. Among our colored people who have been long free, there are many who are intelligent and well advanced in arts and knowledge, and a few, who are ebucated [*sic*] and able men. These are free to go where they please, in foreign countries (though it has been guessed by some of our politicians, who are wiser than the constitution, that this government has no power to grant them passports for their protection, in foreign parts.[66])

This class is excellently qualified and might be efficiently used, for guides, instructors, and protectors of those of their race who are fresh from the plantations of the South, where they have been long degraded by the total abolition of the family relation, shrouded in artificial darkness, and studiously kept in ignorance, by state policy and statute law.

Sixth. I think that those of our blacks who go forth under our present efforts, should go as emigrants, not colonists. A colony, in modern political law, means a dependency of the mother country, entitled to its protection and subject to its sovereign power. Emigrants, on the contrary, are incorporated, as individuals, into the body politic which they enter, and are no longer subjects of their former sovereigns. They may still have the sympathies of their former country, but have no right to appeal to its power for protection, except upon grounds of international comity, and of treaty stipulations, made in their favor.

[signed]   Edwd. Bates

Sept. 25, 1862

Note—The President directed that a copy be sent to the Secretary of State, (Mr. Seward) which was done.

Wednesday, Nov. 5. 1862. In C.[abinet] C.[ouncil]
(The question being up, as to getting out *cotton,* under certain proposed regulations of the Secys. of [the] Treasury and Navy, and certain understandings between the Secy. of State and the British Minister,[67] the Atty. Genl. read the following and enforced it orally, at some length.)

" This question of Cotton, by the magnitude and variety of interests involved in it, and by the powerful influences, both domestic and foreign, brought to bear upon it, besets us with dangerous temptations. Feeling the pressure of present evils, both at home and abroad, we are tempted to adopt expedients for present relief, without sufficiently considering the legal and political bearings, of such measures, and the consequences likely to flow from them.

["]We want Cotton badly, for both home use and for European supply. But the Cotton belongs to our enemy [*sic*], and we cannot get it, except by one of two distinct and opposite classes of measures—
1. War—*take* it by the strong hand, and dispose of it, as so much

---

[66] As a matter of fact, prior to the Civil War, it was a fixed policy of the State Department to refuse passports to free negroes, since "by the Constitution . . . free persons of color are not citizens." They were given instead, a certificate to the effect that they were " free persons of color, born in the United States " and therefore under its protection.

[67] Lord Lyons : *supra,* Sept. 26, 1860, note 24.

spoil; or 2nd. Peaceful commerce—*buy* it from the hostile owners and pay them honestly for it.

["]Now, these two classes of measures rest upon principles which cannot be combined together, because they are in direct antagonism—war and peace. War and trade do not naturally work together, in the same harness; and, to compel them to this unnatural co-action, is to disregard a great principle, and break a fundamental law. For, to trade with the public enemy, is to give to that enemy aid and comfort—and if that be a crime in the individual, it is a folly in the Government, for which it will be sure, in the long run, to pay the penalty.

["]The various expedients which have been, at different times, proposed, to ease the *cotton trade*, in spite of the war, are (if not strictly *measures* of *necessity*) measures of convenience, offered under strong external pressure. All of them, it seems to me, are open to very grave objections.

["]1. All the reasons urged in favor of Cotton, apply equally in *kind*, though differently in *degree*, to all of our great staples—rice, tobacco, hemp, and provisions.

["]2. Our relations with foreign powers may be endangered by such experimental measures.

["]Great Britain and France (the two most powerful nations of Europe, our two greatest customers for cotton, and the two whose recognition of the Southern Confederacy, we most fear) are the most urgent in the demand for cotton. If we yielding to their demands, give them advantages special and peculiar to them, then we do give just ground of offence to all foreign Countries with which we have treaties putting them "upon the footting [*sic*] of the most favored nations."

["]3. I am afraid of the effects of these anomelous [*sic*] measures upon the very complicated subject of our blockade. If we begin to make exceptions in favor of particular articles and particular nations, we do, unavoidably, draw into question the existence of the Blockade itself. And that question is cognizable, not by our courts alone, but also by the Courts of all maritime nations; for the subject of Blockade belongs to the Law of Nations. Now, a Blockade, to be lawful and honest, and therefore to be respected by neutral nations, must be enforced, uniformly and strictly. We cannot play the loose game of open and shut, just as may suit our varying policy of the passing time—for other nations will judge of it, as well as we.

["]In this connexion, I beg to say a few words as to the nature and duration of the Blockade itself.

["]Blockade is always *hostile*—hostile by the nation that makes it, and hostile *against* the place blockaded and the nation or power that holds it. Hence, there can be no such thing as a lawful blockade of a *friendly* port. *A fortiori*, a nation cannot lawfully blockade its own port in its own possession. Therefore, if a port be lawfully blockaded, as Charleston, for instance, and be voluntarily surrendered to the blockading power, or captured, with strong hand, by that power, the Blockade is, *ipso facts* [*sic*], ended, as effectually as if the blockading force were withdrawn, with the declared purpose not to return."

It was listened to with profound attention, and, by some of the members, with, apparently, a painful interest. Mr. Chase remained silent and sad, and indeed, no one directly approved or condemned, but each seemed unwilling to commit himself.

Mr. Stanton agreed with me, that there was danger on the blockade question, and that my plan to avoid those dangers was the best and easiest done—i. e. take the Missi.[ssippi] and the Cotton Ports, as soon as possible, and then the cotton would come in freely (For Genl. Butler [68] writes that the day of cotton-burning is over) [.] And he thought *that* would be done before the 1st. of Decr.

All the rest were silent, except Mr. Seward, who spoke, I thought, very vaguely, about taking military possession—and then considering whether we would raise the blockade and admit general commerce or close the port absolutely under the act of Congress.

I reminded him (to make him explicit) that my proposition was that the taking of possession of the blockaded port by us, whether the possession be military or civil, does, *ipso facts* [*sic*], put an end to the blockade—He answered only, "I do not agree to that." Mr. Seward said that he expected L[or]d. Lyons in a few days and expected to be able to make a satisfactory arrangement with him—(I could not see what L[or]d. L.[yons] and M. Mercier [69] had to do with this internal matter of ours (cotton)—But as usual with us in all knotty cases, the matter was past by, without coming to any conclusion.

Nov 7. First snow of the season—passed off quickly[.]

Nov 13. 62.

(Rough Draft) Order about confiscation.[70]

Executive Mansion, November 13. 1862.

Ordered by the President

That the Attorney General be charged with the Superintendence and direction of all proceedings to be had, under the act of Congress of the 17th. of July 1862, entitled "an act to suppress Insurrection, to punish Treason and Rebellion, to seise and confiscate the property

---

[68] *Supra,* Nov. 29, 1861, notes 88 and 1.

[69] *Supra,* Nov. 27, 1861, note 77.

[70] See J. D. Richardson, *Messages and Papers of the Presidents,* VI, 124–125.

of Rebels, and for other purposes" in so far as m[a]y concern the seizure, prosecution and condemnation of the estate, property and effects of Rebels and Traitors, as mentioned and provided for in the fifth, sixth and seventh sections of the said act of Congress.

And the Attorney General is authorised and required to give to the Attornies [*sic*] and Marshals of the United States, ~~all needful~~ such instructions and directions as he may find needful and convenient, touching all such seizures, prosecutions and condemnations. And moreover to authorise all such Attorneys and Marshals, whenever there may be reasonable ground to fear any forcible resistence to them, in the discharge of their respective duties, in this behalf, to call upon any military officer, in command of any of the forces of the United States, to give to them such aid, protection and support, as may be necessary to enable them safely and efficiently to discharge their respective duties.

And all such commanding officers are required, promptly, to obey such call, and to render the necessary service, as far as may be in their power consistently with their other duties.

Nov 24. Monday. This morning, for the first time, I observed *a little ice* in the gutters[.]

At night, S. B. Ruggles [71] called full of zeal in his project to enlist the Prest. in his scheme, about the connection of the Missi.[ssippi] and the lakes, by enlarged canals—also the Pac[ifi]c. R R. (Tho perhaps generally good, in fact I suppose mainly a N. Y. measure.)

Next day I procured Mr. R.[uggles] an audience of the President, wch. was not at all satisfactory to the Mr. R[uggles]. The Prest. told Mr. R.[uggles] that he was not disposed to take any active steps to favor N. Y. while it was so eager to take advantage of the public misfortunes, to raise the pr[i]ce of freight from the west—that the day after the enemy crossed the Potomac, the canal and R Rs of N. Y. raised the price of freight. Mr. R.[uggles] was angry, and threaten[e]d to arouse the legislature against the Prest—But I believe I mollified him.

Nov 28. To night, there called to see me (brot by Mr. Newton [72]) two eminent quakers of New York—Wm. Cromwell and Benj: Tatham—who come here in a representative capacity, to see after and help the (contraband) negro[e]s.—They say that the camp and hospital of the negro[e]s, are in a horrible condition.

[*November*] *29. Note*[.] Mr. Newton tells me that Mr. Tatham tells him, that Gov Letcher [73] of Va. is anxious to escape, and would

71 Samuel B. Ruggles: New York City lawyer; politician; railroad and bank director; state legislator; canal commissioner; trustee of Columbia College and the Astor Library.
72 *Supra*, Jan. 5, 1862, note 12.
73 *Supra*, April 28, 1859, note 41.

gladly surrender himself at Fortress Monroe, if assured of life and safety.

Mr. T.[atham] gets it throug[h] his brother, who [is a] *Mason*, and gets it through him, and by that means.

Mr. Bernard Kock.
Governor of A'Vache Island.
West Indies.[74]

This *Governor* Kock is an errant humbug. He pretends to have a lease of 20 years for *Isle aux Vaches* from the Haytien [sic] Government, and on the strength of that, boldly "pushed a face" for a contract with our Govt. to supply him with some 1000s of negro[e]s, on pretence of making cotton there.

He inveigled Blair, and perhaps 1 or 2 others of the ministry, into the p[r]eliminary of a contract. He came to me (along with Revd. Mr. Johnson) saying that the contract was all agreed, needed only to be written out, and wanted me to do it. I told him that I had not been consulted, and did not choose to play *scrivener* in the business.

I enquired about him, at the White House, and denounced him as a charlatan adventurer.[75]

Dec 5. *Second* snow, followed by cold and now (Dec 7) weather bright and cold. Hard upon the grand armies in Va., on both sides— The rebels are said to be very poorly supplied with clothes &c[.]

Dec: 15. I recd. an odd note from Hon Wm. A. Richardson,[76] enclosing a letter to him from [   ] Hamilton of Ills, attempting to set up, and asking information upon, a fra[u]dulent appointment of a Marshal, at Chicago (successor to Pine[77]). He alleges that Pine[']s securities procured the appt.ment of this man, on condition that he shd. have his living out of the office, and the rest of the emoluments should go to deminish [sic] the defalcation, in favor of the sureties! I ansd. Mr. R.[ichardson] that I found nothing, and did not expect to, as any official who wd. make *such a* bargain, wd. hardly be so imprudent as to leave tracks behind him.

Dec 19 1862 Friday. Special C.[abinet] C.[ouncil] at 10.30. a. m.

---

[74] A calling card inserted in the diary.

[75] Yet in spite of Mr. Bates's warnings, the President and the Secretary of the Interior signed a contract with Kock on December 31, 1862, in which he agreed to colonize five thousand negroes for fifty dollars a head. With this contract he secured the backing of New York capitalists. Before the colonists sailed the Government learned that Bates's judgment of him had been correct, and he was removed from leadership. About 430 negroes finally embarked. After fearful suffering and complete failure, the Government sent relief, and brought the survivors back to the States in March, 1864.

[76] *Supra*, June 29, 1860, note 71.

[77] Charles N. Pine.

The Prest. (enjoining strict secrecy) informed us that on the night of the 17th. senator Preston King [78] and Fredk. Seward [79] called on him and handed in the resignations of W. H. Seward, sec: of State, and Mr. Frederick Seward, Asst. Sec, of State.

They said, substantially, that the Republican senators, had, in caucus, determined unanimously, that the pub[li]c, interest required that Mr. Seward should retire from the adm[inistratio]n.

Mr. King said that, at first, the document prepared, was against Mr. S.[eward] by name, but that afterwards, it was changed to a more general form, but still, in fact, aimed at Mr. S[eward].

That Mr. S.[eward] said that he was no longer in condition to do good service to the Country, and so, was glad to be relieved from a great and painful burden—and did not wish any effort made to retain him.

The Prest. further informed us that the Rep[ublica]n. Seanators [sic] apptd. a com[mitt]ee. of 9. [Collamer, Fessenden, Grimes, Harris, Howard, Pomeroy, Sumner, Trumbull, and Wade] who waited on him and presented the paper agreed to in the meeting— which he read—

It declares that the only way to put down the rebellion and save the nation, is a vigorous prosecution of the war: It did not name any minister of state, nor allude directly to anyone; but said that it was dangerous to have any one in command of an army, who was not hearty in the cause and the policy above set forth. &c[.]

The Prest said that he had a long conference with the Com-[mitt]ee., who seemeed [sic] earnest and sad—not malicious nor passionate—not denouncing any one, but all of them attributing to Mr. S.[eward] a lukewarmness in the conduct of the war, and seeming to consider him the real cause of our failures.

To use the P[r]est's quaint language, while they believed in the Prest's honesty, they seemed to think that when he had in him any good purposes, Mr. S.[eward] contrived *to suck them out of him unperceived.*

The Prest was evidently distressed—fearing that the rest of us might take [it] as a hint to retire also—said that he could not afford to lose us—did not see how he could get along with any new cabinet, made of new materials.

There was a good deal of conversation, not very pointed, when, upon the P[residen]t's suggestion, to meet us at the P[residen]t's to night, at 7.30, to have a free talk [we adjourned].

The P.[resident] understands that Mr. S[eward]'s resignation is irrevocable—But nothing was sd. of his successor. At night, we

[78] *Supra,* May 19, 1860, note 19.
[79] *Supra,* May 13, 1862, note 38.

met the com[mitt]ee. of senators and had a long talk of some 4 hours[.]

The Prest. stated the case and read the Resolves of the senators, and commented, with some mild severity, upon parts of it. Several senators spoke, with more or less sharpness, all of them directing their force agst Mr. S[eward]. *Collomar* [80] and *Fessenden*,[81] mildly; *Grymes*,[82] *Sumner* [83] and *Trumbull* [84] sharply—Grimes especially—

Several of the cabinet spoke[.] Chase spoke a little abt. the finances[,] seemed offended, and said he would n't have come if he had expected to be arraigned here—Blair spoke better than common, tried to shew the genl harmony of the adm[inistratio]n.—defended Mr. S.[eward] &c and objected to the idea advanced by the Senators, that every important measure and app[ointmen]t. shd. undergo strict scruteny [*sic*] in C.[abinet] C[ouncil].

I spoke at some length, agreeing with Blair, and going beyond him on the last item.

Senator Sumner cited some bad passages in Mr. S[eward]'s lately published correspondence. Blamed him for the *publication*, as unnecessary and untimely, and denounced, as untrue S[eward]'s charge that the two extremes had united to stir up servile insurrection.

Upon the whole, the meeting broke up in a milder spirit than [animated] it [when it] met.

Dec 20 Saturday. The town all in a buz[z]—all the Cabinet *to* resign—new schemes and programs in abundance—and several lists actually sent in to the Prest[.]

The hopes of all adverse factions were revived, and the hopes of every leader stimulated— My friend Gen V.[an] A.[len] [85] told me that the peculiar friends of Gen McClellan were confident that he *must* be recalled and put at the head of the army, and insisted (as the price of their adhesion to him[)], that he should *dictate* his own terms, as the Prest could not help himself—and especially that he must demand the disposal of all the *commands* in the army!

[80] Jacob Collamer, lawyer of Woodstock, Vermont: Whig congressman, 1843–1849; postmaster-general, 1849–1850; Republican U. S. senator, 1855–1865; pre-war opponent of the extreme measures advocated by many Republicans; hearty supporter of Lincoln when the War came.

[81] William P. Fessenden of Maine: Whig congressman, 1841–1843; Whig and then Republican U. S. senator, 1854–1864, 1865–1869; chairman of the important Senate Finance Committee; a Radical during the War and early Reconstruction who finally swung to the Conservatives and voted against conviction of President Johnson in the impeachment trial.

[82] James W. Grimes: member of the Iowa Territorial House of Representatives, 1838–1845; Whig governor of Iowa, 1854–1858; Republican U. S. senator, 1859–1869; important member and later chairman of the Naval Affairs Committee of the Senate.

[83] *Supra*, Jan. 7, 1860, note 9.

[84] *Supra*, Nov. 22, 1860, note 85.

[85] *Supra*, Feb. 4, 1860, note 62.

Towards evening, it was said that the Secs. of Treasury and War had resigned—It proved *true* of the former—*false* of the latter.

Note—The attack of the extreme senators (for such it was) failed—the thing *dribbled* out.   The Secy.'s [*sic*] recalled their resignations.

The only effect which I see, properly attributable to the movement, is a closer connexion than before, between the *extreme* Senators and the assailed secretaries *Seward* and *Stanton*—they keep their places, but come up manfully to the *extreme* measures of their assailants.— The chief one is the bill for the formation and admission of *West Virginia.*

That bill was forced thro' Congress rapidly and secretly, and being before the President, he (*at my instance*) called for our opinions, upon two questions made by me—viz

Is it constitutional?

Is it expedient?

[*December 30.*]   On the 30th. of Decr. all of us except Mr. C. B. Smith (who has just retired, having been apptd. Dist Judge in Inda.) gave in our " opinions in writing[.] "

I believe, tho' I have not read the opini[o]ns, that the six are equally divided—Seward Chase and Stanton, *for* the bill—and Welles, Blair and Bates *against* it.

I denounced it on both grounds.   Blair rather waived the con-stitutional question, but was strong on the other.

The views of the others, *as written*, I do not know.   But if the bill pass, I foresee that they will have cause to regret that those opinions are *written*[.]

I think they have bought their peace with the *extremists* by sup-porting that monstrous bill—and by intensifying the Prest[']s. proc-lamation, of emancipation, to come out Jany. 1, 63.

I have taken care to put myself on record, as I choose to stand, on those questions.

In a country of free thought and active motion, *opinion* is never stationary—it advances and retires—it swings from side to side— as driven by the rush of events.

Public opinion is never spontaneous with the people—It is always a manufactured article.

Weak and hesitating men allow their bold and active enemies to *make* public opinion against them.   Bold and active rulers *make* it on their own side.

The evidences of public opinion against the administration, as exhibited in the recent elections in Indiana, Ohio and Pennsylvania, and in various popular demonstrations elsewhere [86] do not disturb me

---

[86] In the fall elections of 1862, New York, Pennsylvania, Ohio, Indiana, Illinois, and Wisconsin among the states that had voted for Lincoln in 1860, had gone Democratic.

as much as they do some wiser and better men. I think I know the causes of that adverse feeling among the people; and I think I know an efficient and not difficult remedy for the evil.

The causes lie upon the surface of our current history: They are cognizable by the lowest capacity; and simple enough to be used effectually against us, by men of every division and every phase of the opposition. They are made available against us, alike by the malcontents who are such because they are the secret friends of the public enemy, and by the *outs* who are against us only because they wish to get *in.*

We cannot deny that the People have extended to this administration a reasonable degree of supporting confidence, and, that Congress with unhesitating liberality, has granted all our demands for men, money, means and appliances—and all this for the avowed and only purpose of enabling us to suppress the rebellion.

But we have not suppressed the rebellion. We have, during the whole of this year, made no important advance toward its suppression. On the contrary, our present position is, relatively, worse than it was last spring.

Note in 1865. It is easy to see and know, *after the fact.* The hand of God is in this thing. It is not according to the co[u]nsels of Divine wisdom that a treason so stupendous, a crime so enormous should be easily or quickly suppressed. It could not be allowed to pass down the cycle of ages, as a mere episode in a nation's history.

It was to be branded upon the memory of the world, and stand as a beacon, for all coming time. *Therefore* the controversy has been prolonged, and marked with many vicissitudes, to keep alive the fears of the Nation, and the hopes of the Traitors, until the latter were ripe for the destruction which they were obstinately dragging down upon their own heads. We were held back from success—sometimes by our own foolish blunders, and sometimes by the obstinate courage and Satanic energy of the traitors—until treason had worn itself out, in men and material, and had accomplished its own punishment—severely just.

The vanquished suffer a punishment next to annihilation—complete exhau[s]tion, without a hope of recuperation, and absolute defeat, without the possibility of further resistance. And these same vanquished are severely revenged upon their victors, by whose presumptuous vanity, utter disregard of principle and cowardly tyranny, the Country is brought to the brink of ruin. Nothing less than than [*sic*] the stirring up of all the fiercest passions of our nature, and the loosening of all bands of society, by actual rebellion, could have so suddenly undermined the foundations of our Government, by destroying all respect for principles, and all obedience to law.

Nothing less than the unreasoning excitement of the public mind, the hot fermentation of all the elements, could have forced up to the surface many of our most frothy demagogues. Stevens [87] has become a leader, and Wilson,[88] and Wade [89] and Kell[e]y [90] and Bingham [91] talk heresy and nonsense, and are accounted wise and *loyal!*

Beggars

See *Jefferson's Notes on Virginia.* p 257.

" I never yet saw a native American beggar in the streets or highways."

Citizens—Ib: pp 259, 260.

" A foreigner, of any nation, not in open war with us, becomes naturalised by removing to the State to reside, and taking an oath of fidelity; and thereupon, acquires every right of a native citizen; and citizens may divest themselves of that character, by declaring, by solemn deed, or in open court, that they mean to expatriate themselves, and no longer be citizens of this State."

A Dictator—*A Despot*—*A Tyrant*—the *One-man power.* Jefferson[']s Notes on V[irgini]a. Beginning at p. 241.

" In December 1776, our circumstances being much distressed, it was proposed in the house of delegates, to create a *dictator*[,] invested with every power, legislative, executive and judiciary, civil and military, of life and [of] death, over our persons and over our properties;[:] and in June 1781, again under calamity, the same proposition was repeated, and wanted a few votes only of being passed.—One who entered into this contest from a pure love of liberty[,] and a sense of injured rights, who determined to meet [make] every sacrifice[,] and to meet every danger, for the re[-]establishment of those rights on a firm basis, who did not mean to expend his blood and substance for the wretched purpose of changing this master for that, but to place the powers of governing him in a plurality of hands *of his own choice* so that the corrupt will of [no] one man might in the future [in future] oppress him, must stand

[87] Thaddeus Stevens: lawyer of Lancaster, Pennsylvania; Whig and then Republican congressman, 1849–1853, 1859–1868; aggressive anti-slavery leader; bitter opponent of Lincoln and Johnson; fanatical persecutor of the South.

[88] Senator Henry Wilson of Massachusetts. *Supra,* Jan. 7, 1860, note 7.

[89] *Supra,* Aug. 10, 1859, note 77.

[90] William D. (" Pig Iron ") Kelley: Philadelphia lawyer and judge; Republican congressman, 1861–1890; delegate to the Chicago Convention which nominated Lincoln; high tariff extremist; leader of Radical aggressiveness during the War and vindictiveness in Reconstruction.

[91] John A. Bingham of Ohio: Republican congressman, 1855–1863, 1865–1873; extremist during the War and Reconstruction whose Radicalism defeated him for reëlection in 1862; special judge-advocate in the trial of Lincoln's assassins; counsel for the House in the Impeachment Trial of President Johnson.

confounded and dismayed when he is told[,] that a considerable portion of that plurality had meditated the surrender of them into a single hand, and, in lieu of a limited monarchy [monarch], to deliver them [him] over to a despotic one! How must we find his efforts and sacrifices abused and baffled, if he may still, by a single vote, be laid prostrate at the feet of one man! In God's name, from whence have they derived this power? Is it from our ancient laws? None such can be produced. Is it from any principle in our new constitution, expressed or implied? Every lineament [of that], impressed [expressed] or implied, is in full opposition to it. Its fundamental principle is, that the State shall be governed as a *commonwealth*. It provides a *republican* organization, proscribes, under the name of *prerogative*, the exercise of all powers undefined by the laws; places on this basis the whole system of our laws; and, by consolidating them together, chuses that they should [shall] be left to stand or fall together, never providing for any circumstances, nor admitting that such could arise, wherein either should be suspended, no, not for a moment."——

" Was it from the necessity of the case? Necessities which dissolve a government, do not convey its authority to an oligarchy or a monarchy. They throw back[,] into the hands of the people[,] the powers they had delegated, and leave them, as individuals, to shift for themselves."

"A leader may offer, but not impose himself, nor be imposed on them. Much less can their necks be submitted to his sword, their breath to be held at his will or caprice."

After stating the pressing exigencies of several of the States—he concludes, at p. 244,

" In all of which the *republican form* had been found equal to the task of carrying them through the severest trials. In this S[t]ate (V[irgini]a.) alone, did there exist so little virtue, that *fear* was to be fixed in the hearts of the people, and to become the motive of their exertions, and the principle of their government![?] The very thought alone was treason against the people; was treason against mankind in general; as rivetting forever the chains which bow down their necks, by giving to their oppressors a proof, which they would have trumpetted [*sic*] through the universe, of the *imbecility of republican government*, in times of pressing danger, to shield them from harm!" [92]

---

[92] The parentheses and most of the italics are Mr. Bates's. The capitalization and punctuation are not accurately reproduced.

CHAPTER V

1863

Jany 25 Sunday—Coalter, just at dinner popped in upon us, all unlooked for. He and Capt. Russell [1] had been sent up from Camp at Frederic[k]sburg, as witnesses agst. Maj: Floyd Jones,[2] now on trial here, before a Court Martial, for cowardice and other crimes. He and the Capt. are both in fine health[.]

. . .

Jan 30. Went, today, to my office and to C.[abinet] C[ouncil].

Several gentlem[en] of St Louis called to see me—Mayor Taylor,[3] Mr. Homer—Also Mr. Eads,[4] and Dr. Tousig [5]—the last of whom I have not seen yet.

I do not yet know Mr. Eads' special business here. He tells me that only one of his iron gunboats is yet afloat and another ready to launch, as soon as he gets back—and

That he has perfected his plan of an ocean Ship of war, as he thinks, the swiftest and the most powerful, to do and to suffer, that ever floated.

Mayor Taylor, representing St Louis, and Dr. Toussig representing Carondalet,[6] are here to urge the establishment of a Navy Yard—Carondalet is urged, as being the best possible place upon the River. And the St Louis men *proper*, propose Arsenal Island—but *faintly*, as the place is manifestly unfit, being only a sand-bank on the river[.]

Feb 5 Thursday. The streets had become very muddy, with the melting of the snow, when two days ago, it became very cold again. . . .

---

[1] Charles S. Russell of Indiana, regimental friend of Mr. Bates's son, Coalter. He was cited for "gallant and meritorious service" at Antietam, Chancellorsville, and Petersburg.

[2] De Lancey Floyd-Jones, originally Delancy F. Jones: first lieutenant in the Mexican War; major in 1861; officer in the Peninsular Campaign. He not only was acquitted in this trial, but in July was brevetted colonel "for gallant and meritorious service." Coalter was soon trying to get transferred from under him after he had testified against him.

[3] Daniel G. Taylor: captain of river-boats until 1849; then steamboat agent; wholesale liquor merchant; banker; Democratic mayor of St. Louis in 1861.

[4] *Supra*, Jan. 28, 1860, note 38.

[5] William Taussig, born in Prague and educated at the University of Prague, came to St. Louis in 1848, moved to Carondelet in 1851, and was elected mayor in 1852. From 1859 until 1865, he was a judge of the St. Louis County Court to which fell much of the financial and administrative work of the Civil War period.

[6] At this time a village on the Mississippi River in St. Louis County—now part of St. Louis.

Yesterday morning, Coalter, under orders from his head Qu[arter]s. instead of going to Camp at Potomac Creek, started for *Oldtown*, (near Cumberland on the upper Potomac) to do some transient duty, as a mustering officer. He took Woody [7] with him, and expects to be back tomorrow[.]

The bad news from Charleston, to the effect that the Rebel Rams had run out, and sunk two or more of our ships, and driven off the rest, is not credited—at least, if there be any truth in it, it is believed to be exag[g]erated[.][8]

Feb 5. Thomas Ewing,[9] of O.[hio] called at my office on business, which done, he spoke very freely of *Gen Curtis* [10] and his *cotton* operations at Helena.[11] Spoke of them as notorious, saying that Curtis had deposited, in a bank at Chicago, his profits in that business, amounting to $100000.

Gen Curtis see Feby. 24–5[.] [12]

Feb 11. Barton Bates' letter of Feb 4. recd. today, contains his a/c with me whereby, it seems he owes m[e] $906.18.

Feb 12. C. D. Drake [13] called at my office, and agreed to dine with me to day—and the rather as I agreed to send Dick to bring (his old sweet heart) Mrs. Brent, to meet him[.]

Gen Butler,[14] also called, said he'd visit me at home.

[February] 13. Mr. Chase asked me about Mr. Drake's fitness for administrative duties, and I think designs to give him a Bureau[.][15]

Lost—dropped out of my carriage unperceived, my Ebony, gold-headed cane, highly valued because a present from my old friend Mde. Cabanné[.][16]

Feb 15. M.[ontgomery] Blair—For some time back Mr. B.[lair] has been very assiduous in his Court to the Prest., and I hear that he

---

[7] Home on leave from West Point.

[8] No ships were sunk. Two were slightly injured and went to Port Royal for repairs. A full report came from Admiral Du Pont to Secretary Welles on February 9 (G. Welles, *Diary*, I, 234). The news recorded by Mr. Bates seems to have been given out by the Confederates for European consumption.

[9] *Supra*, Oct. 6, 1860, note 41.

[10] *Supra*, Oct. 22, 1861, note 23.

[11] An Arkansas cotton-ginning and shipping town on the Mississippi about seventy-five miles below Memphis. See *infra*, Feb. 25, 1863.

[12] Added later in the margin.

[13] Charles D. Drake: St. Louis lawyer; Democratic state legislator, 1859–1860; Republican U. S. senator, 1867–1870; chief justice of the Court of Claims, 1870–1885. He was now busy organizing the Radical wing of the Unionist Party in Missouri in opposition to Governor Gamble, Bates, and Lincoln. He demanded immediate emancipation, a new constitution, and drastic disfranchisement of "rebels." When the Radical Constitutional Convention met in 1865, he was vice-president and one of its chief sponsors.

[14] *Supra*, Nov. 29, 1861, notes 98 and 1.

[15] Drake did not get the Treasury appointment, but was still negotiating with Chase as late as September. *Infra*, April 4, 1863; Sept. 30, 1863.

[16] *Supra*, April 9, 1860, note 70.

is making, *sub rosa*, fair weather with the democrats, trying to smooth the way to make Genl. Butler [17] Secy of War. We are now at the middle of Mr. L[incoln]'s term, and most adm[inistratio]ns., even in good times, wane towards the latter end,[.] Mr. B.[lair] probably thinks it good policy to have strong friends on both sides.

It is a hard game to play, and I doubt whether Mr. B.[lair] has skill to keep his balance even.

Nat: Intelr. Feb 17. 1863

[*A clipping from the* National Intelligencer *gives the resolutions adopted by the Democratic State Convention of Michigan, assembled at Detroit.*

"*Resolved*, That, while we condemn and denounce the flagrant and monstrous usurpations of the Administration and encroachments of Abolitionism, we equally condemn and denounce the ruinous heresy of secession as unwarranted by the Constitution, and destructive alike of the security and perpetuity of our Government and the peace and liberty of the people."]

Thus, it seems the Michi-*ganders* are very equal and impartial—they are just as much against their own govern't as [against] that of the Rebels!

Feb 19   thursday—At 7. a. m. *Coalter* left for his camp near Fredericksburg, in good health, except a bad cold. He has had a pretty long tour of *fancy duty*, as they term it. He came up Jany. 25 (sunday) being sent as a witness in the case of Maj: Floyd-Jones.[18]

That done, he was ordered up the Potomac, on mustering duty, at various points, from near Cumberland, down to Winchester, and having satisfactorily made his returns, has gone back to his sad duties in the field.

I call his duties *sad*, because, seldom has an army so brave, so strong, and so well appointed, had so hard a fate. With victory in its grasp, in the beginning, when McClellan first marched against Richmond, it has been forced, by the stupid slowness and persistent blunders of its commanders, always to "fight backwards" and at disadvantage—to fight, not to conquer the enemy, but to *save itself!*

In C.[abinet] C.[ouncil] today, the Prest. mentioned the question of brevetting the meritorious *regular* officers, among whom promotion is so slow. I spoke as strongly as I could in favor of *Capt. Russell* [19] of the 11th.,—How he had comma[n]ded his Regt. for months, and in several bloody battles—that he and such like, were overlooked and disheartened &c[.]

[17] *Supra*, Nov. 29, 1861, notes 98 and 1.

[18] *Supra*, Jan. 25, 1863, note 2.

[19] *Supra*, Jan. 25, 1863, note 1.

Today, an empty fellow by name *Jewitt*,[20] thrust himself upon me, at my office, pretending to have a message from Mrs. Lincoln about the pardon case of Fowler,[21] the defaulting Post master of N. Y. i. a. said he wanted to have a good long conversation with me about the *mediation of France and England*, to stop our civil war—I said I could not talk with him on that subject—that I was utterly opposed to foreign intervention, and that, with me it was not a debateable question—He replied that he had been in Europe a long time laboring to bring about mediation, wrote letters to eminent persons &c—I told him that I thought he ought to be punished for his inte[r]meddling—that there was a statute against it &c—He (evidently disconcerted) said he was against *intervention*, as much as any man—that *mediation* was not *intervention*. I replied only, it is plain Sir, that you and I dont [sic] understand the dictionary alike—And then he left, apparently in a huff—

Feb 22 Sunday. . . .

Feb 24. Col Ham: Gamble [22] arrived with a letter from the Gov: [23] to Gibson, [24] stating that the Mo. Legislature had past an act requesting the U. S. Govt. to lend Mo. 3.000.000, to support the militia &c[.] <I doubt if he gets it>

In C.[abinet] C.[ouncil] the Prest. produced a Resolution of the senate, [25] asking for a letter [26] of Genl. Scott, written just before his retirement, complaining of Gen McClellan's neglect and disobedience of orders[.]

The P.[resident] doubted the propriety of sending it, and put the question.

He considered it a blow at McClellan, which he thought impolitic and unhandsome on our part.

I gave my opinion agst. sending the letter—partly on the P[resident]'s ground, but chiefly on the ground that it was more a covert attack upon the P.[resident] than an open one upon McClellan.

I understood Mr. Seward and several others to concur in my view. Mr. Chase alone, spoke openly for giving the letter, not on the ground that it was wisely called for, but that we ought not to seem to have secrets. I thought that it wd. be refused.

---

[20] A person calling himself "William Cornell Jewett of Colorado" who professed intimacy with Southern, Northern, and European statesmen, and sought to negotiate peace. It was he who, by claiming to be an authorized Confederate agent, persuaded Greeley to go to the Niagara Falls conference in 1864.

[21] Isaac V. Fowler, corrupt Grand Sachem of Tammany Hall, 1853–1860, appointed postmaster of New York City by President Pierce and reappointed by President Buchanan, embezzled $155,000 between 1855 and his dismissal in 1860.

[22] Son of the Governor.

[23] Hamilton R. Gamble: *supra*, July 23, 1859, note 39.

[24] *Supra*, April 27, 1859, note 27.

[25] See Feb. 19, 1863, *Cong. Globe*, 37 Cong., 3 Sess., 1089.

[26] Oct. 4, 1861. See the *National Intelligencer*, Feb. 26, 1863.

Senator Henderson [27] of Mo. has joined heartily in the effort to relieve Gen Curtis [28] from the command of the Dept. of the Mo. He thinks now (as Gibson and I do) that if he can remove Curtis, and be known as the efficient cause in doing that good act, his re-election to the Senate will be assured. He has gotten the P.[resident] to promise positively, the removal of Curtis; but still there is a difficulty about his successor—He insists on having *Burnside*,[29] and the P.[resident] is strongly disposed to send Sumner [30]—and so, the matter hangs at present.[31]

After—I have reason to think that the Prest. has a design to send Burnside to S.[outh] C.[arolina] to supersede both Hunter [32] and Foster,[33] between whom there is ch[   ]

Feb. 25 wednesday. Mr. Phelps [34] M.[ember of] C.[ongress] of Mo. (titular Military Gov of Arkansas) called at my office—pale and emaciated, worn down with chronic diarroeha [*sic*] (caught at Helena, last Summer, when Curtis' army lay idly rotting there [35]).

Talking of C[urtis]'s cotton and mule speculations, he told me, i. a. that the army took 3 *camels* in Arks., which were shipped up the river from Helena on the same boat that took *Genl. Curtis and his suite*, and were sent, with their keepers, to Keokuk, which he believes to be *Genl. C[urtis]'s home[.]* [36]

At night, Mr. Newton [37] and Mr. Sargent [38] called to see me, and Mr. N.[ewton] (as usual) had *secrets* to tell—He took me aside to say he *must* have a talk with me, but not now—saying only that he had just had a long private talk with the P.[resident] partly about me—That the P.[resident] assured him that he had full and unabated confidence in Me.

---

[27] John B. Henderson: Democratic lawyer and politician of Missouri; brigadier-general in the militia; U. S. senator, 1862–1869. He had vigorously opposed abolitionism, secession, and coërcion, but when the Civil War came, he supported the Union. He *was* reëlected in 1863 but was refused renomination in 1869 after he had voted "not guilty" in Johnson's impeachment trial.

[28] *Supra*, Oct. 22, 1861, note 23, *infra*, Feb. 25, 1863. He *was* relieved in May, 1863, because he and Governor Gamble could not be brought to coöperate. He was given command of the Department of Kansas.

[29] *Supra*, Nov. 29, 1861, note 97.

[30] *Supra*, June 4, 1862, note 62.

[31] He was succeeded by Schofield. *Infra*, May 30, 1863.

[32] *Supra*, Oct. 22, 1861, note 21.

[33] John G. Foster: West Point graduate of 1846; Mexican War veteran; teacher at West Point; then builder and engineer in charge of U. S. fortifications in Charleston Harbor, 1858–1861; officer in the expedition to Roanoke Island in 1862; now commander of the Department of North Carolina. Soon after this he was sent to aid Burnside at Knoxville, Tennessee, and in December was given command of the Department of the Ohio.

[34] John S. Phelps: Democratic congressman, 1845–1863; colonel of infantry, 1861–1862; military governor of Arkansas, 1862; governor of Missouri, 1877–1881.

[35] *Supra*, Oct. 22, 1861, note 23; Feb. 5, 1863.

[36] Keokuk *was* Curtis's home.

[37] *Supra*, Jan. 5, 1862, note 12.

[38] Probably Aaron A. Sargent: California journalist and lawyer; Republican congressman, 1861–1863, 1869–1873; U. S. senator, 1873–1879; minister to Germany, 1882–1884.

This was in answer to my frequent refusals to go to the P.[resident] at his N.[ewton]'s instance, and volunteer opinion and advice, when not asked.   <In fact, for some time I have not recd. the consideration which I thought my due, especially in regard to Mo. affairs—and also, some matters proper to my own office—I do not doubt the P[resident]'s *personal* confidence, but he is under constant pressure of extreme factions and of bold and importunate men, who taking advantage of his *amiable weakness*, commit him beforehand to their ends, so as to bar all future deliberation.>

Feb 26 Thursday. Disposed of several pardon cases to day—Went to see the Prest. about the Mo. cases sent by Judge Ryland [39] and endorsed by the Mc. delegation, but failed, he being out.

Went to the War Dept. to see Mr. Stanton, about the letters of the Wisconsin delegation, concerning the *anti-draft* riot, at *Port Washington* Ozaukee Co. Wis;

I found Mr. Stanton in consultation with the Prest and the Genl. in chief (Halleck [40]) and perhaps I ought to have retired, but, being invited in, I entered and made a brief statement—Mr. S.[tanton]'s manner was impatient and brusque—not to say uncivil—He, plainly, did not understand my object, and answered as if to an accusation—said the draft com[mis]s[ione]r. (Mr. Pors [41]) was appointed by *his* authority, under the *cons.[cript] Law* and the genl. Laws of war. I said there was a statute which perhaps gave the P.[resident] the power. He seemed to acquiesce, referring to the act of [   ] July, 62—and said refer the papers to him, and he'd give full answer.—I said, *well*, and left—But there is nothing to refer to Mr. Stanton.

N. B. When I entered, the Prest rose, and with a bland countenance, advanced and shook [h]ands. The Secy. and the Genl. kept their seats, and I thought looked disturbed and sulky. The Genl. I know "has no love for me," and the Secy. I fear, would break with me outright, if he thought it quite safe.

I shall be prudent with both, taking good care not [to] trust myself in their power—*in any thing*[.]

Feb 26. The Nat[iona]l. Intelligencer of this morning contains a leader upon the letter of Genl. Scott of 4 Octo: 1861, to see Cameron, stating the neglect and disobedience of Genl. McClellan (see back Feb 24) and the letter itself, as part of the proceedings of the H[ouse] of R[epresentatives].

Just as I said—the blow is struck at the *President*, over the Genl's head—A blow hard to ward off, because it is a shameful and ruinous fact, that there is *no discipline* in the army!

---

[39] John F. Ryland: lawyer of Lexington, Missouri; judge of the Missouri Supreme Court, 1852–1858.

[40] Henry W. Halleck: *supra*, Nov. 13, 1861, note 37.

[41] William A. Pors: German immigrant who settled in Wisconsin in 1849; lawyer; district attorney; draft commissioner.

At about 5 oclock, while I was at dinner, Judge Swayne [42] called to see me (on another business) and talking of *Gen McClellan*, and of the recently published letter of *Genl. Scott*, told me of several conversations with Genl McC[lellan], in one of which the genl. said that he had letters (or written communications) from the Prest. which put the P.[resident] in his (the Genl's) power.

I said I did not believe it—that he might have letters (written in Mr. Lincoln's confiding spirit) which the P.[resident] wd. not like to see published, but that I doubted whether he had any, whose publication would not hurt the Genl quite as much as the Prest.—that the P.[resident] tho' a confiding frank man, was still cautious in his writings.

Judge Swayne's special object in calling to see me, was (for himself Judge Davis,[43] and perhaps some other of the Judges) to talk about *Mr. Eames,*[44] who was entrusted by me, with the chief management of the *Prize cases.*[45]

It seems that *Mr. E.[ames]* in the conduct of the cases, made himself very obnoxious to the Court—I am sure that they did him great injustice; for they said that his speech was no argument at all—did no good, but harm, to the cause, acting like a harlequin, and turning a solemn trial into a farce—

That he had never argued a case before—and did not know how—

That C.[hief] J.[ustice] Taney said, that he no longer wondered at Fitz-John Porter's conviction [46]—he deserved to be convicted for trusting his case to such a counsel!

That the other counsel, Evarts [47] and Dana,[48] shared in the feelings of the court.

This is all very unjust, not to say c[r]uel, and shews a degree of passion and prejudice not very creditable to that high court—I am afraid that the feeling may endanger the *Prize cases.*

---

[42] *Supra,* March 22, 1862, note 49.

[43] David Davis: circuit judge in Illinois, 1848–1862; justice of the U. S. Supreme Court, 1862–1877; U. S. senator, 1877–1883; president pro tem of the Senate, 1881–1883; close personal friend of Lincoln; manager of his campaign for the nomination in 1860.

[44] *Supra,* Jan. 13, 1862, note 30.

[45] *Supra,* Feb. 14, 1862, note 59.

[46] Porter, a nephew of David Porter (*supra,* March 15, 1862, note 39) and West Point graduate of 1845, had served in Mexico, on the faculty of West Point, and on the frontier. In 1860–1861 he had gone on missions to Charleston, to Texas, to Florida, and had then helped with the defense of Washington. In 1862 he fought with the Army of the Potomac, but in November was relieved of his command, ordered to Washington, arrested, tried by court martial on charges of General Pope, convicted of disobedience, and cashiered from the Army—though completely exonerated by an investigation in 1879.

[47] *Supra,* April 8, 1862, note 71.

[48] Richard H. Dana: author of *Two Years before the Mast,* 1840; early Free-Soiler; defense lawyer for the rescuers of the negro Shadrach in 1851 and for Anthony Burns, escaped negro, in 1854; now U. S. attorney in Massachusetts, 1861–1866; later U. S. counsel in the proceedings against Jefferson Davis for treason and before the Fisheries Commission in Halifax in 1877. He persuaded the Democratic Court to sustain the blockade in the Prize Cases.

Of course, this conversation was private and *confidential*, between Judge S.[wayne] and me. His *motive* was kind to me, and his object to warn me to *get rid of Mr. E.[ames]* in Govt. cases, because his presence was offensive to the Court.

Judge S.[wayne] in course of conversation, dropped some hints about the New Almaden Mine case [49] (Cala. land) from which I infer that it will probably be determined against the claimants—for he hinted at the contingent propriety of taking prompt steps to secure the interests of Govt. against the rush of squatters, in case the land should turn out to belong to the Govt.—

The court will probably come to its conclusion by next tuesday— Mar: 3. tho' the decision may not then be announced.

I will see to it, by having arrangements with the Secy. of the Interior and Com[mis]s[ione]r of the G.[eneral] L.[and] O[ffice].

He also told me that Judge Davis saw Secy. Seward last night, who told him that, at no time since the rebellion began, were our relations so good with European powers, generally. France has renewedly aroused the jealousy of England, by her proceedings in Mexico,[50] the near completion of the *Suez* canal,[51] and by her threatening aspect, in general.

Mr. Seward, no doubt, avoids a misstatement of facts, but he draws conclusions very boldly, and sometimes, it seems to me, very strangely. I have my own views of that complicated matter: Europe, I think, will be for or against us, just as we are for or against our selves— i. e. just as we win or lose success. In short, we must beat the enemy, or lose the friendship and support of Europe.

" Unity of *Command "*—

Feb 28. The Nat:[ional] Intel[ligence]r. of this date, has a Leader under this head, shewing a deplorable lack of discipline and subordination in the army.

It shews the real conflict of opinion and authority, between Hunter and Foster, in S.[outh] C[arolina].[52]

---

[49] *U. S.* v. *Andres Castillero*, 2 Black 17–371. Castillero claimed title to a rich quick-silver mine under an 1846 grant of the Mexican Government. He had sold most of his rights to the other shareholders in the New Almaden Mining Company of which one probably unscrupulous James A. Forbes was the chief promoter. The mine was under land claimed by José R. Berreyesa (*infra*, Feb. 24, 1864, note 69) whose widow had inherited his claim. By the Treaty of 1848 the United States had recognized private titles in California but had assumed public land formerly held by Mexico. Hence if the Castillero title proved invalid, and the mine did not lie on the Berreyesa ranch, this rich mineral deposit would revert to the United States. Therefore the United States, Castillero, the New Almaden Mining Company, and the Widow Berreyesa were all interested parties. The case was a tangled one. Ultimately the Court decided it in favor of the United States.

[50] After Britain and Spain had withdrawn their forces and abandoned the joint intervention in Mexico, France had remained, had plotted with the Conservatives to overthrow Juárez, and had landed more troops and advanced inland. Now on February 17, 1863, French troops had recommenced their advance on Mexico City.

[51] Construction of the Suez Canal was begun under de Lesseps and a French company in 1859 and was progressing slowly but certainly.

[52] *Supra*, Feb. 24, 1863.

And also, the shameful vaccilation [*sic*] in the govt. here, and most injurious jealousy among the high officers of the army, relative to the attack upon Vicksburg,[53] and other operations on the Miss[issipp]i.

It contains an extract from the Chicago Tribune,[54] giving a detailed account of the orders abt. the command of the forces intended for Vicksburg, with names, dates &c—It contains this statement (which if true, is at once a calamity and a shame)—"It is clear however, that the Prest designed and had ordered that Genl. *McClernand*[55] should have command, and that *Genl. Halleck*[56] *frustrated the design.*"

It does *appear* that Halleck is determined that we shall not take Vicksburg—if he can prevent it—He *refused* to take it when Bouregard evacuated Corinth[.][57] Then, only 8 or 10.000 men were needed to ensure the capture—the gun boats then having full power to silence the Enemy's batteries when they pleased—When sharply question[ed] in C.[abinet] C.[ouncil] he pretended that he had not troops to spare! Yet at that very time, Curtis, with his 20.000, lay demoralizing and rotting at Helena![58]

March 2—N. B. Gold, in my table drawer, $80, in ½ Eagles— In purse $16.

Took from the drawer $50. in fives package J.

Nat.[ional] Intel[ligence]r. Mar: 4

> "Four persons have been convicted of treason in the United States Court of Indiana for resisting the arrest of deserters in that State. These are the first convictions for treason since the commencement of the rebellion."

Mar 6. W[illia]m. H. Taylor of Nebraska City (N.[ebraska] T.[erritory][)] writes to J.[ohn] M. V.[aughan][59] under date Feb 27, urging his claims to be associate judge of the Ter[ri]t[or]y *vice* judge Streeter, who died on the 19 Feb:

He [is] a Kentuckian by birth, formerly of Palmyra Mo., a near friend (I believe a brother in law) of S. T. Glover.[60]

---

[53] *Infra*, July 6, 1863, note 63.

[54] February 23, 1863.

[55] John A. McClernand: Illinois lawyer and journalist; Democratic congressman, 1843–1851, 1859–1861; brigadier-general in the West, 1861–1864. He *was* given a command at Vicksburg but was relieved of it by Grant on June 18, though later restored for political reasons by Lincoln.

[56] *Supra*, Nov. 13, 1861, note 37.

[57] *Supra*, April 9, 1862, note 77; June 4, 1862.

[58] See *supra*, Oct. 22, 1861, note 23; Feb. 5, Feb. 24, Feb. 25, 1863.

[59] A clerk in the Attorney-General's Office and son of Richard C. Vaughan, Mr. Bates's friend who lived in Lexington, Missouri. He resigned his clerkship in April, 1864, intending to move to Montana, but in 1865 was still in Missouri.

[60] *Supra*, Dec. 23, 1859, note 58.

Mar 6. Recd. a letter from *Julian*, of date Feb 23d., in which he says i. a. that he has recd. from Mr. Riggin, on my order $150.00[.] (I cant [*sic*] tell whether it is 50 or 30[.])

In the same letter he speaks of " Poor George Woodson ! " and more than fears that Goody will resign and go over—" George *has gone over* " says he.

Since then, I gather, (from a letter of one of the little girls of Dardenne [61]) that George has courted Betty H.[atcher] and will probably marry her—I will rejoice at that, because it may save him from the ruin of rushing into the ranks of the Rebellion.

Mar 13 Friday—At 10, this morning, Senator Sumner [62] came to my office to talk about *Letters of Marque*, as authorised by the late act.[63] (which act, by the way, he had opposed, in an able speech)

He told me, what I did not know before, that Secy Seward had proposed the immediate issue of letters, and that the subject wd. be up today, in C.[abinet] C[ouncil].

Sure enough, it did come up, and was talked over at some length; but nothing definitive was done—as the C.[abinet] was not full (Chase and Stanton being absent, at N.[ew] Y.[ork])[.] Being forewarned, I was very guarded, objected, in a mild tone, stating some of the grounds—i. a.

[*Marginal Note.*]   See forward, March 17.

Privateering is only a milder sort of piracy, softened and legalized by the practice of nations, and only from the policy of weakening the enemy by plundering him—That our enemy has no marine commerce, and so offers little temptation to privateersmen, whose sole object is booty—That, as all the enemy's trade upon the ocean is in neutral bottoms, it is very dangerous to trust Privateersmen with the delicate power to overhaul and seize neutral ships, endangering constantly the peace of the nation; and that without any great temptation to incur such a risk.   That, as to what seemed to be the real, but not avowed object, the practical increase of the Navy, as agst the enemy's armed cruisers, at present at sea, or soon expected from England, it was not likely that many wd. offer, strong enought [*sic*] to cope with them—the object of privateers is not to *fight* but to *capture* &c[.]

Mr. Blair, at first, seemed pointedly, against the measure—saying that it was equivalent to war with England, and wd. certainly lead to war.   But afterwards, when the Prest. said, (answering Mr. Seward) that he supposed that we wd. have to come to it, in some form, Mr. Blair seemed to assent that [it] wd. have to be done, war or no war.

---

[61] One of the seven children of Barton who lived on a farm near Dardenne.
[62] *Supra*, Jan. 7, 1860, note 9.
[63] March 3, 1863, *U. S. Statutes at Large*, XII, 37 Cong., 3 Sess., chap. LXXXV, p. 758.

N. B. I have observed lately that whatever opinion Mr. B.[lair] starts with, he yields a ready assent to the final conclusion of the Prest., whether brot about by the influence of Chase Seward or Stanton. Mr. B.[lair] takes special care of himself, his family and special friends, determined not to differ much with the *appointing power*[.]

The matter of letters of marque is again to come up on next tuesday, by which time Mr. Seward will have ready printed, the regulations and instructions, prepared, under the act.

I intend to make a memorandum in writing of my objections, believing as I do, that the measure is full of danger, and unpromising of any important advantage.

Mar: 14. Saturday—Cassius M. Clay[64] (late Maj: Genl) Minister to Russia, now for the 2d. time, called at my office to take leave, on the eve of his departure for his mission.

He seems disappointed and from our brief conversation, was not instructive nor interesting.

I told him that if we had war with England (which I did not expect) his wd. be far the most important of our missions, for, in that case we *must* have Russia for an ally &c[.]

Mar: 15. Sunday—Went to church with Julia, and heard Dr. Smith preach a sermon, very dull, even for him, on the words—" I pray not for the world &c " John xvii.

. . .

[*A newspaper clipping reprinted from the* Washington Star *of March 18, about the arrest of Antonia J. Ford of Fairfax Court House, a spy in the service of J. E. B. Stuart.*[65]]
Gen: Stuart's *female* honorary aid[e] de camp.

Mar 17 Tuesday—Jno. M. Vaughan[66] paid me *$50.* for his father (R.[ichard] C. V.[aughan][67]) in part of *$100*, advanced by me, for his travelling expenses, when he first came on to Washington.

Mar 17. Wm. H. Clarke, son of M. L. C.[larke] of Mo.—Dr. H. W. Pitman, of Loutre Island Mo. Revd. Wm. A. Taylor of Mo.—

The first a prisoner of war, the last two banished, by Provost Martial [*sic*]—referred their letters, respectively, to the Secy of War.

Mar 17. In C.[abinet] C.[ouncil] Privateering again[.]

Since the subject was partially considered, last Friday, I have thought much upon the subject, and am confirmed in the belief that it is a very hazardous experiment.

[*Marginal Note.*]   see back—Mar 13[.]

64 *Supra*, Jan. 13, 1862, note 26.
65 *Supra*, April 21, 1859, note 20.
66 *Supra*, March 6, 1863, note 59.
67 *Supra*, Dec. 9, 1859, note 25.

The only national reason for issuing letters of Marque, is to weaken the enemy by capturing his ships and seising his goods, *in transitu*, on the ocean. But our enemy has no merchant ships and no goods in transitu, in international trade. His only ships are *men of War* cruising against our commerce. And they are stronger than our Privateers (fitted out to prey upon commerce) are likely to be. Fighting is not the vocation nor the intent of Privateers. It is only an undesired incident, that may happen when the Prize is found to be stronger than was expected, or when forced to defend against hostile cruisers.

If the object really be, under the name of letters of Marque, to increase our Navy, in disguise, to fight against the enemy's cruisers, then it would seem to me that there is a far better way—&c[.]

Note[.] Mr. Seward has gotten his instructions printed, and has furnished us all with copy.

Mar 26 Thursday. This morning, Julia recd. a letter from *Dick*, dated last Sunday, stating that next day he was to marry *Ellen Woodson.*

All right—I'm glad that he has given that bond and security for his good behavior.

Mar 29. Recd. a letter from Gov Gamble, stating that Dick *is* married[.]

Mar 29. Got a letter from Coalter, informing that Maj Floyd-Jones [68] is in command of the Brigade, and that he (C[oalter]) is anxious for a change, to get from under him.

On the 30th. Gen Hooker [69] was here, in Washington, and I was anxious to see him, but could not, he was so busy at the War office. I meant to try to get him [Coalter] some staff app[oin]tm[en]t.[70]

[*March*] *31st.* recd. a letter from Dr. Lieber [71] about *our sons'* promotion—wch. I m̶ s handed to the Secy of war[.]

Apl 1. Recd. Telegraph from Dick, that he (and Nelly [72]) will be here Friday, the 3d.

S. T. Glover [73] dined with me today. At night we called on the Prest. but cd. have no talk abt Mo. affairs, on a/c of company—Secy

[68] *Supra,* Jan. 25, 1863, note 2.

[69] Joseph Hooker: West Point graduate of 1837 who had served in Florida, Maine, Mexico, and on the Pacific Coast, but had left the Army in 1851; brigadier- and major-general of volunteers in the Army of the Potomac under McClellan, Pope, and Burnside; commander of the Army of the Potomac from January until June, 1863; leader in the disastrous defeat at Chancellorsville, May 3–5; officer under Grant in the West.

[70] He did get it. See *infra,* May 5, 1863.

[71] *Supra,* April 5, 1862, note 62.

[72] Ellen Woodson Bates, daughter of a cousin of Mr. Bates, whom Dick had married on March 23. *Supra,* March 26 and 29.

[73] *Supra,* Dec. 23, 1859, note 58.

Seward and a Mr. Oakford (a native of Pa. and for long resident of England[)]. Mr. O.[akford] was in consultation, abt. the English furnishing ships to the rebels, and the means of counteracting them[.]

Apl 4. Dick arrived, at 6. a m. with his young wife.

Mr. 2d. Comptroller *Cutts* [74] came into my office to shew me the papers in the case of the late *Purser* Josiah Tatnal Jr. (I had asked him for copy of the bond).

That done, he stated, at cruel length, his difficulty with the Q.[uarter] M.[aster] Genl's office [75]—They want him to give opinion in advance, upon the difficult question, whether the ninety odd new clerks (appointed, but no appropriation for their pay) may not be paid out of a specified fund—I advised him not to commit himself, but to decline, in as few polite words as possible.

He is a polite man, and I think means well, but [is] excessively dull and vain. I really pity him. It is a great misfortune to any gentleman to have no sense.

Mr. Drake [76] (C. D. of St Louis) is here—was at our house last night. His business is, ostensibly, professional. But ? [I question] whether he expects an auditorship in the Treasury?

Sometime ago, Mr. *Chase* asked me how he wd. do for such a place; and lately, Mr. C.[hase] was very anxious to make a vacancy, by making making [sic] Mr. Underwood,[77] Judge of the Eastern Dist. of Va.

Apl 4. At 5. p. m. joined the President's party and started for "Hooker's [78] Camp" army of the Potomac—Took boat at the Navy yard, about sunset, in the midst of a snow-storm. Laid by in the night for some hours, so as to get to Aquia Creek [79] abt breakfast.

Found a train waiting for us, and at Falmouth station,[80] found carriages, which took us to Genl Hooker's head quarters[.]

The party consisted of the Prest., his wife and son, little Tad—Dr. Henry of Washing[ton] Terr[itory]—Capt Crawford of Oregon and Mr. Brookes of Cala.—and myself.

---

[74] James M. Cutts, originally from Maine.

[75] Montgomery C. Meigs was quartermaster-general. *Supra*, Dec. 31, 1861, note 68.

[76] *Supra*, Feb. 12, 1863, note 13.

[77] John C. Underwood, a New Yorker who moved to Virginia in 1832, became a Republican, and was forced by public dislike of his views to return to New York. He was appointed fifth auditor in the Treasury Department in 1861, and in 1863 judge of the Eastern District of Virginia where he defended confiscation of property of "rebels" and civil rights for negroes, and refused Jefferson Davis bail when he was indicted for treason in his district in 1866.

[78] *Supra*, March 29, 1863, note 69.

[79] *Supra*, Oct. 22, 1861, note 13.

[80] A village on the north bank of the Rappahannock, across from Fredericksburg.

At my request, Genl. Butterfield[81] (chief of staff[)] sent me over in fine style, to the of the [*sic*] 11th. Infty. where I staid the night with Capt Russell,[82] (and his mess, Capt Ames,[83] Lieut Higbee[84][)]— I missed Coalter on the way. He went up to pay a last visit to the family, while I went down to see him.

Monday morning I returned to H[ea]d. q[uarte]rs., and attended the review of Cavalry—in grand style, Coach and four, all alone— over 10.000 cavalry—the grandest sight I ever saw[.]

Apl 15. Wrote a note to the Prest recommending *Allen A. Hall*[85] of Tenn: for the vacant Mission to ~~Venezuela~~ Bolivia. And if any special reason against him, then recommending John B Kerr[86] of Md.—

(Judge) *M. M. Jackson*[87] U. S, Consul at Hallifax [*sic*] N. S., called, with another letter from Revd. Edwin. G. Booth, and a statem[en]t abt him[.]

Apl 21. West Virginia! The President's proclamation[88] (*dated Apl 20*) is published in this morning's *Nat[iona]l. Intelligencer.* It announces that the People of the new State have complied with the requirements of the act, and therefore the act will go into effect 60 days from the date of the Proclamation!

The end is not yet! I am convinced that this is but a new complication of our troubles.

Yesterday the news came by telegraph—authentic, from Adjt. Genl. Thomas[89] and from Genl. Grant—that R.[ear] A[dmira]l. Porter's[90] fleet,—7 gun boats and some transports—had run the blockade at Vicksburg, with a loss unexpectedly small—and now have complete command of the River below. It seems to me that this must force the enemy to evacuate Vicksburg; and as soon as

[81] Daniel Butterfield, New York lawyer, business man, and militiaman, who rushed to the defense of Washington at the outbreak of war and served as brigadier- and then major-general under McClellan, Burnside, Hooker, Meade, and finally Sherman. He was Hooker's and later Meade's chief-of-staff.

[82] *Supra*, Jan. 25, 1863, note 1.

[83] John W. Ames of Massachusetts was brevetted lieutenant-colonel "for gallant and meritorious service" at Gettysburg.

[84] George H. Higbee of New Jersey was cited "for gallant and meritorious service" in the Wilderness in 1864 and at Petersburg in 1865.

[85] A Nashville journalist who had been chargé d'affaires in Venezuela, 1841–1845, and assistant secretary of the Treasury, 1849–1850. He got the appointment as minister to Bolivia and remained there until his death in 1867.

[86] A Maryland lawyer who had been a Whig congressman, 1849–1851, and chargé d'affaires to Nicaragua, 1851–1853. As Hall got the appointment, Kerr was not considered, but Bates later appointed him solicitor in the Court of Claims, 1864–1868, and he served as solicitor to the sixth auditor of the Treasury, 1869–1878.

[87] Mortimer M. Jackson: Democratic attorney-general of Wisconsin, 1842–1847; circuit court judge, 1848–1853; consul at Halifax by appointment of Lincoln as reward for services in the election of 1860.

[88] J. D. Richardson, *Messages and Papers of the Presidents*, VI, 167.

[89] *Supra*, Oct. 1, 1861, note 9.

[90] *Supra*, March 15, 1862, note 39.

we are masters of the River, the tide of the war must turn, and the enemy must soon run down.[91]

It will make Hooker's conquest of Va. all the easier,[92] and soon will follow the fall of Charleston [93] and Mobile.[94]

[*A clipping of April 21, 1863, copied from the* New York Evening Post *giving the contrasts in prices in New York and Richmond.*]

Apl 22. Gov Gamble [95] has called the Mo. Convention, avowed to pass an emancipation ordinance. And Glover [96] writes me that it will certainly be done.

See Cicero's Letters (Melmoth)[97] vol: 1. Letter 12. p 51—note two.

The highest *bribe* that I read of in history, is that promised to *Cæsar and Pompey*, by *Ptolemy Aulites* [*Auletes*], King of Egypt,[98] for procuring his acknowledgement as an ally of the Roman Republic=£1.162.500, English[.]

And after that, Ptolemy had to give, to Gabinus, proconsul of Syria, 10.000 talents, for restoring him to his throne after the People had expelled him—And this was done on the advice of Pompey and Marc Anthony[*sic*], and without the Senate's authority.[99]

May 5. The pressure of business and the rush of events, since Apl. 22, have prevented me fro[m] making a single note—

On the 27th. of April—the day that the army of the Potomac struck tents, to march against the enemy, across the Rappahannock—My son, L[ieutenan]t J. C. Bates, was ordered to service on Genl Hooker's [1] staff. On the 28th., he repaired to Head Q[uarte]rs., and has, ever since, been in the most active and dangerous service. There has been a constant succession of fierce and bloody battles—and they are still going on, without as yet, any decided result. I still confidently hope for a great and *valuable* victory.

We have taken many prisoners—perhaps 2000 have arrived here. Just now, I saw, passing my office, under guard, a body of them, from 800 to 1000. They were, in the main, very good-looking men—

---

[91] The tide did turn then. But Vicksburg did not fall until July 4. *Infra*, July 6, 1863, note 63.

[92] Before Vicksburg fell, Hooker (*supra*, March 29, 1863, note 69) was disastrously defeated at Chancellorsville, May 3–5.

[93] Charleston did not fall until February 18, 1865.

[94] Mobile fell even later—April 11, 1865.

[95] *Supra*, July 23, 1859, note 39.

[96] *Supra*, Dec. 23, 1859, note 58.

[97] *Letters of Marcus Tullius Cicero to Several of His Friends*, William Melmoth, ed., 3 vols., Lackington, Allen & Co., London, [1800].

[98] King from 80 to 51 B. C. Crassus, Cæsar, and Pompey were ruling Rome under the Triumvirate when the bribe was paid.

[99] In 55 B. C. while Pompey was consul in Rome and Mark Antony, having fled from Rome in 58 to escape creditors, was serving as a soldier in Egypt and Palestine.

[1] *Supra*, March 29, 1863, note 69.

variously dressed, material, cut and color, but not so ragged and dirty as reported. They seemed to have very little baggage—many without knapsacks, and not a few without coats or hats.—I saw no uniform dress—chiefly home made and home died [*sic*][.]

May 7. I was disappointed. Hooker's army had to retire behind the Rappahannock—Still, our army insists that they hurt the enemy more than they were hurt, in killed, wounded and prisoners; and are ready to try it over.

I hear that Capt. *Russell*[2] behaved very gallantly (as usual)[.]

Capt. Ames[3] (a noble fellow) was badly wounded in the *coat* and *breeches*—a narrow escape—a shot went through his pants without touching him, and one cut open the whole breadth of the back of his coat, barely abrading the skin on the shoulder.

Last Friday, May 8. Gov Gamble[4] and his son (Col Ham:) being in Phila.[delphia], ran down here, to enquire the truth of Hooker's army—They returned saturday, I think in better spirits.

May 10 Sunday night—Isaac Newton[5] called to see me and tho' he talked, at first, abt. the common news and unimportant matters, I perceived that there was something heavy on his mind—He then detailed a long conversation that the P.[ost] M.[aster] Genl. had sought and had with him.

It disclosed no less than a plan to revolutionize and remodel the entire Cabinet—Seward and Stanton and perhaps Bates, indeed all except Welles, to be displaced—Chase to have Seward's place—and if that cd. not be, then Sumner[6] to have it—Holt[7] or Butler[8] or Banks[9] to have Stanton's—and Preston King[10] Chase's[.] And all this to be accomplished by a very simple operation i. e. old Mr. Blair[11] to be the private counsellor—not to say dictator—of the President.

Mr. B.[lair] complained that his father had not, of late, been admitted as much as he desired, to private conferences with the Prest. And he urged Mr. N.[ewton] to use his influence with the Prest. to

[2] *Supra,* Jan. 25, 1863, note 1. He was brevetted lieutenant-colonel on May 3 " for gallant and meritorious service."

[3] *Supra,* April 4, 1863, note 83.

[4] *Supra,* July 23, 1859, note 39.

[5] *Supra,* Jan. 5, 1862, note 12.

[6] *Supra,* Jan. 7, 1860, note 9.

[7] *Supra,* Feb. 2, 1860, note 49.

[8] *Supra,* Nov. 29, 1861, notes 98 and 1.

[9] *Supra,* July 27, 1859, note 57.

[10] *Supra,* May 19, 1860, note 19.

[11] Francis P. Blair, Sr.: Kentucky lawyer, journalist, banker, politician; originally a follower of Clay, but after 1825 a devoted Jackson Democrat; contributor to the Frankfort (Kentucky) *Argus of Western America* until 1830 when Jackson called him to Washington to edit the *Globe;* publisher of the *Congressional Globe;* member of Jackson's " kitchen cabinet." He had resigned his editorship in 1845 but from his home in Silver Spring, Maryland, had continued to wield great influence, had helped to organize the Republican Party, and was a close friend and adviser of both Lincoln and Johnson.

bring about more intimate relations.   That the old man was, beyond all question, the ablest and best informed politician in America—and was known to be such!   That, under his advice, the Prest. wd. be saved a world of trouble, and the Nation far better served, than in any other way!

Mr. B.[lair] spoke in the bitterest terms of the Secs of State and War—that the former was an unprincipled liar—the truth not in him: and the latter a great scoundrel—making all sorts of fraudulent contracts, to put money into his own pocket—that, in that way, "Cameron was a fool to him."   And a good deal more of that sort— Being asked, I advised Mr. N.[ewton] to have nothing to do with the intrigue,—to take care of himself and his own Department—and let Mr. Blair manage his hazardous plot in his own way, and at his own risk—He seemed to see the absurdity of trying to make old Mr. B.[lair] the governing power behind the throne, and the great likelihood that the attempt wd. recoil upon the heads of the contrivers.

Evidently the p.[ost]m.[aster] g.[eneral] is in dead earnest; for I have abundant other proof that he is full in the faith that Wisdom will die with his father and him!

I knew before, his very bad opinion of Seward and Stanton, and his jealousy of Chase.   And as to me, I knew that he was disappointed and dissatisfied because I declined from the start, to be an agent of "the Blairs."   In fact, that clique, has mistaken cunning for wisdom, and they believe fully in trick and contrivance.   They believe me, a mere mar-plot—and, that, as Cardinal Wouley [Wolsey] said of Bishop Gardener—"He was a fool, for he would needs be virtuous.   I'll have none such near his Highness!" [12]

True, I have no confidence in Seward, and very little in Stanton; but that does not make me confide in tricky politicians, who have not the first conception of statesmanship.

Mr. Lincoln has been overburdened with the weight of public affairs.   But, if our arms should soon be crowned with great successes (as I fondly hope) he will then become more independent and self-reliant, and less likely to submit to the dictation of any clique. Now, the *extreme* leaders have subordinated every thing to the negro—Law, justice, policy—the War itself to their mania for abolition[.]

---

[12] Again Mr. Bates quotes incorrectly.   It was of Dr. Pace, Gardiner's predecessor that Shakespeare made Wolsey say:

> "He was a fool;
> "For he would needs be virtuous."

Of Gardiner in contrast he added:

> "that good fellow,
> "If I command him, follows my appointment:
> "I will have none so near else."

Henry VIII, Act II, Scene 2, lines 129–132.

May 11. Mr. Henderson [13] and Gov King [14] of Mo. are here, urging upon the Prest the necessity to make a change of commander in Mo., and at once.

Today, Henderson tells me that the Prest. talked as if he'd do it at once. Mr. Foy [15] is also ostensibly on p.[ost] o.[ffice] business, but I hope doing his best, in the matter of Curtis.[16]

May 11. A letter came from Coalter today—dated saturday, the 9th., in which he says the officers of H[ea]d. Q[uarte]rs. ware [*sic*] ordered to be ready, at short notice, to march with 3 days['] rations.

So, I suppose the rumor is true that Hooker [17] is again crossing the River—And now, I feel confident that he will overwhelm Lee's army.[18]

[*Marginal Note.*] *May 12. tuesday*—On leaving C.[abinet] C.[ouncil] the P.[ost] M.[aster] G.[eneral] staid behind. And I [have] notice[d] the same thing, several times lately. He seeks, as often as possible, to be alone with the President.

May 12. Coming from C.[abinet] C.[ouncil]—Mr. Chase remarked to me " There is not an unpaid requisition in my Department."

That is an extraordinary state of things: The Treasury, it seems, for the first time during the war—is full.

May 16 Saturday. There are growing signs of a general distrust of each oither [*sic*], among leading men and politicians. Each one, statesman or General, is secretly working, either to advance his ambition, or to secure something to retire upon.

At present, abolition seems to be the strongest rallying point, and men who dont [*sic*] care a fig about it, have become all of a sudden, very zealous in that cause—*Seward* and *Stanton* [19] are as hot as Chase. And even Adjt. Genl L. Thomas,[20] has become a very zealous proselyte—He is out on the Missi.[ssippi] straining his little powers in the effort to organize black battalions, but thus far, with little success, tho' the raw material is abundant, all around him.

There is now no mutual confidence among the members of the Govt.—and really no such thing as a C.[abinet] C.[ouncil]. The more ambitious members, who seek to control—Seward—Chase—

[13] *Supra*, Feb. 24, 1863, note 27.
[14] Austin A. King: state legislator, 1834–1836; judge of the Circuit Court, 1837–1848; governor, 1848–1853; again circuit court judge, 1862–1863; Democratic congressman, 1863–1865.
[15] *Supra*, May 31, 1860, note 37.
[16] *Supra*, Oct. 22, 1861, note 23; Feb. 5, 1863.
[17] *Supra*, March 29, 1863, note 69.
[18] Lee was resting his army preparatory to the invasion of Pennsylvania in June.
[19] The underscoring was done later in blue pencil.
[20] *Supra*, Oct. 1, 1861, note 9.

Stanton—never start their projects in C.[abinet] C.[ouncil] but try *first* to commit the Prest., and then, if possible, secure the *apparent* consent of the members. Often, the doubtful measure is put into operation before the majority of us know that it is proposed.

This was especially so in case of the prize ships *Labuan*[21] and *Peterhoff*.[22] In those cases, the Sec of State gave pointed instructions to Dis[tric]t: Att[orne]y at N.[ew] Y.[ork][23] without consulting me—and, as soon as I found it out (but after much of the mischief was done) I, *without consulting any one*, gave instructions flatly to the contrary.

[*A clipping reprints from the* Fall River News *an account of the capture of the English steamer*, Labuan, *at the mouth of the Rio Grande as it was loading with cotton.*]

May 23. Gen: Halleck[24]—Today Isaac Newton[25] told me, as a great secret, that Gen H.[alleck] was a confirmed *opium-eater*— as he is very credibly informed.

That he is something bloated, and with watery eyes, is apparent. But whether from brandy or opium I cannot tell.

May 24. Sunday—Good news from the S.[outh] W[est]. Grant has beaten the enemy in a series of battles. After taking Jackson[26] and the neighboring towns, he drove Pemberton[27] to and across the Big Black. P.[emberton] having destroyed the bridge, G.[rant] built others and pursued him to Vicksburg—taking the batteries and rifle pits on the upper or northern side of the town, so that his (G[rant]'s) right flank rests upon the river, and the town is completely invested by land and confronted on the water by the gunboats.[28] G.[rant] has possession also of Haines' bluff[29]— Pemberton is in the town, with some 20.000 troops.

---

[21] *The Labuan*, May, 1862, District Court, Southern District of New York, *Federal Cases . . . Argued and Determined in the Circuit and District Courts . . .*, XIV, 906. The vessel and cargo were restored.

[22] *The Peterhoff*, May 7, 1863, District Court, Southern District of New York, *ibid.*, XIX, 314. The *Peterhoff* was proceeding to a Southern port with contraband of war on board and false ship's papers when she was captured as a prize and taken first to Key West and then, in the absence of Federal officers, to New York. Both vessel and cargo were condemned.

[23] Edward D. Smith of New York City, U. S. district attorney, 1861–1865.

[24] *Supra*, Nov. 13, 1861, note 37.

[25] *Supra*, Jan. 5, 1862, note 12.

[26] An important railroad center forty-five miles east of Vicksburg. It fell to Grant on May 14.

[27] John C. Pemberton: West Point graduate of 1837; Mexican War veteran who, though born and bred in Philadelphia, joined Virginia's troops in 1861; commander in the Southeast in 1862; lieutenant-general in the lower Mississippi Valley where he led the Confederates at Vicksburg.

[28] Porter had run the batteries at Vicksburg during the night of April 16, and had stationed his boats above the city.

[29] A landing of great strategic importance on the Yazoo River twelve miles northeast of Vicksburg. Sherman with gunboats and soldiers had made feints against it on May 6 and 7, and then, by taking the high bluffs known as Walnut Hills between Haines Bluff and Vicksburg, had cut off the garrison at Haines Bluff.

The number of prisoners and guns taken is said to be very great, but the precise amt not given.

It is confidently believed that Vicksburg *must* surrender (if not already done)[.] Then, of course, Port Hudson [30] *must* fall—and then the River will be open, and will only need to be diligently patrolled by gun boats—with a few strong points garrisoned—to be kept open and made safe.

May 27. Coalter was up from Camp, with Gen Hooker,[31] staid a day and returned[.]

[*May*] *28 Thursday*—Woodson left us today, his leave of absence from the Academy being nearly out, and having to report himself at West Point, on the 1st. of June—next monday.

[*May*] *29.* Down to this day, no decisive news—Rumors of much hard fi[gh]ting—frequent assaults by our troops, taking some redouts, but repulses, and great slaughter on both sides.

May 30 Saturday—The appointment of Gen Schofield [32] to succeed Gen Curtis [33] has produced great excitement among the *jacobins* in Mo. and some among their radical sympathisers and supporters at the north. But, a little patient firmness, prudence, and steady conduct, with the People at home, and active, aggressive war upon the armed enemy, will make all right.

It was the only course that could save Mo. from Social war and utter anarchy. The Radicals seemed to have come to the conclusion that Mr. Lincoln's plan of emancipation was all wrong, too slow and cost too much money; and that the best way to abolitionize Mo. was by violence and fraud—And [if] the state were thrown into anarchy, all the better. It would depopulate the State, by death and banishment. And they could settle it anew, getting improved lands, for nothing!

These devilish designs, I trust, will all be frustrated by the appointment of Schofield, and the expected harmony between him and Gamble.[34] The capture of Vicksburg and opening of the Missi.[ssippi] will secure the peaceful result[.]

[30] A village on a high bluff commanding the Mississippi twenty-two miles above Baton Rouge. It did fall to Banks's army on July 9.

[31] *Supra,* March 29, 1863, note 69.

[32] John M. Schofield: West Point graduate of 1853 who had served in South Carolina and Florida, 1853–1855; professor of philosophy at West Point, 1855–1860, and of physics at Washington University, St. Louis, 1860–1861; chief-of-staff to General Lyon in Missouri in 1861; commander of the Department of the Missouri, 1863–1864.

[33] *Supra,* Oct. 22, 1861, note 23. There had long been pressure from Bates and Bates's Missouri friends for his removal.

[34] The Governor; *supra,* July 23, 1859, note 39.

May 31. The first *negro* knight that I ever read of is "*Sir Edward Jordon*[35] Mayor of the City of Kingston, and *Prime Minister* of Jamaica." [J. Dennis] Harris, in his book, published in 1860, entitled "A summer on the borders of the Caribbean Sea," at p. 131. informs us that, Her Brittanic Majesty had then lately conferred that dignity upon the said Edward Jordan—*Note.* I cant [*sic*] find him in Burke's Peerage and Baronetcy[.]

Head of the Nile

I see, in the papers, that Capt. *Speke*[36] (an Englishman) has discovered, the wonderful secret of all past ages—the source of the *White Nile.*

Washington Hunt[37] of N. Y. a democrat! In the Mo. Rep: of June 4, in its springfield letter of June 1, speaking of a Mass meeting of *Democrats*, says Several *prominent Democrats* are invited—among them *Washington Hunt!* I've a great mind to send him a pocket mirror, that he m[a]y see how he looks, *as a Democrat.* "O! wad some power the giftie gee us" &c[.][37a]

Richard Bates

June 5. On friday *the 5th. of June*, at six oclock, p. m, he left our house, in Washington, to return to Mo. Circumstances seem to make it necessary for him to quit his position, as deputy solicitor of the Court of Claims, and, by the kind interposition of Mr. Gibson,[38] he expects to receive a military appointment in Missouri.

He leaves his young wife with us—a sweet, affectionate girl, who remains with us, (awaiting events) as a *daughter* of the house—on the same footing, in heart and outward act, as Nancy and Matilda.

In regard to Dick, my heart had failed me—When I wrote to Mr. Gibson, disclosing my views, I had despaired of his restoration, in this wicked town. But, this new arrangement, brought about by the active friendship of C. Gibson, opens up a new vista, and inspires me with new hope. May God add his blessing—perfect the change—and crown it with a full restoration to self-respect, to confidence of friends, to honorable labor, and to the consciousness of usefulness to the country!

---

[35] Agitator for political rights for free negroes and emancipation for slaves; newspaper editor who had escaped conviction for treason by the vote of only one juryman; member of the Jamaica Assembly; privy councillor; prime minister; speaker of the House; receiver-general; colonial secretary. He was created commander of the Bath in 1854.

[36] John H. Speke, British colonial soldier and explorer, found the source of the Nile on July 28, 1862, but did not get the news to England until May 11, 1863 after he had reached Khartoum.

[37] *Supra*, Oct. 26, 1859, note 15. He had been an old-time Whig.

[37a] Robert Burns, *To a Louse.*

[38] *Supra*, April 27, 1859, note 27.

June 7 Sunday—I have been confined to my home 3 days, by indisposition, but expect to attend office, tomorrow.

Note. Klopfer [39] told me this morning, that, last evening, some rebel prisoners were brot. in, and among them an officer, " in bran[d] new uniform " just like the dress of our our [*sic*] own officers, except that the belt bore the letters *C. S. A.* instead of *U. S. A.*—If that trick be devised as a disguise or stratagem, it is a *felon* act—and verily, it will meet its reward.

No definitive news from Vicksburg or [Port] Hudson—Yet the news is such as to afford strong hope of the speedy capture of both those places [40]—Then the Missi.[ssippi] will be open to our arms and our commerce—and that will break the heart of the rebellion.

That done, surely the Govt will at last perceive the propriety of occupying the lower *Rio Grande*, with a force strong enough to protect itself, and to prevent all contraband com[m]erce in that quarter. The land forces, I think, need not be large; and two gunboats, of lighest draft, would command the river.

From the very first, I always told the Govt., that the Rebellion would triumph or be crushed on the Mississippi, and that opinion is stronger in me now, than ever. [41]

If, at the beginning, we had seised the great River, when there was nothing to prevent it—fortified a few strong points, and with armed boats, patrolled its whole length, we might have restored the Union, without destroying the Country—we might have spared rivers of blood, and great heaps of ashes.

June 8. The Nat:[ional] Intel[ligencer]: of today, contains a striking " *Historical Parallel* " between great events in 1646 and 1862-3. In the former, the English Parliament promptly rejected the offered mediation of the French King (Louis 14) in the Civil War.

In the latter, our prompt rejection of the offered mediation of the French Emperor (Napoleon 3) in our present Civil War. [42]

June 8. To day recd. a letter from Barton of June 4. enclosing *two* duebills of Dick's to Mr. Eads [43] = $450. How is this? I thought the whole amt. was $750.

[39] Henry A. Klopfer, head messenger in the Attorney-General's Office.

[40] *Infra*, July 6, 1863; *supra*, May 24, 1863, note 30.

[41] *Supra*, May 27, 1859; March 16, April 15, Aug. 27, Nov. 27, Nov. 29, 1861.

[42] On January 9, 1863, Drouyn de Lhuys, French Foreign Minister, wrote Mercier, the French Minister in Washington, a note (Notes from the French Legation, vol. XIX, State Department Archives) in which he suggested mediation. Mercier presented this note in person on February 3, 1863, to Secretary Seward, who apparently did not reply directly but declined the offer of mediation indirectly in the form of an Instruction of February 6 to Dayton, the American Minister in France (Instructions, France, vol. XVI, 321-337, State Department Archives), which he told Dayton " You will be at liberty to read . . . to M. Drouyn de Lhuys." See also the concurrent resolution of Congress declining all such offers of mediation, March 3, 1863, *Cong. Globe*, 37 Cong., 3 Sess., 1497-1498, 1541.

[43] *Supra*, Jan. 28, 1860, note 38.

June 17. Still at home, very unwell.

For some days, I have done no serious work, but read only, for amusement. "*Melmoth's Cicero*" (letters to and from his friends) seems to me a model, almost perfect, of epistolary correspondence: and besides, the notes of the learned editor are replete with solid, historical instruction. Sometimes I find in them striking facts and incidents which, to me, seem wholly new; and constantly, I find in them, pleasant reminders of the half-forgotten reading of my youth.

In Vol 1 p. 430, is a characteristic letter of *Marcus Cato*[44] (he of Utica) to Cicero, and a note which declares that it is "the only composition that has been transmitted to us, from the hands of Cato."

Strange, that a man who acted so conspicuous a part in the history of his country (and that co[u]ntry the mistress of the world); whose name fills so broad a space in history; who lived at a time when the arts and literature of Greece, and the power of Rome, had just culminated—it is strange to me, that such a man should leave no literary remains, but a single letter to a friend! And our surprize is only increased by the letter itself; for it is manifest that he who could write *that* letter, might have written volumes (as his friend did) for the instruction of posterity.

This Cato (unlike his great grandfather[45]—the old brute of a Censor) seems to have been severe, only in his principles and morals; but in his manners displaying the wise and prudent statesman, the bland and amiable *gentleman*, (if they had in Rome, such a thing as a *gentleman*.)

And as for Cicero! I am almost sorry to read this beautiful book of his private correspondence, this sad developement [*sic*] of his inward littleness and corruption. It is like tearing away the cerements, in the mausoleum of some deified hero of the old time, and displaying to the vulgar gaze, the disgusting spectacle of his blackened and worm-eaten carcase [*sic*] of carrion!

Pope writes of Bacon—"The greatest, wisest, meanest of mankind."[46] And Young writes of humanity, itself,

> "How poor, how rich, how abject, how august,
> How complicate, how wonderful, is man![47]["]

But Cicero, I think, stands foremost of mankind, as the exponent of our contradictory nature. No man has exhib[it]ed our nature,

---

[44] Roman statesman (95–46 B. C.) of great integrity who supported Cicero in his attack on the Catiline conspirators and tried to defend the old free state against the ambitions of Cæsar and Pompey, but failed.

[45] Marcus Cato "The Censor" (234–149 B. C.), Roman statesman noted for his integrity, his cruelty, and the severity of his justice. He tried to maintain the simplicity of Roman life and to prevent the spread of Hellenic culture. It was he who decided that "delenda est Carthago."

[46] Alexander Pope (1688–1744), *Essay on Man*, "Epistle IV," lines 281–282.

[47] Edward Young (1683–1765), *Night Thoughts*, I, "On Life, Death, and Immortality," lines 68–69.

in bolder contrast with itself: No man had united in his own person, more of the excellences and the vileness, the majesty and the meanness of human life.

If it were not for the most cogent proofs, drawn from his own authentic writings, it would be incredible, that a man of the highest rank in the dominant nation of the world; the most learned man of a learned age; the master-orator in the lapse of ages; and (theoretically) the purest and sublimest of moral philosophers; could, at the same time, be a fawning sycophant and a lying hypocrite!

If History be really (as has been said) " philosophy teaching by example," [48] is it not a pity that history should be *true*? Would it not be a better teacher, if it were only a *fable* of virtue and consequent happiness, rather than the appalling *truth* of crime and consequent misery?

June 18. Speaking against time. This abuse, I find, prevailed in the *Roman Senate*, as well as in the *American Congress*. See 2. *Melmoth's Cicero* p. 31, note 1. upon Letter VI. from Marcus Coelius [49] to Cicero.

Newspaper. In the same letter at p. 35. this passage occurs—" You will find the several opinions of the Senators, in relation to this affair, in the *newspaper* which I herewith send to you. I leave you to select such articles as you may think worthy of notice." &c[.] And so, it seems that Debates in the Roman Senate were *Reported*, and sent, in *newspaper form*, from Rome into distant provinces.

So, in popular meetings in Rome, *hissing* was a mark of contempt, indulged by the populace, just as it is in our town meetings. Ib: p. 36. note 9.

Then, a *Newspaper* was what its name imparts, a collection of *news*. *Now,* it means *a teacher of Politics*, and Critic of the Government—See Proceedings of an Editor's Convention, in N. York June 8. 1863.

2. Melmoth's Cicero. p 67. Letter from Coelius to Cicero—" You are sensible, I dare say, that so long as the dissentions of our Country are confined within the limits of debate, we ought ever to join the more righteous side; but that, as soon as the sword is drawn, the *strongest party is always the best.*" and note 2. on same.[50]

---

[48] This is an expression of Bolingbroke (*On the Study and Use of History, Letter 2*) who quoted Dionysius of Hallcarnassus (*Ars Rhet.* XI. 2) who in turn was quoting Thucydides (I. 22), the original author.

[49] Marcus Coelius (or Cælius), a Roman youth who was committed to Cicero's care, caused Cicero trouble through his licentiousness, but became an orator of note, a tribune, and finally prætor. These letters were written to Cicero from Rome while Cicero was proconsul in Cilicia.

[50] In these passages, punctuation and capitalization are inaccurately copied, and the italics are Mr. Bates's.

Such was the utter corruption, in morals and politics of bloated and festering Rome, that its ablest and best men, were not ashamed to avow such abominable principles. This Coelius writes more pointed and beautiful letters than Cicero himself. Truly, the Republic was not worth preserving!

June 19. Late at night, all unlooked for, Dick came in.

June 20. Recd. another letter from Barton—date June 16. with Dick[']s 3d. and last due bill to Mr. Eads [51] $350, in all=$800. Barton's letter is, on several points, reserved, perhaps artificially ambiguous, thus shewing a conflict between his desire to be frank and true, and his equally strong desire to spare my feelings. It leaves me in painful doubt—rather almost full conviction that Dick is utterly lost, hopeless of reform—that he has ceased to strive against temptation, and that he is sinking, without a struggle, into the abyss of voluntary meanness and self-contempt. Till now, I could never believe the possibility that a son of mine could sink so low.

He seems beyond the reach of human effort: God's mercy alone can reach his case.

June 20. At night, Dick returned from St Louis, restored (for trial) to his office. His promises were so fair and his resolutions, apparently, so strong, that, by the persuasion of Mr. McPherson,[52] we determined to start west on the 23d. McPherson kindly taking all the trouble of our journey—

June 23. Left Washington in the morning, reached Phil[adelphi]a. to dinner— At 11. p. m. left Phil[adelphi]a., breakfasted at Altoona—passed thro' Pittsburg at 4 or 5. p. m.—Next morning (the 25th.) breakfasted at Indianapolis (the Bates House) and arrived at St Louis at 8. p. m. lodged at the Planters House— Spent friday, 26th. in St Louis, and on Saturday 27th. went up to Chenault. having gone to Florissant (Julian's) friday evening.

All our immediate friends well. The grand children especially, delighted me—Barton's 7 [53] and Julian's 2—are charming children— healthy cheerful, docile, and most of them handsome.

July 1. Returned to St Louis, with Barton who had to open court [54] in St Louis on the 2d. (for delivery of opinions[)], and then to be at Jefferson on the 6th. all which was done.

---

[51] *Supra,* Jan. 28, 1860, note 38.

[52] Probably J. D. McPherson, assistant solicitor in the Court of Claims under Lincoln.

[53] He was apparently following the example of his father who had had seventeen children.

[54] Barton was judge of the Supreme Court of Missouri.

July 4. Launch of the great Iron Gun boat *Winebago*,[55] at Eads' Navy Yard—I was present, with Eads,[56] and Com[modor]e Hull [57]— Miss Bell Holmes christened the boat, with a bottle of champaign [*sic*].

The Workmen of the yard gave Mr. E.[ads] a beautiful flag which, at their desire, I presented. Of course, I made a speech, and Eads an answer—which were printed—Eads took occasion to make a statement of the origin of Missi.[ssippi] gunboats, attributing the original project to me (which is strictly true). This has called forth a denial, attributing the origin to Genl. Fremont—who, in fact, had not returned from Europe, when I first brought Eads to Washington. and put him in communication with the Navy Dept.[58]—in consequence of which, Commander John Rodgers [59] was sent West to begin the construction of gun boats, and Eads made his contract, with Qu.[arter] M.[aster] Genl. Meigs [60] for the first 7. boats.[61]

July 6. Monday evening—returned to Dardenne prairie [62]—and on tuesday, 7th., heard of the capture of Vicksburg [63] and the battle of Gettysburg [64] &c[.]

July 12 Monday—Matilda has not come up but is expected this evening—*We* Julia and I start down this evening. and Expect to start home in a week. taking Sarah [65] with us.

note Matilda remained in St Louis—reaching St Louis, Barton consents that Onward [66] shall go with us, and will bring him down, in time.

Did bring him, Monday 19th.

July 23. Thursday. Left St Louis (exactly a month since we left Washington) at 5. p. m—self—wife—Tilly—Sarah Julian—

---

[55] The *Winnebago* participated with effectiveness in the Batte of Mobile Bay, August 5, 1864.

[56] *Supra*, Jan. 28, 1860, note 38.

[57] Joseph B. Hull of Connecticut who had served in the Navy since 1813, commanded the *Savannah* in the Southern Blockading Squadron in 1861 and from 1862 until 1864 superintended the building of gunboats at St. Louis.

[58] Bates did " put him in communication with the Navy Department," and he probably did it independently of Frémont whom neither of them liked, but though Bates himself had urged operations on the Mississippi from the first (*supra*, June 7, 1863, note 41), it was not until December 31, 1861—six months after Frémont's return from Europe—that Eads visited the Navy Department (*supra*, Dec. 31, 1861) unless there was an earlier trip to Washington not mentioned in the diary, which seems unlikely.

[59] *Supra*, May 9, 1862, note 31.

[60] *Supra*, Dec. 31, 1861, note 69.

[61] *Supra*, Dec. 31, 1861, note 70.

[62] *Supra*, July 30, 1859, note 61.

[63] The largest city in Mississippi, commanding the lower river. It was surrendered by Pemberton to Grant on July 4 after a siege that had lasted since the middle of May.

[64] Fought July 1–3. Gettysburg and Vicksburg together proved the turning point in the War.

[65] One of Barton's daughters.

[66] Thirteen-year-old son of Barton Bates.

and Onward—Got good sleeping Cars—and ran very comfortably to Chicago, 6. a. m.

Mr. Fogg (of Barnum's [67]) introduced me to Mr.[   ]Cook, agt. [   ] R. R. who took good care of us all the way to Chicago, and there, procured tickets for us as far as Niagara falls—i. e. for the propeller Oneida, round to Detroit, and thence by the (Canada) grand trunk R. R—

[July] 24. Remained in Chicago, at the Sherman House, till 5. p. m. Then embarked in the good Propeller Oneida, Capt Parmer, and, at 8. p. m, left the Garden City.[68]

During the day, rode round, for an hour or two, to see the notabilities—with much pleasure to the ladies, and [the] delight of Onwy.[69] O. H. Browning [70] called to see me. Interesting conversation—He seems deeply concerned, and fearful of trouble from the extreme wing of our Rep[ublica]ns. that they will attempt to treat the *returning* states, as conquered provinces, imposing terms upon their *re*-admission. I endeavored to quiet his fears, by urging the extreme folly of such a course and the enlightened character of some of the leaders, who will not fail to see, in such a course, their own defeat and downfall. Our time being short, Mr. B.[rowning] promised to write me more fully, upon the subject—

Left Chicago (in the good propeller *Oneida*, Capt Parmer) at 7. p. m. and reached Milwaukee in the [morning] of *saturday 25 July*. Remained there, taking in freight, the greater part of the day—Notwithstanding the rain, our party (including Mr. Clymer and wife) rode over a good part of the City, in an omnibus—I was surprised at the large [n]umber of beautiful houses—

<Made a pleasant acquaintance with Wm. B. Clymer and wife—of Wellsburg, North Penna.—Mr. C.[lymer] is a grandson of Geo Clymer, the *Signer* of the Declaration of Independence—a very pleasant and well-informed gentleman, and is agent of the great Bingham estate, outside of Phil[adelphi]a.—We travelled together from Chicago to Mackinaw, where we parted—He for L.[ake] Superior, we for Niagara Falls *via* Detroit.

On the way from Milwaukee, we had cloudy and drizzly weather, with cold wind—Stopped some hours to wood, at *Oneida*—on the main land of Mich[igan]: and also at big Beaver Island—Arrived at Mackinaw, 6. a. m. Monday 26th. July[.]

---

[67] Barnum's City Hotel at Third and Vine Streets, St. Louis.

[68] In her early days Chicago surpassed other cities in the extent of her parks and acquired the title "garden city," which she retains on her coat of arms though other cities have far surpassed her in per capita park acreage.

[69] His grandson, Onward.

[70] *Supra*, Sept. 21, 1859, note 97.

July 26 monday. Left Mackinaw, between 8 and 9 a. m. Had a delightful run down to Detroit, where we landed late in the afternoon. Spent the night, pleasantly, at the Michn. Exchange Hotel, kept by Mr. [   ], (who volunteered to give me a note of introduction to Mr. [   ] who keeps the *International,* at N.[iagara] Falls).

[*July*] *27.* After early breakfast, crossed the river, and took the (Canada) Great Western R. R. to " Suspension Bridge[.]"

Note—The Canada peninsula is, by no means so good a Country as I though[t]—much swamp sand and gravel—Level until you approach the hills that border the upper end of Lake Ontario— Dined at *London*—a poor dinner for " the London Tavern[.]"

Dwindass [Dundas] is a pretty place, surrounded by picturesque scenery—Hamilton (at the head of Lake Ontario) is a handsome, th[r]iving looking City—We did not stop there. Remained at the falls two nights and a day.

The trip, all the way around from Chicago, to the falls, was cool and pleasant, and pleased us all very much—

The trip from the falls to Washington, was hot, dusty and disagreeable—

Reached home at noon, saturday August 1, and found all in good health.

[*August 7.*] For a week after my return I did little official work —In fact. there was nothing pressing, and the weather being very hot, I made no great effort.

There is a lull in Public business. On the surface at least, every thing seems seems [*sic*] quiet, yet I apprehend that great efforts are making to arrange plans for future political action, and quietly to establish positions to govern future consequences.

There is, in fact, *no Cabinet*, and the show of Cabinet-councils is getting more and more, a mere show—Little matters or isolated propositions are sometimes talked over, but the great business of the country—questions of leading policy—are not mentioned in C.[abinet] C[ouncil]—unless indeed, after the fact, and when some difficulty has arisen out of a blunder.

Aug 7. This morning visited L[ieutenan]t. Geo. P. Bryan (son of Jno. H. B.[ryan] of Raleigh) at Lincoln Hospital—He is quite well, tho' the pistol shot wound on his head is not quite healed.

Saw also there L[ieutenan]t Mills of Missi. The stump of his leg is almost well.

I offered both of them to supply any necessaries—At present they needed nothing, saying that their comforts were well attended to.

Both of them behaved like polite and self-respecting gentlemen.

Aug 7. Lent Capt C. DeWitt Smith [71] $135, to enable him to go away on his leave of absence, to be paid out of his first accruing salary—He left with me a paper to that effect.

Aug 7. Sent to L[ieutenan]t Henry. T. Coalter (son of St. Geo: C[oalter]) rebel prisoner of War at Johnson's Island [72]—$50— T.[reasury] N.[otes] in a letter written in answer to his of July 25.
Note. My letter was forwarded by Col Hoffman,[73] Com[mis]-s[ione]r. of Prisoners.

Aug 7. Gov Pierpoint [74] of Va. dined with me alone today, and talked pretty freely abt. men and things in Va. and W. Va. He seems to have very loose notions about the principles of Govt. in these disjointed times. And especially in the matter of the Prest's emancipation proclamation.
He promised to bring to see me " Port[e] Crayon "—Col Strother.[75]

[*A note from J. M. Vaughan [76] dated August 7, 1863, says that Mr. Wallace [77] wants him to urge Bates and the President to do something about appointing a district attorney in western Missouri. Capt. Smith [78] asks a short note from Bates " to protect him against Provost Martials [sic] on his trip."*]

Aug 11 Tuesday. In C.[abinet] C.[ouncil] brought up and read to the Prest: a newspaper article containing Genl. Halleck's [79] *false* telegram [80] to F. Billings,[81] and denounced it in plain terms.

[71] Clerk in the Attorney-General's Office whom Bates used as a confidential messenger and personal agent. In 1864 Bates secured him the secretaryship of the Territory of Idaho.

[72] An island in Lake Erie a mile or two inside the entrance to Sandusky Bay, Ohio. Confederate *officers* were imprisoned there.

[73] William Hoffman, West Point graduate of 1829, served in the Black Hawk War, in Mexico, and on the frontier. While still on frontier duty he was made a prisoner by Confederate Texans and held until 1862. He was commissary-general of prisoners at Washington, 1862–1865.

[74] Francis H. Pierpont: Virginia anti-slavery lawyer; governor, 1861–1868, over the loyal remnant of Virginians who maintained a Unionist state government throughout the Civil War.

[75] David H. Strother ("Porte Crayon"): Virginian artist and writer whose sketches first appeared in *Harper's Magazine* about 1850; officer under McClellan and Pope in Virginia, and Banks in the Southwest; chief-of-staff of David Hunter.

[76] *Supra,* March 6, 1863, note 59.

[77] Thomas B. Wallace: merchant of Lexington, Missouri; Federal marshal of the Western District of that State, 1862–1865, 1866–1869.

[78] C. DeWitt Smith.

[79] *Supra,* Nov. 13, 1861, note 37. Halleck was formerly " superintendent-general of the mine, and principal agent of the company " and in one of the early contests over the title to the mine was attorney for the company. He was therefore keenly interested in seeing the present controversy settled in favor of the company.

[80] July 13, 1863, *War of the Rebellion,* series 1, vol. 50, part 2, serial no. 106, p. 522. Halleck assured Billings that " the order for a military occupation of New Almaden was surreptitiously obtained. The Secretary of War has directed General Wright to suspend operations, to restore everything as he found it, and to obey no orders which do not come through the proper channels."

[81] Frederick Billings: young Vermont lawyer who went to California in 1849, where he acquired wealth and political power; later, president of the Northern Pacific Railroad.

And, that same night, wrote to Genl. H.[alleck] informing him what I had done.

Note—A day or two after, he wrote me a silly letter, trying to be cunning and evasive, but evincing very bad judgment and [w]orse taste, and leaving himself open and bare to my reply, wch. he is sure to get, tho' I put off; for the present, for further developements [*sic*]—especially to see what use is made in Cala. of his false testimony. He, foolishly (in his letter to me) reaffirms that the order was *surreptitiously* obtained, as charged in his telegram to Billings. Now, the papers bring us his telegram to Parrot[t] [82]— *two days older* than that to Billings! Truly, "a liar ought to have a good memory."

Aug 18. The Nat:[ional] Intel[ligence]r. of today, contains an able leader upon the history, principles and object of the war, entitled "Wh[e]re are we?"

Aug 24. How they captured *fugitive slaves* in old times—Cicero writes to his friend *Publius Sulpicius* Gov of Illyricum, to catch and return to him his Librarian *Dyonicius* who had stolen some books, and run away, and was lurking in his Province—says the great Tully,[83] "I shall look upon myself as highly indebted to you, if I should recover *this fellow* by your assistance." Melmoth's Cicero, Vol 2. p. 398—Letter 36. of book 9.

No doubt he got his "run[awa]y mi[?] nigger" and probably served him as the accomplished Pollio [84] did his head-waiter, for carlessly breaking a fine glass vase—i. e. chopped him up, and threw the pieces into the Fish-pond—human flesh being thought a fine fattener of fish! In Rome, a master had the same power over his slaves as [over] his pigs.

Aug 27. Recd. from the Navy Dept. (date 26) Appointment of Henry W Sprole (son of my friend W. S. [prole] [85] d. d. of Newburg[h]) to be a midshipman, if he pass Examination—and at once, sent it to his father.

Free negro confederate soldiers

Aug 27 The Nat[ional] Intel[ligence]r. of today, copies from the Nashville Union of Aug 22., an Act of the Tenn: Legislature, passed

---

[82] John Parrott was the American consul at Mazatlán, Mexico, on the Gulf of California, who in 1842 told Admiral Jones that war had been declared with Mexico and urged him to seize California. In the 1850's he became a capitalist and banker in San Francisco and acquired an interest in the New Almaden Mine. This telegram (July 11, 1863, *ibid.*, 518) had assured Parrott that "there has been no military order to interfere with New Almaden Mine. No such military interference is authorized by the War Department, nor will any be permitted."

[83] Marcus Tullius Cicero.

[84] Gaius Asinius Pollio (76 B. C.–5 A. D.), Roman orator, politician, soldier, poet, historian, supporter of Julius Cæsar.

[85] The minister who coached Woodson Bates prior to his entry into West Point.

June 28 1861. for enlistment, as *volunteers* or by *impressment*, of *free negro[e]s* into the army.[86]

Note. Louisiana had done it before.[87] E B.

Also, Professor Parsons'[88] review of the recent English decisions upon the Neutrality Law—case of the *Alexandra*.[89]

Sept. 1st. Today, several of my family—Nancy, Sarah, Ellen, and Onward, escorted by John M. Vaughan[90]—and accompanied by Dick, who goes on business, as far as Cinc[inna]ti—left for Mo. They went to Phil[adelphi]a.—today—thence by Pittsburg, Crestline and Indianapolis, to St Louis.

Note—They were in St Louis on the 4th. "all right" so John Vaughan telegraphs.

Sept. 4. This is my birth-day. I have filled the al[l]oted term of human life—"three score and ten years"—and, taking a fair average of good and evil, in this "checquered scene" of our existence I have great cause of gratitude to God, for the large share of good that has been vouchsaved [*sic*] to me.

My physical powers, and, as I hope, my mental faculties, are better preserved, than in most men of my age. My constitution, naturally robust, is unimpaired by any definite disease, and the gradual decay of time, comes on so slowly, that I hardly perceive its approach. Sight and hearing (blunted and deminished [*sic*] no doubt) are still comfortably available, for all the purposes of business and pleasure; and I still eat and drink and sleep as pleasantly as in my youth.

As happens with old men, generally, I shall probably be the last to perceive my own mental decay. But, with this monition before me, I think myself *now*, as capable of moral and intellectural [*sic*] perceptions, and as able to bear mental labor, as at any period of my life. Thought is as free and locomotion as easy to me, as at any former time—inter[r]upted however, at this moment, by a severe cold, transient, I hope, in its cause and consequences.

My life has been crowned with many blessings, and, comparatively few crosses, especially in my personal and domestic relations. As

---

[86] *Public Acts of the State of Tennessee,* 33 General Assembly, extra session, chap. XXIV, pp. 49–50.

[87] "An Act to authorize the Governor . . . to press into the service of the State, Slaves and other property, for the public defences . . . ," *Acts Passed by the Twenty-Seventh Legislature of . . . Louisiana, in Extra Session . . . , December, 1862, & January 1863,* No. 10.

[88] Theophilus Parsons: son of the Massachusetts chief justice and framer of the Constitution; Dane professor of law at Harvard, 1847–1882; author of numerous legal treatises.

[89] The English court decided that the British Government could not stop an English ship about to sail from an English port to be converted on the high seas into a Confederate warship. *The Attorney-General* v. *Sillem and Others,* E. T. Hurlstone and F. J. Coltman, *Exchequer Reports,* II, 430–640

[90] *Supra,* March 6, 1863, note 59.

a citizen and publicist, I have reached a position quite as high, and have gained a reputation, for knowledge and probity, quite as good as I deserve. And in my *domestic* relations, no man has been more blessed. I have been married more than 40 yrs, and can truly say what I think few men can, that my wife, in all that time, never did an unkind act nor spoke a rep[r]oachful word to me. And my children (with only two exceptions in a large family [91]) have so de-meaned themselves as to make my respect equal to the love I bear them. I have not a wide circle of *friends*, but I have *some*, as true, as ste[a]dfast and as highly valued, as any man is blessed with. I am richly over-paid for all that I have done or can do.

Sept 12, Saturday. Mr. R. B. Carnahan [92] Dist Atty, W.[estern] D.[istrict of] Pa. (of Pittsburg) dined with me—

In the evening, Mr. Price Dist Atty, [of] Md., called, and staid the night, and breakfasted[.]

Much rain in the night.

Sep 13. Sunday—Dick arrived from Cinc[inna]ti, this morning via the B. & O. R. R.—reports the road good and smooth.

Sep 14.—A 11. a. m. C.[abinet] C.[ouncil] (by special call) to consider the difficulties arising out of the frequent and increasing issue of writs of Hab:[eas] corp:[us] for soldiers and military pris-oners. At first there seemed to be very various opinions. The Prest. was greatly moved—more angry than I ever saw him—declared that it was a formed plan of the democratic copperheads, deliberately acted out to defeat the Govt., and aid the enemy. That no honest man did or could believe that the State Judges have any such power [93] &c.

Some (e. g. M. Blair) suggested that a *case be made*, before a Federal Judge, so that we might have a *legal* judgment on our side.

I objected that *no judicial* officer, had power to take a prisoner or soldier, out of the hand[s] of the Prest, by Hab:[eas] Corp:[us] and proposed that we act purely upon the defensive—i. e. inform the judge who issued the writ, of the cause of imprisonment, refuse to deliver the body, and retain possession, by force, if need be. And in case of attempt to punish the officer, for contempt, protect him, by force if need be.

---

[91] He had seventeen children, eight of them still living.

[92] Robert B. Carnahan, after defeat for the Legislature as a Whig, had early joined the Republican Party, and was district attorney, 1861–1870.

[93] In the case of *Ex parte Milligan* (4 Wallace 1–142) in 1866, the Supreme Court decided that state judges did have the right to release a "military prisoner" and that neither President nor Congress could deny him the privilege of the writ of *habeas corpus* if he were "a citizen not connected with the military service and resident in a state where the courts [were] open and in the proper exercise of their jurisdiction."

I resisted the idea, held out by some, of vengeance, or penal justice, by imprisoning the judge who issued the writ.

Sep 15. Again C.[abinet] C.[ouncil] met, and, after some consultation, the result was that an order was to be issued to refuse obedance [*sic*] to the writ, and protect the officer refusing—Also to issue a proclamation suspending the privilege of the writ of Hab[eas] Corp:[us] *in such cases*, under the act of Congress [94] of Mar. 3. 1863.

For the Proclamation,[95] see Nat[ional] Intel[ligence]r. of Sept 16.

Sept. 16. Wednesday—Col Leatherman of Memphis, Tenn: called, with a friendly message from Col A. D. Stuart, of N. Y. who, it seems, is very anxious for [that] the Prest. should issue a proclamation of amnesty. &c[.]

I had a free conversation with Col L.[eatherman] who professed to be highly pleased with my scheme of policy to end the war, and restore the states to their proper functions in the union[.]

[*Marginal Note.*] Col L.[eatherman] expressed surprise at a conversation he had with Mr. Holt,[96] who, he sd. was much excited, and insisted upon a *convention* to settle the terms of peace.

Robt. Dale Owen [97]—Last night, Mr. Barrett [98] (Com[mis]s[ione]r. of Pensions) promised to get me a letter of Mr. O.[wen] proving him a secessionist, *before* the war began.

Saturday night—19. Sept. My niece, Mrs. Flementine Ball,[99] of Lancaster Co.[unty] Va., arrived at our house, very much fatigued, having been delayed in her trip from Baltimore, by a broken bridge.

Sep 21. Last friday, 18 Sep. there was a flood of rain which swept away many small bridges, and did other damage—I fell sick with the storm, and have been confined ever since.

Yesterday, died *Albert Klopfer* my little friend—a very fine boy, and assistant to his father, who is chief messenger in my office[.]

[*September*] *23.* Called to see Genl. Hooker [1] and met also Genl. Butterfield[.][2]

Sep 23. Mr. Mason of St Louis (Taylor & Mason) called at the office, and told me i. a. that there was to be here in a few days,

[94] *U. S. Statutes at Large,* XII, 37 Cong., 3 Sess., chap. LXXXI, pp. 755–758.
[95] Sept. 15, 1863. J. D. Richardson, *Messages and Papers of the Presidents,* VI, 170–171.
[96] *Supra,* Feb. 2, 1860, note 49.
[97] Son of Robert Owen, wealthy British manufacturer and reformer; resident of his father's Utopia at New Harmony, Indiana, in 1825; Indiana state legislator, 1835–1838, 1851; Democratic congressman, 1843–1847; chargé d'affaires and then minister resident to the Two Sicilies, 1853–1858; reformer; abolitionist. He was now serving as chairman of a commission set up by Stanton to study the condition of the recently-freed negroes.
[98] *Supra,* Nov. 19, 1861, note 55.
[99] Daughter of Mr. Bates's brother Fleming.
[1] *Supra,* March 29, 1863, note 69.
[2] *Supra,* April 4, 1863, note 81.

a Delegation of radicals of 1000? to carry the adm[inistratio]n by storm. And that Jim Lane [3] was here to make arrangements for them, &c[.]

Sep 26. saturday. Last night we recd. letters from Broadhead [4] and Rollins,[5] on the subject of the Radical Delegation. This morning called on the Prest, gave him the letters, and had a free and pointed conversation—i. a. he said he *wd. not* remove Schofield,[6] unless something new and unexpected shd. be made out agst. him. I wrote back, to both B.[roadhead] and R[ollins].

Sept. 27. sunday— . . . This morning, I noticed hoar-frost upon the slate of the neighboring roofs.

Last night, recd. a note from Dr. Lieber,[7] with an article of his, in the Ev[enin]g. Post of Sep 19—entitled "Slavery, in point of Social economy," in which he proposes the suppression of Slavery, in the process of *re-construction.* He refers, with praise, to *Jos: Kay's* new work, "Social condition and Education of the People in England." [8]

The Dr. *theorises* very well, he suggests ends, perhaps good in themselves, but wholly ignores the principles and means of their attainment.

Sept. 30. At night Mr. Eads [9] dropped in all unlooked for—His family is at Willard[']s.

Today, the Jacobin Delegation of Mo. and Kansas had its audience of the Prest. I saw him afterwards in a good humor. Some of them he said, were not as bad as he supposed—He really thought some of them were were [sic] pretty good men, if they only knew how! Of course, they did not get Schofield's [10] head.

Mr. Chase invited me to his house to night, *to meet Mr. Drake.*[11] But I declined. I did not wish to meet him *there.* Mr. D.[rake] when last here was a frequent visitor, both at my office and house: This time he has not called at all—conscious, I suppose of his ill-behavior, both to me and [to] my friends.

---

[3] *Supra,* Feb. 3, 1862, note 44.

[4] *Supra,* Dec. 26, 1859, note 66.

[5] *Supra,* Dec. 1, 1859, note 1.

[6] *Supra,* May 30, 1863, note 32. The Missouri Radicals were trying to secure his removal.

[7] *Supra,* April 5, 1862, note 62.

[8] Published in New York by Harper and Brothers in 1863. Joseph Kay was a widely-traveled British economist, sociologist, barrister, and judge of the Salford Hundred Court of Record.

[9] *Supra,* Jan. 28, 1860, note 38.

[10] *Supra,* May 30, 1863, note 32.

[11] *Supra,* Feb. 12, 1863, note 13. He was organizing the Radical faction in Missouri against Bates and his Conservative friends.

Oct 15. The good old *Nat[iona]l. Intelligencer* still struggles
on painfully, to keep itself alive. For some time past it has been
full of able articles upon several of the important questions which
now occupy the public mind. The No. of yesterday, the 14th. is
especially rich. It contains *Rd. H Dana's*[12] admirable speech delivered at Cambridge, against the wild theories of Sumner,[13] Boutwell,[14] Whiting,[15] and the like—that the revolted States being *out
of the Union,* and to be ruled as conquered territory—and that we
must fight (not for the original cause of the war, but a new cause[)]
"the holy cause of civilization and christianity." Also, a fine *leader*
upon the same subject—also Mo. Affairs. and a letter to the Prest.
from Messrs. Rollins[16] and Gibson.[17]

All day there have been rumors of a great battle between Meade[18]
and Lee. I had expected it and in fact, hoped it. To night (Col)
Ulric Dahlgren,[19] came in, on his crutches, to see us, and reported
that Meade had fallen back farther than I supposed with his H[ea]d.
Qu[arte]rs. at Fairfax C.[ourt] H[ouse]. <afterwards, got a
pencil-note from Coalter—H[ea]d. Q[uarte]rs. at Centreville, not
Fairfax C.[ourt] H[ouse].—He (C[oalter]) seems anxious for a
general battle between the two armies, and afraid that Lee will again
be suffered to escape. He seems confident in both the army and the
general. No wonder that he (having fought and suffered through
all the campaigns of the army of the Potomac) should long to see
that army have one fair chance in the field. Heretofore, it has
always been made to fight at disadvantage, and even when winning
bloody victories, to get no fruits.[>]

Note. Coalter has recd. his promotion, and is now a captain, to
date from *May 1. 1863.*

Oct 16   Friday—At C.[abinet] C.[ouncil] the Prest read to us
his answer to the *Radical* delegation of Kansas and Mo.[20] Altho'

---

[12] *Supra,* Feb. 26, 1863, note 48.

[13] *Supra,* Jan. 7, 1860, note 9.

[14] George S. Boutwell: a leader of the Radicals; governor of Massachusetts, 1851, 1852;
member of the Washington Peace Convention of 1861; commissioner of Internal Revenue,
1862–1863; now Republican congressman, 1863–1869; U. S. senator, 1873–1877.

[15] William Whiting: Boston lawyer; solicitor of the War Department, 1862–1865; author of a book in which he upheld the most extreme powers of president and congress over
"rebels."

[16] *Supra,* Dec. 1, 1859, note 1.

[17] *Supra,* April 27, 1859, note 27.

[18] George G. Meade: West Point graduate of 1835; Mexican War veteran; officer of
engineers until 1861; brigadier-general with the Army of the Potomac, 1861–1863; commander of the Army of the Potomac, 1863–1865; Union commander at Gettysburg.

[19] A Philadelphia law student who volunteered on the outbreak of war and served as an
aide to Generals Sigel, Burnside, Frémont, Hooker, and Pope. He had lost a leg at
Gettysburg and was just recovering. Later he was again to do active service and lose his
life in battle. He was the son of John A. B. Dahlgren (*supra,* May 13, 1862, note 39).

[20] Oct. 5, 1863, *Complete Works of Abraham Lincoln,* II, 419–423.

too long, and not phrased in the pointed language I could wish, still, it denies every thing they ask, and is a flat rebuff.

He also read his letter to Genl Schofield,[21] which, tho' in some of its parts, lacking in precision and speciality, still, with a good understanding between the Gov[22] and the Genl., all our legal and legitimate ends may be easily accomplished.

In course of the conversation, I drew the Prest.'s attention to Gov Gamble's last letter—I said it was a formal *demand*, under the constitution, upon *this* government, to protect the State Govt. against local insurrection, wch. was the simple *duty* of this govt. to do &c. The Prest. admitted the duty, but he did not know that there was any such insurrection &c. I answered, substantially, that the Gov's demand was the only evidence *required by the constitution*. The President then said, that certainly he wd. protect the Govt. of Mo., just as he wd. the Govt. of Pa., neither more nor less.

Oct 17 Saturday—I'm afraid Mr. Chase's head is turned by his eagerness in pursuit of the presidency. For a long time back he has been filling all the offices in his own vast patronage, with extreme partizans, and contrives also to fill many vacancies, properly belonging to other departments.

In the *Judiciary, his* appointments seem to me particularly unfortunate, made without any reference to legal and judicial qualification. e. g. Chief Justice *Cartter*[23] of the Sup[rem]e Court, D.[istrict of] C.[olumbia,] is a fierce partizan, an inbred vulgarian and a truculent ignoramus. Ch:[ief] Justice Turner[24] of Nevada Ter-[ritor]y., I do not personally know, but I hear from others, that he is an abridgement of Cartter.

His course in regard to the Dist. of S.[outhern] Florida greatly surprised me. 1. He caused Mr. Bingham[25] of O.[hio] to be apptd.— I tho[ugh]t well of B.[ingham] and made no objection. He was apptd. (to succeed Marvin,[26] resigned) on the *4th of June*, and he, neither accepting nor declining, hung on, higgling and negotiating for leave of absence till Nov 1. tho it was notorious that the public service was suffering for lack of a judge. At last (I insisting that we *must* have a judge) early *in Sept.*, he declined *still with a*

[21] Oct. 1, 1863, *ibid.*, II, 416–417. See *supra*, May 30, 1863, note 32.

[22] Hamilton R. Gamble. *Supra*, July 23, 1859, note 39.

[23] David K. Cartter: Democratic congressman from Ohio, 1849–1853; delegate to the Republican Convention of 1860; minister to Bolivia, 1861–1862; chief justice of the Supreme Court of the District of Columbia, 1863–1887.

[24] George Turner, appointed from Ohio.

[25] *Supra*, Dec. 20, 1862, note 91. He had been defeated for reëlection to Congress in 1862. William W. Lawrence of Ohio was finally appointed.

[26] William Marvin: New York lawyer; U. S. district attorney, 1835–1839, and judge, 1839–1863, of the Southern District of Florida; provisional governor of Florida, 1865–1866.

condition. I told the Prest that the condition was inadmissible. and the declention absolute[.]

Octo 19. Judge R. K. Williams,[27] (Court of Appeals, Ky) of Mayfield Ky—dined with me today. Had a good deal of conversation abt affairs of Ky and Mo.

Oct. 20. The Nat[ional] Intel[ligence]r of today contains Mr. Chase's late speech at Cincinnati (and another at Indianapolis). in which he supposes that our successes are due to the *Proclamation of Freedom.*[28] <It is in striking contrast to Senator Sherman [29] of O.[hio] and various other authorities quite as high, and to the facts of history.> In other parts of those speeches, Mr. C.[hase] attributes the salvation of the country to his own *admirable financial system,* quite as intelligibly, but in language not quite as plain as Cicero's—who swore " By the immortal Gods, I have saved my country." That visit to the west is generally understood as Mr. Ch[a]ses' [*sic*] opening campaign for the Presidency. At all events the war is openly begun between Mr. C.[hase] and the Blairs. see Genl. Frank Blair's [30] answer to Mr. Blow's [31] speech in the St Louis Union of Octo 19.

Octo 22. Mr. A. Burwell of St Louis (formerly of Vicksburg Missi.) dined with me today (introduced by Genl. Coalter [32]) he seems an intelligent man, Virginia born, driven from Missi. by the war, now practising in St Louis.

Octo 22. Recd. a letter from J. O. Broadhead [33] who says that W. W Edwards *is* a candidate for C[ircui]t. Judge in St Charles C[ircui]t., and intimates that he ought to be turned out.

He also passes a high eulogy upon Prest Lincoln's reply to the Mo. Radicals[.] [34]

Oct 26. The Mo. Rep:[ublican] recd. today, contains an extract from one of the German papers printed there, accusing Mr. Seward of delivering to Mr. Mercier,[35] for the use of the French Govt., all the maps, charts &c of various parts of Mexico, which were deposited by

[27] Rufus K. Williams: supporter of Breckinridge for President in the Democratic Convention of 1860; unionist when the War came; supporter of Lincoln's renomination in 1864; judge of the Kentucky Court of Appeals, 1862–1870.

[28] Issued Sept. 22, 1863; Jan. 1, 1863.

[29] John Sherman: Ohio delegate to the Whig conventions of 1848 and 1852; an organizer of the Republican Party in Ohio; Republican congressman, 1855–1861; U. S. senator, 1861–1877, 1881–1897; secretary of the Treasury, 1877–1881; secretary of State, 1897–1898. He had helped Chase secure passage of the bills issuing greenbacks, but unlike Chase, he was conservative on the negro issue.

[30] *Supra,* April 27, 1859. note 25.

[31] *Supra,* Sept. 20, 1859, note 95.

[32] *Supra,* Dec. 20, 1860, note 16.

[33] *Supra,* Dec. 26, 1859, note 66.

[34] *Supra,* Oct. 16, 1863.

[35] *Supra,* Nov. 27, 1861, note 77.

Genl. Scott in our public archives, on his return from the Mexican War.

Coincident with this, Mr. Coffey [36] told me, privately, today, that, last night, Count Gurowski [37] shewed him a letter from Mr. Wilk[e]s,[38] editor of the Spirit of the Times, containing the same charge.

This Mr. Wilk[e]s has lately written an article on " *the conservative plot* " which is copied into the Mo. Democrat. They say he is a *smart fellow*, but that does not make him a wise man. He edits a *Sporting* (gambling) paper, and as *jockeying* is his trade, we need not be surprised at any lie he tells. And as for the *conservative plot*, I hope there is some truth in it; for, it is high time that all honest conservative men should lay their heads together and contrive the best schemes they can, to save something from the wreck which the unscrupulous radicals are conspiring to bring upon the country.

German Radical Convention

Oct 29.   The Nat[iona]l. Intelligence[r] of this morning contains an excellent leader upon the Prest's answer to the Mo. Radicals.[39]

Also—Platform of the *German Radical Convention*, lately held at *Cleveland*.[40]

See forward, p. 217—for the R G. Convention at Indianapolis— in 1865[.] [41]

This German combination is the more to be wondered at, because some of the members of the Convention have good reputation for talents and learning, and stand high, at least in literary circles. Men of their transcendental philosophy, and dogmatic theories of Government, especially when coupled with practical ignorance of our political institutions and of the very meaning of the phrase "Liberty by Law," might be pardoned some of the absurd errors of their platform. But their grotesque egotism, personal and national, is hard to be endured. They are, I suppose, naturalized citizens of the U. S;

---

[36] *Supra,* March 5, 1860, note 18.

[37] *Supra,* Nov. 27, 1861, note 65.

[38] George Wilkes: politician; traveler; author; editor of the New York *Spirit of the Times* since 1850.

[39] *Supra,* Oct. 16, 1863.

[40] The platform demanded: (1) the integrity of the Union, (2) the unconditional suppression of rebellion, (3) abolition of slavery, (4) revision of the Constitution "in the spirit of the Declaration of Independence," (5) application of the "conquered territory" theory to the Southern states, (6) confiscation of "rebel" lands for the benefit of loyal men, (7) "realization of the Monroe Doctrine," (8) alliance with European revolution against foreign intervention, (9) "protection of the freedom of the press and speech against military usurpation," (10) universal military service, (11) support of candidates for office who will support this platform.

[41] *Infra,* July 19, 1865.

and yet, they ignore the laws which made them such, and the oaths which bind them to be, not *Germans*, but *Americans*.

Here, in America, they band themselves together into a cabal, avowedly political, and to control, if possible, the Government of the Country, *as foreigners*. They openly do it, in a fereign [*sic*] name and with no bond of union but foreign ties. They ostentatiously proclaim that they stand aloof from all *American* parties, having for their only object the concentration of the entire *radical German* strength, so as to enable them to wield this avowedly *foreign* power, to turn the scale, in all doubtful elections among *Americans!*

Our naturalization law does all it can to make them *Americans;* and they, in seeking to get the benefits of that law, begin by taking an oath of abjuration against all other countries. Then, after a few years of probation, required for the very purpose of changing them into *Americans*, they are allowed to take the oath of allegiance to this Country, and thus become the political equals of natural-born citizens. And yet these forgetful men, in spite of laws and oaths (all the benefits of which they enjoy) *refuse to be Americans*, and insist upon being *Germans!*

Their motive lies upon the surface, and is obvious. Their leaders believe that they can lead at pleasure, the ignorant masses of their country men in America; and with such a following at their heels, they hope to be able to sell themselves and their deluded *foreigners*, to good advantage, to the leaders of *American* parties and factions. They forget that, *as Germans*, they have no rights in this country— that all their rights here, have been granted to them upon the express condition that they cease to be Germans, and become Americans.

Their platform <I have the platform, as printed, filed away some where>[42] is a strange mixture of impudence and absurdity. They (being *Germans*) insist upon the *Monroe Doctrine* (without knowing what it is) and will have us go to war with France, for intruding into Mexico.

But the very madness of their absurdity is found in their dogma that this country must be in alliance (not with the nations or governments of Europe, but) with the *Revolutionists* of Europe! And the wise and consistent object of that *holy alliance* is declared to be *to prevent foreign intervention!*

Even Kossuth's foolish impudence did not equal this—for he did not pretend to be an *American* citizen.[43]

---

[42] Added in the margin.

[43] Hungarian nationalist and leader of the Revolution of 1848–1849 who, on his visit to the United States in 1851–1852, received an enthusiastic welcome in the North as an opponent of European "tyranny" and then demanded that the United States aid the Hungarian revolt and form an alliance with Great Britain to prevent foreign intervention to suppress revolution in Hungary or elsewhere.

Nov 10. . . .

Yesterday came *Frederick Roever* <He brot. me a letter of introduction from G. F. Filley [44] > [45] of St Louis—a very intelligent German—He bears a commission of Gov Gamble [46] of Mo., as State agent for emigration in Germany. I introduced him to the President and Mr. Seward. Asked a small consulship in Germany, but Mr. F. Seward [47] said that cd. not be, for, as consul *he must* be instructed to have nothing to do with emigration. but offered to give him a general, official, recommendation to all our ministers and consuls in Germany, which is a far better *personal* voucher.

I gave him a copy of the acts of the last Congress, and at his special request, several copies of my Opinion on Citizenship, [48] which he desired to distribute in Germany.

He promised to write to me from abroad.

Nov 11. Talking with Mr. Hodge, in my office, this morning, about the starving condition of *our* captured soldiers at Richmond. He said he had spoken with S[t]anton about it this morning, and proposed that we should reduce to the same condition, the enemy's *officers* whom we hold as prisoners; and that Stanton told him that he had already issued orders to that effect!

Afterwards, on the same day, Coffey [49] told me what the order really was—i. e. that we propose, immediately, to the enemy, to victual our men held as prisoners, at Richmond; and if the enemy refuse to allow it, then threaten the enemy, to treat their men, held prisoners by us, just as they treat ours.

<[*Note.*] [November] 13th. I hear that provisions and clothes, to a large amount, have already been forwarded to our men.>

I denounced retaliation, in the form of starvation and lingering death, as a disgraceful barbarity, that would stink, in the nostrils of the world, through all time!

Nov 12. Thursday night—Attended (with Matilda) the wedding of Senator (Ex Gov.) Sprague [50] with Kate Chase, eldest daughter of Secy Chase.—a large and brilliant crowd.

[*November*] *13. The Canada plot*—Quite a sensation was produced by a letter from Lord Lyons [51] to Secy Seward, to the effect

---

[44] Giles F. Filley: crockery merchant of St. Louis; manufacturer of Excelsior stoves; Free-Soiler in 1848; supporter of Frémont in 1856; now an active Radical Unionist and associate of B. Gratz Brown and F. P. Blair, Jr.

[45] Added in the margin.

[46] *Supra,* July 23, 1859, note 39.

[47] *Supra,* May 13, 1862, note 38.

[48] November 29, 1862, *Official Opinions of the Attorneys-General of the United States,* X, 382–413. Bates maintained that "free men of color, if born in the United States, [were] citizens of the United States."

[49] *Supra,* March 5, 1860, note 18.

[50] William Sprague: wealthy Rhode Island manufacturer; governor, 1860–1863; Republican U. S. senator, 1863–1875.

[51] *Supra,* Sept. 26, 1860, note 24.

that the Govr. Genl. of Canada had discovered evidences of a plot contrived by our malcontents who have taken refuge in his province, to make a sudden invasion of certain of the Lake towns, Buffalo &c, and especially, to surprise Johnson's Island [52] and liberate the rebel officers (over 2000) whom we hold prisoners there.

The different Departments were busy, sending instructions to their several subordinates. I lost no time in putting upon their guard, the Dist. Attornies and Marshals, all along the Lake frontier.

I dont [sic] think there is any thing of importance in the matter. Indeed, I suspect that it is a *'cute* trick, gotten up by the enemy, with the hope that it might operate as a diversion, in favor of the enemy in Va. and N.[orth] C[arolina].

[*Marginal Note.*] 1864. Sept. 21. There is another *Canada* plot just now. Two Steamers have been seised by *some* body.

Nov 15 Sunday. . . . .

Again we are cast into deep sorrow—almost despair—about Dick. We had indulged the hope that his mortification and shame, and his loss of prestige by his ill conduct, followed by a painful sickness, would have led him to repentence [sic] and reformation. But all our hopes of that sort are blasted.

Thursday, the 12th., he left the house after breakfast, as if to go as usual, to his office work, under promise to return, at 3, and go, with Matilda, to a wedding reception, to Col Gardner's. He did not return till the latter part of the night—2 or 3 oclock. Then, finding the house closed, he would not ring, but tried to enter clandestinely, by the rear. He was heard and let in. Having rested only a few hours, he got his breakfast and went away—and has not since been heard of—How he is wasting his time, means and character and in what vile company, we are ignorant. But the terrible conviction is forced upon us, that he has abandoned himself to shame and ruin, and is no longer worthy to be a husband or a son. I have so written to Barton, and advised that his wife should remain in Mo.

(*Nov 22, Sunday*—He came home Sunday night—made a sort of confession—felt prostrate and debased. I shewed him the letter I wrote Barton—Yet, on thursday evening, he again left the house, as if only to take a walk—and has not yet been heard of! now, 11. a m.)

(—*Nov 25. Wednesday*—Tonight, Matt. Pleasants brot. him home in a nervous and agitated state (and brot Dr. Bulkley,) no doubt he has drunk himself into that condition and probably will be better tomorrow.

We have not yet seen him, thinking it wiser to let him sleep and calm himself first.

---

[52] *Supra*, Aug. 7, 1863, note 72.

Nov 17. This day I paid Coalter's draft in favor of (Capt) A. G. Mason (a.[ide-]d.[e-]c[amp] of Genl. Meade [53]) for $125—date Nov 9. Paid to James Trainer.

Nov 18. To day Genl. Millson,[54] of Norfolk, called on me[.]

Nov 19. Today is the consecration of the Military Cemetary [*sic*] at Gettysburg. The President and most of the Cabinet are gone—I could not go[.]

The Nat[iona]l. Intel[ligence]r. of today, contains an account of the late military *abuses of election,* in Md. under the orders of Genl Schenck[.] [55]

Also, a notice of Judge Underwood's [56] decision (in E.[astern] Dis[tric]t. of Va.,[)] that confiscation of land is of the Fee simple[.]

Today, calls upon me, Mr. *Richd. Busteed* [57] of N. Y. lately ap-ptd. U. S. Judge for the Districts of Alabama, *vice* Lane [58] Dec[ease]d.—I m [*sic*] afraid its [*sic*] a " slim chance " for he seems to me, "a slight, unmeritable man." (see forward Dec 26.[)]

Heeren [Arnold H. L.,] [*Reflections on the Politics of Ancient Greece*] [59] p 24. the City of *Sicyon*—its territory divided Achaia from Corinth. This state was one of the smallest in Greece—" But the importance of a commercial state does not depend upon [on] the extent of its territory. Venice was never more flourishing or more powerful, than at the time [at a time] when it did not possess a *square mile* on the continent. Wealthy Corinth[,] not more than *four miles* in extent " &c[.] [60]

p. 35. "And yet the Ætolians and the Acarnanians [61] remained bar-barians[,] after the Athenians had become the instructors of the world.—How difficult it is, to comprehend the history of the culture of nations !"

---

[53] *Supra,* Oct. 15, 1863, note 18.

[54] John S. Millson, Democratic congressman, 1849–1861. His title of general must have been an honorary one, or a mistake of Bates's.

[55] Robert C. Schenck: Ohio lawyer; Whig congressman, 1843–1851; minister to Brazil, 1851–1853; brigadier-general of volunteers in Virginia and West Virginia, 1861–1862; now major-general in command in Maryland, 1862–1863; congressman, 1863–1871; minister to Great Britain, 1870–1876.

[56] *Supra,* April 4, 1863, note 77.

[57] Irish-born New York lawyer; supporter of Douglas in 1860; brigadier-general of volunteers, 1862–1863, who resigned because of a political attack upon him. He held this Alabama judgeship until 1874 and in 1865 declared the "test oath" prescribed by Congress unconstitutional in the U. S. courts.

[58] George W. Lane: lawyer of Huntsville, Alabama; state legislator, 1829–1832; judge of the County Court, 1832–1834; circuit judge, 1834–1846. Lincoln appointed him U. S. district judge in 1861 but his strong unionist sentiments forced him to leave Alabama and he was never able to hold court.

[59] Translated by George Bancroft, Boston, 1824. Heeren was a German historian (1760–1842) who pioneered in the economic interpretation of history in his studies of the institutions, economic relations, and financial systems of ancient states.

[60] In these quotations, as usual, Mr. Bates has freely changed punctuation and capitalization, has added italics, and has copied inaccurately.

[61] Ætolia and Acarnania lay north of the Gulf of Corinth, west of Mt. Parnassus. Their inhabitants were geographically isolated and were constantly fighting each other.

The Ætolians and Acarnanians were in close proximity to both Athens and Corinth, and yet long after the latter had become rich powerful and polished, the former remained, poor, weak and barbarous.

The learned, Dr. [J. R.] Macduff [62]—speaking of the Journey of St Paul to Damascus, to punish the Christians, says—" Footprints of St Paul " p 52—" It must be borne in mind that the Roman emperors, though ever jealous about giving their own power to others, had (since the reign of Julius Cæsar) invested the Jewish High Priest, as head of the Sanhedrim, with full authority over all Israelites who might be living in foreign cities—[and] at least to the extent of excommunication, scourging and imprisonment." citing Lewin.

Heeren, [Reflections on the] Politics of [Ancient] Greece. page 6[-7].

" No European nation ever lived in tents[;] . . . Its soil and climate were peculiarly fitted to accustom them [men] to that regular industry[,] which is the source of all prosperity."

Ib: p. 8   " No Nation where Polygamy was established, has ever obtained a free and well-ordered constitution."

Ib: p 10.   " The distinction still continues apparent, between the Roman part of Europe[,] and that which never yielded to the Romans."

Ib: p 135 [136] <speaking of confederate governments in ancient times, our author says> " We find traces of such Amphictyonic Assemblies,[63] in Greece itself and in the Colonies."—Citing St. Croix, *Des Anciens Gouvern[e]men[t]s Federatifs*, p 115 etc: who gives a list of them.

[" The Peril and Duty of the American People, with Respect to the Foreign Relations of the Country, impending War with England and France, and the Threatened] *Humiliation and Partition* [of the United States] *of America.*["]

The Danville Review, for June, 1863, at p.p. 217–254, see a very striking article with the above title, by Revd. R. J. Breckenridge [64] D. D.[65]

[*A clipping giving:* (1) *an order of the Confederate Secretary of War that all money sent to prisoners should be paid over to them;* (2) *a denial by General Graham that this order had been carried out*

---

[62] A prolific British writer on religious subjects.

[63] Amphictyonic assemblies were gatherings of communities or states associated in a loose federation for festivals or worship at a shrine.

[64] Robert J. Breckinridge: Kentucky lawyer, 1824–1831; state legislator, 1825–1828; Presbyterian minister in Baltimore, 1832–1845; president of Jefferson College, Pennsylvania, 1845–1847; superintendent of public instruction in Kentucky, 1847–1851; professor in the Danville Theological Seminary, 1851–1869. He worked for emancipation before the Civil War, and was a vigorous unionist and adviser of Lincoln on Kentucky affairs.

[65] All of the above citations and quotations are on a separate sheet which is bound into the diary.

up to the time that he left Libby Prison; (3) the vote of Rhode Island refusing to give the suffrage to aliens who had enlisted or might enlist in the Union Army.]

Nov 25. Last night Genl. John. S. Millson,[66] of Norfolk called and sat with me alone, for some hours of pleasant conversation. And today, called on me, at the office, and had a long talk. I think he is a good man, and, in the main, not unwise. Yet he has some strange cranks—e. g. he seems to me absurdly sincere in his old Virginia ideas of *State rights.*

News comes today from Chattanooga that we have gained important successes over the Enemy. Driven him from Lookout mountain[67] and several other important positions—taken two thousand prisoners. It is believed that Bragg[68] is in full retreat.

We hear also to day, that Meade[69] is advancing upon Lee. Coalter writes, Monday, that they were all packed up, ready for the march next morning. So we look for stirring events in the next few days. As it rained hard monday night I suppose the assault was delayed.

[*November*] *26.* Last night, of the 25, I was waked up, abt. midnight by a messenger from the War Office, with [a] copy of Telegram, announcing great successes near Chat[t]anooga, the capture of several strong positions and over 2000 men.

This is thanksgiving day, and the good news comes opportunely. Worshiped at Dr. Smith's church. The Dr. particularly dull— dined at Carrington's[.][70]

At 11. p. m. comes a messenger from the War office, with copy of telegram that Bragg is in full retreat burning his depots, and destroying bridges behind him.

Nov 27 Friday. Today my niece, Mrs. Flementine Ball,[71] left for home, to be landed in Coan river.[72] Com[modor]e Harwood[73]

---

[66] *Supra,* Nov. 18, 1863, note 54.

[67] Hooker attacked the Confederates on Lookout Mountain on November 23 and captured their intrenchments on November 24, while W. T. Sherman took the extreme right of Missionary Ridge, and George H. Thomas drove back the Confederate center.

[68] Braxton Bragg: West Point graduate of 1837; army officer until 1856; Louisiana planter; commissioner of public works who designed the drainage and levee system of Louisiana; brigadier-general in the Confederate Army who served on the Gulf coast in 1861, in Kentucky, at Corinth, at Shiloh in 1862; victor over Rosecrans at Chickamauga in September, 1863. Grant now took command and disastrously defeated Bragg at Chattanooga on November 23–25. Bragg retreated into Georgia and yielded his command to Joseph E. Johnston.

[69] *Supra,* Oct. 15, 1863, note 18.

[70] Edward C. Carrington, Virginia state legislator, 1850–1851; now U. S. district attorney of the District of Columbia.

[71] Daughter of Bates's brother, Fleming.

[72] A tributary of the Potomac in Northumberland County, Virginia, adjoining Lancaster County where she lived.

[73] Andrew A. Harwood: officer in the Navy since 1818; assistant inspector, 1843–1852, and inspector, 1858–1861, of ordnance; chief of the Bureau of Ordnance in 1861; commandant of the Washington Navy Yard and the Potomac Flotilla, 1862–1864.

sent her down in the most respectful manner—in a Government Steamer, the King Philip, (as I since learn, sent special). She was accompanied by Capt. Smith,[74] who attended her with delicate assiduity. On Sunday the 29th. she was safely landed, at the house of her friend, Col Claybrooke.

[*Note.*] Today, monday the 30th.—Cap[tain] Smith returned, and reports all right[.]

[*Marginal Note.*] Sarah J. Bates arrived from Wheeling, on Saturday Nov 28.

Nov 30. The President has been sick ever since thursday—I saw him, saturday, and he was then a little better. Today, monday, he is still improving, as I hear.

Meade [75] having crossed the Rapidann [*sic*] on friday, there has been some sharp fighting, in detached columns, but with no important result. I hear nothing to day, and only wonder that there is not, ere now, a general engagement.

George Smizer tells me that he saw *Fleming* [76] a few weeks, ago, at Montecello [*sic*] Arks: He [Fleming] had been sent from Price's [77] head Q[uarte]rs. in Arks., to Mobile, in pursuit of an absconding quarter master (Beltzehoover, formerly of Pittsburg—and then of St Louis) and was that far on his returner, having the prisoner in charge.

Smizer also says that *Genl. Frost* [78] has escaped, joined his mother in law, Mrs. Graham, and his own wife and children, and gone to Europe.[79]

[*Marginal Note.*] March 19, 64—I read in the news papers that Mrs. Frost has returned to St Louis taken oath and given bond.

. . .

Dec 1. I took a severe cold, by the change of temperature, am confined at home, sick, this day, so bright and beautiful.

Dec 5 Saturday. This day the *Potomac* water was let into the Washington Aqueduct,[80] for the first time. Heretofore the water has been supplied from a creek only. <The Nat[iona]l. Intel[ligence]r. of the 7th. contains a full account of the public ceremonies, dinner &c—I was invited to attend, but could not.[>]

[74] *Supra*, Aug. 7, 1863, note 71.

[75] *Supra*, Oct. 15, 1863, note 18.

[76] Mr. Bates's third son, who was in the Confederate Army.

[77] *Supra*, Nov. 27, 1861, note 70.

[78] *Supra*, Nov. 25, 1860, note 92.

[79] His wife had been banished from St. Louis for Confederate activity.

[80] The aqueduct of stone and brick was twelve and a half miles long and carried water from the Great Falls of the Potomac to the reservoir above Georgetown. The ceremonies included a trip by carriage to the Cabin John Bridge which carried the water across a deep ravine.

Dec 7 (1st. Monday of Dec) Congress, the Supreme Court, and the Court of Claims all met today.

In the H[ouse of] R[epresentatives], there was great apprehension of a disturbance, in consequence of a prevalent belief that Mr. Etherage,[81] Cl[er]k of the late House, would exclude many members from the list, on account of insufficient credentials. But no serious difficulty occurred. The organization was quietly effected, and *Sc[h]uyler Colfax* [82] of Inda., elected Speaker, on the first ballot.

In the Supreme Court, all ten of the Judges were present.

In the Court of Claims, present only Casey [83] C.[hief] J.[ustice] and Judges Loring [84] and Peck[.] [85]

—The solicitor, Mr. Gibson,[86] absent, his family being very sick.

—I forgot to mention in the proper place that Nancy returned home, from St Louis, in company with Mr. and Mrs. Eads, Dec 3d. Thursday.

Mr. and Mrs. E.[ads] staid with us some days (Mr. E[ads] very unwell) and then left, for home. *Note.* Mr. E.[ads] [87] was called here specially, to consult with the Navy Dept. about a contemplated, enormous Iron ship. I expect *He* will build it, in the West.

[*Marginal Note.*] Wednesday, Dec: 16. Coalter came in this morning, unexpectedly, being sent up by his Genl. (Meade) with dispatches. He staid the day and one night, with us, and left thursday morning, for camp. He is in high health and vigor.

Dec 19 Saturday. I have been very unwell (with a cold) for some days past, and very busy withal; and so, have neglected to enter passing events.

Today Dick left us, to begin a new experiment for his reformation and redemption. I had urged his resignation of his place. [88] (Deputy Solicitor of the Court of Claims) A few days ago he sent in his resignation. The President declined to accept it, until he

---

[81] Emerson Etheridge: Whig congressman, 1853–1857, 1859–1861. When Tennessee seceded he remained loyal and served as clerk of the (National) House, 1861–1863. McPherson (*infra*, July 27, 1866, note 63) was chosen clerk in his stead the day after this entry.

[82] *Supra*, April 27, 1859, note 28.

[83] Joseph Casey: Pennsylvania lawyer; Whig congressman, 1849–1851; reporter of the Pennsylvania Supreme Court, 1856–1861; judge, 1861–1870, and chief justice, 1863–1870, of the Court of Claims.

[84] *Supra*, Jan. 7, 1860, note 5.

[85] Ebenezer Peck: twice member of the General Assembly of Lower Canada; King's counsel before he moved to Chicago in 1835; Illinois legislator; clerk, 1841–1845, and reporter, 1850–1863, of the Supreme Court of Illinois; personal friend of Lincoln who appointed him to the Court of Claims in 1863.

[86] *Supra*, April 27, 1859, note 27.

[87] *Supra*, Jan. 28, 1860, note 38; Dec. 31, 1861, note 70.

[88] Because his habits were distressing his father who wanted to get him away from the city temptations. Cf. President Johnson's experience with his son, Robert.

consulted me. I told him that it was done by my advice, and informed him, in general terms, the reason why.

I was willing for him, even to enlist in the army or go before the mast, to sea. But not so my untiring friend, Eads—He brought the matter before Mr. Welles (Secy Navy) and they agreed to get him a place as Secretary or clerk in the Navy, and to that end, Secy Welles has furnished him with a letter to Admiral Lee [89] commanding, the N.[orth] Atlantic fleet, I believe (now at Hampton Roads)—He understands (from Asst. Secy Fox [90]) that he will be apptd. *acting Ensign*, and then be detailed for special duty as under Secy (or writer) to the Admiral, or Captain[']s clerk.

If that be so, he will have the rank and pay of Ensign.

I advanced him $50, for present use, and he has arranged to have the residue of his pay due here (perhaps abt. $500) sent to him, through me.

This is a far better arrangement than I had hoped to make. It breaks his fall and gives him a fair chance to redeem and restore himself—He is very competent to the duties of the place—His associates will be *gentlemen*, and he and they will be under constant and strict discipline.

Just before he left, conjoi[n]ed him to take care only of his own reform and restoration—not fear about support of his wife, that I wd. see that, as if she were my own child. For which he seemed very grateful.

The Radicals vs Gov Gamble [91]

Note—The *Washington Morning C[h]ronicle* of Dec 17. contains violent speeches of Messrs. Blow [92] and Boyd [93] (M.[embers of] C[ongres]s of Mo.) against Gov Gamble—Delivered at a meeting of the Union League.[94] The speeches abound with coarse abuse, gross falsehood and vulgar ignorance, for which, if I had time, I would trounce them soundly.

The radicals are making great efforts to create the belief that they are *the* Union men, and all others are against the Union. And they

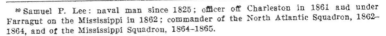

[89] Samuel P. Lee: naval man since 1825; officer off Charleston in 1861 and under Farragut on the Mississippi in 1862; commander of the North Atlantic Squadron, 1862–1864, and of the Mississippi Squadron, 1864–1865.

[90] *Supra*, March 9, 1861, note 40.

[91] *Supra*, July 23, 1859, note 39.

[92] *Supra*, Sept. 20, 1859, note 95.

[93] Sempronius H. Boyd: lawyer and politician of Springfield, Missouri; colonel in the Union Army, 1861–1863; now Emancipationist congressman, 1863–1865; Republican congressman, 1869–1871; minister to Siam, 1890–1893.

[94] The Union League had originated in 1862, and had now spread into eighteen Northern states. Its purposes were largely political—the suppression of opposition, first to the War and later to the Radical Republican Party. It was raising troops, sending supplies to the field, distributing political pamphlets, and denouncing opponents of extremism.

succeed in driving on some *cowardly patriots*, who reluctantly go along with them, for fear of being denounced by them.

A proposition has been introduced into the Senate by Mr. Harlan [95] of Iowa, to create a *retired list* (similar to that in the Army and Navy) of Judges of the Supreme Court, under which a judge, over 70 may withdraw from active duty, on a scale of pay according to his length of service.

The principle is right, but the details all wrong. 70 years is no proper time; for a Judge may be much younger than that, yet, mentally or physically incapable of the duties, and still too poor to give up his salary. There ought to be no *retired list* of *Judges;* but worn out Judges ought to be respectably provided for, by allowing them to *resign,* upon a competent pension.

Dec 20 Sunday. . . .

Dec 21. Still too unwell to go out—weather raw and gusty, threatening snow.

The Monroe Doctrine, again

The Nat[iona]l. Intel[ligence]r. of today, contains a very valuable editorial upon the *Monroe Doctrine*—all the more valuable because short and pointed—

It is a sharp (and crushing) criticism upon a large pamphlet lately put out by *Joshua Leavitt* [96] (first contributed to the *New Englander* Magazine[ )].

The Nat[ional] Intel[ligence]r has heretofore, more than once, fully explained the origin, history and true effect of the *Monroe Doctrine.* But biassed partizans and "half-formed witlings" in political history, still persist in falsifying both the principle and the facts. Some do it wickedly, to set up a false doctrine; and some do it in ignorant egotism, with the conceited vanity of being teachers of what they do not at all understand.

The same paper contains an a/c of a "Great Excitement at Halifax" on account of the Am :[erican] Steamer *Chesapeake*, which had been, practically, seised, and then recaptured by our vessels, in British waters, near Halifax. Our commander gave up the vessel

---

[95] James Harlan : Iowa City lawyer ; president of Iowa Wesleyan University, 1853–1855 ; Republican U. S. senator, 1857–1865, 1867–1873 ; close friend of Lincoln ; father-in-law of Robert Lincoln ; secretary of the Interior, 1865–1866 ; Radical opponent of Johnson.

[96] Vermont lawyer ; Congregational clergyman in Connecticut and Massachusetts ; first secretary of the American Temperance Society ; a founder of the New York Anti-Slavery Society ; editor of several religious and anti-slavery magazines and newspapers in New York and later in Boston. Leavitt's pamphlet has the title, *The Monroe Doctrine.* See the *New Englander,* XXII (October, 1863), 729–777.

to the British authorit[i]es, and a mob of *citizens* rescued the prisoners [" Rebel pirate mutineers "].[97]

Of course, this will lead to diplomatic reclamation, and probably a demand of the prisoners, under the extradition treaty.[98]

Dec 22   tuesday—Still too unwell to go out—or do much at home. Recd. a letter from Dick, (dated yesterday, on board A.[merican] R.[ear] Adml. Lee's Flag ship *Minnisota* [*sic*], Hampton Roads)— Both the facts he states and the tone of his letter cheer me very much. He wrote in a cheerful, confident way, asking for certain necessary things be sent him.

He says that the Admiral treated him with marked kindness— takes him with him, on a tour of inspection, as far south as the Wilmington Blockading squadron, and intends (as soon as he gets his Com[mis]s[io]n. as acting Ensign,[)] to detail him for duty, as Judge Advocate of the Squadron.

I sent his letter to Ellen [Dick's wife], with a note just written.

Dec 23   Wednesday. Still confined. This morning Tilly and Sadie, at 8. a. m. went to Balt[imor]e., to call on Revd. Mr. Dixon (Sadie's friend) and do a little shopping—Expected back to night.

Dec 24. Matilda and Sarah returned from Baltimore, all right.

Yesterday, or last night, died Mrs. Seaton, wife of my venerable friend, W. W. S.[eaton] [99] of the Nat[iona]l. Intelligencer. I am requested to attend, as pall-bearer, tomorrow, 1. p. m.

I was out today, for the first time this week. Called on the President. He has written to O. D. Filley [1] in answer to the application of some of our best men, to relieve Revd. Dr. McPheeters [2] from Provost Martial [*sic*] Dick's [3] *decree of silence* (order not to preach). The Prest had no idea that the *Provost* had assumed to " run the church." I hope the letter will be sufficient[.]

Edwin. C. Claybrook, of 9. Va. Reb[el] Cav[alr]y. is a prisoner of war, at Point Lookout. He is a youth [of] 18 or 20 son of Col [   ] Claybrook [4] of North[umberlan]d. C[ount]y. Va.—The Prest,

---

[97] " The [Union] steamer Chesapeake, seized by Rebel pirate mutineers, [had] been captured by a [Union gunboat *Ella and Annie*] at Sambro, some twenty miles from Halifax." G. Welles, *Diary*, 1, 490. Welles immediately wired orders to surrender the *Chesapeake* to British authorities since she had been captured " in British waters."

[98] The *Chesapeake* and the prisoners taken on it were turned over by the British to the United States, and were brought in March, 1864, from Halifax to New York.

[99] *Infra*, Dec. 25, 1863.

[1] Oliver D. Filley: stove manufacturer and tinware merchant of St. Louis; bank director; mayor in 1858; friend of Thomas H. Benton and Francis P. Blair; staunch unionist, but an opponent of persecution of Southern sympathizers. For Lincoln's letter to him see Dec. 22, 1863, *Complete Works of Abraham Lincoln*, II, 463.

[2] *Supra*, April 24, 1859, note 24.

[3] Franklin A. Dick, of St. Louis: formerly a good friend of Mr. Bates; provost marshal general of Missouri under General Curtis. He was superseded by J. O. Broadhead when General Schofield succeeded Curtis in command in Missouri.

[4] R. A. Claybrook who represented Lancaster and Northumberland Counties in the lower house of the Virginia Assembly in 1855–1858.

being abt. to send for young Linder [5] of Ills: at my instance, ordered up young Claybrook also, with the view, in both cases, to release them, if they will only accept the boon, on any reasonable terms.

The Prest: is anxious to gratify Linder, the father, who is his old friend; and I am very desirous to make a New Year's gift of Claybrook, to his father and family.

Shewed the President, Mr. Gibson's [6] telegram requesting the appointment of Jno. Bozeman Kerr, [7] as Deputy Sol[i]c.[itor] [of the] C[our]t. of Claims. I think it will be done, tho' the Prest said that Senator Harris [8] had proposed a man for the place, he also said that, for a long time, he had wished he had something to give Mr. Kerr.

Dec 25. Attended the funeral of Mrs. Seaton, wife of my ancient friend, W. W. S.[eaton] [9] of the Nat[iona]l. Intelligencer. I was one of the *bearers,* and the weather being very cold, and I barely convallescent [*sic*], I was apprehensive of a backset. But no evil came. Poor Mr. Seaton! Having lived, in great love and harmony with that excellent woman, for more more [*sic*] than Fifty years, I know not how he can bear the loss of such a companion. His grand children are now men and women, having associations and sympathies of their own, and, as to him, respect and reverence only, he will be alone in the world, and very desolate. He is a philosopher, and will shew no signs of impatient and clamorous grief; but this calamity will silently sap the foundation of his existence—And I am prepared to see him sink rapidly and die soon.

Dec 26 Saturday. Wm. Cuddy [10] of St Louis (late Surveyor Genl. there) called at the office, to see me, and came home with me to dinner.

He has closed up the business of the office, at St Louis, very creditably (for which he has the Com[missio]n[e]r's [11] strong voucher[)]. He expects to be appointed Surveyor Genl. of Idahoe [*sic*] Territory.

Conversed with *Secy Welles* upon several interesting topics—
1. Senator Dixon [12] of Con[necticu]t., has gotten the blind side

[5] The son of Usher F. Linder, Illinois lawyer, former state attorney-general, legislator, pro-slavery advocate. The son had enlisted in the Confederate Army.
[6] *Supra,* April 27, 1859, note 27.
[7] *Supra,* April 15, 1863, note 86.
[8] *Supra,* Jan. 4, 1862, note 11.
[9] William W. Seaton: editor of the *Halifax* (North Carolina) *Journal;* associate on the *Raleigh Register,* 1807–1812; co-proprietor with Gales of the *National Intelligencer,* 1812–1866; co-publisher of the *Annals of Congress* covering the period 1798–1824, the *Register of Debates* (of Congress), 1825–1837, and the *American State Papers,* 1832–1861.
[10] Surveyor-general of public lands for the District of Illinois and Missouri, 1861–1863. He apparently did not get the Idaho appointment or else he soon resigned.
[11] James M. Edmunds's of Michigan.
[12] *Supra,* June 24, 1859, note 11.

of the Prest and screwed out of him the nomination of Hammond [13] (a protegé of Mr. D.[ixon] and very obnoxious to most of the Connecticutters) to be Marshal of Conn[ecticu]t. It is understood to be a mere salve to Dixon, and that his pride and apparent influence being safe, *Hammond is to decline*—" *nous verron* " [*sic*].

2. It seems that among " *Lemar's papers* " [14] lately captured by one of our cruisers, there were letters implicating divers persons in New York—i. a 4 letters from one *Trowbridge* to Lemar, I think, which state pretty fully how he " fools the government " here, and communicates freely with his rebel friends.

The writer tells how familiar he is with " *Dick Busteed* " (our newly appointed Dis[tric]t: Judge for Alabama); and mentions a good many others, who will be sorry to find their names published in such connexion.

<Busteed, I think is not yet confirmed, and this perhaps, will *blow* him> [15] *see back Nov 19.*

There was a conference abt these papers, called by the Secy of War, at which were present the Secs. of War Navy and State. The Secy of the Navy had sent the letters to the press, for publication, and that perhaps was the reason for the conference. One of the letters of Trowbridge to Lemar, speaking of a particular venture in Blockade-running, says he will take hold of *that*, because a *nephew of Mr. Seward* is interested, and that will make it *a sure thing.*

Of course, whether true or false, Mr. S.[eward] did not want such letters published—and so they were withheld.

During the conference it was remarked by one of the Secs—I think Mr. Welles s[econde]d., by the sec of war— that Busteed and Trowbridge were here together, a few weeks ago, vouching for each other, mutually, in strong terms.

Mr. Welles thinks that Busteed's appointment was procured wholly by Mr. Seward. Certainly, it was not known to me till after the fact.

<I hear since (at Mr. Pruyn's dinner,[16] Mar 19.) that Busteed wa[s a]ppointed by *Penna.* influence[.]>

To night, Saturday Dec 26. Mr. Welling [17] called on me and among other topics of free conversation, we talked of the strange fact that Mr. Greel[e]y [18] and some other leading editors and politicians at the north, whose secessionism has been frequently avowed, now claim

---

[13] Henry Hammond: formerly a blacksmith; in after years a banker; now a leading politician of Connecticut; anti-slavery agitator who had entered the Republican Party via the Liberty Party and Know-Nothingism. Hammond apparently did decline, but was appointed collector of Internal Revenue of his district by President Johnson. See G. Welles, *Diary*, Jan. 15, 1864 (I. 510).

[14] Col. C. A. L. Lamar, a Confederate agent in England, who later returned and was killed in battle on April 16, 1865, while serving on Howell Cobb's staff in Alabama. Some of his letters were captured on the *Ceres.*

[15] He was confirmed and held the judgeship until 1874.

[16] *Infra*, March 19, 1864, note 32.

[17] *Supra*, June 20, 1859, note 3.

[18] *Supra*, Feb. 2, 1860, note 47.

to be the exclusive friends of the President and the staunchest supporters of the war.

He told me confidentially, that he was told, very lately, by Mr. Riddle,[19] (late M.[ember of] C.[ongress] and recently appointed Counsul [sic] to Matansas) that the Prest. told him that, a few days after the first battle of Bull Run, he received a long letter from Horace Greeley, urging him to make the best peace he could—peace on any terms, with the rebels ! [20]

On Saturday 26 [   ]

—*Civil War*—Rowe's *Lucan*,[21] v. 7. p 231. [Book VII, p. 235]

> " But random shafts too scanty death, afford,
> A *Civil War* is business for the *sword:*
> Where, face to face, the *parricides* may meet,
> *Know* whom they kill, and make the crime complete."

Dec 30. To day was delivered to me, by written order of the President, *Edwin C. Claybrook*, a young man, about 21., son of Col [   ] Claybrook of Northumberland County, Va., a prisoner of war (9. Va. Cav[a]l[r]y[.]) [22]

At my request, he was brought up here, from Point Lookout [23] (by L[ieutenan]t. Heywood of [   ] N.[ew] H.[ampshire] regt. Infty.) and being brot. before the Prest., he ordered him to be bro[ugh]t to me and put under my control, which was done; and I gave my written receipt for him.

He was warmly, but I thought shabbily, dressed, in coarse, grey cloth, with no clothing or baggage of any kind. I took him home to my house, and after free use of the bath room, clothed him, as well as could be, at the moment, in garments of mine and Dicks [sic]. And I intend to put him upon parole and send him home decently, to his family. He seems an ingenuous young man.

<Afterwards, Jany. 5., I took his parole, q.[uantum] v.[is] and sent him down the Potomac, in charge of Commander Parker [24] of the Pot[oma]c. Flotilla—and I hear since that he got home on the 9th. on which day, he wrote me a very manly and gentlemanly letter.[>]

---

[19] Albert G. Riddle : vigorous abolitionist; Republican congressman from Ohio, 1861–1863 ; consul at Matanzas, Cuba, 1863–1864 ; Washington lawyer, 1864–1902 ; law officer of the District of Columbia, 1877–1889.

[20] H. Greeley to A. Lincoln, July 29, 1861, John G. Nicolay and John Hay, *Abraham Lincoln*, IV, 365–366.

[21] Lucan's *Pharsalia* translated into English by Nicholas Rowe, *Works of the English Poets*, Samuel Johnson, ed. (J. Buckland, J. Rivington & Sons, London, 1790), XXVIII, 255–336, and XXIX. In this and the following passage from Lucan. the punctuation and capitalization are inaccurately reproduced. The italics are Mr. Bates's.

[22] *Supra*, Dec. 24, 1863.

[23] Maryland village at the mouth of the Potomac.

[24] Foxhall A. Parker : navy man since 1839 ; executive officer of the Washington Navy Yard, 1861–1862 ; officer in the New Orleans expedition of 1862 ; captain of a gunboat in Atlantic Coast operations, 1862–1863 ; commander of the Potomac Flotilla, 1863–1865.

Cato's [25] Speech on hearing of *Pompey's* death Lucan's Pharsalia (Rowe, Book IX. p 306.)

" We've lost a Roman citizen (he said) :
 One of the noblest of that name is dead ;
 Who[,] though not equal to our fathers found,
 Nor by their strictest rules of justice bound,
 Yet from his faults this benefit we draw,
 He, for his Country's good, transgressed the [her]law,
 To keep a bold, licentious age in awe." &c[.]

A German paper in St Louis says that the President's answer to the Mo. Jacobins [26] (Drake,[27] Lane,[28] Soan & Co.) is " *foolish* and *indecent*[.]"

Perhaps the President has been studying King Solomon's proverbs, and has, thus, learned that it is sometimes the better part of wisdom to " answer a fool according to his folly " *lest he be wise in his own conceit.*[29]

   " The Aristocracy of learning—

" The untaught look on learning
 As a philosopher's[-]stone, a talisman,
 That gives the wearer power and consequence,
 Invests him with mysterious distinction,
 With attributes whose realness can be scanned
 But by his peers. Howe're, among themselves,
 These may divide and wrangle, they uphold
 The common cause against outside assailants—[,]
 Let no profane hand touch their ark. Believe me
 'Tis not so much the intrinsic worth of learning,
 As its contingencies, inspires the crowd
 Of votaries, real or seeming. Fashion some,
 Others ambition leads, or vanity."

     Tragedy of Errors.[30] p 60[.]

---

[25] *Supra,* June 17, 1863, note 44.

[26] The Radical Republicans who were attacking Governor Gamble, Secretary Bates, and President Lincoln.

[27] *Supra,* Feb. 12, 1863, note 13.

[28] *Supra,* Feb. 3, 1862, note 44.

[29] *The Bible,* " Proverbs," XXVI, 5.

[30] Written by Mary L. Putnam ; published anonymously in Boston, in a private edition in 1861, in a public edition in 1862.

CHAPTER VI

1864

1864. Feb 5.

Death of Gov Gamble![1]

[*Obituary notices of Governor Gamble from the* Missouri Republican, *the* Missouri Democrat, *the* St. Louis Evening News, *and the* Union.]

On the next page, I have pasted clips of se[ve]ral St Louis papers, giving brief notice of the, not unexpected, event.

To the Public, his death, especially now, is a calamity; for he stood, like a lighthouse on a rock in the edge of a stormy sea, not only to give warning of the danger, but to resist its violence.

And to me, his loss is a sore grievance—far greater than I had supposed—We have been friends for Forty years, and yet I did not know how highly I prized him, nor what a blank his death would make in both my heart and mind.

His tone was stern—not to say harsh—and he had little about him to wooe [*sic*] those tender emotions commonly called *fondness*. But his great characteristics—strong will, uprightness, courage, devotion to truth and principle—these, guided by his superior talents, gave him a title, long ago, to my unwavering confidence and unqualified respect. In fact, I learn only by his loss, how much I admired and loved him.

The Mo. Rep[ublican] of Feby 4, contains the proceedings of the Bar Meeting, consisting mainly of the Resolutions (drawn by Judge Breckenridge,[2] and uncommonly expressive, chaste and apparently sincere) and excellent speeches, by Gantt,[3] Glover[4] and several others—And the funeral ceremonies in the 2d. Presbyterian Church, with the sermon delivered by Revd. Mr. Brookes.[5]

I do believe that the expressions of respect and sorrow upon the occasion of Gamble's death, are more real and sincere than I have

---

[1] *Supra*, July 23, 1859, note 39.

[2] *Supra*, Dec. 26, 1859, note 67.

[3] Thomas T. Gantt: former St. Louis law partner of Montgomery Blair; U. S. district attorney, 1845–1849; staunch unionist in 1861; colonel on McClellan's staff, 1861–1862; provost marshal general of Missouri, 1862; now a leading Conservative Republican who joined with Bates in opposing extreme measures on either slavery or Confederate sympathizers.

[4] *Supra*, Dec. 23, 1859, note 58.

[5] *Supra*, July 17, 1859, note 30.

ever known attend the demise of any eminent man. The services he has done the state, in patiently and successfully resisting the revolutionary violence of headlong jacobins,[6] are now seen and appreciated; and purity of his personal character now shines all the brighter, because of the clouds of wicked calumny with which his and the State's enemies have so long labored to obscure him.

And now perhaps, in the article of death, he serves his country as effectually as in the best actions of his life. Death has fixed a seal not only upon the man, but his acts and policies also; and so, desperate factionists, seeing small hope of success in their schemes, will, I hope, in a good degree, cease from troubling.

I notice one significant fact. The name of Mr. *Drake*[7] does not appear in any part of the proceedings—neither in the bar meeting, nor in any of the funeral ceremonies. I am a little curious about the motive of his absence—Whether he staid away, because he could not, *conscientiously* join in honoring to so *bad a man as Gamble*; or was he frowned away, by those who thought him unworthy to mingle, on a solemn occasion, with Gamble's friends!

Poor Drake! There is more hope of a fool than of him! He has sold his birth right, without even securing his mess of pottage.

Feb 9. The Nat[iona]l. Intelligencer of today contains a very able article—"A Historical Study." A famous point in the history of Athens, giving the Radical speech of *Cleon*[8] and the conservative speech of Diodotus,[9] thus shewing off, in bold relief, our own demented *Radicals*.

Feb 9. I have been sick—confined to the house—for more than two weeks, with the worst cold upon my lungs than [that] I ever had.

The weather has been very fine for the last two weeks and more. The frost is out of the ground, and the roads are drying fast. And so we may expect an early spring, and consequently, an early beginning of active military movements.

Coalter, yesterday morning, returned to camp, having spent his ten days['] leave with us. He is in perfect health and high spirits, hoping for a chance for distinction, when the campaign opens.

Feb 10 Wednesday. A bright and beautiful day, but, they tell me, rather cold, out of doors. I am still very unwell, taking some

---

[6] The Radical Republicans led by Drake.

[7] *Supra*, Feb. 12, 1863, note 13.

[8] An Athenian demagogue and imperialist, leader of the ruthless war party, who was in power from the death of Pericles until his own death in 422 B. C. The speech referred to was one in favor of exterminating the inhabitants of the conquered "rebel" city of Mytilene.

[9] Diodotus was the conservative leader who opposed this treatment of conquered "rebels" as injurious to Athens and certain to prolong the war. He succeeded in getting the vote of extermination rescinded on the day after its passage, before it had been carried out.

physic, under Dr. Eliot's prescription, and with my breast very sore, by the use of Croton oil, to produce counter-irritation.

The Nat[iona]l. Intell[igence]r. of to day has several very striking articles, as shewing the drift of policy in Congress, and the rapid changes of opinion, in individuals, even upon the most momentous questions of government[.]

1. <in Senate, Feb 8> [10] Senator Sumner's resolutions,[11] for the exterpation [sic] of slavery—Declaring the power to be in Congress and that it is wise to use it.

2. Senator Anthony's [12] resolution [13] to repeal the joint resolution approved Ma[r]ch 2d. 1861, to amend the Constitution. ("Art[icle] 13, No amendment shall be made to the constitution which will authorise or give to Congress the power to abolish or interfere, within any state, with the domestic institutions thereof, including that of persons held to labor or service, by the laws of said State."[)]

Note. This joint resolution, proposed by Mr. Anthony to be repealed, is an *offer* by Congress to the States—not repealable, I suppose, by Congress—If already accepted by a sufficient number of the States, it is it is [sic] now a part of the constitution—If *not yet* accepted, it is a legal and regular proposition to amend, and is still open to acceptance by the States. It is not a statute, which congress can make and enforce by its sole power; but a *proposition* only, which Congress can propound, but the States only can enact and make effectual.

3. Mr. Sumner introduced a bill to repeal all laws for the rendition of fugitive slaves.[14]

Also, a Joint Resolution to amend the constitution thus—

" Every where within the [limits of the] United States, and of each State or Territory thereof, all persons *are equal before the law, so that* no person can hold another, as a slave." [15]

> *Note.* 1. What is *equality before the law?*
>
> 2. Does *that equality* necessarily prevent the one from becoming the slave of the other? The ordinance of '87, and all the constitutions made in pursuance thereof, provide that persons may be sold into slavery *for crime*—Is that repealed?

[10] Added later in the margin.

[11] *Supra,* Jan. 7, 1860. note 9; *Cong. Globe,* 36 Cong., 1 Sess., 523. The resolutions were printed and laid on the table.

[12] Henry B. Anthony: editor of the conservative *Providence Journal;* governor of Rhode Island, 1850–1851 ; Radical Republican U. S. senator, 1859–1884.

[13] The resolution to repeal is in the *Cong. Globe,* 38 Cong., 1 Sess., 522. It was referred to the Committee on the Judiciary.

[14] Feb. 8, 1864, *Cong. Globe,* 38 Cong., 1 Sess., 521. It was referred to the Committee on Slavery and Freedmen.

[15] *Ibid.,* 521. It was referred to the Committee on the Judiciary. The italics are Bates's.

4. Senator Carlile's speech [16] upon the *occasion* of Mr. Henderson's [17] amendment to the enlistment bill[.]

It is more manly and conservative than I thought was in him.

Mr. Henderson's amendment is a curious composition—It runs thus—

" That whenever [when] any person of *African descent* whose services or labor is claimed *in any State* under the laws thereof, shall be mustered into the military or naval service of the United States, he shall *forever thereafter* be free, any law, usage[,] or custom to the contrary notwithstanding; and his mother, his wife[,] and Children shall also be free, provided that by the laws of any state, they owe service or labor to any person or persons who have given aid or comfort to the existing rebellion against the Government, since July 17, 1862; and all laws and parts of laws inconsistent herewith, are hereby repealed." [18]

Surely Cicero was right when he said that " in every Civil war, Success is dangerous, because it is sure to beget arrogance and a disregard of the *laws of the Government—*" (i. e. the Constitution)[.]

These men, flattered with a little success, have opened up to themselves a boundless sourse [*sic*] of power. When the constitution fails them, they have only to say "this is a time of war—and war gives all needed powers "!

I am afraid that this Congress is becoming perfectly Radical and revolutionary.

[*Note.*] In the Intelligencer of the 12th. Feb, there is a resolution (by Senator Sumner) and considerable debate, to redress at least, if not punish the *outrage* of excluding a *colored person*, from the street R. R. Car.[19] Several Senators [20] announced very clearly, their determination to recognise no civil or social distinction[.]

In course of the debate, Mr. Sumner read a letter of "*A. T. Augusta M. B.* [*sic*] Surgeon Seventh U. S. colored troops " date Feb 1, complaining that he had been excluded from the car and forced to *walk* in the mud &c[.] [21]

This letter is addressed to *Captain C. W. Clippington*, Judge Advocate. and concludes with the " request that the offender may be *arrested* and *brought to punishment!* "

It seems not to have occur[r]ed to the dark doctor (nor to the grave senators either) that the *outrage* was personal to himself,

[16] John S. Carlile: Virginia state legislator, 1847–1851; Know-Nothing congressman, 1855–1857; Unionist congressman, 1861; Unionist senator, 1861–1865. For the speech see Feb. 8, 1864; *ibid.*, 524–526.

[17] *Supra*, Feb. 24, 1863, note 27.

[18] Jan. 27, and Feb. 8, 1864, *Cong. Globe*, 38 Cong., 1 Sess., 362, 524.

[19] Feb. 10, 1864, *ibid.*, 553–555. The resolution was agreed to, 30–10.

[20] Pomeroy, Wilkinson, Grimes, and Wilson.

[21] *Ibid.*, 554.

and done by a *civil* carriage-driver, and that it might be quite as legal and proper for Dr. A.[ugusta] to bring his civil action for the wrong, as to call upon a *Judge Advocate* to *arrest and punish the offender.* But so we go—The civil law is too weak and too slow to suit the hot haste of our new patriots—Every thing must be done by military power; and every petty subaltern imagines *himself master of the horse,* to the *Dictator.* If these men have their way a little longer, there will be nothing left of law but final judgment, and no process of justice, but Execution.

Feb. 11. Dr. Lieber [22] (in his Reminiscences of [an intercourse with Mr.] Niebhur, the Historian, p. 151) cites a pamphlet of one Mr. Von Vincke,[23] on the minute division of land, in some parts of Germany, in which it is stated as a fact, that law suits have been brought in the courts on the Rhine, for *half a square foot of land.*

Same book. p 158 [153]. *Nieber* [Niebuhr] says of *Carnot* [24]

" Carnot invented new tactics and showed how to fight and conquer with them. While he was engaged in making the giant-plans for the five armies, he wrote a mathematical work of the highest character, and composed at the same time, some very agreeable [little] poems. He was a mighty genius indeed.[!] "

Feb 11 Thursday—Mr. Gibson [25] returned to the city.

Nat[ional] Intel[ligence]r. Feb 13.

> ["In one of his early orders in Kansas Gen. Ewing [26] announced a determination to put an end to the operations of the anti-slavery patriots in that State who were 'stealing themselves rich in the name of liberty.' On recently acceding to the command . . . Gen. Curtis [27] . . . sa[id]:
>
> "'You may rely on my doing all in my power to prevent border strife and sectional animosities; and I hope you will use your efforts to the same purpose. There is no reason for it. We are all in the same boat; there is not enough of the negro left to quarrel about, and *I am not going to allow loyalty to be a license for horse stealing.*'"]

Well, if Gen Curtis will, in good faith, do *that*—if he will really abridge the privilege of of [*sic*] *Loyalty,* so that it shall no longer steal and rob and mu[r]der, " in the name of patriotism, and for the public good," I will retract some hard things I have said of him.

---

[22] *Supra,* April 5, 1862, note 62.

[23] He was High President of the " Province of Westphalia " in 1824, when he wrote the pamphlet *Report to the Minister of the Interior on the Parcelling of Farms and Cutting-Up of Estates in the Province of Westphalia.*

[24] Lazare N. M. Carnot, 1753–1823, great French general of the Revolutionary and Napoleonic wars.

[25] *Supra,* April 27, 1859, note 27.

[26] Thomas Ewing, Jr.: private secretary to President Taylor, 1849–1850; member of the Kansas Constitutional Convention, 1858; delegate to the Washington Peace Convention, 1861; chief justice of the Kansas Supreme Court, 1861–1862; now brigadier-general of volunteers, 1862–1865; member of the Ohio Constitutional Convention in 1873 and 1874; Democratic congressman from Ohio, 1877–1881.

[27] *Supra,* Oct. 22, 1861, note 23.

Feb 13 Saturday. A beautiful spring day, bright and warm.

I was tempted out, the first time, after a confinement of two weeks and more.

Saw, for the first time, Brutus [J.] Clay [28] (who strongly resembles *Grand Hal*—only larger and han[d]somer) and his kinsman, Green Clay Smith,[29] his nephew I think both K[entuck]y M.[embers of] C[ongres]s[.]

Also, saw and conversed awhile with Gen Sickles.[30]

Called on the President and had a private conversation, of some ½ hour, chiefly about the presidential election. He is fully apprehensive of the schemes of the Radical leaders. When I suggested some of their plots, he said they were almost *fiendish*. He is also fully aware that they would strike him at once, if they durst; but they fear that the blow would be ineffectual, and so, they would fall under his power, as *beaten enemies;* and, for that only reason the hypocrit[e]s try to occupy equivocal ground—so that, when they fail, as *enemies*, they may still pretend to be *friends.*

He told me (what I partly knew before) that the extremists (Chase men?) had called several caucuses in the hope of finding it safe to take open ground agst L[incoln]'s re-nomination, but had never found one in three of the M.[embers of] C[ongres]s that would go against him—<I tried to impress upon him the important fact, that they need him quite as much as he does them—that they are cunning and unscrupulous, and when they find that they dare not openly oppose him, their effort will *then* be to commit him to as many as possible, of their extreme measures, so as to drive off his other friends, until he is weakened down to their level, and it becomes *safe to cast him off*—I think he sees it plainly[.]>

He told me also, that the Editor of the Mo. Democrat ([   ]) sometime ago, wrote a letter to Jim Lane,[31] sharply censuring him for voting for the confirmation of Gen Schofield[32]—and declaring that *Lincoln* must be *defeated, at all hazards*—But that it is not *prudent yet, to declare openly against him!!* This letter, *Lane* himself shewed to the President—Such is the faith that those knaves keep with each other!!

[28] A Kentucky farmer; state legislator, 1840, 1860; president of the Bourbon County Agricultural Association, 1840–1870, and of the Kentucky Agricultural Association, 1853–1861; now a Unionist congressman, 1863–1865.

[29] A lawyer; lieutenant in the Mexican War; brigadier-general of volunteers, 1862–1863; state legislator, 1861–1863; Unionist congressman, 1863–1866; governor of Montana, 1866–1869; and finally a Baptist minister, 1869–1895.

[30] Daniel E. Sickles: lawyer; state legislator, 1847, 1856, 1857; secretary of Legation in London, 1853–1855; minister to Spain, 1869–1875; Democratic congressman, 1857–1861, 1893–1895; brigadier- and then major-general of volunteers in the Army of the Potomac, with which he fought in the Peninsular Campaign, at Antietam, at Fredericksburg, at Chancellorsville, and at Gettysburg where he won a Congressional medal of honor. Though he had lost a leg at Gettysburg, he remained in active service until 1865.

[31] *Supra,* Feb. 3, 1862, note 44.

[32] *Supra,* May 30, 1863, note 32.

The Democrat is now working hard to shew that the attempt now making in St Louis, to get up a *Lincoln Club*, is *premature*, and insinuating that at the *proper time*, all union men will support him!! So, the News is taking the same course.

[*A clipping which publishes a call for a mass convention of Independent Republicans to meet at Cleveland, Ohio, on May 31, 1864.*] [33]

[*Marginal Note.*] These same fellows who thought the aggitation [*sic*] of the question *premature* are now calling for mass convention (at Cleveland) to forestal[l] the Baltimore convention [34] in June!

I remarked to him [Lincoln] that if he stood out manfully against the unprincipled designs of the Radicals, I thought it would be easy to bring all the old Whigs to his support—He answered—1 suppose so, and added that many of the better sort of Democrats were in the same condition—saying that Govr. Hall [35] of Mo. had written to his brother, Judge Hall, [36] M.[ember of] C.[ongress] that the Dem[ocrat]s. of Mo. would go for L.[incoln] of necessity, and that he, the Judge, wd. have to take the pill, however bitter.

Upon the whole, the President seems very hopeful that the machinations of the Radicals will fail, and that, in the matter of the nomination, his friends will be able to counteract them effectually.

I rather think so myself. My chief fear is that the President's easy good nature will enable them to commit him to too many of their extreme measures, so that the wall of separation between them will be too thin to stop the fire of their bad principles, and save the constitution and laws, from the universal conflagration, which their measures plainly portend.

[*A clipping telling of (1) a case of rape among the Germans of St. Louis County, and (2) a meeting of the St. Louis Horticultural Society.*]

[*A sheet giving an " illustrated history of ' The Stars and Stripes.' "*]

[*A clipping headed " Rebel Disaffection Wide-Spread."*]

Nat[ional] Intel[ligence]r. Feb 15

[*A clipping from the* National Intelligencer *printing the names of the delegates to a Virginia Constitutional Convention at Alexandria.*]

[*February 15.*] 16. in all!! And they, for the most part, without constituents!<[*Marginal*] note. Judge Wyley [37] says that all

---

[33] Bates has marked the names of all the Missourians and of one Mississippian who signed the call.

[34] The National Union Convention which renominated Lincoln.

[35] *Supra*, Feb. 21, 1862. note 96.

[36] William A. Hall: judge of the Missouri Circuit Court, 1847; Democratic congressman. 1862–1865.

[37] Andrew Wylie, judge of the Supreme Court of the District of Columbia.

of them put together, have not 5000 *bona fide* constituents.>And the men themselves, nameless, at least unknown!

A pretty convention this to reform the great old commonwealth, and bless her with a new and better constitution! The whole farce is gotten up by a few a few [*sic*] reckless Radicals, who manage those helpless puppets (the *straw* "Governor[38] and Legislature of Virginia") as a gamester manages his marked cards. They are grown very bold, and seem no longer to feel the necessity of disguise, nor even to claim legality and authority for patching up new constitutions for old States.

I have warned one Member of W.[est] V.[irginia] of the fate preparing for his misbegotten, abortive State. These Jacobins,[39] as soon as they get, by the Alexandria juggle, an anti-slavery constitution for *Virginia*, will discover that *West Virginia* was created without authority[40]—and then, having no further use for the political bantling, will knock their blocks from under, and let it slide. For, already, they begin to be jealouse [*sic*] of the double representation in the Senate[.]

Feb 15. The Nat[iona]l. Intel[ligence]r. has a strong leader entitled "Amendment to the Constitution." It does not give the proposition of Mr. Henderson of Mo. offered some time ago,[41] because it is substantially the same as Mr. Sumners[42] [*sic*] (both abolishing slavery in the States and Territories.)<Of course, the Radical Leaders were not green enough to allow so new a convert as Mr. Henderson to engross the *honors of Freedom*, and be hailed, like Bolivar,[43] the *Great Liberator!*[>]

Nay, verily—that would be over-pay to Mr. H.[enderson] considering how good a bargain he had already driven with Mr. Brown.[44] Besides, that would be little better than robbery of Mr. Sumner, thus to snatch the bread out of the mouth of labor.

And so, to have a better division of the honors the Senate's Com-[mitte]e. on the judiciary (Mr. Trumbull[45] Ch[airma]n.) reported the following.

---

[38] Francis H. Pierpont: *supra*, Aug. 7, 1863, note 74.

[39] The Radicals in Congress.

[40] West Virginia became a separate state on June 19, 1863, by vote of Congress and the consent (required under the Constitution) of this "straw" government of Virginia loyalists.

[41] *Supra*, Feb. 10, 1864.

[42] *Loc. cit.*

[43] Simon Bolivar, 1783–1830, Venezuelan liberator of Bolivia, Colombia, Ecuador, Peru, and Venezuela from Spanish rule.

[44] B. Gratz Brown: St. Louis lawyer; state legislator, 1852–1858; Free-Soil founder (in 1854) and editor of the *Missouri Democrat* which Bates so often quotes; an organizer of the Republican Party in Missouri in 1860; strong unionist in 1861; colonel of Missouri volunteers, 1861; Radical emancipationist, 1862; U. S. senator, 1863–1867; Liberal Republican governor, 1871–1873.

[45] *Supra*, Nov. 22, 1860, note 85.

"Art[icle] 13. Neither slavery nor involuntary servitude, except as a punishment for crime, whereof the *offender* shall have been duly convicted shall exist within the United States, or any place subject to their jurisdiction.

Sec[tion] 2. Congress shall have power to enforce this article by appropriate legislation." [46]

[*Note.*] *Offender*—Why was this word substituted for the word *party*, as used in the famous ordinance of 1787 and copied, I believe, into many State constitutions? Now, both the *ordinance* and the and the [*sic*] *amendment* admit of slavery, as a punishment of crime. If the word *party*, as used in the ordinance, mean the person held as a slave, the *party* must be the criminal. But if the *offender* be a woman, reduced to slavery for crime, what is the condition of her child, born in slavery? Does the general maxim *partus sequitur ventrem*, apply, or is the case anomalous and *sui generis*? Was the change accidental, or designed to meet some possible con[tin]gency, in the future?

[*Marginal Note.*] I expected to have gone out today. But the [weather] became raw and damp, clouded up and snowed, more or less, all day[.]

Feb 16 tuesday. This morning the weather is raw and gusty, with glimpses of sunshine between the snow-showers. And so, I dare not go out. My cough is mitigated but still, I have violent spells, to throw off the bad secretions upon the lungs. The excoriation of the breast (by the use of Croton oil) is drying up, and is very uncomfortably stiff[.]

Feb 19 Friday. Ever since last date, the weather has been, and still is intensely cold. . . . I intended to go out to day, but, as advised, abstain.

Last night, called to see me and spent an hour or so, in pleasant conversation, three North Carolinians, Mr. Goodloe [47] (Daniel R), Mr. Hedrick [48] (Profsr. B. S.) and a Mr. Dibble, a *downeaster*, who has however been long settled in business in eastern N.[orth] C.[arolina] and is familiar with the geography, trade and people of

---

[46] Feb. 10, 1864, *Cong. Globe*, 38 Cong., 1 Sess., 553. It was originally introduced by Senator Henderson (*supra*, Feb. 24, 1863, note 27) on January 11, 1864. *Cong. Globe*, 38 Cong., 1 Sess., 145.

[47] North Carolina abolitionist; Washington newspaper editor, 1844–1861; the Washington correspondent of the *New York Times*, 1861–1862; chairman of the commission to emancipate slaves in the District of Columbia, 1862–1863; now an editorial writer for the *Washington Chronicle*, 1863–1865; U. S. marshal for North Carolina, 1865–1866; a leading advocate of congressional reconstruction, 1867–1868; thereafter an independent.

[48] Benjamin S. Hedrick of North Carolina; descendant of back-country German stock; undergraduate at the University of North Carolina; graduate student at Harvard; professor of Chemistry at the University of North Carolina, 1854–1856, who was persecuted and finally forced out because of his anti-slavery views; examiner in the Patent Office after 1861.

the region of the *sounds*. Tho' introduced by by [*sic*] Mr. Goodloe as a Carolinian, I recognized, at once, his northeastern nativity—His *speech bewrayeth* him, for he says *ben*, and *had ought*.

They all represent N.[orth] C.[arolina] as ready to come back, if only supported by a sufficient federal force, to protect them while the effort is being made.

They regret that Genl. Butler [49] is in command there. He is, they think, the last man to soften and conciliate. His name is a fear, not a hope—The people have a vague dread that makes them shrink from contact with him.

[*Marginal Note.*]   N. Carolina Dr. *Tull* recommended for *Marshal*[.]

The *President's* proclamation, of Feb 18, opens, in part, the port of Brownsville, Texas.[50]   see Nat:[ional] Intel:[lingencer] of to day.

Texas—Proposition to Colonise negro[e]s there—There is a bill pending in the Senate, to set apart a portion of the state for that purpose; [51] and Senator (Jim) Lane has made a speech in its favor [52]—assuming that the two races *must* have separate locations.

Feb 19.   Called to see me, and to talk about *another* parden [*sic*], and things generally, *Stephen Dillingham*, of West Falmouth, Massts.—He is an influential "Friend," a worthy man, I think, and [would] be very pleasant, if he only had a little less of the *gift* of *continuance*.

Capt. Smith [53] called to see me. He has heard, i. a. that E. C. Stedman [54] has *come out* for Mr. Chase. *I doubt it.*

Feb 20.   The weather having moderated, and being bright and sunny, I ventured out today, and spent several hours, in business, at the office—I am afraid that E. C. Stedman (who came and dined with me) has been i[n]veigled into politics—a strong Chase man—and now in deeper water than he can wade in.

He tells me that *to him* was assigned the organization of machinery in New York—*ward clubs* &c[.]

As yet, it is simple *opposition*, for he says there is no committal to any one in particular, "and there is no telling how the cat will jump."

Said I "then, so far, it is only an effort to unite all the *outs* against the *ins*"—said he "you shew your sagacity by hitting the

---

[49] *Supra,* Nov. 29, 1861, notes 98 and 1.
[50] Feb. 18, 1864, J. D. Richardson, *Messages and Papers of the Presidents,* VI, 216–217.
[51] Introduced by Senator Lane on Jan. 11, 1864, *Cong. Globe,* 38 Cong., 1 Sess., 145.
[52] Feb. 16, 1864, *ibid.,* 672–675.   For Lane see *supra,* Feb. 3, 1862, note 44.
[53] *Supra,* Aug. 7, 1863, note 71.
[54] *Supra,* March 15, 1862, note 27.

nail upon the very head "—I answered—" there's no need of sagacity to see the sun at noon."

Today comes news that George A. Coffey [55] is dead—His brother
started at once to Phil[adelphi]a.

I hear today for the first time, that a bill has been introduced into
the Senate (and, of all the world, by John Sherman [56]) to *allow appeals from the Commissioner of Internal Revenue!!* to the *Supreme
Court.*

[*Note.*] *Feb 26*[.]   <Senator John Sherman's bill—I have copy
now>

Stedman says that *Swett* [57] and *Laman*,[58] made a great deal of
money in the *New Almaden* S[t]ock,[59] immediately upon *Swett's*
return from Cala.—That Swett's arrangement for the possession of
the mine, [is] expressly to that end, and with stipulations to suit—

That the " Fossatt People " [60] have bought out all the ~~Bergara~~
(perhaps Parrott [61] et al) claim,—And that if Black [62] should lose
this case, he is ' *flat broke.*'

Feb 21 Sunday. Staid close at home. Though the weather is
pleasant, I am afraid to venture out to church, lest *cold feet* might
bring on a coughing spell.

Feb 22. Went to the office and was closely employed, til[l]
4. p m[.] Saw the President. Talked about Mo. affairs—suggested the R. R. (S. W. Branch)[63] good *in itself* for the nation and
the State. and would be sure to unite the state for him.

In Maryland, the fiery new converts to Radicalism—Goldsborough &c—have held their convention. They go, fiercely for immediate emancipation—and declare their sympathy for *Mo. Radicals*—and deplore the conservative element in the Cabinet—meaning
Blair and Bates—

Their intermed[d]ling impudence in Mo. politics is not unlike
the affiliation of the *Radical German* Convention, at Cleveland,
with the *Revolutionists* of Europe.[64]

---

[55] *Supra*, April 6, 1862, note 63.

[56] *Supra*, Oct. 20, 1863, note 29.

[57] Leonard Swett: lawyer of Bloomington, Illinois, who had practiced on the same circuit as Lincoln; an organizer of the Republican Party in Illinois; intimate friend of Lincoln; in 1860 one of his managers. Welles (*Diary*, II, 390) also reports Swett's participation in the Almaden Mine venture.

[58] Probably Joseph B. Lamar, later a Democratic politician in California.

[59] *Supra*, Feb. 26, 1863, note 49.

[60] The men whom Charles Fossat represented in the Fossat case. See *infra*, Feb. 24, 1864, note 68.

[61] *Supra*, Aug. 11, 1863, note 82.

[62] *Infra*, Feb. 24, 1864, note 66.

[63] The Pacific Railroad later became the Missouri Pacific system; the Southwest Branch, the St. Louis and San Francisco system. Though begun in 1851 the tracks had not yet reached the western border of Missouri. See *infra*, March 9, 1864.

[64] *Supra*, Oct. 29, 1863, note 40.

Feb 24. Wednesday, Yesterday the case (No. 111.) Charles Fos-satt v The U.[nited] S.[tates] [65] (with certain intervenors) came on, for argument—The Atty Genl. and Wills for the U[nited] S[tates]— Ex Atty Genls Black [66] and Cushing [67] for Fossatt,[68] the claimant— and Williams and Carlilse [*sic*] for Berr[e]yesa,[69] intervenor—Ex Atty Genl, Rev.y. Johnson [70] who had been of counsel for Parrot[t][71] and others intervenors, moved to dismis[s] the appeal, as to them.

Strenuous efforts were made my mressrs. [*sic*] Black and Cushing (especielly [*sic*] the former, who seemed greatly excited and agi-tated) to exclude the U.[nited] S.[tates] from the case, as no party— having no status, no interest at stake, and no right to be heard. But the court overruled them, and determined to hear all, and upon all the questions involved in the record, and leave open all the points for final *judgment.*

Mr. Cushing opened for Fossatt, and made an effort which greatly disappointed me. It was far below the standard of his reputation. I have suspected for some time, that he is a little, narrow-minded unprincipled man. No doubt, he has a good deal of *learning*, but very little *knowledge;* as indeed, no man can have much useful knowledge (which is wisdom) who is destitute of morals.

Mr. Cushing continued for some time to day (wednesday) flowndering [*sic*] on, from one blunder to another, doing his case more harm than good. [*February 25.*] He was followed by Mr. Wills (with me for the U. S.) who spoke with great ability and effect, during the remainder of that day, and a good part of the next—thursday 25. Feb—

Feb 25 Thursday. Mr. Wills' speech was very attractive, hold-ing the eager attention of the court for hours.

A number of *Wall street* and other speculators in *Fossatt Stock*, were present, eagerly watching the efforts of counsel, who, like

[63] The Fossat or Quicksilver Mine Case, 2 Wallace 649–728. This was another com-plicated California land title dispute. The conflict was between the United States and Fossat over the southern boundary of Fossat's grant, and between Berreyesa and Fossat over the eastern boundary. Berreyesa's claim had been confirmed by a line drawn by the District Court which left the New Almaden Mine on his property. But in 1860 the Surveyor-General had drawn a line which gave the mine to Fossat. The Court finally upheld Fossat's claim against both the United States and Berreyesa.

[66] *Supra*, Oct. 28, 1859, note 22. Black had been counsel for the United States in *U. S. v. Castillero (supra*, Feb. 26, 1863, note 49). In the present case Bates believes he has great pecuniary interest in a decision for Fossat.

[67] *Supra*, Dec. 6, 1861, note 7.

[68] Charles Fossat was the owner of a ranch in the Valley of the Little Captains fifteen miles south of San Francisco upon which he claimed the New Almaden Mine lay. In this case Fossat represented the group who had derived rights in the New Almaden Mine from Larios, the former owner of the Fossat ranch. The settlement of both boundaries in their favor involved title to the rich mineral deposits.

[69] José R. Berreyesa had owned the ranch under which the New Almaden Mine was located until a U. S. survey of 1860 threw the claim to ownership of this land into dispute. Berreyesa had died, but his widow had inherited his claims.

[70] *Supra*, Nov. 26, 1859, note 85.

[71] *Supra*, Aug. 11, 1863, note 82.

bulls and *bears* on change, were pawing up or tearing down their *Fancy Stock.*

Wills' argument to prove that both Fossatt and Berr[e]yesa claims *must* be located in the valley struck terror into the Speculators [72]—I hear that Swett [73] of Ills. (who made the shameful arrangement about the mine, last year) incontenently [*sic*] sold out his stock, at a loss of $30.000.

<*Note*—It is clear now, that I acted prudently, in waiving all Mr. Swett's efforts to get employed in the case[.]>

Feb 26 Friday. Mr. Williams and Mr. Carlisle spoke on the Berr[e]yesa side—*n'emporte* [*sic*]; but they could not help that— their case did not allow a good speech.

Reverdy Johnson told me this morning that he wd. speak in the case—the C[our]t. wd. hear him, as on his motion to dismiss appeal of his clients, Parrott and others.

And *Judge Wayne* [74] told me that my time to speak wd. hardly come on before tuesday—as Johnson would speak monday—He sd. Johnson was very anxious to get the last speech, but he wd. not allow it, that I ought to have a chance to answer *him,* and that Black was entitled to the close[.]

Feb 26 Note. In the quicksilver case, it is a remarkable fact that, besides private counsel of high reputation—Williams and Carlisle—, there are three ex Atty. Genls against the U[nited] S[tates]—Johnson, Cushing and Black.

By the way, *Cushing* has sunk immeasurably. He seems to have excited the implacable disgust of the whole court—Judge Wayne (who is habitually bland, and never forgets that he, himself is a gentleman) said to me privately, that Cushing's effort was a perfect failure—Swaine [75] sd. that C[ushing]'s attack upon Wills (about the map) was a *brutal outrage,* and the court had determined to let W.[ills] answer as he pleased, and not allow C.[ushing] to reply! But that W.[ills] had ansd. most effectually and in good taste.

Judge Grier [76] said to me, in a loud whisper, that every body in ten feet, must have heard—"*E*f you speak, give that damned Yankee hell." I need not say that I was disgusted at his grossness; but Mr. Justice Grier is a natural-born vulgarian, and, by long habit, coarse and harsh.

---

[72] Fossat and the New Almaden Mine owners claimed that their title included on the south a large part of the mountain ridge in which lay the rich mineral deposits. The United States claimed that the ranch included only the land in the valley and that the mountain ridge was public property.

[73] *Supra,* Feb. 20, 1864, note 57.

[74] *Supra,* Nov. 27, 1861, note 74.

[75] *Supra,* March 22, 1862, note 49.

[76] Robert C. Grier: Democratic lawyer of Pennsylvania; judge of the District Court of Allegheny County, 1833–1846; justice of the U. S. Supreme Court, 1846–1870.

Feb 26. Last tuesday night, Nancy and Matilda started for West Point, where they arrived wednesday at 12. m. well[.]

Feb 26. Yesterday, Judge Frayser (of St Charles, Mo.) arrived here, on his way to City Point, trying to get his daughter out of Virginia—I procured him a pass, and he started via Baltimore. I wrote to Genl. Butler,[77] at F[ortres]s. Monroe, asking his aid and kindness. <*Note*[.] Genl. B.[utler] acted handsomely, and wrote to me.>

[*February*] *28 Sunday.* Royston Betts[78] died today, at 3.30. p m[.]

Nancy and Matilda have not yet returned from N. York. Think they will come by the night train, and arrive in the morning.

. . .

Friend Newton[79] is full of news. He tells me today, that a *secret* pamphlet has been gotten up (he thinks, by the machinations of Secy. Usher[80] and Senator Pomeroy[81]) levelled agst. Mrs. L.[incoln] in reference to the infamous *Watt* scandal. He expects to get a copy tomorrow; and if it turn out to be what he supposes, thinks it will produce an explosion.

. . .

Mar 1 Tuesday. Yesterday, in the Quicksilver case—Fossatt v the U. S[82]—I began my argument, and spoke an hour and a half[.] Today I spoke two hours—and concluded.

Then Mr. Black,[83] began his concluding argument, for Fossatt, and spoke an hour, when Court adjourned.

The day is very inclement—rain, hail and high wind—in so much that I could not attend the funeral of my poor friend, Betts,[84] tho' I was specially invited to be one of the pall-bearers.

Mar 2. Nancy and Matilda returned this morning, from their trip to West Point—well and well-pleased.

At the opening of the S.[upreme] C.[ourt] this morning, Judge Wayne[85] (presiding) announced that judge Grier[86] was detained from Court by illness (having had a dangerous fall, as I hear other-

---

[77] *Supra*, Nov. 29, 1861, notes 98 and 1.

[78] A Virginian who was disbursing clerk in the Department of Agriculture.

[79] *Supra*, Jan. 5, 1862, note 12.

[80] Caleb B. Smith had resigned the secretaryship of the Interior in December, 1862, and John P. Usher (*supra*, Feb. 17, 1860, note 77) had been appointed to fill his place.

[81] Samuel C. Pomeroy of Kansas: Massachusetts state legislator, 1852–1853; organizer and agent of the New England Emigrant Aid Society; member of the Kansas free-state Constitutional Convention of 1859; delegate to the Republican national conventions of 1856 and 1860; Republican U. S. senator, 1861–1873.

[82] *Supra*, Feb. 24, 1864, note 65; *infra*, March 2.

[83] *Supra*, Oct. 28, 1859, note 22; Feb. 26, 1864.

[84] *Supra*, April 5, 1862, note 61.

[85] *Supra*, Nov. 27, 1861, note 74.

[86] *Supra*, Feb. 26, 1864, note 76.

wise) and that, consequently the argument of the Fossatt case must be suspended, until tuesday next—the case being too important, in the new aspects it has assumed, to be heard by less than the whole Court—so Mr. Black [87] *lies over.*

Note. Yesterday, after the close of my argument, Several of the Judges, including acting C.[hief] J.[ustice] Wayne, expressed a wish to have my points in answer to Mr. Black's new ground, assumed in his supplemental brief—i. e. that the U. S. is no party here, and has no right to be heard—printed, for use of the Court.

Of course, I'll have it done.

This Fossatt case is the first, of any magnitude, that I have argued; and I do believe that my leaving most of the cases to be argued by *retained* counsel, had spread pretty widely at the bar and perhaps to some members of the Court, the belief that I was unable or afraid to encounter the leading members of the bar. But I am satisfied that this case has dispelled that illusion, both at Bench and Bar.

Mr. Black and his colleagues had laid a very pretty plan to get the management of the case wholly into their own hands. And I am sure that Mr. B.[lack] was taken wholly by surprise by both the matter and the manner in which I sought to counteract him.

His clients ·(by his advice of course) had, at great cost, bought out all the *Intervenors,* [88] who had appealed, except a portion of the adverse claim of *Berr[e]yesa* [89]—and that interest is identical with Fossatt's,[90] as to the principles of the Survey and the method of proceeding, and differed only about a dividing line between them— That done, if he could only exclude the U. S. from the case, of which he seemed very confident, he had the cause in his hand, a plastic lump, to be moulded at pleasure.

My proposition is that if there were a case here at all, the U. S. was a necessary party. But I proceeded to shew, by analysis of the Statutes, that there is no case here.

[*A clipping giving President Lincoln's "Amnesty Proclamation" of March 6, 1864.*]

Rich[mon]d. Enquirer Bro[ugh]t to me by Tat: Paulding.

["*To the Editors of the Enquirer:*

"Gentlemen—When the Yankees made their late raid in the Northern Neck, it was feared they had come to stay, as it was reported, on what seemed to be good authority, that Attorney General Bates had so stated to a relative in Northumberland, and given certain advice, &c.

"It is now known that the report was wholly erroneous. No such declaration was made by Attorney General Bates, and it is proper that this should be

---

[87] *Supra,* March 1.

[88] José R. Berreyesa, represented by J. B. Williams and Carlisle; John Parrott and others, represented by Reverdy Johnson.

[89] *Supra,* Feb. 24, 1864, note 69.

[90] *Supra,* Feb. 24, 1864, note 68.

made known, and any causeless alarm removed. Attorney General Bates is a Virginian by birth, and although identified with the Lincoln dynasty, yet, there are some circumstances known to the writer of this, which cannot be given to the public going to show that there is yet left in his breast some of the feelings of a Virginian.

" 28th January, 1864.   Observer."]

Claybrook [91]

Mar 9. I have been too busy, with pressing official duties, for some time, to ma[ke a]n entry in this book.

Govr. Hall [92] and a good many other Missourians are in the City. The Govr., along with Mr. Gibson [93] and Capt [Silas] Highly of St Jo, dined with me. Highly wants me to make an effert [*sic*] on the Prest. to get a discharge for his son, who is a prisoner of war, at Alton.[94] And I'll try to do it.

The Govr. and Gibson are not content with the President[']s letter to Genl. Rosecrans,[95] about completing the S. W. Branch of our Pacific R. R. and want me to try to get him to make it stronger—It only directs the Genl. to enquire into the subject and report. We want it to authorise the Genl. if he find that the road would be advantageous to the military service, to act definitively, and furnish the iron, as fast as the company can lay it down.

I hope to convince the President that the latter is the better course—better for the service, better for the State and better for himself.[96] <[*Marginal Note.*] Mar 10[.] The Prest has changed his letter to Genl Rosecrans, so as to allow him to proceed at once.[97]>

If he let Stanton have anything to do with it he will mar the enterprise. <If the President had a little more *vim*, he would either control or discharge Mr. S[tanton]. If I were in his place, I would never submit to have the whole influence of the two most powerful Departments, Treasury and War, brought to bear upon the election—against the Prest. and for the aspiring Secretary[.]>

The Prest, no doubt, sees the evil and the danger, but lacks the nerve to apply the remedy.[98]

---

[91] *Supra,* Dec. 24, 1863, note 4.

[92] *Supra,* Feb. 21, 1862, note 96.

[93] *Supra,* April 27, 1859, note 27.

[94] *Infra,* March 15, 1864.

[95] William S. Rosecrans: West Point graduate of 1842; instructor at West Point, and Army engineer until 1854; civil engineer and manufacturer, 1854–1861; aide to McClellan in Ohio, 1861; brigadier-general in command of the Department of the Ohio, 1861, and of the Department of West Virginia, 1861–1862; officer under Halleck before Corinth in 1862; commander of the Army of the Mississippi, 1862, and of the Department of the Cumberland, 1862–1863. He was removed after losing the battle of Chickamauga in September, 1863, but was put in charge of the Department of the Missouri in January, 1864.

[96] See *supra,* Feb. 22, 1864.

[97] March 10, 1864, *Complete Works of Abraham Lincoln,* II, 494.

[98] This sounds strangely like Welles's comments upon President Johnson's failure to remove Stanton. Cf. *Diary of Gideon Welles,* II, 480–482, 581–583, 606, 611, 613, 630; III, 45, 49, 90–91.

Mar 9. The demoralising effect of this civil war is plainly visible in every department of life. The abuse of official powers and the thirst for dishonest gain are now so common that they cease to shock[.]

And all branches of the Government seem to forget the constitutional divisions of power, and the lines and landmarks which separate them—Even pretty good men fall into the error, unconscious of the mischief they are doing. For instance—there is a bill pending, introduced by Senator John Sherman of Ohio, to grant an appeal from the decisions of the *Commissioner of Internal Revenue*, in regard to Stamp duties, directly to the Supreme Court!! [99]

<*Note.* Mar 13. Last night, [at] Gov Morgan's [1] dinner the subject was mentioned by me to Senator Wilson,[2] as a striking instance of heedless legislation. He called Sherman's attention to it, who seemed wholly unconscious of the blunder—I told him that I had no thought, that if the bill did pass, the S.[upreme] C.[ourt] would submit to have the jurisdiction thrust upon it, in that way.>

[*A clipping dated Baltimore, March 9, announcing the arrival at Annapolis of the* City of New York *bringing 660 prisoners from Richmond, and reprinting from the Richmond papers accounts of the death of Colonel Dahlgren* [3] *and the indignities to which his body was subjected. The* Richmond Whig *is quoted as saying: these captured Union soldiers " should not be treated as prisoners of war, but this day's sun should not go down before every scoundrel taken is blown from the cannon's mouth."*]

That is not an economical plan. It costs a charge of powder for each man! All the powder might be saved, and the ferocious temper of the editor of the Whig gratified, if he were indulged in the luxury of cutting their throats with a dinner knife!

[*A clipping quoting an expression of regret by the* New York Evening Post *" that the National Convention of its political friends " has been called for the early date of June 7, because " the longer we wait the better we shall be able to discern the right man for the times."*]

It is not unnatural that [the] Post should wish delay. It needs all the time it can get, to hunt up some candidate to supersede Lincoln. Since Mr. Chase retired,[4] the anti-Lincoln men fear nothing more

---

[99] *Supra,* Feb. 20, 1864.

[1] Edwin D. Morgan: wholesale grocer of New York City; state senator, 1850–1855; state commissioner of immigration, 1855–1858; vice-president of the Republican National Convention in 1856 and delegate in 1860; chairman of the Republican National Committee, 1856–1864, and 1872; governor of New York, 1859–1862; major-general of volunteers, 1861–1863; Republican U. S. senator, 1863–1869.

[2] *Supra,* Jan. 7, 1860, note 7.

[3] *Supra,* Oct. 15, 1863, note 19.

[4] Chase had announced on March 5 that he was not a candidate for the Presidency.

than to be forced to choose, until they have tried all chances for a new candidate. The N[ew] Y[ork] Tribune begs for time.

[*Two clippings printing letters of Salmon P. Chase written on January 18, and March 5, 1864. In the first, he asks for the support of his friends if the party leaders decide that his nomination will best serve the interests of the country, but says that he will support any candidate who may be nominated. In the second, he definitely withdraws his name in the interest of unity in suppressing the rebellion.*]

This forced declention of Mr. Chase is really, not worth much. It proves only that the *present* prospects of Mr. Lincoln are too good to be openly resisted, at least, by men within the party. The extreme men who urged Mr. Chase, afraid to array themselves in *open* opposition to Mr. L[incoln], will only act more guardedly—get up as many candidates as they can, *privily*, with the hope of bringing in Mr. C[hase], at last, as a compromise candidate.

And, in the mean time, strain every nerve to commit Mr. L.[incoln] to as many as possible of their extreme measures.

Mar 12.   Called to see R. Aml Lee [5] and old Mr. Blair. [6]

Also, called, for a few minutes, at Mr. Prest.'s Reception[.] Tilly invited Mrs. Barton Able and Miss Magune, and *chaperoned* them to " the Reception "—They called at my office, on their return.

Note.   Capt Bart:[on] Able [7] (being in my office, with James Archer of St Louis,) examined the pictures of the Atty Genls, which adorn the walls, noticed the fact that there does not appear to be a *bald* man among them, tho' several of them look somewhat old. <Randolph [8] and Lee [9] are the only two who shew any decided baldness—*Black*,[10] no doubt, was painted *in his wig*—the rest, down to me, wear *some* of their own hair, on the top of the head[.]> Some of these men were old—I am 70. Let thoughtful men ponder upon the moderate Living and *conservative* habits of *Lawyers*.

Dined (7. p. m.) at Gov (Senator) Morgans [11] [*sic*] with a select party, among whom were—two foreign ministers, Mr. Stoekle [Stoeckl],[12] Russian, and Count Piper,[13] Swede and Schleiden (Hambourg[)] [14]—Senators Foot [15] (now Prest pro tem[pore]:)

[5] *Supra*, Dec. 19, 1863, note 89.

[6] *Supra*, May 10, 1863, note 11.

[7] *Supra*, May 3, 1860, note 90.

[8] Edmund J. Randolph: aide-de-camp to Washington; attorney-general of Virginia, 1776; member of the Continental Congress, 1779–1782; governor, 1786–1788; framer of the Constitution, 1787; first U. S. attorney-general, 1789–1794; secretary of State, 1794–1795.

[9] Charles Lee: Virginia state legislator; member of the Continental Congress; U. S. naval officer of the Potomac District, 1789–1795; attorney-general, 1795–1801.

[10] *Supra*, Oct. 28, 1859, note 22.

[11] *Supra*, March 9, 1864, note 1.

[12] *Supra*, Nov. 27, 1861.

[13] *Loc. cit.*

[14] He represented Bremen, not Hamburg.   *Supra*, Dec. 25, 1861. note 53.

[15] Solomon Foot, Republican senator from Vermont, 1851–1866.

Wilson,[16] Sherman [17] Nesmith.[18] Rear Admls. Stringham [19] and Paulding [20]—H[ouse] of R.[epresentatives] Washburn[e] [21] of Ills, Davis [22] of Md., Davis [23] of N. Y. and [   ] Genl. Wadsworth,[24] Dr. Cuyler[.]

The only ladies at the table were Mrs. Morgan and her young friend, Miss Jarvis of Hartford Cont.

[*Marginal Note.*] Mar 13. At night, R. Adml. Lee [25] (and wifes [*sic*]) called to see us. Was very pleasant and friendly. Spoke, in high terms of Dick and said he wd. detail him as Judge Advocate of the squadron—was trying to have that office established by law, with the [r]ank of commander.

Mar 15. I and Matilda dined at Mr. Romero,[26] Mexican minister, with a pleasant party, among whom were Secy Stanton, Senator Grimes,[27] Mr. (and Mrs.) Justice Field,[28] M.[embers of] C.[ongres]s Griswold [29] of N. Y. and Cox [30] of Ohio, and their wives.

March 15. I have succeeded, at last, in getting the order for the discharge of young Silas Highley, of St Joe, a prisoner of war, at Alton's [*sic*] and his father, the old Captain, has gone home rejoicing, with the order in his pocket.[31]

Mar 19 Saturday. Dined at Mr. Pruyn's [32] (M.[ember of] C.[ongress] of N Y.) I did not know Mr. P.[ruyn] before, and, from what I had heard of him, expected a *political* dinner, but was agreeably disappointed in finding it *legal* only—4 Justices of [the] S.[upreme] C.[ourt] 3 Senators and 2 or 3 members of the House.

---

[16] *Supra*, Jan. 7, 1860, note 7.

[17] *Supra*, Oct. 20, 1863, note 29.

[18] James W. Nesmith: Democratic senator from Oregon, 1861–1867.

[19] *Supra*, March 9, 1861, note 39.

[20] Hiram Paulding, retired naval officer in command of the Brooklyn Navy Yard.

[21] Elihu B. Washburne: Republican congressman, 1853–1869; secretary of State under Grant.

[22] *Supra*, Dec. 17, 1859, note 39.

[23] Thomas T. Davis: Unionist congressman from New York, 1863–1867.

[24] James S. Wadsworth, wealthy New York land-owner, former military governor of the District of Columbia, now a brigadier-general in the Army of the Potomac, killed in the Wilderness in May.

[25] *Supra*, Dec. 19, 1863, note 89.

[26] Matias Romero, secretary of the Mexican Legation; then chargé d'affaires, 1859–1863; minister, 1863–1868, 1881–1898; secretary of the Treasury under Juárez, 1868–1873, 1876–1879; senator, 1876; postmaster-general, 1880.

[27] *Supra*, Dec. 19, 1862, note 82.

[28] Stephen J. Field: New York City lawyer, 1841–1848; California state legislator; judge of the California Supreme Court, 1857–1863; Democratic unionist in 1861; justice of the U. S. Supreme Court, 1863–1897.

[29] John A. Griswold: Democratic congressman from New York, 1863–1865; Republican congressman, 1865–1869; builder of the *Monitor* and six more ships like it.

[30] Samuel S. ("Sunset") Cox: Democratic congressman from Ohio, 1857–1865, and from New York, 1869–1885, 1886–1889; a supporter of every effort to bring peace and reconciliation between the sections; opponent of the arbitrary use of war powers.

[31] *Supra*, March 9, 1864.

[32] John V. S. L. Pruyn: lawyer and railroad director; state senator, 1861; Democratic congressman, 1863–1865, 1867–1869; chancellor of the University of New York, 1868–1877.

[*A clipping which prints a letter signed "S. H. Boyd," said to have been written from the House of Representatives. "Chase,"* it says, *"will, by G—d, get Lincoln down; . . . Lincoln is a d—d old fool."*]

I hear that even the *Radicals* are getting ashamed of Boyd.[33] He is as unprincipled as they are, but he has no sense.

[*A clipping which prints a letter from the Washington correspondent of the* New York Tribune *originally published in the* Tribune *of December 14, 1863. It tells how John Covode* [34] *of Pennsylvania, James M. Ashley* [35] *of Ohio, and George S. Boutwell* [36] *of Massachusetts called upon President Lincoln as a Committee representing the Union League* [37] *to urge the dismissal of Bates and Blair from the Cabinet and Halleck* [38] *and Schofield* [39] *from their high positions in the Army.*]

These newspaper letter writers are the most shameless liars under the sun. It is only the brazen impudence of a few revolutionary radicals, to betray the Union leagues and steal their strength, which is really great, and *dead* against the Radicals.

[*General Order No. 32 of the District of North Carolina issued at Newbern, on March 11, 1864, by order of Major-General Peck explaining that Northern philanthropy has provided for the education of "colored children," and directing that "free schools be organized at once" for "poor white children," paid for from the "Civil Fund, on orders from these Head Quarters."*]

This document, I suppose, was sent me by the Genl.[40] himself, for it comes from Newburn, with this indorsement [41]—[John J. Peck Maj Genl]

It would seem that Genl Peck is, like Dr. Francia of Paragua,[42] both "King and constable," Pope and Curate— Minister of Instruction and District School master. All power, military and civil, are

---

[33] *Supra*, Dec. 19, 1863, note 93.

[34] *Supra*, April 2, 1860, note 44.

[35] Formerly a clerk on river-boats; then editor of the *Dispatch* and the *Democrat* of Portsmouth, Ohio; a wholesale druggist; now a Republican congressman, 1859–1869, from Ohio; governor of Montana, 1869–1870; railroad president, 1877–1893. In Congress he was an abolitionist, an extreme Radical, a persecutor of the South, a severe critic of Lincoln, and a leader in the impeachment of Johnson.

[36] *Supra*, Oct. 15, 1863, note 14.

[37] *Supra*, Dec. 19, 1863, note 94.

[38] *Supra*, Nov. 13, 1861, note 37.

[39] *Supra*, May 30, 1863, note 32.

[40] John J. Peck: West Point graduate of 1843; army officer in New York, in Mexico, and on the frontier, 1843–1853; railroad promoter and banker of Syracuse, New York, 1853–1861; brigadier- and then major-general of volunteers in Virginia, 1861–1863; commander in North Carolina, 1863–1864, and on the Canadian frontier, 1864–1865.

[41] I. e., with the frank of John Peck, major-general.

[42] José Gaspar Rodríguez Francia of Paraguay: a Catholic priest; sometime professor of theology in the University of Cordova in Spain; later a lawyer; secretary of the revolutionary Junta of Paraguay in 1811, then in 1813 one of two consuls, in 1814 dictator for three years, and in 1817 dictator for life—dictator not only in name but in cruel fact.

[*sic*] concentrated in his person. The *little blacks* being liberally provided for, in the whole state of North Carolina, he now, kindly, make[s] provision for the *little whites*.

[*General Peck gives as the reason for his order his belief that ignorance, resulting from lack of a system of general education, had been " one of the leading causes of the existing revolution."*]

Therefore the Genl (who was sent to N.[orth] C.[arolina] to beat the enemy in the field) generously assumes to legislate for posterity, and to " train up (the *Poor, white children*) in the way they should go."

I think this is the first instance of the establishment of *Free Schools*, at least in America, by *Military order*! Fortunately, the Provost Martil [*sic*] is restricted to the procur[e]ment of ' suitable rooms.' It is very kind in the Genl. not to subject the ' poor white children ' to martial law, as administered by his Provost!

The expence is to be paid out of the *Civil fund*. Lucky General! He can squeese [*sic*] civil blood out of a military turnip. He has, it would seem, *a civil fund*, to be disposed of by military orders from *these Head Quarters*!

The Genl. appoints School Inspectors for the seat of his *civil* government at Newburn. Yet they are military men!

"At an early day, schools will be opened at Washington, Beauford [*sic*] and perhaps other places,"—in his dominions.

I see by the papers that Gen Banks [43] also, has issued an order to establish *common schools* in La! A new branch this, of *military command*![44]

[*A newspaper reprint of a letter of March 7, 1864, from G. C. Eisenmeyer [45] of Mascoutah, St. Clair Co., Illinois, saying that his first, second, and third choice for President at the coming election will be Abraham Lincoln.*]

This letter of Mr. *Eisenmeyer* proves that the extreme Radicals cannot control all the Germans.

This letter is running the rounds, and is quite the talk. A few days ago it appeared in the Nat[ional] Intel[ligence]r., introduced by some commendatory paragraphs.[46]

[*A newspaper copy of a letter of Edward Bates dated February 2, 1862, printed with hearty approval by the* New York Journal of Commerce, *March 10, 1864.*]

---

[43] *Supra*, July 27, 1859, note 57.

[44] These comments are written upon the Order which is bound into the diary.

[45] George C. Eisenmayer: Bavarian-born immigrant to Illinois in 1837; now a successful grape grower and wine manufacturer; an active Republican from the organization of the party.

[46] "A Sentiment for the Times," in the issue of March 15, 1864.

Washington City, Feb. 2, 1864.

To. ——,

Madam: Being confined to my sick room, I have an opportunity which neither my public office nor the court room affords, to acknowledge your note of Jan. 30, written in behalf of the Brooklyn and Long Island Fair, and in aid of the Sanitary Commission.[47]

You ask for an autograph, unconditionally, and for a sentiment, "if agreeable." Now my dear lady, an autograph is a cheap thing and can be easily furnished, whether sick or well; but a sentiment is quite another affair, and does not sort very well with the nauseous physic which I am required to take to-day.

Nevertheless, the cause being so good, and withal its advocate a lady (to which high authority I habitually bow), I must strain a point and try to give you something sentimental, but not of the sickly kind.

I am beginning to grow old, and am a very old fashioned man; for in spite of the rushing current of new opinions, I still believe that we once had good old times, good old principles, and good old men to profess them and act them out, and a good Constitution worthy to be preserved to the latest posterity.

In fact I begin to suspect myself to be little or nothing better than an *old fogy;* for I can't help believing, with Jackson, that the constitutional Union of the States *must* be preserved; and I still have undoubting faith in Washington when he warns us that we cannot preserve our free institutions without a frequent recurrence to the first principles of our government.

That is my sentiment, Madam. I fear it is growing very unpopular, but I can't help that. God knows that I would help it if I could, for I have little hope of improvement from the efforts of men who fancy themselves so much wiser than their fathers were, and so much better than the laws which they made for our good.

With love for your cause, and respect for yourself, I remain,
　　　Your obedient servant,

EDWD. BATES.

[*A clipping from the* Missouri Republican *of March 19, 1864, giving a reprint from the* Boston Journal *which describes the split in the Unionist Party of Missouri, and the threat that the Radical faction will vote Democratic if Frémont is not nominated by the Republicans.*]

---

[47] A voluntary organization that provided cleanliness in camp and hospital, food and medical supplies, and what comforts and cheer it could, for the soldiers in the Civil War.

Mar 22. . . .

I know very little of what is going on in politics and election-eering. As I am not identified with any extreme party, nobody approaches me, to make interest, nor thinks it worth while (or perhaps safe) to tell me what he is aiming at.

I take no part in the schemes of electioneering. But in my own quiet way—by letters to friends, and by the inculcation of principles, in my opinions and other public documents—I give Mr. Lincoln the best support I can; and I believe that, in some quarters, it is not without effect.

My support of Mr. L.[incoln] is not grounded upon an affirma-tive approval of all that is done in his name. There are many things done, especially under the Departments of Treasury and War, which I do not approve[.] In fact I often remonstrate against them. But he is immeasurably preferable to his opponents—Our only chance of a return to law and order—our only means to keep down the reckless, revolutionary spirit of the Radicals.

I hold no terms with the extreme Radicals, but denounce them openly—and in that we are even.

The office I hold is not properly *political*, but strictly *legal;* and it is my duty, above all other ministers of State, to uphold the Law. and to resist all encroachments, from whatever quarter, of mere will and power, upon the province of the law. I am often mortified at being obliged to witness such encroachments, without the power to resist successfully. Still, I remonstrate, and make ' continual claim ' for the right. It is only yesterday, that I sent to the Secretary of War, a strong remonstrance against a sweeping order of confiscation issued by a Provost Martial [48] [*sic*] at Norfolk Va., against one [   ] Williams.[49]

I have never interfered with military seisures for mere military purposes; but I feel it to be my duty to denounce, if I cannot pre-vent, the frequent instances of needless, groundless and wanton in-terference of the military, in matters which, in no wise concern them, as if the object were to contemn and degrade the civil power.

The recent interferences (by the Secy of War and several of the Generals) with both the property and the discipline of the Churches, will not fail to excite a deep and general feeling of dissatisfaction and disgust. The President's opinions (known and published) are against these arbitrary proceedings, and yet they are boldly prac-ticed. The President does not wish it to be so. But I fear he has to say, in his heart, like king David—" These sons [of] Zeruiah be too hard for me! " [50]

---

[48] Brigadier-General Edward A. Wild: *infra*, April 13, 1864, note 93.
[49] *Infra*, April 13, 1864.
[50] *The Bible*, " 2 Samuel," III, 39.

Mar 23. Today called at my office (introduced by Revd. J. N Davis of this city) Bishop *Edwards*, and two of his ministers, of the *United Brethren*, of Ohio. They wanted to talk abt Bishop *Ames'* [51] monopoly of churches in the South (under Secy S[t]anton's order [52]) and seemed to have a hankering after a share of the plunder. I spoke to them very plainly—told them that there was not a shadow of law for what was done; and that, in my opinion, there was little display of christian principle in thus coveting their neighbors['] land—and that I expected the proceeding would break down Bishop Ames, even with his own people.

We parted good friends.

Recd. a letter from Revd. Mr. Foreman of Mo. complaining of Genl Rosecrans' [53] order, governing church assemblies. Ansd.

March 24. Lately, I am pestered every day, with demands for autographs, letters, sentiments, and the like—Here is one of them.

" Republics never grow better; and for the plain reason that beginning at the purest and highest point of civil liberty, every departure from the first position is, necessarily, a progress down hill.

["] Republics always begin poor and weak; and then they honestly invoke, because they need, the protection of, good principles. But when they become rich and powerful, they, too often, resist those same principles, because they are obstacles in the way of ambition and glory.

["] We, Republicans, have no king but the Law. And he who despises the Law and wantonly breaks it, is not a loyal man."

(signed)　　　　*Edward Bates.*

(Written in *somebody's* album, at the request of T. J. Coffey [54])

[*A clipping from the* Missouri Democrat *of March 25, 1864:*

" The Chicago *Tribune* sharply says it admires Attorney General Bates's late letter to the Brooklyn Sanitary Fair, ' just as we admire a cow's head by Rosa Bonheur—for its faithfulness, not for its brains.' It adds:

" ' Mr. Bates says he is " beginning to grow old." We congratulate him on the long postponement of the event. Most men begin to grow old the moment they are born. He is a very " old fashioned man." Very well, then let his attention be confined to old fashioned matters. We can't put old wine into new bottles. He does not seem to be aware that a " rushing current of new events " will bring a " rushing current of new opinions," unless men are under a stupor. He is mistaken in supposing that we fancy ourselves so very much wiser than our fathers *were*, though we trust we are a little wiser in some things, else we had better not lived.' "]

[51] Edward R. Ames: itinerant minister, 1830–1852; after 1852 the Methodist bishop of Indianapolis; strong unionist; for a time an army chaplain.

[52] Nov. 30, 1863, *War of the Rebellion*, series 1, vol. XXXIV, part 2, serial no. 62, pp. 311, 452.

[53] *Supra*, March 9, 1864, note 95.

[54] *Supra*, March 5, 1860, note 18.

Mar 26. Saturday. This morning, Gov Bramlette,[55] ex senator
Dixon,[56] and Mr. Hodges [57] (of the Frankfort Commonwealth) of
Ky: called on me at my office. I introduced them to the President,
with whom I believe they made arrangement for a special audience. [58]
The Governor's mission here is to have a better understanding with
the Genl. Govt., about *negro* enlistments in Ky. The Govr. says that
the draft will not be opposed, if conducted in a simple and honest
way—i. e. enlist the men and march them off, without making it a
pretence to insult, and rob, and dominate every neighborhood—as in
Maryland!

[*Marginal*] *Note.* Mar 28. The President tells me that he made
an arrangement with Gov Bramlette that seemed to be satisfactory,
all around.

They dined with me—Unluckily, Mr. Dixon was so *fatigued with
liquor,* that he wd. do all the talking; and so, I lost the useful conversation which I had hoped to hold with the Governor.

Note. Judge Williams,[59] of the Ky C[our]t. of Appeals, called
to see me—A very good man, I think. He wd. like to change to a
Federal District Judg[e]ship[.]

Mar 27 Sunday. Day before yesterday, Lt. Genl. Grant went to
the front—Hd. Qrs. A.[rmy of the] P[otomac]. It seems not
known whether he will supersede Genl. Meade,[60] or only supervise
him, as all the rest.

. . .

It is currently rumored, and published in some newspapers, that,
in *exchanging prisoners* with the enemy, we *give* more than we *get—*
i. e. we *give* 100, and *get* 75— 80— or 90.

I cannot believe the degrading charge; yet it is confidently affirmed,
and I see no official contradiction. If it turn out to be true, and no
one is brought to condign punishment for the shameful offence, I
shall not be able longer to resist the imputation of cowardly imbecility in the administration of the war.

[55] Thomas E. Bramlette of Kentucky: state legislator; state's attorney, 1848–1850;
judge of the Kentucky Circuit Court, 1856–1861; officer in the Union Army, 1861–1862;
U. S. district attorney, 1862–1863; Unionist Democratic governor, 1863–1867. He supported Lincoln until 1864, but then turned against him and opposed his reëlection because
of the extreme measures adopted by the Federal Government—one of them this matter of
enlisting negro troops.

[56] Archibald Dixon: state legislator, 1830, 1836, 1841; lieutenant-governor of Kentucky,
1843; Whig U. S. senator, 1852–1855; war-time advocate of peace.

[57] Albert G. Hodges of Frankfort, Kentucky: assistant and later owner and editor
of numerous journalistic ventures, 1815–1833; state printer, 1833–1858(?); editor of the
Frankfort Commonwealth, 1833–1872; a Whig, a Know-Nothing, a Unionist during the
War, and finally a Republican.

[58] For an account of what Lincoln told them, see *infra,* May 1, 1864.

[59] *Supra,* Oct. 19, 1863, note 27.

[60] *Supra,* Oct. 15, 1863, note 18.

It occurs to me that the rumor may have arisen out of the (probable) fact, that *officers of ours* may have been exchanged for *men of theirs.*

[*A clipping headed " The New Navy Register " quoting some of the naval statistics provided in it.*]

Mar 30. Last night I attended a party at Secy *Usher's.* Tho' the weather was very stormy, there was quite a gay company, and sufficiently numerous for pleasure.

Among the guests was Mrs. Genl. Grant—who was confided by the host, to my special care.

None of the ministers of State were present, but the Messrs. Seward (Father and son [61]) and myself.

[*An autograph letter from J. M. Vaughan,[62] presenting Mr. Bates with a pair of silver buckles once owned by General Stark of Revolutionary fame.*]

The writer, my young friend, John M. Vaughan, has been a clerk in my office, for nearly three years. He now resigns his office to go West, to seek his fortune—probably in Montana Territory— In going, he leaves me these silver buckles (once worn by *Genl. Stark* [63]) as a memorial of his attachment and fidelity to me.

God speed him. He has my best wishes " in health and wealth long to live."

March 31./64.   *Edw[ar]d. Bates*

[*A clipping from the* Daily Chronicle *of March 29, 1864, which gives: (1) the call of the Union National Convention to be held at Baltimore on June 7; (2) an editorial on " The Last Raid into Kentucky "; (3) a reprint from the* Richmond Sentinel *headed " The Treatment of Negro Soldiers.*"]

Apl 2 Saturday. [*A newspaper reprint of the Senate yeas and nays on a proposition to change " white male " to just " male " in the qualifications for the suffrage (and presumably for office-holding) in the new Territory of Montana.*] [64]

I attach this vote for negro suffrage for two reasons—1. to shew that the Radicals will let no opportunity pass, to assert their principle of equality, and 2d. and chiefly, to shew that Mr. Henderson [65] of Mo. is not wholly sold to the Radicals.

The majority—only 5—22 agst. 17—is not large, and yet I am sure some of them voted under *duress.*

---

[61] Frederick Seward. *Supra,* May 13, 1862, note 38.

[62] *Supra,* March 6, 1863, note 59.

[63] John Stark, a Vermont farmer who served as captain in the French and Indian War and as brigadier-general in the Revolutionary War.

[64] March 31, 1864, *Cong. Globe,* 38 Cong., 1 Sess., 1361. See also *U. S. Statutes at Large,* XIII, chap. XCV, sec. 5, p. 87.

[65] *Supra,* Feb. 24, 1863, note 27.

A late act of Congress creates the office of Warden of the jail in the District of Columbia, and transfers all the powers and duties of the marshal, over the jail and the prisoners, to the Warden of the jail.[66] At the instance of the President, I gave an opinion, to the effect that the marshal could not execute sentence of death, upon two convicts in the jail. And now, Marshal Laman [67] tells me that there is quite a buz[z] among Senators, on finding out the legal effect of their act establishing the Warden, which, in fact, was intended only to cut down the marshal's profits, by taking from him the jail. He says that some of them are very sour agst. me.—
N' importe.

" God was not [yet] pleased to think us fit for deliverance, and we must attend his leisure."

　　　　Evelyn's Diary,[68] vol 3. p 14.

April 5 Tuesday. Yesterday the *Sup[rem]e. Court* announced that it would adjourn monday the 18th. and consequently, there will be no arguments, after tuesday the 12th.

In the Fossatt v The U. S.[69] (the Quicksilver case, on the survey) Judge Nelson [70] delivered the opinion of the Court, in favor of Fossatt, in every point. <Vide infra Apl 10>

Clifford [71] J[ustice] gave a dissenting opinion, with a great deal of point and unction.

I was surprised at the judgment, and confidently believe that it is dangerously erroneous, in several particulars—It assumes that the proceeding upon the survey is a continuation only of the action on the title—in the nature of Execution, and therefore proper for the juditial [*sic*] action of the court. That the act of 1860 gave power to the District Court to direct the survey, and expressly *gave appeal* to *this Court!*

I fear that this judgment will cost the court a great deal of mortification, and that it may be many years before it can retrace its steps back to good doctrine.

Apl 6. . . .

To day, there were but six Judges on the Sup[rem]e. bench. Taney, Wayne,[72] Grier [73] and Catron,[74] all absent, from indisposition—I fear

---

[66] Feb. 29, 1864. *U. S. Statutes at Large,* XIII, chap. XVI, p. 12–13.

[67] Ward H. Lamon : *supra,* Dec. 6, 1861, note 12.

[68] *Diary and Correspondence of John Evelyn, F. R. S.,* in 4 volumes, William Bray, editor (Henry Colburn, London, 1854).

[69] *Supra,* Feb. 24, 1864, note 65 ; Feb. 20 to March 2, 1864.

[70] *Supra,* March 6, 1861, note 32.

[71] Nathan Clifford : Maine lawyer ; state legislator, 1830–1834 ; attorney-general of Maine, 1834–1838 ; Democratic congressman, 1839–1843 ; U. S. attorney-general, 1846–1848 ; commissioner to Mexico, 1848–1849 ; justice of the U. S. Supreme Court, 1858–1881.

[72] *Supra,* Nov. 27, 1861, note 74.

[73] *Supra,* Feb. 26, 1864, note 76.

[74] John Catron : Nashville lawyer ; justice of the Tennessee Supreme Court, 1824–1834 ; justice of the U. S. Supreme Court, 1837–1865 ; staunch unionist. When war came he tried to continue holding court in Tennessee, but was driven out.

it is probable that T.[aney] W[ayne] and G[rier] will never sit again [75]—Yet the Ch.[ief] J.[ustice] told me tonight, that he might go to court tomorrow, if a good day; he says he cant [*sic*] walk, is weak in the knees, and I advised him not to expose himself, as the term is almost over—only three more days for argument.

[*Marginal Note.*] Ch[ief] J[ustice] Taney was again on the bench, friday Apl 8[.]

Apl 7. 1864. [*Clippings from the* National Intelligencer *of April 6 and 7, 1864, about an alleged letter dated 1834 said to have been written by George Thompson* [76] " *late a member of the British Parliament," about a projected uprising of slaves in Tennessee. The letter expressed the opinion that " the dissolution of the Union is the object to be kept steadily in view." In April, 1864, Mr. Thompson, then visiting Washington, asked permission to use the Hall of Representatives for an evening anti-slavery address. The old letter was used as an argument against allowing him the use of the hall, but the permission was granted none the less.*]

Mr. Thompson delivered his address last night, in presence of a great concourse (the President included) and took occasion to deny emphatically and with circumstance, the writing of any such letter.

Apl 9. . . . Dick left us today. He came up from the squadron two days since, with *Fleet Captain* Barnes, on a short visit—Capt B.[arnes] dined with us yesterday.

Dick[']s conduct of late, gives us great hope and comfort.

Apl 9. Evelyn's Diary, Vol 3. p 45. In a letter to his father in law, Sir Richard Browne,[77] he recommends a young man to him, to be his private Secretary, in this quaint and expressive manner—" I have herein enclosed you a cursory proof of the youth's writing, which truly he performs with a wonderful facility and strange sweetness of hand, nor can you be so fitted, in every respect. He is young, humble, congruously literate, very apprehensive and ingenuous, and may be of great use to you &c. . . . His person is not very gracious, the small pox having quite put out one of his eyes: but he is of good shape: . . . Truly[,] I am of opinion you will be very proud of him, and may make him your secretary, with a great deal of reason; however, if you do not like him, I am now resolved never to part with him, so long as he is willing to be with me; and above all, he is admirably temperate."

---

[75] Taney did sit for the rest of this term, but died October 12. Wayne sat until he died, July 5, 1867, and Grier continued a justice until he died, September 26, 1870.

[76] A leader in the movement for abolition of slavery in the British Colonies. In 1834–1835 at the danger of his life he toured New England preaching abolitionism. He returned to America in 1851 and again in 1864. From 1847 until 1852 he sat in Parliament.

[77] The letter was written from London, April 5, 1649. Sir Richard Browne was ambassador from England to the Court of France.

Apl 10. . . .

The Supreme Court. Every day I am pained (sometimes shamed and disgusted) at witnessing the proceedings in this highest of all courts—both the substance and the mode—.<Vide supra Apl 5>

Heretofore, the maxim *stare decisis*, was almost ostentatiously announced; but now, it looks as if cases were determined on grounds of policy only, and upon local and transient reasons. Former (recent) decisions are simply ignored or flatly overruled; and the scales of justice rise and sink by some motive power, unknown to me, which, if not interested, seems to me a capricious will.

In the California Land cases the court evinces a remarkable infirmity of purpose and instability of judgment—veering from course to course, and swinging from side to side, all the way down from the Mariposa gold mines [78] (Fremont's) to the New Almaden Quicksilver mine.[79] At this term two cases have been decided differently upon the very same grounds. One claim was rejected for *lack of Registry*—that seeming to be the only ground—and another claim was confirmed in spite of that objection!!

In the Fossatt case I urged the want of jurisdiction—that the making of the survey is an executive act merely, not proper for the courts; and that the District court having taken jurisdiction, under the act of 1860, if an appeal lay at all, it lay, by express provision, to the Circuit Court. Still, the S.[upreme] C.[ourt] assumes the jurisdiction, and passes upon the survey!

And yet, the Court is even now, itself, raising the question whether it has jurisdiction in any case of appeal from the Court of Claims; and that too as far as I can learn, upon the sole alleged ground that when the Court has pronounced judgment, it cannot enforce execution!

(Note. The court has formally set down the question for argument—not *inter partes*, for no party has made objection, but—*but free for argument by all comers!*)

The great, and now c[h]ronic, error which has well nigh destroyed the dignity and is impairing the usefulness of the court, is the extreme looseness and irregularity of practice in the courts below, allowed and encouraged here; and this has gone to such a pitch that no man—not the Ch[ief] Justice—knows what is the *true record* from the Court below, it is so hidden and smothered with the *hotch potch* matter, thrust into the miscellaneous collection miscalled the record of the case.

---

[78] *John C. Fremont* v. *U. S.,* 17 Howard 542–576. In this case the title of Frémont to the land was confirmed in spite of unquestionable failure to comply with the terms of the grant.

[79] *Supra,* Feb. 26, 1863, note 49. In this case the claim of the Almaden Mine Company was rejected because of lack of proper registry of the title.

And in this court the good old law of pleading is silently ignored—for I do not know that it is repealed—No assignment of
errors is required, and consequently, there can be no specific issues of
law for the court to try, but the court must hunt thro' the incongruous
mass of the so called record, to find, if it can, what errors may *lurk
and wander* there.

Every lawyer who brings a case here, by writ of error or appeal,
knows of course, what errors he complains of, and it is no hardship
to require him to plead them.

[*A clipping from the* Missouri Democrat *of April 5, 1864, re-
porting a meeting of the St. Louis City Council called by Acting
Mayor A. W. Fagin* [80] *to consider an opinion given by Charles A.
Drake, City Counselor.*]

This Mr. Drake seems to have a great faculty to stir up dirt,
whatever water he dabbles in.

[*A comment of "Anti-Traitor" in the* Missouri Democrat *of
April 5, 1864, on a prayer offered by Dr. McPheeters* [81] *that God
might " grant us a peace that would be honorable and safe."*]

The Democrat, it seems, objects to a " safe and honorable peace."

One of two conclusions would seem to follow: Either the Democrat does not want peace at all; or, if we must have pe[a]ce, he wants
some kind of peace *that is not safe and honorable.*

The Dem:[ocrat] has *made money* rapidly during the war!

Mo. Dem:[ocrat] Apl. 6

> ["The Presbytery of St. Louis, O.[ld] S.[chool] will meet in Kirkwood
> this evening. We are authorized to state that an officer will be present
> to administer the prescribed oath, for the accommodation of such members
> as cannot conveniently come to the city."]

At my instance, the Prest. has written to Genl. Rosecrans [82] to
stop thise [*sic*] useless and wanton interference with the churches. [83]
And I wrote to Revd. Mr. Foreman exp[r]essing the hope that
our judicatories would not degrade themselves by sitting under a
Provost Martial [*sic*][.]

[*A clipping from the* Union *of April 6, 1864, reporting a meeting
of the Directors of the Union Pacific Railroad.*]

This looks like *progress*[.]

Apl 11 monday. In Sup[rem]e. Court today, I argued two
revenue cases, from Boston, the one the *Almond* case, [84] so called,

[80] Aaron W. Fagin: wealthy St. Louis commission merchant; mine owner; flour miller,
who during the War made handsome profits selling flour to the Government.

[81] *Supra*, April 24, 1859, note 24.

[82] *Supra*, March 9, 1864, note 95.

[83] April 4, 1864, *Complete Works of Abraham Lincoln*, II, 507.

[84] *Homer* v. *the Collector*, 1 Wallace 486–490. The question was whether almonds
fell in the Tariff Act of 1857 under " fruit, green or ripe " or under " almonds, currants,
dates," etc. If the former, as the importer claimed, they were subject to an import duty
of only eight per cent; if the latter, as the United States claimed, the duty was thirty
per cent. The Court decided in favor of the United States.

against Mr. Welch;[85] the other the *Wool* case,[86] against Mr. Bartlett.[87]

These two were the last cases for argument this term. The court adjourned over till next Monday, when the opinions will be delivered and the term be closed[.]

Ch: [*ief*] *J.*[*ustice*] *Taney* was in his seat again to day, and I was much pleased to find that he seemed even more cheerful and active than last friday.

All the Judges were present except Mr. Justice *Grier*,[88] who has gone home sick. The *4* seniors, Taney, Wayne,[89] Catron[90] and Grier, are evidently failing, being, obviously, less active in mind and body, than at the last term. I think all four of them would gladly retire, if Congress would pass the proposed bill—to enable the justices to resign, upon an adequate pensi[o]n.

But most of them, if not all, cannot afford to resign, having no support but their salaries.

[*Note.*] I might perhaps, as well have said *5*, as 4; for Mr. Justice Nelson[91] shews as plainly as the other 4 signs of decay. He walks with a firmer step it is true, but I do not see that his *mind* stands more erect than theirs, or moves onward with a steadier gait.[92]

Apl 12. Cataclysis [*Catalysis*]—I never observed this word, till now. Yet, it is used by as great authorities as *John Evelyn* and *Jeremy Taylor* (see Evelyn's Diary and correspondence p.p. 65–69 [67–69]. Vol 3)[.] Warcester's [*sic*] Dic:[tionary] defines it by the single English word, *Dissolution*. And it is not in Richardson's Class[ica]l. Dic[tionary]:

Apl 13, Wednesday. Just as I began to write to the President (as he suggested I should) about Genl. Wilde's[93] *confiscation* order,

---

[85] The lawyer who argued the case for Homer, the importer.

[86] *Iasigi et al.* v. *the Collector*, 1 Wallace 375–384. A shipment of wool had been appraised at the Port of Boston and delivered to Iasigi & Goddard, importers. While it was still in their warehouse, it was reappraised and a duty assessed. They paid the duty under protest and then sued the Collector for recovery. The Court decided in favor of the Collector's right of reappraisement.

[87] Sidney Bartlett, counsel for the Importers, a leading lawyer of Boston who frequently argued cases before the U. S. Supreme Court.

[88] *Supra*, Feb. 26, 1864, note 76.

[89] *Supra*, Nov. 27, 1861, note 74.

[90] *Supra*, April 6, 1864, note 74.

[91] *Supra*, March 6, 1861, note 32.

[92] Bates had predicted before that three of these five would never sit again. But though Taney died on October 12 of this year, Catron served until his death in 1865, and Wayne until he died in 1867, while Grier sat until 1870 and Nelson until 1872, after Bates himself had died in 1869.

[93] Edward A. Wild of Brookline, Massachusetts: officer in the Army of the Potomac, 1861–1863; major-general of volunteers who recruited colored troops in North Carolina, 1863–1864; now commander at Norfolk.

at Norfolk, comes a package from the War Department (Genl. Canby[94]) with the Report of Genl. Wilde to Genl. Butler,[95] and Genl. B[utler]'s to [the] sec: [of] war, upon the case of the confiscation of Williams' estate.

I am astonished at both the matter and the manner—I knew that some upstarts in power, entertained such thoughts and did such things, in fact, but I never knew before, such monstrosities deliberately reduced to writing, and embodied in formal official reports.

Gen Wilde affirms that Martial law rules all that Dept., and that there is no Civil law there, except as *tolerated* by the Military. And Gen Butler says that Gen Wilde, *being no lawyer*, made a mistake of a word—He did not mean *confiscate*, but *sequestrate!*

Both the Generals, however, disclaim all intention to *confiscate*— and as that is the only point of conflict with the powers and duties of my Department, I shall not go out of my way, to raise a quarrel with the military, about powers and assumptions which (however questionable) do not, specially, impinge upon me.

Besides as to Genl. Butler—howeve[r] others denounce him— my personal relations with him are altogether courteous and friendly. Indeed, he has been very kind, in granting every request of mine to facilitate my friends who had lawful business across the lines—especially in the cases of Mr. Frayser of Mo. and Dr. Bates of Ohio.

"A strong will without a good heart, is even worse than keen logic without sound judgment."

Lieber,[96] in Washington and Napoleon.[97]

[*April*] *20 Wednesday.* Attended a pleasant party at Secy Welles'[.]

Apl 23. Evelyn's Diary and Correspondence, Vol 3. p 102.

Here is a very striking letter of Jeremy Taylor to John Evelyn (Feb 17. 1657–8)—It is for consolation upon the death of a very precocious child (in fact 2).

The letter abounds with astute and winning arguments, and engaging passages—among them, this—

" Remember, Sir, your two boys are too [sic] bright stars, and their innocence is secured, and you shall never hear evil of them again.

[94] Edward R. S. Canby: West Point graduate of 1839; officer in Florida, Mexico, California, Washington, and on the frontier; commander of the Department of New Mexico, 1861–1862; assistant adjutant-general in Washington and New York, 1862–1864; commander of the Division of West Mississippi after May, 1864.

[95] *Supra*, Nov. 29, 1861, notes 98 and 1.

[96] *Supra*, April 5, 1862, note 62.

[97] A *Fragment* printed for the Metropolitan Fair, held in behalf of the Sanitary Commission in New York in April, 1864.

Their state is safe, and heaven is given to them upon very easy terms; nothing but to be born and die. It will cost you more trouble to get where they are; and, among[st] other things, one of the hardnesses will be, that you must over come even this just and reasonable grief; and indeed, though the grief hath but too reasonable a cause, yet it is much more reasonable that you master it." &c[.]

<And see my letter to Mrs. Wharton,[98] upon the death of her grandson, *Robert Frayser.*>

[*Marginal*] *Note.* J.[eremy] T.[aylor']s letter to Evelyn—p. 98—upon the Immortality of the Soul, is [a] good sample of the logical, subtlety of the learned, of that day.

Apl 23 Saturday. JOHN M. BOTTS, *and his secret history of the Rebellion.*[99]

Today, Genl. Ingalls,[1] Ch:[ief] Q[uarte]r. Master of the Army of the Potomac delivered to me a sealed package (folio size), sent by Mr. Botts (called, in pencil, *1.st. Instalment*) marked Secret history of the Rebellion, for thirty years before it began—Confided to me, for safe keeping, till called for by the author—J.[ohn] M. B[otts].

I deposited it with my private valuables, of course, still sealed up. And have written to Mr. Botts (through my son, Capt. J. C. Bates, of Genl. Mead[e]'s[2] staff) that I will sacredly keep that and all other "instalments" which may follow, subject to his call.

<*Note.* Afterwards, C. Douglas Gray, late of Augusta Co. Va. a fast friend of Mr. Botts, comes and says that he is specially authorised by Mr. B.[otts] to say to me that I may open and read it. I have done so, s[t]ill keeping it private.>

Apl. 25. Monday. Today, the Army of Genl. *Burnside*[3] passed through the City, in a constant stream, for many hours—Horse, Foot and Artillery—supposed 40.000 strong. The troops moved down 14th. street, and crossed the Potomac, by the Long Bridge, into Va. This army has been, for some time, in course of formation, at An-[n]apolis. It is said to be composed entirely of new troops, except a nucleus of 10.000 veterans, part of Burnside's old corps.

I have no certain information, but I conjecture that Burnside, with his army, will be charged with the defence of this capital; and that the army of the Potomac (relieved from that embarrassing and par-

---

[98] Mr. Bates's sister: *infra,* Dec. 11, 1865.

[99] *Supra,* July 15, 1859, note 22. The book appeared under the title, *The Great Rebellion: Its Secret History, Rise, Progress, and Disastrous Failure,* Harper & Brothers, N. Y., 1866.

[1] Rufus Ingalls: West Point graduate of 1843: officer in Mexico, California, Oregon; officer of reënforcements for Fort Pickens in 1861: aide-de-camp to McClellan, 1861–1862; chief quartermaster of the Army of the Potomac, 1862–1865.

[2] *Supra,* Oct. 15, 1863, note 18.

[3] *Supra,* Nov. 29, 1861, note 97.

alysing duty) will, henceforth be free to devote itself to all exigenc[i]es of the war, farther south. It is a noble army, enured to hardships and dangers, well disciplined, and full of patient courage. Now, for the first time, it will have a fair chance to show what stuff it is made of. And I doubt not, it will make a glorious answer.

[*April*] *26*. <I hear this morning that a number of troops came in last night, from the *west*, and passed on to the front.>

[*April*] *26*. Mr. Clarke,[4] M.[ember of] C.[ongress] of N.[ew] Y.[ork] called to pay his respects, and told me some facts, which I had not heard before, about the surrender of Plymouth N.[orth] C[arolina] by Gen Wessells.[5]

He says (repeating the news of the morning) that Wessells surrendered 25.00 men: and that after the surrender, the enemy deliberately shot [not only] all our black soldiers, but also, several hundred of *our* North Carolina troops—executing these last *as traitors!* How many of them he did not say.

For the sake of humanity, I hope that this is not true. But if it be true—superadded to the massacre at Columbus,[6] it will give to the closing scenes of the war, a brutal ferocity, unknown to modern times. For such barbarity can hardly fail to produce a corresponding barbarity, in retaliation.

[*Marginal Note.*] At cabinet today, I find that this horrid story is not believed.

Apl 28. Today I make a great change in the conduct and person[n]el of my (Atty Genl's) office. I have agreed with Mr. Titian. J. Coffey[7] (my assistant) at his earnest instance and for his advancement in general practice, to accept his resignation of his office, of Ass[istan]t. A.[ttorney] G.[eneral] and appoint *J. Hubley Ashton*[8] of Phila.[delphia] in his stead. And to employ him, Coffey, to aid me in the management of the cases in the Supreme Court, at $6000— all of which is to be reduced to writing.

John M. Vaughan[9] has resigned—in consequence of some unfounded suspicions against him, in the war office (which I have, I suppose satisfactorily, explained to Chs: A Dana,[10] Ass[istan]t. Secy of War[)]—I have determined to appoint in his stead, young

[4] Freeman Clarke: bank, railroad, and utility company director and president; formerly a Whig; an organizer of Republicanism in New York; congressman, 1863–1865, 1871–1875; comptroller of the currency, 1865–1867.

[5] Henry W. Wessells: graduate of West Point in 1833; veteran of the Seminole and Mexican Wars and of the Pacific Coast and frontier service; officer on the Missouri border, 1861–1862, in the Army of the Potomac, 1862–1863, and in North Carolina in 1863–1864. He had surrendered Plymouth to the Confederates on April 20, 1864.

[6] I. e., at Fort Pillow near Columbus, Kentucky. *Infra*, May 9, 1864, note 32.

[7] *Supra*, March 5, 1860, note 18.

[8] *Supra*, Feb. 5, 1862, note 52.

[9] *Supra*, March 6, 1863, note 59.

[10] *Supra*, July 27, 1859, note 51.

John Rowland [11]—a boy of 17, son of Dr. R.[owland] [12] already a clerk in the office, to be *my confidential.*

He is a precotious [*sic*] boy, now actually engaged as a short-hand writer (phonographer) in the trial of Admiral Wilkes,[13] and I cant [*sic*] get him till that is over.

Apl 29. This is the *fiftieth* anniversary of my landing in St Louis; and I gave a dinner to the gentlemen of the office—and a bottle of wine, each, to the messenger and laborer—Klopfer [14] and Brown—The Dinner was attended by the *whole office* except Dr. Rowland, who was sick—Present T. J. Coffey Ass[istan]t.; Theo: Field ch:[ief] clerk; C. DeWitt Smith,[15] Opinion and letter cl[er]k; Matt: F. Pleasants, pardon cl[er]k; Andrew [L.] Kerr, Cal[iforni]a. L.[and] C [laims] cl[er]k; J. M. Vaughan's [16] vacancy (my private and confidential) not filled.

The meeting was cordial and pleasant.

[*May 1.*]   [*A newspaper reprint under the heading " The Negroes and the war " of a long letter of President Lincoln to A. G. Hodges* [17] *of Frankfort, Kentucky.*] [18]

[*A cutting from the* Baltimore Clipper *of April 29, 1864, giving a telegraphic report of an evening session in the House of Representatives, when Thaddeus Stevens introduced his bill disfranchising the seceded states.*]

" Uncle Thad:" Stevens [19] always full of whims and oddities. He is, at once ignorant and careless of the constitution. He thinks of it only as a bar of Juniata Iron—that may be forged into any shape, and cut into any pieces, to suit the fancy of any Pa. blacksmith.

But, it was at an "*Evening Session*" when no one can guaranty the sobriety of the House.

[*An editorial headed " Working guns by steam."*]

Eads' Turret.[20] This invention bids fair to revolutionize the art of War—in so far, at least, as concerns the defence of ports and harbors. *E. Bates* May 1. 1864[.]

---

[11] It should be Hugh A. Rowland. Bates did appoint him to a clerkship at $1,200 a year.

[12] John A. Rowland, opinion clerk in the Attorney-General's Office.

[13] *Supra*, Nov. 16, 1861, note 46. Wilkes was on trial for insubordination.

[14] Henry A. Klopfer, head messenger.

[15] *Supra*, Aug. 7, 1863, note 71.

[16] *Supra*, March 6, 1863, note 59.

[17] *Supra*, March 26, 1864, note 57.

[18] April 4, 1864, *Complete Works of Abraham Lincoln*, II, 508–509. This letter gives " the substance " of what Lincoln had already told him verbally: *supra*, March 26, 1864.

[19] *Supra*, Dec. 20, 1862, note 87.

[20] *Supra*, Jan. 28, 1860, note 38; Dec. 31, 1861, note 70. The Eads turret, unlike the Ericsson turret on the monitors, did not revolve and therefore did not have to be fastened to the deck by a joint that was highly vulnerable. Furthermore, the guns in Eads's turret were operated by steam.

May 1. The weather cloudy and drizzly, and cold for the season, in so much that I feel very unwell this morning.

The spring, generally, has been cold, and the season unusually backward. The street trees are just beginning to put out their leaves, and it is only in the last week or so, that the peach and plum trees are in full bloom.

Note. There have been virulent disputes in the H[ouse] of R.[epresentatives] abt Gen F. P. Blair.[21] The House called upon the Prest., by resolution, about Genl. Blair's civico-military position [22] and the debate arose, mainly upon his answer. <Genl. B.[lair] just before leaving the House and going to the army, made a fierce onslaught upon Mr. Chase, which angered the Radicals generally, and especially Mr. C[hase]'s peculiar friends.>

N. B. Yesterday, Gov A. A. King [23] of Mo. told me that a M.[ember of] C.[ongress] of Ohio told him (in presence of 3 or 4 others) that the Ohio Delegation would call on the President in a body, and demand the dismission of Genl B[lair]—and if refused, wd. call on Mr. Chase and demand his resignation!

But they were angry then, and will probably think better of it, when *sobered* by a night's sleep and a comfortable breakfast.

May 5. For some days past, I have been very unwell, occasioned as I think, by my sedentary habits, and continued, unremitting mental labor, for some months past. It has told upon me dangerously, in the derangement of my nervous system—Indeed I suffered a slight paralysis, in so much, that for two or three days, my speech was, sensibly impaired—I could not articulate distinctly and continuously.

<[*Note.*] May 8. Thank God, the symptons [*sic*] have disappeared and my nerves are steady, again>

May 8. Sunday. For some days past, the City has been in a nervous excitement about the war, it being understood that a great battle was imminent, in Virginia. For some days, we knew that [the] Army of the Potomac had crossed the Rapidan with out opposition, [24] and that Lee must fight or flee or be cut off in the rear. And we supposed that Grant (having cleared his camp of pestilent news-writers) had stopped communication, for good reasons. We

---

[21] *Supra,* April 27, 1859, note 25.

[22] Blair held the rank of major-general and served under Sherman on his campaign in the South. While he still held this commission he served as a congressman from March 4, 1863, until the Radicals whom he had attacked unseated him on June 10, 1864, in favor of Knox who had contested his election. He then returned to his post in the Army.

[23] *Supra,* May 11, 1863, note 14.

[24] General Meade's army crossed the Rapidan on May 4, and Grant followed him on May 5. Lee attacked and the bloody Battle of the Wilderness began. It was fought on a thickly wooded plateau south of the Rapidan on May 5–6.

are now (this evening) credibly informed, that Grant has sent up orders for the instant preparation of Hospital accom[m]odations for 8000 wounded—That there has been hard fighting, for two day[s]— the most prolonged and obstinate battle of the war—That Lee has been beaten, leaving 10.000 dead and wounded upon the field—That he is in full retreat and Grant in hot pursuit.

There may be mistakes in de[t]ails—numbers &c[.] But the government believes that we have gained a great victory: probably the turning point of the war. [25]

I am now growing impatient to hear from the column under Gen (Baldy) Smith,[26] said to have landed at City Point, last Friday, with the intent to operate, *rapidly*, agst. Petersburg, and generally on the south of Richmond. If Smith's column be successful, and Lee be badly beaten north of James river, then the war is, in fact over in Va., for there will be no escape for Lee's remnant, to the south, and no chance for reinforcements and supplies, from that direction, even if the enemy [had them] there to send.

But they have them not, for I take it for certain that Sherman [27] is, even now, pressing down into Georgia, from Chattinooga [*sic*], with a gallant army, superior to his antagonist Gen Joe Johns[t]on.[28]

And when they hear the news of Lee's defeat (if the fact be indeed so) I think the hearts of the leaders will fail them, and their armies will crumble, every where.

May 8. see for *Ship-money*, a passage in Evelyn's Diary, Vol 1. p. 17 speaking of a great ship then lately built <1641>—

" But what is to be deplored as to this vessel is[,] that it cost his Majesty the affections of his subjects, perverted by the malcontent great ones, who took occasion to quarrel for his having raised a very slight tax for the building of this and equipping the rest of the navy, without an act of Parliament; though[,] by the suffrage[s] of the major part of the Judges[,] the King might legally do in times of imminent danger[,] of which his Majesty was best apprised. But this not satisfying a jealous party, it was condemned as *unprece-*

---

[25] The Battle of the Wilderness was a draw—not a great victory, but it did begin the fierce persistent fighting with heavy losses on both sides which eventually wore down the Confederates. Failing to dislodge Lee, Grant withdrew toward Richmond in an effort to flank him.

[26] William F. Smith: West Point graduate of 1845; officer in Texas, in Florida, and in the coast service; professor of mathematics at West Point; brigadier- and then major-general of volunteers in the various Virginia campaigns, 1861–1863, at Chattanooga in 1863, and again in Virginia in 1864–1865.

[27] William T. Sherman: West Point graduate of 1840; officer in the South, in California, and in Missouri, 1840–1853; California banker, 1853–1857; business man in New York, 1857; Kansas lawyer, 1858–1859; superintendent of the Louisiana Military Academy, 1859–1861; one of the few who foresaw the seriousness of the War; commander in Kentucky, 1861, 1862; officer under Grant at Shiloh, Corinth, Vicksburg, and Chattanooga, 1862–1864; commander in the South in 1864–1865. He had taken Atlanta and Savannah and was headed northward on a victorious campaign when Lee's surrender ended the War.

[28] See *supra*, May 8, 1862, note 26.

dential,[29] [. . . .] and[,] accordingly[,] the Judges were removed of their places, fined[,] and imprisoned."

[*Marginal Note.*] *Unprecedential.* This word is new to me. I never saw it before.

May 9. Note. The sub: committee of Congress (Senator Wade[30] of O.[hio] and Rep:[resentative] Gooch[31] of Mass:) sent West to enquire into the facts of the massacre of Fort Pillow,[32] have made their report,[33] shewing a cruel barbarity on the part of the enemy, even worse than had been reported.

Thereupon, the President addressed a circular note, (dated May 3d.) to all the members of the Cabinet, requiring the written opinion of each one of us as to what measures the government ought to take in relation to the said massacre.[34]

Last friday, May 6, all of us, in full council, read and handed to the Prest. our respective opinions; and the President has the subject in deliberation.

I think there was very little communication among the members—for the opinions were very diverse. I, for one, had no understanding with any person—I wrote my opinion with too much haste perhaps—being pressed with business and sick. Its faults and its merits are all my own, for I did not consult flesh and blood about it.

[*A notice of a meeting of the Washoe Agricultural, Mining and Mechanical Society, held in Carson City, March 28, 1864.*]

I did never expect to hear of an *Agricultural* Society in Nevada. For all my information had led me to believe that there were not 10.000. acres of arable land, in the whole Territory.

But it seems that Agriculture is put *first*, before the mining and mechanical.

Seeing that my friend *Clemens*[35] is cor:[responding] sec. I have already sent him some garden and flower seeds.

<*Note. Afterwards he wrote me that he had planted the seeds I sent him, in a friend's garden, some of which grew very well, but that the season was too short for the gigantic cucumber, which in-

---

[29] The italics are Bates's.

[30] *Supra*, Aug. 10, 1859, note 77.

[31] Daniel W. Gooch: Boston lawyer; state legislator, 1852; Republican congressman, 1858–1865, 1873–1875; Navy agent, 1865–1866; Pension agent in Boston, 1876–1886.

[32] On April 13, Confederate General Forrest captured Fort Pillow on the Mississippi above Memphis, Tennessee. The Union garrison was about half black and half white. Of 557 men, 39% were killed and 24% wounded, largely after the fort was taken; the slaughter of the black troops was particularly heavy.

[33] May 5, 1864, *House Committee Reports*, 38 Cong., 1 Sess., 1, ser. no. 1206, doc. no. 65.

[34] *Complete Works of Abraham Lincoln*, II, 518–519.

[35] Son of Judge John M. Clemens, slave-holder of Virginia, then of Kentucky, then of Tennessee where Orion was born, then of Hannibal, Missouri, after 1839. Orion was secretary of the Territory of Nevada, 1861–1864. His brother, Samuel, accompanied him westward and while there began contributing to a Virginia City newspaper under the pen name "Mark Twain."

deed, flourished very well. but the fruit did not attain a greater length than *three feet*, before it was caught by the frost.>

May 14 Friday. Ja[me]s Brooks [36] of N. Y. M.[ember of] C.[ongress] called to talk about Mrs. [Lydia] Howard (now in the old capitol prison, charged with unlawful intercourse with the enemy). She is, it seems, a daughter of Tho[ma]s. Mason Randolph,[37] of Tuckehoe [*sic*] V[irgini]a and niece of Hy. L. Patterson [38] of St Louis. Mr. Brooks tells me that Mr. Howard,[39] the husband, was a *fast young* man of Balt[imor]e.—that he was an officer—perhaps Major in the rebel army—reduced to the ranks for *Drunkenness*—That she is akin to his [Brooks's] wife, and therefore he takes an interest in her. I told him what I had [d]one, with the Secy of War, about her, and wrote it to him—That I had written to Mr. Patterson &c[.]

He told me further, that she had two or three brothers in N.[ew] Y.[ork] engaged in business.

May 15. For the last 8 or 10 days, the most terrible battles of the war have occurred in Virginia.[40] The carnage has been unexampled. I know not the number of our *dead*, but the *wounded* amount to nearly if not quite 15.000! And the enemy is supposed to have suffered much more severely, in both dead and wounded. And now, it [is] almost certain that Richmond must fall in a few days, and probable that Lee's grand army must be captured or utterly dissolved. For he has lost immensely in material as well as men.[41] His cavalry, I think is nearly exhausted, and our cavalry has scoured his rear, every where, destroying his supplies, and cutting his communications, in every direction. The R Rs are destroyed between him and Rich[mond].—Between him and Charlott[e]sville—between C.[harlottesville] and Lynchburg (and, of course, the James river Canal is in our power.)

All this is on the *North* side of James River—On the *South* side, the same work is going on—The great S.[outh] W.[estern] R. R. is broken in many places, especially the bridge of New River is burned. The road between Rich[mon]d. and Petersburg cont[inue]s in our possession—and S.[outh] and E.[ast] of Peter[s]burg,—to

---

[36] *Supra*, Sept. 20, 1860, note 12.

[37] Thomas Mann Randolph, the father of Mrs. Howard, was a half-brother of Jefferson's son-in-law of the same name who was governor of Virginia.

[38] Mrs. Howard's mother had been a Miss Patterson.

[39] Frank Key Howard.

[40] Hard fighting had continued from the Battle of the Wilderness (*supra*, May 8) May 5–6, until this Battle of Spotsylvania Court House, May 10–12. Here again losses were heavy and again after failure to dislodge Lee, Grant withdrew in a flanking movement toward Richmond.

[41] Lee was far from beaten. Richmond did not fall nor Lee surrender until after eleven months more of fighting with casualty lists that aroused the North to sharp criticism of Grant.

Weldon and to Suffolk, destroyed,　And, at the last advices, a force deemed sufficient, sent to cut the Danville road—So, I think the fate of Lee is inevitable[.]　Our troops are driving him slowly, as it [at] the point of the bayonet.　His troops fight with desperation, and ours with the most obstinate and persistent courage.　The loss in high officers is very great on both sides.　The last account from the enemy is, that Genl. J. E. B. Stuart [42] is killed, and Longstreet [43] and Hill,[44] *hors du combat*, with their wounds[.]

Butler,[45] who holds the R. R. between Richmond and Petersburg, is investing F[or]t. Darling,[46] expecting to reduce it soon.

If all these successes come, the rebellion will have lost all prestige, and must crumble.

The news is very good also, from Sherman,[47] in Geo[rgi]a.　He is pressing upon Joe Johnston,[48] whose army, already beaten back, from post to post, will lose all heart, when they hear that Virginia is conquered and their capital taken.

Note.　Coalter is still without a wound, in all this carnage.

Still May 15.　Saturday night, Charley Russell,[49] (no longer *Captain* [)] stepped in upon us (with sister Carry)[.]

He is now Lt. Col of the 28.　"U. S. Colored troops" and has, camped at Alexandria, a battalion—6 companies of stalwart blacks. He is eager to get to the front, before Grant *cleans up* his work.

He is a brave and skilful officer, and I only wish (as in fact, he does) that he commanded *white* troops.

Precocious children—Evelyn, in his Diary, Vol:1. p 323 [324], notices the death of a little son of his, only five years old, whom he describes as a prodegy [*sic*], for goodness, beauty and attainments— Says he—

"He had learned all his Catechism: at two years and a half old[,] he could perfectly read any of the English, Latin, French[,] or

[42] *Supra*, April 21, 1859, note 20.　Stuart was not killed, but he had been mortally wounded on May 10 and removed to Richmond, where he died on June 12.

[43] James Longstreet: West Point graduate of 1842 ; officer in Missouri, Louisiana, Texas, Florida, Mexico, 1842–1861 ; Confederate brigadier-general (1861) and later major- and then lieutenant-general who fought at both the Battles of Bull Run, in the Peninsular Campaign, at Fredericksburg, at Gettysburg, in 1861–1863 ; at Chickamauga in 1863 ; and under Lee again in 1864.　He *was* wounded in this battle by his own men, and was disabled for two months.

[44] Ambrose P. Hill: West Point graduate of 1847 ; officer in Mexico, in Florida, and then in Washington with the Coast Survey, 1847–1861.　When Virginia seceded he entered the Confederate Army, became a lieutenant-general, and fought in the Peninsular Campaign, at both Battles of Bull Run, at Fredericksburg, at Chancellorsville, and at Gettysburg.　He continued to serve under Lee until he was killed in action April 2, 1865.

[45] *Supra*, Nov. 29, 1861, notes 98 and 1.

[46] On the right bank of the James, at Drury's Bluff, nine miles south of Richmond.

[47] W. T. Sherman had been making preparations since April 10 to attack Atlanta. Early in May he had moved from Chattanooga into Georgia, and on May 14 had driven Johnston out of Dalton.

[48] *Supra*, May 8, 1862, note 26.

[49] *Supra*, Jan. 25, 1863, note 1.

Gothic letters, pronouncing the three first languages exactly. He had, before the fifth year, or in that year, not only skill to read most written hands, but to decline all the nouns, conjugate all the verbs regular, and most of the irregular[;]—learning [learned] out "*Puerilis*," got by heart, almost the entire vocabulary of Latin and French primitives and words, could make congruous syntax, turn English into Latin, and *vice versa*[,"]—&c &c thro' a long list of accomplishments.[50]

And Dr. Lieber,[51] in his remeniscences [*sic*] of *Niebuhr* tells of a little son of N[iebuhr]'s, only three years old, who could, fluently read *Tacitus, in Latin!*[52]

When I mentioned that to Baron Gerolt,[53] the Prussian Minister, he told me he knew young Niebuhr, a protegé of the King, as son of his friend, holding an honorable office—That he was an immature, imbecile person, misshapen and with an enormous, disproportioned head[.]

No wonder that Evelyn's smart child died, and Niebuhr's grew up rickety and useless—their intellect was over taxed, at the expense of both mind and body.

May 17.   Dined at Mr. Eames'[54] with (the literary) Mrs. Howe,[55] Mr. Jourdan, and Count Gurowski[.][56]

In the evening, with Matilda, visited Douglass [*sic*] hospital, to take some comforts to the wounded, both officers and soldiers—Capt. Lowe[57] and his companions—Maj Bruen,[58] and Capts. Keyes[59] and Anderson,[60] are d[o]ing well.

So many wounded are coming here, from the field, that all who can well bear transportation, are sent farther north.

Got a letter from Coalter, dated 16th. No fighting that day— getting up, food, stragglers, and reinforcements—Of the latter I hear that at least 20,000, have gone forward. A few days now, will tell the tale, in Virginia.

---

[50] Inaccurately copied, especially the punctuation.

[51] *Supra,* April 5, 1862, note 62.

[52] Francis Lieber, *Reminiscences of an Intercourse with Mr. Niebuhr the Historian* (Philadelphia, 1835), 66.

[53] *Supra,* Nov. 27, 1861, note 82.

[54] *Supra,* Jan. 13, 1862, note 30.

[55] *Infra,* May 20, 1864.

[56] *Supra,* Nov. 27, 1861, note 65.

[57] William B. Lowe of Ohio. He did recover from his wounds.

[58] Luther P. Bruen of Ohio, who had been wounded in the Battle of Laurel Hill, Virginia. He died on June 21.

[59] Hamlin W. Keyes of Massachusetts had been cited for "gallant and meritorious service" in the Wilderness. He, too, had been wounded at Laurel Hill and died on June 18.

[60] Probably Thomas M. Anderson of Ohio who had been cited for gallant service both in the Wilderness and at Spotsylvania. He was wounded at Spotsylvania, but recovered, remained in the Army, and became an Indian fighter and writer.

Fashions of Dress—Hoop-petty coats and long-tailed dresses are not inventions of the present age. More than 200 years ago (1644) the ladies of Genoa wore enormous hoops " which being put about the waist of the lady, and full as broad [on both sides] as she can reach with her hands, bear out her coats in [such] a manner, that she appears to be as broad as [long."]she is long[.]"

> Evelyn's Diary, Vol 1. p 88.

And long, draggle-tails are of much older date, as we learn from Homer. Hector answers his loving wife Andromoche [*sic*],

" How would the sons of Troy, in arms renow[n]ed,

　And Troy[']s proud dames, *whose garments sweep the ground*,

　Attaint the lustre of my former name,

　Should Hector basely quit the field of fame[?]."[51]

In the garden at Florence, Evelyn saw a Rose grafted on an Orange tree—Diary [vol. I,] p 92.

[*A clipping giving " Richmond Prices Current."*]

Serf. 2 Bouv: Dic:[52] 516.

> "A predial laborer only bound to the soil"

" The *slave*, on the contrary, is the property of his master, who may require him to act as he pleases, in every respect, and who may sell him as *a chattel*. Citing *Lepage, Science du Droit* C. 3. art. 2. § 2.

And yet, *modern* slavery is greatly mitigated from the unlimited power and unrestrained caprice of the ancients. They (the ancient masters) had absolute power of life and death, with no restraints upon the most whimsical cruelties.

The mother of King Cyrus ordered a once favorite eunuch to be *skinned alive;* and even the accomplished Pollio, the most classic and graceful courtier of Augustus Cæsar, caused his head-servant to be chopped up and thrown, as bait, into the fish pond, for the grave offence of breaking a glass vase, by careless handling![63]

But now, the wanton killing of a slave is murder; and the penalty of death has (in our own times) been inflicted for it, *upon gentlemen,* by both English and American judges—In the Vergin [*sic*] I[s]les and in So: Carolina. E. B.

Evelyn's Diary. Vol: 1. p 155. (Feb 7. 1645) Speaking of a beautiful plain, near Baia, in Italy—says i. a.

" The Summer is here eternal, caused by the natural and adventitious heat of the earth, warmed through the subterranean fires, as was shewn to us by our guide, who alighted, and[,] cutting up a turf

---

[61] Bates took this from *The Iliad of Homer; Translated by Alexander Pope,* I, Book 6, p. 21, in the *Works of the British Poets, Including Translations from the Greek and Romun Authors,* edited by Thomas Park (John Sharpe, London, 1828).

[62] John Bouvier, *Law Dictionary Adapted to the Constitution and Laws of the United States.* . . .

[63] *Supra,* Aug. 24, 1863.

with his knife, and delivering it to me, it was so hot, I was hardly able to hold it in my hands. This mountain is exceedingly fruitful in vines, and exotics grow readily."

I have not read in any other book, so minute an account (inventory, rather) of the gorgeous display, and wanton waste of wealth as Evelyn tells us of, in Churches, Palaces, Gardens, Fountains, Sculptures, Paintings, Libraries and Jewels, ostentatiously displayed in Rome, Naples and other parts of Italy.

This is proof, I admit, that the country is good and most desirable; but it [is] also [proof] of, what we know to be historically true, that the *people* of Italy have been opp[r]essed for cycles of ages, by Kings, Priests, and nobles, who have been able to aggregate in their own hands, all power, wealth art and taste, leaving the People poor, degraded and vile. As in the latter days of the corrupt Republic, the cry of the populace still is—*br[e]ad and the games!*

"While nought remains of all that riches gave
   But towns unmanned, and Lords without a slave[.] " [64]

Evelyn tells us that there were when he was at Naples (1645) there were [*sic*] in that city, no less than 30.000 co[u]rtezans, [65] *licensed and paying tax!* [66]

May 20. Truffles—What are they? See Evelyn's Diary Vol. 1. p. 78 (Sept 30. 1644) At Avignon—

"Here we supped and lay, having[,] amongst other dainties, a dish of *truffle*, which is a certain earth-nut, found out by a *hog* trained to it, and for which those animals are sold at a great price."

He says of the truffles—"it is [in truth] an incomparable meat."

MRS. HOWE [67]—Wife of Dr. Howe,[68] of Boston, famous as a teacher of the deaf and dumb. This lady is here, giving a course of private lectures, on quaint subjects—e. g. "*moral triganometry* [*sic*] " *alias* "practical ethics."

I dined with her, by special invitation, at Mr. Eames' [69]—She is a smart, educated, travelled lady, a little touched, 'tis thought, with *strong-mindedness*. Complacent, and well satisfied with her peculiar theories.

[64] The verse was added in the margin.

[65] *Diary and Correspondence* (1854, Wm. Bray, ed.), I, 153.

[66] Everything from the definition of "serf" to this point is written on a separate sheet and bound into the diary.

[67] Julia Ward Howe, daughter of a New York banker; master of several ancient and modern languages; a prolific contributor of essays, reviews, and travel sketches to periodicals; author of several volumes of poems; in later life, a lecturer and active worker for women's rights.

[68] Samuel G. Howe: surgeon to the Greek revolutionists, 1824–1830; relief worker in Greece and in Prussia; founder and director of the Perkins Institution for the Blind in Boston; teacher of the deaf and dumb; Union reformer; advocate of asylums for the demented; anti-slavery agitator; director of the U. S. Sanitary Commission, 1861–1864; chairman of the first (the Massachusetts) board of state charities, 1865–1874.

[69] *Supra*, Jan. 13, 1862, note 30.

I thought I, unwittingly, "trod upon her corns" by talking to her about *moral and intellectual Chemistry!*

She seems to have some pretty just ideas of what our Radical monomaniacs mean by *Progress* and *Philanthropy*. And that is shewn by a sharp hit she is said to have given *Mr. Sumner*,[10] the other day, as thus—

Mrs. H. "Ah! Mr. Sumner, have you heard young Booth yet? he's a man of fine talents and noble hopes, in his profession."

Mr. S. "Why, n-no madam—I, long since, ceased to take any interest in *individuals!*" Mrs. H—"You have made great *progress* Sir—*God* has not yet gone so far—at least *according to the last accounts!*"

It seems that God makes but *slow progress*, as compared with these self-sufficient, blatant philanthropists. But they, perhaps, know best.

[*May 26.*]   On the 26th. of May happening to meet Mr. S.[umner] at the President's, he asked me if I had heard what was thought at the North, about my recent opinion upon the pay of *black* chaplains in the army. I said, no, I have *not* seen in the news papers, any mention of the Opinion (which was true). He then said that at some great meeting at the north, Wm. Lloyd Garrison [11] had praised me very highly, for that opinion and the one on Citizenship—I answered, "Perhaps Mr. Garrison mistakes me for an Abolitionist." And then I told him that a learned friend (German) at St Louis (I did not tell him that it was Dr. Chs. L. Bernays [12]) had written me that the *Radicals* of Mo., would never forgive me for proving that negro[e]s had some rights *by law*, whereas they insist that all the rights of negro[e]s are derived from their bounty!

I thought Mr. S.[umner] seemed a little chagrined—He replied only—Your correspondent is a very witty man.

May 29. This is the *forty first* anniversary of my marriage: And I can say what not one man in 1000 can—that, in all these forty one years, my wife has never given me one angry look or one reproachful word. On the contrary, this day our mutual affection is as warm, and our mutual confidence far stronger, than in the first week of marriage. This is god's blessing.

The day is bright and beautiful—the air cool and refreshing. Commissioner Newton [73] (head farmer of the Country) says that

[10] *Supra*, Jan. 7, 1860, note 9.

[11] Editor of reformist papers in Newburyport, Boston, Bennington (Vermont), and Baltimore, and finally of the famous *Liberator* which he founded in 1831. His militant abolitionism had made him an ardent disunionist and opponent of Lincoln until the Emancipation Proclamation was promulgated.

[72] *Supra*, Sept. 20, 1860, note 9.

[73] *Supra*, Jan. 5, 1862, note 12.

this *May* for vegitation [*sic*] [is the best] that he remembers—
that all fruit trees, grain and grass are in far better condition
than usual, and promise an abundant crop[.]

This morning, the news from the army in Va. is that Grant and
Meade [74] finding Lee in very strong position on the South anna
(with grant's accustomed Strategy) by a sudden movement to the
rear, recrossed the *North Anna* and crossed the Pamunky, below
the junction of the north and south Anna—thus again flanking
Lee, on his extreme right. This movement will, I suppose, force
Lee to abandon his works on the South Anna, and either fight us
in the open field, or fall back upon Richmond.[75]

Mean while our army gains great facilities, in the great matter of
communication and supplies—commanding York river, and in easy
communication with Butler's [76] position on James River—not more
than 25 or 30 miles, and a plain country between.

The report is that Lee's cavalry is greatly deminished [*sic*] in
numbers, and much demoralized and broken down, and not able to
stand before ours.

The Rebels fight desperately, and with great skill and courage.
Still, I think they must soon succumb, in Va. at least, for they have
to cope with superior numbers and means, and now, for the first
time, with a skill and strategy quite equal to their own.

This afternoon Lt. Col C. S. Russell [77] (with his father) called to
take leave. He is just starting to the front, with his black Battalion.
He is confident that he has them so disciplined, that, even after a
severe repulse, he can rally them and bring them again to a brave
charge, and promises to report to me.[78]

June 4. Several days ago, Ja[me]s B. Eads [79] arrived here, and
lodges with us, having left his family at N York, on the way to
Europe—He is still in feeble health, and comes here to close up some
money accounts with the Government.

He is in the highest esteem at the Navy Dept. His late inventions, especially the one for working great guns by steam, are deemed
of the greatest importance. Since the trial of his apparatus, on the
Winnebago, at St Louis, the Dept., charmed with the success, has
ordered one of the Monitors on the sea-coast to be fitted up in that
way.

For some days past, many Delegates to [the] Baltimore convention (to nominate Prest.) have arrived. I have seen several from

---

[74] *Supra,* Oct. 15, 1863, note 18.
[75] The Battle of the North Anna was fought May 23–27. Lee did fall back on Richmond
and Grant then was able to make only a frontal attack. He did so unsuccessfully, in the
Battle of Cold Harbor, with terrific losses, June 1–3, and then withdrew on June 12.
[76] *Supra,* Nov. 29, 1861, notes 98 and 1.
[77] *Supra,* Jan. 25, 1863, note 1.
[78] See *infra,* Aug. 2, 1864.
[79] *Supra,* Jan. 28, 1860, note 38.

Cala.—one from *Nevada Ter*[*ritory*]—Dr. Labuski—It is surely a bad precedent, to admit delegates in the conv[entio]n. to nominate, when the people of the *Territories* have no voice in the election. Mo. has a double delegation—Conservative and *Radical*, and some of both parties are here.

Of the conservatives, Govr. W. P. Hall,[80] Marshal Wallace,[81] Eads and McPherson—and Broadhead [82] and Sam Breckenridge,[83] are, daily, expected.

The *Radicals* are here in great force (a list of them is published, whereby it appears that C. D. Drake [84] is at their head. <[*Marginal Note.*] Mistake. Drake does not come>) Some of them I think, are in an awkward quandary—Mr. Blow,[85] for one, tells Mr. Eads that he will not go to the convention—he will reserve his judgment, as to the Presidency, till September! He is really in a pinch—The Radical leaders of his District are very exacting; if he fail one jot in their extreme measures, he may no longer be M.[ember of] C[ongress].[86] And if he go with them "a whoring after " Fremont, and after[ward] Lincoln by [be] elected, he has *forfeited his stock* in that concern, and can no longer *draw dividend*!

Senator Gratz Brown [87] too—He headed the call for the Fremont convention at Cleveland,[88] yet now he tells Mr. Eads that he keeps himself aloof from political controversy!

June 7. This day's Nat[iona]l. Intelligencer, contains *Fremont's* acceptance of the *Cleveland* nomination for the *Presidency*. Is ready to yield if a proper nomination is made at Baltimore, but will run against *Lincoln*.[89]

Also a letter of Jefferson Davis to Gov Vance [90] of N.[orth] C.[arolina] in (indignant) answer [91] to V[ance]'s proposition [92] to treat for peace.

---

[80] *Supra*, Feb. 21, 1862, note 96.

[81] *Supra*, Aug. 7, 1863, note 77.

[82] *Supra*, Dec. 26, 1859, note 66.

[83] *Supra*, Dec. 26, 1859, note 67.

[84] *Supra*, Feb. 12, 1863, note 13.

[85] *Supra*, Sept. 20, 1859, note 95.

[86] He *was* reëlected in 1864.

[87] *Supra*, Feb. 15, 1864, note 44.

[88] A group of anti-Lincoln Radicals, western Germans, and abolitionists met in convention at Cleveland on May 31, and nominated John C. Frémont for the Presidency and General John Cochrane of New York for the Vice-Presidency.

[89] Support of Lincoln proved so strong that Frémont "ungracefully" withdrew his candidacy privately in a letter of September 17, publicly in one written on September 21 and published on September 22.

[90] Zebulon B. Vance: North Carolina lawyer; state legislator, 1854; Democratic congressman, 1858–1861; colonel in the Confederate Army, 1861–1862; governor of North Carolina, 1862–1866, 1876–1878; Democratic U. S. senator, 1879–1894. Vance had opposed secession until it was accomplished. As early as December, 1863, he urged peace negotiations with the North, though he continued to support the Confederate Government. After the War he became a leader of moderate and more reasonable Southerners.

[91] Jan. 8, 1864. *Jefferson Davis, Constitutionalist, His Letters, Papers, and Speeches*, (Dunbar Rowland, ed.), VI, 143–146.

[92] Dec. 30, 1863, reprinted in the *National Intelligencer*, June 7, 1864.

Arguelles affair

June 9. [The] Nat[iona]l. I[n]telligencer of today contains a long and able article (editorial) against the secret arrest and extradition of *Arguelles*,[93] the Spaniard who, it seems, was very privately arrested, hurried on board a Spanish vessel and sent off to the Capt. General of Cuba. He was claimed by the Spanish minister [94] (not as of right, but [of] comity) to answer for some crime connected with the slave-trade in Cuba. The article is a very full historical and legal view of the subject, and concludes very pointedly, and with great show of authority, against the the [*sic*] right and legality of the proceeding.

It is strange that a step so important and delicate should have been taken without any Cabinet discussion. I was wholly ignorant of the proceeding until after the fact; and the first man that told me of it was *Murray*,[95] the Marshal at N.[ew] Y[ork], who was evidently proud of the adroitness with which he did the job, and not much alarmed by the indictment in the State court, for kidnapping, though he had to flee, for the present, to avoid arrest.

I think the Secy. of State, Mr. Seward, was led to the hazardous measure (of very doubtful policy, at least, if not clearly illegal) by his belief that it would be a capital hit, to win the favor of the extreme anti-slavery men. But in that he is likely to fail; for Usher tells me that the Senate's Com[mitte]e. on Foreign affairs, with Sumner its head, is prepared, unanimously to denounce the measure. And I do not doubt that this matter will figure largely, in the approaching canvass.

June 10. The Baltimore Convention (*National Union* I believe, it[']s called itself) has surprised and mortified me greatly. It did indeed nominate Mr. Lincoln, but in a manner and with attendant circumstances, as if the object were to defeat their own nomination. They were all (nearly) instructed to vote for Mr. Lincoln, but many of them hated to do it, and only "kept the word of promise to the ear" doing their worst to break it to the hope. They *rejected* the only delegates from Mo. who were instructed and pledged for Lincoln, and admitted the *destructives*, who were *pledged against*

---

[93] As Lieutenant-Governor of Colon, Cuba, José A. Arguelles had seized a cargo of slaves, had received praise and a portion of the prize money therefor, and had then moved to New York to enter business. Subsequently it was discovered that he had sold one hundred forty-one of the slaves (after reporting them dead of small-pox) and had pocketed the money. There was no extradition treaty with Spain to give them authority, but Lincoln and Seward instructed the U. S. Marshal to arrest and return him as an act of comity. Cf. Gideon Welles, *Diary*, II, 36, 45–46.

[94] Gabriel Garcia y Tassara: *supra*, Nov. 27, 1861.

[95] Robert Murray, Federal marshal of the Southern District of New York. For seizing Arguelles, Murray was indicted on the charge of kidnapping. He sought to have the case transferred to a Federal court because he had acted on the President's order. The state court refused to transfer the case, but the indictment was finally quashed.

Lincoln, and, in fact, voted against him, *falsely alleging* that they were instructed to vote for Grant! The *conservative* was chosen in a manner more legitimate and regular than the destructive Radicals; for the Radical convention in Mo. (which appointed those delegates) was, substantially annulled, by the defection of the whole German element, they preferring to go to Cleveland [96] and support *Fremont,* rather than go to the "packed Lincoln gathering, at Baltimore." Their rep[resentative]s did desert the Mo: Convention; and every[one] knows that the Germans constitute the heart and nucl[e]us—the body and strength of the Radicals of Mo. The remaining part of the convention (about ⅔ in no.) resolved to send delegates to Baltimore, because they could better serve the destructive cause, and support Fremont, at Baltimore than at Cleveland. And they judged rightly—for they "are wiser, in their generation than the children of light."

[*Marginal Note.*] I shall tell the Prest: in all frankness, that his best nomination is not that at Baltimore, but his nomination spontaneously, by the People, by which the convention was constrained to name him. That if he choose to unite with his enemies, he and they can easily accomplish his defeat.

Note. July 13. Handed to the President an extract of my letter to T. J. Coffey,[97] expressing my views pretty plainly, of the Convention.

To day, unexpectedly, Coalter made his appearance, being sent up by his Genl. (Meade [98]) with despatches, and trophies (27 colors) taken from the enemy in battle. He [is] well and stout, but weather-beaten, and talks confidently of getting into Richmond before long[.] ([*Note.*] He returned to the army, this morning Sunday 12th. thinking it probable that the base is changed to James River[.])

June 11. Yesterday and today remarkably cool for the season— Fine fighting weather.

Called on me, part of the La. delegation to the late Baltimore convention, viz Cuthbert Bullitt,[99] Col R. V. Montague, Dr. M. F. Bourgano,[1] J. W. Thomas. R. W. Taliaferro.

I gave them a plain, strong old fogy talk, with which they seemed well pleased.

Also, Allen S. Richardson, of Mo.

---

[96] *Supra,* June 4, 1864, note 88.

[97] *Supra,* March 5, 1860, note 18.

[98] *Supra,* Oct. 15, 1863, note 18.

[99] A Louisiana loyalist whom Bates made U. S. marshal in 1864.

[1] Maxmilian F. Bonzano, German-born physician of New Orleans; melter and refiner in the mint, 1848–1861. He opposed secession and fled to the North, but returned in 1862, and became a politician. He was elected to Congress under Lincoln's reorganization of the State, but was not seated.

June 12 Sunday. Dr. Rob. J. Breckinridge [2] (he says this is the right spelling) preached this morning, in the Hall of the H[ouse] of R[epresentatives]. The crowd was so great that I could not get in—He, with his little son John [3] and Edw C. Carrington [4] and his two boys, spent the evening with us, and we had a pleasant time for some hours. We arranged to meet at West Point two weeks hence, if I can go.

June 13. Chf Engineer Wm. H. Shock [5] has a son (Wilton G.) abt. 18, who was seduced off to the rebels, and is now a prisoner and sick and very repentant. I succeeded, to day, in getting an order for his discharge on taking the oath. The father was so overcome as to be unmanned. He seemed to have a sort of *hysteria*, and thought himself sick of influensa [*sic*]. He dined with us, and went [to] Baltimore much better.

Last saturday, the 11th., I laid before the Prest my correspondence with Genl. Wallace [6] (com[mandin]g. the Middle Dept. <Balt[i-mor]e>[)] relating to his *confiscation orders*, nos. 30 and 33—I told the Prest that the orders were not only without law, but flatly against law and against his orders; and that the Genl's letter of justification was wor[s]e than the orders, in that it avowed the illegal act, knowingly done, and defended it, upon grounds the most absurd.

I told him that the General was putting weapons in the hands of the enemies of the adm[inistratio]n., by assuming arbitrary and illegal powers, without a pretence of military necessity—That, regretting any conflict of jurisdiction, I must and would protect my office and myself, and, to that end, if Genl Wallace's proceeding be not stopped, I wd. leave of record, in the office, my solemn protest against the military usurpation.

On Monday, the 13th. the Prest. directed me to give to the Secy. of War, Genl Wallace[']s two orders no. 30 and 33, and telling me that the Secy. would issue an order revoking them, on the ground (not touching the legal merits of the question) that they relate to a subject about which the Genl. ought not to give any order, without consulting the head of the Dept.

---

[2] *Supra*, Nov. 19, 1863, note 64.

[3] John R. Breckinridge was murdered in 1874 at Lebanon, Tennessee, while a law student at Cumberland University.

[4] *Supra*, Nov. 26, 1863, note 70.

[5] Chief engineer of the Navy; 1851–1864; superintendent of the building of river monitors at St. Louis, 1862–1863; fleet-engineer under Farragut before Mobile and later under Thatcher, 1863–1865; inventor of numerous naval devices.

[6] Lew Wallace; Indiana lawyer; first lieutenant in the Mexican War; state legislator; governor of New Mexico, 1878–1881; minister to Turkey, 1881–1885; colonel in West Virginia in 1861; brigadier-general of volunteers at Fort Donelson, major-general at Shiloh and Corinth, 1862; commander at Cincinnati, 1863–1864, and at Baltimore, 1864–1865.

I called on the Secy. and delivered the orders.   He was evidently
gruff and out of temper—talked harshly of Senator Johnson [7] of
Md., and of rebels and sympathize[r]s—and was barely civil to
me—I told him that it was an easy thing to denoun[c]e men as
rebels and disloyalists, and sometimes done to screen usurpation
and oppression &c.   That if all the persons and property aimed at
by Genl W.[allace] were tainted with rebellion that would give
the Genl. no power of confiscation.

He evidently hates to give the order, and if done at all, it will
be very ungracefully.

Note.   Friday, June 17, I do not know that the order is yet given.
Afterwards the P[r]es[iden]t. told me that the Secy. of War
had *written a letter* to Genl. W[allace] (which he saw and was
satisfied with) to stay the order; and that he had seen Genl.
W[allace]'s telegram admitting the rec[eip]t of it.   <the order
has *not* been enforced.>

June 17.   The Nat[iona]l. Intel[ligence]r. of this morning con-
tains a very sharp letter of *Thurlow Weed*, [8] against the N.[ew]
Y.[ork] Evening Post and the Radicals generally, and in favor of
Mr. Seward[.]

Maximilian Emperor

[*A copy of the Manifesto of Maximilian*, [9] *dated May 28, 1864, at
Vera Cruz.*]

This manifesto of the new Emperor is an extraordinary document,
and the more so when we remember that it is issued by a prince of
the house of Hapsburg.

In several particulars, it strongly resembles a party platform, of
our own Country, only better written than most of them, and probably quite as hollow and deceptious.   I think just such a proclamation, the Emperor might have had " made to order,["] in New York
or Boston.

[*A clipping dated Carson City, July 7, 1864, and signed by Orion
Clemens,* [10] *President of the Ormsby County Sanitary Commission,* [11]
giving a statement of contributions to the Sanitary Fund.]

How true is it that failure of our present wish, is often the success
of our real interest.   I refused to help Mr. Clemens to get a little

---

[7] *Supra*, Nov. 26, 1859, note 85.

[8] *Supra*, July 27, 1859, note 58.

[9] Maximilian, archduke of Austria, had become head of the Austrian Navy at 22, had
been governor-general of Lombardy-Venetia, 1857–1859, and had gone as an explorer to
Brazil, before he accepted the Emperorship of Mexico in April, 1864.   He arrived in
Mexico in June, 1864, and was executed in June, 1867.

[10] *Supra*, May 9, 1864, note 35.   On the front cover of the diary Bates has pasted the
official seal of Nevada.

[11] *Supra*, March 19, 1864, note 47.

German consulship, but did get him the Secretaryship of Nevada—
and now, he is in good position, a valuable and rising man.

Vast variety of Tulips—Says Evelyn—Diary vol 1. p. 266—
speaking of Mr. Morini [Morine, naturalist], a great vertuoso [*sic*]
at Paris—" He told me there were 10.000 sorts of *tulips* only."

June 25.   Yesterday and the day before far the hot[t]est of the
season, and this morning gives token of another scorching day.

The President returned, night before last, from his visit to the
army in Va. He is perceptably [*sic*], disappointed at the small
measure of our success, in that region; but encouraged by Grant's
persistent confidence. He visited personally, all positions about
Petersburg and Bermuda Hundred.

A few days ago, Mr. [   ] Bowden [12] Atty Genl of Va. wrote me
a letter complaining of the unlawful conduct of the military at
Norfolk, in arbitrary control of individuals, and in interfering with
the courts of law. And yesterday, 24th. came Gov Pierepoint
[Pierpont] [13] of Va. and Judge Snead [14] and Mr. Porter [15] of Norfolk
(respectively Judge and Pros[ecutin]g. Atty there) to make complaint on the same subject—I told them that oral complaints are of
no avail, and they, all, promised to reduce their allegations to
writing.

[*Marginal*] Note. In the afternoon, they and Mr. Bowden (Atty
Gen of Va.) brot. to my *house* their and Gov. Pierepoint's [Pier-
pont's] written statements.

Mr. Porter, I fear, is a noisy *yorker*, very brave in the *absence* of
enemies[.]

Poor Pierepoint! [Pierpont!] He ought to be, and I suppose is
ashamed of his former subserviency to the Radicals. He begins to
find out that my advice to him and the M.[embers of] C[ongres]s of
W. Va. to beware of those heartless demagogues, was sound and true.
He begins to feel mean, in discovering how he has been fooled, used
and betrayed.

In the Assistant's room, at the office, met Judge Underwood,[16] and
Mr. Chandler [17] Dist Atty. Va.

[12] T. R. Bowden was attorney-general in the "restored government" of Virginia with
its capital at Alexandria.

[13] *Supra*, Aug. 7, 1863, note 74.

[14] Edward Snead, later a Radical lleader in the Reconstruction convention called by the
military authorities in 1867 to remodel the state constitution.

[15] Charles H. Porter, another of the Radical leaders of Reconstruction days.

[16] *Supra*, April 4, 1863, note 77.

[17] L. H. Chandler represented the Conservative Republican faction of Virginia. This
group who had maintained a loyal government in Virginia during the War suffered
alike from Confederates who hated them because they were "loyal" to the Federal
Government and from Radicals because they resisted extreme measures which the Army
was trying to impose.

Mr. C.[handler] gave me a pitiable a/c of how he was abused by
Brigr. Genl. *Wilde*,[18] at Norfolk.

That *Wilde* is the same ruffian that caused a gentleman to be
stripped and whipped by his own slaves, and called it *poetic justice!*
(I heard the President quote his words). The wretch ought to be
punished in emphatic *prose*.

Still June 25. In conversation with the Prest., I told him that I
had not yet learned that the Secy. of War had issued the promised
order, revoking Genl. Wallace's confiscation orders, at Baltimore—
I only knew that no public steps were taken to enforce them. He
said yes, it had been issued—Stanton read him the letter to Wallace,
and he (the P[resident]) approved it; and he saw Gen W[allace]'s
telegram, acknowle[d]ging the rec[e]ipt of it[.] [19]

And so, it seems, that Genl. W.[allace] ostentatiously publishes
his orders, assuming very broad jurisdiction, and now, silently ab-
stains from executing them—saying nothing about the *revoking
order!* And thus the Government lies under the odium of assuming
the power, without the spirit to enforce it!

June 26 sunday. Evelyn's Diary, Vol 1. p 310 (Aug: 1655)
" On sunday afternoon, I frequently stay[ed] at home to catechise
and instruct my family, those exercises universally ceasing in the
Parish churches, so as *people had no principles*, and grew very ignorant of even the common points of Christianity; all devotion being
now placed in hearing sermons and discourses of speculative and
notional things."

Again, page 315 (At Ipswich) says he " I had the curiosity to visit
some Quakers here in prison; a *new fanatic sect, of dangerous principles*, who show no respect to any man, magistrate[,] or other, and
seem a melancholy, proud sort of people, and *exceedingly ignorant*.
One of these was said to have fasted twenty days; but another, en-
deavoring to do the like, perished on the 10th., when he would have
eaten, but could not."

p 316—The process of *Coking* mineral coal, it seems, was not then
understood.

June 26. Evelyn 1. p 318—" The Ambassador of Holland["]
laughed at our committee of trade, as composed of men wholly
ignorant of it, and how they were the ruin of commerce, by gratifying some for private ends."

I dare say the same thing is going on here *now*—the Minister from
Holland,[20] and even my learned friend Schleiden,[21] from honest

---

[18] *Supra*, April 13, 1864, note 93.

[19] See *supra*, June 13, 1864.

[20] T. M. Roest van Limburg, Minister Resident, 1858–1859; Envoy Extraordinary and Minister Plenipotentiary, 1860–1867.

[21] *Supra*, Dec. 25, 1861, note 53.

little Bremen, laugh at *Thad: Stephens* [22] [*sic*] and his com[mitt]ee.
of Ways and Means—and for the same cause.

June 27 monday—Dined with me, (to meet Mr. Eads [23]) Mr.
Welles, Secy. [of the] Navy and his ass[istan]t. Mr. Fox. [24] Expected Adml. Davis [25] and Professors Bache [26] and Henry [27] but all
3 were absent from the city[.] Mr. Welling [28] also dined with us,
also [*sic*].

In the evening called Mr. Fendall, [29] Col Chipman, [30] Maj. Hoer-
ner, [31] Geo: Coffey, Mrs. Laman, [32] and perhaps one or two more.

. . .

June 28. . . .

[*A clipping from the* National Intelligencer *of June 28, 1864,
giving the resolution offered by Mr. Davis* [33] *of Maryland from the
Committee on Foreign Affairs, that* " *Congress has a constitutional
right to an authoritative voice in declaring and prescribing the foreign policy of the United States, as well in the recognition of new
Powers as in other matters.*"] [34]

Mr. Davis is a bold man. Having turned Radical, for a purpose,
he seems to ignore all former doctrines, and stake his all on the
struggle for the leadership of his faction. This resolution is sufficiently peremptory, as to Doctrines and powers, and conveniently
vague as to *subjects*, objects, and " other matters."

I predict that Mr. Davis will " kill himself off "[.] The original
radicals will not trust him—His knavery is of a different sort from
theirs.

---

[22] *Supra*, Dec. 20, 1862, note 87.

[23] *Supra*, Jan. 28, 1860, note 38; Dec. 31, 1861, note 70.

[24] *Supra*, March 9, 1861, note 40.

[25] Charles H. Davis, scientist and naval officer; fleet captain at Port Royal in 1861; commander on the Upper Mississippi in 1862; now chief of the Bureau of Navigation in Washington, 1862–1865.

[26] Alexander D. Bache; physicist; professor at the University of Pennsylvania, 1828–1836, 1842–1843; president of Girard College, 1836–1839; superintendent of the public schools of Philadelphia, 1839–1842; superintendent of the U. S. Coast Survey, 1843–1867; regent of the Smithsonian Institution, 1846–1867; first president of the National Academy of Sciences; vice-president of the Sanitary Commission.

[27] Joseph Henry; physicist; inventor; professor at Princeton. 1832–1846; first secretary and director of the Smithsonian Institution, 1846–1878; founder of our system of weather predictions; an organizer of the American Association for the Advancement of Sciences; original member and president of the National Academy of Sciences.

[28] *Supra*, June 20, 1859, note 3.

[29] Philip R. Fendall: lawyer of Washington, D. C.; district attorney, 1841–1845, 1849–1853.

[30] Norton P. Chipman of Iowa, colonel of volunteers, 1862–1865.

[31] Probably Caleb W. Hörnor of Pennsylvania, surgeon and major of volunteers, 1862–1866.

[32] Wife of Ward H. Lamon (*supra*, Dec. 6, 1861, note 12).

[33] *Supra*, Dec. 17, 1859, note 39.

[34] June 27, 1864, *Cong. Globe*, 38 Cong., 1 Sess., 3309.

June 30. Today about noon, I was surprised to hear that *Mr. Chase*, Secy. of the Treasury had resigned, and that David Tod,[35] ex Govr. of Ohio, was nominated to fill the vacancy. Of course, the town is full of rumors of the cause and motive of Mr. C[hase]'s resignation—One is that he and the Prest disagree as to who shall be Sub-treasurer at New York—Another is that Mr. C.[hase] hopes for the nomination by the Democratic convention to meet at Chicago, and that Fremont and his friends will waive the nomination at Cleveland,[36] in his favor—And yet another (and [t]he most pro[ba]ble) is that his present position is very irksome, in many respects,

1. his social and political relations do not seem to be cordial with the other ministers, except perhaps Staunton [*sic*].

2. his scheme of finance is pretty well played out—and seems now to be generally considered a puffing machine that must soon burst by inflation—for gold is at 240 and still rising.

I have not conversed with many; but as far as my information goes, there seems to be a vague feeling of relief from a burden, and a hope of better things.

I should not be a bit surprised, if Stanton soon followed Chase. In that I see no public misfortune, for I think it hardly possible that the War Office could be worse administered.[37]

<I fancy that I see in this movement another effort of the Radicals to bolt the Baltimore nomination—If they could find a *feasible* candidate I'm sure they would do it[.]>

Mr. Lincoln, I hope, will find out, in time the danger of leaning upon that broken reed.

July 1. David Tod of Ohio was, yesterday nominated by the President, to fill Mr. Chase's vacancy, as secy of the Treasury. It took all by surprise, and the Senate, I hear, was reluctant, and doubtful whether or no to confirm him. Luckily, he declined, by telegraph.

Then, Wm. Pitt Fessenden,[38] Maine Senator, was nominated, and confirmed, as by acclamation. This seems to be generally acceptable.

This Evening Mr. *Eads*[39] and Genevieve left for New York, to start for Europe on the 6th.

---

[35] Ohio lawyer; state legislator, 1838; minister to Brazil, 1847–1852; vice-president of the Democratic Convention at Charleston in 1860; an advocate of compromise before the War, but a strong supporter of the Government when civil war came; Republican governor of Ohio, 1862–1864.

[36] *Supra*, June 4, 1864, note 88.

[37] Stanton finally "relinquished charge of the War Department" only on May 26, 1868, after various unsuccessful efforts of Johnson to remove him, and after the failure of the impeachment trial of Johnson by Stanton's Radical friends became certain.

[38] *Supra*, Dec. 19, 1862, note 81.

[39] *Supra*, Jan. 28, 1860, note 38.

Mrs. E. H. CARRINGTON (mother of E. C. C[arrington] [40]) arrived, fresh from Va.—Her son Edward brot her from Harper's ferry— I procured an order from the President.

July 3. Very lucky that Mrs. Carrington got down so soon; as it seems that Genl. Segel [41] got scared again, and incontenenly [*sic*], ran away from Martinsburg to Harper's Ferry and took safe refuge upon the Maryland heights.

The cause of this flight was that some guerillas made a show of attacking the B[altimore] and O. R R at or near Martinsburg " with an overwhelming force."

Now it seems to me very plain, that the enemy cannot have a *great force* in that region. But " the wicked shall flee when no man pursueth ! " [42]

Poor Sigel ! he seems foredoomed to be whipped and laughed at— His reputation is good *for retreat.*

> " He, like the hindmost chariot wheels, is curst,
>   Still to be near, but ne'er to be the first."

July 4. Last evenening [*sic*], had a sharp attack of dysentery, . . . To day staid quietly, at home, to rest and refresh.

In the forenoon, comes Cuthbert Bullitt,[43] to have a talk about La. affairs. I propose to make him Marshal, in place of Graham,[44] and some other good man Dist Atty vice *Waples.*[45]

How the President will take it, I know not; but if he'll just let me " take the responsibility," I'll make short work of Mr. Chase's knot of ignorant and rapacious swindlers, from the Balise to C[a]iro.[46]

Mr. Bullitt tells me that the officers (of Revenue &c) down to clerks, occupy the best houses, (ready furnished) in N.[ew] O[rleans]—without contract or rent, as far as he knows—Mr. Flanders,[47] for instance, lives in Mrs. Fiske's palace, furnished with great magnificence.

To day, at 12.30. Congress adjourned—God be thanked ! Of course, they passed some necessary and proper laws—they could not help it. But, both house[s] being destitute of a *leader*, every thing is in confusion, and every little clique and faction aspires to rule. It

[40] *Supra,* Nov. 26, 1863, note 70.

[41] *Supra,* June 4, 1862, note 60.

[42] *The Bible,* " Proverbs," XXVIII, 1.

[43] A Louisiana loyalist. Bates did appoint him U. S. marshal.

[44] James Graham, loyalist, U. S. marshal of the Eastern District of Louisiana, 1862–1864.

[45] Rufus Waples, loyalist, U. S. district attorney in the Eastern District of Louisiana, 1862–1864. Jonathan K. Gould was appointed in his stead.

[46] I. e., from the mouth of the Mississippi to the mouth of the Ohio.

[47] Benjamin F. Flanders : New Hampshire-bred lawyer of New Orleans ; editor, educator, alderman, railroad official, 1843–1861 ; fugitive in the North, 1861–1862 ; military treasurer of New Orleans, 1862 ; congressman, 1862–1863 ; now special Treasury agent, 1863–1866 ; governor of Louisiana, 1867–1868 ; mayor of New Orleans, 1870–1872 ; assistant U. S. treasurer, 1873–1882.

is, as Lord Coke[48] says, "Parliamentum indoctum "—it has no
settled purpose, no consistent plan, no acknowledged policy.

The *Radicals* own no constitutional restraints, and seek to govern
by the whim of the moment—reckless of future consequences. They
are doing their worst, by practical facts, to put all the revolted States
out of the Union—no part of the U. S. so that they may govern them,
as England governs India. The last Congress freely admitted
Rep[resentative]s: from Tennessee—Va. and La. (at the instance
of the Prest.) But *this* House refuses. The Senate indeed, still has
a member from Va., Mr. Carlile,[49] and senators are not quite so
barefaced as to move his expulsion.

Les amis des noirs, seem to me absolutely mad. The negro is
ever uppermost in their thoughts, and is sure to give a sable tinge
to every subject of legislation that comes before either house. And
yet, strange to say, there has not been a single proposition calculated
in the smal[l]est degree, to give any substantial advantage to the
freedmen, by establishing their *status,* and giving to them locality,
stability and consistent social relations. The subject is used only as
a topic (very sensitive) for electioneering—not at all for the good
of the negro. [*Marginal Note.*] The bill to establish a Bureau
for the affairs of the freedmen is no exception for that bill really
proposed no good for the negro. And it has failed.[50]

My Friend C. DeWitt Smith,[51] is confirmed Secy. of Idaho, at
the last moment of the Senate, and after a sharp struggle.

July 10. For several days past there has been great excitement
here and in Maryland and Penna. in consequence of a renewed
invasion of the rebels, into Md.

At first it was made light of, as a mere raid, by a light party;
but now, it is ascertained to be a formidable army, of some 20.000,
or more, commanded by Brackenridge[52] [*sic*], Ewell[53] and Early.[54]

---

[48] Edward Coke, great English jurist, authority on the common law, defender of the
independence of judges under Elizabeth and James I.

[49] *Supra,* Feb. 10, 1864, note 16.

[50] A Freedmen's Bureau bill, establishing a military bureau to aid the former slaves,
was introduced on December 14, 1863 (*Cong. Globe,* 38 Cong., 1 Sess., 19). After long
consideration the bill was postponed on July 2 until December (*ibid.,* 3527). It was
then taken up again and passed, and became law on March 3, 1865, *U. S. Statutes at
Large,* XIII, chap. XC, pp. 507–509.

[51] *Supra,* Aug. 7, 1863, note 71.

[52] *Supra,* Oct. 26, 1859, note 19.

[53] Richard S. Ewell: West Point graduate of 1840; officer in Mexico and on the
frontier, 1840–1861; Confederate brigadier- and finally lieutenant-general at the first
Bull Run, then in the Shenandoah, at Gettysburg, in the Wilderness, and at Spotsylvania. He could not have been leading this raid into Maryland as he had been permanently
incapacitated for field service by a fall at Spotsylvania and had been sent back to command the Department of Henrico.

[54] Jubal A. Early: West Point graduate of 1837; lawyer of Rocky Mount, Virginia;
volunteer in the Mexican War; state legislator, 1841–1842; opponent of secession until
Virginia seceded; colonel and eventually lieutenant-general, in the Army of Northern Virginia, 1861–1864, and in the Shenandoah, 1864–1865. He very nearly captured
Washington in this raid.

How an army so great could traverse the country, without being discovered, is a mystery. There must have been the most supine negligence—or worse. Segel [55] commanded at Martinsburg—was *surprised*, fled precipitately, leaving his Qr. master and Com[mis]-s[ar]y stores, a prey to the enemy. Kell[e]y [56] was at Cumberland and Weber [57] at Harper's Ferry. Yet the enemy crossed the Potomact [*sic*], took Frederick and Hagarstown [*sic*], and defeated poor Lew Wallace,[58] on the banks of the Monocacy,[59] and drove him back, in haste to Baltimore. And now, the enemy has his scouting parties and foragers, all over the Country around Baltimore and Washington. They have cut the Northern central, near Balt[imor]e. and probably, by this time, have cut the RR. between Balt[imor]e. and Wilmington. I have not heard yet of our taking a single one of their roving parties. And I fear that our Generals, Wallace, Segel &c. are helpless imbiciles [60] [*sic*].

Some of our townspeople are in ludicrous terror, lest Washington itself should be taken.

Notwithstanding the supine folly which has invited and allowed this invasion still, I have good hope that the invaders will not be allowed to re-cross the Potomac. They will not be able to go much farther, north, and troops are pouring in behind them, to bar the retreat.

July 14. Alas! for the impotence or treachery of our military rulers! The raiders have retired across the Potomac, with all their booty safe! Nobody seems disposed to hinder them.

[*Marginal Note*] 14. To my surprise, Dick popped in at the office—Went home and dined, and staid an hour or two—then repaired on board and steamed down the river. He came up in personal attendance upon Adml. Lee,[61] who made a flying trip.

[*A clipping headed "Military Interference with Elections" which reprints from the* Memphis Argus *a letter of John Park,*

[55] *Supra,* June 4, 1862, note 60.

[56] Benjamin F. Kelley, merchant, 1826–1851; freight agent of the Baltimore and Ohio at Wheeling, 1851–1861; brigadier-general of volunteers in command of the Department of Harper's Ferry and Cumberland, 1861–1862, and the Department of West Virginia, 1863–1865; collector of Internal Revenue in West Virginia, 1865–1869. He was brevetted for his services in defending Cumberland during this raid.

[57] Max Weber: German soldier and revolutionist who immigrated to New York in 1849; colonel of volunteers at Fort Hatteras in 1861; brigadier-general at Norfolk and Antietam in 1862, and in the Shenandoah Valley in 1864; assessor of Internal Revenue at New York, 1870–1872; and collector, 1872–1883. He had just repelled an attack of General Early, July 4–7, 1864, at Harper's Ferry.

[58] *Supra,* June 13, 1864, note 6.

[59] The Battle of the Monocacy, fought on the river of that name a few miles from Frederick, Maryland, on July 9, was a severe defeat for the Federal Troops and exposed Washington to attack.

[60] As a matter of fact, though Wallace was defeated, the resistance he offered delayed Early long enough for Grant to send the reënforcements to Washington which saved that city from capture.

[61] *Supra,* Dec. 19, 1863, note 89.

candidate for mayor, complaining because the rumor that the Military would take over the government if he were elected was prejudicing his chances, and asking if ' Washburne ' [62] really intended to do so; and a letter from Major-General " Washburne " declaring that he certainly would take over the rule of the city if Park or any other not thoroughly loyal man were elected.]*

[Clippings giving (1) a poem on Meade [63] *and Lee found in a confederate soldier's note-book; (2) an Address from C. D. Drake* [64] *to the Radicals of Missouri; (3) the " Peace Resolution " " recently offered in the Senate " by Garrett Davis* [65] *of Kentucky:*

" *Resolved by the Senate and House of Representatives of the United States of America in Congress assembled*, That three years of civil war, in which the enormous expenditure of blood and treasure has no parallel in the world's history, and whose widespread rapine and diabolical cruelties have shocked Christendom, and which, from alternating success, has produced no essential results, prove that war was not the proper remedy for our national troubles.

" *Resolved*, That if the people of America would save and restore their shattered Constitution, and avert from themselves and their posterity the slavery of a military despotism and of a public debt, the interest upon which all the avails of their labor and economy will never meet, they must bring this war to a speedy close.

" *Resolved*, That the President of the United States be and he is hereby authorized to propose a cessation of arms and an amnesty to the authorities of the Confederate States of America, with a view to a convention of the people of all the States to reconstruct their Union; and if that cannot be effected, then that said convention agree upon the terms of a separation of the States without the further effusion of blood and of a lasting peace among them." [66]]

July 15. The *National Intelligencer* contains a long leader entitled " *The late National humiliation*." Some may think the picture drawn of the imbecility of the *War administration*, is " too severely true." It is more plain and direct, in its censures, than any previous article I have noticed in that paper. There are some passages in the article which shew the old tendency to McClellan[.]

—To day, I spoke my mind, very plainly, to the Prest. (in presence of Seward, Welles and Usher) abt the ignorant imbecility of the late military operations, and my contempt for Genl. Halleck. [67]

---

[62] Cadwallader C. Washburn of Wisconsin: lawyer, lumber- and flour-mill owner; Republican congressman, 1855–1861, 1867–1871; delegate to the Washington Peace Convention in 1861; officer in Arkansas, at Vicksburg, and in Texas, 1861–1864; now commander of the District of West Tennessee, 1864–1865; governor of Wisconsin, 1872–1874.

[63] *Supra*, Oct. 15, 1863, note 18.

[64] *Supra*, Feb. 12, 1863, note 13.

[65] Kentucky lawyer; state legislator, 1833–1835; Whig congressman, 1839–1847; Whig and then Democratic U. S. senator, 1861–1872; supporter of the War until 1864, but thereafter a vigorous opponent of the arbitrary acts of the Government both in war and in reconstruction.

[66] These resolutions were not printed in the *Congressional Globe* of 1864.

[67] *Supra*, Nov. 13, 1861, note 37.

July 16 Saturday. Today, like yesterday, is bright and cool with
a pleasant breese—Fine time for the rebel raiders to retire into Va.,
at ease, with their spoils, gathered all over Maryland! Small danger, I trow, of their being disturbed in the retreat, seeing that
Halleck is in command of the forces which ought to intercept or
pursue—No news today, from pursuers or pursued.

No news from Sherman, except that he had reached the immediate
defences of Atlanta[.]

Nothing from the War in Va.

The President does not yet answer my demand [68] for the revocation
of the arbitrary orders of Genls Shepley [69] and Butler,[70] for ab[o]l-
ishing civil law at Norfolk, Va.

Day before yesterday, I introduced Genl. Millson,[71] of Norfolk,
who had an audience on the subject, but I think Gov Pierpoint
[Pierpont] [72] (with Judge Snead [73] and Mr. Porter [74]) failed yesterday to get a hearing.

The President, I fear, is in a most unpleasant dilemma. I am sure
he sees and feels the wrong done, but cannot pluck up the spirit to
redress the evil, much less to punish the wrong-doers. Well may he
say, with King David—" These sons of Zeruiah be too hard for me." [75]

Theo: W. Field, ch[ief] cl[er]k, returned from N.[ew] Y.[ork]
to day.

Wrote to Tilly, to come home fr:[om] Wheeling.

[*A clipping headed " Ice a Life Prolonger," and another headed
" Violence to a Member of Congress " which tells of the stoning of
Mr. King* [76] *by Radical militia on the streets of Richmond, Missouri.*]

July 20. Yesterday, in C.[abinet] C.[ouncil] The President
brought up the matter of the military proceedings at Norfolk [.]
Made a long statement, [of] the quarrel between Gov Pierepoint
[Pierpont] and Genl. Butler—say ~~nothing~~ little, about the orders of
Shepley and Butler, and nothing at all about *my* letter [77]—Some conversation took place in which the Prest. said he was much perplexed
to know what to do &c[.] Mr. Stanton, sec [of] War said it was a

[68] *Supra,* April 13, 1864. Bates had also protested in writing to Stanton. *Supra,*
March 22, 1864.

[69] George F. Shepley: U. S. district attorney for Maine, 1853–1861; delegate to the
Democratic National Conventions of 1860; officer before New Orleans, 1862; military governor of Louisiana, 1862–1864; now commander of Eastern Virginia, 1864; later an officer
of the Army of the James, 1864–1865; military governor of Richmond in 1865; and U. S.
circuit judge in Maine, 1869–1878.

[70] *Supra,* Nov. 29, 1861, notes 98 and 1.

[71] *Supra,* Nov. 18, 1863, note 54.

[72] *Supra,* Aug. 7, 1863, note 74.

[73] *Supra,* June 25, 1864, note 14.

[74] *Supra,* June 25, 1864, note 15.

[75] *The Bible,* " 2 Samuel," III, 39.

[76] *Supra,* May 11, 1863, note 14.

[77] *Supra,* April 13, 1864.

high-handed measure—In answer to some question of Mr. Fessenden, Sec [of the] Trasy. I said " I[t] is a bald usurpation." afterwards Mr. F.[essenden] said it was clearly against law, and Gen Butler ought to be ordered to be ordered [*sic*] to revoke the orders, and abstain from doing any thing under the mock election[.]

Mr. Seward, Sec of State, (who always shuffles around a knotty point, by some trick) thought that *as It was a question of military necessity*, it ought to be refered to Genl. Grant! (just to stave it off) *I* ansd. that the Secy of State could not have read Gen Shepley's order, which put it on a different footing—*I* told the prest that, in my judg[men]t, it was a simple question of jurisdiction—whether the military should put down the civil law—I was only the *law-officer* of the Govt. without any power, but would protect my office and my self, by putting of record, the opinions and views which I had on these subjects, &c[.]

All admitted that the Govt. of Va. was fully recognized by every branch of the U. S. govt. (referring to the W. Va. act) &c—I do not remember that Welles and Usher said any thing, except that Mr. Welles said that Genl Butler had given permits to trade in the N. C.[arolina] sounds—and some of them had been detected in trading with the agent of the enemy—selling whisky, shoses [*sic*] &c[.]

I think the Prest : can[']t get over revoking the orders, but I fear, reluctantly and ungracefully[.]

[*Marginal Note.*] July 31. I am mortified that the President has not yet announced his determination on this important business. It ought not to have occupied an hour. The Genls proceedings are flat usurpation, and ought to have been put down instantly. The admm[inistratio]n. cannot but feel the evils of such barbarous government.

July 20. On one of the last t[w]o days of June—I think the 29th.—it was the day I went with Miss Eads[78] to the State Dept., to get her passport—I expressed to Mr. Seward my desire to have a conversation with him, about political affairs, saying that neither he nor I had time that day, and requested him to name a day soon, when I could have the conversation.

More than three weeks have passed, and I have not heard from him. I asked for that meeting chiefly because Mr. S.[eward] as it seemed to me, carefully concealed his views of the gravest public questions from me. I noticed that, even in C.[abinet] C.[ouncil] when I was present, he never declared his principles and measures in a straightforward manly way, but dealt in hints and suggestions only, as if to keep open all availab[l]e subterfuges, for future use. And now, he declines the direct request of a conversation. Of course, he has a

---

[78] Daughter of James B. Eads : *supra*, Jan. 28, 1860, note 38.

reason for declining—I think it is one of two—Either he has a contempt for my knowledge and ability in such matters, or he is *afraid* to talk with me freely, lest I find out more surely, his hollow foundations and equivocal policy. Perhaps it is my vanity which makes me believe the latter.

July 21. . . .

[*July*] 22d. called on me, at the office Jno. H Rankin of St Louis (with Capt. Aikin) abt. som[e] Steam Boat business. I gave him a note to the 3d. Auditor.

Also called Charles Jones,[79] of Franklin Mo.

July 22. In C.[abinet] C[ouncil]—present, Welles, Usher, Blair, Bates, and part of the time, Fessenden. absent Seward and Stanton—

The Prest. gave a minute account of the (pretended) attempt to negotiate for peace, thro' George [N.] Sanders,[80] Clem. C. Clay [81] and Holcolm[be] [82] by the agency of that meddlesome blockhead, Jewitt [Jewett] [83] and Horace Greel[e]y.[84] He read us all the letters.[85]

I am surprised to find the Prest. green enough to be entrapped into such a correspondence; but being in, his letters seem to me cautious and prudent.

Jewitt [Jewett] a crack-brained simpleton (who aspires to be a knave, while he really belongs to a lower order of entities) opens the affair, by a letter and telegram to Greel[e]y; and Greel[e]y carries on the play, by writing to the President, to draw him out, and, if possible, commit him, to his hurt—while the pretended Confederate Commissioners play *dumby,*—wa[i]ting to avail themselves of some probable blunder, on this side.

I noticed that the gentlemen present were, at first, very chary, in speaking of Greel[e]y, evidently afraid of him and his paper, *the*

[79] Democratic state legislator, 1844–1862; a slave-holder who sympathized with the South but opposed secession, who remained loyal to the Union, yet opposed emancipation.

[80] Kentucky Democrat who moved to New York City about 1844; editor of the flamboyantly democratic *Democratic Review;* consul at London under Pierce; agitator for the imperialism of the Ostend Manifesto; author of a consular letter urging the assassination of Louis Napoleon; Navy agent in New York City, 1856–1859; advocate of secession for Kentucky, 1859–1861; unofficial agent of the Confederacy in Canada, 1861–1865.

[81] Clement Claiborne Clay of Huntsville, Alabama; lawyer; state legislator, 1842, 1844, 1845; County Court judge, 1846–1848; Democratic U. S. senator, 1853–1861; Confederate senator, 1861–1863; Confederate commissioner in Canada, 1864–1865.

[82] James P. Holcombe, professor of law at the University of Virginia, 1851–1861; secession member of the Virginia Convention of 1861; Confederate congressman, 1862–1864; Confederate commissioner in Canada, 1864.

[83] *Supra,* Feb. 19, 1863, note 20.

[84] *Supra,* Feb. 2, 1860, note 47.

[85] John G. Nicolay and John Hay (*Abraham Lincoln,* IX, 184–200) give extracts from this correspondence.

Tribune; and so, I said "I cant [*sic*] yet see the color of the cat, but there is certainly a cat in that mealtub." The contrivers of the plot counted largely on the Presidents [*sic*] gullibility, else they never would have started it by the agency of such a mad fellow as Jewitt [Jewett]—perhaps they used him prudently, thinking that if bluffed off, at the start, they might pass it off as a joke.

I consider it a very serious affair—a double trick.—On the part of the Rebel Commissioners (now at Niagara, on the Canada side) the hope might have been entertained that a show of negotiation for peace might produce a truce, relax the war, and give them a breathing spell, at this critical moment of their fate. And as for Greel[e]y, I think he was cunningly seeking to make a pretext for bolting the Baltimore nomination. <see p. 1. [August 17, 1864]>

The President, I fear, is afraid of the Tribune, and thinks he cant [*sic*] afford to have it for an enemy. And Usher tries to deepen that impression. But Blair says there is no danger of that; that Greel[e]y is restrained by *Hall,*[86] who controls the paper, *and Greel[e]y* too, owning $\frac{6}{10}$ of the stock, and is a fast friend of the President—(of that? [I question.])

<[*Note.*] Oct [   ]. It appears that Greel[e]y is now *ruled in,* as Blair said. He is now a *sound* (?) Lincoln man—Elector *at large,* for the State of N. Y! Having, vainly, exhausted his strength against Mr. Lincoln's *candidacy,* he now, adopts the *candidate* (manifestly forced upon him, by popular demonstration) and plays the next best game, i. e. tries to convert him to his own use, by making him as great a Radical as himself.>

July 23. The National Intelligencer of today, is rich—it contains—

1. the "*curious negotiations for peace,*" above referred to.

2. *How to destroy Caterpillars*—by Coal oil.

3: *Spirit of the religious press*—with long extracts from the *Independent* of N.[ew] Y.[ork] (H.[enry] W.[ard] Beecher[87]) upon the invasion of Md. and the siege of Washington—Deservedly sharp on the on the [*sic*] whole affair, and especially contemptuous of that poor thing—*Halleck.*[88]

And from the N.[ew] Y.[ork] Observer—This last is upon *the Raid,* and the war generally—severe.

---

[86] Henry Hall, son of a leading New York jurist, was connected with the *Tribune* for twenty-six years during eighteen of which he was business manager.

[87] Connecticut-bred Presbyterian clergyman in Indianapolis, 1839–1847, and at Plymouth Congregational Church in Brooklyn, 1847–1887; anti-slavery leader. He was dissatisfied with Lincoln because he did not emancipate the slaves sooner and prosecute the War more vigorously.

[88] *Supra,* Nov. 13, 1861, note 37. The underscoring was done later in red pencil.

Among other things, it contains a statement of all the calls for troops, from the beginning, viz

April 16. 1861	75.000
May 4. 1861	64.748.
July to Dec 1861	500.000.
July 1. 1862	300,000,
Aug 4. 1862	300.000
Summer of 1863	300.000
Feb 1. 1864	500.000

2.039 748

See Nat[ional] Intel:[ligencer] July 9, for "*Number of our troops*"

(And now, we have a recent call for 500,000 more[.)]

([*Marginal Note.*] Nat[iona]l Intel[ligencer] July 9. and see Nat[iona]l. Intel[ligence]r. of Monday July 25.[89] President's Proclamation [90]—and the Bill to guarantee Republican form of Govt. to certain states.[91])

4 The Maryland Convention [92] proposes that the *President and the commanders* of the military *departments* (which include Md.) do levy on the *Sympathise[r]s*, the amt. of the losses of the *Loyal* men, by the late raid!!! [93]   <Why did they not do it themselves?   The Mo. sages, I think would[.>]

5: The act of Congress of July 2d. 64—No. 194, relating to commercial intercourse with insurrectionary States,—captured and abandoned property &c.[94]

July 25. Monday—9. a. m. It rained gently all night, and is still raining.

In *politics*, every thing seems restless and unsettled. I am more glad than ever, that I belong to no party—When the Whig party committed suicide, in 1856, and thereby left the nation without a *bodyguard*, I died with it—There are in fact, no parties now, united by any common principle. Party-ties are so weakened that they no longer amount to an obligation; and party names are used only

---

[89] The editorial headed "The Point of Inquiry" criticizes the "weakness or negligence" which made the raid possible, and demands a Presidential inquiry.

[90] July 8, 1864, J. D. Richardson, *Messages and Papers of the Presidents*, VI, 222–223. The proclamation replies to the H. Winter Davis reconstruction bill.

[91] A bill presents a plan of reconstruction. It was introduced into the House on January 18, 1864 (*Cong. Globe*, 38 Cong., 1 Sess., 259) by H. Winter Davis (*supra*, Dec. 17, 1859, note 39). Davis made a notable speech advocating it on March 22 (*Cong. Globe*, 38 Cong., 1 Sess., 1243; Appendix, 82–85). It passed the House on May 4 (*ibid.*, 2108) and the Senate on July 2, 1864 (*ibid.*, 3491). Lincoln "pocket vetoed" it.

[92] Maryland held a convention in July, 1864, which adopted a new constitution abolishing slavery without compensation to the owners. By excluding all sympathizers with the South through a rigid test-oath, by allowing absent Union soldiers to vote, and by securing Lincoln's active advocacy, the sponsors secured approval by popular vote in October with a majority of 375 in the entire state.

[93] This item appeared in the issue of July 23.

[94] *U. S. Statutes at Large*, XIII, chap. CCXXV, p. 375.

by crafty politicians, to juggle with, for electioneering purposes. Individuals seem bent only on the great work of taking care of themselves, and are ready to change sides, at short notice, and to enlist under any banner that promises higher pay and better hopes of plunder. There is much speculation as to the probable course of the Democratic convention to meet at Chicago, the last of August. Some think Mr. Chase will be nominated. I do not; unless indeed, those who made the Baltimore nomination should abandon it—which is not likely, for those who made it have not time to form and arrange another plan. In fact, political parties are in a transition (almost revolutionary) state.

Called at the office, today, Genl. Gantt [95] and Wm. M. Randolph [96] of Arks. Mr. Randolph has been pardoned by the Prest. but erroneously, as *Willard*, and wishes it changed.

To night, Captain Smith [97] brought to see us, Robt. M. [W.] Bates (a clerk in the Bureau of Int[erna]l. Revenue [98]) a good looking, intelligent, Methodist man, of middle age—a native of Fairfax Co. Va., now much reduced, by these sad times.

. . .

July 26. There is a rumor this morning that the Enemy has again taken Martinsburg.[99]

July 29. [*A newspaper rumor that the rebels show signs of falling back toward the Shenandoah Valley.*]

And yet, we hear on the 30th. that the *advance* of the enemy has taken (and *burnt*) Chambersburg [1] and the country round about.

And nobody here seems surprised, for nobody doubts the ignorance and improvidence of the military administration. And all can see the vaccilating [*sic*] imbecility of such men as Stanton and Halleck [2] and such like[.]

July 30. Told Johnny Rowland [3] that I should watch him closely during the month of August, and that if his conduct pleased me exactly, at the beginning of September, I would raise his salary, from 1200 to $1400.

---

[95] *Supra*, Feb. 5, 1864, note 3.

[96] Lawyer of Little Rock, Arkansas, 1858–1862; Confederate district attorney, 1862–1864; a resident of Memphis, Tennessee, after 1865.

[97] *Supra*, Aug. 7, 1863, note 71.

[98] Clerk from 1863 to 1865—born in Virginia, appointed from California.

[99] A West Virginia town at the outlet of the Shenandoah Valley on the Baltimore and Ohio Railroad about one hundred miles west of Baltimore. Early had taken it on July 4. He took it again on another raid across the Potomac at the end of July.

[1] Pennsylvania town in the Cumberland Valley, fifty-two miles southwest of Harrisburg. It was burned by McCausland (infra, Aug. 14, 1864, note 31) sent by Early (*supra*, July 10, 1864, note 54) who was then making a successful raid across the Potomac, terrifying Maryland, southern Pennsylvania, and West Virginia.

[2] *Supra*, Nov. 13, 1861, note 37.

[3] It should be Hugh A. Rowland, clerk in the Attorney-General's Office.

Called to see me, and had a long talk, B. Rush Plunly[?] a scatter-brained zealot that teaches negro[e]s in Loua. Avows himself an *extremist* and *radical*, yet quarrels with other Radicals, whose peculiar stripe don[']t suit him[.] <For his letter to T. J. Coffey see New Letter Book, Aug 1.>

[*A clipping with the caption* " *Resignation of Solicitor Gibson* [4]— *He thinks his* '*retention of office* ' *under President Lincoln,* '*would be wholly useless to the country* '—*The President thinks so too."*]

Here is Mr. Gibson's resignation, and the President's answer (by the hand of John Hay [5]). I regret to be obliged to say that *both* of them seem to me in bad taste—and uncalled for in fact; and hardly justifiable on any motive (that occurs to me) of prudence and Policy.

July 31. Sunday morning. Klopfer,[6] in bringing the morning mail, brings also a verbal report to the effect, that Grant had succeeded in blowing up (by mine) the enemy's principal Fort at Petersburg—the one that commands the town—so effectually that only 4 men escaped, out of a whole Regt. (of S. Carolinians).

Sed quære. Klopfer hears a great many big stories.

Afternoon's Extra—Explosion terrific—a genl. assault following, and in progress, at last a/c.

note. A shameful business. Somebody ought to be punis[h]ed—but wont [*sic.*]

3. p. m. Dick left on his return to the fleet *via* Balt[imor]e.

Note. The weather, today and yesterday, very hot. Sever[e] drought still prevailing. Even the trees in the streets are wilting; and copious rain, tho' very desirable, on many a/cs, wd. be too late to save the corn crops, in many parts.

Thus closes *July,* not exactly the month of wonders, yet remarkable—some of its days very cool and some very hot. We are disgraced by the imbecility of some of our war office[r]s, in permitting two successive invasions of Md. and Pa.,[7] and unless Grant be eminently successful in Va., we stand disgraced, at the end of the month.

Aug 1. The news of the morning makes it probable that the present raid into Penna. is a small affair, as to the numbers of the invaders. But that, it seems, matters not: Big or little, they go where they please, and retire when they please. They seem to have full faith (justified by experience) in the imbecility of our War administration, and in the obstinate errors and persistent blunders of certain of our generals.

---

[4] *Supra,* April 27, 1859, note 27.
[5] *Supra,* Jan. 13, 1862, note 29.
[6] Henry A. Klopfer, head messenger in the Attorney-General's Office.
[7] Early's two raids across the Potomac during July (*supra,* July 10, 14, 26, and 29. 1864).

My office, unavoidably, brings me sometimes into conflict with that class of military commanders whose egotism prompts them to use their power whenever they get a chance. And I find, by long observation, that those who are most the terror of unarmed, helpless individuals, are most the scorn of the armed public enemy.

Aug 2. There were but three of us at C.[abinet] C.[ouncil] to day—Welles, Blair and I—The Prest: explained some particulars of G[r]ant's and of Sherman's positions, making affairs more favorable to us, than they seem on the outside.

The Prest. is incensed at, Gibson's letter of resignation [8]—and strikes back, I think, in blind impetuosity agst Welling [9] as well as Gibson. I repeated to him my clear opinion that he had no chance of Mo. from the Radicals—Unless he backed his friends there, the state is inevitably lost.

[*A clipping from the National Intelligencer reporting a charge by a Colored Division in which these troops were routed.*]

At Petersburg

That is a sad blow to my friend *Charley* Russell (Lt. Col. C. S. Russell, commanding a battalion of "colored troops.") [10]

On his way *to the front*, he asked me if I thought his men would really fight. I answered "yes surely—They'll *charge* as bravely as any troops; but once repulsed and broken, they cant [*sic*] be rallied; because they have no habit of *moral discipline*."

And so it proved—and so we lost the day!

Aug 4 Thursday. This is, under the Prest's procla[ma]tion, a day of humiliation, fasting and prayer; [11] and surely no people ever stood more in need of self-abasement, for our persistent wickedness and perverse obstinacy in wrong. The whole scheme of individual and social morality seems to be reversed. Our men who seemed to be the best among us, seem to have lost the *moral sense*—argument and logic are wasted upon them, for, yielding a stupid assent to your propositions, they no longer do any thing *because it is right*, nor leave any thing undone *because it is wrong*.

<The President knows as well as I do, that Genl. Butler's proceedings to overthrow the Civil Law at Norfolk, and establish his own despotism in its stead, is unlawful and wrong, and without even a pretence of military necessity, [12] and yet, he will not revoke the usurping orders, for fear Genl Butler will "raise a hubbub *about it*." Alas! that I should live to see such abject fear—such small stolid

[8] See *supra,* July 30, 1864.
[9] *Supra,* June 20, 1859, note 3.
[10] *Supra,* May 29, 1864.
[11] July 7, 1864, J. D. Richardson, *Messages and Papers of the Presidents,* VI, 221–222.
[12] See *supra,* March 22, April 13, July 16, 1864.

indifference to duty—such open contempt of constitution and law—
and such profound ignorance of policy and prudence!

My heart is sick, when I see the President shrink from the correction of gross and heinous wrong because he is afraid " Genl Butler
will raise a hubbub about it.">

Attended Dr. Smith's church, in the forenoon, and heard a passible
good sermon, but not as st[r]ong as the occasion called for, with such
rich material at hand.

At night fall, Matilda returned from Wheeling, bringing with
her, *Ada* Bates.

Aug 5 Friday. Delivered to the President J. O. Broadhead's [13]
sad letter on Mo. affairs (a fair copy of it). He read it *in silence*,
and seemed deeply moved. But I foresee that no good will come
of it. The Prest knows what is right, as well as any man, and
would be glad to *see it done*, but, unhappily, lacks the nerve to do it.

I had a pretty long conversation with him, about the appeal of
the Govr. (Pierepoint [Pierpont] [14]) and other officers of Va.
against Gen Butler's proceedings to put down civil law in Norfolk.[15]
I was ashamed when I found that he had done nothing upon the
subject—slurred it over in silence, only because he is afraid Gen
B.[utler] " will raise a *hubbub about it.*" I reminded him that it
was a formal appeal by the Governor of a state, backed by the
official opinion of his own Atty Genl.,[16] to the effect that Genl.
B[utler]'s proceeding was a mere usurpation, and a grave offence.
That is *a case pending* which must be decided—that not to revoke
the order is to approve and sanction it—&c[.]

But all in vain—He was impassive as water.

Aug 6. . . .

Called to see me, at the office, *Gov. Michael Hahn*,[17] of La. Had a
long talk with him—Tho' in fact, *I* did most of the talking—and
this on purpose, for I wished him to hear some of my views, distinctly and emphatically expressed, before disclosing his. When he
comes to see me again—which he says will be Monday—I will be the
listener.

Today's Nat[iona]l: Intel[ligence]r.—contains a long article,—
apparently, a running history of " General Grant's Campaign."

[13] *Supra*, Dec. 26, 1859, note 66.

[14] *Supra*, Aug. 7, 1863, note 74.

[15] See *supra*, March 22, April 13, July 16, Aug. 4, 1864.

[16] T. R. Bowden: *supra*, June 25, 1864.

[17] German-born New Orleans lawyer; Unionist congressman, 1862–1863; prize commissioner of New Orleans, 1863–1864; governor of Louisiana, 1864–1865; U. S. senator-
elect, 1865; editor of the *New Orleans Republican*, 1867–1871; state legislator, 1872–1876;
superintendent of the Mint, 1878; district judge, 1879–1885; Republican congressman,
1885–1886. He had been a vigorous opponent of slavery and secession, and was now a
leading Southern Unionist.

[*A clipping from the* National Intelligencer *of August 6, 1864, headed " Local Matters " giving two items under the captions " Humiliation and Prayer " and " The Negroes' Jubilee." The latter states that the grounds of the White House were opened to the colored people on the day appointed for national humiliation and prayer, with a speaker's stand, benches, and swings, provided for their use in order that they might show their appreciation of " the much-desired and highly appreciated privileges they are permitted to enjoy since the freeing of the slaves and abolishing of the black laws of the District of Columbia." The grounds were full; and " ardent as the desire was among these colored people to religiously observe the day, they yet contrived to render a considerable amount of amusement not inconsistent with the religious programme."*]

It seems by this that the *white* and the black understand the Proclamation differently, and use the day for different and opposite purposes.

The Whites humble in fasting and prayer, as well they may, in view of their great and many sins, which have called down God's vengeance, and has [*sic*] brought upon us this desolating war, and still continues [*sic*] it.

But the Blacks rejoice exceedingly, over the results of the war, already accomplished in their favor, and exult in the hope of the continuance of the war, in all its desolations. And this is reasonable *in them;* for they are taught by those at the North, who, ostentatiously claim to be their only friends, that the war is waged solely for their emancipation, and for wiping out the blot of negro slavery, from this continent. I do not believe that the negro[e]s desire that the Whites shall be reduced to slavery; but if, by the destructive processes of the war, their own personal freedom can be accomplished, we cannot expect them to reject that consummation, because, by the same processes, all the civil, social and political rights of white men may be destroyed.

Note. The thoughtles[s], not to say foolish, zeal of our *amis des noirs* is well shown in this one fact.—Recent acts of Congress make elaborate provision for the enlistment of ~~Bla~~ *Colored* troops, but there is no law providing specially for the enlistment of *White* troops.—Nay more—the law makes no provision about *the color* of Generals and Admirals in the Army and Navy.

Aug 8. Dined with *Mr. M[i]chael Hahn*, Govr.<see Aug. 10> (titular) of Louisiana. He thinks that La. has had great success (!) in the effort at re construction. And this, with the double despotism and complicated plunder by the military, and the Treasury agents staring him in the face.

This evening Nancy took the seven oclock train for N.[ew] Y.[ork] to visit Woody at West Point.

Aug 9. Comes Judge *J. S. Whitaker* [18] of N.[ew] O[rleans]—(ex Probate judge) introduced by Mr. *J.[oseph] Ad:[olphus] Rosier*, in strong terms (stronger than, after inspection of *the article*, I thought well warranted.) He dined with me and sat, some hours, in various conversation, about war, politics &c. He may be, as Rosier supposes, a worthy and reliable man—But he seems to me an inferior man, both in talents and acquirements, of coarse manners and habits[.]

Aug 10. I see by the newspapers that J. *Madison Day* [J. Madison Wells?] and others strongly denounce *Mr. Hahn* as having held office (Notary) under the Rebel govt., and some other offences— And (what seems very strange to me, in such a *lawyer* as Mr. Day claims to be) they call upon the *President*, to *punish him!* These men seem to have a strange notion of *legal* Government. If he be guilty of perjury, as they surmise, why not prosecute him?

Aug 11. Heard from Nancy. She was safe in N.[ew] Y.[ork] on tuesday morning, intending to go to West Point in the evening. <She did not go till Wednesd[a]y evening>

Called on me, introduced by Jas Harrison [19] of St Louis, Mr. McDonald, merchant of Montreal, who is here about *cotton*, in which he has [in]vested largely, in Texas and La. I gave him a card to Mr. Harrington.[20]

[*Marginal Note.*] The Weekly Nat:[ional] Int[elligence]r. of the 11th. contain[s] important matter—i. a. Ben Wade's [21] and Winter Davis' [22] manifesto agst. the President.[23]

Aug 11. This day I found on my official desk, among some, apparently, waste papers, a letter signed J. Fowlkes, dated Memphis Ten Feb. 26, 1863—addressed—A. S. Mitchell Esq.[24]—and marked *Private.*

It is about furnishing supplies to the enemy and getting cotton in return. There is, enclosed in the letter, a paper (copy I suppose) purporting to be a permit of Lt. Genl J. C. Pemberton [25] to Saml. P. Walker and Dr. J. Fowlkes, to introduce *supplies* and take proceeds back in cotton.

---

[18] John S. Whitaker, born in Massachusetts, bred in Charleston, South Carolina, was a New Orleans lawyer who became judge of the state District Court, 1863–1864.

[19] A wealthy Kentucky-born merchant of St. Louis who carried on extensive commercial enterprises in Missouri, on the western rivers, in Mexico, in Arkansas; part owner of the Iron Mountain mine; iron manufacturer; railroad organizer and director.

[20] *Infra*, Sept. 16, 1864, note 78.

[21] *Supra*, Aug. 10, 1859, note 77.

[22] *Supra*, Dec. 17, 1859, note 30.

[23] The Manifesto appeared in the issue of August 10, not that of August 11. Lincoln had announced a program of moderate restoration of the South and had begun to put it into practice. In opposition to this H. Winter Davis had introduced a bill embodying the Radical plan of reconstruction. Lincoln had "pocket vetoed" it, and then had answered it in a proclamation (*supra*, July 23, 1864). This Manifesto of Davis and Wade was the Radicals' defiant reply to the President's proclamation.

[24] *Supra*, Nov. 9, 1859, note 33.

[25] *Supra*, May 24, 1863, note 27.

It is evidently, part of a contrivance of illicit trade with the enemy: and, possibly, may have been, largely, carried out.

. . .

Aug 13. Saturday. Staid close in office—very hot—Came *Rufus Waples*,[26] late Dist Atty at N.[ew] O[rleans], with divers papers shewing that he is "a marvellous proper man" for the place from which he has just been removed. *Joseph Adolphus Rosier* writes, declining the attorneyship to which he has just been appointed, *vice* Waples.

. . .

[*Under the caption "Spirit of the German Press" the* Missouri Republican *of August 11, 1864, prints an article from the* Westliche Post *denouncing the Military for allowing an old "Copperhead" leader to return; an item from the* Anzeiger *accusing the Provost Marshal at St. Louis and Postmaster Foy* [27] *of opening letters of Radicals; and a long reprint from the* Boston Pioneer *repudiating the Chicago Convention's program and announcing that the "Radical Democracy" will never give up the Cleveland platform, and will not relinquish the Cleveland candidate until a better is provided.*]

[*August*] *14 sunday.* . . .

The last news which I have heard from Genl. Sheridan [28] (down to friday) is that he was pursuing Gen Early [29] up the Shenendoh[*sic*] vall[e]y above Winchester, now and then skirmishing.

That is always the way. When the enemy has done his pleasure, north of the Potomac he withdraws at his leisure, up the Va. Valley, leaving us to repair damage upon the Canal and B[altimore] and O.[hio] R R, and skirmish *in the rear*—the only exception, I believe is, the late rough handling which Averel[l] [30] gave McCausland, [31] at Moorfield.

I heard yesterday, that large bodies of troops—chiefly cavalry—are on the [march], to the support of Sheridan. But with small

---

[26] *Supra*, July 4, 1864, note 45.

[27] *Supra*, May 31, 1860, note 37.

[28] Philip H. Sheridan, West Point graduate of 1853, who served on the frontier, 1853–1861, in Missouri, 1861–1862, at Corinth, Nashville, Stone River, Chickamauga, and Chattanooga, 1862–1864. In 1864 he was placed in command of the Cavalry of the Army of the Potomac, and fought in the Wilderness, at Spotsylvania, at Cold Harbor, and in the Shenandoah Valley, from April until August, 1864. He commanded the Army of the Shenandoah from August, 1864, until he joined Grant before Richmond early in 1865.

[29] *Supra*, July 10, 1864, note 54.

[30] William W. Averell: West Point graduate of 1855; officer on the frontier, 1855–1861; cavalryman on the Peninsula, at both Battles of Bull Run, at Fredericksburg, 1861–1863; in West Virginia, 1863–1864, and in the Shenandoah, 1864–1865.

[31] John McCausland, graduate of the Virginia Military Institute of 1857 and professor there until 1861; officer in western Virginia in 1861, in Kentucky, 1861–1862, at Donelson in 1862, and in western Virginia and the Shenandoah, 1862–1864. He was made brigadier-general under Early in the Shenandoah in 1864, and participated in the raid of early July and the victory of the Monocacy. He burned Chambersburg, Pennsylvania, in late July, opposed Sheridan in the Valley until early 1865, and then fought under Lee before Richmond.

chance I fear of doing any thing more than *Skirmish in the rear!* But perhaps nothing better ought to be hoped for from the improvidence (not to say imbecility) of such men as Stanton and Halleck. [32]

Apropos of Stanton—There is a violent outcry against him, especially in Pa. and N. Y. On Friday last, I saw Cameron—come over special to demand an audience of the President, abt. the late raid into Pa., burning of Chambersburg &c [33] and in general, the shameful conduct of the War in that quarter. No doubt, he had a hearing yesterday, but I have not heard the result. Probably, the Prest. may be forced to do *something;* and likely enough poor *Couch* [34] (commanding in Pa.) may be made the scape goat, leaving the great offenders unpunished—as usual.

[*A clipping from the St Louis Union of August 1, 1864, headed "Something New. Colonel Fletcher to Come out for Lincoln; the Whole State Ticket to Follow Suit.*"]

Wonders!—The Mo. Rep[ublican] says *C. D. Drake* [35] is about to take the stump for *honest ole Abe!* and is sharp upon the Radicals, in a long article.

I see, by the St Louis papers that Dr. *S. W. Anderson* and *D. H. Armstrong* [36] have been tried by a military com[mis]s[io]n (for some *disloyalty*) and sentenced to banishment. But the matter [is] all set aside by reason of the illegal constitution of the Court.

> —" I nulled [t]he jointure with a flaw,
> Which I beforehand had agreed
> To have inserted in the deed ! "

Extract from Evelin's Diary.

vol. 2. p 96. March 1675.

" The Map of Ireland, made by Sir W[illia]m. Petty is believed to be the most exact that ever yet was made of any Country. He did promise to publish it; and I am told that it cost him near £1000, to have it engraved at Amsterdam. There is not a better *Latin* poet living, when he gives himself that diversion; nor is his excellency less in Council and prudent matters of State, but he is so exceeding nice in sifting and examining all possible contingencies,

---

[32] *Supra*, Nov. 13, 1861, note 37.

[33] See *supra*, July 29 and Aug. 1, 1864.

[34] Darius N. Couch: West Point graduate of 1846; officer in Mexico and on the Atlantic Coast until he resigned in 1855 to enter business; brigadier- and major-general of volunteers in the Peninsular Campaign and at Antietam, Fredericksburg, Chancellorsville, and Gettysburg. After Chancellorsville he asked to be relieved of serving under Hooker and was transferred to Pennsylvania. Late in 1864 he fought at Nashville and in 1865 in the Carolinas.

[35] *Supra*, Feb. 12, 1863, note 13.

[36] David H. Armstrong; teacher in New Bedford, Massachusetts, 1833–1837, at Lebanon, Illinois, 1837–1838, and in St. Louis, 1838–1847; comptroller of St. Louis, 1847–1850; postmaster, 1854–1858; Democratic U. S. senator, 1877–1879.

that he adventures at nothing that [which] is not demonstration. There was not, in the whole world his equal, for [a] superintendent of manufacture or [and] improvement of trade, or to govern a plantation. If I were a prince, I would [should] make him my second counsellor, at least. There is nothing difficult to him. He is[,] besides[,] courageous,[;"] &c[.] "

Again, at p 119—*Grenadiers.*

" Now were brought into service a new sort of soldiers, called *grenadiers,* who were dextrous in flinging hand grenados, every one having a pouch full; they had furred caps with coped crowns, like Janizaries, which made them look very fierce, and some had long hoods, hanging down behind, as we picture fools. Their clothing being likewise piebald, yellow and red." [37]

Aug 17. Rev. Dr. Stimson, of Batavia N. Y. comes, introduced by *Woody*—I[n] trouble about his son, in danger of losing his place in the Academy, for *black marks* capriciously given—I gave him a note to the Prest.

Mr. J. H. Ashton [38] telegrap[h]s, from *Schooley Mountain* N. J., that he'll be here monday—*now* wednesday—

Aug 17. 64. Here is a sample of Mr. H. Greel[e]y's [39] hand writing, on an envelope.[40] And as far as I can make out the letter enclosed, it reads thus—

Office of the Tribune, New York, Aug 14. 1864.

" Dear Sir

You are doubtless aware that Mr. James Graham [41] U.[nited] S.[tates] Marshal for Louisiana has been superseded—Mr. Cuthbert Bullitt [42] being designated to succeed him. Mr. Graham is known *to me* as an honest, capable, patriotic citizen, whose removal is a *declaration of war* by *the Government* on the truest and staunchest unionists of Louisiana. I trust therefore that if Mr. Bullitt has not accepted the post, Mr. Graham may be retained in it.

Yours (and something illegible)

HORACE GREEL[E]Y "

" Hon E BATES "

And this is a sample of Mr. Greel[e]y's modesty, and of his delicate forbearance *against* the Administration! I told the prest: at the time of Jewitt and Greel[e]y's manoeuve[r]ing for a pretended negotiation for peace, at Niagara, that the latter was only

---

[37] The first italics were Bates's, the second Evelyn's. Bates's punctuation and capitalization are inaccurate.

[38] *Supra,* Feb. 5, 1862, note 52.

[39] *Supra,* Feb. 2, 1860, note 47.

[40] On the back of Greeley's envelope is printed the " Union Party Platform."

[41] *Supra,* July 4, 1864, note 44.

[42] *Supra,* June 11, 1864, note 99.

scheming to find or make a pretence to bolt the Baltimore nomination. <see p 105. July 22.>

Note. I ansd. Mr. G[reely]'s letter somewhat " in King Cambyses' vein "[.] [43] see Letter Book.

Aug 18 Thursday. This day *Chief Justice Taney* (as he promised last week) sent me his photograph picture, with name and direction thereon, in his own hand writing. The chirography, both on the card and on the envelope, is remarkably good, for a man of his age— 88.

. . .

Jos. H. Gamble has returned here, with strong vouchers, hoping to get a treasury agency, from Mr. Fessenden. Mr. F.[essenden] has not returned from his trip home, but is expected in a day or two.

[*A clipping from the* New York Herald *of August 19, 1864, reports that Judge Black,* [44] *Jake Thompson,* [45] *and General Hooker* [46] *are all stopping at hotels in Niagara Falls, and wonders whether Stanton upset Greeley's negotiations* [47] *with the Southern commissioners in order to initiate his own.*]

Aug 20. Rained all the forenoon. Much water fell.

Calls to see me at the office, John D. Daggett,[48] of St Louis[.] He comes on business in the Treasury; and has a daughter with him— Will call, with her to see us. I introduced him to Gov Pierpoint [Pierpont] [49] and Judge Snead,[50] of Va., who happened to meet there.

Aug 20. Saturday (see back, Aug 5.) Govr. Pierpoint [Pierpont] <I thought the name *Pierpoint*, was a corruption of *Pierrepont*. But I find it an old English name of great respectability. see 2. Evelyn's Diary p 266.>[51] and Judge Snead called to see me, in the office, with cheerful faces. Said they had had a pleasant talk with the President, and had, good hope that he would reverse Gen Butler's arbitrary proceedings, and set things right at Norfolk.[52]

They tell me however that the same sort of factious *military* speculators are getting up a movement like that at Norfolk, to put down the civil law by *military power*, and a mock election at Alexandria. If need be the Govr. will write me upon the subject—and if I find it needful, I will *force* the subject upon the consideration of the Government.

---

[43] Shakespeare, *King Henry IV*, Part 1, Act II, Scene 4.

[44] *Supra*, Oct. 28, 1859, note 22.

[45] *Supra*, April 22, 1862, note 9.

[46] *Supra*, March 29, 1863, note 69.

[47] *Supra*, July 22, 1864.

[48] Commission and retail merchant and steamboat owner of St. Louis; insurance company director; founder and president of the St. Louis Gas Light Company; mayor in 1841.

[49] *Supra*, Aug. 7, 1863, note 74.

[50] *Supra*, June 25, 1864, note 14.

[51] The name in Evelyn was Pierpoint.

[52] *Supra*, March 22, April 13, June 25, July 16, Aug. 4–5, 1864.

I have heretofore forborne too much, to avoid a conflict of jurisdictions, but it only makes the military usurpers more bold and insolent—Hereafter, in open, gross cases, I will press the matter *to issue.*

I find, by close observation, that the best soldiers are the most respectful to the law; and that those of our officers who are least dreaded by the public enemy, are the greatest terror to women and unarmed men both friend and foe.

Extract from Evelyn's Diary Vol 2. p 245.   Nov [Dec.] 13. 1685—

" Dining at Mr. Pepys's, Dr. Slayer showed us an experiment of a wonderful nature, pouring first a very cold liquor into a glass, and super fusing upon it another, to appearance cold and clear liquor[,] also; it first produced a white cloud, then boiling, divers coruscations and actual flames of fire mingled with the liquor, which being a little shaken together, fixed divers suns and stars of real fire, perfectly globular, on the sides of the glass, and which there stuck, like so many constellations, burning most vehemently, and resembling stars and heavenly bodies, and that for a long space.   It seemed to exhibit a theory of the eduction of light out of the chaos, and the fixing or gathering of the universal light into lumenous [*sic*] bodies.   This matter[,] or phosphorus, was made out of *human blood* and urine, elucidating the vital flame, or heat[,] in animal bodies.   A very noble experiment ! "

Sexes of Plants.   Notes to Evelyn's Diary II. 385, where it is said that Dr. Grew [53] was one of the first who advocated the theory of different sexes in plants.

Evelyn's *Diary. Vol: 2. p. 264.*   Mar: 16. 1687.

" I saw a trial of those devilish, murdering, mischief-doing engines called *bombs*, shot out of the mortar-piece on Blackheath." *Note.*   Those mortars of 187 years ago, would seem paltry pop guns, alongside of our 200 lb. Parrot[t]s [54] and 15 inch Dahlgrens. [55]

Ibid: p 298—An: 1689.

" Public matters went very ill in Ireland ; confusion and dissention amongst ourselves, stupidity, inconstancy, emulation, the governors employing unskilful men in greatest offices, no person of public

---

[53] Nehemiah Grew, 1641–1712, English plant anatomist and physiologist.

[54] Rifled cast-iron cannon and projectiles, invented by Robert P. Parrott, West Point graduate of 1824, professor at West Point, 1824–1829, officer on duty in the West, in Florida, in the Ordnance Bureau in Washington, 1829–1836, superintendent of the West Point Iron and Cannon Foundry at Cold Spring, New York, 1836–1867. Parrotts were first used at the First Battle of Bull Run, and continued in extensive use throughout the War.

[55] Smooth-bore guns, popularly called " soda water bottles," invented by John A. B. Dahlgren (*supra*, May 13, 1862, note 39) and used by the Navy throughout the Civil War and for several years thereafter.

spirit and ability appearing[,]—threaten us with a very sad prospect of what may be the conclusion, without God's infinite mercy." [56]

How like our own times!

Aug 22. Mr. Ashton [57] returned home, not much bettered by his trip of two weeks, and more.

Aug 24. The Nat[iona]l. Intel[ligence]r.—"Peace breaking and Peace making" a Resumé of the N.[ew] Y.[ork] Tribune's *Secession* doctrines.

Sept. 5. Yesterday, Sunday, Sept. 4. was my 71st. birthday, and I have great cause to t[h]ank a benign Providence for the measure of bodily health and mental vigor which I am still permitted to enjoy.

I have been on a visit, for a week or so, to West Point—chiefly to see Woody, and bring Nancy home—she has been there several weeks—

Travelling is now very convenient and quick—Down to N.[ew] Y.[ork] in that excellent S.[team] B.[oat] the Mary Powell—Capt. Anderson—and then, at 7. p. m. take the cars (sleeping) and reach Washington, at 6.30, in the morning!

At the point, made sundry new acquaintances Genl. Z. B. Tower,[58] the Supe[rintenden]t. is an old bachelor, badly wounded in [the] knee, some months since. He seems to be a plain, sensible, con[s]cientious man—Col Tidbal[l].[59] of Artillery (Capt in the old line) seems a good fellow, but, I fear, very dull—Several younger office[r]s, I got slightly acquainted with—as Maj Platt [60]—Capts. Randall,[61] Farqu[h]ar,[62] Smith,[63] but none very striking. If I had my way, I would not send to *the Point*, of choice, disabled or supernumerary office[r]s—but the very best I had—I would make it a promotion and an honor—So that *the boys* might always have before them, for imitation, the best models of soldiers and gentlemen.

---

[56] The italics are Bates's: the punctuation is inaccurately copied. These extracts from Evelyn are written on a separate sheet which is pasted into the diary.

[57] *Supra,* Feb. 5, 1862, note 52.

[58] Zealous B. Tower of Massachusetts: superintendent of the Military Academy, July 8–September 8, 1864; brigadier-general of volunteers. He had been brevetted for "gallant and meritorious service" at Cerro Gordo, at Contreras, at Churubusco, and at Chapultepec in 1847, and at Fort Pickens, and Cedar Mountain during the Civil War.

[59] John C. Tidball: of Ohio, commandant of cadets and instructor of infantry, of artillery, and of cavalry, July 10–September 22, 1864; colonel of volunteers.

[60] Edward R. Platt of Vermont: acting professor of Spanish, July 27, 1864–March 4, 1865; major of volunteers.

[61] Alanson M. Randol of New York: assistant instructor of artillery, August 27–December 12, 1864; captain.

[62] Francis U. Farquhar of Pennsylvania: treasurer and assistant professor of engineering, August 22, 1864–July 16, 1865; captain of engineers.

[63] Alfred T. Smith of Illinois: assistant instructor of infantry, 1863–1865; assistant professor of mathematics, 1862–1865; first lieutenant.

Made pleasant acquaintance with Mrs. Thomas, (wife of the Genl.[64] of Chattamaugua [Chickamauga] renoun) and her sister, Miss Kellog, both ladies of plain worth and dignity.

Also, Mrs. Farragut (wife of the famous Admiral[65]) and her sweet little protagé [sic], Miss Draper, (daughter of Professor Draper[66]). Mrs. F.[arragut] is a handsome, vivacious lady, and very young looking, to have a grown-up son, a Cadet, at the Academy. And Miss Draper is a very charming little girl—abt 16, I suppose. I promised her a copy of verses, wh[i]ch. I'll get Tilly to copy and send.

Evelyn's Diary, of Augt. 25. *1695* [II, 337].—["]Bombarding of Cadiz; a cruel and brutish way of making war, first begun by the French."—Again, after speaking of the capture of Capt. Gifford's[67] ship, by the French, and the loss of a great sum—" The losses of this sort to the nation have been immense, and all through negligence and little care to secure the same, near our own coasts; of infinitely more concern to the public than spending their time in bombarding and ruining two or three paltry towns, without any benefit, or weakening our enemies, who, though they began, ought not to be imitated in an action totally adverse to humanity[,] *or* Christianity[.] "[68]

Sept. 8. Mrs. Mary. J. Clark (daughter of Chapman. J. Stuart) has written me several letters, first urging [me] to get [her] a pass to return into Va., (the promise of which I succeeded in getting from Genl. Augur,[69] two days since)[.] Now she writes me that she is a prisoner in Baltimore. I hope she will soon be discharged and allowed to go. For, besides commiserating her condition—having a poor lame child—her *absence* will relieve me. My position subjects me to constant appeals, which Humanity forbids me to ignore— Born in Va., and living in Mo. (both border and belligerent [sic] States) applications are constantly made to me by old acquaintances

---

[64] George H. Thomas: West Point graduate of 1840; officer in the Seminole and Mexican wars, in California, and on the frontier; a Virginian whose sense of duty kept him loyal to the Union when his State seceded; major-general. He fought in the Shenandoah, in Tennessee, in Kentucky in 1861, in Kentucky, Mississippi, and Tennessee, 1862–1865. His greatest fame came from his part in the Battle of Chickamauga.

[65] *Supra*, March 15, 1862, note 38.

[66] John W. Draper: English-born chemist, inventor, and historian; professor of chemistry at Hampden-Sidney College, 1836–1838, at New York University, 1838–1850; president of the New York University Medical School, 1850–1882; author of the *History of the Conflict between Religion and Science.*

[67] Captain Gifford was a friend of Evelyn's who had ventured all he had in a voyage of two years to the East Indies, only to be captured by the French almost within sight of England.

[68] The italics are Bates's; the punctuation is inaccurate.

[69] Christopher C. Augur: West Point graduate of 1843; officer in Mexico, on the Far Western frontier, and at West Point; brigadier-general of volunteers in Washington, 1861–1862, in Virginia in 1862, at Baton Rouge and Port Hudson in 1863, and in the Department of Washington, 1863–1865.

and the children and grand children of friends of my youth, who are sick or in prison, impoverished or otherwise distressed by the calamities of war. These various calls occupy more of my time than I can well spare—in hearing sorrowful tales, reading sad letters and answering them, visiting various office[r]s and corresponding with them.

Besides, it costs me a considerable sum, in money—I have expended, in that way, more than $500.

[*A clipping from the* Missouri Republican *of September 8, 1864, which, under the caption " Spirit of the German Press," quotes the* Boston Pioneer *as saying that Lincoln " has brought even honesty into disrepute," and as announcing that " Radical Democrats " do not like McClellan, but will under no circumstances vote for Lincoln. The Indiana correspondent of the* Westliche Post *reports Indiana opposed to Lincoln and Morton* [70] *both, and says that " the only way to redeem the State for the Republican party would be to throw* LINCOLN *overboard." The* New Yorker Democrat, *" a Lincoln paper," admits that Lincoln is a weak candidate, believes Frémont a stronger one, but prefers to have both withdraw in favor of a still stronger Radical.*]

[*Marginal Note.*] Sept. 9. I procured a pass for Miss Gordon of Va., to come to Balt[imor]e., and sent it to her aunt, Mrs. Jno. Hanson Thomas.[71]

Sept. 9. In C.[abinet] C.[ouncil] today, Mr. Fessenden produced his plan for getting out *cotton,* under the late act of Congress.

His plan seemed to me well enough, if confined to his own Statutory duties, i. e. the appointment and instruction of agents to purchase cotton, at certain points within our lines. But he embarrassed himself by trying also to regulate the method of *getting the cotton in,* ready to be bought—That is outside his province, and can only be controlled by the President as commander in chief.

I stated the intrinsic difficulty of carrying on *war and trade,* against and with the same people, at the same time. But, that difficulty overcome, I thought the measure might be made effectual, to a considerable extent, by refusing permits to all of our people, to go into the enemy country, to get cotton—as leading to corrupt speculation and odious monopoly—and allowing all cotton to be brought in *to our military posts,* asking no questions, to be forwarded to the Treasury agents, to be bought and paid for under the act.

And the Prest: directed the Secy. of the Treasury to try his his [*sic*] hand, in drawing up the details of such an intercourse.

---

[70] Oliver H. P. T. Morton: Indiana lawyer, circuit court judge, 1852–1853; lieutenant-governor, 1860; governor, 1861–1867; U. S. senator, 1867–1877. Through the use of arbitrary power as War Governor, Morton had aroused vigorous opposition. In 1862 Indiana had elected a Democratic legislature, and Morton was now governing without a legislature by executive edict as a practical dictator.

[71] *Supra,* April 14, 1862, note 91.

This discussion (if an informal, disjointed conversation can be called discussion) convinced me, more than ever, of the evil tendency of times like these, in removing the land marks of power, and breaking down the barriers which ought to [stand.] between the different authorities. There would be no difficulty if the Sec of the T.[reasury] wd. content himself with his own duties, under the act i. e. appoint agents, at proper places and instruct them how to act in buyin[g] the cotton brought in to them, to be sold, without meddling with what he has no power to control—*the bringing in* of the cotton, to be sold. Having fulfilled *his own branch* of the business, he might, I think, without impropriety, suggest to the President, his views as to the most prudent method to get the cotton *in*, so that his agents might buy it.

[*Marginal Note.*] This night, Maj Burr (Judge of the Levy court) sent me a basket of fine peaches.

[*A clipping from the* Missouri Republican *of September 9, 1864, reprints an article from the* Westliche Post *which reports general dissatisfaction with all of the candidates for the Presidency—Lincoln, McClellan, Frémont—and hopes that the " Cincinnati Convention, which has been called for this . . . purpose" will unite the " honest Union men " who want none of the three, behind a suitable candidate.*]

Sept 10. Rained again this morning. There has hardly been a day, for the last ten, without rain, more or less; and the cloudy weather has renewed my cold, from time to time, and made me quite unwell.

[*A broadside entitled "Aphorisms on Government" written by T. M. Jacks, member-elect of Congress from the First District of Arkansas who speculates on the purposes of government and opposes military rule.*]

Dr. Jacks, claiming to be M.[ember of] C.[ongress] of Arks.

[*September 11*]. And so—*sund*[*a*]*y the 11th.*—there was a thunder storm and very heavy rain, beginning this morning, before day and continuing till abt 9. a. m.

Aristotle

Equality—Citizenship.

Aristotle's *Politics* [72]—Book 3. Chap 13. p. 109—" The rectitude of any thing must be assumed to consist in [its] *equality;* that therefore, which is equally right, will be advantageous to the whole State[,] and to every member of it, in common. Now, in general, a *citizen* is one who *shares in the Government*, and also, in his turn, submits to the Government [to be governed]; but his condition is

---

[72] *The Politics and Economics of Aristotle*, Edward Walford, ed. (Henry G. Bohn, London, 1853). The punctuation and capitalization are inaccurately copied. The italics are Mr. Bates's.

different in different States; the best is that in which a man is enabled to choose, both to govern and to be governed, *with regard to virtue*, during his whole life."

So too, our Declaration of Rights holds it to be a self-evident truth "*that all men are created equal!*" But what Aristotle meant, and what our declaration meant, by *Equality*, is understood by each individual, according to his own preconceived notions, and applied, in practical argument, to any form of social and political existence which may serve his turn, for the present purpose.

The word, used, generally, as in both the above quotations, is a mere abstraction, very convenient for the use of those who wish "to point a moral or adorn a tale," [72a] and yet avoid committing them selves to any thing in particular. It is often used as a pretty, ear-catching apothe[g]m, which may satisfy shallow thinkers and evade the necessity of logical anaylsis. For instance, several learned chancellors have tersely said *Equality is Equity;* and the pretty saying has run into some good books, for doctrine.

Doubtless the phrase may be true, when applied to a specific State of facts; but, as a general proposition, it is always false. It cannot be predicated of any two sentient animals, man or beast, that they are *equal*, in all things. Therefore, it is an abuse of language and a perversion of though[t] to apply the term to any two persons or things, without stating the particulars in which they are equal, and thus admitting their inequality, in other particulars. And this applies to all entities—to physical nature as well as to mental, moral and legal relations and aptitudes.

Equality, in some particulars, may exist, while the *inequalities* in other and more important particulars make a striking contrast. Men may falsely say that mice and elephants are equal, because they have an equal number of feet; and yet, even their feet are very far from being equal, and they differ widely, in many other particulars.

As to the Declaration of Independence, on which some zealous enthusiasts harp so strongly—Suppose it be literally true that "all men are *created* equal," what then? I remark——

1. The declaration does not say how long nor on what conditions they remain equal after their creation. Adam was created holy and good, and consequently, happy; but he soon sinned and got the wages thereof—lost his place and privileges; and his first descentents [*sic*] took to murder and idolitry [*sic*]; and we see what consequences followed.

2 *When* can a man be said to be *created*—at conception or birth? At the latter, I suppose, for he cannot be *created* after birth—he can only be altered, improved, added to or deminished [*sic*]. He was *created* then, helpless in body and imbecile in mind, without volition,

---

[72a] Samuel Johnson, *The Vanity of Human Wishes*, line 221.

judgment, action and wholly dependent on others for food and locomotion and consequently, for life itself.—in fact, a poor little slave,
incapable of asserting, or even of comprehending any right or interest. If created equal, then it is an equality in ignorance, impotence
and absolute dependence. As the poor little slave (man) is, when first
created, incapable of self-suppor[t] and protection, it is (if we would
but heed the voice of nature) the blessed providence of God that
plants in the heart of some more capable person, an instinct of love
and mercy which prompts to, and in a manner compels the support
and protection of that helpless *beginning of a man.*

Yet some zealous Optimists, wiser (as they think) than God, will
not allow him to create man as he chooses—and as we, in fact, find
him—but will have him made after some fashion of their own, and
will have him endued with certain rights, powers and faculties, required by their self-made theory, but contradicted by all the facts
of nature and history.

3. The declaration of independence, like all other written instruments, must be judged by its words. It means what it says; and does
not mean what it does not say. It says that all men are *created*
equal; but it does not say that men, after creation and in the concrete of society, *are* and *continue to be* equal. For that would be an
egregious falsehood, contradicted by every man's daily experience.
I have as good right to say that the declaration does not mean what
it says, in this regard, as any other man has to say that it means
something more, or something other and different from what it does
say.

4. Yet some zealous persons (and good withal) in order to in-
tensify (and *Frenchify*) the thought, will have it (adding unwar-
rantably, to the words of the declaration) that men are created equal
"*before the Law.*" Now, it is precisely *before the law*, that men are
not equal; because, independently of their intrinsic qualities, the law
takes special pains to make them unequal. The son of 24, though,
possibly, a wiser and better man than his father of fifty, is not eligible, as his father is, to either house of Congress or to the Presidency. And why not? Simply because the Law says *no.* Whatever he may be, by nature, nurture and virtue, *before the law*, he is
not his father's equal.

5. But the declaration goes on to say of men "that they are endowed by their creator with certain unalienable rights; that among
these are life, liberty, and the pursuit of happiness."

Now, I do not assume to have a precise understanding of all that
is meant by these words. I know however, that they do not purport
to be the enactment of a law, or the prescription of a human rule,
for the government of men in society. They amount, only to a
declaration of what the authors supposed to be the exercise of a

super-human power, for the good of men. The rights mentioned
are declared to be unalienable; and the en[d]owment of them made,
not by man, but by God, the Creator. Therefore, the premises being
true, it is impossible that subordinate man can have any right to
annul the Divine grant, by alienating or destroying any one of those
God-given rights.

The proposition is universal, applying to all created men; and
yet men, always and every where do "refuse the awards of Providence, and will not rest in Heaven's determination." They do, under
a pretence of some kind of justice better than God's, and for reasons
and motives satisfactory to some local legislature, and with all the
forms and mockeries of human law, destroy that unalienable life,
which God has given. They do habitually, take away a man's unalienable liberty, and shut him up in a loathsome prison, and
perh[a]ps for no better reason than that he stole a horse. They do,
daily, interfere with men's unalienable right to "the pursuit of
happiness" in their own way, by compelling them, either to abandon
the pursuit altogether, or to follow it, under great difficulties, and
through fields of carnage—i. e. by the draft of soldiers.

Sept 14 Wednesday. This evening, my little cousin Ada, of
Wheeling, left us, after a visit of some weeks. Matilda took her as
far as Baltimore, where she met a Revd. gentleman, who will escort
her home[.]

(Note. Tilly returned friday evening, bringing with her our
young friend, Cornelia Dorsey[.])

Sept 16. To day, I handed to Mr. Nicolay [73] my check for $250,
my contribution to the National Union Comm[itte]e., towards the
pending election. I believe all the other cabinet ministers have done
the same.

(Note, Yesterday, I sent $25, to John. S. Fleming, a young pris-
oner of war, at Camp Chase, Ohio. I never saw the young man, but
he needed the money and asked for it, and is a son of *John. S.
Fleming*, of Goochland, Va. with whom I had friendly relations
when we were young.)

This evening Mr. Welling [74] called to see me, and I could not help
feeling, with some sorrow, that it was the first time since the Na-
t[iona]l. Intel[ligence]r. came out openly for McClellan. I do not
doubt that Mr. W.[elling] has acted conscienciously [*sic*] in this
thing. But I think he has committed an unfortunate error, both for
himself and for the paper.

The McClellan movement,[75] I believe *must* fail. The man himself,
has no prestige—no reputation, nor the chance to have one, as a

[73] *Supra,* Feb. 28, 1862, note 18.

[74] *Supra,* June 20, 1859, note 3.

[75] The Democratic Convention had met in Chicago on August 29; and on its first ballot
had nominated McClellan for the Presidency.

politician, and certainly no renoun in arms. And as for the Democratic party, it no longer exists, as a distinct, organized body. More than half its former members have gone into open rebellion, and a large portion of the remnant having strong sympathy with its departed friends. There is not a leader among them, not a man of such marked talents for civil life, or such glory in war, as to attract popular favor, by giving any assured hope of success. I am convinced that the *man* cannot support the party, nor the *party* the man.

I fear that my friend Welling has made a sad mistake, in so far as concerns himself personally. And for the glorious old Intelligencer, I grieve when I fear that it will lose, in its old age much of that high reputation which it has long maintained for wisdom, principle, moderation and prudence.

Doubtless the able men of the Intelligencer will be able to show many and great errors in the men of the present administration; but they offer no certain or even probable, remedy for the evil, either in McClellan, or in the demoralized and effete Democratic party.

The Chicago convention calls itself the *Democratic* convention, and Gen McClellan, in his letter of acceptance, confirms the name and character; yet several writers who support the cause, I observe, call it (prepost[e]rously enough) *Conservative;* forgetting that Democracy has always heretofore, claimed for itself the title of *Progressive*, as the very opposite of *Conservative;* and affected to despise and hate conservatism, as, at once, a weakness and a crime.

[*An article in the* Railroad Record *upon " The Public Debt—How to pay it " advocating an ad-valorem export tax " of at least one hundred per cent. if not more " on cotton, and a similar tax on tobacco.*]

This is not the only writer who thinks he has found the means to pay the national debt. Most of the schemes have perhaps, some merit, but all seem to me over-sanguine.

I have an idea which no one seems willing to elaborate. I do not doubt that the gold and silver lands might be so managed as to produce a revenue more than enough to pay the interest upon our public debt, or any that we are likely to have.

[signed] Edw Bates

[*Note.*] 1865. Feby—Here is another plan to pay the Debt and save the Nation, by Mr. Thomas Allen. [76]

[*A half-column article " for the* Missouri Democrat," *signed Thomas Allen of St. Louis. Mr. Allen suggested that two hundred thousand citizens give the government $10,000 each in order to end heavy taxation. If not enough altruists responded the public lands might be withdrawn from sale, carefully re-surveyed, and each man*

---

[76] *Supra*, Feb. 4, 1860, note 71.

contributing $10,000 toward the payment of the public debt be given the privilege of drawing five thousand acres of land, and smaller contributors be rewarded in proportion.]

Col Elliott. F. Shepard [77]—of 16. Wall St. N. Y.

The other day I received a letter from him, stating a question and asking my opinion upon it, and enclosing his *check for $500*. The question is whether the 10.30 notes are, *by law*, receivable in payment of duties?

From the first, I had a strong impression that it was not right for me to give opinion on that subject, to any private person, lest it might conflict with the interest of, and my duty to, the public. I examined the question somewhat, so as to have (without forming a definitive opinion) a pretty clear impression in the affirmative. The question, I knew, had been formally submitted to the Treasury (by R. A. Whitthaus, merchant, N.[ew] Y[ork]) and I thought it prudent to converse with Mr. Fessenden upon the subject. I did so, stating my fears that the Govt. might be legally bound to redeem the notes in that way, and that the question might be started, at any moment, in the courts. I knew before, from Mr. Harrington, [78] that the Treasury had refused to receive the 10.30s for duties; and now, Mr. Fessenden expresses the positive opinion that the law is against their receivability—and moreover that hoping soon to absorb the most of those notes, it was very desirable that the question should not be stirred at present, I determ[in]ed at once, to let the matter drop.

And consequently, I could not give an opinion upon the subject, to any private person; and I have returned to him his check for $500.

[*Marginal*] Note. Captured or abandoned property. The act. March 3. 1863. [*U. S. Statutes at Large*,] ch: C.XX.—*Vol* 12. p. 820. Act July 2. 1864. [*ibid.*,] ch: C.C.XXV—Vol 13. page 375.

Sept. 17. Spec[i]al meeting of C.[abinet] C.[ouncil] call[e]d, to consider of claims of certain persons in Louisiana to have restored to them, their plantations, which had been seised by the Military, and, after being sometime in possession of the Quarter Master, turned over to a Treasury agent (Mr. Flanders [79]). It evidently appeared that the President and the Secs. of Treasury and War had never considered how and by what authority those plantations were held—Mr. Fessenden insists that Flanders has no authority under *his Department*, and considers him, in that regard, the agent of the War Dept. But Mr. Stanton says no—the War office, having turned over the plantations to a treasury agent,

[77] New York lawyer, 1858–1861, 1865–1884; president of the American Sabbath Union; owner of the *New York Mail and Express*, 1888–1893. During the Civil War he served as aide-de-camp to Governor Morgan of New York with the rank of colonel.

[78] George Harrington: clerk in the Treasury Department, 1845–1861; assistant secretary of the Treasury, 1861–1865; minister to Switzerland, 1865–1869.

[79] *Supra*, July 4, 1864, note 47.

had nothing more to do with them. Still, the question remained how to dispose of them; and there seemed to be no sensible understanding upon the subject—Nobody had considered the elements of the case—under what right or power, they were seised, for what uses and purposes held, or by whom to be controlled and disposed of—

The subject being tangled in this manner, I suggested several thoughts, to bring the case to more definite issues—i. a—I asked what is meant by a *plantation?* to which I was sarcastically answered, "Why, of course, *the place where planting is done*"— which raised a laugh at my expense—Then, said I, being only the *place*, my question is fully answered—It is *land* only—not stock, implements, machinery, nor any outfit, beyond the land. That will do—the act of, 63 relates to personal property—and these plantations were seised and these transactions occur[r]ed long before the act of July 2d., 64, which is the first that gives power *to the treasury agent*, to lease (and there is now [no] power given to any one else[)].

It was suggested by the secy. of War, that as these plantations were originally seised by the military power, so they ought now to be disposed of by military order.

To that I answered, that military seisure could only be for military use—that it was no claim of title, but is possession only, and continues so long only as the possession is needed, and continues in fact—and that it applies to friends as well as foes. And, besides all this, that these plantations were actually and formally surrendered and turned over to the *Treasury* agent—and so the military connection with them had ceased.

I then suggested the difficulties of making any Executive order, civil or military, as to the delivery of possession, and that the best way would be to leave the parties entitled, to assert their claims, in the courts. Mr. Stanton said the courts might give the possession to traitors in arms. I replied that the laws had made provisions of their own for the forfeiture and confiscation of land of rebels; and that I did not know that [the] question of confiscation could be tried, collaterally, in an action for possession. He rejoined that a Judge could not, in any case, give possession to a rebel—I said, how is he to know that [the] plaintiff is a rebel, till he is tried and convicted? If the Judge decide a case otherwise than according to law, he ought to be impeached and broken—He resumed (rather *in furore*) if the Judge should give the land to a traitor *he ought to be shot* and *I would give the order!* I could not help replying—You might have *force* enough to ensure impunity for the crime, but, by law, you would be subject to be hanged for the murder![")]

Sept. 22. For the last two or three days, we have been getting the particulars of Sheridan's great victory [80] over Early,[81] in the valley of the Shenandoah. I think it looks like the beginning of the end. If the flying remnant of rebel army, can be pursued to Staunton and Charlottesville, the Central Va. R. R. and the James River canal will be broken. That event, I think will soon be followed by our occupation of Cape Fear river, which will effectually close Wilmington. And then, the war (at least with great armies) will be at an end.

([*September*] *23d*.—We learn this evening that Sheridan has defeated Early <and this time very effectually> driving him from his strong position, at Fisher's Hill, near Strasburg, and capturing many prisoners, guns &c—and still pursuing hotly) [82] *Note.* Reinforcements are going to Sheridan, with all secrecy and celerity and I think our flag will be pushed on, even to Charlot[te]sville and Lynchburg.

Sept. 23 Friday. To day, on coming out from C.[abinet] C.[ouncil] I was surprised to learn the *retirement* of P.[ost] M.[aster] G.[eneral] Blair. He shewed to Mr. Welles and me the President[']s letter (recd. this morning) suggesting his resignation. The letter is couched in very gentle and friendly terms—reminds Mr. B.[lair] of his often-expressed willingness to withdraw, whenever the Prest should think the Adm[inistratio]n. could be better or more harmoniously conducted, in his absence &c. I[t]. declares that there has never been the slightest *personal* dissatisfaction &c.

Mr. Blair says he will publish the letter—having Mr. L[incoln]'s leave to do so.

He thinks that this is the result of a compromise with the leaders of the Fremont party—the extreme Radicals. And circumstances seem to warrant the conclusion, for Fremont's letter of declention,[83] while it professes to oppose the McClellan democrats, and thus indirectly support L[incoln], haughtily dictates the line of policy and measures to Mr. L[incoln].

Also, it is announced that *Ben F. Wade* and *H[enr]y Winter Davis* (notwithstanding their fierce manifesto [84]) are to take the Stump for Lincoln.

The result will, probably, be to ensure Mr. L[incoln]'s election over McClellan; and the Radicals, no doubt, hope that they will constitute the controlling element in the new party thus formed, and as such will continue to govern the nation. In this view it is their shrewdest policy to abandon their separate organization, for in that

[80] *Supra,* Aug. 14, 1864, note 28. Sheridan had taken command at Harper's Ferry on August 7. On September 19, he drove Early out of Winchester and pursued him up the Valley. *Infra,* Sept. 23, Oct. 11, 1864.

[81] *Supra,* July 10, 1864, note 54.

[82] *Supra,* Sept. 22, 1864. Sheridan pursued Early's fleeing troops beyond Staunton. *Infra,* Oct. 11, 1864.

[83] [*Appleton's*] *American Annual Cyclopaedia,* IV (1864), 795.

[84] See *supra,* Aug. 11, 1864.

they were foredoomed to defeat. But perhaps, their success is a melancholy defeat for their Country.

I think Mr. Lincoln could have been elected without them and in spite of them. In that event, the Country might have been governed, free from their *malign influences*, and more nearly in conformity to the constitution.[85]

Sep 24 Saturday. The morning papers contain accounts of Sheridan's successes [86] and that he is still pressing on[.]

See, in this morning's Chronicle the correspondence between the Mayor of Atlanta and Gen Sherman about the order expelling the inhabitants.[87]

[*September 29.*] *Reverdy Johnson* [88]—The Nat[iona]l. Intelligencer of Sept. 29, contains his letter to the Com[mitte]e. of the Baltimore ratification, *McClellan* meeting.

It is not long, but more terse and pointed than his letters usually are, and is, in fact, more calculated to damage Mr. Lincoln, than any one document that I have seen.

John B. Henderson.[89] I notice also in the St Louis papers, that Senator Henderson was to make a *Democratic* speech (McClellan) at Troy Mo.—at the time of the unseemly riot there.

Note. Both Johnson and Henderson were *Douglas Democrats,* at the last Presidential election, and therefore do but follow their proclivities, in taking the side of Genl. McClellan, whose only merits, as *president*, consist in the *party name*, for he has no *civil* and *political* history; while Mr. Lincoln is plausibly assailed for all the imputed errors in fact and doctrine, of his administration.

McC.[lellan] should be elected, they think, not because he has any qualifications; but because L[incoln], has many faults.

Sept. 30. This morning, Jno. Minor Clarkson came to my house with a letter from his father. His sister, Josephine, wife [of] Genl. J. J. Clarkson, C. S. A. is here with him, asking a pass to go to her husband, at Richmond.[90] I gave him a letter to Genl. Hitchcock.[91]

To day, at C.[abinet] C.[ouncil] I was surprised to hear Mr. Seward insist that the Prest. should issue a proclamation declaring Nevada a state in the union, upon no better evidence than a short

---

[85] In view of the history of Radical-controlled reconstruction and economic policies, this speculation of Bates's is most interesting.

[86] *Supra*, Sept. 22–23, 1864.

[87] W. T. Sherman had occupied Atlanta on September 2, 1864, and on November 15 was to begin his march to the sea.

[88] *Supra*, Nov. 26, 1859, note 85.

[89] *Supra*, Feb. 24, 1863, note 27.

[90] The Clarkson family were old Virginia friends of Mr. Bates.

[91] Ethan A. Hitchcock: West Point graduate of 1817; officer at West Point, on the frontier, in the Seminole War, in the Indian service, in Mexico, and on the Pacific Coast; major-general of volunteers in Washington where he revised the military code. He served on the commission for exchange of prisoners, and advised Lincoln.

telegram [92] of Gov Nye,[93] and in the teeth, as I think, of the act of Congress, which requires the adoption of the constitution, by popular vote, and also a certified copy of the constitution to be sent to the Prest.

Mr. Fessenden declared, flatly, against it, and so did I. The Prest told Mr. S.[eward] to prepare [a] draft of a proclamation, and that he would think of it.

Mr. Welles shewed me a strange order of the Prest to authorize Mr. [   ] Hamilton,[94] of Texas to bring out cotton, from certain ports in Texas, and send it to a govt. agent at N.[ew] O[rleans].[95] Mr. W.[elles] thinks that it amounts to an abrogation of the blockade, and tells me that his commanding officer, on that coast, says he will not regard the order. He also tells me that Fessenden declares that *he* does not recognize the order!

It gives me pain to see so many instances of Mr. Seward's extreme looseness in practical politics, and his utter disregard of the forms and the plain requirements of law. He is constantly getting the President into trouble, and unsettling the best established policies of the the [sic] Government.

It was he that procured the Prest's *cotton* order, in favor of Hamilton; and nobody knows what fortunes some of his friends and protegés will make out of it. Mr. W.[elles] mentioned the matter, complainingly, to the Prest., who said he rec[k]oned it was all right; it had been arranged by S.[eward]!!

Octo 1 Saturday. Cold, driz[z]ly weather all day, with wind N. E. Now—9.30. p. m. still raining slowly. No wind storm, at or since the equinox.

Now is the time when our fleet off the N.[orth] C.[arolina] coast most need[s] vigilance, and I suppose most practice[s] it. That is our most dangerous coast—Wilmington is the only port for the Blockade runners—and now the equinox and the dark of the moon come together.

I got an interesting letter from Dick, giving the difficulties of the blockade and good information of the topography of the neighboring shores.

---

[92] The state convention was held so late that it was necessary to telegraph the constitution to Washington in order that Nevada might be admitted and her electoral vote counted to help reëlect Lincoln.

[93] James W. Nye : lawyer, county judge, district attorney of Madison County, New York ; then a lawyer in Syracuse, 1848–1857 ; president of the metropolitan board of police, New York City, 1857–1860 ; governor of Nevada, 1861–1864 ; Republican U. S. senator, 1864–1873.

[94] Andrew J. Hamilton : Texas lawyer ; state attorney-general, 1849–1850 ; state legislator, 1851–1853 ; Independent Democratic congressman, 1859–1861 ; unionist leader who tried to prevent Texas secession ; brigadier-general of volunteers, 1862–1865 ; military governor of Texas, 1862–1865 ; provisional governor, 1865–1866 ; justice of the Texas Supreme Court, 1866–1868.

[95] A. Lincoln to General E. R. S. Canby (*supra*, April 13, 1864, note 94), Aug. 9, 1864, *Complete Works of Abraham Lincoln*, II, 560.

I have reason to hope that Eads' river gun boats,[96] now in Mobile Bay, will be sent round to the N.[orth] C.[arolina] coast—perhaps they have already arrived—They, I think will secure the Cape Fear River, and then Wilmington will be sealed up, as tight as Mobile.[97]

Yesterday, Mr. Newton [98] went down to his Va. farm, without informing his wife, and I cannot help sharing in her anxiety, lest he be surprised by guerillas.

The news from Mo. is still very bad.   The enemy has cut the Iron Mountain R. R.[99] at at [sic] Big River bridge and other points—Have entered Fredericktown, Farmington and Potosi; [1] and have even cut the S.[outh] W.[est] branch, some distance East of Rolla.[2]   What a sagacious, provident Genl. Rosecrans [3] must be!   For many months past, there was no embodied enemy in or near the state.   He had nothing to do but put down a few Scattering Marauders, and keep the peace, and that he failed to do, perhaps, just because it was an easy job.   And now the enemy comes upon him unaware, and strikes the state, at once, from the extreme South up to near the centre, while he, ignorant of their coming, and wholly unprepared, is in no condition to attack the foe, but is every where, on the *run or on the defense.*

He has indeed (the papers say) issued an *eloquent* appeal to the militia—*after the enemy is in the heart of the State!* Maryland has been shamefully be-Sigeled [4] and be-Wallaced,[5] while Mo. is be-Curtised [6] and be-Rosecransed,[7] to her ruin.

The frequent recurrence of this ignorant imbecility or criminal negligence, gives a plausibility to the accusation made by some angry men (which I cannot yet believe) that it is the policy of some of our generals, to grind down the border states, and break the spirit of their people, by repeated devastations and constant military rule.

---

[96] *Supra*, Jan. 28, 1860, note 38 ; Dec. 31, 1861, note 70.

[97] Fort Fisher which protected the entrance to Wilmington fell to the combined naval and land forces of Admiral Porter (*supra*, March 15, 1862, note 39) and General Terry (*infra*, Aug. 21, 1865, note 18) January 16, 1865, and thereafter Wilmington was effectively closed to blockade runners.

[98] *Supra*, Jan. 5, 1862. note 12.

[99] A railroad running from St. Louis about ninety miles south to Iron Mountain, and eventually on to Arkansas as part of the St. Louis, Iron Mountain, and Southern Railroad.

[1] The nearest of these towns, Potosi, was only sixty-five miles south of St. Louis.

[2] The Southwest Branch, when completed, was to run to the southwestern edge of the State. It became part of the St. Louis and San Francisco Railroad. Rolla was only fifty miles southeast of Jefferson City, the capital of the State.

[3] *Supra*, March 9, 1864, note 95.

[4] Sigel had at first commanded the Department of West Virginia, but in June, 1864, had been relegated to a subordinate position near Harper's Ferry. He was swept out of the way in July by Early and driven to Maryland Heights where he remained in useless security while Early moved on toward Washington.

[5] Wallace commanded in Maryland from March 12, 1864, until the end of the War. *Supra*, June 13, 1864, note 6.

[6] Curtis commanded in Missouri from September, 1862, until May, 1863. *Supra*, Oct. 22, 1861, note 23.

[7] Rosecrans commanded in Missouri from January 28, 1864, until December 9, 1864.

Oct 5. Things worse and worse in Mo. The Guerillas all up, no doubt, by concert with Price's invasion;[8] and I see nothing on our side but sheer impotence and fear. The rebels go where they please, through the State, and as far as I hear, we attack them no where.

It seems that Genl. Rosecrans appointed Genl. F.[rank] Blair[9] to command in St Louis County, when Mayor *Thomas* (Ja[me]s. S.)[10] [objected] on the ground of Blair's unpopularity! and Genl. R.[osecrans] reversed the order and appointed Genl. Pleasanton.[11]

Octo 5. Owen Deveny. In compliance with his letter I have this day purchased for him Government stocks to the amount of $250, with int[erest] from the 15 Augt (which I paid—being 2.50). I have left the bonds in deposit, at Jay Cook & Co.'s till I can hear from Owen.

[*Note.*] Afterwards—(one of the last days of Octo) I withdrew the bonds and have them in my private custody. I have written to Owen (now in Nevada) stating the exact condition of his interests now in my hands—substantially—the bonds above named, and abt $43, in currency.

St Louis, Dec [   ] 1864.

Oct 6 Thursday. Miss Eliz[abe]th. T. Wilson[12] (called Betty) of Boon[e]ville Mo. called to get my aid to procure a pass to go into Va. Her Sister, (wife [of] Willis Wilson of Cumberland Cy Va.) is lately dead, leaving several Orphan children, and she is urged by the family to go and take care of them—passes are refused just now, but I hope to make out hers to be an exceptional case. She is staying with us till it can be known whether or no she can go.

Note. Sunday the 9th. I got her pass, from the Prest. direct, as a special favor, and she started in the mail boat, at 3. p. m. better accom[m]odated than I had hoped.

Oct 7. Friday night. Mrs. Hebb, my old friend, came to stay the night with us.

---

[8] Price invaded the State in September and October, 1864. See *supra*, Nov. 27, 1861, note 70.

[9] *Supra*, April 27, 1859, note 25.

[10] St. Louis banker, 1825-1864, mayor, 1864-1869, who was a vigorous Unionist during the War.

[11] Alfred Pleasonton: West Point graduate of 1844; officer in Mexico, on the frontier, in Florida, and in Washington and Oregon, 1844-1861; major in the Peninsular Campaign; brigadier-general of volunteers in the cavalry at Antietam, Fredericksburg, Chancellorsville, and major-general at Gettysburg. In 1864 he was transferred to Missouri and drove Price from the State.

[12] Sister of John Wilson, later successful physician of Kansas City, but now a Confederate captain under Price engaged in a destructive raid into Missouri (*supra*, Oct. 5).

To day I heard some further accounts of [the] *Sons of Freedom*[13] conspiracy—It seems that *Dodd*,[14] being on his trial before a military commission in Inda., and proof enough given to hang him, has effected his escape.   These developements [*sic*] exhibit a terrible amount of disaffection and lurking treason in the north-western states, if the testimony be not a fabrication—a Titus Oat[e]s plot[15]—According to the testimony, the conspirators claimed *40.000* in Inda. 50.000 in Ills and 40.000 in Mo.— and, apparently, it is plainly a *Democratic* plot.

Oct 9   sunday. . . .

Today I found my winter overcoat very comfortable, in the open street.

Tomorrow Mr. Ashton,[16] my assistant, goes to Phil[adelphi]a. to attend the election, tuesday—thence on to N.[ew] Y.[ork] to be married Thursday.   I know not how long he will be absent. In the mean time, I am very busy in the office, having, among other things, to give opinions upon several important questions—i. a. whether our great Lakes are "the high seas," and whether piracy can be committed on Lake Erie.[17]   My private correspondence, must, of course, be postponed.

I regretted to lose Mr. Walters' lecture upon Solomon's Temple, but I was so engaged in seeing Miss Wilson[18] fairly off, that I could not attend.

Oct 11   Tuesday   Comes Col Ch[arle]s H. Lewis[19] (brother of John F)[20] of Rockingham Co. Va.   He and several of his young relatives—brothers, sons and nephews—were seised and sent down, *as*

---

[13] The Sons of Liberty, formerly the Knights of the Golden Circle and then the Order of American Knights, was a secret society in the Northwest which opposed the War, and sought to defeat Lincoln and other Republicans.   During the summer of 1864 some of the society's hot-heads plotted an armed rising.   More responsible leaders, when informed, put an end to the project, but Republican Governor Morton of Indiana, in danger of defeat for reëlection, found evidence in the possession of one Dodd of which he made political capital.

[14] H. H. Dodd, an Indiana printer who was grand commander in Indiana of the Sons of Liberty.   About August 20 the police seized in his office thirty-two boxes labeled "Sunday-school books" but containing 400 navy revolvers and 135,000 rounds of ammunition, supposedly paid for by money furnished by Jacob Thompson, the Confederate agent in Canada.

[15] Inventor of tales of wide-spread Popish plots in England, 1678–1680, and forger of evidence to incriminate those he accused.

[16] *Supra*, Feb. 5, 1862, note 52.

[17] "Lake Erie Pirates," *Official Opinions of the Attorneys-General of the United States*, XI, 114–115.

[18] *Supra*, Oct. 6, 1864.

[19] Virginia lawyer and editor who remained loyal to the Federal Government during the War; secretary of the "restored government" of 1864; minister to Portugal, 1870–1874.

[20] Virginia lawyer and planter; member of the Convention of 1861 who refused to sign the ordinance of secession and remained loyal throughout the War; Republican lieutenant-governor, 1869–1870; U. S. senator, 1870–1875; U. S. marshal of western Virginia, 1878–1882; Readjuster lieutenant-governor, 1881.

129742—33——28

prisoners nominally but really, for their protection, by Genl. Sheridan[.] [21]

He dined with me. And he told me, i. a that Early's [22] troops after the defeat at Fisher's hill,[23] were demoralized, and straggling through his neighborhood, by squads and singly, declared that they were tired of the war—would fight on till the Presidential election, in hopes that if McClellan is elected, he would give them peace and independence but if Lincoln were elected they would fight no more, but give up, in despair.[24]

[*Articles from the* Washington Daily Chronicle *of October 11, 1864, giving cheerful war news from all sides, telling of a Union meeting in Baltimore, announcing that the enemy has been driven off in Missouri, and reprinting from the* Richmond Enquirer *of October 6 a discussion of* " *Negroes as Rebel Soldiers* ".]

Oct 12. News of elections coming. Very fair in Ohio and Inda., but rather doubtful in Penna.[25]

Oct 13 Thursday. Chief Justice Taney died last night, in ripe old age—88. The event has been long expected and takes no one by surprise. I called at his house last evening, and was told that he was *no better*, and I was prepared, at any moment, to hear of his death.

He was a man of great and varied talents; a model of a presiding officer; and the last specimen within my knowledge, of a graceful and polished old fashioned gentleman.

The lustre of his fame, as a lawyer and judge, is for the present, dimmed by the bitterness of party feeling arising out of his unfortunate judgment in the Dred Scott case. That was a great error; but it ought not and will not, for long, tarnish his otherwise well earned fame.

He has filled many offices, and generally, with applause—i. a. Atty. Genl. of Md.—and, under the U. S, Secy. of the Treasury, Atty Genl and Chief Justice [of the] U. S.

He cannot be forgotten, for his life is interwoven with the history of his country, and, in a greater or less degree, must give tone and color to the eventful age in which he has lived.

Some men—adopting the Hindoo dogma, that *inanition* is the perfected state of man—that *not to be* is better than *to be*—pretend that the thing most to be desired is perfect seclusion, isolation from the world—that man is happ[i]est when most ignorant of the world, and

---

[21] *Supra,* Aug. 14, 1864, note 28.
[22] *Supra,* July 10, 1864, note 54.
[23] *Supra,* Sept. 22, Sept. 23, 1864.
[24] This paragraph except for the " He dined with me " was crowded in later, partly in the margin.
[25] These states held their state and congressional elections in October.

least known to his fellow men in it! To this purpose some of our poets have written—

> " Thus, let me live unseen, unknown ;
>   Thus, unlamented, let me die ;
>   Steal from the world, and not a stone
>   Tell where I lie.'[26]

A, Pope

But all this is affectation, springing from disappointed ambition and wounded pride. The true, God-given state of man is *action;* His stimulus is ambition and his support is hope. His instinct is to live, to act, to know and to be known. By nature, he prefers even a miserable life to annihilation. Most men, if brave enough to be honest, would say —

> I'd rather be a snail, and crawl
> Upon some loathsome prison wall,
> To leave a trail which might make known
> That I once lived—when I am gone,
> Than waste, in sloth, this life of mine,
> And, dying, leave the world no sign.

This is the natural out-growth of earthly hope and human passion. All men long for *continuance. Duration* is implied in the idea of human happiness, even confined to this world. And surely the *Christian,* who hopes continually for " that rest which is reserved for the people of God "[27] takes Eternity into his vision. All long *to be*, and all fear *not to be.*

[*Marginal Note.*] Saturday, Oct 15. I attended Judge Taney's funeral, from his dwelling in Washing[ton] to Frederick Md. High Mass was sung in the Jesuits' church at Fred[eric]k. and I saw his body placed in the grave (beside his mother, as he had ordered) in the old church yard there. The Atty: Genl's office was closed to day, by my order. *Note.* The Prest. Sec.y. Seward and the P.[ost] M.[aster] Genl. Gov Den[n]ison,[28] attended the body, from the dwelling to the cars. I returned home at night.

Octo 17 monday. Called to see me in the afternoon, Robt. A. Gray of Rockingham, Va. (a refugee) and will call again tomorrow, on some business of his own.

<Note—Oct 19. Mr. Gray agrees to [s]top at our house for a few days, going out [going out or not], as suits his convenience, both to eat and to sleep>

---

[26] Alexander Pope (1688–1744), *Ode on Solitude.*

[27] *The Bible,* " Hebrews," IV, 9.

[28] William Dennison : Cincinnati lawyer ; bank president ; railroad promoter ; steel manufacturer ; Whig legislator ; an organizer of the Republican Party in Ohio ; governor, 1860–1862 ; chairman of the National Union convention of 1864. He had been appointed postmaster-general when Blair resigned in September, 1864 and held office until disagreement with President Johnson forced his resignation in 1866.

Octo 18. I obtained a pass from the Prest: for *old* Mrs. Carrington, to return South [29] (Charlott[e]sville) she to have transportation to our lines, and to be accompanied by her son (Genl. C.[arrington] of Washington) as far as Martinsburg.

<[*October*] 22d. I had begun to fear that the old lady would after all her anxiety, decline to go—but I learn, to day, that tuesday the 25th. is fixed for her departure.>

Octo 22 Saturday. Mr. Gray staid with us several days, and left, this evening for N. York. I gave him a letter to Genl. Van Alen.[30]

Within the last few days, Sheridan has won another great victory over the rebel army in the vall[e]y of the Shenandoah. It seems that Long Street had superseded Early in command of the rebs: [31] and finding Sheridan absent (he had come down to Washington and was just returning) made a furious attack on us, at cedar creek, near Strasburg—drove in our lines and captured some 20 pieces of our artillery.

Just at that time, Sheridan [32] arrived upon the field, and at once, turned the tide of battle [33]—drove the enemy at all points—killed and captured a great many, and took some 50 guns, including our 20 lest [lost] in the morning.

From Mo. there is no decidedly better news. Price [34] is retiring up the Mo. on the south side; and our Genl.[35] (recovering a little from his panic) is pursuing. But Price crosses with detachments, where he pleases, and sacks the towns on the north side.

Even as low down as Warren [36] and St. Charles,[37] the guerillas and other straggling bands roam the country at pleasure—The mail is stopped, even at Wentzville.[38]

Oct 23 Sunday. The St Louis newspapers bring us, this morning, account of the death of *John. D. Coalter*, the last brother of my wife.

We were prepared for it, by information of his protracted illness; and yet, it strikes as a sudden blow. I fear the effects upon my wife. Her once numerous family [39] has faded away, until she and her sister Fanny (widow of Dr. Means of S.[outh] C.[arolina]) alone remain. And Mrs. Means' life (if indeed she still lives) is dark and sorrow-

---

[29] *Supra*, July 1, 1864.

[30] *Supra*, Feb. 4, 1860, note 62.

[31] It was Early, not Longstreet, who commanded. *Supra*, July 10, 1864, note 54.

[32] *Supra*, Aug. 14, 1864, note 28.

[33] It was in returning to take command of his routed army at the Battle of Cedar Creek that Sheridan made his famous " ride."

[34] *Supra*, Nov. 27, 1861, note 70.

[35] W. S. Rosecrans: *supra*, March 9, 1864, note 95.

[36] A village about one hundred thirty miles northwest of St. Louis.

[37] A town on the north bank of the Missouri only twenty-two miles from St. Louis.

[38] A village twenty-one miles west of St. Charles.

[39] David Coalter of South Carolina and Missouri had had seven children : Mrs. Bates, Mrs. Means, Mrs. Hamilton Gamble, Mrs. W. C. Preston, Mrs. William Harper (*supra*, June 29, 1860, note 69), John D. Coalter (*supra*, Dec. 20, 1860, note 16), and Beverly T. Coalter, a Missouri physician.

ful, in view of the death of her sons who have fallen in this cruel war.

Genl. Coalter died, at his own house, in St. Louis, on wednesday, Oct: 19. 1864. In one view, he is rather to be envied than mourned. He had no wife nor child, nor, in fact, any helpless dependent. His nephew *John* Coalter—son of Beverly—is nearest to that condition, and doubtless, fair provision has been made for him. He was nearly alone in the world—and now that death has sadly thinned the ranks of his and my old acquaintances, in the last few years, and that the events of this horrid war have broken up society and alienated the oldest and closest associates. Perhaps he only escapes, in good time, from greater calamities impending. If he have only made his peace with God, all is well—and of that I have good hope, for besides his own repentence [*sic*], I have great reliance upon the unceasing prayers of his sainted mother.

Oct 24 monday. I see, in the Chronicle, an account of a new movement in Politics, to weaken the Democratic nomination. It is headed by many of the most prominent democrats in the city and State of New York—such as F. B. Corning,[40] Moses Taylor,[41] Edwards Pierrepont,[42] John A Dix,[43] and the like.

This movement is not only formidable to the McClellanites for the names enlisted against them; but the *fact* of such a move at New York and at this time, is proof that the Democracy has no power of unity and cohesion[.]

It is a call for a " Convention and mass meeting of the *Democracy opposed to the Chicago Platform.*["]

There is nothing that more surprises me, than the habitual abuse of words and perversion of language and sense. Heretofore and until lately, the Democratic party gloried in calling itself *the party of Progress*, and in denouncing its adversaries as *Conservatives.*

---

[40] Probably Erastus Corning of Albany: iron manufacturer; president of the New York Central Railroad; mayor, 1834–1837; state senator, 1842–1846; congressman, 1857–1859, 1861–1863; member of the Washington Peace Convention of 1861; War Democrat who supported the Government but protested against its arbitrary acts, notably in the arrest of Vallandigham.

[41] Foreign trader, merchant, banker of New York City; railroad and mine promoter; sponsor of the first Atlantic cable; president of the City Bank, 1855–1882; chairman of the bankers' loan committee which floated war-bonds among New York banks.

[42] New York lawyer; judge of the Superior Court of New York City, 1857–1860; Federal commissioner to try prisoners of state during the Civil War; government prosecutor of John H. Surratt, 1867; U. S. district attorney, 1869–1870; U. S. attorney-general, 1875–1876; minister to Great Britain, 1876–1878. He did active service in 1864 in organizing the War Democrats in support of Lincoln.

[43] Soldier, 1812–1828; lawyer; secretary of the Democratic Convention of 1832; U. S. senator, 1845–1849; assistant U. S. treasurer, 1853; postmaster of New York City, 1860–1861; secretary of the Treasury, 1861; minister to France, 1866–1869; Republican governor of New York, 1873–1875; sometime president of the Chicago and Rock Island Railroad, the Mississippi and Missouri, the Erie, and the Union Pacific; major-general of volunteers in command of the Department of Maryland, 1861–1863, and of the Department of the East at New York, 1863–1865; a leading War Democrat; later, a supporter of Johnsonian moderation toward the South.

All conservatism was, in their eyes, a crime. But now their presses and public orators claim for them the merit of *conservatism*—Even Mr. Pendleton [44]—one of the most radical of progressive democrats—is now declared a conservative!

But, it is not alone in party politics that this kind of *moral forgery* is constantly perpetrated. Respectable writers on government and constitutional law lay down their propositions in terms which are not only not necessary to the success of their main design, but false in fact, and laying them open to easy refutation and ridicule. They say, habitually, what they do not mean—They falsely say (what if it were true, proves nothing, under our constitution) that all men are *equal*. And, as falsely, that the majority of the *gove[r]ned* do and ought to rule.

The most popular news-writers, wantonly, abuse language, by using words in a false sense. In recounting a battle in which one of the armies left half of its number dead on the field, they will have it that the army was *literally* DECEMATED [*sic*]! And when they undertake to portray a man very shabbily dressed, they say that his clothes are *dilapidated*. And yet the frenchman (just learning to speak English was laughed at for saying—"*Extinguish* dat dog," when he only wanted the dog *put out* of the room.

Even the dictionaries have cought [*sic*] the mania for *cant phrases*, and are doing their worst to render our language vague and indeterminate, by digging up its very *roots*.

Oct. 27. Called on me, in the office, *J. S. Bradford*, Asst. Coast Survey, a mess mate of Dick, on the Flag Ship Malvern—came home and dined with us, but declined to stay the night, having an engagement.

Oct 28 Friday. Attended C.[abinet] C.[ouncil] and [was] not a little surprised, to hear nothing talked of but election matters, and those minor points. Neither great *principles* nor great *facts* seem, at present, to have any chance for a fair consideration[.]

Even matters of the gravest intrinsic importance are, just now, viewed and acted upon only in their relations to the pending election—e. g. the prosecution of Dodd et al (*Sons of Liberty!*) in Inda.,[45] and the trials of Ferry and Donahue, in Baltimore, for fraud and forgery, in the vote of the N. Y. soldiers.

I wish the election was over. The President, I think, as soon as re elected, will be a freer and bolder man.

---

[44] George H. Pendleton: Cincinnati lawyer, state legislator, 1854–1856; Democratic congressman, 1857–1865; president of the Kentucky Central Railroad, 1869–1879; Democratic U. S. senator, 1879–1885; minister to Germany, 1885–1889. He was now a candidate for reëlection to Congress and for election to the Vice-Presidency on the ticket with McClellan, but he was defeated for both offices.

[45] See *supra*, Oct. 7, 1864.

[*A clipping describing Vermont as a state where they have no soldiers, only one city, no theaters, no mobs, no police, and no murders in the past ten years.*]

That is comfort and happiness[.]   Let Glory go to grass!

[*A clipping describing a meeting of the highest Masonic Council.*]

I wonder if the Count of Kneiphausen is one of the newly chosen honorary members[.]   Their *High Mightinesses*, with the *illustrious* Albert *Pike* [46] at their head!

[*An announcement in the* Cincinnati Daily Times, *October 24, 1864, that the Louisiana Legislature has chosen R. K. Cutler to fill the unexpired term of John Slidell* [47] *in the United States Senate, and Charles Smith to fill the short term of J. P. Benjamin.* [48]]

These La. Senators will hardly be allowed to take their seats.   The last congress was very liberal in admitting the Senators and Reps: of disturbed States.   But the Radicals who rule the present Congress seem determined to press their false doctrine to the extremity of *Secession.* [49]

[*A pamphlet entitled " General McClellan's Record.   His Sympathy with the South.   Read for Yourself; " and a clipping headed* " McClellan the Traitor, Again."]

These fierce denunciations do no good, but great harm.   McClellan has faults enough, both negative and affirmative; and his party is in the same condition.

These charges of treachery and treason, not well established by proof, do but take off the edge from other accusations which cannot be defended, thus, discrediting the best-founded objection against him, and exciting a popular sympathy for him, as a *persecuted man*. And thus men are often *lied* into a consequence which the *truth* could not give them.

Quakers.   On the night of Friday, Oct 28, a " travelling Friend " Eliz[abe]th *Comstock,* [50] widow, (introduced by Isaac Newton [51] and

[46] Since 1859 the grand commander of the supreme council of the thirty-third degree Masons for the southern jurisdiction of the United States and head of the Royal Order of Scotland in the United States.   Previously he had been an Arkansas school-teacher, a trapper, a writer, a lawyer, a soldier in the Mexican War, a railroad promoter.   He was Confederate agent to the Indians during the War.

[47] *Supra*, Nov. 26, 1859, note 89.

[48] Judah P. Benjamin: New Orleans lawyer; Whig U. S. senator, 1853–1859; Democratic U. S. senator, 1859–1861; ardent advocate of secession; Confederate attorney-general, 1861; secretary of War, 1861–1862; secretary of State, 1862–1865; London lawyer, 1866–1883.

[49] Between 1861 and 1863 all members elected by a loyal portion of the voters in a Unionist district of seceding states were admitted to seats in both Houses of Congress, because the official theory was that the states had not seceded.   But after December, 1863, no member was recognized from any portion of a state that had seceded.

[50] An English-born minister of the Society of Friends who had moved in 1858 to Rollin, Michigan.   She was a vigorous advocate of abolitionism, of peace, of temperance, of prison reform, and of women's rights.   During the War she ministered to prisoners and the wounded in camps and hospitals.   On this trip to Washington she visited Lincoln and " held worship " for him in the White House.   Her first name was inserted into the diary in blue pencil after this entry was made.

[51] *Supra*, Jan. 5, 1862, note 12.

wife) visited us, and held worship, in our house. She was accompanied by Mr. G[r]innell [52] ex M[ember of] C.[ongress] of Massts., her special escort, and her " r[e]ligious friends,["] Samuel and William Bettel, and Martha B.[ettel] daughter of William.

Mrs. C[omstock]'s speech or sermon was excellent—especially correct, in style and language—and Sam[ue]l. Bettel's prayer was good, *per se*, but strange, to us, in manner.

The whole proceeding was so novel to my family that it seemed to them queer, not to say affected, and, in effect, ran out of the *solemn* into the ludicrous.

[*Marginal Note.*]   Afterward, monday night, she spoke to a crowded audience, at the Methodist church, cor[ner] of F. and 5th.—a most excellent discourse, remarkable for its chaste beauty and purity of Style.

[*Marginal Note.*] [53]   Again, Sunday night, Nov 6, heard Mrs. C.[omstock] deliver a very affecting and touching prayer and sermon, to a vast audience. She seems to me as true an " ambassador of Christ " as I ever saw.

Nov. 1.   I happened today, to hear Mr. Seward read to Mr. Lincoln a draft of [a] dispatch to one of our Ministers abroad, in which he stated the success of the new Maryland constitution.[54] And, putting this in contrast with the *Dred Scott* decision, the dispatch affirms that the Supreme Court affirms, in that case, that Congress has no power to restrain the spread of slavery.

That is a plain error. And it seems to me strange that Mr. S.[eward] should go out of the way to cite the case, as if just to blunder over it. The case *decides* no such doctrine; and I distinctly so declared in my opinion on " Citizenship." [55]

And so, the issue is direct between Mr. S.[eward] and me— *He* tells one of our ministers abroad, that the court *did so decide* and this, in a letter that must come out some day. And *I* tell all the world in a printed opinion, that the court *did not so decide.* The difference between us is that he had no occasion to cite the case at all, while I was under the unavoidable necessity to discuss it and declare its true legal import.

And, in this way false views are propagated, for many will read the short letter who will never read the long case.

---

[52] Joseph Grinnell: New Bedford merchant; bank president; railroad president and director; cotton manufacturer; Whig congressman, 1843–1851.

[53] The note is in red ink.

[54] A convention met at Annapolis from April 27 to September 6, 1864. The Constitution it drew up was ratified by popular vote, October 12 and 13.

[55] November 29, 1862, *Official Opinions of the Attorneys-General of the United States*, X, 382–413.

Nov. 1. This evening I, with Matilda, dined with Mr. Romaro,[55] Mexican Minister, to meet Genl. *Doblado,*[57] lately driven out of Mexico by the French. Officials present, the ministers of Spain (Tassara)[58] and Chile (Aster-Bernago,[)] [59] Secretaries Seward and Usher and Asst Secy Seward.[60] *Ladies,* the wife of the Chelean [*sic*] Minister (a very striking and beautiful young woman) Mde. Potestad,[61] wife of the Spanish Secy of Legation—an American and very handsome—and Mrs. and Miss Seward and our Till.

Genl. Doblado is not very prepossessing. But as he speaks no English, he may be cleverer than I could see.

Nov 2. to day I ansd. *Augus. L. Langham,* on board [the] U. S. St[eame]r. Gettysburg, and sent his letter of Oct 12, to his sister Mrs. Barcklay.

Today also, I spoke (to Mr. Fendall[62] and) Judge Wayne,[63] about *Mrs. Stephenson,*[64] daughter of Judge Taney, and at night, Saw Mrs. S.[tephenson] herself.

Anthony Trollope's " North America " [65] is, I believe (for I have not read it thoroughly) a very good book, in which may be found a great deal of shrewd sagacity, honest truth and sound logic[.]

Chapter 13. of Vol 1. p. 268, entitled "An apology for the war," will well pay any American for the reading. In fact, I doubt whether there is one American in 50.000, who, by writing a short chapter, can place our side of the controversy in a fairer light. His book will, assuredly, make its impression on the English mind.

Nov 5. Called to see me, with Mr. Com[missione]r. Newton,[66] *Henry Dickenson* and *wife.* English people evidently of the *well-to-do class*—Quakers, very intelligent, affable and well bred. I wish we had thousands such.

---

[56] *Supra,* March 15, 1864, note 26.

[57] Manuel Doblado: Mexican lawyer and liberal leader; revolutionist, 1853–1855; minister of Foreign Affairs under President Comonfort, 1855–1856; member of the Congress which drew up the Constitution of 1857; again a revolutionist in company with Juárez; governor of Guanajuato, 1859–1861; negotiator of the treaty under which the English and Spanish withdrew from Mexico in 1862; leader in Juárez's armed opposition to Maximilian and the French. He soon returned to Mexico and died of a malignant fever.

[58] *Supra,* Nov. 27, 1861, note 78.

[59] F. L. Asta Buruaga, Chargé d'Affaires of Chile, 1860–1867.

[60] Frederick W. Seward: *supra,* May 13, 1862, note 38.

[61] Signor Don Mariano Potestad was First Secretary of Legation, 1864–1865; Signor Don Luis de Potestad was Second Secretary of Legation, 1864–1865, and First Secretary of Legation, 1866–1874.

[62] *Supra,* June 27, 1864, note 29.

[63] *Supra,* Nov. 27, 1861, note 74.

[64] Elizabeth Taney Stevenson, wife of William Stevenson, a Baltimore merchant.

[65] English novelist, 1815–1882, son of Frances Trollope, who after an unhappy and financially unsuccessful sojourn in Cincinnati, had published her unpleasant impressions in *Domestic Manners of the Americans* in 1832. His book was the result of a visit to the United States in 1862. The edition Bates used was published in 1862 in two volumes by Chapman and Hall of London.

[66] *Supra,* Jan. 5, 1862, note 12.

Nov 6 sunday forenoon. Attended Revd. Geo: Smith's church, on the Island. He preached specially to the children, on the text (Prov[erbs]: 20) "The sluggard will not plow, because of the cold, *therefore*, he shall beg in harvest, and have nothing.["] As yet, preaching to *children* is *not his forte*[.] But he will come to it, for he is a ready man, of good feelings and fine talents. He tells me that the Genl. Ass[embl]y. (N.[ew] S.[chool]) directs a sermon *to children*, once, at least, in two months.

There is a fine field for usefulness—and also, for that sort of fame which eminent usefulness is sure to bring.

At night, again heard Eliz[abet]h. Comstock,[67] at the Methodist church, cor:[ner of] 5th. and F. (She was unwell, and had not eaten a mouthful that day) yet she made no complaint, and her prayer was sublime and beautiful, and her sermon excellent, tho' I thought not quite equal to that of sunday se[ve]n. night.

Nov 7. Comes Corder Fine, of St Louis, to solicit the discharge of his two young sons, prisoners of war at Camp Morton Inda.——At my request, the President grants it.

Poor Fine was melted with gratitude, and returns rejoicing.

Nov 7. All unexpected *Coalter* (Capt. Jno. C Bates) pops in upon me—He comes, on a week's leave, to visit us, before the family goes West [68]—of which intention he was privily informed.

Nov 9. The election of yesterday is no longer doubtful. The news, this morning, from New York and Penna., ensures the success of Mr. Lincoln.[69]

On Friday, Nov 11. Coalter paid me (insisted on paying) the money I lent him last year, to buy a horse from Capt. Maxon —$125—promising to let me know whenever he got into a strait for money, and apply to me *first of all.*

Nov 11 Friday. Many Virginians are fleeing, to escape conscription. Robt. A. Gray [70] (who was with us some 2 weeks ago) returned from the North, this morning. And during the day his brother, C. Douglas Gray and Beverly Botts came in, accompanied by Miss Rosalie Botts, and Mrs. Wager, an elderly widow (neighbor of Mr. Botts, in Culpeper)—They [came] to escape conscription— the women, to buy necessaries—

I presented them to the President, who received them kindly, and granted their request.

---

[67] *Supra*, Oct. 28, 1864, note 50.

[68] Bates had determined to retire after the election, and did so at the end of November. *Infra*, Nov. 30, 1864.

[69] Lincoln carried all non-Confederate states save Kentucky, Delaware, and New Jersey The electoral vote stood 212–21.

[70] See *supra*, Oct. 17, Oct. 22, 1864.

Nov 14. monday. Miss Rosalie Botts is still with us, and does not know certainly, when she will be able to return home.

Nov 19. saturday—She expects to go to Balt[imor]e. this evening—return tomorrow—and go home monday.

. . .

[*November 20.*]   [*A newspaper reprint of Lincoln's proclamation of November 19, 1864, raising the blockade of certain southern ports.*] [71]

This proclamation is another striking instance of Mr. Seward's vague, indistinct style of composition.

He hates a positive committal, and is, studiously, dark. It is hard to tell, by this proclamation, whether the intention is to *raise the blockade* or *open the ports*—two very different things. I have constantly held (more than once, in C.[abinet] C.[ouncil]) that a nation cannot blockade its own port, in its own possession—because *Blockade is an act of war*, which a nation *cannot* commit agst. itself. Mr. S.[eward] silently, dissented, but never ventured to discuss the subject.

The President also has power, by law, to *close the ports*. In that case, the party attempting to to [*sic*] bring in goods, can be punished only as a smuggler. But the attempt to break bloc[k]ade, works a forfeiture of ship and cargo—must be adjudged under the law of nations, and constantly imperils our relations with neutrals.

It is hard to tell whether this is an *opening of the ports* or a *raising of the blockade*, two very different things.

Nov 22   night. The rain continues, with no sign of abatement.

Klopfer [72] has just packed for me another large sack of books and documents, to go by mail to Julian.

Miss Rosalie Botts returned to day from Baltimore, was met here by Va. friends e g Col Ch[arle]s [H.] Lewis [73] and C Douglas Gray[.] [74]

Lt. Post dined with us and starts for home[.]   He is honorably restored—Shame upon Gen Rosecrans,[75] that he was ever put in peril of office and honor.

I shall resign—to take effect at the end of this month.   As the time shortens, I feel a sensible relief, as the lifting of a burden.

This morning, Mr. Newton [76] told me that he had had a free conversation with the President, who if not overborne by others would

[71] J. D. Richardson, *Messages and Papers of the Presidents,* VI, 230.
[72] Henry A. Klopfer, head messenger in the Attorney-General's Office.
[73] *Supra,* Oct. 11, 1864, note 19.
[74] *Supra,* Oct. 17, Oct. 22, Nov. 11, 1864.
[75] *Supra,* March 9, 1864, note 95.
[76] *Supra,* Jan. 5, 1862, note 12.

gladly, make me Ch.[ief] J[ustice]—That Chase was turning every stone, to get it, and several others were urged, from different quarters [77]—And, (!) that the leading *Friends* would urge me.

I am happy in the feeling that the failure to get the place, will be no painful disappointment for my mind is made up to private life and a bare competency. If I get it, it is a mere gratuitous addition, to be held only for a little while, and as a crowning and retiring honor.

[*A clipping from the* National Intelligencer *headed "Conflict of jurisdiction in Kentucky," describing a dispute between Governor Bramlette* [78] *and General Ewing.* [79]]

This is but one of a thousand instances, in which our military commanders forget the principles of our Govt. and the limitations of power.

It is one of the worst evils of this civil war, that it has destroyed all reverence for Law, and introduced in its stead the arbitrary will of *commande[r]s*. Only think of Hugh Ewing *ordering* the *Courts* of Kentucky what to do !

[*Note.*]   And see forward—Feb 24/65. page 162—Gen Tom Ewing *levying a tax* ! !

[*A pamphlet sermon by Christmas Evans of Wales.*]

Nov 24, 1864.   Given to me today, by *John. W. Tatum* of Wilmington, Delaware—a somewhat famous Quaker.

[*November 30.*] I resigned my office of Atty Genl. [of the] U. S. to take effect Nov 30. 1864, having served just 3 years and ¾.   Some months before[,] I made known to the President my wish to retire as soon as he should be reelected and thus, out of doubt and danger, endorsed by the nation.   I remained about the office for two days longer—closing up my private affairs and in pleasant intercourse with the subordinates—all of whom seem to regret my departure, as all of them have done their best to oblige me.   I part with them all with regret, and in great kindness.

Dec 1.   We had an action [auction] sale of household goods, which sold very well—Instead of 6 or $800, the net proceeds amounted to $1445.96[.]

Nancy relieved me of all trouble in the sale—as she had done about the packing and transportation of our goods sent home.

---

[77] Chase (*supra*, March 5, 1861, note 27) was appointed on December 6.

[78] *Supra*, March 26, 1864, note 55.

[79] Hugh B. Ewing, son of Thomas Ewing (*supra*, Oct. 6, 1860, note 41), brother of Thomas, Jr. (*supra*, Feb. 11, 1864, note 26), and foster-brother of General W. T. Sherman, had gone to California in the gold rush of 1849, but had returned and practiced law in St. Louis, 1854–1856, and in Leavenworth, Kansas, 1856–1858. He fought in West Virginia under McClellan and Rosecrans in 1861–1862, at Antietam, at Vicksburg, and then under Sherman in the West until he was ordered to North Carolina in 1865.

At night, many people calle[r]s to [see] us—Nancy and me—we having rooms at the Metropolitan Hotel, i. a. Mr. and Mrs. Newton [80] and their [friends] Isaac Barton and [   ] Shaffer, quakers of Phil[adelphi]a.

Dec 2. Closed the a/c of our sale, shewing the result above stated. We expect to start tomorrow morning for Phil[adelphi]a. to meet *Ma* and Tilly, returning from West Point.

I have the following means in hand

    1 Cash _____about_____ $545. 00
    2 Draft on New York_____ 2478. 39
                                               _____
                                               $3023. 39

During the day, called on a good many—head officers &c—Gov Dennison (p.[ost] m.[aster] g.[eneral]) seems anxious that I should write to him—Mr. Stanton, Sec [of] War, was especially civil— Told me to write to my sons, in the army [81] and assure them that he would [do] any thing for them that they would expect me to do.

Met Messrs. Seward, Well[e]s and Usher at the Prest's and had a pleasant leave-taking. The President's manner was affable and kind. At parting, he took me aside and said he would write to me soon at St Louis.

(Note. Dec. 21. not heard from yet.)

At night we had many visitors—Mr. and Miss Fendall,[82] Capt. Smith [83]—just returned, leaving Ma and Tilly a[t] Phil[adelphi]a.— Several clerks of the office—Mr. Newton,[84] Mr. Justice Miller,[85] Mr. Coffey [86] &c[.]

[*December 3–19*] Dec 3 Saturday morning—Left Washington and reached Phil[adelphi]a. at 2. p. m. all well.

At 11 oclock sunday night, Dec 4. left Phil[adelphi]a. and reached St Louis, at 4 a. m. Wednesday Dec 7[.]

The weather was very mild during the whole trip; but changed just as we arrived, and became very cold, and so so [*sic*] continued for some days.

(Note, I took a severe cold and am still confined to the house—Dec 21. A snowstorm today)

Col Thos. A. Scott [87] of the Pa. Centran [*sic*] R R gave us a free pass to Pittsburg and telegraphed to help us further on. And Capt.

[80] *Supra*, Jan. 5, 1862, note 12.
[81] C. Woodson Bates at West Point and J. Coalter Bates with the Army of the Potomac.
[82] *Supra*, June 27, 1864, note 29.
[83] *Supra*, Aug. 7, 1863, note 71.
[84] *Supra*, Jan. 5, 1862, note 12.
[85] Samuel F. Miller: Kentucky physician, 1838–1847; lawyer, 1847–1850; emancipationist; Iowa lawyer, 1850–1861; justice of the Supreme Court, 1862–1890.
[86] *Supra*, March 5, 1860, note 18.
[87] *Supra*, Dec. 25, 1861, note 37.

G. Bolton Newton was particularly kind and serviceable, in getting us forward.

We lodge at Julian's, where we are crowded and neither we nor the family as comfortable as might be.

[*A clipping from the* National Intelligencer *publishing two letters written by General R. E. Lee on April 20, 1865, one to General Scott, the other to his sister, explaining his resignation from the United States Army, and declaring:* "*save in defence of my native State, I never desire again to draw my sword.*"] [88]

Alas! for the blindness of human judgment, and for the perversity of human morals! This man, reared, from a boy, by his Country's bounty, and pledged, in a thousand ways, to his country's flag and to the support of its laws, in a moment joins the *grand rebellion* and strikes at the very life of his country!—and all under the false pretence of *defending* his *native State!*

[*A newspaper reprint from the* Boston Journal *which describes the congestion in transportation facilities between the East and West and tells that with corn above two dollars a bushel in Boston it is being burned as fuel in parts of the West. The* Journal *urges coöperation between East and West in the improvement of means of transportation.*]

Washington Daily Morning Chronicle Dec 4. 1864.

["The public has already been informed of the resignation of Mr. Bates, the Attorney General. Yesterday terminated his official labors. He has filled his high functions with great ability and with unspotted integrity during a period of unparalleled importance in the history of the country, and he retires to the repose of his quiet home in Missouri with the respect and confidence of his late associates, and the grateful esteem of all whose fortune it has been to have official business with his department of the Government. Though esteemed by many as more conservative than the majority of his countrymen at the present day, Mr. Bates has given opinions involving the rights of the colored race which have been quite abreast with the times, and which will henceforth stand as landmarks of constitutional interpretation. He accepted without soliciting the office which he lays down, has retained it at the sacrifice of his ease and comfort, . . . It is fortunate for America when she is served in her high places of power by men like the retiring Attorney General, who combines with high intelligence an irreproachable life, and perfect simplicity of character and demeanor."]

Dec 20. Almost every day I see some new proof of the absolute infatuation of the leading me[n] of S.[outh] C.[arolina] and the *cotton* States.

This day, Barton Bates, (who is Ex[ecut]or: of his Uncle J. D. Coalter [89]) handed to me two [letters] written to Gen C.[oalter] while

[88] For the letters see J. William Jones, *Life and Letters of Robert Edward Lee*, 132–133.
[89] *Supra*, Dec. 20, 1860, note 16.

he was a member of the " Peace Convention," [of] 1861, by two eminent S. Carolinians, *Hammond* [90] and *Hayne*.[91]

They had no doubt at all that *Cotton is King* and that the Cotton
States could dictate their own terms, not only to the U. S. but to the
world also.[92]

They were wild enough to expect " Peacible [*sic*] Secession "
while nothing doubting their power to accomplish their end by war.
Slavery was the one predominant principle that was to rule all
others, and they were to rule slavery!

How is it now, when Sherman's desolating march has tracked the
whole length of Georgia,[93] and Thomas [94] has, well nigh annihilated
Hood's [95] army in Tennessee!

Definitions

Loyalty n.[oun] adhesion to *my* clique.   <*note*[.] the rights of
loyalty are in danger—Its privileges are assailed—Even Gen Curtis [96] declares that he will no longer permit *loyalty* to be a justification for Ho[r]se-stealing! Bravo General—stick to that, and you
may yet ' do the State som[e] service.'>

Radical n.[oun] a rooter (and, figuratively, a *scratcher* or *digger*)
<Note. The ' *Digger* ' Indians are the lowest and vilest upon the
continent. They inhabit the most sterile regions of the Rockey
[*sic*] mountains, and, sinking back into primitive nature, get a precarious living by digging roots, along the mountain gorges.[>]

In France, both hogs and dogs are carefully taught to hunt, and
root or *scratch* up, truffles (? trifles)—a kind of edible root that
grows under ground, without any stem or leaf, above the surface.
And so they cannot be found by any human sense or reason, but
only by *brute instinct*.

Politically, a *Radical* is a man who is always dealing with the
root—the origin and foundation, of society. He appeals, for every

[90] James H. Hammond, states' rights, free-trade congressman, 1835–1836; governor of
South Carolina, 1842–1844; Democratic U. S. senator, 1857–1860; a leader of secession
in 1850–1852 who came in the late 'Fifties to doubt its wisdom.

[91] Arthur P. Hayne: Charleston lawyer; soldier in the War of 1812 and the Florida
War; state legislator; U. S. naval agent in the Mediterranean; Democratic U. S. senator,
1858.

[92] To a boast of Seward in 1858 that the North would rule the South as conquered provinces, Hammond had replied, " You dare not make war on cotton—No power on earth
dares make war upon it. Cotton is king."

[93] Sherman had left Atlanta on November 15 and entered Savannah, December 22.

[94] *Supra*, Sept. 5, 1864, note 64.

[95] John B. Hood of Kentucky: West Point graduate of 1853; officer in California, on
the frontier, and at West Point until he entered the Confederate Army in 1861. He
fought on the Peninsula, at Second Bull Run, Fredericksburg, Antietam, and Gettysburg,
and then at Chickamauga where he lost a leg. When Joseph E. Johnston was removed
in July, 1864, Hood was given command of the Confederate Army in the West, but was
badly defeated by Sherman at Atlanta in July, August, and September, and by Thomas at
Nashville on December 16. After this Nashville defeat he was relieved of command.

[96] *Supra*, Oct. 22, 1861, note 23.

thing, great and small, to the primitive principles of man's nature, *as he understands them;* and boldly assumes (in spite of apparent facts) that man was created, not according to the counsels of Eternal Wisdom, but according to the radical theory. He always claims to act in the name of the *Sovereign People,* and armed with all their powers. Of course then, he is above all constitutions and laws: For he is the fountain of all law, the source of all power and right; and, of necessity therefore, must be above the stream of legal justice which flows from that fountain. With him, "the good of the people is the *Supreme law,*" and *he* is the only judge of what is good for the People! with full power to determine what part—of the *population* compose *his* people.

Convention. a gathering of Demagogues, designed to throw society into anarchy, and then to gamble for a better system.

Guizot's Democracy in France—p. 19.

"The U[nited] S[tates] of America are universally admitted to be the model of a Republic and a Democracy. Did it ever enter the head of the American people to call the U.[nited] S.[tates] a Democratic Republic?"

"No; nor is this astonishing. In that country there was no struggle between Aristocracy and Democracy; between an ancient aristocratical society, and a new democratic society: on the contrary[,] the leaders of society in the U.[nited] S[tates], the descendants of the first colonists, the majority of the principal planters in the country and the principal merchants in the towns, who constituted the natural aristocracy of the country, placed themselves at the head of the revolution and the Republic. The devotion, energy and constancy which they shewed in the cause[,] were greater than those displayed by the people. The conquest of their independence[,] and the foundation of the Republic[,] was not[,] then, the work and [the] victory of certain classes over certain other classes; it was the joint work of all, led by the highest, the wealthiest[,] and most [the] enlightened, who had often great difficulty in rallying the spirit and sustaining the courage of the mass of the population." [97]

Aristotle's Politics. Book 4. Ch: 4. p. [133] 134.

"Since[,] then these things are necessary for a State, to the end that it may be happy and just, it follows that citizens who engage in public affairs should be men of abilities therein. Many persons think it possible that different employment[s] may be allotted to the same person, as that of a Soldier, a husbandman[,] and an

---

[97] This quotation is copied onto a large letter-sheet and pasted into the diary. It is taken from the edition published by Appleton in New York in 1849.

artificer; and [; as] also that others may be both Senators and Judges: *but all men lay claim to political ability, and think themselves qualified for almost every department in the State.*"

Most true. And here is another proof of the common saying that man is always and every where the same. As it was in the far east, in the semi-barberous [*sic*] times of Aristotle, so it is in America, in my day—Egotism, Vanity, self-conceit are as veritable parts of our nature, as blood and bones.

" But (says our author, continuing) the same person cannot, at once, be *poor* and *rich*." And yet, our poet hath it—

"How *poor*, how *rich*, how abject, how august—
How complicate, how wonderful is man ! " [98]

[THOUGHTS ON THE TIMES] [99]

[Tyranny is better than Liberty, if one saves a nation and the other destroys it."]

Which one?   Either?

[If a nation by dissention and division loses its strength, it must submit to any fate that may befall it.]

With or without dissention, we *must* submit to what *befalls us*.

[People are but poorly fitted for free government if they know not the duties to their agent, government, or are unwilling to perform them.]

(L'Empi[r]e, c'est la paix.)

[How illy fitted are people to be freemen who give to party and faction the service they should give to their country.]

Then who are fit to be freemen?

[If free institutions are simply great nurseries for politicians and demagogues, who set the people wrangling so they may profit, then there is something wrong in such institutions.]

Something rotten in the State of Denmark.

[Should the insanity of the present time permit this country to be dismembered, could it continue so for half a generation with so many natural interests so linked together?]

[Do people who are proposing to cut up this country in pieces or States ever reflect on the burdens they are preparing to impose on themselves? First the cost of a separate government for each part, and then the armies and navies they will each have to support, to be always prepared for one part of the present country to fight against the other part.]

[If this country is to be divided in two or more parts each as a matter of course seeks to be the strongest. How can such a contest cease?]

[The natural condition of man is to live by the sweat of his brow.]

or die for lack of sweat.

[The unnatural is to live by the compulsory labor of others. Too many desiring to live in this way has helped to cause the present national strife.]

---

[98] Edward Young (1683–1765), *Night Thoughts*, I, " On Life, Death, and Immortality," lines 68–69.

[99] The following is a copy of a broadside dated 1864 with interlineations and comments by Mr. Bates.

Then you, being wise, show the remedy.

[*All free governments* are predicated *on* kindness and forbearance of one portion of the people to the other; and as a last resort, majorities to decide differences. But if in a country, large or small, each portion of it insists on having their own way, then free government better be dispensed with for such people.]

[Free government is in thought a beautiful thing to contemplate, but in practice there is much vice about it, owing to the vast number it engenders of so-called politicians, office holders and office seekers, of whom so many are constantly leading astray and demoralizing the people. To gain their ends are many, alas, willing to do worse than Judas, betray their country for less than the "thirty pieces."]

That's right, catch wisdom and virtue as you do the itch[.]

[If the rebels have a right to Richmond, then they must have the right to plant their guns opposite Washington—consequently one or the other must fall.]

Non sequitur[.]

[Hannibal and his Numidians afflicted the Romans a long while; but Roman firmness withstood all. So must the American people, with unabating resolution, hold out against the *slave holders*.]

The only *slaveholder* in Eastern Va. *now*, is the Genl. of the Department. He (or his underlings) binds and scourges whom he will, and calls it—*poetic justice*[.]

[and their deluded followers.]

Hannibal was a naughty fellow to afflict the Romans; but the Romans did not grow free by whipping Hannibal[.]

[How short-sighted are those who imagine they can hold property and have prosperity, independent of a good and stable goverument.]

What is a good and stable Government?

[If people divide in three or four Presidential parties, and employ themselves entirely in opposing and pulling against each other, what resistance would they make against the common enemy.]

Dont [*sic*] know sir. But make them all follow *me* for I am wise and virtuous—any how, if they all follow *me* they wont [*sic*] be divided[.]

[If a house was attacked by murderers and robbers, and the inmates instead of defending themselves *sat* [*sic*] to fighting against each other, how would they be situated in a short time? So if a people quarrel among themselves instead of being united against the common enemy, where will they be in a short time?]

Ans: In the vocative!

[We laud the freedom of a people, but unless it leads them to the preservation of their power and self-preservation, it is but a chimera—a dream. Without power what is a nation or people?]

Without *power* they will certainly be *powerless*, *Ergo*, they ought to labor for the *preservation* of their *preservation!*

[Are people now-a-days so demented as to suppose they can retain their individual property without supporting their government? It overcome, what barrier or bulwark have they against any wrong or outrage?]

They are rather silly I believe; but what of that, Mr. Wiseacre. Do you deny to a *free people* the right to be *foolish!*

[Can there be any compromise with a malignant enemy short of conquest or surrender? Some people fancy by truckling to our unprincipled enemies they might make terms. Would it not result in the end *by* their subjugation and slavery? Who would surrender in a death struggle with an enemy a mortal weapon, except with life? So can any possession we now hold be given up.]

Some people are foolish enough to do (or write) any thing.

[It is necessary for the loyal people of this country to conquer or be conquered. Any division of the country is only the beginning of new wars. It is the interest of both the North and South to be one people, whether under a President, King, Emperor or Czar?

Which will you choose, Solomon—King, Emperor or Czar,?

[To try to work a machine twenty different ways, it would fail to work at all. So to try to carry on government in many ways, to suit every one's notions, would be an entire failure.]

Very likely. Government, I guess, is easiest tilled when planted in straight rows.

[If twenty millions of people, under a free government, (that is every one to do as they like,) cannot protect their country from the attacks of five millions under a harsh and tyrannic rule, then free government for general good had better give way to despotism.]

Fine Government that—Every one " a law unto himself."

[Tyranny is a blessing *in disguise* for a people who are too corrupt or too stupid to govern and defend themselves.]

Why *disguise* it, if it be a blessing?

[If there is ever to be planted alongside of us a nation of people delighting in war and fighting, the sooner American freemen shall excel in that line of business (as they have in most other things) the better—else they will be liable to be much imposed on.]

Oh yes! Every man should know his own trade.

[Our progenitors fancied free government and majorities could adjust human disputes. This system seems to have no effect with those who are determined to have their own way.]

Does the learned author know any nation governed by majorities?

[A *strong* government that gives people security, and thereby prosperity, is better than a *free* government that gives free license to mischief-makers and disturbers of the public peace, whose only desire is to thrive by anarchy and discord.]

Yes surely. Every one but the Czar, would rather have security *than* liberty[.]

[*All* man's comforts are obtained by *his* labor and industry; whoever interferes with or interrupts this labor and industry without just cause is a public enemy, not only to a few, but the whole world. They are of the same order of people as the former Algerenes.]

Not *all*, for some men live very comfortably on other men's labor.

[For a nation to be great and prosperous, her citizens should be brave and valiant, and her government firm and stable, so as to restrain the evil disposed from creating factions and disorder.]

What becomes of freedom then? if a man cant [*sic*] be factious?

[Let the people of this country always fight, not to do wrong to others, but to prevent others doing wrong to them. And when they do take up the sword let it be in earnest, by a firm and *united* people. In union there is happiness and prosperity. In disunion misery and ruin.]
[UNITED STATES, 1864.]   [C.]

But, suppose they a'nt *united*, what then? Wont [*sic*] you allow them to fight, just because they are *divided?* Why, being divided, they wont [*sic*] agree to any thing but to fight.

" It is a great misfortune to any gentleman not to have tolerably good sense " *Lincum Fidellius.* The astute writer of these apothe[g]ms is a man of *progress.* He has just discovered that all men *ought to be* wise and virtuous; and yet the Scriptures inform us that " there is none that *doeth good*, no, not one " [1]—and again—" he is a propitiation for our *sins*, and not ours only, but for sins of the whole world " [2]—and the Savior himself declares that he came to call " not the *righteous*, but *sinners*, to repentence [*sic*]." [3] Besides, in civil government, there are penal laws and penal magistrates. Why? Because they all know that " sin *will* abound " and that they *must* be prepared to restrain and punish it. " Free Government " what is it? Is not that government the *freeest*, which has the best laws, the best executed, for the restraint of *Freedom*—which is power?

This wise and virtuous author seems to have a high opinion of *majorities*, assuming that they have control in *Free Governments.* This is a great mistake, but very common. It is a cunning lie, invented by crafty demagogues, to gull the multiude. The majority of the People did never, even for a day, control the government of any country on the globe—no, not since the fall of Adam. In despotisms, the king's upper servants govern, and in governments *mis*called *free*, the selected *few* govern[.]

" *Constitutional guarantees* " This phrase is familiarily used by thousands of persons who have no definite idea of the thing they, thus vaguely, attempt to express. A *guarantee*, is never original and primitive, but always *relative*, and *collateral to something else.* It is a *warranty*, a *security*. The body of the constitution is not a *guarantee*, but simply a *law*, to be reverenced and obeyed, as such, and to be enforced, if need be, by all the sanctions provided in it or under it.

A guaran*tor* is not a ruler nor a judge; he cannot, at his own mere will, enforce the guarantee, against the will of the parties interested. If A. guarantee a debt due from B to C, he cannot insist upon paying the debt, in spite of the wish and protest of C, the creditor, and thus, constitute himself the *forced* creditor of B. C. may, if he will, forgive the debt to his friend B; or, in the

[1] *The Bible,* "Matthew," XIX, 17.
[2] *Ibid.,* " 1 John," II, 2.
[3] *Ibid.,* "Matthew," IX, 13.

mean while, he may have become the debtor of B. in a larger amount. And so, among nations: A guarantee by one nation for the fulfilment of a treaty between two other nations, does not make the guaran*tor* nation the severeign [*sic*], the judge, the arbiter, of the other two nations. Our *treaty guarantee* to *Venezuela* (now "The United States of Colombia")[4] of the possession and neutrality of the Isthmus of Panama, does not vest us with the sovereignty, nor any control whatever, over the Isthmus. A *guarantor*, has no independent power of his own, and no obligation (nor even right) to act in the premises, until properly called upon to *fulfil his guaranty*. He has only a *contingent duty*, and no *rights* at all in the subject matter.

Our treaty-guarantee of the Isthmus was a plain departure from the old and settled policy of the nation, against entangling our country in the affairs of other nations. The treaty was privately (not to say secretly) negotiated and ratified by the senate.[5] The treaty attracted little attention at the time, and that little was directed, chiefly to the better transit from sea to sea, for trade and travel, supposed to be secured by the treaty. The *guarantee* seems to have been kept studiously in the dark. Nobody seemed to rem[em]ber it, and very few ever knew it. A very good lawyer lately, expressed his astonishment, when I referred to the treaty, and thought that I must be mistaken as to its existence.

In fact, I had forgotten it myself, until Mr. Seward, Secretary of State, applied to me (as Atty. Genl.) for my opinion on a practical case arising under the treaty.

The case was about this—Spain, being at war with Peru, was desirous to convey troops and munitions across the isthmus, and would have done it, in spite of the weak power there; but Venezue[l]a (or the U. S. of Columbia [*sic*], demanded of us the fulfilment of *our guaranty*, and the Secy. of State wanted my opinion whether or no, we were bound to do it.

As much as I disliked the treaty, and strongly as I suspected the injustice and fraud of the motive which led it, I could do no less than tell Mr. Seward that there were no two ways about it—we must ful-

[4] Dec. 12, 1846, William M. Malloy, *Treaties, Conventions, International Acts, Protocols, and Agreements*, I, 302–314. Article XXXV deals with Panama. The Treaty was with New Granada, which then included Colombia and Panama. Venezuela had been a part of the federal state of Colombia from 1821 to 1829, but had then become a separate state. In 1861 New Granada had assumed the name, United States of Colombia.

[5] The archives of the State Department contain fourteen despatches and two enclosures on the negotiation of the treaty (Despatches, II, Colombia) and the *Senate Executive Journal* (VII [1845–1848], 191–193, 278, 423, 424) gives among other documents, the President's message transmitting the Treaty to the Senate. But no information is available concerning the debate on the Treaty or its rejection, as it was considered in executive session. There is no apparent reason, other than this statement of Mr. Bates to believe that the negotiation and the Senate debate were any more *secret* than is usual with such treaties.

fill our contract.[6] And I suppose that Mr. Seward so informed Mr. Tassara,[7] the Spanish Minister, for I heard no more of the affair, and the war soon dwindled to nothing, for Spain could not wage much of a war around the horn.

I remembered afterwards, that at the time of the treaty, I wrote an article against it, in the Mo. Rep[*ublican*].

[*A clipping which reads:*

"Not a single right of the State of New Jersey has been yielded, and not one of her citizens, during my administration, has been deprived of his liberty without due process of law."]

Gov Parker's[8] valedictory.

A noble boast, and if true, goes far to prove that New Jersey is the best governed state in the Union, and its people the best and happiest in the world.

In most othe[r] parts of the U. S. the rights of the States are abandoned, in despair, and the freedom of the people constantly outraged, by irresponsible power. Every where else, Provost Martials [*sic*], Military commissions and underlings of the Freedmen's Bureau do what they please, without any law to guide or restrain them.

Happy New Jersey!

[*A newspaper cutting announces the marriage of Hannah J. Duke, an Iowa giantess weighing 585 pounds to Mr. Rein, a German-American whose weight is about 140 pounds. The bridal party consisted of Siamese twins and other museum celebrities.*]

Miss Hannah is surely a fortunate woman. She had already grown great, by her own internal resources, and now, by foreign alliance, from the position of a simple *Duke*, she has come to Reign.

And Mr. *Rein* is hardly less fortunate; for, like a Pennsylvania millionaire, he has "struck ile," and now, he may retire from the labors of taming wild horses, and live at ease, in the unstinted enjoyment of the fat of the land.

[*A clipping giving a military directory of St. Louis, and another* "Concerning the Wilmington Failure and its Causes" *reprinted from the* Cincinnati Gazette.]

---

[6] "Neutrality of the Isthmus of Panama," August 18, 1864, *Official Opinions of the Attorneys-General of the United States*, XI, 67–69.

[7] *Supra*, Nov. 27, 1861, note 78.

[8] Joel Parker: New Jersey lawyer; state legislator, 1847–1851; prosecuting attorney, 1852–1857; opponent of coërcion of the South until the War came when he supported the Government, though he favored complete amnesty for Southerners in Reconstruction. He was Democratic governor of New Jersey, 1863–1866, 1872–1875.

CHAPTER VII

1865

[January 12.] *[A clipping from a Missouri newspaper giving "The Emancipation Ordinance. The votes for and against."]*

Jany: 12. This is the Missouri ordinance of emancipation,[1] with votes of the Convention, for and against—passed January 12. 1865.

Every effort is being made to give eclat to the occasion, and make the most of it, for partizan purposes. In this state, there was not the slightest need of such a measure, at this time, for the object—the abolition of slavery within the State—was already, substantially, accomplished.

The former convention, two years ago, had practically done the work, by its ordinance for *gradual* emancipation,[2] whose operation would be complete five years hence, in 1870. But the subject was persistently agitated, because it was a sensitive and passionate subject, to get a convention called,[3] under the false pretence that its only object was to erace [*sic*] the blot of slavery, but with the real object to remodel the whole constitution so as [to] secure the ascendency and permanency of the *Radical Party*, (if that may possibly be done) and, at all events, to secure to themselves, for the present at least, all the offices and emoluments of the state and all the patronage of the general government. This, I have no doubt they will do; but I am inclined to think that they will be so extreme as to draw their patriotism and wisdom into serious question. It is said, that they intend to vacate all the judg[e]ships and other offices of profit or honor, and give the appointment to their puppit [*sic*], Govr. Fletcher.[4]

I am credibly informed that they refuse to take any oath of office, not by accident or forgetfulness—for Switzler[5] of Boone, made a formal motion to take the oath, which was voted down.

[1] January 11, 1865, *Journal of the Missouri State Convention Held at the City of St. Louis, January 6—April 10, 1865,* 25–27.

[2] This ordinance had provided that on July 4, 1870, slavery should be declared abolished, slaves who were past forty years of age continuing in bondage for life, those under twelve until they were twenty-three, and all others until July 4, 1876. *Journal of the Missouri State Convention Held in Jefferson City, June, 1863,* Appendix, 15.

[3] The convention was called for January 6, 1865.

[4] Thomas C. Fletcher: lawyer; land agent; colonel in the Union Army, 1862–1864; Republican governor of Missouri, 1865–1869.

[5] *Supra,* April 7, 1860, note 57.

And now, it is generally believed, that they will not venture to submit their work to a vote of the People![6]

note. Since then, they have thought better of the *oath*—and took it, on motion of a *Rad*:[*ical*.]

Jany 14. [*Marginal Entry.*] This morning the newspapers inform us that the Tennessee convention has declared emancipation[.][7] It is much more proper there than here. For *there*, there might be need for it—here none. This Tennee. convention I understand is rather a meeting of volunteers than of the Peoples' deputies.

[*January 18.*] " Give 'em rope " &c—The [Missouri] convention, Jany. 17—One Mr. Newgent,[8] introduced the following—
"An Ordinance to protect citizens and soldiers [9]

["] Be it ordained by the People of the State of Missouri[,] in Convention assembled : That no soldier nor citizen *of this State* shall be liable to any action *by* the Civil Authorities, for any act heretofore done, or that may hereafter be done, *under*—the authority of *any military commander* [command] *in* this state.

Mo. Dem:[ocrat] Jany. 18./65

Mr. Bonham's [10] motion agst offering terms of Peace.[11]

Messrs. Gilstrap [12] and Switzler.[13] spoke against it at some length. Mr. Strong [14] offered an amendment, indo[r]sing the President's plan [15]—But before action on the amendment—Mr. Krekel [16] (Mr. Drake [17] in the chair first announcing the fall of Fort Fisher [18]) offered the following resolution—

---

[6] The constitution was submitted to a popular vote on June 6 in an election in which the drastic restrictions on voting of the *new* constitution were enforced. This limited electorate ratified it by a majority of only 1,862 out of 85,478 votes. The count was 43,670 to 41,808.

[7] A Tennessee convention had assembled at Nashville on January 9. It adopted an amendment very much like the Thirteenth Amendment to the Federal Constitution, immediately and completely abolishing slavery subject only to a popular vote on February 22.

[8] Andrew G. Newgent : Baptist preacher, 1836–1861 ; Cass County merchant, 1854–1861 ; colonel in the Union Army, 1861–1862 ; lieutenant-colonel of state militia, 1862–1864 ; Jacksonian Democrat, 1832–1861 ; Radical Republican throughout Reconstruction.

[9] *Journal of the Missouri State Convention Held at the City of St. Louis, January 6– April 10, 1865*, 41. The italics, punctuation, and capitalization are all inaccurately reproduced.

[10] David Bonham : farmer ; quartermaster in the Union Army, 1861–1865 ; county court judge, 1869–1870 ; state legislator for five terms beginning in 1879.

[11] *Ibid.*, 42.

[12] Abner L. Gilstrap, lawyer of Macon City, Missouri.

[13] *Supra*, April 7, 1860, note 57.

[14] George P. Strong, St. Louis lawyer.

[15] *Ibid.*, 42. Lincoln had declared in his annual message on December 6, 1864, that Southerners could " have peace at any moment by laying down their arms and submitting to the national authority under the constitution," leaving any questions which remained, to be adjusted " by the peaceful means of legislation, conference, courts, and votes, operating only in constitutional and lawful channels."

[16] *Supra*, June 6, 1860, note 46.

[17] *Supra*, Feb. 12, 1863, note 13.

[18] *Supra*, Oct. 1, 1864, note 97.

"*Resolved*, That this convention looks with apprehension to the preparation now making, on the part of the Southern States to return to their allegience[*sic*] as States, by separate State action, because of the claim of State Sovereignty *implied* therein, as well as the danger to the *cause of freedom* to the slaves yet held in bondage; and we call upon the Government [, the Congress,] and the People of the United States, not to expose the people of *the South* to that fearful ordeal of *gradual emancipation* through which the people of Missouri has [have] passed which has laid waste her fields, [and] expelled from their homes and caused the murder of many of her best citizens."!! [19]

Mr. D'Oench [20] submitted a proposition "for winding up the Missouri State Bank and branches" [21]—And urged the necessity of it "because of the disloyalty of many of those connected with the institutions affected." And then

Mr. Housmann,[22] offered a resolution to speed the Com[mitt]ee. on the *loyalty* of the members!! [23]—So they go.

Jan 22 Sunday— . . .

The convention now sitting evidently believes that it is composed of the true "High Mightinesses," and I suppose the members are ready to adopt Mayor Thomas' description, that—"Saving the power of God Almighty, they are omnipotent!"

Called, ostensibly, to enfranchise the slaves and to punish rebels, they assume to remodel the State and dispose of all its interests. They do not condescend to *amend* the constitution, but assume to make a new one—the *Declaration of Rights*. Now, a *Declaration* of rights is not an enactment of any new law. It is as it purports to be, simply, a recognition of existing rights,—natural, primitive, God-given—if indeed, there be a God!—Which seems to be an open question, freely debated in this learned, humane and virtuous convention! In debating whether an *atheist* might be a witness, several of the members gave their opinions freely [24]—Krekel did not *directly* deny the existence of God, but reserving his opinion on that point, insisted that govt. had no right to enquire of the witness, his opinion on that point! But several others, e. g. Owen [25] of Franklin and one Mr. Hughes [26] boldly said (like the fool mentioned in Scrip-

---

[19] *Journal of the Missouri State Convention Held at the City of St. Louis, January 6–April 10, 1865*, 42.

[20] William D'Oench, Prussian-born merchant of St. Louis.

[21] *Ibid.*, 42.

[22] George Husmann, German-born nurseryman of Hermann, Missouri.

[23] The speech of Mr. D'Oench and the resolution of Mr. Husmann do not appear in the *Journal*.

[24] This debate is not recorded in the *Journal*.

[25] James W. Owens, lawyer of Washington, Missouri.

[26] Benjamin F. Hughes, physician of Sedalia, Missouri.

ture[)] "there is no God!"[27] As these Godless men seem not to
have been called to any account, nor subjected to any denunciation, for
the blasphemy, and hence I infer that there are in the Convention,
atheists enough to make their party *respectable* (?)—*Strong* enough
at least, to be feared and courted. Even Messrs. Drake and Strong
(who are both elders of the Presbyterian church) took the discussion
very meekly, as a difference of opinion on some minor question of
policy!—not half so important as being "sound on the nigger."

One thing is certain, according to these *new lights*—We are not a
part of *Christendom*, and this nation of ours is not a *Christian
Nation!*

Note—wrote to J Hubley Ashton,[28] to the same effect.

Extract from Mde. D'Arblay's [29] (Miss Burney's) Jany/65 Diary.
vol 1. p 288—A. D. 1780—concerning *Chatterton*,[30] the greatest impostor, or the greatest genius of that age—Perhaps both.

"We had much talk among us, of *Chatterton*, and, as he was best
known in this part of the world, I attended particularly to the opinion of Dr. Harrington concerning him; and the more particularly
because he is uncommonly well versed in the Knowledge of English
antiquities; therefore was I much surprised to find it his opinion that
Chatterton was no imposter, and that the poems were authentic, and
Rowley's. Much indeed he said, they had been modernised in
the copies; not from design, but from the difficulty which attended
reading the old manuscript—a difficulty which the genius of Chatterton urged him not to confess but to redress. A book however, is
now publishing that is entirely to clear up this so long-disputed and
very mysterious affair, by *Dr. Mills, Dean* of *Exeter*."

[*A clipping headed "Everybody's Words" giving a long list of
familiar quotations, and another headed "Things Worth Knowing
about Horses" listing a number of books on the subject.*]

[*A newspaper clipping which gives an extract from a letter of
General W. T. Sherman written on January 8, 1865.*][31]

That is the true, clean doctrine of the constitution and the law.
There is no such thing as re-*construction*—The idea is seised
upon by radical dema[go]gues only to revolutionize particular
States, under the pretense of resisting attempted revolution! In-

---

[27] *The Bible,* "Psalms," XIV, 1; LIII, 1.

[28] *Supra,* Feb. 5, 1862, note 52.

[29] Frances Burney D'Arblay, 1752–1840, was an English novelist who, when young, was
a friend of Dr. Samuel Johnson.

[30] Thomas Chatterton, 1852–1870, English poet who wrote much of his verse under the
name of Thomas Rowley, a fabrication of his own, who he claimed had been a Bristol
priest and poet of the Fifteenth Century whose work he had found in manuscript. At
seventeen Chatterton committed suicide.

[31] The clipping gives only the latter part of the fourth paragraph of the letter. Mr.
Bates later inserts the whole letter in the diary. *Infra,* Sept. 18, 1865.

surrection and rebellion do not put a State out of the Union. And this [is] not only demonstrably true, as a principle, but declared and practically acted out, by the Federal Govt. and every separate branch thereof (see Krekel's resolution at p. 155—Jan 17) [.]

[*Later Addition.*] And see "Genl. Sherman's official account of his great March through Georgia and the Carolinas "[.]

[*A clipping giving the members of the Supreme Court and the division of circuits among them in January, 1865.*]

Jan 25 Wednesday—With Sarah [32] and Matilda, attended the marriage of *John Dillon*—son of P. M.—and *Blanche Vallé*—daughter of Nere—at the R.[oman] C.[atholic] Cathedral—and the reception at Mrs. Henry Chouteau [33]—grand mother of the bride.

All unlooked for, *Coalter* arrived this morning[.] He is on *leave* for 20 days (which may be extended 10). He came by West point, to see Woodson—W.[oodson] has passed his examination and is, for the present, safe. C.[oalter] looks in perfect health, and thinks that nothing will be done, towards the taking of Richmond, until more is done further south. ([*Note.*] This proved literally true—Sherman's march was part of the plan.) [34]

Note. Saturday the 28th. Coalter went up with Barton and returned to St. Louis, with Fred: Hatcher. all well.

Jan 27, Friday. This day, Barton concluded a bargain for a dwelling place for us. It is a lot of about 100 feet front, on the South east corner of Morgan Street and Leffingwell Avenue: A very eligible place with a good house, large enough for our family, and arranged with many conveniences, and now in good order.

There is ground enough for a garden as large as I am able to cultivate; and the house affords a good room for my Library and Study.

The place costs $23.000, more than I am able to pay, by my own means, but the generous, filial piety of Barton makes all easy on that score. We pay down $18.000, and assume to pay off an incumbrance of $5000.

<Note. [*January 31.*] The deed executed Jany 30. and $18.000 *paid*, and $5000, (secured to Mr. Todd, by deed of trust—) assumed by me—of course including the interest notes. The place is ensured

---

[32] Sarah Woodson Bates, Julian's wife.

[33] Henry Chouteau: cousin of Pierre Chouteau (*supra*, April 9, 1860, note 68); descendant of an early fur-trader; and member of one of the oldest and wealthiest families of Missouri. He had been clerk of the County Court and recorder of St. Louis County, 1827–1842, and head of Chouteau and Vallé, sugar, coffee, and produce merchants, from 1842 until his death in 1855.

[34] Sherman had captured Savannah on December 22. He began to march northward on February 1 spreading destruction as he went. He entered Columbia, South Carolina, on February 17, and was in North Carolina when Lee surrendered in April.

for $8000—$5000 in the Home Mutual and $3000 in the Mound City Ins:[urance] Co., and the policies are assigned to me.[>]

To day, went to see our new place. The garden ground is in fine order, well enclosed, manured and spaded: a good many fruit and shade trees planted, and among them 8 pears and 6 peach—all select.

Feb 2. (*Thursday*). . . . Coalter and Matilda started, early this morning, [for Dardenne,[35]] expecting to return monday.

[*A newspaper slip headed* " *Senate—Evening Session. Movement for a New Convention.*"]

The Mo. Democrat of this day contains a matter likely to have a marked effect upon the proceedings of our radical and *rabid* Convention. In the State senate a resolution has been offered—and passed 18 to 2—requiring a com[mitt]ee. to consider the propriety of calling *another Convention!* [36] to amend the constitution of the State! The measure was introduced by senator Müller [37] and sustained, in warm speeches by several—i. a. *Moench* [38] and Anderson [39]—

The existing convention was openly denounced, as impudent usurpers, assuming unlimited poweres [*sic*] over every thing in the State, and meddling with matters, never intended to be submitted to [t]hem.

It is pleasant to hear them denounced by such tran[s]cendental radicals as Moench, and such time-serving demagogues as Anderson. It is a good sign, and good may come of it.

[*A clipping containing boasts of the Missouri Convention that it is the master of the Legislature and could even abolish it.*]

Judge Moody [40] told me today that Mr. Krekel [41] has matured a plan, and is zealously pushing it, for a complete reform of our judiciary system viz—elect Judges of the Sup[rem]e. C[our]t., by popular vote, and give to them (the Supreme Judges!) the election of all the Circuit Judges! Poor Krekel!—"the higher a bear climbs the plainer he shews his tail—"

---

[35] *Supra*, July 30, 1859, note 61.

[36] A Missouri state convention controlled by Radicals had assembled in St. Louis on January 6 and continued sitting until April 10.

[37] Madison Miller: soldier in the Mexican War; then a resident of Carondelet, Missouri, and president of the St. Louis and Iron Mountain Railroad; colonel of volunteers captured at Shiloh; now a state senator.

[38] Frederick Muench: German-born Missouri farmer; writer on agricultural subjects; contributor to the *American Agriculturalist*; state senator, 1861–1865.

[39] *Supra*, June 22, 1860, note 63.

[40] James G. Moody: St. Louis lawyer; judge of the St. Louis Circuit Court; opponent of the Radical Constitution of 1865. He was finally removed from office by the Legislature in 1866 for refusal to apply the test oath to jurors.

[41] *Supra*, June 6, 1860, note 46.

The Mo. Democrat of Feb 2. also contains the long letter of Mr. Blow (H. T.) [42] in favor of the recognition of Arkansas,[43] with her present organization[.]

It is praised for ability, which I do not find in it; and yet I do not think that Mr. Blow could have written it—If he *could*, it would have taken the form of a *speech* in the House. In the form of a *letter*, he could easily get some Arkansas man to do it for him. And I have no doubt that, in substance, it is all the work of another hand.

Feb 3 Friday, Judge Henry Clover [44] has made a speech in the Convention *against* negro suffrage. Whether it be that Mr. Clover is beginning to wake up, a little, to common sense, or that the German element [45] is beginning to fear that negro[e]s and dutchmen are like to be antagonists, I cannot say; but whatever the motive, the fact may be of some use, in disabusing the vulgar mind in regard to the absurd theory of the exact equality of men.

This morning early, the clouds dispersed, and we have a bright and warm forenoon. To day Nancy begins to collect our goods at the new house[.]

[*February 9.*] We got possession of the House, bo[ugh]t. of J. L. Garrison, monday, Feb: 6—Nancy and Eliza Woodson slept there, and next day—tuesday the 7th. [the family] moved to the place, and slep[t] there that night. Tuesday and wednesday were very cold, so that the getting in of furniture and fixing, was much retarded.

Monday night, Tilly and Coalter returned from Dardenne,[46] bringing Onward.

Feb 9 Thursday. Dick is expected down today, bringing his wife and child. They would come *here* certainly, but for the supposed necessity of having *Charley F.* in care of *Mammy*, who is at Julian's.

. . .

On Monday *Feb 6* came into my service, as House servant, and man of all work [   ]. He seems to be a practised servant (waited on both Gov Gamble [47] and Mr. Coalter,[48] in their last illness) was a

---

[42] *Supra*, Sept. 20, 1859, note 95.

[43] A loyal government had been organized in Arkansas, and slavery abolished, the Confederate debt repudiated, and the ordinance of secession declared null, by a Convention which met at Little Rock in January, 1864.

[44] A St. Louis lawyer who had come from New York City in 1844; city attorney, 1849; circuit attorney, 1852–1856; state legislator, 1856; judge of the County Criminal Court, 1856–1863; city counselor, 1863–1865. Originally a Democrat, he had become a Republican in 1856, and was author of the "Ousting Ordinance" in this Convention.

[45] The Germans were generally Radical Republicans, particularly extreme on the negro question.

[46] *Supra*, July 30, 1859, note 61.

[47] *Supra*, July 23, 1859, note 39.

[48] Mrs. Bates's father, David Coalter.

slave at Vicksburgh, when captured by Grant, and thereby made free. He is serving this month on trial—nothing yet said about the amt. of wages.

He is a bright mulatto, about 30, I think[.]

Note. He left, of his own accord, Monday, March 6. Paid him $25.

Feb 12, sunday. Beautiful, moderate weather, for the three days. Julian and Dick, with their wives and children, and Coalter and Onward dined with us today. I am quite unwell, having taken a fresh cold.

I hear no news and have seen no newspapers, for several days.

Feb 13 Monday. Coalter started early this morning, returning to the army of the Potomac.

[February] 16 Thursday. Dick started early this morning, returning to the Navy, at Cairo.

[A clipping giving a dispatch from Hilton Head,[49] which tells of the "burning of the mansion in which John C. Calhoun was born," and in which he had lived until within four years of his death.[50]]

And such it seems are the materials which compose our history, and such the freedom of a lying press!

John C. Calhoun never lived at "the southern extremity of Hilton Head island" nor [with]in 100 miles of it.

He lived at his own mountain home, in the upper part of So: Carolina[.]

The bold ignorance of the writer is inexcusable. he ought to have known better, for Calhoun habitually dated his writings at *Fort Hill,* his plantation and residence, in the mountains of South Carolina.

[A clipping publishing a " Letter from the Chief of the Cherokee Nation " on " The Cherokee Indians and the War."]

Wilmington N.[orth] C[arolina].

Feb 24. The papers of today announce that Wilmington is in possession of our troops [51]—No particulars are given.

Feb 24. Came *Edward Bredell,*[52] to ask advice about a curious Doc[umen]t.—a military assessment for $1000. Genl. T. Ewings [53]

---

[49] A South Carolina village on the sea-coast seventeen miles south of Beaufort.

[50] Calhoun did die in 1850, but he had always lived in the up-country.

[51] The fall of Fort Fisher on January 16 had permitted a close blockade of Wilmington (*supra,* Oct. 1, 1864, note 97). That city itself was captured by General Schofield (*supra,* May 30, 1863, note 32) on February 22. The news did not appear in the St. Louis papers until February 25.

[52] St. Louis merchant, mine operator, glass manufacturer, president of the school board.

[53] *Supra,* Feb. 11, 1864, note 26.

[*sic*] order of Feb 4/65—levying a tax on rebels and rebel sym[p]a-thisers, for the support of refugees and contrabands.

I gave him a note, stating that the proceeding is illegal and void; and advising him to appeal to Gen Pope.[54]

Note—It was by the order of this same Genl. *Tom Ewing*, that several of the western counties of Mo. were, laid waste! <see back, page 150 [November 22, 1864]—Gen Hugh Ewing in K.y.>

[*A newspaper account of the " Thirty-eighth Day " of " The State Convention."*]

Feby 24. The convention[55] seems to be running the same career as the French *Legislative Assembly*, and The *Turners' Hall*[56] begins to assume the powers of the *Jacobin Club.*

There is this difference however, between the impudent upstarts of the French Assembly and our impudent upstarts—The French had at least sincerity, courage and zeal, with some touch of knowledge and science; but ours are, for the most part, mere igno-ramusses [*sic*], destitute alike, of sincerity, zeal, courage and know-ledge. They are only playing an impudent game of *bluff*, against what they believe to be the cowardly impotence of their adversaries.

Such men are the easiest of all, to be *bluffed* off, if met with any show of sense and courage.

Mr. St. Gem[57] can never act the part (nor die the death) of his prototype, *St. Just*,[58] for he lacks all the high qualities of that *moral tiger*—sense, courage and self-devotion to his cause, howev[e]r bad.

Mr. St. Gem freely spouts at the *Jacobin Club* (The Turners' Hall); boldly urges the violent suppression of the *usurpers*, his own colleagues; but, as soon as called to account in the Convention, for his insolent talk, he, incontenently [*sic*], *caves in*—To be sure, he *did* use the naughty words—but he did not mean any harm!—not he!—he only swaggered about the powder-house, flourishing a flaming torch, only to show how big and bold a man he was—But he had no notion of blowing up the concern—He only wanted to curry favor with the Jacobins!

And so they let him off. But whether because they were afraid to punish him, or because they thought him *doli non capax*, does not yet appear.

---

[54] *Supra*, March 15, 1862, note 33.

[55] The Missouri Constitutional Convention which had convened in St. Louis on January 6.

[56] The Turnhalle of the St. Louis Turnverein, the local branch of the Nord Ameri-kanischer Turnerbund which spread organized gymnastics through America. The mem-bers of the gymnastic society were locally called " Turners " and in their hall the Con-vention met.

[57] Gustavus St. Gem, merchant of Ste. Genevieve, Missouri.

[58] Relentless revolutionist, organizer of the Terror against all moderates, called the " St. John of the Messiah of the People." He was guillotined with Robespierre on July 28, 1794, in the rising against his terrorism.

[*A newspaper paragraph on "The new anti-slavery rule in the Methodist Discipline."*]

New—It is a mistake to say that the anti-slavery rule, in the Methodist discipline is *new*. It is as old as the first little book of discipline—published in the very words of *Wesley* [59]—" What shall be done for the exterpation [*sic*] of the *sin* of Slavery? "

The title of the little book is—" The Doctrines and Discipline of the Methodist Episcopal Church "—Printed at Cincinnati, in 1840. And vouched for by six of the most eminent Divines, whose names are signed to the address to the members—viz—Robert R. Roberts,[60] Joshua Soule,[61] Elijah Hedding,[62] James. O. Andrew,[63] Beverly Waugh [64] and Thomas. A. Morris [65]—All of them, I think, then or since, Bishops. <See [Part Second] Section X page 195, for the title *Of Slavery*>

—" it is impossible to allay *with arguments*, either the animosities or the fears of parties."

So says Monsr. *Thiers*,[66] in his History of the French Revolution, Vol 1. p 216. And I have always found it so; and indeed, upon the soundest principles of logic, it *must* be so. For, it were absurd to hope to change, by logical argument, opinions adopted in spite of sense and reason. The only way to correct an obstinate fool, is to let him suffer the consequences of his folly.

[*An editorial from the* Missouri Democrat *of February 24, 1865, on " Revision of the laws."*]

I hope the result may show that the gentlemen named are as well fitted for the duties assigned them,[67] as the Mo. Dem[ocrat] supposes. I do not know the gentlemen well enough to enable me to pass any satisfactory judgment, in advance. But I am sure that the editor

---

[59] John Wesley, 1703–1791, founder of Methodism, was originally an Anglican clergyman who had traveled throughout Britain as an itinerant preacher and had lived for a time in Georgia where he saw slavery at close range.

[60] Minister in the Baltimore Conference, 1802–1816; pioneer-bishop in Indiana, 1816–1843.

[61] Minister in the New England Conference, 1799–1816, then in New York and Baltimore, 1820–1824; Methodist Book Concern agent, 1816–1820; bishop in Ohio, 1824–1842; bishop of the Southern Methodist Church in Tennessee, 1844–1854.

[62] Circuit-riding minister of the New York and New England Conferences, 1801–1824; anti-abolitionist bishop, 1824–1852.

[63] Minister in Georgia and the Carolinas, 1812–1832; bishop, 1832–1866. It was over the ownership of slaves by Andrew's second wife that the Methodist Church split into a Northern and a Southern communion in 1844.

[64] Minister in the Baltimore Conference, 1809–1828; agent of the Methodist Book Concern, 1828–1836; bishop, 1836–1858.

[65] Minister in the Ohio Conference, 1814–1834; editor of the *Western Christian Advocate*, 1834–1836; bishop in Ohio, 1836–1872.

[66] M. J. L. Adolphe Thiers, 1797–1877; Liberal cabinet minister in France, 1832–1836, 1840; President of France, 1871–1873; historian. Bates used the third American edition of his *History of the French Revolution*, 4 vols., translated by Frederick Shoberl (Carey and Hart, Philadelphia, 1842).

[67] The Legislature had appointed a committee of three to carry out the constitutionally required decennial revision of the laws. The members were C. C. Simmons, a St. Louis lawyer, Mr. Currier, also of St. Louis, and Walter Lovelace, Speaker of the House.

of the Democrat has no correct idea of the degree of learning and character of mind and habits suitable for the task.

As far as I can see, by this publication, the Genl. Assembly does not intend (as has been the habit) to re-enact the revised laws, but only to have the statutes collated and arranged, by a committee.

Extract of Thiers' Hist:[ory of the] French Rev:[olution, I, 229.]

" The court then conceived a hope—for people cannot help forming hopes, even in the most gloomy conjunctures [conjectures]—[,] that Louis XVI, by taking *incapable* and *rediculous* [*sic*] demagogues (for ministers)[,] would ruin the reputation of the party from which he should have selected them." The hope proved fallacious at that time, in France; [68] and I find myself guilt yoft he folloy of repeating the same idle hopes, about the promotion of certain heartless and brainless Radicals; forgetting that, while the *fool-fever* still rages in the multitude, it is sure to be acc[o]unted a wicked folly, to be *virtuous* and *wise.*

Thiers thus, grap[h]ically, depicts *Dumouriez* [69]

" He had neither the dignity of a profound conviction, nor the pride of a despotic will, and he could command none but soldiers. If, with his genius, he [had] possessed the passions of a *Mirabeau*[,] or the resolution of a *Cromwell*, or merely the dogmatism of a *Robespierre*, he might have directed the course of the Revolution, and France."

Hist French Rev: vol 1. p. [229–]230.

" Parties always put *persons* in the place of *circumstances*, that they may throw upon some one the blame of the disasters which befal[l] them." [70]

Ib. p. 244.

Feb 26 Sunday . . .

Mr. Nichols, (an Englishman) (a job carpenter[)] is still working for us—chiefly under Nancy's direction—He is putting up bookshelves and fixing chests and boxes for my *Study;* and my books and papers are ready, on the spot, to be arranged; and with Matilda's valuable help, this will not be a great labor.

---

[68] This was in 1792 when Louis had dismissed Narbonne and had been forced by the Assembly to part with the rest of his moderate ministers, and then had to accept a ministry of Girondists who sought more strictly to limit the monarchy though they had not yet become republicans.

[69] Charles F. du P. Dumouriez, 1739–1823 : soldier Girondist in the French Revolution ; minister of Foreign Affairs (1792) who declared war on Austria and tried to bring Louis XVI and the Assembly together under the Constitution. Later he became a Revolutionary general but fled to the enemy in 1793 to escape being guillotined for defeat and moderate views.

[70] In these four quotations, the punctuation and capitalization are inaccurate ; the italics and the parenthetical phrase are Mr. Bates's.

And thus, in a very short time, I hope to have a pleasant retreat, where, undisturbed by outward cares, I can read, write and ruminate, controlled only by my own free propensities. And then—if I can escape pecuniary difficulties (of which I have a cheering hope, mainly thro' Barton's practical wisdom and generous devotion) my position will be very fortunate—almost realizing the poet's dream of a happy old age—

"Ease and alternate labo[u]r, useful life,
    Progressive virtue[,] and approving Heaven[!]."[71]

Appropos [*sic*] of work. Several of my friends are urging me to turn author. They insist upon my compiling a book, to consist of memoirs of myself and the times; notices of individuals and of particular events, correspondence, &c. And some of them (perhaps flattering my vanity) express the decided opinion, that such a work, besides being useful to the public, might be made profitable to the writer.

I am not yet resolved upon the subject. For some years past, I have been trying to *study myself*, and to form a just and cool judgment of my own capabilities; well knowing that a man who cannot make a reasonably fair estimate of his own faculties, is too partial to pass a just judgment upon the faculties and powers of other men. By that course of self-examination, I am clearly convinced that I am not qualified to write a general History. *That* requires an accurate survey of the whole field of action, a precise knowledge of details, and a mind, so practiced as to weave each one into its appropriate place, so as to harmonize with the general whole, and exert its proper influence upon the final result.

But I think that I am reasonably well qualified to state a principle, in accurate terms, and maintain it by logical argument; and to pass judgment upon a man or a measure, and support it with such power as the facts of the case and the principles involved in it, may warrant.

I once had a strong desire to write sketches of some of the earlier inhabitants of Missouri. But I have never had the leisure. Some of them were "men of mark" and character, whose superiors, (in intelligence, integrity and manhood) have not yet appeared among us. If I write at all, for the press, *they* will not be forgotten.

It is, I believe, a fact, now avouched by history, that, in all the States of the West, there were, among the first settlers, (who organized society and gave tone and character to the infant community) men whose superiors have not yet been found among their successors, albeit those successors have every apparent advantage,

---

[71] James Thomson (1700–1748), *The Seasons. Spring.*

in numbers, wealth, and all the means and appliances of education
and general advancement in Art, Science and taste.

Feb 27 Monday. . . .

Feby. 28 tuesday morning—Comes my grand-son, *Onward Bates*
who arrived in town last night, with his aunt Sarah—Julian's wife.
He comes, by previous arrangement of his father (Barton Bates), to
enter himself *Apprentice to Gerard. B. Allen* [72] (Allen & Filley) to
learn the trade of a *Machinist* [*sic*]. He is a very ingenuous youth,
of good, solid parts: Not brilliant, but uncommonly heedful and *apt
to learn*, and retentive of all he learns. He is well advanced, for a
boy of 15—Has read more than most lads (perhaps without much
method)—Is, as I hear, pretty well versed in Geography, Grammar,
Arithmetic and Algebra—Knows a little Latin, and perhaps a smat-
tering of German. In temper, he is docile and tractable, and in
manners, respectful, orderly and moral—Yet of a firm and independent character of mind.

I have high hopes that he will avail himself of all his opportunities, and make himself a man of whom his near kindred may be
proud.

He will live with us—that is, spend his nights and spare time at our
house. And so, we hope to be able to exercise a fair degree of care
over his habits and associations[.]

[*A newsaper clipping giving the text of "An act to prevent officers of the army and navy . . . from interfering in elections in the
States."*]

Better late than never—

The Radical demogogues have carried elections as the[y] please,
in Maryland, Missouri, and else where, by military means, and perhaps now think that the[y] no longer need military force to secure
their ascendency. Whether that be the reason for passing this
law; or whether they be "pricked in their conscience" and are
ashamed of their former sins in this way—in short, whatever be
the cause, I am glad of the *fact*. It is clear now, that *military
interference* in elections, *is a crime* punishable by law.

In reading anew, the History of the French Revolution,[73] and
in contemplating, with painful doubts and fears, the present critical
condition of our own country, I am more than ever, convinced of the
truth of an old thought of mine (often expressed, and in various
forms)—viz—A *Republic* whose Officers have power to disregard
the law, and to violate the rights and liberties of individuals, with-

---

[72] Irish-born St. Louis contractor, lumber miller, iron manufacturer, insurance company
president, bank director, vice-president of the North Missouri Railroad, and director of
steamship companies.

[73] He was at this time reading Thiers's *French Revolution*.

out the fear of legal punishment, is a far worse Government than any hereditary, absolute monarchy, can be. Because, although both are despotic, and therefore to be feared and guarded against, yet such a Republic is a universal, permiating [*sic*] tyranny. It is *Despotism multiplied by Republican forms.* And we are taught by history, that the single-handed despotism of Pissistratus [Peisistratus] [74] was not half so injurious to the people of Athens, as the multiplied oppressions of the Thirty Tyrants.[75]

March 1. . . . After several days confinement to the house, I was out last afternoon, on a necessary errand—found the streets a *slush* of mud—Came home, with cold feet and aches all over—and am very unwell today.

By reason of my ill health lately, and the want of a convenient place to read and write (which last, I hope will be reformed in a few days, and my study put in right order) my correspondence has been sadly neglected. Some letters I *owe*, and some others I had special reasons for wishing to write. I owe letters to Mr. Newton,[76] Com[mis]s[ione]r. of Agricultural Dept. and to Mr. Dennison, Post Master Genl.—And I ought to write to the President, to T. J. Coffey,[77] to Richd. H. Dana,[78] Mr. Forbes and one or two others at Boston—to Dr. Lieber[79] and Hiram Ketchum,[80] at New York and divers others, scattered over the land.

[*Newspaper accounts of the proceedings of the forty-second and forty-third days in the Missouri State Convention.*]

When this convention first met, it had an unqu[e]stioning conceit of its own omnipotence. In stolid egotism, it did not doubt that it held in its hand, the State and all its rights and interests, to be disposed of at its own will and pleasure. And as all the members (except a timid and helpless few) were "free of the craft of Radicals," they expected that the party could act with unanimity, and effectually carry out the *Secret* object of the convention—which was, to consolidate the power of the *Radicals*, and exclude all others from office and honors—Even if they had been right, in the impudent assumption of of [*sic*] unlimited power, still, there were inherent defects which would ensure their defeat and degradation, if opposed by any reasonable degree of sense and prudence:

---

[74] Athenian statesman who succeeded in ruling Athens under a wise and benevolent dictatorship during most of the period from 561 to 527, B. C.

[75] The government set up by Lysander in Athens in 404 at the close of the Peloponnesian War was known as that of "The Thirty Tyrants."

[76] *Supra*, Jan. 5, 1862, note 12.

[77] *Supra*, March 5, 1860, note 18.

[78] *Supra*, Feb. 26, 1863, note 48.

[79] See *supra*, April 5, 1862, note 62.

[80] See *supra*, April 20, 1859, note 19

1. The essential mode of a *radical*—without which he cannot exist—is that he is always dealing with the *root*, the *foundation*, of Society—always appealing to the original source of power—always wielding the sovereign majesty and irresistable [*sic*] force of the People. That power can, at pleasure, abrogate all former laws and constitutions—And so, constitutions and laws are no obstacles to *radicals*. They sweep them out of the way, as they do all other *obsolete institutions* of human society. They do not condescend to *amend* old systems, but think it easier and better to *destroy* them, and *make* new ones, in their stead! *Conservatism* is their horror; and they consider it an evidence of weakness, a confession of their own inferiority, to *conserve* any thing, not originated by themselves. Their principles, then, (if they have any) *must* lead to wrangling and rivalry among themselves—and finally, to anarchy.

2. This particular convention was required by no legal or political necessity. The subject was started and agitated purely as a party measure, to consolidate and continue the Radicals in power. The false pretence, for calling it into being, was to emancipate the slaves and punish the rebels. (*Note.* Mr. Moench [Muench] [81] and other prominent radicals, publicly declare this to be the *only* motive for the convention; and censured the convention severely, for presuming to go into a general change of the constitution[.]) This false pretence is simply absurd. For as to emancipation, *it* was already accomplished, by the ordinance of the former convention.[82] And as to punishing rebls [*sic*], that is foreign to the office of a Convention—which consists only in the *making* of the fundamental law, and not in the administration of penal justice. A convention is not a *court of correction*. But they have no idea of either the divisions or the limits of power.

3. The convention is composed of inferior materials. There is not a man in it, of high and general reputation for talents or learning or virtue; and therefore, there is no acknowledged leader. And hence, every little upstart *claims to be a leader*, and hopes to win something, by an *odd trick*. And, in this way, a great variety of wild and foolish propositions are put forward, not as parts of any system, but as mere gambling experiments in radical politics. And this state of things cannot but engender mutual suspicions and personal rivalries. And we see now, that, almost every day, the debates consist, mainly of personal wrangling—charges and recriminations.

But the members seem to have lowered their tone a good deal, since the first meeting. They begin to doubt their omnipotence—They

[81] *Supra*, Feb. 2, 1865, note 38.
[82] *Supra*, Jan. 12, 1865, note 2.

begin to fear one another *within*, and the clubs and factions *without*—*Drake*[83] accuses a clique *within* of a plot to defeat the Bill of rights—*Krakel* [Krekel][84] charges another clique of a conspiracy to withhold the new constitution from the judgement of the People. *Note.* The demagogue Anderson,[85] of Pike—M.[ember of the] a.[ssembly] and M.[ember of] C[ongress] elect—(in *virtuous* indignation at the convention, for treading upon the toes of the Assembly) has been heard to declare that the Convention ought to be deposed by *military power.* And one of its own members—Mr. St. Gem[86] of Ste. Genevieve—in [a] public speech, at the *Jacobin Club*, i. e. The Turners' Hall[87] urged the dispersion of the usurpers, by mob violence !

But, fortunately, the Convention has no character or reputation sufficient to enable it to control public opinion, and thus, act out its own bad designs; and [it] is deficient in that personal courage which alone can inspire a wholesome fear in adversaries generally, and ensure the power necessary to punish those who openly contemn and assail it. By tricks and subterfuges, the Convention may cheat us into much evil. But it has not the nerve to attempt domination, by open violence. It has not even the vim to protect itself: A motion was indeed made, to expel St. Gem, for his factious violence among the Jacobins, but the hearts of the members failed. They quailed before a refractory member and the mob that backed him; and durst not attempt to punish an offender who attempted the life of the convention, by violence !

The convention is an *annoyance* only, not a serious evil, to be dreaded for its caprices, or *respected* for its power. And I should not be surprised, if, in less than a year, it should be deemed a popular reproach, to be called *a member of that convention.*

[*Marginal Note.*] March 3. /65 Pd. Bill of Bridge, Beach & Co. for stove = $23.65[.]

March 3d. Last night, called to see me Messrs. D. R. Garrison[88] and Col A. R. Easton,[89] and spent some hours pleasantly.

Also, Barton Bates came in, unexpectedly, about 10 p. m—having come down hastily, on business, for a few days.

. . .

[83] *Supra*, Feb. 12, 1863, note 13.

[84] *Supra*, June 6, 1860, note 46.

[85] *Supra*, June 22, 1860, note 63.

[86] *Supra*, Feb. 24, 1865, note 57.

[87] *Supra*, Feb. 24, 1865, note 56.

[88] Daniel R. Garrison : St. Louis manufacturer of steam machinery ; vice-president and general manager of the Missouri Pacific Railroad ; later, a manufacturer of Bessemer steel.

[89] Alton R. Easton : officer in the Mexican War ; assistant treasurer of the United States, 1853 ; judge of the County Court, 1860–1864 ; inspector-general of Missouri, 1861–1864 ; later, assessor of internal revenue and pension agent under President Grant.

March 4 Saturday—Inauguration day—heralded for celebration with great pomp, in New York and other places; and I hear that considerable efforts at display will be made in this city. I cannot go out to day, being still confined to the house, by serious sickness.

March 4, Saturday. I am still confined at home. Inauguration day. There seems to have been some effort (beginning in N. York to awaken enthusiasm, by military, and other, displays.

In this city, I understand, the display was somewhat imposing—procession, music—and the various societies marching through the mud, under their respective flags—But cold and inanimate. The day of enthusiasm is past; and now I see nothing active in St Louis politics, but the struggle (languidly continued) to secure the *spoils* of the *Radicals*.

The newspapers are especially dull, of late, and cautiously reticent—as if wholly unresolved what grounds to take on new questions, as they arise, and afraid to give offence to somebody who may be strong enough to do mischief.

I am thoroughly disgusted with the imbecile cowardice of the St Louis press—that part of it at least, which pretends to have some lingering respect for law, truth and conservatism! Their highest effort, in the way of politics, is an occasional joke—an awkward attempt to ridicule some particular man or clique. But they do not venture to make a serious charge against any public offender—nor to assert and maintain any settled doctrine of the government—nor to discus[s], calmly, any good principle, now daily assailed by the demagogues. <Oct 23d. 1865. Some of them have altered a good deal, for the better[.]>

If there were any press here, in whose conductors I had the slightest confidence, I would venture before the public, upon several questions which seem to me of much moment, and which I believe would interest the people. But I know of no Journalist here of any enlarged views of public law, or depth of knowledge or boldness of spirit, to recognize a true principle and efficiently maintain it.

[*A newspaper clipping containing a rhymed satire on Drake's Plantation Bitters.*]

To Dr. Drake

Dear Doctor, your bitters are good,
    And I think it no hardship to take 'em;
And so would your rhimes, if you could
    Invent a good *recipe*, to make 'em.
There's your coz: Charles D. who rehearses
    His Dullness, 'til all are in titters,
Can[']t for life, manufacture such verses,
    Nor hold a light to your Plantation Bitters.

March 7. This day Julia and I gave receipts, in duplicate (the written date I think, is anterior) to *Barton Bates* Ex[ecut]or of *John D. Coalter*, for $15.000, the [amount] of legacy of J. D. C[oalter] to J.[ulia] D. B.[ates]. This to square the a/c of the legacy, before the Probate Court.

Part of this sum consists of Gas Light Bonds, bearing interest, at 10 pr. ct—with coupons—say $97.

Another part—say $4500—is in gold, yet to be exchanged[.]

Barton is, in fact, largely in advance—e. g. He paid $18.000, on the house we live in.

Robespierre. Mignet [90] says of him (see note in Thiers' Hist[ory of the] Fr:[ench] Rev:[olution] Vol 1. p. 434)
" This man, whose talents were but of the [an] ordinary kind, and whose disposition was vain owed to his *inferiority* his late *appearance* on the stage, which, *in revolutions*, is always a great advantage. It is a trite old saying that " those who sow revolutions seldom live to reap the harvest "—" Had Timri peace, that slew his master? " . . . He was a living proof that[,] in civil troubles, obstinate mediocrity is more powerful than the irregularity of genius.[91] It is not only in *civil troubles* but in all the affairs of life, that *obstinate mediocrity* triumphs over *irregular genius*, and enjoys the fruits of victory. Genius may sometimes win success, by a *coup de main*—a lucky hit. But this is the exception. The rule is the other way. God's moral government of the world has ordained the law of prosperity—i. e. that labor, patience, courage, constant attention to the common things of life, shall surmount all obstacles, subdue all opponents, and rule the world.["]

Allison [92] says of the Girondins [93]—" They were too hono[u]rable to believe in the wickedness of their opponents; too scrupulous to adopt the means [requisite] to crush them." [94]—*vide* conservatives and radicals, at Home.

[*A clipping giving the derivation of certain "Americanisms".*]

? It is more nearly true as to *Creek* (a small river) than the rest. *Dipper* is generic—both English and American. It is anything to *dip up* with; and not another name for *ladle*—(which is, itself, only one sort of *dipper*.)

Pail and *Pitcher* are old English words.

[90] François A. A. Mignet, 1796–1884 : friend of Thiers ; leader in the Revolution of 1830 in France ; archivist of the French Foreign Office, 1830–1848 ; historian of the Middle Ages.

[91] The punctuation is inaccurate and the italics in both passages are Mr. Bates's.

[92] Sir Archibald Alison, English historian, 1792–1867.

[93] The Girondists—at first constitutional monarchists, later republicans—represented moderate opinion among the French Revolutionists, and were finally overthrown and guillotined by the radical Jacobins.

[94] *History of Europe from the Commencement of the French Revolution in 1789, to the Restoration of the Bourbons in 1815*, 1842 ed., I, 146.

In America certainly, and I believe in England, the practical difference between *pail* and *bucket* is that the pail has an upright handle on one side, while the bucket has a *bale* spanning the top. The occasional use of the two words *pail* and *bucket*, as synonimous [*sic*], is carelessness only, a mere abuse of language.

March 8. . . .

The negro boy, *George Curtis*, comes on trial, as a house servant.

March 9   Thursday, . . .

[*A newspaper reprint of the proclamation of Governor Thomas C. Fletcher,*[95] *restoring civil law in Missouri.*] [96]

I am very glad to find Gov Fletcher, thus resolved to try to restore the *practical* power of the *law*, in Missouri. But it seems to me that he labors under a mistake in supposing that there ever was any *other law* established here.

It has been, erroneously assumed that *martial law* existed here, by some unexplained means. Those who desired to use the arbitrary power of military commanders, against their enemies (whether the public enemies, or only the objects of their private suspicion or cupidity), insolently demanded it; and those who were suspected of complicity with the enemy (whether real[l]y guil[t]y or not), and those who were intimidated by threats and violence, and the failure to get redress, for the grossest wrongs, quailed, and patiently submitted to the usurpation.

I have, constantly and openly, held—Officially at Washington and personally, every where—that *martial law* was not established in Mo. That the military and *provotal* government, actually used here, was a bald usurpation of power—and every instance of its exercise, which concerned the civil rights of individuals and the jurisdiction of the Courts, was a manifest wrong, aggravated by the false pretence of lawful authority.

I have always contended that the Law, rightly administered, has amble [*sic*] power to protect itself, to vindicate the constitution, to uphold the Government and to subdue and punish the public enemy. And therefore, that it is not only a crime, but a gross folly, to *break the law*, in order to serve or save the country! That is the false pretence of ambitious ignorance and revolutionary violence.

Many people, ignorantly or wantonly, confound *military* law and *martial*, as if they were one and the same, while, in truth, they are the exact opposites of each other.

Martial law is the *will* of the military chief. *Military* law is the ordinary law of the land which relates to *military* affairs—We desig-

---

[95] *Supra,* Jan. 12, 1865, note 4.

[96] March 7, 1865, *Messages and Proclamations of the Governors of the State of Missouri* (Grace G. Avery and Floyd C. Shoemaker, eds.), IV, 257–258.

nate portions of the law, according to the subject-matter—as *Criminal* law, *Land* law, and the like.

Genl. Pope[97] has written a strong letter in answer to Govr. Fletcher, for the reestablishment of *law*, and against military usurpations; laying the blame justly on the people of Mo.

I attach the letter, and mean to write about it.

Genl. Pope's letter to *Gov: Fletcher* March 8. 65 on Martial Law *and* Civil Law with comments by the Ed:[itor] [of the] Dispatch, and Gen Pope's order of March 17, 1865[.] [98]

[*A clipping giving the March 8 letter and the editorial.*]

This is exactly what I proposed to Genl. Sumner and he adopted.[99]

[*A clipping giving the March 17 letter.*]

Note—I have not read, as I ought to have done, the current proceedings of the Convention, and so it escaped me, until I saw, in the 'Dispatch' of Mar: 9—in the editorial comments on Genl. Pope's letter to Gov Fletcher—that the Convention had passed a resolution declaring that the removal of Martial law, "would be inexpedient and dangerous."

This declaration of the Convention, foolish and wicked as it is, nevertheless, abounds with useful information, proper to be known to the public, and which ought to be pressed, continually, upon the attention of the people. It not only proves the ignorance and folly of the members of that body, but it shows, also, to what destructive and wicked measures they resort, for the sole purpose of consolidating and continuing their hea[r]tless and brainless party! They want *Martial law* (that is military despotism) while they pretend to be *civil officers*! They want military protection *against the people*, while they are carrying out their scheme to engross all the civil offices of the State and all the patronage of the Genl. Govt.!

[*Marginal Insert.*] Surely there must be some men in the Convention who are not so ignorant as not to know the difference between *Martial* law and *Military* law. Krekel[1] and Clover[2] *ought* to know it, and Strong[3] and Drake[4] *do* know it.

[*A clipping reporting a discussion in the Convention of a motion to strike the word "white" out of the Constitution.*]

In [the] Mo. Convention, March 7. Subject, negro suffrage. There must be some mistake in this report; for Mr. Krekel is reputed an

[97] *Supra,* March 15, 1862, note 33.
[98] This paragraph is written on an envelope which contains the two clippings. The envelope is pasted into the dalry.
[99] Probably when he was about to take command of the Department of the Missouri. See *supra,* June 4, 1862, note 62.
[1] *Supra,* June 6, 1860, note 46.
[2] *Supra,* Feb. 3, 1865, note 44.
[3] *Supra,* Jan. 18, 1865, note 14.
[4] *Supra,* Feb. 12, 1863, note 13.

intelligent man, and reasonably honest. He was quoting from various State Constitutions, and professed to know them all, for otherwise he could not state that " South Carolina was the only State that *had* the word *white* in its constitution." If he really said so, believing that he spoke the truth, then he was grossly ignorant of the constitutions of the States, and very bold, to affirm a matter about which he was ignorant. But, if he dishonestly said it, knowing it to be untrue, then he presumed very largely, upon the ignorance of his hearers; and perhaps, this presumption was justified, for verily, they are *parliamentum indoctum*[.] [5]

Thiers' Hist:[ory of the] Fr:[ench] Rev.[olution] Vol 2, p. 27.

" Can Louis 16. be tried? "

["]What Tribunal shall pronounce judgment? " The author gives a brief summary of the argument, on both sides, which I think may be read and pondered, with much instruction, by all lovers of constitutional government.

[*A clipping describing the* Richmond Examiner *as furious in denunciation of Governor Brown's message,*[6] *which it declares is a* " *recommendation to Georgia to abandon the Confederacy.*"]

How absurdly foolish is it to object to Georgia's right to " abandon the Confederacy ! " It is of the very essence of Secession that each State has the right to withdraw, at pleasure.

And besides, the right is expressly recognized and affirmed in the constitution (or League) by which their Confederation exists. On ourside, the President and all the Government, have, at all times, been anxious to get the rebels back, State by State, as fast as possible. Yet it seems that the Richmond Examiner has kindred spirits in the Mo. Convention, who dread the restoration of peace and order, by the return of Separate States, to their allegiance.—See Mr. Krekel's resolution in convention, Jan 17—Back. p. 155 [January 18, 1865].

[*A clipping from the* St. Louis Daily Dispatch *describing Judge Clover and Thomas B. Harris under the caption* " *Convention Sketches.*"]

St. Just,[7] in his speech, in the French convention, against Louis 16. says—i. a. " . . . for, when a nation is so base as to suffer itself to be ruled by tyrants, dominion [domination] is the right of the first comer, and is not more sacred, more legitimate on the head of one[,] than on that of the other.[!] " [8] And his partizans, the Jacobins, acted out his doctrine, in blood, and shame and misery.

Thiers' Fr:[ench] Rev.[olution] vol 2. p 38. in note.

---

[5] A phrase of Sir Edward Coke. See *supra*, July 4, 1864, note 48.

[6] Joseph E. Brown of Georgia : *supra*, Dec. 2, 1859, note 8. For his message of February 11, 1865 see [Appleton's] *American Annual Cyclopaedia,* V (1865), 391.

[7] *Supra*, Feb. 24, 1865, note 58.

[8] M. J. L. A. Thiers, *op. cit.,* II, 32.

Here is a sketch of the two sides or parties in [the] French convention, drawn by *Garat*,[9] in a very masterly and graphic style, but rather *too French*, for my full comprehension. It abounds with terse and cutting phrases, and the description of the monster, Marat,[10] is perfectly horrible.

Mar 10, Friday. The weather a good deal softened. Barton left, for home, after early breakfast.

I spent a good part of the day down town. Conversed freely with several gentlemen—Breckinridge,[11] Reber,[12] Hickman [13] and heard a good many things—i. a. Mr. Hickman tells me, that Judge Edwards [14] (being advised from Washington, that Krekel [15] could not be Judge of the Western District,[)] was disposed to apply for it *himself*(!) on the ground that, as he was turned out of the Dis-[tric]t: Attorne[y]ship because he was a Radical, and as the *President* is now, as great a radical as he, his chance might be good!—and that both Mr. Hickman and Judge Treat,[16] advised him against it.

<Mr. Edwards forgets that if the Prest. have really sunk into a *Radical*, still, he has never betrayed his superior officer nor reviled and resisted the State authorities, nor persecuted the most honest and patriotic men of Mo.>

At night, come Genl. Vaughan [17] and his son George and Wm. H. Letcher,[18] and spent the evening pleasantly.

Again, in the evening of the 11th, comes Genl. V.[aughan] under promise to spend the night, but cannot as he has just heard that the Bushw[h]ackers are very bad about Lexington, and so, he must hasten home.

March 13 Monday. Last night, I was quite sick, and staid within all day. Weather warm, with gusty clouds.

---

[9] Dominique J. Garat, 1749–1833: member of the Legislative Assembly and of the Convention during the French Revolution; reporter of their proceedings in *Le Journal de Paris;* minister of Justice, 1792–1793; minister of the Interior, 1793; ambassador to Naples, 1798; president of the Council of Ancients, 1799; senator under Napoleon.

[10] Jean P. Marat, 1743–1793: physician, 1775–1788; extremist in the French Revolution; editor of *L'Ami du Peuple,* 1789–1792, which he wrote from hiding-places in cellars and sewers; member of the Convention, 1792–1793; bitter opponent of the moderate Girondists. He was murdered in his bath by Charlotte Corday in July, 1793.

[11] Judge Samuel M. Breckinridge: *supra,* Dec. 26, 1859, note 67.

[12] *Supra,* June 4, 1859, note 74.

[13] Ben. L. Hickman, a St. Louis attorney.

[14] William W. Edwards: St. Charles lawyer; prosecuting attorney, 1858–1862; U. S. district attorney, 1862–1863; Missouri circuit court judge for many years after 1863.

[15] *Supra,* June 6, 1860, note 46.

[16] Samuel Treat: St. Louis lawyer; editor; judge of the Court of Common Pleas, 1850–1857; judge of the U. S. District Court, 1857–1887.

[17] *Supra,* Dec. 9, 1859, note 25.

[18] *Supra,* Dec. 19, 1859, note 48.

March 14. . . .

Last night, after we had gone to bed, comes *Mr. Eads* [19] (with Miss Eliza Dillon) to make us a call[.]   I was very glad to see him look so well—better I thought, than for several years past.

He is in high spirits—being eminently successful in his new inventions—in naval architecture—in the structure of iron turrets—and especially, in the manoeuvering of great guns, by steam power.[20] All these have have [*sic*] attracted very lively interest and not a little admiration, among military and naval men, on both sides of the atlantic.   Thus, his fame is made, and the amount of his fortune rests with himself.

He will sail again for Europe—to join his family in Switzerland—taking Miss Eliza Dillon with him.   In the mean time, he is pressed with business.

[*A clipping quoting Maximilian's decree of religious toleration in Mexico.*]

Notes—

1 Maximilian,[21] it seems, is Emperor of *Mexico—not the Mexicans*—whereas Louis Napoleon is Emperor of *The French*—not of *France*.   There may be a greater difference than, at first, strikes the casual eye.   Napoleon. 1. meant something when he took the title Emperor of *the French*.

2. The Empire *protects* the R.[oman] C.[atholic] church—but *how*, is not said.

3. Toleration, ' free and simple ', is granted to all other religions. But let them take care to do nothing opposed to " morality, civilization and good habits ''; for, if the Empire be once well established,—*itself being the judge*—it will be apt to find out that whatever is against *Mother church* (which it "*protects*,") must also, be against morality and good habits.

4. The *Police*, it seems, is to superintend the *exercise* of Religion ! In that particular, we, here in Mo., are a little in advance of the Emperor; for, by a certain General *Order*, every Synod and Presbytery must sit under the eye of a *Provost Martial* [*sic*] *!*

[*Marginal Note.*]   On Monday, the 13th. March Removed to my new Study, in the front room, 2d. Story—not yet quite furn[i]shed.

Calls to see me, Mrs. Davis (widow of Peter Lindell jr.) and had a long talk about old Mr. Lindell [22] and his will.   She, evidently thinks that Levin H Baker stole and destroyed the will, with the connivance, if not the direct aid of *B. A. Hill*.[23]   She insists that

---

[19] *Supra,* Jan. 28, 1860, note 38.

[20] See *supra,* May 1, 1864.

[21] *Supra,* June 17, 1864, note 9.

[22] *Supra,* May 3, 1859, note 44.

[23] *Supra,* Dec. 28, 1861, note 56.

"Lev:" stole the *safe key*, before the old man's death—and makes a strong show of circumstances.

She lives at 230. Locust street, between 11th. and 12th.

Mar 15. . . .

I have written several letters of late importing that I shall probably write for publication, and that I do not like to devote my whole time to that labor, without some pecuniary reward. I have just written a long letter to T J Coffey [24] on that subject.

The same letter contains remarks about Ch[ief] J[ustice] Chase[.]

[*A newspaper reprint of an order of March 14, 1865, issued by the State Department for the arrest of all persons, citizens or aliens, who are or have been engaged in blockade running.*]

Mar 17. Friday and St Patrick's Day, with a great display of Irish piety and patriotism—

Called on *Bosse & Steinlich*, who are making for me a fine writing desk. It is not yet done and will not be, for some weeks. <see *infra* p 183 [April 21]>

Had a long talk with *Judge Treat*,[25] who told me, in detail, how Genl. Pope [26] and Govr. Fletcher [27] came to issue, respectively, their letter and proclamation, in favor of re-establishing and enforcing the *civil law*, in the teeth of the vote of the *Convention*, in favor of *Martial Law.*

Capt. Woodson (Geo. T.) came, and staid the night, (and is still here today   Mar 18)[.]

[*A clipping from the* St. Louis Daily Dispatch *of March 20, 1865. which prints General Pope's Order No. 15 and a long editorial upon it.*]

This St. Patrick's day is marked by two very important facts, whether so arranged, on purpose to do honour to the occasion, or a merely accidental coincidence, I know not.   But so it is, that on this very day, Genl. John Pope, the [commander of] Grand Division of the Missouri, issued his "General Order, No. 15," which is in humiliating contrast with his letter of the 8th. of this month,[28] written in answer to a note of Gov Fletcher, on the subject of *Martial Law* in Missouri.   This order is a mortifying proof of Genl. Pope's ignorance, alike, of the laws of the land and the principle of our institutions.

And on this same day, the Convention (in eager pursuit of their main object, i. e. the engros[s]ment of all the offices, profits and powers of the Government—and to secure the impunity of their

[24] *Supra,* March 5, 1860, note 18.
[25] *Supra,* March 10, 1865, note 16.
[26] *Supra,* March 15, 1862, note 33.
[27] *Supra,* Jan. 12, 1865, note 4.
[28] *Supra,* March 9, 1865.

partizans, for past crimes) passed an Ordinance to vacate the judg[e]-ships and other civil offices—estimated at some 400 to 600—and provided for the filling of the vacancies by the *Governor*[.]

And providing that no proceedings shall be had in the civil tribunals, against any offender who acted under the authority of any *military comma[n]der*[.]

And thus, they hope to secure aggrandizement now and impunity hereafter for all past crimes.

Genl. Pope displayed in *his letter* some show of sense, justice and law. But *his order* shews him totally ignorant of law and principle, or that he has quailed to the truculence of the Convention!

And as for Gov Fletcher, he may, by his timidity, degrade himself into the mere cat's paw of a few demagogues in the Convention, to his own ruin: This *submission* of Pope and apprehended submission of the Governor, is an absolute abandonment of their principles and policy. Their course was taken on mature consideration, and the letter of the Genl. and Proclamation of the Govr. deliberately issued, in pursuance of a formed purpose,—This is well known to others besides me—e. g. Judge Treat.

March 18 saturday—Another bright warm day, urging me to get ready for gardening—already, I have procured a beginning supply of garden tools and *Friend Newton*[29] has sent me a good variety of seeds[.]

Seeds sent by Mr. Com[mis]s[ione]r. Newton—recd. Mar 15. 1865

1 Large white *Lima Beans* 1. paper

2. Boardman's improved, blue *Imperial Pea* 3 packages

3. White Kidney Beans 2 packages

4. *Paul's prolific peas*—1. pack

5 Champion of England *peas* 1. p

6. Blue Prussian *Peas*

7 Tuscarora *corn*. 1. p

8 A[d]ams' Early corn

9 Napoleon Peas 1. p.

10 Black Spanish Watermelon 2. p

11 Mountain Sweet Watermelon 2. p.

12. Early White Spine cucumber 1. p

13. Short Green prickly cucr. 2. p

14. Scarlet *Turnip* Radish 1. p

15 *Long* scarlet Radish 1 p

16. Yellow Turnip Beet 1. p. and 2.

17. Spanish *white* onion 3. p

18. White Solid Celery 3. p

19. White Cabbage Let[t]uce 2. p

20 Tripoli *flat Onion* 3. p

21. Strasburg *Onion* 2 p

22. *Blood red* Onion 4. p

23. Thyme 2 p

24. Summer *crook-neck squash* 1. p. & 1

25 Boston Marrow Squash 3. p

26 Early curled Siletia Lettuce 1. p

---

[29] *Supra*, Jan. 5, 1862, note 12.

27. Double curled Parseley [sic] 1. p

28 Late London Cauliflower 1. p —

29. Extra early, flat *Bassam Beet* 1. p

30 Giant, Victoria Rhubarb 3. p

31. Hollow-crown Parsnip 2 p

32 *Solid Giant celery* 1. p

33 Sweet Marjoram 1. p

34 Christina Melon 1. p

To day, *Mrs. M A Childs* paid me the *face* of her due-bill, for money lent, a year and [a] half ago. She would have paid *interest*, but I declined—paid *$125*.

Mar 19   Sunday. Cloudy and drizzling—Comes *Jerry* and proposes to put in some little crop at Grape Hill, and I promised, if I sell the place, to make some arrangement to protect him.

We arranged for his work for me there, in taking up and bringing in certain trees, trees [sic] posts and other cedar timber.

I handed him *$15*. on a/c [f]or work done and to be done[.]

[*A broadside inscribed by Richard Bates with "Post marked, St. Louis May 30. 1862 recd. June 3. 1862 Rd. B." and by the sender with the admonition "Read and Ponder Well." signed "Patriotism":*

"MESSAGE OF OLD 'ABE'
"TO THE FEDERAL CONGRESS,
"FOURTH OF JULY, 1861.

"The Richmond (Va.) Whig received the following by 'special electric telegraph,' and, of course, published it exclusively:

"Once more, Representatives, Senators, all,
You come to my capital, swift at my call.
'Tis well, for you've something important to do
In this most disagreeable national stew.
For, since I came hither to 'run the machine,'
Disguised in Scotch cap and full Lincoln green,
There's the devil to pay in the whole d——d concern,
As from Cameron, Seward, and Chase you will learn
Yet, though everything here of a burst-up gives warning,
I'm certain you'll put it all right in the morning,
So do as I tell you, be on the alert,
For the panic's fictitious, and nobody's hurt.

"I have started up war of invasion, you know,
Let who will pretend to deny it—that's so!
But I saw from the White House an impudent rag,
Which they told me was known as Jeff. Davis' flag,
Waving all above Alexandria high,
Insulting my government, flouting the sky,
Above MY Alexandria (isn't it Bates?
Retrocession's a humbug—what right have the States?)
So I ordered young Ellsworth to take the rag down—
Mrs. Lincoln she craved it to make a new gown.
But young Ellsworth, he kinder got shot in the race,
And came back in a galvanized burial case.
But, then, Jackson, the scoundrel, he got his desert,
The panic's fi[c]titious! 'there's nobody hurt.'

" It is true, I sent steamers, which tried for a week
  To silence the rebels down there at the Creek,
  But they had at Game Point about fifty or more
  Rifled cannon set up in a line on the shore,
  And six thousand Confederate practised to fire 'em,
  (Confound these Virginians, we never can tire 'em!)
  Who made game of our shooting, and crippled our fleet,
  So we prudently ordered a hasty retreat,
  With decks full of passangers, DEAD heads indeed,
  For whom of fresh coffins there straightway was need,
  And still later, at Gresham's they killed Captain Ward,
  In command of the Freeborn—'twas devilish hard—
  But in spite of all this, the rebellion's a spurt,
  The panic's fictitious and ' nobody hurt.'

" Herewith I beg leave to submit the report
  Of Butler, the General, concerning the sport
  They had at Great Bethel, near Fortress Monroe,
  With Hill and Magruder, some four weeks ago—
  And here, let me say, a more reckless intruder
  I never have known than this Colonel Magruder
  He has taken the COMFORT away from Old Point,
  And thrown our peninsular plans out of joint.
  While in matters of warfare, to him General Butler
  Would scarcely be able to act like a sutler.
  And the insolent rebels will call to our faces
  The fight at Great Bethel the " Newmarket races."
  Then supersede Butler at once with whoever
  Can drive this Magruder clean into the river,
  And I shall be confident still to assert
  This panic's fictitious, and ' nobody's hurt ! '

" 'Tis my province, perhaps, herein briefly to state
  The State of my province, surely late
  Missouri and Maryland—one has the paw
  Of my Lyon upon her, and one has the law
  Called martial, proclaimed through her borders and cities.
  Both are crushed out—I make bold to say it is.
  St. Louis is silent, and Baltimore dumb,
  They hear but the monotone roll of my drum.
  In the latter vile seaport I ordered Cadwallader
  To manacle freedom, and though the crowd followed her,
  Locked up in McHenry, she's safe, it is plain,
  With Merryman, habeas corpus and Kane,
  And as for that crabbed Old Dotard, Judge Taney,
  For much I would put him on board of the Pawnee,
  And make his decisions a little more curt,
  For the panic's fictitious, and nobody's hurt.

"And now I'll just say what I'd have you to do,
In order to put your new President through—
First, three hundred millions is wanted by Chase,
He cannot run longer the government's face.
And Cameron wants, for the use old Scott,
Some four hundred thousand more men than he's got.
Then Sixty new iron-plate ships, to stand shells,
Are loudly demanded—must have 'em—by Wells.
For England, the bully, won't stand the blockade,
And insists we shall not embarrass her trade.
But who fears the British? I'll speedily tune 'em,
As sure as my name is ' E Pluribus Unum.'
For I am myself the whole United S[t]ates.
Constitution and Law—if you doubt me, ask Bates.
The Star Spangled Banner's my holiday shirt—
Hurrah for Abe Lincoln—there's ' nobody hurt.' "]

Mar: 1865. In 1862, this was the tone of contempt and ridicule in which the rebels habitually indulged. Then " *One* Southron could whip *five* Yankees." Then " The yan[k]ees were cowards, and could not be coaxed or kicked across Mason and Dixon's line." Then their Editors and orators boasted how they would march over and devastate the whole north—That they would " make grass grow in Broad Way N.[ew] Y.[ork] and pasture their horses in Boston Common !"

How is it now? The fragments of their armies are fleeing before our forces, every where, from the Mississippi to the Potomac; and the same *editors* and *orators* are whining over the wasteful and unresisted march of *Sherman*[30] through the whole length and breadth of Georgia and the Carolinas !

[*A clipping listing the committees of the U. S. Senate at the extra session of 1865; another discussing Stanton's shattered health.*]

[*An editorial from the* Missouri Republican *of March 23, 1865, on* " *Powers of the Convention.*"][31]

Note. B. *Gratz Brown*[32] in his long letter to the convention (see M[iss]o.[uri] Dem[ocrat], about Jany 6. /65) claims for the convention *unlimited power*. But he, (if not mad) is very illogical—One conspicuous point in his argument in favor of *Negro Suffrage*, is that " *Freedom and Franchise are inseparable!*" If he meant that as a mere flourish of rhetoric, it is a poor conceit, for it is not otherwise witty than the two f. f.s—and not a whit truer or smarter than if he had said *fire and fat are inseparable!*

---

[30] Sherman started northward on February 1 and was now marching through North Carolina to meet Schofield (*supra*, May 30, 1863, note 32) at Goldsboro on March 23.

[31] Opposite the phrase " the people," Bates wrote " Who are they?" Opposite " body of men selected from among the people," he inserted " Selected by whom."

[32] *Supra*, Feb. 15, 1864, note 44.

[*A newspaper paragraph relating to Grant's capture of "rebel armies" under Buckner*[33] *at Fort Donelson, Pemberton*[34] *at Vicksburg, and Lee at Appomattox.*[35]]

Grant captures 3 armies[.]   The only three we ever took.

Mar 23   Thursday.   Paid *Reuben Nicholls* for work done about my house—shelving office and other jobs, and some materials (see his bill) $132.77.

This day (tho' in my 72d. year) I was enrolled as a *militiaman!* This was done under the new act of Assembly, which, as I am told (for I have not read it) requires the enrol[l]ment of all *male inhabitants*, without regard to age or color![36]

Note.   A man came into one of the enrolling offices in this City, bearing in his arms, his two little sons, infants, and said to the Enrolling Officer—Sir, "*We three* have come to be enrolled as *militiamen*."—And the Officer, was a good deal *posed*—hesitated, hemmed and hawed, and finally, refused to give the *babies* certificates of enrol[l]ment!

Wise Legislature that!   And the Governor[37] too —Moderate and law-abiding man that he is—I hear that he has, *by proclamation*, repealed that part of the law which requires *aliens* to be enrolled!

Mar 24.   Asa Wilqus is dead.   I attended his funeral to day—Also, visited Mrs McGhee, who lies very low.

Mar 25   Saturday.   I have resolved to write something upon the political questions now of greatest interest to our state, and intend to address a note to the Mo. Democrat asking to have my articles published in that paper.   Went down town to consult Breckenridge,[38] Broadhead[39] and Glover[40]—saw <seen>[41] only the first named—

(Saw Glover sunday night—Broadhead monday and all three of them approve the *plan*.   Yet they all seem struck with my *boldness*, in declaring that the Convention is simply *revolutionary*, and has no powers at all, *granted by law*.[)]

---

[33] *Supra,* Dec. 31, 1861, note 61.

[34] *Supra,* May 24, 1863, note 27.

[35] Mr. Bates had a habit of filling up blank pages in his diary with newspaper clippings. This one is manifestly inserted out of its proper place.

[36] Section 1 of the militia law, passed on February 10, 1865, required military service of all males regardless of color but Section 2 exempted men under eighteen and over forty-five.   Section 11, however, required the *enrollment* of *all* males presumably regardless of age, though it did not say so, and Section 16 provided a penalty for *all* (again without exemption) who failed to enroll.   *Laws of the State of Missouri Passed at the Regular Session of the Twenty-Third General Assembly* . . . *Held* . . . *December 26, 1864,* 51–58. See also *infra,* "Appendix," Letter Number Three.

[37] Thomas C. Fletcher: *supra,* Jan. 12, 1865, note 4.

[38] *Supra,* Dec. 26, 1859, note 67.

[39] *Supra,* Dec. 26, 1859, note 66.

[40] *Supra,* Dec. 23, 1859, note 58.

[41] Inserted in margin.

Mar 28. S. T. Glover hands to me his written statement, about Col *Harding's*[42] order to *Circuit Atty.* John. F. Ryland Jr.,[43] to dismiss certain indictments pending in Jackson Co. Circuit. Court.

Mr. G.[lover] says that he read it to *Genl. Pope*[44] yesterday, who said that it had already come before him, and that he had ordered an *investigation*—(which, probably, will never happen)[.]

Here is another Sample of *Martial law*, which the Convention thinks so necessary for the preservation of the *liberties* and *institutions* of the country!

If Col Harding, a District commander, can domineer over the circuit Court and suppress the laws of the state, what is there to prevent Pope, or any subordinate commander, from *ordering* the Convention, to cease their babbling about human rights, and stop their clumsey [*sic*] efforts at constitution making.

Judge *Krekel*[45] (now U. S. judge of that District) being a staunch believer in *Martial law*, will, doubtless, be happy to receive the *orders of the District commander*, in all things touching the discharge of his *judicial duties.* Col Harding may tell him who[m] to try and punish and who[m] to set free, and also, may furnish him with better opinions than his own, to be delivered from the bench!

<Appropos [*sic*]—I am credibly informed that *Halleck*,[46] when in command of this Department, once ordered Mr. Clover,[47] Judge of the St Louis criminal court, to charge the grand jury in a particular way. I believe that Clover had the spirit to decline obedience to the order—but how he got out of the scrape, I do not know—

Mr. Glover can tell all about it[.]>

Mar: 30 thursday— . . .

Last night Zenas Smith called to see me, to ask my influence to get a pass for Mrs. Giles to return from Richmond. I declined, for good reasons.

(A year or more ago, Mrs. Giles went from St. Louis to Washington, and there solicited a pass for herself and daughter, to go through to Richmond. Their object, understood at the time, was for the daughter (a very pretty, flaunting, human butterfly) to marry a rebel Officer, one Colonel or general Pollard, who, it seems *engaged* with the young lady, while he was, sometime a prisoner of war, here, in St Louis. But the *General's* love, it appe[a]rs, melted

[42] See also *infra*, June 2, 1865.
[43] John E. Ryland of Lexington: teacher; lawyer; major in the Missouri militia, 1862–1863; circuit attorney, 1863–1865; mayor of Lexington, 1868. Though his term as circuit attorney continued until 1868, he was removed in 1865 under the "Ousting Ordinance."
[44] *Supra*, March 15, 1862, note 33.
[45] *Supra*, June 6, 1860, note 46.
[46] *Supra*, Nov. 13, 1861, note 37.
[47] *Supra*, Feb. 3, 1865, note 44.

away, with the waning fortunes of Rebellion, and he *repudiated*. And thus, the object of the journey failing Mrs. G.[iles] wants to come back. Her native home is near Richmond, she being a daughter of Sam Branch.[)]

Mar 31. Today I recd. a note from McKee, Fishback & Co.[48] (Mo. Dem:[ocrat]) agreeing to publish my articles but they must be *short*.

Note. The letter is dated the *28th.*, but [　　]

Lately, there has been a trial before a military commission, at Chicago, of certain conspirators, indifferently called *American Knights* or *Sons of Liberty*.[49] Clement L. Vallandingham [*sic*] [50] had been chosen chief of the gang, and it seems was called as a witness *for the defence.* He made a poor show, as a witness—just such as might be expected from a man vain enough to aspire to be, in his locality and circumstances, a democratic apostle, wicked enough to plot treason but too timid to execute it.

They abandoned the name of *Knights*, because, besides being absurd, it smacks of aristocracy. But what can they mean by *Sons of Liberty?* Is it the bastard children of *Free Love?*

Apl. 3. Richmond is evacuated by the enemy, and we (Genl. Weitzel [51]) have possession. Lee, of course, left in great haste, leaving much of his heavy material, and covering his retreat by fierce and disastrous battles at our lines, near the Appomattox—in which, I hear, we took 12.000 prisoners. Lee retreats from Rich[mon]d. by the line of the Danville R. R. while Grant is hard after him, and can hardly fail to strike his flank and rear.

The retreat seems to me needless and cruel. I suppose it is hopeless of success, and designed only to get certain great leaders—Davis and others—out of the falling capital and in some place, whence they may hope to escape immediate capture, and save their persons, by flight.

During the day, comes Bartons [*sic*] wife and little Cora—at night, Dick, with his wife and child.

In the afternoon, Barton Able [52] and Geo: A. Maguire—Mr. Maguire, wants recommendation to be consul at Bordeau[x].

[48] Publishers of the *Democrat*. George W. Fishback, formerly an Ohio lawyer, 1851–1854, and then a reporter for the *St. Louis Evening News* and the *St. Louis Intelligencer*, 1854–1855, had been editor and part owner of the *Missouri Democrat* since 1855.

[49] *Supra*, Oct. 7, 1864, note 13.

[50] *Supra*, Jan. 13, 1860, note 26.

[51] Godfrey Weitzel: West Point graduate of 1855; an engineer at New Orleans and at West Point before the War, at Fort Pickens, Cincinnati, and Washington in 1861, and under Butler at New Orleans in 1862; brigadier-general of volunteers in Louisiana and at Port Hudson, 1862–1864, and in the Army of the James, 1864–1865.

[52] *Supra*, May 3, 1860, note 90.

Admiral Lee [53] and Mr. Simmons [54] took tea with us; and later, Mr. Janvier ([the] Adm[ira]l's. Secy) and Mr. Cochrane,[55] L[ieutenan]t. of Marines, made a pleasant visit[.]

Apl 4 Barton handed me *$700*—

To day, I shall hand in, my *first*—introductory—article,[56] to be published in the Mo. Democrat.
(which was done)

Visited the Flagship of A[d]m[ira]l. Lee—with most of my family, and had a pleasant time.

At night, comes John. M. Vaughan,[57] and brings with him Mr. *Davis*, the editor at Lexington,[.]   He seems much pleased with my undertaking to write in the *Democrat*, and promises to furnish me with much material, touching men and facts, during my absence at Washington.

Apl 5 . . .

[*News of military matters printed over Stanton's signature.*]

Reports are coming in rapidly, of the results of Lee's abandonment of Richmond and the consequent destruction of all kinds of property connected with the army.   His army must be demoralized, and I have no doubt that his retreat will soon become an utter rout.   I suppose that he would have capitulated at Richmond, but for the supposed necessity of saving from surrender, the ringleaders of rebellion, civil and military, by taking them a little way out of Richmond, and thus, giving them a last hope of fleeing to some place of personal safety.

[*An order signed by Seward offering a reward for the capture of* " *evil-disposed persons* " *who have entered the United States* " *from a country where they are tolerated.*"]

This covers both England and Mexico; and I suppose is politic enough, as a means of keeping those incendiaries out of the country.

" It is always idle ambition, ardent minds, superior talents, that are the *first* [58] to engage in revolutions."   Thiers French Rev.[olution] vol 2. p 142.

But those who are first to " fire the public heart " and light up the conflagration, are often the first also, to be consumed by its flames. Few survive to witness the catastrophe.   And hence, almost always. some man arises after the first fury of the revolution is past, who reaps the harvest and secures the crop for himself.

---

[53] *Supra*, Dec. 19, 1863, note 89.

[54] Probably C. C. Simmons, a St. Louis lawyer, who in February of this year had been appointed by the Legislature of Missouri to a Committee to revise the laws of the State.

[55] Henry C. Cochrane had served in the Navy since 1861, was commissioned lieutenant in 1863 when only twenty-one, and then continued in the Marine Corps until 1905.

[56] See *infra*, "Appendix."

[57] *Supra*, March 6, 1863, note 59.

[58] The italics are Mr. Bates's.

To day Dr. Bernays [59] called to see me and staid some hours, talking with more than his accustomed vehement enthusiasm. He read to me Moench's [Muench's] [60] atrocious letter and his own scorching answer.

This letter of Moench [Muench] is useful as a link in the chain of evidence to prove the wide-spread conspiracy to revolutionize the state, not only in its Government and laws, but also in its population and property—to drive out the present people, and fill their places by a new importation from *Hessen* [61] and elsewhere.

This *Revd.* Mr. Moench [Muench] resembles, in some particulars the Revd. *M. Chabot* [62]—the secularised Capuchin Monk who figured in the french revolutionary convention.

Apl 7—Note. The *Mo. Rep:*[*ublican*] republishes, from the Mo. Dem:[ocrat] my introductory essay [62a] upon the misgovernment of the State, but without any allusion to the letter or the subject, in *small print* and *hid away* in an obscure part of the paper. Also (by accident I suppose) it falsified my position that the *Laws* DO give ample power to the officers to bring the war to a successful close, and to govern the country in peace, by incerting [*sic*] a gratuitous *not*, after the word *do*.

[*April 10.*] But that is cured by my letter published in the Mo. Rep[ublican] of Apl. 10.—Here it is. [63]

ST. LOUIS, April 8, 1865.

To the Editor of the Missouri Republican:

SIR: Yesterday you republished from the Democrat my preliminary address to the people of Missouri, intended as an introduction to a series which I design to write, concerning the misgovernment of this State. And I regret to find that, by some strange mistake, one of my main propositions of law is not only erroneously stated, but exactly *reversed*. In that short address I stated *four* distinct propositions, which I assumed to maintain in after essays. In the *third* proposition I affirmed that the laws "*Do* confer upon the officers of Government, national and State, all the powers which are necessary to the successful prosecution of the war, and to the peaceful rule of the country." But your paper makes me say that the laws *do not* confer these powers.

---

[59] *Supra*, Sept. 20, 1860, note 9.
[60] Supra, Feb. 2, 1865, note 38.
[61] The Duchy of Hesse-Darmstadt in Germany.
[62] François Chabot: Franciscan friar, Revolutionary leader, member of the extreme left in the Legislative Assembly, and the Convention, who was finally tried and executed on April 5, 1794, for part in a bribery plot.
[62a] *Infra*, "Appendix."
[63] This paragraph and the letter which follows were added on or after April 10.

I beg that this error may be corrected, for, as printed, it falsifies my position, and contradicts what I shall labor to maintain—that is, that the powers of the Government and the liberties of the people can be easier and more successfully maintained by upholding and obeying the laws, than by despising and trampling them down.

Very respectfully,

EDW'D BATES.

[*A clipping from the Missouri Democrat telling of the "rout of Lee's army."*]

Apl 10 monday. News comes this morning that Lee has been compelled to surrender, with all his army. I suppose [this] means the army under his immediate command, and not the armies generally of the confederacy, of all of which he is the commander in chief. As yet, the details have not reached us.

. . .

Apl 11. Charles McDonald comes on trial for a month as man of all work, at $30. Both to stop at the end of the month.

[*A long clipping from the St. Louis Daily Dispatch of April 14, 1865, giving the "Address of the Minority of the Convention" under the caption "Shall the New Constitution Be Adopted?"*]

Apl 15. The Mo. Rep[ublican] of this day contains a pretty long list of appointment[s] made by Gov Fletcher,[64] to fill vacancies made by the corrupt Ordinance of the Convention.[65]

Let it be remembered that the members of the convention while committing this spoliation for themselves, nevertheless, lacked the nerve to vote others *out* and themselve[s] *in*—and so, required the Governor to fill the vacancies, thereby assuming the responsibility of declaring upon the loyalty of the present holders. It was publicly announced, in the convention, by Mr. Strong[66] of St Louis, that the Governor told him that he would re-appoint *all the officers who were loyal.* And so, every one not reappointed, is *adjudged to be disloyal.* Judges Moody[67] and Lord[68] and Reber[69] have gotten the Governor's *certificate of loyalty.* Poor *Prim[m]*,[70] of the Crim-

---

[64] *Supra,* Jan. 12, 1865, note 4.

[65] The so-called "Ousting Ordinance" which declared vacant all judgeships and clerkships of the state and county courts, provided for their refilling by gubernatorial appointment, and required the test oath of the new appointees. *Journal of the Missouri State Convention Held at the City of St. Louis January 6–April 10, 1865,* 282.

[66] *Supra,* Jan. 18, 1865, note 14.

[67] *Supra,* Feb. 2, 1865, note 40.

[68] Charles B. Lord: lawyer in Buffalo, New York, 1833–1843, in St. Louis, 1843–1855; judge of the Land Court for two terms; judge of the Circuit Court, 1866–1868.

[69] *Supra,* June 4, 1859, note 74.

[70] Wilson Primm: St. Louis lawyer who read law under Bates; a former partner of the Radical leader, Drake (*supra,* Feb. 12, 1863, note 13); member of the Board of Education; alderman; clerk of the Circuit Court; judge of the St. Louis Criminal Court, 1862–1875.

inal Court, may be adjudged *a traitor knave*—and "his bishopric
be given to another."

Apl. 15. This morning we have the astounding news, by various
telegrams that last night, *President Lincoln* was *murdered*, in a
public Theatre, in Washington! and that the assassin escaped, in
the stupid amazement of the crowd, by leaping from the box to the
stage and disappearing behind the scenes. One account says that
as the assassin ran across the stage, brandishing a knife, he ex-
clamimed [*sic*]—"I am avenged—*sic semper tyr[a]nnis.*" [71] *Sic
semper tyrannis* is the motto on the shield of *Virginia*—and this
may give a clue to the unravelling of a great *conspiracy*, for this
assassination is not the act of *one man;* but only one scene of a great
drama.

Also that about the same hour, Mr. Seward, being ill in bed, was
assailed by another (or the same) assassin, and received several
stabs, but it is not yet known whether or no they are mortal!

It is also said that two of his sons (in attendance on a/c of his sickness—his severe hurt [72] lately, at Richmond—) were dangerously
wounded by the assassin: Fred: W. [73] Asst. Secy, was knocked down
by a billet, over [the] head; and Major S. [74] paymaster, U. S. A. was
severely stabbed. [75]

This day was appointed by authority, for displays of rejoicing
and thanksgiving over the recent great victories of the national
arms. I presume it is turned into a day of mourning.

We will thank God as heartily, for the solid benefits derived by
the nation, from those great achievements, but at such a time, any
boistrous display of joy would be contrary to good feeling and
good taste.

I shall abstain from all ostentacious [*sic*] displ[a]y of exuberant
emotion, for besides a deep sense of the calamity which the nation
has sustained, my private feelings are deeply moved by the sudden
murder of my chief, with and under whom I have served the country, through many difficult and trying scenes, and always with
mutual sentiments of respect and friendship.

I mourn his fall, both for the country and for myself.

---

[71] Theatrical though it sounds, this account is accurate.

[72] Seward's horses had run away from the coachman on April 5, and Seward, in attempting to jump from the carriage, had been knocked unconscious with a broken jaw and
dislocated shoulder, and had lain several days in delirium. This happened in Washington, not Richmond.

[73] *Supra*, May 13, 1862, note 38.

[74] Samuel S. Seward: captain of volunteers, 1862–1863; major, 1863–1865. It was not,
however, Samuel but another son, Augustus, who was wounded by the assassin who
attacked his father and his brother, Frederick.

[75] Both Mr. Seward and his son Frederick were precariously ill for a number of days,
and Mr. Seward was not able to go out to a cabinet meeting until June 9.

[*A reprint in the* Missouri Republican *of April 18, 1865, of a circular signed by L. C. Matlack, Major 17th Illinois Cavalry and District Provost-Marshal in St. Louis, announcing that "no complaints nor claims of the negro will hereafter be entertained or prosecuted at this office."*]

That's a "bully" Major! He declines further jurisdiction of *black cases,* by assuming jurisdiction to judge and determine upon the laws of the state! Wise *Provost Marshal* that! There *was,* he asserts, *a necessity* which required the *District Provost Martial* [*sic*] to exercise *civil functions*—and he, *being judge of necessities,* performs the miricle of of squeesing [*sic*] *civil* blood out of a military turnip!

The former law, it seems, did not suit him—and so he took *martial* jurisdiction—"But that is all changed now"—The law is altered for the better, and so, he will allow the civil officers to execute it!

He has learned, it seems, *from the Secretary of State,* that blacks and whites are *equal before the* law! What will Mr. Krekel [76] say to that? He labored hard in the Convention (and finally succeeded,) to make them *unequal* before the law, in the matter of suffrage. "The inequality of the negro before the law was alike the occasion and the justification"—of his assumed jurisdiction. And so he grasped the power over the subject, to reverse the law, just because *the law was wrong!*

Apl 18. night—I am greatly surprised at the dearth of information concerning the assassins of the President and the Secretary of State. Neither of them, it seems, is yet captured, (tho' frequent rumors have come that they were) and the longer the time, the greater the chance of the escape of the wretches.

Note. the Mo. Rep[ublican] of today, republishes (with several typographical errors) my letters to [t]he people, Nos. 1 and 2.

Apl. 19 Wednesday. This day was observed here (as I suppose every where) with great solemnity, being the funeral of the murdered President.

I attended the 2d. Presbyterian church, where there was an immence [*sic*] crowd, in so much that many could not get seats, either in ailse [*sic*], stair case or gallery.

Most of the prayers, and speeches were impressive and in good taste; but I could not help feeling [regretful] at the tone and manner of Dr. Post [77]—Harsh, vindictive and out of keeping with his usually bland and amiable character. This cry for vengeance, is not his natural temper, and I cannot help fearing that his ardent tem-

[76] *Supra,* June 6, 1860, note 46.
[77] *Supra,* Jan. 31, 1860, note 44.

perament has been worked upon by crafty partizans, to make him
seem to be one of them.   For I know that it is the present scheme
of the extreme radicals (who never were Lincoln's friends) to make
party capital out of his flagitious murder.

Apl 20.   Completed my contract with Alex[ande]r. Cameron,
for the lot in Carondalet.[78]   He surrendered his lease for the 100
f[ee]t.—I conveyed him 50 f[ee]t. on the corner, containing his improvements and he paid $30, a foot=1500, and $150 back rents, so
that, after paying Leffingwell's [79] costs, I recd. in gross, $1611.

No tidings yet of the arrest of the assassins.

Apl 21. Bosse & Gieslich,[80] cabinet makers, brought home my
desk, an excellent article of handsome oak, for which I paid
them $90.

[*A clipping headed " The New Constitution—Protest of Gov.
Fletcher.*"]

" The rats are running from the burning house."   Govr.
Fletcher [81] and Mr. Johnson [82] have waked up, from the drunken
dream of radicalism, just in time to smell the smoke of the kindling
fires, and save themselves, by timely flight, from the coming conflagration.

If, efficiently and successfully, they resist this crowning iniquity,
let all their past errors be forgiven and forgotten.   This is not a
time for vengeance.   Let it suffice for justice, that the heartless
and brainless demagogues, who planned the mischief, and still persist in carrying it out, sink to their proper level of obscure impotence,
in the bottom of the pit which they have digged.

[*Special Order No. 2 issued on April 7, 1865, by B. K. Davis,
Major commanding at Lexington, Missouri, decreeing that on Sunday morning April 9 public thanks be offered in all the churches
for the recent Union victories.*]

There's a pious Major, for you!   And, he speaks as one that has
authority, and not as the Pharasees [*sic*].   By virtue of his position, as *post* major of Militia, at Lexington, he undertakes to issue
his special orders to all the Churches in the City, when and where,
and for what they *must* thank God!   It is but charity to suppose

[78] A village near St. Louis which became a part of that city in 1870.

[79] Hiram W. Leffingwell: real estate promoter who laid out some of the city's parks
and boulevards; deputy county surveyor; deputy U. S. marshal.

[80] See *supra*, March 17, 1865.

[81] *Supra*, Jan. 12, 1865, note 4.

[82] Charles P. Johnson: St. Louis lawyer admitted to the bar in 1857; Free-Soiler; city
attorney, 1859–1860: lieutenant of Missouri Infantry, 1861; state legislator, 1862–1863,
1865–1866, 1881–1882; an advocate first of Lincoln's proposal of conpensated emancipation, then of unconditional emancipation; defeated Radical candidate for Congress in
1864; circuit attorney of St. Louis, 1866–1872; Liberal Republican lieutenant-governor,
1872–1874.

that the man is demented.   For if not " There is more hope of a fool than of him." [83]

This incident, by itself is of no great importance, but it is a sad proof of the full triumph of military despotism over the laws of the State (and worse, over the spirit of the people)[.]   Harding commands the Circuit Court,[84] and Davis commands all the parsons and congregations of Lexington.   They must pray now by *Special orders.*

Apl. 24.   Barton came down, bringing his wife, and staid two days, closely employed at work.   They returned this morning, all well.   Apl 26[.]

Also, Dr. Davis (with his wife, Julia Coalter,[)] left this morning—they have been with us some days.

Apl. 25.   I delivered at the office of the Mo. Dem[ocrat] my third letter to the people.[85]   I am a little afraid that they will decline to print it, on the pretence that it is too long.   If they do refuse, the real reason will be *fear;* for they are ha[r]d pressed just now, in regard to the new constitution.   Gov Fletcher [86] and Johnson,[87] and many other leaders of the party, great and small, are coming out against the new constitution.   Mr. Drake [88] is writing a series of frothey [*sic*] articles in support of the constitution; and he is very severely handled, in the papers, by Dr. Linton [89] and others.   ([*Note.*] Thursday Apl 27.   The Mo. Dem[ocrat] has not yet published my No. 3.[)]]

Apl 26.   I am very unwell—feel worn out and stay at home all day—fine, warm weather[.]

Apl. 27.   The Mo. Rep[ublican] of today has much good matter. i. a. (under the head of *Spirit of [the] German Press*) *Fredk Moench* [Muench][90] comes out flat *agst. the new Constitution.*   [*A clipping giving a reprint of his article in the* Westliche Post.]

2d.   A good editorial—" Wanted—a policy."

3.   Genl. Sherman's terms of peace, &c[.] [91]

Note.   I subscribed to the Mo. *Democrat* and paid one years[*sic*] subscription $12.   And also arranged to have 10 Nos. of each Edition which contains a letter of mine, put up separately, for me.

---

[83] *The Bible,* " Proverbs," chap. XXVI. verse 12.

[84] *Supra,* March 28, 1865; *infra,* June 2, 1865.

[85] See *infra,* "Appendix."

[86] *Supra,* Jan. 12, 1865, note 4.

[87] *Supra,* April 21, 1865, note 82.

[88] *Supra,* Feb. 12, 1863, note 13.

[89] M. L. Linton, founder and editor of the *St. Louis Medical and Surgical Journal,* 1843–1871, professor of medicine at St. Louis University.

[90] *Supra,* Feb. 2, 1865, note 38.

[91] Those granted by Sherman to Joseph E. Johnston.   The item appears in the issue of April 25, not in that of April 27.   See also [*Appleton's*] *American Annual Cyclopaedia,* V (1865), 68.

Apl. 28 (Friday). The Mo. Dem[ocrat] of this morning, contains my letter to the People of Mo., No. 3.[92]

Today the paper is full of matter, besides my article,[;] it [prints] Mr. Drake's [93] No. 7 (the last, he says) upon graveyards and Orphans' asy[l]ums—

Genl. Sherman's official report [94] of his southern campaign—And Halleck's [95] orders, very stringent about Sherman[.]

And Gratz Brown's [96] adhesion to the New Constitution[.]

May 1   Monday. Retained *John Murray*, (a brother of Dan) as a servantman of all work. He is to lodge and have his washing done at his brother Dan's, and I am to pay him $30, for this month—Each party is free to stop the contract at the end of the month, giving to the other a few days['] notice.

Dr. Warner and Dr. Barclay called, in the forenoon.

[*May 4.*] [*A newspaper reprint of President Johnson's proclamation* [97] *offering rewards for the arrest of Jefferson Davis and others.*[98]]

May 4. This proclamation surprises me very much; for Prest Johnson would not lend himself to a party trick to make temporary capital out of the *assassination*. Therefore I infer that there there [*sic*] is some evidence—enough to show probable cause—that the men named in the Proclamation are implicated in the detestable plot.

Note. The proclamation does not charge them as officers or members of the C.[onfederate] S.[tates of] A.[merica] but only thus "*Jeff. Davis* late of Richmond Va:" &c[.]

Note again—It appears that the evidence on which the proclamation is founded, is " the bureau of *military* justice "—and I infer that if the culprits be caught, they will be dealt with sum[m]arily, by a *military tribunal*, and not be remitted to a civil court, to be tried either for treason, or for conspiracy to commit murder.

Probably also, *this further policy* had a controlling influence. We have extradition treaties with many of the nations; but these treaties do not bind either of the parties to deliver up persons charged with *political offences;* and so, the surrender could not be demanded, to answer for *treason*, but *murder* and the attempt to com[m]it it, are among the enumerated crimes[.]

---

[92] *Infra,* "Appendix."

[93] *Supra,* Feb. 12, 1863, note 13.

[94] Published in book form. See also Appleton's *American Annual Cyclopaedia,* V (1865), 69.

[95] *Supra,* Nov. 13, 1861, note 37.

[96] *Supra,* Feb. 15, 1864, note 44.

[97] May 2, 1865, James D. Richardson, *Messages and Papers of the Presidents,* VI, 307–308.

[98] Clement C. Clay (*supra,* July 22, 1864, note 81), Jacob Thompson (*supra,* April 22, 1862, note 9), George N. Sanders (*supra,* July 22, 1864, note 80), Beverley Tucker, and William C. Cleary.

And thus, it may become very important, to fix upon the high traitors, who make good their escape to foreign countries, the charge of murder, in preference to treason.

May 6.

" Of all the people in the world, the Americans are the most [are most] disposed to forget the past and its lessons."—Mo. Dem[ocrat]. May 6./65[.]

This is taken from a bitter editorial urging proscription and vengeance.

The proposition however, is true. We have, utterly, forgotten the lesson so solemnly taught by Washington—that the only way to preserve our liberties, is " *a frequent recurrence to the first principles of the government.*"

May 8.

[*A newspaper reprint of an order of Major-General George H. Thomas,*[99] *attempting to suppress the guerillas in Tennessee.*]

Good, very good. Genl. Thomas, as all the world knows, is a true soldier and a wise and safe commander. But also, as this order proves, he is a man of good sense and practical wisdom.

[*A newspaper reprint of a letter from General Sherman to the Governor of Louisiana,*[1] *dated April 5, 1865.*]

Sherman, tho' sometimes a little wayward and eccentric, is, undoubtedly, a sincere, brave man; a man of agile mind, of great depth and breadth of thought.

See back, at p 157 [January 22, 1865], his compendious plan for reorganizing the Union.[2]

And see next page, about *him and Halleck.*[3] If I had not known before that Halleck was both knave and fool. I would have found out the latter by his pert insolence, in trying to snub and belittle Sherman, about the terms offered to Johns[t]on's[4] army.

May [ ] " Reverses are, in fact, of little consequence provided that successes be mingled with them, and impart hope hope [*sic*] and courage to the vanquished. The alternative has but the effect of increasing the energy[,] and exalting the enthusiasm of the resistence [*sic*]."

Thiers' Fren:[ch] Rev:[olution] vol 2. p 294.

May 10 Wednesday. The Mo. Dem[ocrat] has not yet published, my letter to the people, No. 4. I will enquire to day why not.

---

[99] *Supra,* Sept. 5, 1864, note 64.

[1] J. Madison Wells : sugar and cotton planter ; lieutenant-governor of Louisiana, 1864-1865 ; governor, from 1865 until General Sheridan removed him in 1867 ; surveyor of the port of New Orleans under Grant and Hayes.

[2] See also *infra,* 505–506.

[3] *Infra,* May 10, 1865.

[4] *Supra,* May 8, 1862, note 26.

E. B. *Dorsey* and his sister Cornelia, left our house early this morning, homeward bound, *via* Chicago.

I gave him letters to *Nicolay* [5] the consul at Paris—and Eads,[6] any where in Europe[.]

Genl. Sherman

[A long editorial headed "Progress of Snubbing."]

Only think of it! Such a poor thing as *General* Halleck, presuming to *snub* and belittle such a real General as Sherman! But so it is: " This world is grown so bad, that wrens make prey, where eagles dare not perch." [7]

That viper has bitten a file, and, no doubt, upon inspection, his teeth will be found broken.

May 11. The Mo. Dem :[ocrat] publishes my letter No. 4. unusually accurate.[8]

. . .

May 12. Went down to hear *Sarah Beresford* read her thesis before the High School, but missed it, being a few minutes too late— Courteously treated by P[r]of[esso]r. Childs.

Note. Met *Greene Erskine* [9] in the street (not having seen him before, for several years). He tells me that *the new constitution gives* all *school lands to the State.* I must look to that.

<*Postea.* I do not find it so—§ 9 of Art 9. is a knavish attempt in that direction, but I think does not reach the object. It provides that " The Gen Assembly shal[l], *as far as it can be done,* without *infringing upon vested rights,* reduce all lands, moneys[,] and other property, used or held for school purposes, in the various counties of this State, *into the Public School fund* [10] &c "—

Wherever the rights are *legally vested,* they are safe against the plundering ordinance—for the whole constitution *is but an Ordinance*—not only so, in truth and substance, but so declared by name— The Convention says, We the People &c do *ordain* this constitution—

I have heard it surmised that a good deal of the *Roman Catholic* property, within the State, is not, in strictness, *legally vested*—e. g. the old Cathe[d]ral Square and several others that might be named. If

---

[5] *Supra,* Feb. 28, 1862, note 18.   He was consul at Paris, 1865–1869.

[6] *Supra,* Jan. 28, 1860, note 38.

[7] W. Shakespeare, *Richard III,* Act I, Scene 3.

[8] *Infra,* " Appendix."

[9] Formerly a New Hampshire sailor ; then a resident of Montreal, Boston, Norfolk, Richmond ; finally a merchant in Danish St. Thomas, in New York City, 1826–1832, in St. Louis, 1832–1841 ; now a retired and wealthy citizen of St. Louis.

[10] The italics are Bates's.

that be so, the Radicals will have a fine chance to spoil the R.[oman]
C.[atholic] he[i]rarchy! Let Arch Bishop Kenric[k] [11] look to it.

[*A newspaper reprint of President Johnson's proclamation of
May 9, 1865, that the laws of the United States are in force in
Virginia.*] [12]

This proclamation of the President has not been as much considered by the Press and the People as its vast importance deserves.
When I am a little more at leisure, I design to draw attention to
several parts of it[.]

[*An editorial from the* Missouri Democrat *of May 12, 1865, titled
"The Adoption of the New Constitution Is a Party Question."*]

May 17 Wednesday—Took Mrs. Bates, Mrs. Woodson and Mrs.
Walton (Emely) to visit Mr. Shaw's [13] garden, and had a pleasant
time.

[*May 18*] [*A clipping from the* Missouri Democrat *of May 18,
1865, which tells that in 1864 a bill passed its second reading in the
Confederate Congress "legalizing the starvation of prisoners, the
murder of negroes, the burning of Northern cities, and the assassination of the heads of our Government."*]

I doubt whether there is a word of truth in this. No reference is
made to any source of information: It stands alone in the paper
as it stands here. If *unfounded*, it is a base and cruel charge.

May 18. The papers of this morning—Mo. Rep[ublican] and
Mo. Dem[ocrat]—both contain the decision of Judge Moody,[14] of the
St Louis circuit court, in the quo warranto case of Conrad vs Bernoudy—(Recorder of St Louis Co.[unty]) under the ordinance of
the Convention vacating offices, Conrad being appointed by Govr.
Fletcher, to succeed Bernoudy, brought his writ; and it is against
that that Judge Moody decides.

One Mr. Ousley (an acquaintance of S. Blood [15]) called to see me
about his condition, being under bond, and under order (provo[s]tal)
confining him to limits. I rated him soundly, about the cowardice
of people in his condition—telling him that I did not pity people
much who would make no effort to vindicate their rights &c. He
bore it me[e]kly, and left apparently cheered up.

---

[11] Peter R. Kenrick, ordained in Dublin, Ireland, in 1832, was a Catholic priest in
Philadelphia in 1833, editor of the *Catholic Herald* in 1835, bishop of St. Louis, 1843–
1847, archbishop, 1847–1893. He forbade his priests to take the "test oath" of the
Missouri Constitution of 1865,—an oath later declared unconstitutional. In Rome in
1870 he opposed the promulgation of the dogma of papal infallibility.

[12] "Executive Order," J. D. Richardson, *Messages and Papers of the Presidents*, V,
337–338.

[13] *Supra,* June 4, 1859, note 71.

[14] *Supra,* Feb. 2, 1865, note 40.

[15] Sullivan Blood settled in St. Louis in 1817, became deputy sheriff, alderman, ship-
captain, and a founder, director, and president of the Boatmen's Savings Institution,
1847–1870.

[*A pamphlet entitled* R. H. Wendover's Views on the New Constitution of Missouri, St. Louis, May 18th, 1865.]

R. H. Wendover *agin* the new Constitution[.]   Strong as *pizen*[.]

May 18.   Trial of the Assassins at Washington, by secret *military*
court.   Some one sends me the Phila. "Ledger" of May 12, containing copious extracts from the N. Y. *Post*, the *Tribune* and the
Times—all denouncing bitterly, the proceeding, as, at once, a dangerous b[r]each of law, and a gross blunder in policy.

Some days afterwards, I notice a paragraph in the N. Y. *Post*,
from which I infer that the N. Y. *Times* (scared, perhaps, at his own
boldness, in daring to assert a principle contrary to the dictatorship
of the war office) is easing off and backing down, into its normal
condition of abject dependence upon power—*Raymond*[16] has capacity, and would rather be a statesman, and a good citizen than a
sycophant—*if it were convenient*, and consistent with the pecuniary
interest of his paper.

Note, I wrote to Ashton,[17] the other day, to tell me how the government fell into the blunder of insisting upon trying the conspirators, by a military court.

[*A clipping from the* Missouri Democrat *headed* "*Spirit of the
German Press.   Judge Moodey's Decision*" *which reprints articles
from the* Anzeiger *and the* Westliche Post.]

"True as preaching."   Alas! for poor *Bay*[18] and *Dryden*,[19] I
despise them almost too much to pity them.

They lose their offices *now*, because they abandon their duty;
and they can hope for nothing hereafter, because they abandon
their duty *now!*

I now regret deeply that Barton Bates did not hold on, till now.[20]
He wd. have saved us from this pitiable shame.

Bay and Dryden have signed their death warrant.

" A *brave* Recorder of Deeds!

" Oh! most valiant flea, that takes its breakfast on the lip of a
lion! "[21]

---

[16] *Supra*, Feb. 4, 1860, note 61.

[17] *Supra*, Feb. 5, 1862, note 52.

[18] William V. N. Bay of Union, Missouri: state legislator, 1844–1848; Democratic congressman, 1849–1851; judge of the Missouri Supreme Court, 1862–1865. He had just
been removed under the "Ousting Ordinance" (*supra*, April 15, 1865, note 65) by Governor Fletcher (*supra*, Jan. 12, 1865, note 4) and Bates was disgusted because he had
not resisted the removal as unconstitutional.

[19] John D. S. Dryden: Virginia-born Missouri lawyer; judge of the Missouri Supreme
Court, 1862–1865. He, too, had been removed and had submitted to it as Bay had.

[20] Barton, Mr. Bates's eldest son, had been appointed in 1862 and elected in 1863 to a
judgeship of the Missouri Supreme Court along with Bay and Dryden, but had voluntarily
resigned in February, 1865.

[21] " . . . that's a valiant flea that dare eat his breakfast," etc. W. Shakespeare, *Henry
V*, Act III, Scene 7.

May 23. [*A newspaper clipping headed " Fraud and Corruption,"
reprinting an article from the* St. Joseph Herald *dealing with cases
involving persons in trouble with the military authorities.*]

I am heartily glad that these miscreants are beginning to be un-
earthed, and their crimes brought to light. It may be well perhaps,
to begin with the caitiff attorneys, becausese [*sic*] it may be easier to
handle them, at first, than to bring to condign punishment the
more powerful Commanders and Provosts; but, let their fingers
be fairly caught by the machinery of the law, and they must be
drawn in, to their very shoulders! One thorough trial of such a
villainous case, will give a clue for the developement [*sic*] of a score
of similar rascalities.

May 25   Thursday. . . . .

The Mo. Dem[ocrat] of this morning, contains my *fifth* letter to the
People of Mo.[22]

By the way, my vanity cannot help being, more or less, tickled
by the many letters which I receive, thanking me for my addresses
to the People. Some of them are from eminent men in the East.
And I must confess that my modesty is offended, and the value of
their praise deminished [*sic*] by its exuberance.

One of those letters is from *T. J. Coffey*[23] of Phil[adelphi]a.
from which I here copy a paragraph—says he
" it is my deliberate judgment that your last letter, on Rosecrans[24] and
the administration of law by Provost Martials [*sic*], is better than
any thing in *Junius*[25]—with as much vigor and clearness of stile
[*sic*], it has more than his pointedness and effectiveness, without any
of his acrimony and malignity. It is therefore, more dignified and becoming, and better suited to instruct the popular mind. . . . —Your
contrast between Rosecrans' relations with the *loyal people,* and his
want of relations with the *disloyal people under Price*[26] cannot be
beaten."

In that same letter, Coffey gives me *privately,* a pitiable account of
my successor, Mr. Speed.[27] It seems, that when he came into office
a new man, with not much reputation as a lawyer, and perhaps,

---

[22] *Infra,* "Appendix."

[23] *Supra,* March 5, 1860, note 18.

[24] *Supra,* March 9, 1864, note 95.

[25] *The Letters of Junius,* originally printed in the *London Public Advertiser,* between
January 21, 1769, and January 21, 1772, were savage pseudonymous attacks upon the
Government of the Duke of Grafton and upon George III, noted for their stylistic
perfection.

[26] *Supra,* Nov. 27, 1861, note 70.

[27] James Speed: Louisville lawyer; a state legislator; opponent of slavery in Kentucky; friend and supporter of Lincoln who helped organize the Unionist sentiment of
Kentucky to keep that State loyal in 1861. He served as attorney-general from December, 1864, until in 1866 his resignation was forced by Johnson's friends because of his
failure to support the President.

no strong confidence in his own opinions, he was caressed and courted by Stanton and Seward, and sank, under the weight of their blandishments, into a mere tool—to give such opinions as were wanted! Tho' my indignation rises at seeing the corruption and degredation of the *Law Department* of the Government, I cannot help pitying my poor imbecile successor! "Alas! poor Yorrick [*sic*]!" [28]

[*A long editorial from the* Philadelphia Public Ledger *of May 12, 1865, on* "*Secret Military Tribunals*" *and a reprint of an editorial from the New York Tribune of May 11 on the same subject.*]

<See forward, 222—Aug 21.>

Military trials for civil offences.

The three leading *Republican* papers in New York,—the Post, the Tribune and the Times—come out boldly, against the trial of *the assassins* of the President and the Sewards, by a *Military Commission*.

I am pained to be led to believe that my successor, Atty Genl. Speed, has been wheedled out of an *opinion*, to the effect that such a trial is lawful. [29] If he be, in the lowest degree, qualified for his office, he must know better. Such a trial is not only unlawful, but it is a gross blunder in policy: It denies the great, fundamental principle, that ours is a government of *Law*, and that the law is strong enough, to rule the people wisely and well; and if the offenders be done to death by that tribunal, however truly guilty, they will pass for martyrs with half the world.

I do not doubt that that unwise determination was the work of Mr. Stanton. He believes in mere force, so long as he wields it, but cowers before it, when wielded by any other hand. I think however, that Prest. Johnson is awakened to a true perception of the danger; and the result may be that the *Military Commission* will dwindle down to a mere *court* of *Enquiry*, and that when all the testimony has been taken, the prisoners may yet be turned over to the *Civil Courts*! [30]

I have no doubt, that first, Stanton's intention was to try Davis in the same way [31]—But his heart fails him—For I see, by the papers, that Davis and Breckenridge [32] [*sic*] have been indicted for *Treason*, in the *Circuit Court* of *the District of Columbia*. [33]

---

[28] W. Shakespeare, *Hamlet*, Act V, Scene 1.

[29] July, 1865, *Official Opinions of the Attorneys-General of the United States*, XI, 297–317.

[30] They were not turned over to a civil court, but were executed on order of the military court. For Johnson's connection with the episode see George F. Milton, *Age of Hate*, 205–211.

[31] Cf. Gideon Welles, *Diary*, II, 335, 337–339.

[32] *Supra*, Oct. 26, 1859, note 19.

[33] Chase, in whose circuit Virginia lay, refused to sit on this case until civil order was restored, and by that time feeling had subsided, and the cases against Davis and Breckinridge were ultimately dropped.

(*Note.* Mr. Ashton [34] informs me that great efforts are making, to force the trial of Jeff Davis, in the same illegal manner. Apprehensive of that result, he urges me to write my views of the subject, so as to get them before the Atty Genl's office) [.]

May 29 Monday. This is the 42d. anniversary of my marriage. We have had a long lease of happy intercourse, and, as I think, a sum of blessings far above the common lot of married life. Age has come upon us, with its consequent infirmities, yet still, the intercourse is as sweet as ever, and more necessarity [*sic*] than ever, to mutual comfort.

> "And evening comes at last, serene and mild,
> When after the long, vernal day of life,
> Enamored more, as more rememberance swells
> With many a proof of recollected love;
> Together down the[y] sink, in social bliss,
> Together freed, their gentle spirits fly,
> To scenes where love and joy promiscuous reign !"

May 30. This morning's Mo. Rep[ublica]n. contains the Amnesty proclamation of *Prest. Johnson.*[35] I like it very much, both in matter and style.

It is *attested* by Secy. Seward, but evidently not *written* by him— The style is altogether too precise and pointed, to be his composition.

The same paper contains another proclamation of the President, relative to the reestablishment of government in *North Carolina*[.] [36]

This contains some questionable doctrines, about [which] I cannot express a positive opinion, because I have not yet considered the subject maturely.

The Mo. Dem[ocrat] of May 29, contains a correspondence between the Revd. Dr. H. A. Nelson and Mr. Drake,[37] in which the former objects to "the Oath of Loyalty"[38] on the ground that it requires us to swear to maintain the union, *under any circumstances,* thus taking away the *right of rebellion* as asserted in the Declaration of Independence. Mr. D[rake] answers and explains that the oath *does not mean what it says,* whenever the *swearer* shall find out that the oath is against his essential interests, which interests, the *higher law of Selfpreservation* makes it his *right and duty to defend,* against all other laws !

[34] *Supra,* Feb. 5, 1862, note 52.
[35] May 29, 1865, J. D. Richardson, *op. cit.,* VI, 310-312.
[36] May 29, 1865, *ibid.,* VI, 312–314.
[37] *Supra,* Feb. 12, 1863, note 13.
[38] Missouri Constitution of 1865, Article XIII, Section 6. This oath had to be taken not only by voters (Article II, Section 3) but by all public office-holders, by officers and managers of private corporations, by officers of churches, and by all teachers.

Note. The higher law of *self-preservation* applies to States and Nations, as well as to men and mice.

> "Treason has never prospered. What's the reason?
> When it prospers, none dare call it *treason.*" [39]

Note 2. The Mo. Rep[ublican] of May 30, comments, with appropriate severity, upon the correspondence.

May 30. I recd. today The Lexington weekly Union, of May 27. which contains the *protest* of *Jesse Schofield* and *N. W. Letton*, judges of the County court of Lafayette against their unlawful arrest, by one Capt. Holmes (with negro militia under him—*backed by Govr. Fletcher* [40]) to compel them to surrender their offices and mun[i]ments to the Gov's new appointees, the two judges—Schofield and Letton, being removed by the sweeping ordinance of the convention. [41]

It seems, that they were twice arrested—On the first arrest they were discharge[d], by Judge Tutt, [42] on hab[eas] corp[us.] On the 2d. arrest— [   ].

I wonder if men will tamely submit to this. The Governor ought to be *sued* instantly—and impeached as soon as the Assembly meets[.]

<June 2d. I hear today, from Mr. Sharp [43] (of Sharp & Broadhead [44]) that there are men from the upper county, here taking legal counsel what to do. It seems that Col Harding [45] was applied to, to *oust* some of the officers holding over in spite of the Convention[.] That he sent to Genl Dodge, [46] for authority, who answered that the U. S. troops had nothing to do with it—Still, that *Gov Fletcher* had sent an order to *any troops* at Sedalia, [47] and that certain *U. S. troops* there, had executed it seising the records in hands of the *old* officers and giving over to the *new* ones[>].

June 2. Syfax—(E S. Woodson) Lent him $15. to be returned, positively, next Monday week.

---

[39] Sir John Harrington (1561–1612), *Epigrams*, Book IV, no. 5. It is not accurately quoted.

[40] *Supra*, Jan. 12, 1865, note 4.

[41] *Supra*, April 15, 1865, note 65.

[42] John A. S. Tutt, Virginia-born lawyer of Lexington, Missouri, formerly a county attorney and probate judge, now judge of the Missouri Circuit Court, 1862–1869. Tutt though opposed by the Radicals, was reappointed under the " Ousting Ordinance."

[43] Fidelio C. Sharp, Kentucky-born St. Louis lawyer.

[44] *Supra*, Dec. 26, 1859, note 66.

[45] See also *supra*, March 28, 1865.

[46] Grenville M. Dodge of Council Bluffs, Iowa : civil engineer and railroad builder in Illinois and Iowa, 1851–1861; officer under Frémont and then Curtis in Missouri and Arkansas, 1861–1862; brigadier-general of volunteers under Grant and then under Sherman in Mississippi and before Atlanta, 1862–1864; commander in Missouri. 1864–1865, again a railroad builder; congressman, 1867–1869.

[47] A railroad junction on the Missouri Pacific one hundred eighty-nine miles west of St. Louis.

June 2. This Day, my letter to the People. No. 6, was published both in the Mo. Dem:[ocrat] and the Mo. Rep:[ublican.] [48]

[*A clipping from the* St. Louis Dispatch *of June 3, 1865, printing a long letter of "Jacob Jonsing on Senator N. B. Jonderson" in the style of the Bigelow Papers.*]

June 5   Monday—Went to Dardenne Prairie,[49] under care of Miss Palm Hatcher—to see my sister, Mrs. Wharton [50] and other friends— Barton very kindly, took me round the neighborhood, wherever I wished to go.

Came home, thursday evening, the 8th., bringing with me Mr. Woodson, to stay a few days.

Found at our house three sweet girls—Mary Walton of St Charles, my grand niece, and two sweet daughters of Dr. Bates, of Wheeling— Sarah J. and Ella.

The vote on the Radical constitution!—We have carried St Louis and St Charles [51] by good majorities—and to all appearance, the nuisance will be abated.[52]

Whatever may be the result of the whole vote, the convention has made itself odious, and the leaders of sections have sunk into contempt—beaten at their own homes: In St Louis, where *Mr. Drake* [53] hoped to reign supreme, the majority against the constitution, is I hear, about 6000, and Cha[rle]s. P. Johnson,[54] a *reformed Radical*, is elected, to fill a vacancy in the Legislature, by an overwhelming vote.   And so, Mr. Drake is plucked bare, and cast down upon his own dunghill.   In St Charles, *Krekel* [55] fares no better; we beat them largely in the town, and in the whole county, 5 or 600.   And even in Warren,[56] where " Father Moench [Muench] " [57] opposed the constitution, a majority voted *for* it, to make sure of being *against him.*

In fact all the prominent members of the convention are sunk into contempt and the whole party in this state, I think has received its death-blow[.]   Mr. Krekel is the only prominent man of the party who has secured a safe retreat—U. S. Judge of the Western District—He is wholly unfit for the place, and will not

[48] *Infra,* "Appendix."

[49] *Supra.* July 30, 1859, note 61.

[50] Bates's only surviving sister, aged eighty years, who lived at Oakland near Dardenne Prairie.   See *infra,* Dec. 11, 1865.

[51] The County northwest of St. Louis County ; south of the Mississippi and northwest of the Missouri.

[52] The Radicals carried the State for the Constitution, 43,670–41,808, but that was only after great numbers of voters were disfranchised by the new voting clause of this very Constitution upon whose adoption the vote was being taken.

[53] *Supra,* Feb. 12, 1863, note 13.

[54] *Supra,* April 21, 1865, note 82.

[55] *Supra,* June 6, 1860, note 46.

[56] The County just west of St. Charles County and north of the Missouri River.

[57] *Supra,* Feb. 2, 1865, note 38.

fail to display in it, his ignorance and his perverse notions of law and government. He owes his appointment wholly to *Senator Henderson*[58] who got badly bitten in supposing that by making Krekel a judge he had "bought the Dutch."

Note. After all, Krekel is as good a *District* Judge as *Chase* is a ch[ief] Justice—The latter has a more enlarged association and a broader field, but is equally destitute of the requisites of his office— a competent knowledge of Law, Political history, and the ground-principles of our institutions. Mr. Chase never thinks of obeying the constitution *because it is so written*, but makes it bend to his groundless notion of universal Democracy. And besides, he is eaten up with his preposterous ambition to be President, which he eagerly pursues, by means as preposterous as the thought itself—e. g. his late foolish blunder of making a political speech to a *negro meeting* in Charleston.[59]

June 12. This day retained Cornelius McGrannighan to serve in my family—servant generally—He is on trial for a month, at the end of which, either party is free to quit—I pay him $35, and he [is] to procure his own lodging.

Thiers' French Revolution. Vol 2. p. 410.

"On that day <Dec 23. 1793> the column was utterly destroyed, and the great war of La Vendée[60] was truly brought to a close."

and then the historian remarks—

"If we take a general view of this memorable campaign of 1793, we cannot help considering it [as] the greatest effort that was ever made by a nation threatened with civil war."

Perhaps it was true at that day: But, after the efforts made by the U. S. for the last 4 years and the crowning efforts of the Spring of 1865, to put down the great rebellion of the *South*, the Vendean war is cast into the shade by the far-greater carnage and the far-wider spread desolation of the American civil war.

And all this has happened in my own time. When La Vendée succumbed, I was *3 months* old—and now, I am *72 years!*

Patois—Provincialism. Local phrase[.]

The word *chores*, is familiar in New England, meaning *little jobs*, running errands and the like. I thought it was a mere *patois*—a vulgar cant—but since Shakespear uses it, in the mouth of as great a person as Cleopatra, I must suppose it a *creditable* word. See Anthony and Cleopatra, Act 4. Scene 13—[15] [line 75]—and Act 5. Scene 2 [line 230]—Both times in the Queen's mouth.

---

[58] *Supra*, Feb. 24, 1863, note 27.

[59] See Appleton's *American Annual Cyclopaedia*, V (1865), 765.

[60] The region in northwestern France whose inhabitants—largely peasants—rebelled against the Revolution in 1793 and were finally suppressed only by terrific bloodshed.

True, S[h]akespeare spells it *Chare;* but that makes no odds, for the context plainly shows the meaning.

I forget whether, L[or]d. Campbell (in his little book on Shakespeare's law learning) [61] has mentioned the phrase, found in this same play, of *praying in aid*—an English law technic, which I dont [*sic*] rem[e]mber to have seen elsewhere, except in law books.

June 14. The Supreme court—Judges Dryden [62] and Bay [63] held an extra session on Monday the 12th. of June, which session cont[inue]d. till this day, when the judges were arrested as stated in the hand bill below. <see back p. 174 [March 9.].>

[*A broadside headed "Dispatch! Extra. Arbitrary Violence and Usurpation. Supreme Judges Taken Off the Bench. Gov. Fletcher Assumes to Decide a Question of Law. The Judges Taken before the Recorder's Court! Excitement in the City."*]

Gov Fletcher [64] must be a very mean, *little* man, and under the influence of very poor advisers (I hear that Knox [65] & Field [66] are his chief counsellors, *at law*)[.]

The affair has produced an effect upon the public mind, the most solemn and profound; and the best men in society, seem, at last, resolved to act in earnest, for the support of the law, against these violent proceedings of a reckless faction. The oppos[i]tion is no longer characterised by wordy denunciation and ribald abuse, but by plain solid accusation of crime, and a fixed purpose to enforce the law against the criminals.

[*June 17.*] On the night of Saturday, June 17, there was a grand meeting in front of the Court House, sober, thoughtful, solemn, at which Broadhead [67] made an excellent speech—others spoke also—and some solid resolutions were passed,—practically useful, if acted out.

On the same day—Saturday, June 17—of course, before the meeting—I published, in the "Evening Dispatch," a letter addressed to "The People of Missouri, and especially, to the People of the City and County of St Louis." designed to quiet the *passions* and excite the judgment and resolution of the People to enforce *the law* against Gov F.[letcher] and his accomplices.

I think that Gov F.[letcher] by this last wicked folly, has struck the death blow of his insensate party in this state.

[61] John Lord Campbell, *Shakespeare's Legal Acquirements Considered*, John Murray, London, 1859. The phrase occurs in Act V, Scene 2, line 27. Campbell does not mention it.
[62] *Supra*, May 18, 1865, note 19.
[63] *Supra*, May 18, 1865, note 18.
[64] *Supra*, Jan. 12, 1865, note 4.
[65] *Supra*, Nov. 2, 1859, note 30.
[66] *Supra*, Oct. 26, 1859, note 14.
[67] *Supra*, Dec. 26, 1859, note 66.

[*A clipping which prints a call for a meeting of Missouri Radicals on June 29, 1865, to approve the action of Governor Fletcher in removing Judges Bay and Dryden from the Supreme Court.*]

See back. p. 174 [March 9, 1865.]

June 21. [*A letter from S. P. Chase to a committee of colored men, June 6, 1865, reprinted from the* New Orleans Times *of June 9, 1865.*] [68]

When a friend at Phila[delphi]a. wrote me some months ago that a new party organization of Radica[l]s was in progress, with a view to the Presidency, whose distinctive principle would be, *negro suffrage*, I was inceredulous [*sic*], not believing that any considerable number of aspiring men could be so demented as to make *negro suffrage* the basis of a *National Party*. I knew that Mr. Chase was animated by a restless and unreasoning appetite for distinction, and so yearned after the Presidency, that he would stoop to any thing which promised success; but I did not think that he was weak enough to lean upon that broken reed.

But his Charleston speech,[69] and this N[ew] Orleans letter have undeceived me: He is a weaker man than even I, had supposed. He is evidently of opinion that the Radical party at the North, now bent on making *negro suffrage* their war cry, for the next campaign are strong enough to make him a feasible candidate for the next presidency.

[*A clipping which states:*

"The negroes of Cincinnati are about to present Chief Justice CHASE with a piece of silver plate in commemoration of his act of swearing into office a Mayor, who was elected by negro votes at Fernandina, Florida."]

Poor man! The eagerness of his appetite makes him eat poison; and if I am any prophet, he will die of it.

The worst feature of it is that those headlong partizans are upsetting the constitution and destroying the States. What right has Ohio and R[hode] Island to meddle with suffrage in Va. and Florida?

[*A clipping headed "The Question of Negro Suffrage" describes the proceedings at the New School Presbyterian Conference in New York:*

"The principal theme of the discussion was negro suffrage. The last speaker . . . stated that it became, at this time, an absolute necessity to give the negro the ballot, to counterbalance the Irish vote, and to keep out of Congress and the Senate, men from the South. The time has come, when such influences as Irish and Southern politicians should be held in check. The motion on the adoption of the memorial was put and carried."]

---

[68] S. P. Chase to Messrs. J. D. Rudanez, L. Golls, and L. Banks, Committee, June 6, 1865, Appleton's *American Annual Cyclopaedia*, V (1865), 515–516.

[69] See *supra*, June 5, 1865.

Military treason! I confess my ignorance. I never heard of it, till I read just now, a sketch of Reverdy Johnson's argument [70] (in Mrs. Surrat[t]'s case [71]) before the *Military* Commission, at Washington—He says (and cites Lawrence's Wheaton, Supp: p 41) that, in March /63, *Genl. Halleck* [72] gave an order to our General commanding in Tennessee, in which he undertakes to define *Military Treason!* as contradistinguished from *legal* treason. *Halleck's treason*, seems to me a new invention. It certainly is not Treason *against the U. S*, which (says the constitution—Art 3. § 3) shall consist *only* in levying war against them, *or* adhering to their enemies giving them aid and comfort."

Halleck's treason!!

June 27. . . .
Called to see us Revd. Mr. Foreman.

June 29. Aarchibald Gamble [73] called to see me[.]

June 30. Paid the man for wartering [*sic*] the street $2.50[.]

July 3. This day, I received and read a speech deliver[e]d by *Rich[ar]d. H. Dana* Jr.,[74] of Boston, at Faneuil Hall, June 21. 1865, concerning the 'Re-organization of the Rebel-States."

This speech fills me with sorrow and alarm. For long, I have been in the habit of looking upon *Rd. H. Dana* as among the most enlightened publicists and soundest statesmen in the country. But this speech subverts the very foundations of *American Government*— The fundamental principles upon which our fathers built the superstructure of our complex institutions.<[*Marginal Note.*] The U. S. have [*sic*] no *constitutional* power to *conquer* a state[.] On the contrary the U. S. is bound to suppress insurrection therein, and guaranty to each state in this Union. a Republican form of government, and that is inconsistent with conquest.> I must needs write upon this subject; and, considering the high honor in which I hold Mr. Dana, I think I will write, directly to him, and as soon as I have time and health to collect and arrange my thoughts.

July 5. . . .
Barton has been with us for several days and expects to go home friday (this is wednesday) [.]

---

[70] *Supra*, Nov. 26. 1859, note 85. For the argument see Benn Pitman's *Assassination of President Lincoln and the Trial of the Conspirators*, 251–263.

[71] Subsequent opinion has tended to support Senator Johnson in his defense of Mrs. Surratt, but she was hanged none the less with the other conspirators for Lincoln's death.

[72] *Supra*, Nov. 13, 1861, note 37.

[73] Virginia-born lawyer who settled in St. Louis in 1816, for eighteen years clerk of the Circuit Court and recorder of deeds.

[74] *Supra*, Feb. 26, 1863, note 48. His speech was published in pamphlet form.

The Miss Bates of Wheeling are still with us [75]—for how long, we don[']t know.

[*A clipping purporting to give part of Holt's testimony at the secret trial of Lincoln's assassins.*]

[*A copy of a long letter from Governor Crapo* [76] *of Michigan in which he refuses to turn certain murderers over to the military authority.*]

I am rejoiced to find that the Civil authorities are beginning to assert the law and their own rightful powers, against the insolent usurpations of the *Military*. This *Governor Crapo* writes good law and common sense; and if the Sec. of Ware [*sic*] be yet capable of shame, he must feel severely rebuked by the Govr.'s manly answer.

It is but a part of the revolutionary scheme which is even now, trying the *conspirators* [77] at Washington, by a *Military Commission*, and urging the trial of [*Jefferson*] *Davis*, by the same means.

<Since the above was written, the telegraph informs us that the *Military Commission* has condemned *all* the accused—4 of them to death, and the others to long terms of imprisonment.

I hoped to the last, that Prest. Johnson would set aside the finding, and remit the prisoners to the civil courts. But, the 4 condemned to death, were executed on the 7th. of July[.]> [78]

I see by the papers, that the Sec of War has, by his simple fiat, prevented the opening of Fords Theatre—the scene of Prest. Lincoln's assassination.

After that, what may he not do? What is to hinder him from from [*sic*] transferring estates from one man to another, annulling land titles and dissolving the tie of marriage?

July [ ]. On friday, the 7th., Barton took me up to his house, I being very unwell—On monday the 10th., Julia and Matilda followed—taking little Fanny [79] with them. Wednesday 12, Matilda came home bringing Hester [80])—Thursday, 13—both Julia and I being very unwell, Barton brought us home where we arrived at nightfall, rejoiced to find that Coalter had arrived, in high health, and, as he requested, [had been] ordered to St. Louis, on recruiting duty.

Note—Coalter says that Gen Meade [81] told him that he was brevetted *Lieut. Col.* but that he had recd. no official information of it. <He got it soon after[.]> [82]

---

[75] See *supra*, June 5, 1865.

[76] Henry H. Crapo: farmer, land surveyor, militiaman in Massachusetts until 1856; lumber miller at Flint, Michigan, 1856–1864; mayor; state senator; governor, 1865–1869.

[77] Those involved in the assassination of Lincoln.

[78] The parenthetical paragraphs were added later.

[79] A grandchild of Mr. Bates.

[80] A grand-daughter of Mr. Bates—Barton's child.

[81] *Supra*, Oct. 15, 1863, note 18.

[82] The parenthetical sentence was added later than the rest of the note. The brevet was antedated April 9, 1865.

My own health is very bad, my throat and lungs being badly implicated. Julian thinks, and so do I, that I might be carried off at any time, and at very short notice. This gives me no uneasiness—not the slightest alarm. I have lived already, beyond the allotted time of man. God has been very merciful to me, in my own person and in my family, and I am ready to go cheerfully whenever called. Indeed, I hope that I will not be allowed, in this world, to Outlive my faculties and my affections.

[*A reprint from the* Black Republican [83] *which predicts that the colored race will be extinct in the United States in three hundred years unless Congress grants the negroes a place in which to live by themselves.*]

This black editor is something of a ph[i]losopher, and, evidently, has more practical sense—which is wisdom—than most of his white brethren. *He* is dealing with realities of concrete life, while they are dogmatizing with their own fanciful theories.

July 18.   Sarah J. and Oella Bates, of Wheeling,[84] started home this [morning?], after a visit to us of 5 or 6 weeks—Julian and Matilda saw them fairly off.

July 19. . . . .
My health is very feeble: Went down town this morning, and returned very tired.
Radical German Convention at *Indianapolis.* . . .
[*A pamphlet containing the resolutions passed by the Radical German Convention which met at Indianapolis in May, 1865.*

The first resolution demands complete civil rights and the suffrage for the negro; the second demands that the "monarchical system of Executive power" be destroyed by abolishing the separate executive and putting all executive power into the hands of a committee of Congress; the third demands that the Monroe Doctrine be maintained by meeting "monarchical intervention in America" with "republican intervention in Europe"; the fourth insists upon complete freedom of religion and faith which must include (1) abolition of "the appointment of days for fasting and prayer, the Sunday constraint, the oath on the Bible, the opening of legislative assemblies with prayer," and (2) suppression of the power of the Papacy; the last demands provision of "a stronger representation in the Legislature" for "the laboring and neglected classes" and the assertion of "the principle that the State's help in all cases must come to the relief, where, for any individual, his own help is not sufficient for the satisfaction of just demands, and for securing an existence worthy the dignity of man."]

<see back, p. 15 [October 29, 1863]—the G.[erman] R.[adical] convention, at Cleveland in 1863>

---

[83] The editor was a negro minister in New Orleans.
[84] See *supra*, June 5, and July 5, 1865.

These *Radical Germans!* They are as mad as [   ] Anacharsis Clootz.[85] They are not satisfied with the anarchic opinions of their brethren—The Radical German convention, which sat at Cleveland some two years ago—they, among other monstrosities, of principle and policy, insisted that this Government ought to be in sympathy and action, united with *the Revolutionists of Europe!*—That dont [*sic*] satisfy these last, *progressive Radicals.* They are for destroying the constitution, thus annulling the *United States*—for without the Constitution there can be no U. S, and establishing a *Democratic Empire* in its stead! If they must have an *Emp[i]re* France, pe[r]haps would be their best model, but they, being not only *Radicals*, but German radicals, may have a traditionary preference for the *Holy Roman Empire!*

Still, they are no worse than many of our home-born *Radicals*, who, in that destructive name, despise all constitutional restraints, and laugh at the idea of *liberty by law.*

Revd. Stuart Robinson [86] D. D.

[*A ten-page pamphlet entitled* Infamous Perjuries of the " Bureau of Military Justice " Exposed.—Letter of Rev. Stuart Robinson to Hon. Mr. Emmons.]

(See forward, Aug. 7, 1866.)[86a]

The Revd. Stuart Robinson, D. D., does not seem to me to have made the most of his case. He gives way to his indignation, at the expense of his logic. And yet he has matter enough, if perspicuously and tersely stated, to overwhelm both the witnesses with shame.

From all I have heard of Dr. Robinson, I am inclined to think him rather a theoretical rebel than a practical traitor. He has hard measure. Like many other *smart*, silly men, who are wise in their own conceit, he excites more practical and less brilliant minds to the commission of crimes from which he, himself, would recoil with horror. There is a sort of social justice which I have often observed in the concrete of life—Men often escape the condign punishment of the offences of which they are really guilty, and yet are brought to shame and sorrow, for crimes imputed, of which they were really innocent[.]

I once defended a man charged with the homicide of his brother: True, he killed the man, but under justifiable circumstances; yet he

---

[85] Jean B. du V. de G. Cloots, 1755–1794, known as Anacharsis Cloots, " orator of the human race," a revolutionary philosopher of noble Prussian birth who went to France to join in the Revolution in 1790, gave money to the cause in 1792, was elected to the Convention, and finally was guillotined March 24, 1794, as an Hébertist.

[86] Irish-born Presbyterian minister and school teacher in western Virginia, 1841–1847, in Kentucky, 1847–1852, and in Baltimore, 1852–1856; professor in the Theological Seminary at Danville, Kentucky, 1856–1858; minister in Louisville, 1858–1862, 1866–1881. In 1862 his pro-slavery and secession activities led to the suppression of a paper he edited, and forced him to leave the State and live in Canada until 1866.

[86a] See the marginal note, *infra*, 494.

was convicted and sent to the penetentiary [*sic*], because (as I verily believe) *he was an old horse thief!*

[*Marginal Note.*] *Aug 7. 1866.* I have just read, in the Mo. Rep[ublican] of this day, the Report of the minority of the Judiciary com[mitt]ee. of the H[ouse] of R.[epresentatives] [87] (Mr. *A. J. Rogers* [88] of N.[ew] J.[ersey])] on the same vile plot. He discloses the perjury of the witnesses and the wicked subornation of certain high officials, to the point of nausea.

[*A newspaper reprint of a letter of Archbishop Kenrick* [89] *written on July 28, 1865 to the Catholic Clergy says:*

> " Since under the new Constitution a certain oath [90] is to be exacted of Priests, that they may have leave to announce God's word, and officiate at marriages, which oath they can in no wise take without a sacrifice of ecclesiastical liberty, I have judged it expedient to indicate to you my opinion in the matter, that you may have before your eyes a rule to be followed in a case of this delicacy. I hope that the civil power will abstain from exacting such an oath. But should it happen otherwise, I wish you to inform me of the particular circumstances of your position, that I may be able to give you counsel and assistance."]

In my own mind, I was satisfied, from the first, that the Roman Catholics would never submit to the foolish and unjust requirement of the new constitution; but now, this letter of Archbishop Kenrick, makes the matter certain, that the R.[oman] C[atholic]s resist the oppression. And that will embolden all the weaker sects to do the same. And not only so, but secular persons, teachers, lawyers and the like will be apt to follow the example; and I thank [think] that such an array of opposition, will test the courage of the Radical leaders[.]

<see back p 215 [August 30, 1865], the archbishop agst the *Fenians*>

July 22. Saturday. Robert. B. Frayser, adm[inistrato]r. of Sarah Bates, [91] Sent me a check for $1800. of which I am to send $500, to *Flementine Ball* [92] and $500 to *Eliza B. Hudnall*, [93] being heirs—the 1st. a child, the 2d. grand child—of Fleming Bates dec[ease]d. And the remaining $800, for myself.

July 28 Friday. [94] Father being too unwell to write requests me to make entries here for him to bring his Diary down to the above date.

---

[87] " Minority Report " on the " Assassination of Lincoln," July 28, 1866, *House Reports,* 39 Cong., 1 Sess., vol. I, ser. no. 1272, doc. no. 104, pp. 30–41.

[88] Andrew J. Rogers: originally a New Jersey lawyer, 1852–1863: Democratic congressman, 1863–1867; New York lawyer, 1867–1892, 1896–1900; lawyer and police commissioner in Denver, Colorado, 1892–1896.

[89] *Supra,* May 12, 1865, note 11.

[90] The test oath; see *supra,* May 30, 1865, note 38.

[91] Mr. Bates's sister who had died on August 12, 1859.

[92] Mr. Bates's niece—daughter of Fleming Bates.

[93] Mr. Bates's grand-niece—grand-daughter of Fleming Bates.

[94] This whole entry is in a feminine hand—written by one of Bates's daughters.

Sunday the 23rd. being a bright pleasant day he and Mama and Sister and Coalter and Onward and Hester and myself went to the central church, Father seemed rather oppressed in church though:, and Dr. Anderson's [95] sermon was not specially attractive. He and Mama rode home in Mr. Booth's carriage—In the afternoon he went to Judge Reber's [96] to dine and meet Gen Sherman, and returned home about 6½ very much fatigued by the unusual exercise taken during the day—He was soon attacked by a painful fit of suffocation and we thought for hours that each labored breath would be his last—Julian was out of town attending a very ill patient and we could get no physician until near midnight when Mr. Merriman brought Dr. Timothy Papin [97]—in the meantime we applied such remedies as we knew of, his breathing could be heard a half square, Mr. Merriman heard it at his house, and the pain was so great that he almost wished for death—he, and we all thought he was dying he took leave of us and left parting words for the absent children, Brother, Julian, Fleming, Dick and Woody—he said he was not afraid to die, he was "at peace with Jesus"—(God help me I dont [sic] know what that means, I thought then I would be willing to die if I could have that feeling) [98]—but God in his mercy permitted this cup to pass from us, his breathing gradually became free, but it was not until three o'clock that exhausted by so much suffering he fell into a restless troubled sleep.

He is much weakened and recovers slowly. The neighbors and friends have been very kind in proffers of assistance[.]

Monday the 24th. Coalter telegraphed the Sec'y of War asking leave for Cadet Bates and rec'd a very kind response expressing regret at Father's illness asking to be informed as to his condition and saying that leave had been forwarded Woody[.]

[*An editorial from the* Missouri Democrat *of August 2, 1865, on* "*Our Immigration Movement*," *and an article reprinted from the* London Daily News *telling* "*How British Emigration is Encouraged.*"]

The Mo. Dem:[ocrat] while praising highly, in general terms, the plan to encourage emigration, seems carefully to avoid giving particula[r]s. Nothing is stated to lead to the belief that the plan is any thing more than a scheme of electioneering, by by [sic] speeches and newspaper and pamphlet articles, in common form.

It does not even mention the high premium offered in the new constitution—i. e. the right of suffrage *without naturalization!*

---

[95] *Supra*, July 17, 1859, note 26.

[96] *Supra*, June 4, 1859, note 74.

[97] A native of St. Louis (1825) who studied medicine in Paris, founded St. John's Hospital, and taught in the St. Louis Hospital and the Missouri Medical College.

[98] This is the daughter's interjection.

The extract from an English paper, below, discloses a far more efficient aid to immigration.

[*Two clippings giving reprints of military orders which declare a Richmond municipal election null and void, provide for close military supervision of a state election in Kentucky, and disfranchise large classes of citizens in Kentucky.*]

I am but wasting my time and labor and foolishly, " fretting myself, because the wicked prosper."

It is idle to invoke principles and prate about the Constitution and the law, when every day, we see, ostentatiously displayed, such practical examples as these, of absolute despotism, avowed, in the name of *Martial Law.*

[*A clipping which states that returned rebels have been shot in Missouri.*]

As far as I can learn, these murders are committed chiefly, by the cowardly militia, who took good care to keep out of gun-shot of the Rebels, when they came as avowed Enemies, with arms in their hands[.]

[*A clipping telling how a German professor has carefully counted the hairs of the human head.*]

[*A newspaper statement that the people of Lancaster, Pennsylvania, have annoyed Ex-President Buchanan by electing him three years in succession to the undesired office of constable.*]

Prest Buchanan a constable!

Aug 4. Since then, I have sent to Flementine and Eliza, each, $500, drafts on the B[an]k of America N[ew] Y[ork].[99]

This money will be a very opportune supply—as Flementine writes me that she has *no money*, and no prospect of getting any for a year to come.

[*Note.*] Aug 20. I am getting uneasy at not hearing from my nieces, Flementine and Eliza. The drafts were sent them in a letter addressed to them *jointly*, and sent to the care of Mrs. Clarke, of Baltimore.

[*Additional Note.*]—I have recd. a letter since, announcing the safe arrival of the drafts—

Aug 7. See Lives of the L[or]d. Chancellors,[1] Vol 1. p. 235. In vit. Sir Robert Thorpe.[2]

" It is to be deeply deplored that of a virtuous magistrate. like *Thorpe*,[3] such slender memorials remain, as it is so much more agreeable to relate what is hono[u]rable than what is disgraceful to

---

[99] See *Infra*, July 22, 1865.

[1] John Lord Campbell, *The Lives of the Lord Chancellors and Keepers of the Great Seal of England*, 7 vols., Blanchard and Lea, Philadelphia, 1851.

[2] Master of Pembroke College, Cambridge, 1347–1364 ; chief justice of the Court of Common Pleas, 1356–1371 ; lord chancellor, 1371–1372.

[3] The italics are Mr. Bates's.

human nature—to praise [rather] than to condemn; but I find, from my laborious researches, that while a Chancellor is going on in the equal and satisfactory discharge of his duty, little notice is taken of him, and that he is only made prominent by biographers and historians, when he takes bribes, perverts the law, violates the Constitution, oppresses the innocent, and brings ruin on his Country:—[''']

> "The evil that men do lives after them;
> The good is oft interred with their bones."[4]

Alas! it is always so. As it was with Lord C[h]ancellor Thorpe, so it is with all other public functionaries—As it was in the fourteenth century, so it is in the nineteenth! Jeffreys is more famous than Mansfield,[5] and Chase[6] eclipses Marshall!

Aug 9. Wednesday. This morning, Woodson returned from Dardenne.[7]

This evening, the Gas Lamp was lighted for the first time, at the corner of Morgan Street and Leffingwell Avenue.

We have had gas in our house, for more than a month.

[*A clipping which reports a rumor that Judge Edwards[8] of St. Charles will only permit those attorneys to practice in his circuit who have taken the constitutional oath.[9]*]

Judge *Edwards* is not very smart, but I think he has too much sense for that.

[*A clipping asking what the Radicals will do about the opinion of Judge Sprague[10] of the U. S. District Court in Boston in the* Amy Warwick *case[11] in which he said:*

> "'It has been supposed that [. . .] after the rebellion is supressed the Government [it] will have the rights of conquest; that a State and its inhabitants may be permanently divested of all political privileges,

---

[4] W. Shakespeare, *Julius Caesar*, Act III, Scene 2.

[5] George Jeffreys was advocate of the Crown in the state trials of England from 1678 to 1683, and the judge who as chief justice of the King's Bench (1683–1685) condemned several famous state prisoners and conducted the "bloody assizes" at Winchester in 1685, whereas William Murray, first earl of Mansfield and chief justice of the King's Bench (1756–1788), was a moderate judge whose decisions over a long period of years brought order out of chaos in the realms of commercial law and the law of contract.

[6] Possibly Samuel Chase (*supra*, April 2, 1860, note 46), a contemporary of John Marshall, but more probably Salmon P. Chase, the actual chief justice, for whom Bates had little respect.

[7] *Supra*, July 30, 1859, note 61.

[8] *Supra*, March 9, 1865, note 14.

[9] See *supra*, May 30, 1865, note 38.

[10] Peleg Sprague, Maine state legislator, 1821–1822; National Republican congressman, 1825–1829, and U. S. senator, 1829–1835, from Maine; Boston lawyer, 1840–1841; judge of the U. S. district court in Massachusetts, 1841–1865.

[11] *The Amy Warwick* (Dunlop, Moncure & Co., Claimants), 1 *Federal Cases* 808–811. The *Amy Warwick* was captured on August 10, 1861, while running the blockade en route from Rio de Janeiro to Richmond. Dunlop, Moncure & Co. was a Richmond firm who sued for the portion of the cargo which was its property. The property was condemned and the claim dismissed. The quotation from the clipping is not accurate.

and treated as foreign territory acquired by arms. This is an error[,] —a grave and dangerous error.[. . .] Under despotic Governments[,] the power of municipal confiscation may be unlimited; but under our Government the right of sovereignty over any portion of a State is given and limited by the Constitution, and will be the same after the war as it was before. . . .'"]

The *Radicals* are not likely to shew more respect for a decision of Judge Sp[r]ague, than they habitually shew for the Constitution[.]

[*August 12*] [*An editorial headed "Southern Parties" which declares:*

"The regeneration of the South depends upon the progress which Radicalism makes in the rebellious districts. As it secures possession, the Government may withdraw its troops, and leave the law to perform its mission. Until that time the spirit of treason may be expected to predominate. Fortunately for the country, there is, or soon will be, a Radical party organized in every Southern State."]

This [is] an Editorial of the Mo. Dem:[ocrat] of Aug 12. 1865, and sufficiently shewes [*sic*] the settled object of the *Radical Party.* They are determined, by mere brute force, to " secure possession of the Government " in the hands of the *few over the many;* and then, when they have altered the law to suit their faction, they propose to withdraw the troops, and leave *their law* to perform its mission[.]

Aug 21, Monday. For the last two days, I have been very unwell. The disease of my lungs seems to yield readily, in degree, to Julian's prescriptions, but it lies in wait continually, and returns upon me, whenever I fail to take the medicines, according to direction.

[*Marginal Note.*] Barton came down to see me, staid till wed- nesday, 23d., and then returned taking Onward [12] along for a holi- day of a few weeks[.]

Atty Genl. Speed, and Military tribunals.

I have just read a pamphlet (sent to me under the frank of Atty Genl. James Speed) entitled " Opinion on the constitutional power of the Military to try and *execute* the Assassins of the President[.] [18]

By Attorney General James Speed.["]

<see back, 205, May 25.>

This is the most extraordinary document I ever read, under the name of a law opinion—

Mr. Speed states the case, in this short paragraph—

" The President was assassinated at a theatre, in the city of Washington. *At the time* of the assassination a civil war was

---

[12] Mr. Bates's grandson—Barton's eldest child.

[18] July, 1865, *Official Opinions of the Attorneys-General of the United States,* XI, 297– 317.

flagrant, and the city of Washington *was defended by fortifications*, regularly and constantly manned, the *principal* police in the City was by *federal soldiers*, the public offices and property in the city *were all guarded by soldiers*, and the President's House and person were *or should have been*, under the guard of soldiers. *Martial law had been declared* in the District of Columbia, but *the civil courts were open and held their regular Sessions, and transacted business, as in times of peace.*" [14]

These are the only facts stated; and upon these facts alone, the Attorney General proceeds to state his argument, and to announce his opinion, in these words—

" My conclusion[,] therefore[,] is[,] that if the persons who are charged with the assassination of the President committed the deed *as public enemies* ([,]as I believe they did—[,] and whether they did or not is a question to be decided by the *tribunal* before which they are tried)[,] they not only *can*[,] *but ought to be tried before a military* tribunal. If the persons charged have offended against the *laws of war*, it would be as palpably wrong for the *military to hand them over to the civil civil* [*sic*] *courts*, as it would be wrong in the civil court to convict a man of murder who had in time of war, killed another in battle[.]"

Note. This opinion is addressed *To the President* and dated " *July — 1865.*" *After* the sentence, and in fact, after the execution of the accused who were condemned to death! And thus, it is apparent that the opinion was gotten up (a mere fetch of the War Office) to bolster up a jurisdiction, *after the fact*, so generally denounced, by lawyers and by the respectable press, all over the country.

Not here to go into minute criticism—The Atty Genl. does not venture to deny the obligation of the cited clauses of the constitution, but only says that they must be read along with others, which he says, make the Laws of nations part of the Laws of the land; and that the *laws of War*—being part of the laws of Nations—are thus, constitutionally *part of the laws of the land.* And thus, a *part of the law of the land*, established as such, by hypothetical arguments is made to override and annul the plain and repeated provisions of the *constitution!*

The whole substance of the opinion is, that if the accused " committed the deed *as public enemies*,["] they not only *can* but *ought* to be tried by a *military tribunal.*

Well, *Treason* can be committed only by a *public enemy*, for it consists only " in levying war against the U. S. or adhering to their *enemies*, giving them aid and comfort." [15] *Pirates* also are *public*

---

[14] In this and the following quotation, the capitalization and punctuation are faulty, and the italics are Mr. Bates's.

[15] *The Constitution*, Article III, section 3.

enemies; indeed they are often called *enemies of mankind!* Yet, according to Atty Genl. Speed, they can be tried lawfully only by a *military tribunal!* With him, the only question (to give jurisdiction) is did the offender act as a *public enemy,* or only of his *private malice*—If the former, the *military* must *try,* that being the general, public government, and the Civil Courts being designed only to punish *private offenders* and redress *private* wrongs!

This doctrine would be infin[i]tely rediculous [*sic*], if it were not so full of danger to all legal government.

It is a little remarkable that the Atty Genl. does not call his *military tribunals* by the name of *Courts*—nor pretend that there is any *written law* for their existence. They are not *Courts Martial,* created, limited and governed by act of Congress, but the mere creatures of the commander—great or small—with no rule for their consti[tu]-tion—whether they shall consist of one or many—of officers or privates—with no limit as to the kind of cases to be tried excepct [*sic*] that the accused must be *public enemies;* and no legal forms of trial; and no designation of the kind and degree of punishment to be awarded. The constitutional inhibition against "Cruel and unusual punishments"[16] cannot apply to *Military tribunals sitting only under the Laws* of War! They may, if they will, award such tortures as were inflicted upon the assassins of Henry IV, king of France, or William, the Silent, Prince of Orange, or Kleber, general of the French army in Egypt. As there is no known law for their existience [*sic*], there can be no prescribed form for their creation and mode of action, and no written limitation of their powers. But the Atty Genl. is mistaken in one important particular, set down in the very title of the opinion (as published in pamphlet form, by authority of his office). True the Tribunal is unlimited as to the sentence it may pronounce, but the sentence is of no force until approved by the President. The Commission had no power to *execute its sentence;* but the President could annul it, at pleasure, with or without a reason.

<Very lately, two men were convicted and sentenced to severe punishment, by a *Military Commission* sitting in Washington—the alleged crime was a fraud committed *in New York*—The news papers say that Prest. Johnson set aside the whole proceeding, as *coram non Judice,* and remitted the men to the civil authority of N. Y.>

As said before, the Atty Genl. does not call his *military tribunals* courts; nor does he designate them by any particular name, but uses the generic description only of *tribunals;* neither does he describe the *power* that appoints and uses them for its instruments of punishment, as the *Government* or the *President,* but as *The Military*—

---

[16] *Ibid.,* amendment VIII.

thus, assuming that *the Military* is a recognized *power in the State*—a separate and independent political existence, with authority to define and punish offences, to try offenders, to hear and determine accusations, and to pronounce and execute judgment upon the accused.

It is hard to understand what the Atty Genl. means by *the Military*. Does he mean the entire military force of the U.[nited] S:[tates] consisting of the Army, the Navy and the Militia in actual service, as organized by acts of Congress, and of which the President is the constitutional Commander in chief? Is that *The Military* which the Attorney General supposes to be vested with the independent power to charge, *try and execute* all offenders *against the Laws of War*—all offenders who " com[m]it the deed *as public enemies* "—Or must we understand that these exorbitant powers are vested in every commander of a separate army, or Detachment or Post on shore; and in every commander of a separate squadron or detached ship of war, at sea? In either case, the power must be exercised not only without the sanction of any written law, but against the express terms of the constitution and the Statutes. The President, the Commander in chief, and all his subordinates in the Army and the Navy exist only by written law, without which they are nothing; and I affirm it, as a fundamental principle, that he who claims any right or power by virtue of a *written law or grant*, must claim it according to the terms of that writing—and not otherwise.

Our fathers thought, and taught us, to believe, that we lived under a government of law—that it was possible that Law might be a *rule of government* for a nation, as well as a *rule of action* for a man. But now, the *first law officer* of the government assures us that this is all a mistake—That " *in time of war* "—war with any body, great or small—the laws are silenced, and *the military* at its own caprice, can inflict whatever punishment it pleases, upon any person supposed (by " the Military ") to be guilty of some offense against the (unknown) Laws of war, or some offence committed by them as a *public enemy*.

The Laws and usages of war—What are they? Who knows them? Are they written in any book? Are they prescribed by any acknowledged authority? There is no such thing as the *Laws of War*. War is the very reverse of Law—and its existence always implies (as between the parties to the war) the absence or disregard of all law. <*[Marginal Note.]* We say *figuratively*, the *laws of gravitation*—of—of [*sic*] *electricity*, of *matter*—of *mind*—meaning only the course of nature, over which man has no control.> And as for the *usages* of of [*sic*] war, they are not *laws* at all—not *rules of action*, binding on any body,—and there is no means of finding out what they are, without knowing the *practice* of all who have made war, in all time. (Mr. Atty says that the laws of war, are but parcel of the Law of Nations)

But if there be *laws and usages of war*, to set them up, as of authority superior to the constitution and Statutes of the United States, seems to me nothing short of absurd logic and insolent usurpation.

(The most that can be said of them is that there are certain *habits of comity* practised among nations, but of no binding force, and certainly not superior to positive law.[)] [17]

But these *Military Tribunals* (not *Courts*, martial or civil) —Atty Genl. Speed says that they are instituted " in the interest of justice and mercy! "—they are instituted " to save [human] life! " they are instituted to " prevent indiscriminate slaughter! " Still, what are they, and of what materials are they composed? They are committees of enquiry, to find out whether certain persons are guilty of some offense against the *laws of war*, or guilty of some offense, by them committed *as public enemies;* and if they find them guilty, they are to indicate (without any law to guide them) what kind of punishment, and how much, ought to be inflicted. But they can pass no *final sentence;* for (according *to the Laws and usages of war*) that little matter belongs to *The Military* above them. But how are they constituted, and of what material? They are selected by the military commander *from among his own subordinates*, who are bound to obey him, and responsible to him; and therefore, they will, commonly, find the case as required or desired by the commander who selected them. But if their finding happen to be unsatisfactory to the commander, it goes for nothing—He annuls the sentence. *Courts Martial* exist by statute law, and the members thereof have *legal* duties and rights. But these *military tribunals* exist only by the will of their commander, and that will is their only known rule of proceeding.

[*Marginal Note.*] *Instituted in the interest* of *Justice and mercy*, to *save life—*to *prevent indiscriminate Slaughter! The Military* thus become, at once the Judges and dispensers of justice and mercy! Instead of *killing* (which seems to be its special vocation) its office is to save life! And it *prevents itself* from committing indiscriminate slaughter!

It is part of the Attorney Genl.'s statement of his case, that " *Martial law had been declared*, in the District of Columbia; and yet, in his mind, *the declaration of of* [sic] *martial law* was not necessary to support the jurisdiction of the *Military tribunals;* for he asserts the

---

[17] The parenthetical sentence was inserted later.

power in *the Military*, as the necessary result of the bare existence of a state of war. And he assumes that " *the Military* " is not the Creature and servant of the Civil Government, bound to fight its battles and obey its orders but that it is, " in time of war " an independent government of itself, vested with full powers to arrest, try, adjudge and execute all offenders against the laws of War, and all who offend *as public enemies!* And that this extraordinary power is to be exercised not in accordance with any written law of our own country, but under authority of some imaginary code of laws supposed to exist /) only in the usage and practice of Civilized Nations, generally!

Still, it is part of the Attorney Generals [*sic*] statement of the facts of the case on which his opinion is based, that " martial law had been declared in the District of Columbia." That fact must have been stated with some view to its legitimate, legal effect upon the judgment of the Attorney General in regard to the great question submitted by the President for his opinion,—viz " The constitutional power of *the Military* to try and execute the assassins of the President."

Martial Law, says he, has been *declared*, in the D.[istrict of] C.[olumbia]. Then, in his opinion, there is such a thing, known in the jurisprudence of this country, as *Martial law* (but he does not hint what it is) [.] But, whatever it is, it is made effectual, by being *declared*—(and yet he does not tell us who declared it, nor by what authority, nor when declared, nor how.)

[*A newspaper clipping:*

> " Gen. Terry,[18] Commander of the Department of Virginia, has just given the people of that State a very forcible reminder that martial law still prevails there by the issuance of two orders, making provisions for loyal people to recover their property confiscated by the rebel Government, and by putting a stop to all legal proceedings instituted against national officers for acts done in the performance of their official duties. Hereafter, while martial law continues to prevail, the General announces that any person connected with the institution of suits of this character will be arrested."]

Here is a practical proof of the Atty Genl.'s meaning. Gen *Terry* commanding the Department of Va.—any *military* commander, of any district or place, may do just what he pleases—make law and execute it, after his own fashion—or, without any *prescribed* law, do what he pleases, with regard to past transactions—ex *post facto*.

---

[18] Alfred H. Terry: clerk of the Superior and Supreme Courts of Connecticut, 1854–1860; officer at Bull Run in 1861, and under T. W. Sherman at Port Royal in 1861 (*supra*, Nov. 13, 1861); brigadier-general of volunteers on the Carolina coast, 1862–1864, and with the Army of the James in 1864; commander of the successful assault on Fort Fisher in January, 1865 (*supra*, Oct. 1, 1864, Jan. 18, 1865); commander of the Department of Virginia after April, 1865.

[*August 30.*] Archbishop Kenrick [19] aga[i]nst *the Fenians,*[20] (and see forward p 218 [July 19, 1865], agst. the Radical's Oath.[)]

[*A clipping headed " To the Roman Catholics of St. Louis" giving a letter of Archbishop Kenrick of August 30, 1865, in which he forbids a funeral in St. Patrick's church because it had been announced that a Fenian oration was to be delivered in connection with the service. He says:*

> "I use this occasion to state publicly, what I have uniformly stated in private conversation, that the members of the Fenian Brotherhood, men or women, are not admissable to the sacraments of the Church as long as they are united with that association, which I have always regarded as immoral in its object—the exciting of rebellion in Ireland, and unlawful and illegal in its means, a quasi military organization in this country while at peace with England, to be made effective in the event of war with that power."]

[*A reprint from the* Westliche Post *says that President Johnson's letter to Governor Sharkey " shows two things."*

"Firstly, that President Johnson has gone over completely to the Democratic party; and, secondly, that he does not consider his *infamous reconstruction policy* as any longer as an experiment, but as a *fait accompli.*"]

Sept. 2, saturday. I have just read a speech of *Montgomery Blair* [21]—delivered lately at Clarksville, Md. in which he makes heavy charges against Seward, and Stanton and Holt [22]—and in a bold, direct manner, as if conscious of his ability to make his charges good, denounces them, as the real authors of the war—

Note, since then, I have read a statement of Mr. Fox [23] (Asst. Secy. [of the] Navy) ab[ou]t the failure to relieve Ft. Sumter, which I suppose may have some connection with Mr. Blair's speech.

Sept. 4. Monday. This day, I am 72 years old. And there remain now, of the 12 children brought up by my parents, only two of us—my sister Margaret M. Wharton (widow of Dr. Austin Wharton) now 80 years, and myself.

Sept. 4. To day I entered my two grand daughters, Hester and Cora,[24] at the *Stoddard School* (one of the excellent Common Schools of St Louis, of which Miss *Judkins* is *Principal.*

<No. Miss *Judkins* is transferred to another school, and Miss *Walbridge* is principal>

---

[19] *Supra,* May 12, 1865, note 11.

[20] An Irish-American secret society founded in 1858 to aid in the establishment of an Irish republic, partly through political pressure on the American Government, to force it to further the Fenian purpose.

[21] *Supra,* March 5, 1861, note 31. For the speech see the pamphlet: *The Rebellion—Where the Guilt Lies.*

[22] *Supra,* Feb. 2, 1860, note 49.

[23] *Supra,* March 9, 1861, note 40. Probably the statement printed in *Confidential Correspondence of Gustavus Vasa Fox* (R. M. Thompson and R. Wainwright, eds.), I, 38–41.

[24] Barton's daughters who lived with Mr. Bates while they went to school in St. Louis.

Sept. 12. I have been very sick since last date, tho' mending slowly—and the weather continues very hot[.]

Sept 14. Thursday. This morning, Fleming [25] arrived, direct from Washington, Arks; apparently in good health and bodily comfort—dressed (not to my liking) in grey frock and pantaloons. As yet, I know nothing of his circumstances, prospects and purposes.

[September 18, 1865]

[A broadside given Mr. Bates by General Sherman:

Head-Quarters, Military Division of the Mississippi,
IN THE FIELD, SAVANNAH, GA., January 8, 1865.

" N. W. ——, *Esq.,* —— *County, Ga.:*

" DEAR SIR:—Yours of the 3d inst. is received, and in answer to your inquiries I beg to state:

" I am merely a military commander and can only act in that capacity; nor can I give any assurances or pledges affecting civil matters in the future. They will be adjusted by Congress when Georgia is again represented there as of old.

" *Georgia is not out of the Union,** and therefore the talk of ' reconstruction ' appears to me inappropriate. Some of her people have been and still remain in a state of revolt; and as long as they remain armed and organized, the United States must pursue them with armies, and deal with them according to military law. But as soon as they break up their armed organizations and return to their homes, I take it they will be dealt with by the civil courts. Some of the rebels in Georgia, in my judgment, deserve death, because they have committed murder, and other crimes which are punished with death by all civilized Governments on earth. But the great mass probably will never be noticed. I think this was the course indicated by General Washington, with reference to the Whisky Insurrection, and a like principle seemed to be recognized at the time of the Burr conspiracy.

"As to the Union of the States under our Government, we have the high authority of General Washington, who bade us be jealous and careful of it, and the still more emphatic words of Gen. Jackson, ' The Federal Union, it must and shall be preserved.' Certainly Georgians can not question the authority of such men, and should not suspect our motives, who are simply fulfilling their commands. Wherever necessary, force has been used to carry out that end; and you may rest assured that the Union will be preserved, cost what it may. And if you are sensible men you will conform to this order of things or else migrate to some other country. There is no other alternative open to the people of Georgia. *My opinion** is that no negotiations are necessary, nor commissioners, nor conventions, nor anything of the kind. Whenever the people of Georgia quit rebelling against their Government, and elect members of Congress and Senators, and these go and take their seats, then the State of Georgia will have resumed her functions in the Union.

" These are merely my opinions, but in confirmation of them, as I think, the people of Georgia may well consider the following words, referring to the people of the rebellious States, which I quote from the recent annual message of President Lincoln to Congress at its present session:

---

[25] Mr. Bates's third son who had been in the Confederate Army.

* The underscoring was done by Mr. Bates in red pencil.

" ' They can at any moment have peace simply by laying down their arms and submitting to the national authority under the Constitution. After so much, the Government could not, if it would, maintain war against them. The loyal people would not sustain or allow it. If questions should remain, we would adjust them by the peaceful means of legislation, conference, courts and votes. Operating only in constitutional and lawful channels, some certain and other possible questions are and would be beyond the Executive power to adjust, as for instance, the admission of members into Congress and whatever might require the appropriation of money.'

" The President then alludes to the general pardon and amnesty offered for more than a year past, upon specified and most liberal terms, to all except certain designated classes, even these being 'still within contemplation of special clemency,' and adds—

" ' It is still so open to all, but the time may come—probably will come—when public duty shall demand that it be closed, and that in lieu, more vigorous measures than heretofore shall be adopted.'

" It seems to me that it is time for the people of Georgia to act for themselves, and return in time to their duty to the Government of their Fathers.

" Respectfully your obedient servant,

W. T. SHERMAN, Major General."]

Sept. 18. 1865. This day, in conversation with Gen Sherman I referred to this letter (of which I had but an extract) in connection with certain passages of his official reports—fully endo[r]sing his principle, and he kindly gave me this copy.

Edwd. Bates

Monday, Sep 19. After a long spell of dry hot weather the temperature has changed and yesterday and today a[re] cool and bracing and very bright. Julian took me on a ride, this morning, I called on my old friends, the Danials, who seemed to take the call as a favor[.]

MAXATANIMY—the odd name of a grape, obtained, by Nancy, at the Propagation Garden at Washing[ton]. Two samples are growing in our garden, . . .

Sept. 23d. Saturday—Barton came down on wednesday night, (with Onward) and returned home this morning.

I am still very unwell. I eat and sleep pretty well, but cannot renew my strength.

Sept. 28. The Mo. Pacific Railroad has in the last few days, been completed to the State line, at Kansas City. And beyond that point, the R. R. is completed and in actual use, 40 miles, to Lawrence.

Sept. 30, Saturday. . . .

Last night, Fleming and Goody Woodson were here, with Julian and Coalter.

Mo. Dem.[ocrat] Oct 2.

[*A newspaper clipping announces that General Howard,*[26] *commissioner of the Freedmen's Bureau, has established a court for the examination of "difficulties arising between freedmen and their employers."*]

And so the Freedmen's Bureau has become *a Government!* It establishes a *Court* to examine into " all difficulties " &c—see my letter to T. J. Coffey,[27] a few days ago.

[*An editorial from the* Missouri Democrat *of October 2, 1865, headed "President Johnson and the Union Party " speculating upon whether Johnson will break with the Radical Republicans.*]

Oct. 3. I received a prompt answer from the Genl. Post Office (from *Mr. Skinner,*[28] the Asst.) to my letter urging the employment of *Joseph McI[l]waine.* My request was, at once, granted, and Mac appointed Mail Agent on the R. R. Route from St Louis to Ramey (or *Ramsey*), at a salary of $900, per an:[num.]

This was joyful news to the family, for they were getting very poor, and working very hard, for a bare living. And seldom have I so highly enjoyed the luxury of a good deed done, as when I delivered the commission and announced the good news to the family.

This appointment of McI[l]waine, solely on my request, proves the good feeling of Mr. Dennison, the P.[ost] M.[aster] G.[eneral] and his willingness to oblige me; and it also tends to prove that the Radicals have not universal sway in that and other branches of the government. It proves that the St Louis Radicals are no longer considered as speaking the word of power in the city and the state— the Genl P.[ost] O.[ffice] refuses to take the Post office here, from Foy [29] and give it to McKee, and dare[s] to appoint a route agent to gratify an open enemy of the Radicals.

[*A long editorial from the* Missouri Republican *of October 3, 1865, on " More Abuses by the Freedmen's Bureau."*]

[*An editorial reprinted from the* Lexington (Kentucky) Observer and Reporter *of October 7, 1865, criticizing the military trial of Lincoln's assassins under the caption "The Sense of Justice."*]

---

[26] Oliver O. Howard: West Point graduate of 1854; ordnance officer in New York, Maine, and Florida; professor of mathematics at West Point; officer at First Bull Run, on the Peninsula, at Second Bull Run, Antietam, Chancellorsville, Gettysburg, Chattanooga, and with Sherman in Georgia and the Carolinas. He became commissioner of the Freedmen's Bureau after the War, 1865–1874.

[27] *Supra,* March 5, 1860, note 18.

[28] St. John B. L. Skinner of New York.

[29] Postmaster at St. Louis: *supra,* May 31, 1860, note 37.

Oct. 12. [*A newspaper clipping headed "West Virginia Troubles" which describes a proclamation of the Governor* [30] *forbidding an attempt to hold a Virginia election in Jefferson County, West Virginia.*]

Poor, silly dupe! West Va.! It was conceived, as a fraudulent party trick, by a few unprincipled Radicals, and the prurient ambition of a few meritless aspirants urged it, with indecent haste, into premature birth (lest their only chance for personal distinction should be lost forever).

The bill giving the consent of Congress, to the formation of the new State was rushed through precipitately. The friends of [the] bill thought delay dangerous—any little accident, any revival among the M.[embers] of C[ongres]s, of a sense of justice and decency would, probably defeat it: And so, it was pressed through without any of the ordinary care and caution which is due to every legislative enactment—and, in fact, the bill was full of the most glaring blunders. But the friends of the bill dared not attempt to amend it, lest delay and the scrut[in]y of debate might expose its absurdity and defeat its passage—And so it was passed in all its deformity.

The *act* [31] gives the consent of Congress that the 48 N[orth] western counties of Va., *by name*—and *not including Jefferson county*—may form themselves into a state.

The Convention of W. Va. made a constitution in which it was provided, *i. a.* that other Counties than those named in the act of Congress, might become parts of W Va. by consenting thereto, and organizing accordingly!

The terms of the constitution are not fulfilled. Congress has not given its consent to the formation of the State of W. Va., so as to include the County of *Jefferson*, any more than the counties of *Henrico, Campbell, Dinwiddie, Norfolk* and *Fairfax*—so as to include all the chief towns of the "Good old Commonwealth" of Va.

Whether or no the County of Jefferson has ever held any politico military force, to join itself, to the great state of W.[est] V.[irginia] I do not know. But be that as it may Govr. Boreman's course is altogether *Radical*. He seems to have no idea of the authority of his office of Governor, nor of civil authority in any official hand. In *provost martial* stile [*sic*], he orders the arrest of the parties concerned—and, conscious of his own weakness, he invokes the strong hand of *U.[nited] S.[tates] troops.*

---

[30] Arthur I. Boreman of Parkersburg, West Virginia: Virginia state legislator, 1855–1861; opponent of secession; judge of the West Virginia Circuit Court, 1861–1863, 1888–1896; president of the Convention which formed the State of West Virginia; first governor, 1863–1869; U. S. senator, 1869–1875.

[31] Dec. 31, 1862, *U. S. Statutes at Large,* XII, chap. VI, p. 633.

[*Marginal*] *Note.* The Legislature of Va. having given its consent, incautiously, that the counties of Jefferson, Berkely and Frederick, might, if they would, join themselves to W. Va. now, Dec /65 retract and repeal the act.

Oct 15, Sunday. . . .

Oct. 16. Monday—At night, Barton arrived (by R. R) with Caroline and little Peggy.

Note For the last few days, the Synod of Mo. (O.[ld] S.[chool] Pres[byteria]n.) has been sitting in this city. It seems to be understood that the Synod will declare null, the proceedings of that body, last year; and will pass a vote of censure both upon that body and upon the last *General Assembly*, in reference especially, to the proceedings relating to Pastor *Farris*[32] and Elder *Watson*,[33] of St Charles Church[.]

Oct 17 (Tuesday). A continued Storm of cold rain, all day which seemed to renew my disease, and makes me very uncomfortable. In the evening, comes Mr. Pagne of Hannibal, with his wife and two children—The house is already full, and Julia and the girls have the girls have [*sic*] their hands more than full, in trying to accom[m]odate their friends—We have with us this evening—Barton and wife and 4 children; Mr. and Mrs. Pagne and 2 children—Fleming, Dick and Coalter=13.

Oct 18 Wednesday morning. This morning, my old *due bill* note to Peter Lindell[34] (Date, Nov 26 1857, for $500) was presented by young Mr. Baker, son of Robert, and was paid and taken up, with Int 7 yrs. 8 mo[nth]s.=$235 by check for $735.

Note—there is a mystery about this due bill. I feel sure that P.[eter] L.[indell] never intended to receive the am[oun]t. and never mentioned it for years, so that I had really, had [*sic*] forgotten it. It was presented to me some two months ago, by *Robt. Baker.* I was not prepared to pay it, at the moment, but, not long, after, wrote to Leven. H. Baker, the adm[inistrato]r., that I was ready to pay, but not being answered, I called several times at Mr. B[aker]'s office but could not find the note, and sent my son, Coalter, several times, to pay it, with the check in blank (to be filled up by him with the right amt., when ascertained) but he cd. not get a chance to pay it— At last, it is sent this day, by the hand of Young Mr. Baker (a youth).

[32] *Supra*, Dec. 25, 1859, note 63.
[33] Samuel S. Watson: wealthy farmer near St. Charles who had settled in Missouri in 1819; president of Lindenwood Female College; trustee of Westminster College at Fulton; bank director; county court judge.
[34] *Supra*, May 3, 1859, note 44.

There is an evident shuffling about this note, and I cant [*sic*] help thinking that there is something wrong about the transaction. I ought to have the inventory examined, to see whether or no the note is returned among the assets.

This morning, Edward Hall called (with Julian) to see me. He has come to town, to have a painful operation performed—to have cut out a tumor under his arm.—

(*Oct 23.* The operation was expertly performed, and he is recovering finely[.])

Oct 23. Monday—This morning, Barton, with his wife and little Peggy, returned home[.]

. . .

[*A clipping giving a call for a mass convention of Missouri Conservatives to meet in St. Louis on October 26, 1865, to consider means of restoring the Union and supporting the policy of President Johnson. The call is signed by many of Bates's close political friends.*]

[*An item reprinted from the* Westliche Post *denounces the backers of this convention as " Southern sympathizers " and friends of " Jeff." Davis.*]

This insolent German, driven from his own country for rebellion, presumes to denounce, our best men, *as rebels!* Such is our freedom of the press! The *Marats* [85] and Heberts,[86] and Baboeufs [87] are safe here in the name of liberty!

[*A clipping headed "An Outspoken Judge " which tells how Judge Able of the First District Court of New Orleans defied the orders of the officers of the Freedmen's Bureau, denied their authority, defended the independence of the judiciary, and appealed to the people and the President under the Constitution for support.*]

Bravo, Judge *Abell!* I hope you are an *able* judge.

[*Communications from Governor Fletcher* [38] *and Secretary of State Francis Rodman, recalling a writ for an election in the Fifteenth Senatorial District in Missouri, to fill a vacancy which they now say does not exist.*]

And thus, it seems, that Govr. *Fletcher*, after issuing a *legal writ*, recalls it, at will, and orders the officer having charge of its execution, *not to execute it!*

---

[35] *Supra,* March 9, 1865, note 10.

[36] Jacques R. Hébert : fanatical Paris journalist ; leader in the club of the Cordeliers in the French Revolution ; member of the Paris Commune ; vigorous opponent of the Girondists and organizer of the Cult of the Goddess of Reason.

[37] François N. Babeuf, obscure participant in the French Revolution until 1794 when he moved to Paris and became editor of Le Journal de la Liberté de la Presse and later of Le Tribun du Peuple. His interest was economics ; he preached socialism. The Directory had him executed in 1797 for attempts to organize a new revolution.

[38] *Supra,* Jan. 12, 1865, note 4.

So, he appointed *one clerk*, to superesede [*sic*] Vaughan,[39] and then appointed another, to supercede his first appointee!

[*A clipping from the* Missouri Democrat *of October 7 or 17, 1865, giving the dates on which various States have ratified the Constitutional Amendment abolishing slavery.*]

Thus, it seems, that the revolted states are to be counted, in passing the amendment, although the Radicals claim that, for other purposes, the revolted States are not *S*[*t*]*ates in the Union*, but *conquered territory!* [40]

[*A paragraph reprinted from the* La Grange American *of October 12, 1865, about the resignation from the Supreme Bench of the State of Judge Dryden* [41] *and Judge Bates.* [42] *The writer asserts that they resigned positions to which they had no right anyway, because they had already been ousted by the "loyal people" of Missouri.*]

"Dryden and *Bates*" The mendacious fellows are so used to lying that [they] do not even *pretend* to truth—*Bates* resigned in February[.]

[*A clipping on "Jansenist Bishops" of Holland, and another on the disfranchisement of deserters in New Orleans by the Provost Marshal.*]

[*A clipping which asserts that General Palmer* [43] *had overruled the findings of a court-martial that had sentenced several negroes to death for mutiny and for trying to kill an officer on duty.*]

From all I can hear, this Gen Palmer is the maddest Radical of them all. He seems to have the "*black vomit*" of politics.

Tho' daily, trampling down all laws in Ky. he is particularly nice about the court martial—The judg[men]t. is void because a member of the court served half a day after he was mustered out!

He is one who strains at a *gate* and swallows a *sawmill!*

[*A half-column report of a reconstruction speech delivered by Thaddeus Stevens* [44] *at Lancaster, Pennsylvania, on September 6, 1865.*]

(see forward, p 247[)] [44a]

This is the same Mr. Stevens, who has a great dread of being thought a *fool* and *no lawyer!* On the passage of the bill to admit

[39] *Supra*, March 6, 1863, note 59.

[40] Caution dictated inclusion of the late Confederate states in making up the three-fourths of the states necessary to amendment of the Constitution, so that the legality of the Thirteenth Amendment could not later be disputed, and three-fourths of *all* the states could not be secured without ratification by some of the late Confederate states.

[41] *Supra*, May 18, 1865, note 19.

[42] Mr. Bates's eldest son, Barton, was judge of the Missouri Supreme Court until he resigned early in 1865.

[44] Innis N. Palmer: West Point graduate of 1846; veteran of the Mexican War and the frontier service; major at First Bull Run; brigadier-general of volunteers on the Peninsula; commander of camps of drafted men in 1862; officer in North Carolina, 1862–1865.

[44] *Supra*, Dec. 20, 1862, note 87. For the speech see the pamphlet: *Reconstruction Speech . . . Delivered in the City of Lancaster, September 7th, 1865.*

[44a] See *infra*, 523.

the new state of *West Virginia*, he supported and voted for it, but thought it necessary to make a speech in *defence of his own reputation for sense!* He was afraid that if he gave a silent vote in favor of the bill, some body might think him " fool enough to believe the bill constitutional!" And therefore, he openly proclaimed in his place in the H.[ouse] of R[epresentatives], that he *knew* that the bill was *unconstitutional*, but that was no obstacle to the passage of the bill—because *in time of war, the constitution is suspended!* [45]

And yet, Mr. Stevens had no legal warrant for sitting in that House, or making that foolish speech, or casting that wicked vote, but that same *suspended* constitution! And so, without *that*, he was a mere usurping intruder into that House. Yet he is a leader of the Radicals of Pa., and assumes to teach the government in its most important duties of Law, and politics!

The nation is degraded and demoralized, and—" Wrens make prey, where eagles dare not perch." [46]

Oct. 26. This day assembled in St Louis, the Mass convention of all parties and men who are opposed to the Radicals and their new constitution. I do not doubt that the opposition has, on its side, the strength of the State, in numbers talents and personal worth, and yet I am not without fear that they lack the harmony and unity of purpose necessary to success.

We have it in our power, if we can only act with harmony and prudence, to overturn the new constitution and put down its authors. But our very strength imperils our success, by exciting, prematurely, the ambition of individuals and of parties and cliques among us. We have enough to say against the Radicals of Mo., to destroy a party twice as strong as they; but, if we imprudently, stir questions which may excite divisions among us, we may spoil all, and do for the Radicals what they cannot do for themselves—consolidate and continue their power.

The convention [sat] for two days, in good harmony among themselves, and apparently, a pungent and persistent spirit against the Radicals. The resolutions adopted, tho' introducing a few topics which I could have wished avoided, are satisfactory—better than I expected. The *Executive* Committee appointed, may do much, if they will detail (besides speakers) writers carefully selected, and with a view to their adaptation to the various branches of the warfare that we must carry on against the radicals—as a party, and as individuals.

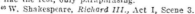

[45] Dec. 9, 1862, *Cong. Globe*, 37 Cong., 3 Sess., 50–51. The portion in quotation marks is, like the rest, only paraphrasing.

[46] W. Shakespeare, *Richard III.*, Act I, Scene 3.

I have begun my part, by handing to General Vaughan [47] (for The Lexington Express) an article upon Senator B. Gratz Brown [48] and Universal Suffrage—and I mean to follow it up.

Oct 29. . . .

[*November 2.*] The weather continued bad . . . until tuesday, Nov 1. It affected me injuriously. And I think I should have had another dangerous paroxism [*sic*] of my disease, but for Julian's well timed application of a blister, which, however kept me in great pain, all of yesterday, Nov 1.

Nov 2. I feel better to day. At last we have a bright sun.

Nov 6—Monday. This morning, my cousin, Col C. F Woodson returned home, after a visit (specially to me) of several days— He came down I think last thursday night, accompanied by his son, Col Rd. G. Woodson. His company was a great comfort to me.

I am growing uneasy on account of not hearing from *Barton*— By last advices, he had been very sick, but was convallescent [*sic*]. We hope to hear today, that he is quite recovered[.]

[*A clipping headed " Glorious News! " which prints the proclamation* [49] *of President Johnson revoking martial law in Kentucky.*]

" Glorious News! " What a pass have we come to, when we must hail, as *glorious news*, the repeal, by *Executive Power*, of *Martial law*, in the once proud State of Kentucky.

Note—This proclamation of President Johnson, while it professes to supersede *Martial law*, still leaves in force the suspension of the privilege of the writ of *Habeas Corpus*.

Some men, apparently, very sensible men too, have, as it seems to me, very strange ideas about the *Hab:[eas] Corp:[us]*—They seem to think that the *suspension of the privilege of the writ*, confers upon the Government, (or the officers of the Government) the lawful power to arrest and imprison whomsoever it will, and for whatever length of time it pleases. This is a great error. The writ of *Hab:[eas] Corp:[us]* is not, and is not designed to be, a full remedy for unlawful imprisonment. In England (from which country we borrow it) it is the *King's prerogative writ*, issued by him, in furtherance of *his right* to know by whom, and why any subject of his, is imprisoned, and to judge of the cause of the imprisonment. The most that can be accomplished by the writ of Hab:[eas] Corp:[us] is the discharge of the prisoner from illegal restrai[n]t.

[47] *Supra*, Dec. 9, 1859, note 25.
[48] *Supra*, Feb. 15, 1864, note 44.
[49] Oct. 12, 1865, J. D. Richardson, *Messages and Papers of the Presidents*, VI, 331–332.

It affords him no redress for the personal wrong done to him—no damages, as his pay or compensation, for the wrong done, and no punishment for the wrong-doer. The writ authorises the Court or Judge, *not* to redress the wrong done, but merely to examine the case, and, if the imprisonment be found illegal, to discharge the prisoner.

The suspension of the privilege of the writ of *hab[eas] corp[us]* then, does not suspend the privilege of the *writ of trespass*. And hence, a man illegally imprisoned and without the right to issue a writ of *habeas corpus*, may, nevertheless issue his *writ of trespass*, and recover damages against his unlawful jailer, *while he is still in prison*. And every continuance of the imprisonment will be a new cause of action[.]

Every imprisonment without " probable cause," will support an action of trespass.

Some of the more ignorant sort, have asserted (without daring to cite the text) that my official opinion upon Habeas Corpus,[50] supports the contrary doctrinee [*sic*]—But that is an errer [*sic*]— an error of ignorance in some and of malice in others.

[*Marginal Addition.*] On one of the last days of *October*, I noticed a fact which seemed to me new and unusual in vegetation. The Purple Flowering Bean, in our garden, after full flowering and maturing its fruit—the pods being quite dry, a spell of wet weather was succeeded by a new growth, and the same bunches, with the dry pods on, produced fresh blossoms, as pretty as those of the early summer.

Nov 8. . . .

Nov 9. . . . This evening I walked out a little, the first time I have ventured off the lot, for a week and more.

Today Mr. Gibson[51] called to see me, the first time for several months. We talked over various questions of politics, and I read him extracts from several of my letters—Also delivered him a letter recd. from E. Etheridge[.][52]

At night, comes Leonard Woods, grown up to be a stout man, big as Coalter—A machiniste [*sic*] by trade[.]

Nov. 12 Sunday. . . .

I hope I am recovering my health. I feel better to day and yesterday, than at any time, for several months past.

Nov 15. The fine weather continues, and with it, my health seems to be improving. This evening took a ride with Maj. Booth—visited

---

[50] July 5, 1861, *Official Opinions of the Attorneys-General of the United States*, X, 74-92.

[51] *Supra*, April 27, 1859, note 27.

[52] *Supra*, Dec. 7, 1863, note 81.

Grape Hill,[53] where we met Nancy and Mrs. Broadhead,[54] gathering roots and plants for Mrs. B[roadhead]'s new garden.

We hear today, that my sister, Mrs. Wharton is very low, and like to die any day. I never expect to see her again—She is 80 years, preserving her faculties remarkably well, yet ready and willing to go whenever called.

Nov 17. Julia went up, with Julian and Richard, and on the *18*th., Julian returned, and reports my sister greatly better, and in no immediate prospect of death. And on the 19th. sunday, I wrote to Julia to stay as long as she pleased, as my own health is greatly improved.

Nov 18. [*A clipping giving details of the vote in the lower house of the Missouri Legislature that defeated a resolution which sought to declare vacant the seats of Messrs. Jameson* [55] *and Barlow.*[56]]

It may be useful to preserve this vote, and watch the voters, for future occasions. The time is not distant when some of the *noes* will be glad to have this vote forgotten.

Note. The result might have been different if all the members had been present, for the absentees are more than the difference between the ayes and noes.

Nov 19/65. [*An editorial from the* Missouri Republican *of November 19, 1865, headed "The Police—The Thieves—The Garoters."*]

I am alarmed at the rapid growth of lawlessness and strong tendency to anarchy. The spirit of disobedience is manifest, in all the walks of life. Nobody relies upon *the law*, for his protection. And it is an evil omen for our country, and *legal government* every where, that the People have lost all confidence in the *law*, as the rule of government and the protector of individuals, and in all public functionaries, legislative, executive, and (alas!) judicial also.

Eads Bates.

Nov 21, tuesday. I have just got a letter from Barton saying that he has another son born to him, last sunday night, "Nov 19th. 1865, at 11.30. p m." and has named him EADS—all well.

This boy *Eads* (doubtless named after our excellent friend *James. B. Eads*)[57] is Barton's 4th. son, and 8th. child.

---

[53] A farm owned by Mr. Bates.

[54] Wife of James O. Broadhead : *supra*, Dec. 26, 1859, note 66.

[55] E. H. E. Jameson, representative of St. Louis in the Missouri House of Representatives.

[56] Stephen D. Barlow : assistant clerk of the St. Louis Circuit Court, 1840–1842 ; deputy clerk of the Court of Common Pleas, 1842–1844 ; county clerk and recorder of deeds, 1844–1854 ; secretary-treasurer, president, 1859–1866, of the St. Louis and Iron Mountain Railroad ; Conservative Republican state legislator, 1865–1866.

[57] *Supra,* Jan. 28, 1860, note 38. Later, Eads Bates is spoken of as a girl.

Nov 22. . . .

Planted today, the following grape vines viz—1st. 2. *Red Elben*, in front of the west porch at the end of the beds on the N. and S. sides of the walk, from the porch, westward.

2d. 1. *Hartford prolific*, diagonally across the paved walk, from the S. W. corner of porch.

3d. 1. *Concord*—S. E. from the last named, about 6 or 8. feet, and near the point of the angle of the waste-water gutter. <*Note*. At the foot of each one of these plants I stuck in slips cut from the vine of each one, respectively.> Also, I planted, along the South side of the lattice screen, two roots of the *Philistrone* grape, which I dug yesterday, at Grape Hill.

Also, I inserted 4 slips of the *Hill* grape, on the north border of the east flat (where we had cantilopes [*sic*] last summer)[.]

Also two small *cherry* scions (red cluster) [(]dug by me yesterday, at Grape Hill) on the border in front of the back building, next west of the brick walk[.]

Also, 4 small roots of the tye [*sic*] vine, around an aspin tree, in the N. W. corner of the garden.

> ["A RESOLUTION offered by Mr. TRUMBULL, against the pardon of JEFF DAVIS and other prominent rebel leaders, has been passed by the Tennessee State Senate."]

A very pragmatical Senate that. Perhaps they have suffered persecution, but it seems, it did not teach them mercy.

That Senate is, beyond a doubt, *Radical*.

[*A notice of a meeting of the Presbyterian General Assembly at Pittsburgh, and the refusal of Cyrus H. McCormick* [58] *of Chicago to give more to the cause of Presbyterian education until the General Assembly shows signs of rescinding its recent action so that reunion of Northern and Southern churches may be possible.*]

Many leaders of the Pres[byteria]n. church have a hankering after noteriety [*sic*], and as politics, for the present, is more blatant than Religion, they seem resolved to show their *loyalty*(?) at the expense of their christianity.

[*A notice of an enthusiastic meeting in Cooper Union of the American Union Commission,* " *organized to aid in the restoration of the Union, on the basis of freedom, industry, education and Christian morality.*]

Some short time ago, I recd. a circular from the president of this *American Union Com*[*m*]*ission*, and altho' it professed to be modelled after the *Christian Commission*,[59] I had some misgivings about it—It

---

[58] Virginia-born inventor of the reaper; since 1848 a manufacturer of farm implements in Chicago; founder of the McCormick Theological Seminary in Chicago.

[59] This was organized by a convention of the Y. M. C. A. with the object of promoting "the spiritual good of the soldiers and incidentally their intellectual improvement and social and physical comfort."

was too broad—had too many irons in the fire, and proposed the employment of too many instrumentalities, to be other than *political*.

[*A newspaper assertion that the western counties of Missouri have been plundered of many miles of fence-rails and much stock—all of which might be found in Kansas.*]

I have reason to think that the devastation of the western counties of Mo. was one of the most wicked and cold-blooded schemes of plunder recorded in history—And yet, it was done, in great part, with the formal sanction of *military orders*.

[*A would-be humorous clipping on deaths of husbands.*]

[*A newspaper statement that President Johnson had issued an order designed to protect the person and property of ex-Senator Trusten Polk.*[60]]

What stupid nonsence is this. If the Prest. has *pardoned* Mr. Polk, very well. That is his right, but he has no power to make such an order[.]

[*A statement that the Legislature of Indiana is considering a resolution to confer full rights of citizenship upon negroes.*][61]

Five cents reward for a definition of the phrase "full rights of citizen*ship*[.]"

[*A statement that Mt. Hood in Oregon is again active after a quiet period of nearly half a century.*]

Long ago, when I was a boy, my old friend *Billy* Pope (who was zealously *loyal*, and did not like to admit that his own country was dependent on any other for any thing) hearing that a *Volcano* had broke out, in North Carolina, broke forth in a transport of Joy[.]

"Ah! (said he) did not I tell you? We are fast becoming independent—We no longer import hominy-mortars and horse-shoe nails from England, and very little madder and no bricks from Holland. And now we are independent of the world, for *volcano*[e]s—for we have one of our own![''"]

[*An article upon the adulteration of gas.*]

I have long thought it possible that gas might and would be debased, but I did not know that the introduction of atmospheric air (or rather the Oxygen which it contains) would make it explosive.

[*A newspaper clipping headed "The Boston Military Commission," which asserts that the commission is to investigate a charge made by Prussia that Massachusetts officials caused Prussian subjects to be imported and enlisted in the army to fill up the quota of the State.*]

---

[60] *Supra,* Sept. 6, 1860, note 91.

[61] It was not passed. In fact, just at this time the Legislature refused to repeal the portion of the Indiana Constitution which forbade free negroes to enter the State.

What can a *Military* Commission have to do with—" try and execute " Gov Andrew ? [62]

I remember that Govr. Andrew was at Washington on that business. He urged that a cargo of his imported dutchmen be required to land at a U. S. station, lest, if they landed at a common wharf they might escape, &c[.]

[*Clippings telling of the trial of a janitor before a military commission for furnishing playing cards and refreshments to prisoners; a summons of a colonel before a military commission in Washington for being absent without leave; the indictment of General Fisk [63] by a Kentucky grand-jury for granting passes to 11,000 negroes to leave Kentucky to emigrate to Indiana and Ohio.*][64]

Nov 24. Friday—evening. . . .

My health is improving, but I still have a troublesome cold and regain my strength very slowly.

To day, called upon Genl. Dodge [65] and had a pleasan[t] talk about old men and old times. He is 83 y[ea]rs. old, and vigorous.

Saw my friend *Eads.*[66] He is just returned from Europe, bringing his [family]—tho' his wife remains behind in New York, putting the two youngest daughters to s[c]hool. His health seems good, and he promised to visit me tonight.

My wife is still absent,[67] but expects to be at home to night or tomorrow, with Fredk Hatcher.[67a]

[*Marginal Note.*]   Killed a mosquito in my room this evening.

Nov 25: . . .

I notice in a newspaper today, what purports to be a chapter from Mr. Buchanan's book,[68] in which the Ex Prest gives his account of the Origin of the *Monroe Doctrine.* I do not know whether his book is yet published, or this extract given by way of ante-past— It seems to be fairly stated, as to the facts of the origin; but (in

[62] John A. Andrew: Boston lawyer; reformer; an organizer of the Free-Soil Party in 1848; Republican state legislator, 1858; governor of Massachusetts, 1861–1866; a supporter of vigorous prosecution of the War, but an opponent of vindictiveness in Reconstruction.

[63] Clinton B. Fisk of St. Louis: small banker in Michigan until the crash of 1857 sent him to St. Louis; brigadier-general of volunteers who fought in Missouri and Arkansas throughout the War; at this time commissioner of the Freedmen's Bureau in Kentucky and Tennessee; later a leader of the Probibition Party.

[64] All of the above clippings and the comments upon them are upon a separate sheet which is bound into the diary.

[65] Henry Dodge: an early settler of Ste. Geneveve, Missouri, 1796–1827; sheriff, 1805–1821; U. S. marshal; U. S. ranger in Wisconsin, 1832–1836; governor of the Territory of Wisconsin, 1836–1841, 1845–1848; Democratic delegate to Congress, 1841–1845; U. S. senator, 1848–1857.

[66] *Supra,* Jan. 28, 1860, note 38.

[67] See *supra,* Nov. 19, 1865.

[67a] See *infra,* Dec. 7, 1865, note 79.

[68] James Buchanan, *The Administration on the Eve of the Rebellion* (Sampson Low, Son & Marston, London, 1865), 276–286.

common with many others) his inferences, of doctrine and fact, are greatly exag[g]erated.

[*Marginal Note.*] Nov 30 another ch:[apter] "*the eve of the rebellion*[."] [*A lengthy excerpt from the* Missouri Republican *printing this chapter*] The last days of Mr. Buchanan's adm[inistratio]n written by himself.

At night, Julia returned home, attended by Dick. The sick in Dardenne[69] seem better.

Also, Mr. Eads[70] and daughters, Eliza and Ada called to see us. Mr. E[ads]'s reception by the Naval authorities in England, was was [*sic*] very flattering. His inventions of the stationary turret[71] and the manoe[u]v[e]ring of great guns, were examined with admiration and great applause.

[*A newspaper reprint of the report to a Caucus of Missouri Radicals of the Committee appointed by that Caucus to consider amendments to the Constitution.*]

Radical Platform.

Here we have it, distinctly and repeatedly avowed, that the New Constitution is but the *party platform* of the Radicals. It is treated throughout, not as the Organic law of the State, but a contrivance to consolidate the strength and continue the supremacy of the present dominant faction; and that, not so much by increasing its its [*sic*] intrinsic force, as by the exclusion of all opposition.

They go, emphatically, for the "*total disfranchisement* of all rebels!"

That is—if they mean what they say—rebels are to have no rights! Ours is no longer a *Government of the People*—a democracy—but an aristocracy of the good people, the *loyal* people, the *Radicals!*

[*A clipping, headed "A Mooncalf in the Missouri Legislature," says that a bill has passed its second reading which makes it an offense punishable by heavy fine for one to address a " rebel," without using his full military title prefixed by the term " rebel."*]

This *mooncalf* shown up here, is *Radical Colonel* Madison Miller,[72] of Vide Poche, a senator from St Louis County.

I hear, upon enquiry, that he has actually introduced a bill "to make treason odious," and that this is one of its provisions. It is a mercy that our radical masters have so little sense, for if they only had a modicum of intelligence, they might do immense mischief[.]

---

[69] Dardenne was the home of Mr. Bates's eldest son, Barton, and his family. Barton had been sick, his wife had been having an eighth baby, and Mrs. Wharton, the eighty-year-old sister, who lived near Dardenne had been critically ill.

[70] *Supra*, Jan. 28, 1860, note 38.

[71] *Supra*, May 1, 1864, note 20.

[72] *Supra*, Feb. 2, 1865, note 37.

[*A clipping prints a letter from Emory S. Foster, " Clerk Johnson Court," to General Sterling Price,*[73] *dated Warrensburg, June 1, 1861:*

> " SIR—We have here a company of about fifty mounted men. We wish to know whether the State can arm us or not. If it cannot, are our services wanted or not?"]

Can this be the same *Foster* who was a member of the Radical convention, and there publicly boasted that *he had burned a woman's house*, because (as he said) she had harbored bushwhackers? I think he is the same. These radicals are extreme and intolerant on every side, howeve[r] often they change. *Note* this letter is dated 2 or 3 weeks after the taking of camp Jackson.[74]

Dec 3. (sunday morning). . . .

My health is decidedly improving, tho' I have a bad cold which stops up my head and throat, very uncomfortably. Yesterday, I took more exercise than on any day for months past. In the morning, I busied myself in planting some little peach trees (white blossom) and some flowering roots; and afterwards, I, I [*sic*] undertook to make a coop for some fowls that Caroline [75] had sent us.

My grand-daughters, Hester and Cora, were perfectly happy yesterday—On friday, the monthly report of their school (the Stoddard school) was made, shewing *Hester* at the *head of the first class*, and Cora *second best* of the 2d. class, and at night, their uncle Fred: came in with their father's waggon, bringing a variety of good things from the Country—and reporting all the sick improving.

Late in the afternoon, Mr. Eads [76] called, in his buggy, took me down to the Southern Hotel and shewed to me his beautiful models of heavy batteries. It is wonderful, and I do not doubt that he has wraught [*sic*] a revolution in the conduct of War, around the globe.

Mr. Eads came home with me, and while we were at supper, the hot-water pipe of our kitchen stove burst, and disconcerted the whole family—we can have no fire in the kitchen, until it is mended.

My long-continued sickness and expectation of approaching death, have made me indolent, or careless of ordinary affairs. I find it very difficult to bring myself to any ordinary business. Hardly any thing excites an interest in me, but the condition of the country, in its political and governmental aspects. I am slow even, in writing an argument against the use of *Martial Law* and *Military com-*

---

[73] *Supra*, Nov. 27, 1861, note 70.

[74] Camp Jackson was the encampment ground where the Missouri state militia of the St. Louis district assembled early in May, 1861, under orders of the pro-Confederate governor, Jackson (*supra*, Jan. 9, 1860, note 15). After one week General Lyon broke it up on the charge that it was a threat to Missouri's remaining within the Union.

[75] Mrs. Barton Bates.

[76] *Supra*, Jan. 28, 1860, note 38.

missions, which I had promised to Reverdy Johnson;[77] and as slow, in answering Mr. Dana and the meeting in Faneuil Hall.[78]

. . .

Dec 4. . . .

Dec 5. . . . At night, comes Barton.

Dec 7 Thursday. . . .
Mr. Hatcher[79] writes that my sister is at the point of death.

. . .

This (Decr. 7.) is the day appointed for Thanksgiving; and, while we have real and great cause of thankfulness to God, we have still greater cause to pray to him for his further mercies, and especially that [   ]
Bible.
" The first *Bible* ever printed on this continent was in *native Indian*—New Testament in 1661, and the old in 1663, both by Revd. John Eliot.[80] They were published at Cambridge." Religious Denominations p 303.

Dec 9   Saturday. . . .
A letter from *Caroline* to Julia states that there is much sickness among our friends in Dardenne prairie, (i. a. little Peggy)—Mrs. Wharton, Gay Hatcher and Eliza Woodson.[81]
So Barton gives up his trip to Granby,[82] and goes home at once.

Dec 11 Monday morning . . .
This morning, Matilda and Julia Woodson go up to attend our sick friends.
Mrs. *Margaret M. Wharton* (the last survivor of my five sisters) died yesterday (*sunday, Dec 10*) at 11. oclock a. m. at the house of her son-in law H.y. Thatcher of Oakland, St Charles County.
She was 80 years old last August, and, to the last she was blessed with the full possession of her faculties and her affections. Her death is no cause of bitter sorrow, but only a pensive regret, for she died as she had long lived, at peace with man and with God.   Her mission in this world was fully accomplished, and she was cheerful and happy in the hope of removal to a brighter and better home than this.

---

[77] *Supra,* Nov. 26, 1859, note 85.
[78] See *supra,* July 3, 1865.
[79] Son-in-law of Mr. Bates's sister, Mrs. Wharton.
[80] Graduate of Jesus College, Cambridge, in 1622; minister of Roxbury, 1631–1690; missionary to the Indians.
[81] The Woodsons were cousins of Mr. Bates.
[82] A town near the lead mines of southwestern Missouri on the Southwest Branch of the Pacific Railroad—now the St. Louis and San Francisco Railroad. Granby developed smelting works and lead furnaces.

Note. This is Nancy's birth day—a bright and beautiful day, and she says is the first for the last 28 or 30 years, that has not been attended with foul weather.

Dec 12 Tuesday. . . .

Capt. Dd. B. Hill (who claims to be weather-wise, and indeed wise, generally) predicts very cold weather before the end of the month. He says that before the new year, the navigation of our rivers, will be stopped by ice.

[*Marginal Note.*]   Dec 13. I'm afraid Capt Hill is right, for it is entensely [*sic*] cold this morning.

Note. Capt. Hill has, for some time back, been engaged in a new line [of] philosophical enquiry. He has suspended his life long labors upon *perpetual motion*, and prepared a treatise upon the *Ocean Wave.* He has a theory of his own, I think perfectly new, and the chief point of that theory is that the theatre of *wave-action*, is at the bottom of the sea, where, he thinks, the waves rush along with a force absolutely irresistable [*sic*] by any art or contrivance of man. Hence he considers it impossible that a telegraphic line can be laid and kept along the bottom of the sea.

Citizen. "This then is sufficient to show what a *citizen* is; for whoever has a right to take part in the *judicial* and *executive* part of government in any state, him we call a *citizen* of that place; and a State, in one word, is the collective body *of such persons*, sufficient in themselves, for all the purposes of life."

Aristotle[']s Politics,[83] Book 3. ch 1. p 84.

A very different idea is expressed in my official opinion (as Atty. Genl. [of the] U. S.) upon *citizenship*.[84] I held (and still hold) that a citizen of the U. S. is neither more nor less than a member of the body politic, no matter whether high or low, governor or governed.

[*A newspaper statement that Secretary of War Stanton has agreed to send a military force to rebuild damaged levees in Mississippi and Louisiana—holding that he can do this because the States are under military government.*]

That can hardly be: Stanton may be despotic enough to do the thing, but I think not foolish enough to avow it.

[*A clipping stating that Senator Anthony*[85] *has called up the House resolution of Mr. Stevens*[86] *for the appointment of a Joint*

[83] *The Politics and Economics of Aristotle,* Edward Walford, ed., Henry G. Bohn, London, 1853.   The capitalization is inaccurate and the italics are Mr. Bates's.

[84] *Official Opinions of the Attorneys-General of the United States,* X, 382–413.

[85] *Supra,* Feb. 10, 1864, note 12.   For his motion see Dec. 12, 1865, *Cong. Globe,* 39 Cong., 1 Sess., 24, 30.

[86] *Supra,* Dec. 30, 1862, note 87.   For his resolution see Dec. 4, 1865, *Cong. Globe,* 39 Cong., 1 Sess., 6.

Committee on the lately rebellious States,[87] *moving to amend the same so as to make it a concurrent instead of a joint resolution.*]

It was a sharp move of *Thad: Stevens,* to commit *both* Houses of Congress to the exclusion of the southern members, by making the resolution *joint;* and still sharper, to tie the hands of both houses, and so exclude the southern members, until the *joint committee should report!* <see back p 235 [October 23, 1865.]>

HONEST *Thad:* pretends not to know that each house *must* be the separate and exclusive judge of its own members. But he knew very well, that if the Senate consented to have its hands tied until *his* honest committee should make a report, they might remain tied forever.

Note. Afterwards, in debate in [the] H[ouse] of R[presentatives] old Thad: amidst other ravings declared that " the *State of Tennessee* is *not known* to this House [n]or to congress ! "[88] A very ignorant House, it would seem—ignorant alike of the constitution and of geography ! He probably, thinks the House as ignorant and vicious as himself.

[*A newspaper story that Mr. Hollister* [89] *has introduced into Congress a resolution endorsing the statement alleged to have been made by General Grant while in Richmond, that " the advent of Maximilian* [90] *to the pretended throne of Mexico is a part of the rebellion, and his immediate expulsion therefrom should be a part of its history."*]

This Mr. Hollister must [be] a bright genius. he is as radical as a ruta baga turnip. Because Napoleon chose to play the despot, and establish a throne in Mexico, *we* also, must play the despot, and establish a republic there. These Radicals are extremely anxious to have the war continued as long as possible, for without a pretence of war, they may find it hard to continue much longer, the use of *martial law,* and hitherto that has been their only dependence for carrying out their tyranny in Missouri. That shift may last the Rad[ical]s sometime yet—It is a pretty conception—say they. The Empire in Mexico is part of the rebellion, and until it is put down the war continues; and so long as we are at war, we must have martial law. q. e. d.

This chimes in exactly, with Thad: Stevens' doctrine that in time of war the constitution is inoperative.

Again—Mr. Stevens called Mr. Davis to order—" The House having nothing to do at present, with the constitution ! " He has no

[87] The Joint Committee of Fifteen on Reconstruction with Senator Fessenden as chairman and Stevens as its motive force, became a great power in Reconstruction. The Radicals dominated the Committee, and no measure concerning the South could get before either House without the approval of this Committee.

[88] Dec. 12, 1865, *ibid.,* 31.

[89] There was no person of this name in Congress.

[90] *Supra,* June 17, 1864, note 9.

use for the constitution but to a seat in Congress.[91]   see Nat[ional] Intel[ligence]r Dec 16 /61[.]

Dec 15 Friday. This day, I have been very uncomfortable in body, and dull withal, in mind—finding it hard to hold my mind upon a plain track of thought, or pursue, with ease and celerity, a train of ideas.

The weather is still very cold, tho' bright[.]

At night come Maj. Booth and Mr. Frayser, to visit us.

Note, gave to Mr. Frayser [92] (as adm[inistrato]r. of my sister Sarah [93]) my receipt for $1800, being the amount of money paid me at different times on a/c of the estate—viz $1000, on the 8th. of January 1861; for which I then gave him my note of that date (by way of security against accident) which note is now returned to me and cancelled—And $800, paid me some months ago, along with certain money to be sent by me, to Mrs. Ball and Miss Hudnall heirs of Fleming Bates dec[ease]d.[94]

Dec 17 Sunday. . . .

This day I wrote to Owen Deviny, that I would immediately, send his funds as directed—see Letter book.

Also, wrote to Geo. T. Curtis,[95] [of] N. Y. on reading in the Mo. Rep[ublican], his letter to Mr. Whittlesey, about the test oath of clergy men.[96]

John O'fallon [97] died this day, at the advanced age of 74. He has, for many years, filled a large space in this society, and dying, much respected and beloved, he leaves behind him a large estate and " the sweet savor of a good name.["]

The Congressional Globe, of Decr. 12 (sent me by Mr. Hogan [98]) contains some very interesting matter—as first *in the Senate* Gar-

---

[91] When a resolution requiring the reference of all questions of admission of Southern members in either House to the Joint Committee of Fifteen (*supra*, Dec. 12, 1865, note 87) was under discussion, Thomas T. Davis of New York said : " I rise to a question of order. In my judgment, it seems that there is another constitutional objection to the passage of this resolution. The Constitution of the United States provides that each House———." Mr. Stevens interrupted : ". . . The Chair has nothing to do with what is constitutional and what is not, in this matter." Dec. 14, 1865, *Cong. Globe*, 39 Cong., 1 Sess., 61.

[92] Robert B. Frayser, son-in-law of Mrs. Wharton, and hence Sarah Bates's nephew.

[93] Mr. Bates's sister who had died on August 12, 1859.

[94] See *supra*, July 22, 1865.

[95] Lawyer in Boston, 1837–1862, in New York, 1862–1888 ; Massachusetts legislator, 1840–1843. He often practiced before the Supreme Court, had defended Scott in the famous Dred Scott case, and was an authority on constitutional law. He had been a Webster Whig, but became a Democrat ; he supported the War but was critical of the Government.

[96] See *supra*, May 30, 1865, note 38.

[97] Wealthy St. Louis merchant ; state legislator, 1821–1825 ; benefactor of the scientific department of St. Louis University and of Washington University, and donor of a dispensary and medical college to St. Louis.

[98] *Supra*, Jan. 9, 1860, note 13.

r[e]tt Davis' resolution on *habeas corpus* [99] and his speech [1] in favor of Prest. Johnson.

Next, the consideration of the *joint* resolution (from the H[o]use) for a *joint* Com[mitt]ee. of re-construction [2] Senator Anthony's amendments thereto,[3] and some debate, i. a. Doolittle's Speech.[4]

In the course of that debate Senator Howard [5] of Mich: fully displayed his rabid radicalism—Says he—

" I [t]hink [,sir,] the country expects nothing less [than this] at our hands. I think that portion of the *loyal* people of the U[nited] S.[tates] who have sacrificed &c . . . have a right to at least this assurance at our hands, that neithe[r] House of Congress will recognize *as States*, any one of the rebel states until the event to which I have alluded." [6]—that [is], until the *joint committee* (not yet in existence) shall have reported, and Congress shall have acted finally on the report, (which might never be).

Not States! what are they then? conquered provi[n]ces?

Also, a letter from Gov Pierepoint [Pierpont] [7] of Va., containing an act of the Legislature of Virginia repudiating West Va.

In the House, various motions were up, in regard to the Tennessee delegation.[8] The minority, (who favor Prest. Johnson's views) could do little more than call the yeas and nays, by that means, has forced the truculent majority of record, and some of them are already uneasy about it (as Hogan writes me) in dread of the wrath to come.

Dec 19 Tuesday. Come Mrs. Dr. Fred: Bates and her little boy. Also Dick and Wm. Rhodes. Crossed, at St. Charles on the ice[.] [9]

Dec 20. . . .

---

[99] *Supra*, July 14, 1864, note 65. For the resolution see Dec. 12, 1865, *Cong. Globe*, 39 Cong., 1 Sess., 23.

[1] *Ibid.*, 23.

[2] *Ibid.*, 24.

[3] *Ibid.*, 24.

[4] *Supra*, Aug. 10, 1859, note 76. For the speech see *Cong. Globe*, 39 Cong., 1 Sess., 25–26.

[5] Jacob M. Howard: Detroit lawyer; state legislator, 1838; Whig congressman, 1841–1843; a founder of the Republican Party in 1854; attorney-general of Michigan, 1855–1861; U. S. senator, 1862–1871.

[6] Dec. 12, 1865, *ibid.*, 24. The italics are Mr. Bates's.

[7] *Supra*, Aug. 7, 1863, note 74.

[8] I. e., in regard to the admission of the duly elected Tennessee members to their seats in the House of Representatives. Until 1863 both Houses had admitted *loyal* members from the seceded states. Then the policy was changed and from 1863 to 1865 seats were refused to these men. Maynard from Tennessee who had sat from 1861 to 1863 and had been as courageously and unquestionably loyal as President Johnson himself, was made a test case. To have seated Maynard would have recognized the Conservative claim—which until 1863 had been the accepted theory and practice of the Government—that states could not secede, that the Confederate States were and always had been in the Union, and that these states were entitled to representation in Congress whenever they should send men personally loyal.

[9] The Missouri River had to be crossed by ferry in traveling between St. Louis and places in St. Charles County where Barton lived.

Dec 21 Thursday. Last night was decidedly, the coldest of the season; yet Matilda did not arrive from St. Charles, til[l] near 11. p. m. escorted by Fred Hatcher. They were detained by the ice, in crossing the river at St. Charles.

. . .

L[or]d. Campbell's Lives of the Ch[ief] Justices,[10] vol 2. p 39. In vit

Pemberton,[11]—" he caused some grumbling among the old stagers, by showing, as they alleged, too little respect for precedent and authority; but he was deeply versed in jurisprudence, as a science, and he thought it better *to be governed by a right principle* than *by a wrong decision.*["]

An upright judge that, and a wise. At p. 49[–50]—Roger North[12] had a grudge against Pemberton " for having a hankering after honesty and independence "—And so, Cardinal Wolsey is made to say of Bishop Gardiner—" He was a fool, for he would needs be virtuous." [13]

[A newspaper copy of Seward's proclamation that the constitutional amendment abolishing slavery has been ratified.] [14]

At the moment when this proclamation is published, and slavery is declared to be abolished throughout the Republic, by the amendment to the constitution—passed *by the votes of the Southern States, lately in rebellion*, the radical leaders in both houses of Congress declare that there are no such states in existence!

Stevens of Pa. says that " The S[t]ate of Tennessee is not known to this house [n]or to Congress! " [15]

And in the Senate, Mr. Howard of Michn., refused to " recognize them *as States* "!! [16]

And so, it seems, they are not *States in the Union*, yet they can enact a constitution for the United States!

Are these men mad?

[A newspaper clipping headed "A Missionary Needed" which tells of a township in Caldwell County,[17] Missouri, with a voting population of 400 (300 of whom voted as Radicals at the last election) where 360 persons had been indicted for gambling and other offences at the last term of the Circuit Court. There was one preacher in the number.]

---

[10] Mr. Bates used an edition published by Blanchard & Lea in Philadelphia in 1853.

[11] Sir Francis Pemberton, 1625–1697: judge of the King's Bench, 1679–1680; chief justice of the King's Bench, 1681–1683; chief justice of the Common Pleas, 1683.

[12] English lawyer, 1653–1734; solicitor-general, 1684–1688; biographer of his family.

[13] See *supra*, May 10, 1863, note 12.

[14] Dec. 18, 1865, *Works of William H. Seward* (Geo. E. Baker, ed., 1884), V, 595–596.

[15] See *supra*, Dec. 12, 1865.

[16] See *supra*, Dec. 17, 1865.

[17] A county in the northwestern portion of the State.

It seems to me, a missionary is not the proper remedy—"a rod for a fool's back" might do better. But if there must be a *missionary*, send that *preacher* on a miss[i]on to the penetentiary [*sic*].

[*An editorial statement that Trumbull*[18] *of Illinois and other Conservative Union men who "voted with the Democrats" on Senator Sumner's "bill*[19] *to confirm land titles to the freedmen settled upon the Sea Islands in South Carolina" are "as 'diabolical Copperheads' as—Edward Bates."*]

It is of the nature of radicalism to "run into the ground."

Extremists always,[;] men of sense and reason, who in a moment of enthusiasm seem to act with them, are soon forced to abandon them, by [reason of] their folly and wickedness.

[*A newspaper paragraph purporting to give the gist of an interview between Napoleon and George N. Sanders on the subject of Mexico.*]

This "needs confirmation[.]" It is not at all likely that *Napolean* [*sic*] would unbosom himself to *George. N. Saunders.*[20]

Dec 23d., Saturday—Our house is much thinned off today. My three grand children, Onward Hester and Cora, accompanied by R. G. Woodson [and] Richard Bates, left, in the morning, for Dardenne Prairie[21]—And in the afternoon, Lavinia[22] and her little boy started home (accompanied by Mr. Spencer, cousin to Lavinia, and by Virgil Conway)[.] And so, our family is, at once, deminished [*sic*] by the departure of seven.

Dec 24. Sunday. . . .

My own health varies a little, from day to day as the weather varies, severe or mild, wet or dry. The affection of the kidneys and bladder is still very troublesome— . . .

. . .

Col Broadhead[23] came to see me,—the first time for several weeks.

Christmas day. I was quite sick last night and all the forepart of today, and supposed I had taken a new cold; but I feel better this afternoon.

Julian and family dined here today, well and happy.

There has been a dense fog all day, and the *thaw* is still going on, even in the shadiest nooks. I dare not go out of the house, for fear

---

[18] See *supra*, Nov. 22, 1860, note 85.

[19] See *supra*, Jan. 7, 1860, note 9. For the bill see Dec. 11, 1865, *Cong. Globe*, 39 Cong., 1 Sess., 17. The vote was not on the bill itself, but on a motion of Senator Doolittle (*supra*, Aug. 10, 1859, note 76) to refer it to the Judiciary Committee instead of to the Committee on Military Affairs as demanded by Sumner.

[20] Because of Mr. Sanders's attacks upon him; see *supra*, July 22, 1864, note 80.

[21] *Supra*, July 30, 1859, note 61.

[22] Wife of Dr. Frederick Bates.

[23] *Supra*, Dec. 26, 1859, note 66.

of taking cold. Indeed my strength is so reduced that I could not go far, if the weather and the ground were ever so inviting.

I may not deny that my vanity is sometimes mortified by the neglect of my old acquaintances. Very few call to see me, and I am "forgotten like a dead man." To day, Maj Booth and Capt. Hill called; and no one else, except Julian and his family, who dined with us. The little grand daughters, Edwa and Winona, seemed very happy, and both Fleming and Coalter called in, late, to dinner.

Old men like me, sick, it may be, and uninteresting, ought not to be surprised that the young do not affect their society. Such as I, are in condition to recite this churlish poetry—

"As I walked by myself, I said to myself, and myself said again unto me,
Look to thyself, take care of thyself, for nobody cares for thee.
Thus I said to myself, and thus answered myself, with the selfsame repartee,
If thou look to thyself or look not to thyself, 'tis the selfsame thing to thee." [24]

Still, there are *some* whose prolonged absence cannot fail to excite some surprise and curiosity. Mr. Charles Gibson,[25] has visited me but once, since the early summer; and then very hastily—a mere call. This gives me some uneasiness, for I really had a strong regard for Mr. G.[ibson] and thought he reciprocated my feelings. I fear that I may, unwittingly, have done something to estrange him from me; and he is too proud or too modest to tell me of it. Surely, I would gladly rectify any such error, if I did but know it.

I thought that the *St Louis bar*, under the circumstances would have recognized me, in some respectful form. Aside from any personal standing at the bar, I filled the post of Atty. Genl., for several years, and thus, by courtesy and usage, taking rank as head of the bar, it might have been expected that some courteous notice would have been taken of me. But no such thing was done. I never even received a line of acknowledgement of divers books and documents which I sent to the library; and do not, to this day, know that they were ever received, except that I, accidently found one or two of the volumes which I had sent, in the library. I was always, however, regularly dunned *for my dues*.

Dec 26. Tuesday: . . .

Saturday, Dec 30. . . .

In searching for reasons to account for the extreme violence of such radicals as Stevens,[26] Wade,[27] Sumner,[28] and the like, and their bold repudiation of all principle, in their efforts to grind and oppress

---

[24] Isaac Ross: *All the Same in the End*, Epitaph in the Churchyard in Homersfield, England.

[25] *Supra*, April 27, 1859, note 27.

[26] *Supra*, Dec. 30, 1862, note 87.

[27] *Supra*, Aug. 10, 1859, note 77.

[28] *Supra*, Jan. 7, 1860, note 9.

the Southern States; one material point seems to be wholly overlooked " Tis conscience that makes cowards of us all,"[.][29]   They
feel that they deserve to be hated by the southern people for their
cruel conspiracy to degrade and ruin the southern States, and, naturally enough, they conclude that their bad passions are imitated,
and their malicious hatred reciprocated at the South."

---

[29] " Thus conscience does make cowards of us all."   W. Shakespeare, *Hamlet*, Act III,
Scene 1.

129742—33——35

CHAPTER VIII

1866

Monday January. 1. 1866. Another year is gone, and I am still mercifully preserved. Three months ago, I little thought that I should live to see this day; and indeed, I did not much regret the expected change. But now, the disease of my lungs and throat seems a good deal mitigated, and the prospect of prolonged life is much improved. Still, I am confined closely to the house; for (besides my general disease) I have . . . I suppose inflam[m]ation of the bladder— . . .

During the day, a number of friends called to see me in my room, and among them Gen: Sherman, Genl. Blair,[1] Capt. Blood,[2] Capt. Bart Able,[3] Dr. Bernays[4] Mr. (Elder) Scott, D R Garrison,[5] C Gibson,[6] A Todd.[7] A. W. Alexander, et al: So that I had more social intercourse this day, than at any time, for many months before.

At night, comes Barton with his three eldest children—Onward returns to his labor in [the] shop, and Hester and Cora to their school. The night was not very cold, but crisp and glassy.

Jan. 2. . . .

[January 5.] [*A clipping reprinting an article from the* Pall Mall Gazette *of January 5 entitled "President Johnson and His Opponents—The Greatness of the Task before Him." The* Gazette *credits Johnson with sagacity and statesmanship.*]

Jan. 10. Ever since the last date, the weather has contin[ue]d. cold—good skating on the ponds (I hear from my children) and the River is tightly bridged with ice, so that the heaviest coal-wagons pass habitually.

. . .

Our house, I believe, is kept comfortably warm; more so, I hear, than most others. The furnace in the cellar, supplies a good degree

---

[1] *Supra,* May 10, 1863, note 11.
[2] *Supra,* May 18, 1865, note 15.
[3] *Supra,* May 3, 1860, note 90.
[4] *Supra,* Sept. 20, 1860, note 9.
[5] *Supra,* March 3, 1865, note 88.
[6] *Supra,* April 27, 1859, note 27.
[7] Albert Todd: St. Louis lawyer; Whig state legislator, 1854; later a Democrat; member of the Constitutional Convention of 1875; a founder and trustee of Washington University.

of heat to the passages and stair ways, even to the third story. My own room, having a good, *wood* stove, is kept at what temperature I please.

Note. A few days ago, Col T. T. Gantt [8] lent me two volumes— *Works of John Stuart Mill*—viz *Liberty* (of thought and discussion) and *Considerations on Representative Government*—

The former—*Liberty*—I have read nearly through with a very mixed feeling. There is much to admire, in the acute perception, the sharp logic, the ready wit, and above all, in the easy, natural style and graceful diction of the composition. But I find in his principles and dogmas, much to doubt, and not a little to condemn and resist. In reading the work, I could not forbear, to pause as I passed along, and write down divers notes and comments. These were written hastily, certainly, and perhaps without sufficient consideration.

The conservatives held their meeting on the 8, January, as announced, for some time passed; but I fear, it was rather a failure. The weather was very cold and bad, and their [there is means neither to] warm nor light the rotunda. But I fear that these physical obstacles to our success in the war which it beho[o]ves us to wage in resisting the tyranny of the Radicals[, are not the only ones which stand in our way]. We need warming and lighting ourselves. Our more eminent men, who are, mainly relied upon to conduct the controversy, are urgently engaged in the pursuits of business, which cannot be neglected, without personal loss and discredit. And hence, they can devote to the public cause, only the scraps and remnants of time and attention which they can snatch, at brief intervals, from the duties of business.

Their opinions may be all right, and their wishes and intentions just what they should be, and yet, it is not possible for them to give their time and mind to [the] public.

[*A clipping which quotes Reverdy Johnson's* [9] *statement that the bill providing for a test oath* [10] *had been unanimously rejected by the Senate Judiciary Committee—yet was passed by the Senate.*]

Time was when any proposition touching law and principle, must have failed in the senate, if opposed by the unanimous opinion of the judiciary committee. But then, it was thought to be decent, at least to *profess* some respect for principle and some obedience to law.

"On the 23d inst. there was great excitement at the Fenian [11] headquarters in New York, said to be caused by orders of an important character from Stephens, the Chief Head Centre. It is said also that the Brotherhood have resolved to declare war against Canada."]

[8] *Supra*, Feb. 5, 1864, note 3.

[9] *Supra*, Nov. 26, 1859, note 85.

[10] July 2, 1862, *U. S. Statutes at Large*, XII, 502.

[11] *Supra*, Aug. 21, 1865, note 20.

This whole Fenian farce seems to me an impudent swindle—an outrage against law, against national comity and against common sense. Only think of an *Irish Republic* established in *America!* with a President and senate sitting in New York, and declaring war against Canada!

[*A clipping which prints a series of replies to invitations to a Mayor's banquet. The first is that of Mr. Bates.*]

[*A paragraph announcing the inauguration of Governor Fairchild* [12] *of Wisconsin, and quoting his opinion that Jefferson Davis should be hanged for treason.*]

This Governor Fairchild seems to be a mere *child*, in law and politics. He is not content that Davis should be tried *by law*, and take his chances, like other men, for justice, as administered by the courts, and mercy, as dispensed by the President. No—That would violate his radical theory of blood and plunder. Davis must be "tried, convicted and *hung*," or the American people will never be content! What right has that simple Child to speak for the American People?

He may be a *Fair*-child, but a *Dark* man
—*Hic niger est—hunc te Romane caveto.*[13]

[*A long article on the "Death of Presidents."*]

Gen Harry Lee [14] delivered the obituary oration in which is found, I think for the first time the famous sentence—" First in war, first in peace, first in the hearts of his country men."

[*A newspaper article on the first bishops in America, on which Bates has carefully indicated which belonged to the "Church of England" and which to the "Roman Catholic" faiths.*]

Coke [15] and Asbury [16] were [the] first *Methodist* Bishops—they [were] consecrated by John Wesley.

[*A reprint of an article in the* Louisville Journal *which lists a number of "reasonable and distinguished" men who are supporters of President Johnson's Southern policy. Among them is Mr. Bates.*][17]

---

[12] Lucius Fairchild of Madison, Wisconsin: gold prospector in California, 1849–1855; an officer (ultimately brigadier-general of volunteers) at Second Bull Run and Gettysburg; secretary of State of Wisconsin, 1864–1866; governor, 1866–1872; later U. S. consul in Liverpool and Paris, 1872–1880; minister to Spain, 1880–1882.

[13] Horace *Sermones* i. 4. 85.

[14] Henry Lee, Revolutionary soldier, 1776–1781; member of the Continental Congress, 1785–1788; state legislator, 1789–1791; governor, 1791–1794; father of Robert E. Lee. It was while a member of Congress, 1799–1801, that he delivered the famous eulogy of Washington for that body.

[15] Thomas Coke: Methodist superintendent, later called bishop, who helped organize American Methodism, 1784–1803.

[16] Francis Asbury: missionary to America, 1771; general superintendent of Methodism in America, 1772–1773; assistant to the superintendent under a Tory named Rankin, 1773–1784; superintendent, later called bishop, who shared with Coke the direction of the new American Methodist Episcopal Church, 1784–1816.

[17] These clippings and the comments thereon are on a large sheet bound into the diary.

Jany. 11. . . .

Jany. 12 Friday. . . .

The River is rising, by the late rain, and hopes are entertained that the ice will soon break up, so as to open navigation, which has been stopped for some weeks. Many boats lying at our [s]hore, will be in great danger, if the ice break suddenly[.]

Julia is quite sick with [a] severe cold, and Nancy far from well; and Matilda still absent, in Bonhomme, on a visit with Lavinia,[18] and is expected home tomorrow.

After sunset—The weather is still mild and beautiful. I went out for a little exercise, this evening—the first [time] for a month.

<Public Opinion.>

Demagogues, and all small politicians who seek their own interest by pretending to be great friends and admirers of the people, assume that the people, always *wise* and *virtuous*, have always, an *enlightened public opinion*—or, at least, that the "sober, second thought" of the people is, always right and wise. I have had occasion several times, to declare the belief that *public opinion* is never spontaneous with the people; that it is always, a *manufactured article*, made by parties, to suit their occasions. This is, *publicly*, a very unpopular belief, but, *privately*, it has the hearty concurrence of 99 in every 100 intelligent men. I observe that Mr. *John Stuart Mill*, in the very last sentence of his book upon *Representative Government*, speaks of—"those, who *supply the English public with Opinions*."

In fact, very few men have the information necessary to form distinct opinions upon political questions as they arise. And of that few, not many have the industry, honesty and courage to form and avow opinions upon grave questions of principle or policy. The mass of mankind follow, blindly, the opinions of some leader who promises to be successful. And hence, the rapid and total changes which we often see in what is called public opinion.

Jan 13 Saturday. A very mild, pleasant day—Feeling better than common, I went out in the afternoon, and rode in the street car, and walked some distance, for exercise—the first time I have been off the lot, for more than a month.

Jany 14. . . .

The ice in the river has given way, and I hear that a great many steamboats are destroyed—15 or 20.

---

[18] Wife of Dr. Frederick Bates of western Missouri who was a nephew of Edward Bates.

Jan 15. As I expected last evening, the atmosphere was in a very unsettled condition, portending great changes. I was very unwell during the night, and did not leave my bed till near 11. to day. . . .

Mo. Dem[ocrat] Jan 16. 66.

[*A clipping which prints a resolution of censure of Congressman Thomas E. Noell* [19] *of Missouri passed by the Radical Union members of the General Assembly from his Congressional District.*]

" For which of those good works do ye stone me? " [20]

Jany 16.   tuesday . . .

Small pox in Jefferson

Mo. Legislature. Mr. *McGee* [21] offered a resolution to adjourn to St Louis, on account of the small pox; and made some fearful statements—" it was raging in Jefferson city, at a terrible rate; no care was taken of the sick; the legislature had already lost one member from that cause, and came near losing another. The senators might all have it, if such exhibitions were continued as he had seen on the streets on yesterday afternoon, when persons afflicted with the disease were walking about in the most frequented places.["]

Mr. Moench [Muench] [22] suggested that the legislature had no such constitutional power &c[.]

Mr. Cox [23] saw small pox patients walking about the streets every day &c[.] He thought it due to families of senators to take care to protect themselves against the this [*sic*] terrible disease. It was so bad here that the *Dogs were in danger of taking it!*

Mr. McGee returned to the charge—" there were 8 or 10 cases of the very worse kind, right on High Street, where we all had to walk walk [*sic*] every day."

Mr. Goebel [24] " had talked with a most eminent physician of Jefferson city, who said he had not had a single patient this winter. There was not a single case *in the penitentiary*, as had been reported. He was of opinion that the matter had been greatly exaggerated." The Senate adjourned—

And so, let us hope, that as the *dogs* and *convicts* escaped, the Senators dismissed their fears, and agreed to forego the pleasures of a session in St Louis; thus giving a striking evidence of their courage and loyalty.

---

[19] Thomas E. Noell: lawyer of Perryville; major of militia, 1861–1862; captain in the U. S. Army, 1862–1865; Radical Republican congressman, 1865–1867.

[20] *The Bible*, "John," X, 32.

[21] E. M. McGee had been elected to the Missouri Senate from the Fourteenth District in 1865.

[22] *Supra*, Feb. 2, 1865, note 38.

[23] John H. Cox, senator from the Fifth District.

[24] Girt Goebel, senator of the Twenty-first District.

At night. comes Barton, on his way to South Carolina; and departed the next [day], in the afternoon, Wednesday, January 17.

Jan 20 Saturday. . . .

To day, the cold continues extreme, and of course, the effects are painfully felt by me.

Jan 21 Sunday. . . .

The Negro suffrage question.

Mr. Kell[e]y [25] of Pa.—formerly a furious democrat, now an extreme radical—has lately made a speech [26] in the H[ouse] of R[epresentatives], claiming for Congress, the power to regulate the right of suffrage, and establish the necessary qualifications for a voter, in the several States. Some days afterward, Mr. Kasson [27] of Iowa, ansd. him; <The Nat[ional] Intel[ligence]r. says Kasson made an able speech and copies largely from it> [28] and that led to [a] chopping little debate between them.[29] Mr. Kell[e]y (absurdly enough) vouched Madison on his side. He was for the constitution in its length and breadth, "*as understood by Washington and Madison.*"[30] Mr. Kasson is for the constitution *as it is*[.] And therein Mr. Kasson has the merit of a[t] least claiming to understand it *for himself*, while Mr. Kell[e]y makes no such claim; he goes for it, only as it is understood by somebody else.

Kell[e]y, though neither learned nor wise, is still a *smart* man, and one would think that his experience at the bar and bench of Phil[adelphi]a., and in congress might have enabled him to express his thoughts, in true and perspicuous language. But in that, he fails notably, but whether by accident or design, I cannot say. He has sense enough, if honestly and prudently governed, but his self-esteem is strong and his party zeal overpowering; and hence, his perceptions are distorted and his ingenuity stimulated. He speaks ambiguously, sometimes because his vision is clouded with interested views, for self and party, and consequently his thoughts must needs be vague and indistinct; and sometimes (perhaps most frequently) he is tempted to speak so cunningly to day, as to answer the present end in view, and yet not conflict with the altered circumstances of

[25] *Supra*, Dec. 30, 1862, note 90.

[26] Jan. 10, 1866, *Cong. Globe*, 39 Cong., 1 Sess., 180–183.

[27] John A. Kasson: Des Moines lawyer; delegate to the Republican National Convention in 1860; first assistant postmaster-general, 1861–1862; congressman, 1863–1867, 1873–1877, 1881–1884; American commissioner at international conferences, 1863, 1867, 1885, 1889, 1897, 1898; state legislator, 1868–1872; minister to Austria-Hungary, 1877–1881, and to Germany, 1884–1885.

[28] Added in the margin.

[29] Jan. 15, 1866, *Cong. Globe*, 39 Cong., 1 Sess., 235–240.

[30] *Ibid.*, 237.

tomorrow. This is a hard game to play. Some succe[e]d at it, but other some ruin themselves, and superadd a load of shame.—

Mr. Kell[e]y said " he was for the Constitution *with the power inherent [inhering] (1) in Congress*, (2) *so* to [to so] regulate suffrage as to give to (3) *every citizen of the country* the right to exercise it, (4) *within the limitation of 21 years of age*, and a citizen[,] either by birth or naturalization! " [31] [*Marginal Note.*] See (t.[ri-]w[eekly]) Nat[ional] Intel:[ligencer] Jan 16[.]

1. I[f] the power claimed, be *inherent* in Congress, then it must be original, innate, " not delegated to the U. S." by the constitution, " nor prohibited to the S[ta]tes " and therefore, (by the terms of the 10th. amendment,) the power *is reserved* to the *States respectively, or to the people.* Congress, in its nature, is incapable of *inherent* powers, for itself is but a derivative being, created by the constitution, and incapable of powers, except such as are granted *by its creator—The power is not given, but reserved to another.*

2. " *so* to regulate " &[c.] Why, the constitution neither gives the power to Congress, nor regulates, in whose hands soever it may be. It is Mr. Kell[e]y's own regulation[.]

3. " Every citizen " &c. Mr. Kell[e]y, surely does not mean what he says. *Every citizen,* includes females, lunatics, paupers, criminals however infamous—even *rebels.* To be sure Mr. Kell[e]y puts in one exception, of his own make—*21. years of age.* The statement of that one exception, excludes all others, and so Mr. K[elly], being a lawyer and a judge, must have intended—if he intended any thing in particular—

Why exclude persons under *21*, when the constitution is silent about it? Such are not excluded, by law, from being soldiers—they may fight but sha'nt vote. Mr. K.[elly] seems to think that voting belongs to *citizens alone*, and therein betrays his gross ignorance. The original constitutions of Massts. and N Carolina did not make citizenship a qualification for voting; and the new constitution of Missouri, grants to a large class of aliens, in express terms, the right of suffrage.

— In fact, the negro-fever has so deranged judge Kell[e]y, as to make him blind to reason and deaf to common sense. He pretends now to believe that congress has power to control suffrage in the States, and labors to degrade Madison, to the advocacy of that absurd heresy.

Jany. 22, Monday—Last night, Genl. Sherman called and sat, with the family, in my study, till a late hour. He is a very social, pleasant man, and we had a pleasant time.

---

[31] The quotation is taken not from the *Congressional Globe*, but from a paraphrase of it in the *National Intelligencer* of January 16, 1866.

When Barton started to the south,[32] the Genl. at my request, gave him a note, addressed to all military officers, in that region [askin]g them to do for him any kindness he might need.

Jan 23. Paid J. L. Garrison's *interest* note for $200, at the Exchange Bank. It is a charge upon our lot, bo[ugh]t. of him, for the deferred payment of $5000.

Recd. from Robt. A. Walton his check in Benoist, for *$2000*, on a/c of my interest in the Florissant[33] farm, lately sold to Reuben Musick.

This day, I recd. a letter from Professor Bartlett,[34] (confidentially) informing me that Woodson has failed in his examination! Poor, thoughtless boy! He has talents enough to have won a high standing in his class, and yet he failed, by sheer idleness and inattention; for I do not know that he is given to any other vice. I could have borne his death, but my courage sinks, in view of his degradation.

Jan 24. Wednesday. . . .

Early this morning, *Dick* left, for the S.[outh] W.[est] part of the State, sent by Mr. Eads,[35] to examine about lands, mines &c, in that quarter.

I think Mr. Eads has a thought of some gigantic project in that direction; and if Dick fulfill his present mission satisfactorily, [   ] Perhaps Mr. Eads has some idea of purchasing the S.[outh] W.[est] branch of the Pacific R. R.[36] and of connecting with it a great operation in lands, mineral and other.

. . . it is still hailing, and the surface, as seen from my windows, is well covered with ice. The foot passengers are sliding to and fro, and often fall outright, and boys and girls are skating on the sidewalks.

Jan 25 Thursday. . . .

Last night, Judge Moody[37] called. He did not speak plainly, but evidently his object was to get from me a letter to Prest Johnson, recommending him for Justice of the Supreme Court, vice Catron[38] dec[ease]d. He tells me that Genl. Grant is warmly for him, and puts it straight to the President—and that Glover,[39] Broadhead[40] &c &c, here have backed him strongly.

---

[32] *Supra,* Jan. 16, 1866.

[33] *Supra,* May 18, 1859, note 52.

[34] William H. C. Bartlett, West Point graduate of 1826, served in the Engineering Corps from 1829 to 1834, and at West Point as assistant professor of engineering, 1827–1829, and as professor of natural and experimental philosophy, 1834–1871.

[35] *Supra,* Jan. 28, 1860, note 38.

[36] The Southwest Branch became a part of the St. Louis and San Francisco Railroad.

[37] *Supra,* Feb. 2, 1865, note 40.

[38] *Supra,* April 6, 1864, note 74. He had died on May 30, 1865.

[39] *Supra,* Dec. 23, 1869, note 58.

[40] *Supra,* Dec. 26, 1859, note 66.

He says that the Resolution [41] of Thad: Stevens [42] to repeal the
test oath of Attornies [*sic*] is a mere trick, to avoid the decision of the
S.[upreme] C.[ourt] in Garland's case,[43] in which case, he says, the
court will certainly decide the act unconstitutional, unless the case
be evaded, by repealing the act.

Jan 26   Friday—. . .

[A newspaper clipping giving the vote—yeas 94, nays 37—on a
resolution passed in the House of Representatives that United States
soldiers should not be withdrawn from the seceded states " until the
two Houses of Congress shall have ascertained and declared that their
further presence there is no longer needed." [44]]

Resolution of the U.[nited] S.[tates] H[ouse] of R[epresentatives]

The insolence of these Ra[d]icals has no bounds.   They no longer
pretend to have any respect for law.   They openly assume the command of the army, over the head of the President, presuming (in
their ignorant egotism) upon his fears.   They are so carried away
with the infatuation, that they think the president will, in awe of
them, shrink from his constitutional duty, to com[m]and the army,
until such time as—" the two houses of Congress shall have *ascer-*
tained and declared that their further presence there is no longer
needed ! "

The mover of this *modest* and *discreet* resolution is one Mr. Williams [45] of Pa., " whom not to know argues myself unknown."   The
conduct of Mr. Williams in offering, and of the House, in passing,
the resolution reminds me of the story of a Virginia Captain of
militia, who had served (as I did) some months in the bloodless war
against the British, at Norfolk.   The Captain was chock full of
high notions of his own military skill and prowess, and doubted not
that, if he only had a chance, he could [46] make himself an Alexander,
a Cæsar or a Bonaparte.   Once his adventurous spirit urged him to
scramble up to [the] summit of the Peaks of Otter,[47] and there,
standing on the highest pinnacle, the ruling passion came strong upon
him, and made him fancy himself Lord paramount of all creation.
And, " filled with fury, rapt, inspired," he gave forth his orders
thus, grandiloquently—*Attention, the world!   By Nations!   to the*
right about, face!

---

[41] Jan. 15, 1866, *Cong. Globe*, 39 Cong., 1 Sess., 234.   It was agreed to in the House.

[42] *Supra*, Dec. 20, 1862, note 87.

[43] *Ex Parte Garland*, 4 Wallace 333–399.   The Supreme Court did declare the law of
January 24, 1865, requiring the test oath of attorneys in Federal courts, unconstitutional—
because it was a punishment " for past conduct " and therefore a violation of the clause
of the Constitution which prohibits " bills of attainder."

[44] Jan. 8, 1866, *Cong. Globe*, 39 Cong., 1 Sess., 137.

[45] Thomas Williams : Pittsburgh lawyer ; state senator, 1838–1841 ; Republican congressman, 1863–1869 ; a manager in Johnson's impeachment trial in 1868.

[46] " Could " was inserted later.

[47] Mountain-peaks of the Blue Ridge of southern Virginia whose elevation reaches 4001
feet.

But the stiff-necked and stupid nations marched right on, and would not face about at his command!

Jan 30 Tuesday. . . .

Julia continues very unwell, from her recent fall; and last night, I had a sharp return of my my [*sic*] maladies—both of them.

The National Intelligencer (tri-weekly) now comes to me pretty regularly, and altho' it has no ostensible editor, it abounds with strong articles; not indeed equal to Gales,[48] in dignity of thought, nor purity of style, nor accuracy of statement, nor to Welling,[49] in classic l[e]arning and elegance of diction; but more bold, and therefore more popular in its tone, than in the good old times of Gales and Seaton.[50] It is justly severe upon the Radicals in Congress, for the free negro suffrage bill, in the D[istrict] of C[olumbia].[51] And as for John W Forney,[52] it has flayed him alive, for his abuse of the people of the district, and his gross falsehoods and tergivers[at]ions.

I dont [*sic*] know how it could have escaped me, but I read yesterday, for the first time, some account of the bill[53] (introduced by Senator How[e][54] of Wis:) to establish *Territorial Governments* for the southern States! The paper states that Rever[d]y Johnson[55] has made a very able speech against the bill—and gives some extracts. Thus these Radicals have cast off all shame and are openly revolutionary. *Howe* in the Senate, assumes to treat what were once the *States of the Union,* as mere property, and govern them despotically—and *Kell[e]y,* in the House (not denying them statehood) assumes to regulate their suffrage, and control their elections.[56] They utterly disregarded the constitution, which is their only warrant for sitting in the seats which they defile.

Feb 3 Saturday. The *first* and *second* days of the month were bright and but moderately cold—indeed, seemed very pleasant, for

[48] Joseph Gales: reporter of Congressional proceedings for the *National Intelligencer,* 1807–1820; proprietor and chief editorial writer of the *National Intelligencer,* 1809–1860; partner of W. W. Seaton; publisher of the *Register of Debates,* 1825–1837, the *Annals of Congress* for the years 1798–1824, and the *American State Papers,* 1832–1861.

[49] *Supra,* June 20, 1859, note 3.

[50] *Supra,* Dec. 25, 1863, note 9.

[51] See *House Bills,* 39 Cong., 1 Sess., H. R. 1. It was introduced by Mr. Kelley (*supra,* Dec. 30, 1862, note 90), on Dec. 5, 1865. *Cong. Globe,* 39 Cong., 1 Sess., 10. It passed the House on Jan. 18, 1866. *Ibid.,* 311. In the Senate it was indefinitely postponed on Feb. 13, 1867. *Ibid.,* 39 Cong., 2 Sess., 1245.

[52] *Supra,* Nov. 20, 1861, note 59.

[53] Jan. 10, 1866, *Cong. Globe,* 39 Cong., 1 Sess., 162.

[54] Timothy O. Howe of Green Bay, Wisconsin: Maine state legislator, 1845; judge of the Circuit and Supreme Courts of Wisconsin, 1850–1855; Union Republican U. S. senator, 1861–1879; postmaster-general, 1881–1883.

[55] *Supra,* Nov. 26, 1859, note 85. For the speech see Jan. 11, 1866, *Cong. Globe,* 39 Cong., 1 Sess., 188–193.

[56] *Supra,* Jan. 21, 1866.

winter, seen through my windows— for I am still too sick to venture
out at all. . . .

Last night (like several nights lately), I suffered a good deal by the
returning symptoms of my *lung* disease. I was kept up a good part
of the night, not being able to breathe freely in a recumbent position. That is a very unpleasant situation, for, besides the *present*
discomfort, it seems constantly to threaten a total suppression of
breath.

A[b]out noon, called judge Watrous of Texas, desiring me to
identify him, to enable him to negotiate a warrant for Judge Williams' salary (in behalf he says, of Mrs. Williams, the judge being
dead, but the warrant endorsed by him.[)] I signed a memo.[ran-
dum] (on the back of an official letter of mine, to Mrs. W[illiams],[)]
to the effect that I saw no reason why the warrant should not be
paid.

In the afternnoon [*sic*] called, successively, *L M. Kennett* [57] and
Logan Stanton. The conversation turned almost naturally, upon
political topics, and (in view of their personal and relative positions)
could not but be piquant.

Feb 4 Sunday— . . .

This morning, my throat feels better, my bladder worse, . . .

I learn for the first time, this morning, from *Julian*, that the
waste material of the body caused by *intellectual* labor, habitually
passes off more freely, *through the kidneys*, while the refuse caused
by *bodily labor* passes *through the skin.*

Feb 5 Monday. . . .

Recd. a pleasant call from Revd. Dr. Eliot.[58] And afterwards,
Revd. Dr. Post.[59]

The Nat[iona]l. Intelligencer (tri-weekly, Feb. 1.) contains a
caustic piece of irony on *Trumbull's bill*,[60] to enlarge the powers of
the *Freedmen's Bureau.*

That bill is the consummation of lawless radicalism, and insolent
contempt of the constitution.

Note—The bill is copied into a former paper (Nat[ional] Intel[ligencer], t.[ri-]w.[eekly] Jany 27) and is the worst sample I
ever saw, of legislative composition, both in manner and in matter,
except the New Constitution of Mo.

§ 1. continues the original act,[61] of Mar. 3. 1865. " and shall extend
to all refugees and freed men, in all parts of the U. S; "—and the

[57] *Supra*, June 16, 1859, note 94.

[58] *Supra*, Feb. 22, 1860, note 79.

[59] *Supra*, Jan. 31, 1860, note 44.

[60] *Supra*, Nov. 22, 1860, note 85. For the bill see *Senate Bills*, 39 Cong., 1 Sess., bill
no. 60.

[61] *U. S. Statutes at Large*, XIII, chap. XC., 507.

Prest. may devide [*sic*] the U. S. into districts of one or more States—not to exceed 12. and with the advice of the Senate, may app[oin]t. an asst. com[mis]s[io]n[e]r. for each District, who &c—" Or the sd. Bureau may, in the discretion of the Prest., be placed under a com[mis]s[io]n[e]r. and asst. com[missione]rs, to be *detailed from the army*, in which event, each *officer* so detailed to duty, shall serve without increase of pay or allowances.

§ 2. The Com[mis]s[ione]r. (with the approval of the prest.) shall divide each Dis[tric]t into sub dis[tric]t[s], (not less than a county *or* parish) and shall *assign* to each sub Dis[tric]t, "*at least* one AGENT, either a citizen, officer of the army, or enlisted man " who, if an officer, shall serve without additional compensation, "and if a citizen or enlisted man shall receive a salary not exceeding $1500 per an[num] "—the agent to be sworn. Each Asst. Com[mis]s[ione]r. may employ " not exceeding *six clerks* " one of the 3d. class and 5 of the 1st. And each *agent* of a sub district *may employ two clerks* of the 1st. class[.] "And the President of the U. S through the war Dept and the com[mis]s[ione]r., *shall extend military jurisdiction* OVER all employé[e]s agents agents [*sic*] and officers of this Bureau, in the exercise of the duties imposed or authorised by this act, or the act to which [this] act is supplementary." (!)

§ *3.* The Secy. of War may issue such supplies " as he may deem needful " for refugees and freedmen their wives and children, " under such rules and regulations *as he may direct.*["]

§ *4.* The President to set apart lands and

§ *5.* Occupants of land under Gen Shermans [*sic*] order of Jany 16. 1865, confirmed in possession for 3 years[.]

§ *6.* The Comm[is]s[ione]r. shall, under the direction of the P[r]es[iden]t., procure lands, and build assiylums [*sic*] and Schools " for refugees and freedmen dependent upon the Government for support, &c (!)

§7. Whenever in any state or District, in which the ordinary course of judicial proceedings *has been* interrupted by the rebellion, and wherein, in consequence of any state or local law, ordinance, police or other regulation, custom *or prejudice* any of the *civil rights* or immunities belonging to white persons, including &c, " are refused or denied to negro[e]s, mulattoes, freed men, *refugees* or any other person, on account of race, color, or any previous condition of slavery or involuntary servitude, except &c " it shall be the duty of the President of the U. S. *through* the *Com[m]issioner*, to extend *military protection and jurisdiction*, over ALL CASES AFFECTING *such such* [*sic*] *persons* so *discriminated aga[i]nst.*

§8. That any person who, under color of any State or local law, ordinance, police or other regulation or custom, shall in any state or district in which the ordinary course of judicial proceedings *has been* interrupted by the rebellion, subject or cause to be subjected any negro, mulatto, freedman, refugee, or other person, on account of race or color, or any previous condition of slavery or involuntary servitude, except as a punishment of crime whereof the party shall have been duly convicted, or *for any other cause* to the deprivation of any *civil right* secured to white persons, or to any other or different or to any other or different [*sic*] punishment than white persons are subject to, for the commission of like acts or offences, shall be deemed *guilty of a misdemeanor* and be punished by a fine not exceeding $1000, or imprisonment not not [*sic*] to exceed one year, or both, " and [62] it shall be *the duty* of *the officers and agents* of this Bureau to take jurisdiction of and hear and determine *all offences* committed against the provisions of this section, and *also* of *all cases* affecting negro[e]s mulatto[e]s freedmen refugees, or other persons who are discriminated against in any of the particulars mentioned in the preceeding [*sic*] section of this act, under such rules and regulations as the President of the U. S. *through the War Department*, shall prescribe.   The Jurisdiction conferred by this section on the *officers and agents* of this bureau to cease and determine whenever the discrimination on acount of which it is conferred ceases, and in no event to be exercised in any state in which the ordinary course of judicial proceedings *has not been* interrupted by the rebellion, nor in any such state after said state has been fully restored in *all* its *constitutional* relations to the U. S. and the courts of the State and of the U. S. within the same are not disturbed or stopped in the peacible [*sic*] course of justice."

I understand that this act has passed both Houses, forced through, by the despotic caucus of the Radicals. I take it for certain that Prest Johnson will put his veto upon the hideous monster. If he yield to that, he yields everey [*sic*] thing—his personal respectability, his official dignity, the lawful powers of his office, and, in fact, the whole government—and becomes the passive slave of his worst enemies, who, henseforth [*sic*], will have no motive to treat him otherwise than with mingled severity and contempt. I will not doubt that he will veto it.

[*Marginal*] *Note. Feb: 20.* The President's *veto* [63] is in our morning papers—dated *yesterday* the 19 of Feby., and sent by Telegraph last night. Now, that the Radicals have have [*sic*] brought *their war* against the President and the constitution to a definitive issue, my hopes for the Republic begin to revive. The Radicals have committed themselves to grossly foolish measures— and the Prest. is committed, stronger than ever, to the constitution.

---

[62] The remainder of this paragraph is written in red ink.

[63] See *infra*, Feb. 20, 1866.

Feb 8 Thursday. . . .

To night, my good friend and kinsman, *John N. Booth* is to marry Miss *Mary Alice Garrison*, daughter of my neighbor Daniel. R. Garrison[.][64]

(P. S. They were married, accordingly.)

Feb 9. Called to see me this morning (father) *E. I. Fitspatrick* Priest, St Bridgets. A pleasant young man who politely, reminded me that he and all his class (the Rhetoric class of St. Xavier's) went to hear me, in defence of the counts de Montesquou [65] (in 1847.)

Mr. Gibson [66] came to interest me to write in furtherance of the views of Messrs. Garrison [67] and Taylor [68] who are going to Washington with the hope of a transfer of the *Overland Mail*, from the northern route to their route [69]—the [Missouri] Pacific and the Union Pacific R Rs[.] [70]

I have just received a long letter from Mr. Coffey,[71] the very weakest and poorest that I ever knew him [to] write. It is a very lame defence of the late Radical measures in Congress—especially Trumbul[l]'s bill [72] to enlarge the powers of the Freedmen's bureau.

He admits that the *rebel states* are *states in the* Union, but suggests that Congress may exercise *unconstitutional powers*, because *the state of war still exists!!* War, it seems, relieves congress from all the restraints of the constitution!! and confers upon congress new powers, not given by the constitution! If war still continues, I wish to know who is our enemy? against whom are we to fight? Oh! says my ingenuous Radical friend, it is not a *fighting* war, it is only a war to enable congress to pass what unconstitutional acts it pleases! I had thought that war was as *lawful* as peace: The constitution provides for *war*—Congress has power to *declare* war; and if by declaring war the constitution is, *ipso facto*, repealed; then Congress, by the very act of declaring war, destroys its own existence, for it exists only in and by the constitution.

---

[64] *Supra*, March 3, 1865, note 88.

[65] *Supra*, May 20, 1859, note 55.

[66] *Supra*, April 27, 1859, note 27.

[67] *Supra*, March 3, 1865, note 88.

[68] *Supra*, Jan. 30, 1863, note 3.

[69] In 1858 John Butterfield established the first mail service across the continent to California. The route lay from St. Louis by the Pacific Railway to Tipton (later to other termini of the railroad farther west), thence to Fort Smith, Arkansas, to El Paso, Texas, to Arizona, to Los Angeles, and finally to San Francisco. The "Overland Mail" reduced the time from the four to six months required by immigrant trains to a twenty-five-day service. In 1861 the outbreak of the War necessitated a change from the southern to the Omaha and Platte River route. Now that the War was over, St. Louis wished the mail route returned to Missouri, using the newly finished Pacific Railway as far as Kansas City.

[70] The Pacific or Missouri Pacific, begun in 1851, ran through Jefferson City and Tipton to Kansas City which it reached in October, 1865. The Union Pacific, begun in 1865 with termini at Kansas City and Omaha, was completed in 1869.

[71] *Supra*, March 5, 1860, note 18.

[72] *Supra*, Feb. 5, 1866.

Feb 10. . . .

Feb 11. . . .

Feb 14 Wednesday. . . .

By 9. a. m. the clouds dispersed and the sun came out brightly.
It turned very cold in the night, and is still so.   The windows of my
room are covered thick with ice, crystalized in fantastic forms and
so thick as to obstruct the view.   And not without beauty—such
beauty as *Cou[n]sellor Phillips* [73] might call "decorated rudeness."

This sharp, changeable weather tells, painfully, upon my ruined
health.   Last afternoon, Revd. Dr. Sc[h]uyler [74] kindly called, and
spent several hours in pleasant conversation. i. a. I read to him my
late letter to Prest. Johnson. [75]

Night. It is still intensely cold—not surpassed in severity, during
the whole of this bad winter.

Our house, I suppose, is warmer than most houses.   The furnace
tempers the air in all the stair ways and passages, and thus makes it
easy to keep the rooms comfortably warm.

Gen Sherman has returned from Washington[.]

Feb 16 Friday. . . .

Recd. today, a letter from Mr. Ashton [76] (Asst. Atty Genl.[)] in
good humor and he says, not at all angry with me, for "rubbing
him against the hair" as I had feared—He thinks that our hair
grows pretty much alike.   In mentioning his wife, he notices, very
modestly, *the baby*, also.

John Stuart Mill is a writer of wonderful variety and *agility* of
thought, and great facility of expression, so as to set forth, with
ease and grace, the faintest tints and minutest forms of ideas.   His
manner of writing is very suggestive of other thoughts in the minds
of his readers, but painfully deficient in definite conclusions of his
own.   While I am charmed with the ease and grace of his style and
the rich variety of his thoughts, in the aggregate mass, in reading
him, I am constantly disappointed and mortified at the lack of
specialty in his propositions and precision in his conclusions.   Sometimes indeed, I cannot understand, at all, what he means—for instance, in Rep[resentativ]e. Govt. p. 34. he talks about giving "the
first commencement of scientific precision to the notion of good government."   That may be very wise, for any thing that I know, but
the sense is wholly hid from me.

---

[73] Charles Phillips, 1787(?)–1859, Irish-born London barrister and writer, noted for
his persuasive appeals to juries, for overstatement, and for a rather florid eloquence.

[74] Montgomery Schuyler, Episcopal clergyman in Michigan, 1842–1844, in New York
1844–1854, and in St. Louis, where he was rector of Christ Church, from 1854 until 1896.

[75] See *infra*, Feb. 20, 1866.

[76] *Supra*, Feb. 5, 1862, note 52.

Moreover, like our own politicians, here at home, he indulges in the bad practice of exaggerated statement—saying what he does not mean, even when setting forth a great principle or a governmental postulate—for instance—Rep[resentativ]e. Govt. p. 64 " There is no difficulty (says he) in showing that the *ideally* best form of Government is that in which the sovereignty, or Supreme controlling power, in the last resort, is vested in the *entire aggregate of the community*, *every citizen* not only having a voice in the exercise of that ultimate sovereignty, but being, at least occasionally, called on to take an actual part in the government, by the personal discharge of some public function, local or general."

Now, it is perfectly certain that Mr. Mill, being a man of sense— a man of ideas—cannot mean seriously, to say what he, actually says. The statement admits that the government he indicates is not *really* the best, but only *ideally* so. What does he mean by the word *ideally*—something grotesquely imagined, contrary to the known and the possible facts? The *ideally* best! Why, no sane man ever had *an idea* that *the supreme controlling power, in the last resort*, ought, or possibly can be vested in *the entire aggregate of the community— every citizen* having a voice, and occasionally, sharing in the actual government—men, women children, lunatics, idiots, paupers and convict felons!

Ah! says Mr. Mill, that is so obviously wrong, that you ought not to suppose that I meant it, though I said it. But, Mr. Mill, suppose that your proposition is not so gross as to be obviously absurd to all mankind, but only foolish and wicked, in the eyes of all wise and just men, yet very popular with knaves and charlatans and radicals. Suppose that case; and you still claim the privilege to repudiate what you please and stick to what you please of your own statements *after the public judgment has passed* upon them. No, Mr. Mill, you cant [*sic*] be allowed that privilege. You are a man of ideas, and of a large and fluent vocabulary. You can speak *truly*, if you choose, and therefore when you speak falsely, you ought to be he[l]d to it. Besides, you are a *volunteer instructor* of mankind, and if you cant or wont [*sic*] say what you mean and mean what you say, you perhaps, would do quite as well, to split your pen and stop short.

It is bad enough for Senator, Gratz Brown [77] to write an elaborate article in favor of *universal* suffrage, at the very moment that he and his faction are denying to a large majority of the people, the right to vote! He and they may be forgiven, because they know not what they do. But not you, Mr. Mill, for—

" You know the *right*, and yet the *wrong* pursue."

---

[77] *Supra*, Feb. 15, 1864, note 44.

[*Marginal Addition.*] Those who exclaim the loudest about *universal suffrage* —the right of *every citizen* to have a share of the power of government, always speak untruly. Their *universal* means very *restricted;* their *every citizen* means *our party;* and their *People* means the *favored few, loyal, like me.*

In Ashton's letter, above mentioned, he states that there are two cases [78] pending in the S.[upreme] C.[ourt] involving the question of the legality of *Military Commissions*, as courts, with power to " try and execute " offenders. He states the array of counsel, and conjectures the division of [the] court—i. e. for the U. S. Messrs. the Atty Genl. Speed [79] and S[t]anbery [80] and Evarts [81]—and for the Relators Messrs. Black [82] of Pa. and Doudley Field [83] (and another) [.]

These gentlemen named, all, have reputation for forensic ability, in private cases, *inter partes;* but, I have never heard of their superiority, as *Publicists* and *constitutional Lawyers.* Some of them, I know, are not such, and I predict a failure in the argument, probably, on both sides. In discussing constitutional questions, it is, of late, the prevailing fashion among the disputants, to ignore the constitution itself, and our entire system of legal government, and to show off their learning in elaborate debate about the conflicting opinions of different individuals.

It seems to be assumed that the judges will decide upon party grounds and personal considerations! And he classifies the Judges pro and con, thus—" I count on the following members being against the Commissions—*Nelson*,[84] *Clifford*,[85] *Grier* [86] and *Davis* [87] (and *perhaps* Ch[ief] J[ustice] Chase.[)] I think *Swayne*,[88] *Wayne* [89]

---

[78] There were *three* cases, Milligan's, Horsey's and Bowles's. The Court's orders in all three were given at this time, but the opinions were not rendered until the next term, and that in the Milligan case covered the other two. See *ex parte Milligan,* 4 Wallace 2–142.

[79] *Supra,* May 25, 1865, note 27.

[80] Henry Stanbery of Cincinnati, attorney-general of Ohio, 1846; member of the Constitutional Convention of 1850; U. S. attorney-general, 1866–1868; counsel for President Johnson in his impeachment trial, 1868; nominee for the U. S. Supreme Court—rejected by the Senate because of his support of Johnson.

[81] *Supra,* April 8, 1862, note 71.

[82] *Supra,* Oct. 28, 1859, note 22.

[83] David Dudley Field: New York lawyer; member of state legal commissions, 1847–1850, 1857–1865; leader in the Washington Peace Convention of 1861; Democratic congressman, 1877. In the period following the War, he frequently argued before the U. S. Supreme Court, not only in the Milligan case, but in the Cummings (test-oath) case, the McCardle (Reconstruction Act of 1867) case, and the Cruikshank (Enforcement Act of 1870) case—in each of which he carried his constitutional point.

[84] *Supra,* March 6, 1861, note 32.

[85] *Supra,* April 5, 1864, note 71.

[86] *Supra,* Feb. 26, 1864, note 76.

[87] *Supra,* Feb. 26, 1863, note 43.

[88] *Supra,* March 22, 1862, note 49.

[89] *Supra,* Nov. 27, 1861, note 74.

and *Field* [90] will be *certainly* in *favor* of the U. S.—Miller [91] is doubtful!" [92]

Alas! Alas! that any judge of the S.[upreme] C.[ourt] of the U. S. should even be suspected of deciding such a case upon party or personal grounds—deciding wrong because otherwise, "some gentlemen *here* will be in a very unenviable position."

If the S.[upreme] Court should decide that Military Commissions are *lawful*, I predict that the judges who give opinion that way, will go down to posterity with characters as black as that of L[or]d. Ch[ief] J.[ustice] Saunders; [93] and that their judgment will be far more odious to this nation, than Saunders' judgment against the chartered rights and liberties of the city of London,[94] ever was to the English people.

Feb 20. This morning the papers contain Prest. Johnson's *veto message* to the Senate, against *Trumbull's* bill—the foolish and wicked bill to enlarge the powers of the Freedmen's bureau. It was delivered yesterday.

Note. (1) On the *10th.* of Feby., I addressed to *Prest. Johnson* a plain, downright letter about the duties of his position, and what the nation expects of him—against military commissions, and denouncing Trumbull's bill of enormities.[95]

St Louis Mo. Feb. 10. 1866

To Andrew Johnson

President of the United States,

Sir,

Perhaps I do but aggravate my offence, in presuming to write to you, a second time, when my first letter has never been recognized, perhaps never seen by you. But I am constrained by considerations far higher than any personal vanity of my own, or any mere forms of courtesy due to a great magistrate whom I respect and honor.

I am past seventy years old, and in very bad health, and therefore, beyond the reach of all the hopes and fears which commonly, actuate

---

[90] *Supra*, March 15, 1864, note 28.

[91] *Supra*, Dec. 2, 1864, note 85.

[92] Justices Nelson, Clifford, and Grier, but also Mr. Justice Field concurred with Mr. Justice Davis in the majority opinion. Chief Justice Chase wrote a minority opinion agreeing to the order of the Court, but basing his decision upon other grounds, and Justices Wayne, Swayne, and Miller concurred with him in this.

[93] Sir Edmund Saunders: London barrister; reporter of the King's Bench, 1666–1672; chief justice of the King's Bench, 1682–1683.

[94] This suit, in which Charles II by *quo warranto* proceedings took away the charter of the City of London, was brought on the advice of Saunders as counsel to the King. In order to win the case, Charles II moved Pemberton (*supra*, Dec. 21, 1865, note 11) to the Court of Common Pleas to vacate the chief justiceship of the King's Bench for Saunders who would favor the Crown.

[95] Mr. Bates's letter to the President is in the Johnson MSS., LXXXVI, 9046. For the veto message see J. D. Richardson, *Messages and Papers of the Presidents*, VI, 398–405.

the conduct of men engaged in the strifes of party politics. I belong
to no political party, now in existence, and sympa[t]hise with no
political organization but that which was ordained by the constitution, and which lives and moves and has its being *only* in, under and
according to that fundamental law. And I have no respect for either
the judgment or the patriotism of any man whose prurient vanity is
strong enough to make him believe that he is justified in attempting
to do good to his country, in ways forbidden by that fundamental
law. I believe, undoubtingly, that if our government be, in any respect, better than the government of any civilized country in Europe,
it is only because it is a government of *law*, and not of the *will* of
those who happen, for the time being, to be in places of power,
whether as Kings, or Presidents or congressmen.

I believe that the constitution, if reverently preserved, obeyed and
acted out in practice, will insure the stability and continuance of the
government, and the liberty and prosperity of the people. And I
believe, as confidently, that, if the constitution be, habitually, broken
and despised, by men in office, the Government will lose all hold upon
the affection and respect of the people, and will become weak, irregular and arbitrary, fluctuating, from day to day, with the changing
passions of men and factions.

I am aware sir (and the fact grieves me deeply) that since your
accession to legal power, you have been constrained, by the novelties
and difficulties of your situation, to give your apparent sanction to
certain arbitrary measures of government dangerous alike to the
liberty of individuals and to the supremacy of the laws of the land.
I mean the use of *military commissions*, instead of *Courts* established
and regulated by law, to try and punish supposed criminals. I do
not allege this as a designed wrong on your part, for I know full
well, how you have been misled into that unhappy position. I know
that there are men connected with the government who affect to believe (and boldly preach it for doctrine) that *the military* is a separate, independent power in the state—in fact, a government in itself,
with authority to constitute courts, and administer penal justice, at
its own pleasure, and without any subordination to the written laws
of the country! Such men pretend to believe, and teach it openly,
that the commander of the army (that is the President) has legitimate power, at his own discretion, and by his mere declaration, to
annul the constitution and the statutes, and establish his own will in
their stead!

Mr. President, I will not trouble you with argument upon this
great theme, involving, as it does, the liberty and laws of a nation,
on the one side, and upon the other side, the power and the passions
of a despot; but content myself with remarking that whoever has
read the constitution *must know* that "the military" is only one

branch or instrument of that "Executive Power" which, by the terms of the constitution, is vested in the President. That the *military* is always and every where, under the command of the President; and that the President himself, is always, every where, and under all possible circumstances, under the command of the constitution. That in fact, if there be, in the nation, any one man who, more than any other man, is the bound servant of the Constitution, that man is the President.

I have spoken freely of what has been done since you came to the Presidency, which in my judgment, is contrary to the constitution and dangerous to liberty and law. I suppose that those wrongs were done, not because you actively approved them, but because, (then fresh in office and surrounded with untried obstacles) you could not at once, perceive that you held in your official hand, the legal means of preventing or curing the evil. And now Sir, I will speak with equal freedom of the altered state of affairs, and of what every law-loving patriot in the nation hopes and expects at your hands. We believe that you are a patriot—an earnest, sincere brave man—determined to fulfill all the legal duties of your station "as you understand them." And that thought gives me great comfort; for I do not doubt that you are armed with all the legal powers which are necessary to maintain the established government, by preserving, protecting and defending the constitution and taking care that the laws be faithfully executed, against all the efforts of a desperate faction, which seems, for the present, to dominate both Houses of Congress, and, in its eagerness to clutch all power into its own hands, has cast off even the outward show of respect for the constitution. And, having these lawful powers in your own hand, I will not allow myself to doubt that you will use them efficiently, for the public good; for I know you to be too good a constitutional lawyer to suppose that official powers may be treated as *privileges*, and waived at pleasure. The powers of the President do not belong to him, as an individual. They are granted to him *officially* and for the sole purpose of enabling him to perform his duties.

As I write this letter only in the exercise of what I suppose to be my right, as a citizen, and not in the character of a counsellor, whose advice has been asked, I will not obtrude upon you my opinions, in detail, upon the special matters which are now so recklessly thrust upon you and the nation. Nor will I dwell, at any great length, upon the coarse insolence with which you and your benign policy towards the southern states, have been treated in Congress. A leading member of the House has, in effect, denied your official existence, and assumed to consider you an alien and a stranger, by declaring that "The state of Tennessee is not known to this House or to Congress!" A prominent senator has introduced a bill to degrade the States which you have invited to resume their constitutional positions in the Union, by ruling them as so much conquered territory, subject to the arbitrary power of Congress. And both houses have recently passed a bill requiring you, in flat contradiction of your constitutional duty "to extend *military jurisdiction* over all employés, agents and officers" of the freedman's bureau, and to "extend *military protection and jurisdiction* over all cases affecting such persons" as are discriminated against by state laws. And the same bill also provides (without any reference to the intermediate or conflicting authority of the President, the War Department, the chief Freedman of the bureau, or the Courts of law) that "it shall be the duty of the *officers and agents* of this bureau (all and each one of them, of course) *to take jurisdiction*, of, and to *hear and determine all offences* committed against the provisions of this section (8); and also of *all cases* affecting negro[e]s, mulatto[e]s, freedmen, refugees or *other persons* who are discriminated against, in any of the particulars mentioned in the preceeding [*sic*] section of this act!"

I shall not weary you sir, with comments upon these legislative monstrosities. But I cannot forbear to remark that the faction which now domineers over the two houses of Congress, is itself, not only utterly regardless of the constitution, but is, apparently, determined to force you to be an accomplice in their crime. And that is not all: They will degrade you, if they can, by forcing you to recant and falsify the wisest and best measures which you have yet devised, for the good of your country and your own historic fame.

These are not new opinions of mine. They were formed long ago—before the Radical leaders had dared to declare open war against you and the constitution. And to show this, I will close the present writing with an extract from a private letter written by me, as long ago as last September, in answer to an eminent friend in Pennsylvania—

The extract—"You express the opinion that a split between the administration and the Radicals is inevitable[.]" I suppose so; and that split may be very formidable if the Radicals be still allowed by the administration to give tone and direction to all or any of the Departments, whereby the Government is, every day, committed to Radical enormities, and thereby pledged against law and truth. But, if we really have *an administration* (and not seven or eight distinct Departmental Governments, each one scheming for its own ends), if President Johnson will assume what lawfully belongs to him—the headship of the nation the actual control of *an administration* all of whose parts are required to operate harmoniously, for the attainment of *one* great end—the restoration of the Union, with peace and order—and by *one* great means, the strict observance of the consti-

tution—if, I say, the President will only do this, and, with a fixed
resolution and a steady hand, perform all his own duties *according
to law*, he will have small cause to fear the Radicals. All the honest
men among them (and I suppose there may be some) will willingly
acquiesce in a course so manifestly just and right, all the timid, the
trimmers, the timeservers, (which I take to be the bulk of the Radical
faction), will hasten to give in their adhesion, rather than renounce
all hope of power and patronage for the next three years. And as
for the few truculent leaders who (like the frogs we read of) hoped,
by bellowing, and blowing, to pass themselves off for bullocks—they
have no substance in them, and may be trodden out, like so many
sparks on the floor."

It was much easier *then* than *now*, to serve the country by putting
down that faction; for then they had not fully organized their conspiracy against the constitution, nor marshalled all their powers for
mischief. But the good end can be accomplished, as effectually, now
as then, and by the sam[e] simple means—the strict observance of
the constitution and the faithful execution of the laws.

I remain, Mr. President,
> With the greatest respect
>> Your friend and fellow citizen

EDW.D BATES

He had time to read it before sending in his excellent veto message;
but I do not flatter myself into the notion that any thing that I could
say would be of any influence upon him, in so great a matter of state.

[*Note*.] (2) On saturday night, the 24th., was held a great mass
meeting of the citizens of St. Louis, called by the " State central com-
[mitt]ee. of the Conservative Union Party," Genl. E. B. Brown [96]
Prest.

I was specially invited, but, of course, could not attend, by reason
of sickness; and the invitation was too late (dated the 24) to allow
me to state my views to the meeting, by way of letter. Nevertheless,
I have stated some of my views of the subject, in a letter addressed
to Genl. Brown, dated Feby. 24.

Feb. 27. tuesday. . . . I hope for some improvement in health as
soon as we get warm, dry air.

Last night, Barton returned from his trip to S. Carolina (having
been absent since the 17th. of Jany.) all well and having accomplished
his business satisfactorily.

---

[96] Egbert B. Brown: mayor of Toledo, 1849; railway manager, 1852–1861; brigadier-
general of volunteers who helped preserve St. Louis to the Unionists in 1861, and served
in Missouri, Arkansas, and Texas from 1861 to 1865; U. S. pension agent at St. Louis,
1866–1868.

Note. The Mo. Rep[ublican] of the *28* contains Prest Johnson's speech to the people, in answer to the great meeting, in his support of which *P. R. Fendall* [97] was ch[a]irman. His *enemies* charge him with letting down his dignity by that speech, making himself "vulgar, common and popular," while his *friends* insist that his enemies mourn over his deminished [*sic*] dignity, only because they are sore under the cuffs and kicks they got from his plebe[i]an hands and feet. What a burlesque it is for such men as Wade [98] and Stevens [99] to whine about dignity.

Mr. Seward's speech, at the great meeting in N.[ew] Y.[ork] lately held at The Cooper Institute,[1] makes me ashamed. The meeting was called to *indorse the veto*—and so it does, after a very equivocal, see-saw fashion. His position forced him upon the rostrum, and his object seemed to be, to get off it, if possible, without incurring the open censure of either party. Perhaps he may gain that point of ignoble security against the blatant anger of either party. But I do not see how he can escape the contempt of both. <*[Marginal Note.]* Nat[ional] Intel[ligencer] (t.[ri-]w.[eekly]) Feb 24./66>

[*A clipping headed "Misplaced Confidence" which states that Speaker Colfax* [2] *wagered and lost a box of cigars on a bet that President Johnson would sign the Freedmen's Bureau bill.*]

Misplaced confidence! All of us are subject, more or less, to that misfortune because all of us are, more or less, blinded by our own inordinate vanity[.] The self-conceit of these brainless radicals amounts to a real mania. They had a *misplaced confidence* in their own power to do mischief, and still protect themselves against the universal law, that "the wages of sin is death." [3] And they had a confidence, foolishly misplaced, in the cowardice of Andrew Johnson; and really seemed to believe that he would quail before them, whenever they chose to frown and shake their fists.

[*A reprint in the* Missouri Democrat *of a letter from J. F. Benjamin,* [4] *dated House of Representatives, Washington, February 20, 1866, in which he calls the veto of the Freedmen's Bureau bill* " *a second edition of the bombardment of Fort Sumter* " *and promises* "*war to the knife* " *on Johnson and the South.*]

---

[97] *Supra,* June 27, 1864, note 29.

[98] *Supra,* Aug. 10, 1859, note 77.

[99] *Supra,* Dec. 20, 1862, note 87.

[1] Separately published as *Speech of W. H. Seward, to the Citizens of New York, at Cooper Institute, February 22, 1866, on the Restoration of Union,* Washington, 1866.

[2] *Supra,* April 27, 1859, note 28.

[3] *The Bible,* "Romans," VI, 23.

[4] John F. Benjamin: Shelbyville lawyer; Democratic state legislator, 1850–1852; brigadier-general in the Union Army; provost marshal in Missouri, 1863–1864; delegate to the Republican National Convention in 1864; Radical Republican congressman, 1865–1871.

This Mr. BENJAMIN, has overstepped the mark of prudence. I wot, he will live to mourn the day that he wrote this foolish letter. And the *Democrat*, (if not past all shame) would for indorsing it.

In nothing—not even the charging Prest. Johnson and his supporters, with *treason*, and assuming for the *Radicals* the name of the *Union* party—is there a greater falsehood than the assertion that *they* are the party which elected him. It is a noteworthy fact of late, such men as Mr. Benjamin are doing all they can, to sink the name of *Radical*, and assume that of *Republican*, and sometimes, they have the hardihood to call themselves *the Union party!*

Mr. Benjamin considers the Prest's veto message against the Freedman's Bureau bill " an open declaration of war," and declares that henceforth, it is *a war to the* KNIFE! Does that mean that Johnson may look out for the fate of Lincoln? Will some *loyal* radical act the part of Booth![5]

[*A newspaper summary of measures under discussion in Congress on March 8—the House bill providing that the Supreme Court shall consist of a Chief Justice and eight Associate Justices,[6] and Senator Henderson's resolutions[7] on the subject of reconstruction.*]

The *Supreme Court* is to be a mere party machine; to be manipulated, built up and pulled down as party exigencies require.

Poor Henderson! What can he mean by saying that the Insurgent states *allowed* their political relations to be *severed?*

They did not sever them *themselves*—that is clear. Then who did? Mr. H.[enderson] and his radical brethren?

[*A clipping telling of the divorce secured in Iowa by the wife of Congressman Kasson[8] on the ground of infidelity in spite of which Mr. Kasson will resume his seat; and another giving statistics on the decrease in inhabited houses in Ireland.*]

March 14—Wednesday, This is *Julia's* birthday—the 59th. And the next *29th. of May* will be the 43d. anniversary of our marriage, and I am devoutly thankful that we have been allowed to spend together so large a portion of our lives, in one unbroken stream of love and confidence.

This morning, *Dick* left us (his wife and child being here, for the present) with a view to settlement there, in business at Granby.[9]

---

[5] John Wilkes Booth, Lincoln's assassin.

[6] It became law on July 23, 1866, *U. S. Statutes at Large*, XIV, chap. CCX, 209. By an Act of March 3, 1863, the number of justices on the Supreme Court had been increased from nine to ten. Judge Catron (*supra*, April 6, 1864, note 74) had died on May 30, 1865. In April, 1865, Johnson nominated Stanbery (*supra*, Feb. 16, 1866, note 80) to fill the tenth place, but he was not approved, and in July Johnson signed this bill reducing the number of justices again to nine.

[7] See *supra*, Feb. 24, 1863, note 27. For the resolution see March 8, 1866, *Cong. Globe*, 39 Cong., 1 Sess., 1252–1253.

[8] *Supra*, Jan. 21, 1866, note 27.

[9] See *supra*, Dec. 9, 1865, note 82.

The particulars [are] not understood by me, but I think the plan is understood and approved by both Barton and Mr. Eads,[10] and therefore, likely to succeed.

[*March*] *15*. . . .

Barton has been here since last monday night, and expects to go home tomorrow.

During the day, come Julia Coalter and her sister Carry (Julia is Mrs. Dr. Davis of Pike Co.)

At night, comes Maj Genl. Meade [11] U. S. A (with his aid[e], Maj Emory) to make me a call, I find [him] pleasant and friendly, as heretofore.

Genl Meade is a frank, fair man. I. A. he told me an incident about his dining with Stevens [12] and Sumner [13] (at Mr. Hooper's). Mr. Sumner was fully convinced that a *northern* person could not safely go to the South—He had letters from various parts, from males and females, civil and military—and they satisfied every body *but the prest.* of the bad state of feeling at the south! The Genl. answered him to the effect that his correspentents [*sic*] were not trustworthy—they were there under strong prejudices and so behaved as to excite the counter prejudices of the people—the school-marms wou[l]d insist upon all *lit nigs* singing old John Brown &c[.]

[*March*] *16* Called Maj. Genl. Thomas,[14] with his wife and her sister, Miss Kellog[g], (whom Nancy and I had meat [*sic*] at West Point and found very pleasant)[.]

I found Genl. Thomas, a plain, quiet man, as reticent as Grant. Genl. Scott (I know, by personal conversation) thinks very highly of him—brags of him, as his native county man—Dinwiddie Co.[unty] Va.

N. b. Genl. T.[homas] tells me that he was indeed, born in Dinwiddie Co. but brot. up in Suffolk.

Mar 27. Mr. Eads, (having just returned from the east,) called to get Barton to go with him and Mr. H. T. Blow,[15] to Granby.[16] Being in haste, it was thought best that Fleming (who offered his services) should go up for Barton, which he did (going up and returning on the 28th.) and Barton is expected down on the 29th.

[10] *Supra,* Jan. 28, 1860, note 38.
[11] *Supra,* Oct. 15, 1863, note 18.
[12] *Supra,* Dec. 20, 1862, note 87.
[13] *Supra,* Jan. 7, 1860, note 9.
[14] *Supra,* Sept. 5, 1864, note 64.
[15] *Supra,* Sept. 20, 1859, note 95.
[16] *Supra,* Dec. 9, 1865, note 82; March 14, 1866.

Since the last date we have had a good deal of raw, uncomfortable weather, and consequently, I have had quite a sick turn, for some days. The weather is now changed for the better.

I shall begin gardening now, as soon as possible and hope to profit, in my bodily health, by the lighter labors of that delightful occupation.

The Radical party is now at open and defiant war with Prest. Johnson. The Prest. has *vetoed* the "Civil liberty bill," and it seems to be expected by some well-informed acquaintances of mine, that the two houses will pass the bill, in spite of the veto.[17] In that event, some who think worst of the Radicals, believe—that the Prest. will soon be *impeached* by the revolutionists of the House, and *condemned*, in short order, by the revolutionists of the Senate.

I do not believe it, because—1. I think they lack the courage to attempt it—2. If they have the courage, they lack to [the] power to do it—And 3. If they have the courage to dare and the power to do it, the result would, inevitably, produce another civil war, which, passing through desolation, could only end in despotism.

April 1. Sunday. A beautiful, mild day—Easter. It is communion day with us, and Julia, Matilda and the grand children are gone to church. Nancy stays at home with me, and Fleming and Col Woodson (Goody) are here.

Yesterday, my old friend, Dr. Simpson[18] came to see me—the first time be [I] believe that he has been in any private house other than his own, for many years—and therefore, I prize the visit, as a special favor.

A few days ago, *Father De Smet*,[19] the famous Jesuit Missionary, paid me a visit—We are old friends.—And yesterday, he sent me two books (his more recent publications) 1st. "Modern Missions and Missionaries"[20] and "Indian Sketches."

Father De Smet is, I think, full of courage, zeal and self-devotion: upon the whole, a very superior man. I have known him for many years, and have always, found him consistent and persistent in what he believed to be right.

Apl. 4. I have just read the President's *Proclamation of Peace*, dated April 2d.![21]

I suppose the Prest thought it proper to issue the proclamation, not because, in fact or in principle, the case required it, but to put

[17] For the bill see April 9, 1866, *U. S. Statutes at Large*, XIV, chap. XXXI, 27. For Johnson's veto see March 27, 1866, J. D. Richardson, *op. cit.*, VI, 405–413. For its passage over the veto see April 6–9, 1866, *Cong. Globe*, 39 Cong., 1 Sess., 1809, 1861.

[18] Robert Simpson: *supra*, Oct. 24, 1860, note 74.

[19] Peter J. De Smet, Belgian-born Jesuit brought to Missouri by Bishop Dubourg about 1823(?); a founder and professor of the University of St. Louis; missionary to the Indians of the Northwest.

[20] Probably *Western Missions and Missionaries* (James B. Kirker, N. Y., 1863).

[21] See J. D. Richardson, *op. cit.*, VI, 429–432.

down the impudent pretence of the Radicals that the war still continued.

It is carefully worded—and does not say that peace now begins to exist—but that the war *is* over and peace *does* exist[.]

Yesterday was the municipal election in St Louis, and the Radicals were badly beaten. The papers say that the Conservative candidates were elected by about 3000.

St Louis August. 18th. 1849.

Mrs. Duke H. Janssen & Christopher Lohmann

1849	*Bought of O. L. Biermann & J. Braches*	
April 16.	45 Bbls raw Whiskey 2186 Gal's at 15¾ cts a Gallon _____	$344[.]29½

This bill [22] is a real transaction. It came into my hands as counsel in a suit at law. It serves to shew the vast change in prices between the years *1849* and 1866. In 1849 the price, it seems, was 15¾ cents, and paid no tax—now, it pays an excise tax of *$2. a gallon*, and the price of a good article (such as I drink) is from $3.50 to $5.00. a gallon! And most other articles of daily living are in the same proportion.

"I think that poor folks mann be witches " (Burns)
Else, how do they manage to live?["]

[*A clipping from the* Missouri Republican *of April 24, 1866, which prints* "A Card " *from C. D. Drake* [23] *denying that he made a speech in St. Louis in 1861 attacking Republicanism, defending the South, and declaring the North* "aggressive, defiant and insulting."]

I think this card must lead to further explanation, for [James] Peckham can hardly be so great a liar or so bold a man as to invent the whole story.

I see that Mr. Drake rests his assertion that Col Peckham's statement is "utterly false in every particular " upon two grounds—place and time—He says—" I made no speech of any kind *in front* of the Court house, in the year *1861*."

Possibly Peckham may be able to verify his facts, as occurring in the C.[ourt] H.[ouse] and *before Jany. 1861*. But if he fail entirely, he ought to be branded[.]

Just as I supposed, Peckham has come out—and says it is all true in *1860*—not '61.

May 4 Friday. For a month past, I have neglected this diary, being in fact, very unwell, and particularly dull and averse to labor. I am *apparently* mending—my symptoms all seem better, and yet, I fail to gain strength and the faculty of breathing freely.

---

[22] This bill is pasted into the diary, written in an exceptionally good hand, on a bit of paper evidently taken from an old account book.
[23] *Supra*, Feb. 12, 1863, note 13.

1-month gap

This day *Fred* Bieser came to live with us, on trial, as servant and laborer. Hee [*sic*] seems to be a cheerful well-disposed boy, but as yet can speak and understand but little English[.]

(Note. On the 12th. I paid him $10)

May 10. Matilda started today (thursday) to visit Dr. Bates' family, and perhaps, attend *Saidy's* marriage[.]

(Note *12th*. arrived safely—as Dr. B[ates] telegraphs me.)

May 13 Sunday—There was a fine rain last night, and now the garden looks smiling.

Yesterday morning, there was a premature birth in Julian's family. The mother is doing well, but the child lived only a little while, and will be buried today, in the family grave yard, near Florissant[.]²⁴

[*A clipping from the* Missouri Republican *of May 24, 1866, which prints a long communication from Washington signed "Unus" commenting favorably upon the Report of Generals Steedman and Fullerton on the Freedmen's Bureau.*]

May 28. Came to see me today two of my very few remaining acquaintances of more than 40 years['] standing—John D Dagget[t]²⁵ and Elihu Shepherd[.]²⁶

May 29, tuesday. This is the *43d*. anniversary of my marriage, and now, in old age, natural decay and sickness, our mutual love burns as brightly as in the days of our youth.

God has dealt most kindly with us—He has blessed us with a large family of children, several of whom are the comfort and honor of our declining life, and he has made the course of our wedded life one unbroken stream of mutual love and enjoyment; for I declare that in the long course of 43 years, there has never been a momentary alienation or the slightest angry passage between us. Today my wife is far dearer to my heart than on the 29th. of May 1823, and, in person she is still as lovely to *my* eye and *my* touch as when first delivered to my arms, in youthful beauty of sixteen.

For some days past, the Genl. Assemblies of the two branches of the Presbyterian Church (*Old* and New Schools) have been in session here; and I grieve to find that they act more like caucusses [*sic*] of Radical Politicians than like courts of christian Churches. They copy, as closely as may be, the opinions and practices of [the] present, dominant faction in Congress—as unscrupulous in assuming forbid-

---

²⁴ *Supra,* May 18, 1859, note 52.
²⁵ *Supra,* Aug. 20, 1864, note 48.
²⁶ Elihu H. Shepard of St. Louis: soldier in the War of 1812; member of the Columbian Expedition of 1819; professor of languages at St. Louis University, 1823–1828; steamboat owner; pottery manufacturer. He joined the Confederate forces in 1861, but surrendered when Camp Jackson was taken, and then served in the Union Army, 1864–1865.

den powers and as shameless [in] exercising them. They (the old school) cut off the Presbytery of Louisville, without citation or trial, for alleged insubordination; and they, *summarily*, expelled a member for writing and publishing a distasteful letter, reflecting upon the body and on some particular [individuals(?)]. In flat violation of the constitution of the church, the G[eneral] A[ssembly] of the *O.[ld] S.[chool]* claims to be the Supreme law-making power, enforcing, by excision, implicit obedience to their mere resolutions. Besides, many of the members (and those among the most prominent) seem to forget that they are gentlemen—Pastors and elders—and indulge freely in *the* low passi[o]ns and vulgar slang of partizan politicians. For instance, an able-bodied member from Ohio (Dr. Thomas,[27] I think, of Dayton), in praise of his own valor in attacking the Louisville Presbytery and the signers of the " declaration and testimony," boasted that he "had taken the Bull by the horns and made the calves of the church bleat ! "

Aside from the nauseous vulgarity of the speech, as uttered by a D. D. in the highest judicatory of the church, it seeme[s] to me that the D.(elicate) D.(octor) is at fault in his bucolical learning: for I never knew before that the calves would *take on and cry* because their *sire*, the Bull was roughly seised by the horns, by some stalwart herdsman, like D D Thomas, tho' I thought it very likely that the calves would bleat, if they saw the tails of their *dams*, the Cows, twisted and rudely jirked [*sic*] about, by the same strong hand.

As the speech of the Reverend (D. D.) Thomas was evidently made, not for a Christian Court, but for " the Militia," it is probable that he had a covert allusion to the famous conundrum—" Why is a gang of calves like the militia?" Answer—" Because it is the Bull-work of the nation." And thus, the Delicate Doctor may be considered about as wise and witty as he is polite and prudent.

The New School G.[eneral] A.[ssembly] had less jarring in the course of its proceedings than the O.[ld] S.[chool] because they were, apparently, all of one mind, being a political association, of the Chase school, well drilled and disciplined by Mr. Stevens [28] and the subalterns of his Committee of Fifteen.[29] The N.[ew] S.[chool] G.[eneral] A.[ssembly] was not a Christian Court in any thing but the name. It was a *political convention*, and the last, crowning act of its session avows and proves that character—The Assembly, doffing its character as *Court Christian*, resolved itself in a Political

---

[27] Thomas E. Thomas, English-born Presbyterian minister in Ohio, 1836–1849; president of Hanover College in Indiana, 1849–1854; professor in the New-Albany Theological Seminary, from 1854 until the Seminary moved to Chicago in 1857 when he was dropped because of his anti-slavery views. He was minister of a church in Dayton, Ohio, from 1858 to 1871.

[28] *Supra*, Dec. 20, 1862, note 87.

[29] *Supra*, Dec. 12, 1865, note 87.

Caucus, ostentaciously [*sic*] praising and censuring particular governmental measures, and erecting a platform for future political action!

They followed exactly the model of the Com[mitt]ee. of 15 in Congress—They stifled debate by the previous question—they denied all time for examination and reflection, and forced it through, in the first hour! The measure had been reported by their " Committe[e] on the *State of the Country*["] (not the *church*), and a member of that comm[i]ttee declared, substantially, that it had been maturely considered by the committee, and that was enough; individual members had no right to know or judge of it—that they must take it blindly, as it came from the hands of the committee, *upon their allegiance to the party!*

[*A clipping describing the political character of the New School Assembly and telling how the chairman of the "Committee on the State of the Country" used a prayer meeting to exhort the commissioners, whatever they might do while together, to vote the Radical ticket when they got home.*]

These two Assemblies have, I fear, well nigh destroyed the Presbyterian Church. They have already destroyed the respectability of its character and its power for good. They have made the subdivisions of the—Synods and Presbyteries—so many political clubs, assuming to themselves the general direction of all their acts, for the good of *the Party.* If the Church can survive the shock of this epidemic madness—this wicked defection of so many of its members,[—]it must be on account of its own intrinsic excellency and the persevering courage of a few of its members who still remain faithful, and whose salt has not lost its savor,[30] in the midst of this general decay.

During the session of the G.[eneral] A.[ssembly] (O.[ld] S.[chool]) Revd. Aaron P. Forman (having his wife with him) lodges with us, and at divers times, has brought home with him certain members of the body, and eminent persons attendant upon it— among them Dr. McGill, the old stated clerk, Dr. Wm. Breckenridge and the famous Dr. McCosh,[31] the Scotch metaphysician, who is a professor in Queen's College, Ireland. Dr. Boardman[32] of Phil[adelphi]a. (who is said to be one of the most mild, learned and able men of the body) has sent word that he is coming to see me.

I have made pleasant acquaintance with a *lay* member, Col Charles Marshall of Mason County Ky. He voluntarily sought me, coming

---

[30] *The Bible*, " Matthew," V, 13.

[31] James McCosh: Scotch Presbyterian minister; professor of logic and metaphysics in Queen's College, Belfast, 1852–1868; president of Princeton College, 1868–1888.

[32] Henry A. Boardman; Presbyterian clergyman; pastor of the Tenth Presbyterian Church of Philadelphia, 1833–1876; moderator of the General Assembly of 1854; trustee of Princeton Theological Seminary.

to my house and introducing himself. I find him a pleasant gentleman, well read, of frank manners and fine powers of conversation.

A day or two after the adjournment, (June 6) Revd. Dr. Boardman, of Phil[adelphi]a., called specially to see me (Mrs. Rob[er]t. Campbell [33] brought him in her carriage). And I enjoyed an hour or two of very pleasant conversation with him. He seems to be a man of excellent partes [*sic*], learned and dignified to be sure, but without learning and dignity enough to stiffen and deform his gentlemanly courtesy and frank demeanor, or to deminish [*sic*] the good effects of his natural good sense and prudent precision and energy of speech. He is very much concerned about the conduct of the Genl. Assembly, deeming it shameful in itself, and calculated to inflict a deep and lasting injury upon the church. He expressed, and repeated several times, the wish that I would criticise the proceedings of the G.[eneral] A[ssembly]; and suggested that I should write it for the "Presbyterian" at Phil[adelphi]a. and enclose to him, who would see it properly published.

June 8. Barton has returned home after a visit of several days. He brought down his wife (with the youngest child, *Eads*, whom I had never seen before) to see me, knowing that I was very anxious to see her, and knowing that I consider the tenure of my life so insecure that every time I enjoy the society of a distant friend, seems to me, probably. the last.

[*A clipping from the tri-weekly* National Intelligencer *of June 2, 1866, headed "Marrying by Squads" describes the marriage ceremony as performed for colored people by the Freedmen's Bureau.*]

The *Freedmen's Bureau* seems to be a *Government* in itself. It is a mighty power surely, and seems to have a wonderful faculty of contracting and expanding itself so as to meet all occasions and cover questions as the[y] arise. It is lucky for the "officers and agents of the bureau" that the law of their creation does not specify their duties nor define their powers and so they assume, with philanthropic logic, that, as their mission is to do "the greatest good to the greatest number" of blacks, they may do what they please!

The act creating the Bureau [34]—Act [of] March 3. 1865—see page 507 [February 5, 1866]—grants no such powers as are habitually exercised over the negro[e]s, and does not authorize any such organization of the means and machinery of power as actually exists— and congress has no power to make such a grant or authorize such an organization. The whole anomalous scheme is a bald usurpation.

The "officers and agents of the Bureau," big and little, have no more *legal* right to do what they are doing every day, than *Dr.*

---

[33] *Supra*, Sept. 26, 1860, note 25.
[34] *U. S. Statutes at Large*, XIII, chap. XC, 506.

Francia[35] had to be the absolute despot—both King and Constable—in Paraguay.

[*A newspaper reprint of General O. O. Howard's* [36] *Circular No. 4, relating to affairs of the Freedmen's Bureau.*]

Here is another sample of the quiet usurpation of the *Bureaurocracy*, as John Stuart Mill calls it[.]

June 18 (monday). This morning a large company of our Dardenne[37] friends started home—From our house Woodson Bates and John D. Coalter[38] and my two grand daughters Hester and Cora Bates—and from Julians [*sic*], the three Misses Hatcher, Betty, Gay and Netty, and the two Misses Woodson, Eliza and Mary. The Schools in the city have just closed their sessions, for summer vacation; and four of the girls,—Mary Woodson, Netty Hatcher and Hester and Cora Bates—are scholars; and they return home rejoicing, for all four stand at the head of their respective classes.

Note. I send to my daughter in law Caroline my *first cucumber* of the season.

June 22. . . . .

[*A newspaper article headed "An important correspondence— Semmes forbidden to act as Judge" gives the correspondence between the commander of the Department of the Tennessee and Secretary Stanton about the election of Admiral Raphael W. Semmes* [39] *to a judgeship in the Probate Court of Mobile.*]

And thus, it seems, " the military " (as Atty. Gen. Speed calls the governing power of the U. S.) has the absolute control of the civil offices of the States!

The *military commandant* is *ordered* that Raphael. W. Semmes " be not permitted to hold or exercise the functions of Probate Judge in the City of Mobile, or any other civil or political office of trust, while he remains unpardoned by the President."

It seems to me, at once, an oppression and an insult to the State of Alabama—She is not *permitted* to decide who may be judge of probate in one of her districts! And Semmes is not permitted to act, so long as he remains unpardoned by the President—for some crime I suppose, not stated.—Suppose he should be tried and *acquitted*, still,

---

[35] *Supra*, March 19, 1864, note 42.

[36] *Supra*, Sept. 30, 1865, note 26.

[37] *Supra*, July 30, 1859, note 61.

[38] A nephew of Mrs. Bates.

[39] Midshipman in the Navy, 1826–1837; commissioned officer, 1837–1861; Confederate commander of the *Sumter* and later of the *Alabama* both of which did damage to Northern shipping; commander of the James River Fleet in 1865; prisoner under a charge of treason, December, 1865, to April, 1866. He was barred from the judgeship because he fell within the class of high officers who were excepted from the general amnesty, and refused to sue for pardon.

the military will not permit him to be a civil or political officer, until pardoned by the President!

Sunday July 1. This day, my grandson, *Onward Bates*, joins the *2d. Presbyterian church*, which is under the pastoral charge of the Revd. Mr. Nichols [40]—On his profession of faith and baptism—Also, my Daughter, Nancy C. joins the same church, *by letter* from the *Central*[.]

Charles. F. Woodson, my cousin, is here, on a special visit to me. He has been down several days, is in good health and pretty good spirits, and his visit is a great comfort to me. Yesterday Col T. T. Gantt [41] called to see him and took him to ride, and promised to come again today. He left for home, July 2d.

Last evening, Revd. Dr. Anderson [42] called, and supped with us. He came to bring Nancy's letter of dismission and to give me a copy of the Address against the late proceedings of the Genl. Assembly.

At night, Genl. Sherman made us a friendly call.

. . .

Note. The first cucumber cut in our garden was on the *18th. of June*, and now, one, saved for seed, *ripe, yellow*.

July 2. . .

My sons, Barton and Julian came in the down train, arriving about 9. p. m. Onward goes up tomorrow evening.

My garden is, in the main, in good condition; especially, the Lima beans, Tomato[e]s, and Gumbo are promising; and the rain, last night, came just in time for them.

July 3. Tuesday. This is the day of meeting of the Conservative Union Convention of the State, and the City is already crowded with its members. Sunday evening, three of them (Genl. Richd. C. Vaughan [43] and Mr. Wallace,[44] of Lafayette, and Wm. H. Letcher [45] of Saline) called, and I see a long list, in the Mo. Rep[ublican] of this morning, of those already in the City. Judging from that list, it is clear that the Convention will contain a large portion of the intelligence, respectability and strength of the State.

If the Convention will act harmoniously and with courage and prudent energy—forgetting old party names and policies, and confining itself strictly, to the few great issues of the present time, there is good hope of a glorious and happy result—the restoration

---

[40] Samuel J. Niccolls: formerly minister of a church in Chambersburg, Pennsylvania, 1860–1864; chaplain in the Army; twenty-six-year-old minister of the church at Broadway and Walnut Streets in St. Louis.

[41] *Supra*, Feb. 5, 1864, note 3.

[42] *Supra*, July 17, 1859, note 26.

[43] *Supra*, Dec. 9, 1859, note 25.

[44] *Supra*, Aug. 7, 1863, note 77.

[45] *Supra*, Dec. 19, 1859, note 48.

of the State to a condition of Law, Order and Peace, and the consequent suppression of the pernicious faction of the *Radicals*.

I think our Convention will be greatly aided in its objects, and especially, in its tone and spirit, by the call for a *National Conservative Convention*, to meet at Philadelphia, Augt. 15, which is now, warmly, answered, in all parts of the Country.

As to our State convention, I have suggested to more than one of its members, a measure which seems to me very important, as a means of manifesting our superior strength, and therefore securing our ultimate victory—I propose that the convention state to the people, a few simple, direct propositions, involving the substance of our cause, and require an election to be held for or against them. At that election, every man be allowed to vote who has the qualifications required by law, before the adoption of the new constitution.

This, necessarily, implies good organization, and some pecuniary expense. But, without these, we can hardly hope for victory. As to organization, I am led to believe by Genl. Brown[46] (chairman of the Central committee) that good progress has already been made in that direction. And as to the expense, that need not be large, in actual money, unless we count the time lost by voters and the agents who conduct the election.

The election ought to be separate and independent [*sic*], not a m[e]re extra voting, of the regular election, for that would leave the whole matter under *Radical* control. And the voting should be strictly confined to the matter proposed by the Convention; for if left at large, there [is] great danger that, in many precincts, the interests of particular parties and individuals will pervert the election, and give tone and character to the whole proceeding.

There need, in fact, be no actual expe[n]se, beyond what may be necessary for stationery and printing.

July 7   Saturday. . . .

Today paid assessment—$18—on my house at the Mound city Mut[ua]l. F[ire] & M.[arine] Ins[urance] Co[.]

Also pd. bill to Wilson & Keach [wholesale Grocers]—$13.50[.]

Matilda—Nancy recd. a letter from her, this morning—date 3d. inst: She is very well but indefinite about coming home.<[*Note.*]

July 14.   Saturday—She arrived, with Saidy[.]>

Johnny Coalter returned from Dardenne, last night,[47] and intends to go up to see his mother and sisters next monday. Nancy and Sarah speak of going up at the same time. (note—they did not go)

Note. The Nat[iona]l: Intel[ligence]r. of July 3d. (triweekly) contains a short article of mine (signed EB) upon the *Legislative Power*, intended to rectify a doctrinal error of the paper (9 June.) [.]

---

46 *Supra*, Feb. 20, 1866, note 96.
47 See *supra*, June 18, 1866.

[*A short paragraph giving statistics on the number of vineyards in the United States.*]

Grapes in the U S

[*A clipping announces the celebration on August 11, 1866, of the centenary of the first land grant made in St. Louis, and the purpose of organizing a historical association on that occasion.*]

July 12 Thursday. Recd. Telegram from Matilda, saying—*We* (who?) *on* Friday[.]

Today mailed a letter to the President recommending *Thomas B. Wallace* [47a] to be restored to the office of Marshal of the Western district of Mo.—and Genl. Rd. C. Vaughan [47b] to be Assessor of his District[.]

(Autograph of Gideon Welles, Secy. of the Navy)

[*An envelope addressed to Mr. Bates with the signature* " *G. Welles* " *upon it.*]

July 21. Saturday. . . .

This morning Mrs. Woodson and Julia started home.

" St. Louis Times. A Democratic Journal, Vol 1. no. 1 " of this date, was dropped at my door this morning. It is *anonymous*—avowing no name of either Editor, proprietor of [or] publisher. From some passages in it, I infer that it will make war upon the Radicals and support Prest. Johnson.

The telegraph says that a resolution has passe[d] the H[ouse] of R[epresentatives] to admit that M.[embers of] C[ongres]s of Tennessee—even *Stevens* voting for it.[48] I am glad that *poor, ignorant* Mr. Stevens has found out at last, that, there is really, such a state as Tennessee !

The morning papers announced that *Genl. Rousseau* [49] M.[ember of] C.[ongress] of Ky., has resigned his seat in the House, to avoid the resolution [50] to expel him, pending there on account of *his caning* the ex Revd. *Grinnell*,[51] M.[ember of] C.[ongress] of Iowa, for his

---

[47a] *Supra*, Aug. 7, 1863, note 77.

[47b] *Supra*, Dec. 9, 1859, note 25.

[48] July 20, 1866, *Cong. Globe*, 39 Cong., 1 Sess., 3980.

[49] Lovell H. Rousseau: lawyer of Louisville, Kentucky; formerly Indiana state legislator, 1844–1845, 1847–1849; captain in the Mexican War; Kentucky state senator, 1860–1861; major-general in the Civil War. He served in Congress from 1865 until this episode with Grinnell. The majority of the investigatory Committee voted to expel (*ibid.*, 3818); the minority to reprimand him (*ibid.*, 3819). The House accepted the minority report (*ibid.*, 3892). He resigned, however, and was reëlected and finished out his own term.

[50] July 14, 1866, *ibid.*, 3818–3819.

[51] Josiah B. Grinnell: Congregational minister; abolitionist who had to leave a Washington church in 1851 because of his views; founder of Grinnell College in Iowa; an organizer of the Republican Party in Iowa; delegate to the National Convention in 1860; state senator, 1856–1860; special agent of the Post Office Department, 1861–1863; congressman, 1863–1867. For the remarks of Grinnell which led to the caning see Feb. 5, 1866, *ibid.*, 648–654; Feb. 6, 1866, *ibid.*, 688; June 11, 1866, *ibid.*, 3096–3097.

coarse abuse and vulgar vituperation, in debate. The Resolution does not pretend to justify the foul-mouthed parson, but propose[s] to expel the Ky. member, for a breach of the privileges of the members, as guaranteed by the constitution, in these words—" For any speech or debate in either House, they shall not be questioned in any other Place " (Con:[stitution] Art[icle] 1. Section 6, clause 1)[.] It occurs to me that Rousseau committed a grave error in resigning. If he had held on to his place, until actually expelled—if the house were mad enough to do it—no doubt that it would have strengthened his position, before his constituents, who would hardly have failed to restore him triumphantly, to the seat from which he had been so wrongfully ejected.

Besides, I think the expulsion of a member for *questioning* another member out of the House, for his vulgar rudeness in it, is on the part of the House, a usurpation of power and a perversion of the constitution. A usurpation dangerous, at once, in the instance and in the principle. The words of the constitution are—" shall not be *questioned* in any other place." I apprehend that these words were directed against the other branches of the government, and not against *individuals;* that their meaning is that no member of either house shall be brought to trial—put to answer—*id est questioned*—before any other branch of the government than the house to which he belongs, for any speech or debate in either house. *Caning* is not, literally, *questioning:* It is only one species of punishment, for wrongs done by speech or debate, in the house; and any punishment or attack upon a member of either house, for speech or debate in his house, done by any other branch of the government, is the wrong intended to be guarded against by that clause of the constitution—not the acts of individuals—the law can punish them—not the justice which men may seek, nor the vengeance which they may try to take for wanton injuries inflicted by members of Congress in their respective houses.

If the *caning* of a member can be punished by the expulsion of the *caning* member, or by fine, imprisonment, stripes or undefined and discretionary chastisement of private persons—and this because the *caned* member was not to be *questioned in any other place*, then it is plain that the meaning of the word *questioned*, as there used, [is] that the member shall be held to answer, tried or punished, as for a public offence, *only* in his own House.

If caning can be punished *by the House*, in that way, so also can any disrespectful words, spoken, written—or printed, concerning any foolish or wicked speech or debate by a M.[ember of] C.[ongress] *in his house.* The debates in Congress can no longer be sharply criticised. Neither the people nor the press will be free to say what they think about the debates—They dare not say that the speech of the Honorable Member proves him to be either a knave or a simpleton. If Senator Benton were alive again, he durst not repeat what he once said about a brother Senator—that he was a great liar and a dirty dog! however true his saying.

The dominant faction in Congress seems determined to stretch its privileges to the utmost limit. It openly violates the constitution, in annulling the essential guarantees of life, liberty and property (see the Freedmen's Bureau bill,[52] and the Civil Liberty bill[53]); It boldly attempts to usurp the legitimate powers of the President and now, it claims the prerogative to punish, *at discretion*, any man who, by *caning*, speaking, writing or printing, *questions* any honorable member, for any foolish or wicked speech he may make *in the house!*

Note—Afterwards (see triweekly Nat:[ional] Intel.[ligencer] of July 19) the resolution of *Expulsion*, failed, for lack of a ⅔ vote.[54] And then the House (on motion of Genl. Banks![55]) juggled around till it passed the resolution of *censure*[56]—which had been formally rejected!

While these latter proceedings were going on in the House, an assault was made by two men, upon a clerk of one of the House's Com[mitt]ees. " within the walls of the Capitol "; the men were in custody of *the Police*, yet the House passed a resolution that "the Sergeant at arms is hereby called upon to take into *his custody* the persons of the assailants, and to detain them until further orders of the House, upon the subject." And thus the House assumes jurisdiction over *strangers* who may assault any of its subordinate employe[e]s *within the walls* of *the Capitol!* I suppose the offenders were properly arrested and in the *legal* custody of the Police officers, to be dealt with according to law—Yet the House directs its Sergeant to take the prisoners out of that *legal* custody and hold them, subject to the discretionary order of the House!

July 22. Yesterday—Saturday, July 21—died *Peter. E. Blow.*[57] [*A newspaper reprint of a telegram from General Thomas*[58] *in Tennessee to General Grant reporting Governor Brownlow's*[59] *request for military assistance in compelling attendance of a quorum*

---

[52] July 16, 1866, *U. S. Statutes at Large*, XIV, chap. CC, p. 173–177.

[53] April 9, 1866, *ibid.*, XIV, chap. XXXI, p. 27–30.

[54] See also July 17, 1866, *Cong. Globe*, 39 Cong., 1 Sess., 3891.

[55] *Supra*, July 27, 1859, note 57.

[56] July 18, 1866, *Cong. Globe*, 39 Cong., 1 Sess., 3892.

[57] Brother of Henry T. Blow (*supra*, Sept. 20, 1859, note 95) with whom he was associated in business.

[58] *Supra*, Sept. 5, 1864, note 64.

[59] William G. Brownlow of Knoxville, Tennessee: Methodist minister, 1826–1838; editor successively of the *Tennessee Whig*, the *Jonesboro Whig and Independent*, and the *Knoxville Whig*, 1838–1861; strong Union man; Radical governor, 1865–1869; bitter enemy of Johnson; U. S. senator, 1869–1875.

of the Legislature; and a copy of Stanton's answer refusing such aid.[60]]

This rowdy " Parson Brownlow " Gov of Tenn[essee] is as foolish a radical as Gov Fletcher[61] of Mo. Neither of them ever had an idea of either Government or Liberty by law. They want the legal means and machinery of government only to make a pretence of law, before the ignorant masses *now*, and to lie about *hereafter*, when the passions of men may be somewhat cooled down.

If we were not so accustomed to monstrous political crimes, as to cease to be shocked at them, we could hardly believe it possible that the governor of a *State* would call upon a general in command of a *Federal army*, to *manage* refractory members of the State legislature, *with the means at his disposal*—to wit, guns and bayonets!!

July 27 Friday. This morning, I recd., under the frank of Hon[orable] John Hogan,[62] M.[ember of] C.[ongress] a document which I take to be very valuable—A large pamphlet of 128 pages— And this is its Title Page—"[A] Political Manual for 1866, including a classified summary of the important Executive, Legislative[,] and Politico-Military Facts of the Period[,] from President Johnson's accession, April 15. 1865, to July 4. 1866; and containing a full record of the Action of each branch of the Government on Reconstruction. By Edward McPherson,[63] Clerk of the House of Representatives of the United States."

[*July*] *28.* [*A clipping giving the population of St. Louis by city wards.*]

And so it seems that, at this day, St. Louis contains over 200.000 inhabitants!

When I first came here, in the spring of 1814, there was no *census*, but the people then chiefly French, were supposed to amount to 2000, or at most 2500!

And those few were poor. They came poor and remained poor, for there was no means of making wealth. No manufactures [at] all, and no commerce except a little trade with the Indians, in furs and peltries. Very little actual money—*argent contant*, as the cre-

---

[60] When Governor Brownlow called the Radicals in the Legislature together to ratify the Fourteenth Amendment the Conservatives absented themselves. It was to compel the attendance of enough of them to obtain a quorum that he appealed to Thomas. Stanton did reply (Order of E. M. S. to Gen. Grant, July 17, 1866, Stanton MSS., XXX) refusing aid, when President Johnson so ordered him, but in the meantime he had withheld Thomas's telegram for instructions from the President for three days until, in the absence of instructions, two members had already been arrested and the Amendment ratified.

[61] *Supra*, Jan. 12, 1865, note 4.

[62] *Supra*, Jan. 9, 1860, note 13.

[63] Edward McPherson: editor of the *Harrisburg American*, 1851, the *Lancaster Independent Whig*, 1851–1854, and the *Pittsburgh Daily Times*, 1855; Republican congressman, 1863; deputy commissioner of Internal Revenue, 1859–1863; Republican National Committeeman, 1860–1864; later clerk of the House of Representatives, 1863–1875, 1881–1883, 1889–1891; author of books on Reconstruction.

oles called it—existed among us.   Shaved deer skins was the *currency*
(as *tobacco* used to be, in Virginia and Maryland)[.]   And, in that
specie merchants contracted and gave their notes, valuing the raw
hides, at 6 lb. for the dollar.

And yet, the people of that day, were, I think, more kind and
affable, orderly and law abiding, and quite as contented and happy
as the more numerous people of this day, with all their higher re-
finement and vast accumulation of wealth.

. . .

Sunday July 29. . . .
[*A newspaper paragraph announces*:

> " By a curious coincidence it appears that the coming year, 1867, has
> been fixed upon by Mahomedans [*sic*], Brahmins, and various other
> sects, as well as by some few Christians, as a period in the history
> of the universe to be marked by some great and marvellous change."]

Perhaps it is but the natural, presumption of humanity—but so
it is that man, the lazy animal, while neglecting the duties of his own
contracted sphere, boldly rushes upon the boundless theatre of action
which God has reserved to himself, and assumes to know things
unknowable, and to do things *undoable*, by any finite creature.

This is indeed, but an outburst of inordinate vanity; but I suppose
it is human nature, for it belongs alike, to the learned (so called)
and the ignorant—to the theologian and the politician—all of them
pretent to comprehend the entire polity of the Divine Government.
They know not only the *will of God*, but also the motives of his
action and the ends which his acts were designed to produce!   They
gauge the *omniscience* of God by the standard of their own ignorance,
and measure his *eternity* by their own hour glass!

The Revd. Dr. Wines,[64] in his pedantic book about Civil Government[65] (or the preface to it) assumes that civil government is an
ordinance of God, and then declares that " the *end which God had
in view*, was the *perfection and happiness* of his rational creatures."
Thus, it would seem that *the end which God had in view*, planned
and settled by eternal wisdom, from everlasting to everlasting, has
failed of its accomplishment!   Has been frustrated, these six thousand years, by the wicked free-will of man!   And yet, Dr. Wines
passes for a pious man and would be shocked at the imputation of
being an unbeliever in either the omniscience or the omnipotence of
God!

It is a common stratigem [*sic*] (so common as to have grown into
use with many pretty good people, who seem wholly unconscious of
the insolent presumption) when we want to give importance to our

---

[64] *Supra*, July 25, 1859, note 43.
[65] " Introductory Essay on Civil Society and Government," in *Commentaries on the
Laws of the Ancient Hebrews*, Geo. P. Putnam, N. Y., 1853.   The quotation appears to be
a paraphrase of a statement on page 20.

proposition or to deter others, from disputing it, to assert that *God ordains it so*—and therefore, to oppose it, is not only unreasonable, but impious. There is great skill and force in this knock-down argument. I[t] frightens off many weak-minded, conscientious opponents, who fear to resist you, "lest, peradventure, they be found fighting against God!" And thus (in monarchies) *Kings reign by the grace of God*, and (in republics) all men are *created equal*, and are endowed *by the creator*, with certain *unalienable rights!*

Milton (who wrote, I think, after king Charles' head had been cut off) says, in his lofty verse, that *God gave to man* "Over beast, fish, fowl, dominion absolute (but) Man over man, *he made not lord:*" He was familiar with the acts and purposes of God, knowing them as well as if he were a privy counsellor of the Most High!

This presumptuous vanity is manifested not only in the supposed facts of God's actual government and the ascertainment of the times and seasons of the fulfilment of his designs (as darkly revealed to man, in prephecy [*sic*]), yet men (even pious good men), in their egregious egotism, undertake to foreknow the time and manner in which God *intends* to fulfil his, yet unexecuted judgments—They are able to give definition and date to the mille[n]ni[u]m, and to tell when and how God wills to bring this world to an end!

I have read the books of some self-conceited writers who laboriously, displayed their own ignorance, under the pretence of explaining a subject, alike incomprehensible to themselves and others; and I know of several pastors who seem to take delight in confusing the minds and unsettling the simple faith of the weaker members of their congregations, by surmises and gu[e]sses and fanciful theories about the millennium—what it is and when it is to come!

I could give several instances of such men—but they are enthusiasts, poss[i]bly sincere, and therefore, in charity, had better be quietly laughed at, than publicly exposed and censured.

[*July 30.*] [*A newspaper reprint of a letter signed by the various members of the National Union Executive Committee asking all delegates to the Philadelphia Convention to call at its headquarters upon arriving.*]

July 30. This list may be useful to all who have occasion to correspond with the active agents of the conservative party.

Besides, it shows the present position of the men named, and therefore, has a historical value, for the future[.]

The Judiciary Com[mitt]ee. H[ouse] of R.[epresentatives] by *Mr. Boutwell* [66] has a long report [67]—referring to letters and other documents—with the view to prove the complicity of the "Richmond

---

[66] *Supra*, Oct. 15, 1863, note 14.
[67] "Assassination of Lincoln," July, 1866, *House Reports*, 39 Cong., 1 Sess., vol. I, ser. no. 1272, doc. no. 104.

Government," and especially, Davis, Benjamin,[68] Walker,[69] Thompson (Jake)[70] and C. C. Clay,[71] in the assassination plot.

The report concludes with two resolutions—The 1st. declares that there is *no defect in the law* for bringing Davis to trial for Treason, or any other crime—The 2d. affirms "That it is *the duty* of the *Executive Department* of the Government. to proceed with the *investigation of the facts*, connected with the assassination of the late President[,] Abraham Lincoln, without unnecessary delay " &c.[.][72]

(see triweekly *Nat[ional] Intel:[ligencer]* of July 28.)

The 1st. resolution, I suppose, is true. There is no obstacle to the trial, now that military commissions are no more.

The 2d. displays only a series of presumptuous blunde[r]s.—In the first place, what right has the *House* to ascertain and declare *the duties of the Executive?* And in the second place, what *right* has the President, and how can it become *his duty* to *investigate the facts* of a case purely judicial?

[*Marginal*] Note. Mr. Rogers[73] of N.[ew] J.[ersey] (the minority of the Com[mitt]ee.) made a scorching report exposing " the conspiracy to to [*sic*] implicate["] Davis and others in the assassination !

(Clipped from the Lexington Weekly Express July 28. 1866[)]

[*Two clippings which give accounts of a shooting in Lexington.*]

Society, in the region round about Lexington, is very fierce and defiant; and no doubt, men, mutually suspecting each other of the worst designs, are very prompt to anticipate the violence which they think they foresee. Formerly, when the *Radicals* were backed by the *military*, they domine[e]red with a high hand, and all their outrages were justified, in their own eyes, by their loyalty, and sanctified by *martial law*. But now, the tables are turned. The *Radicals*, having fixed the statutes to suit themselves, the Conservatives seem determined to *fight for their rights*.

[*A circular of McAllister & Wallis advertising themselves as attorneys and agents for claims arising out of the War.*]

[*A newspaper clipping calls attention to the fact that the Constitution of the United States, " the supreme law of thirty-five States and eight Territories," "contains only 36 sections, and 4,800 words;" while the new Constitution of Missouri has 192 sections and 14,600 words.*]

A fair contrast between the patriots and the Statesmen of the Revolution and the Radical Demagogues of our own time.

---

[68] *Supra*, Oct. 28, 1864, note 48.

[69] Leroy P. Walker: Alabama lawyer; son of the first senator from Alabama; himself a state legislator in the 1840's; state circuit judge, 1850–1853; leader of secession; Confederate secretary of War, 1861.

[70] *Supra*, April 22, 1862, note 9.

[71] *Supra*, July 22, 1864, note 81.

[72] The italics and most of the capitalization are Mr. Bates's.

[73] *Supra*, July 19, 1865, note 88.

APPENDIX

LETTERS TO THE PEOPLE OF MISSOURI [1]

Letter Number One [2]

As one of the oldest among you, (I say not one of the wisest or best, but one of the oldest) I feel it to be my duty to lay before you some of my thoughts and opinions in regard to the terrible circumstances in which we find ourselves, and the danger of utter ruin which now hangs over the State.

I came and settled in St. Louis more than fifty years ago, and from that time forth, my life and conduct have been open to public observation; for during all that time I have lived by the practice of the law, and, at different and distant periods, I have held various public offices. And thus my behavior, as a man and a citizen, and my general character and reputation must be known to the people of Missouri, for good or for evil.

I have brought up a large family of children among you, and had made, as I hoped until lately, many friends and few or no enemies; I came here a youth of twenty and have witnessed all the vicissitudes of this growing country; I have labored in this community for more than half a century—with what propriety of conduct and success in action let others judge—and now, in my age, all that I am and all that I have is inseparably connected with the interest and character of the State.

These facts, I think, give me some right to speak to you in the plain language of sincerity and truth, and to expect at your hands a fair and candid hearing. And besides this, I have a duty yet to perform. I owe a debt of gratitude, as yet unpaid, to a generous people, who received me, in my youth, with great kindness and favor; who upheld and encouraged me, in all the hopes and efforts of my early manhood; and who, for long, honored my riper age with their respect and confidence. My age unfits me to engage anew in the more active strifes of political parties, by re-entering the common field of such controversies, and aspiring to the places of power which political parties alone can give. In fact (as you all do know) I have

---

[1] In these letters, errors that are obviously typographical mistakes of the newspaper have been corrected for the sake of smoother reading.

[2] Published in the *Missouri Democrat* of April 6, 1865.

lately resigned an honorable place in the General Government, and come back to my old home, hoping to enjoy, in privacy and peace, the society of my family and friends. I did not resign, however, until the affairs of the nation were greatly altered for the better. My political chief had just passed through the ordeal of a new election, and the Administration in which I bore a part was then sanctioned by the nation. The success of our arms had turned a hope into a certainty, that the rebellion would be quelled; that the war would be brought to an end; and that, with wisdom and virtue in the civil government, law and order might be once more firmly established.

Such was then the prospect in the nation at large; and in this State the outward appearances were no less cheering. Price's invasion [3] (which ought never to have been allowed, and never could have happened without gross dereliction on our part,) was driven back; there was no embodied enemy within the State, and no enemy at all, but a few marauding outlaws, whose numbers are estimated by General Pope,[4] in his late letter to the Governor,[5] at only twenty for each county.

Such were the outward circumstances when I came home and found, to my grief and shame, that, notwithstanding the absence of all enemies, except the few incapable of any serious mischief, unless by the sufferance of *our* military, the State was ruled only by the arbitrary will of a few men; that the law was trodden down, and too weak to give protection; that the spirit of the people was cowed by threats and violence; and that there was no longer any feeling of conscious security for life, liberty or property, nor any assured hope of stability in the Government or *liberty by law*, in the people.

Under these circumstances, I feel irresistibly impelled to volunteer in the service of the State, pledging myself to do what in me lies, in resisting the revolutionary violence which now threatens to overwhelm all its interests. And I see no way in which I can hope, so efficiently, to serve the people of the State as by addressing you through the press, and in that way giving you my opinion and advice (the best I am capable of forming) of the evils by which we are now beset, and the possible remedies which may yet lie within our reach. And, to that end, I have asked and obtained leave to publish my articles in the *Missouri Democrat*. This essay is intended only as an introduction to others which are to follow, and as an outline of the scope and design of what I intend to write.

Timid friends have advised me to forbear, and urged me not to expose myself to the obloquy and persecution of an active and wiry

---

[3] See *supra*, Oct. 5, 6. and 22, 1864.

[4] *Supra*, March 15, 1862, note 33.

[5] Thomas C. Fletcher: *supra*, Jan. 12, 1865, note 4.

body of partizans, who have nothing to lose and everything to gain, by their projected revolution. They even hinted that armed authority might be invoked to stop my pen. But I rejected that advice—meant, no doubt, in kindness, and full of selfish prudence. I learned a better lesson than that in my youth, and in my age I have not departed therefrom, that is—never despair of the republic, until the last possible effort in its defense has been made and has failed.

I have assumed, and, in the forthcoming articles, shall endeavor to maintain, along with others not now stated) the following distinct propositions:

1. *Martial law* is not the governing rule over this State. It does not exist here; and all that has been done under that pretence and contrary to the laws of the land, was and is a personal wrong and a punishable usurpation.

2. The government of the various sections and districts of this State, by *Provost Marshals*, is an unlawful and dangerous anomaly. Provost Marshal[s] are strictly military, and incapable of civil functions. They are simply military police officers—neither more nor less.

3. The laws of the land (as found in the constitutions and statutes of the United States and the State of Missouri) do confer upon the officers of Government, National and States['], all the powers which are necessary to the successful prosecution of the war and to the peaceful rule of the country. And any attempt to substitute, in place of the *laws*, the *will* of any military officer, is not only an act of *disloyalty*, but is also a dangerous blow struck at the Government's lawful power for good.

4. The Convention now sitting in St. Louis is revolutionary—in its origin, in its composition and character, in some of its proceedings already passed, and in others clearly indicated in the course of its action. Instead of being " omnipotent," as some extremists claim, it has not a tittle of power *granted by law*. And as it has no *granted powers* and written limitation upon the powers assumed, it cannot have any *duties*, and may do, at its own caprice, anything or nothing. But whatever it has done or may do, can carry with it no *legal obligation*, until ratified by the people or acquiesced in by the State.

In the next number, I intend to treat of Martial Law, and the manner in which it is sought to be used and abused in this State. It will follow in convenient time, after this.

EDWARD BATES.

St. Louis, April 3d, 1865.

Letter Number Two [6]

I come now to treat of martial law, and the use and abuse now sought to be made of it, in this State. And my proposition is that martial law is not the governing rule over this State. It does not exist here; and whatever may have been done, under that pretense, and contrary to the laws of the land, is a personal wrong and a punishable usurpation. That is my proposition; and I shall endeavor to maintain it, even at the hazard of differing widely from the opinion and wish of the Convention, now sitting in St. Louis.[7]

The Convention assumes that the State is under martial law, and expresses a strong desire that it so remain; but it has not, in any proceeding that I have seen, informed the people (whom it assumes to govern with absolute sway) what martial law is; nor who made, nor when nor where it was made; nor how it is possible to repeal or annul it. The Convention is prudent in abstaining from any attempted explanation on these points, because the matter is incapable of explanation, upon any grounds consistent with law or reason. The members may pretend ignorance, if they will, in order to save for themselves hereafter, when the day of their shame shall come, the hackneyed plea of convicted offenders—" it was the error of the head and not of the heart." But there are some members of that body who ought to know, and do know, that martial law (as contradistinguished from the law of the land) is simply no law at all; that it is neither more nor less than the suppression of the established government, and the substitution of the will, however capricious, of the military commander, in the vacated place of the laws.

That is *martial law*, pure and simple; and none but the most ignorant are in any danger of confounding it with *military law*, which is not only another and a different thing, but the exact opposite of the despotism of martial law. Military law consists of those parts of the Constitution and statutes which relate to the army and its control and management. In like manner, we have groups of other laws which, for convenience, are classified, and familiarly called by the names of their respective subjects—for instance, we have naval law, revenue law, land law, judiciary law. Yet every one of these is administered in the forms of the constitution, and by constitutional functionaries; and in regard to every one of them, including military law, every man may look into the statute book and there read the measure of his obligations and his rights. But where can you read any *legal* description of *martial law*, any derivation of its powers, or any limitation upon their exercise? No where: and for the simple reason that it has *no legal existence;* and the very term *martial law* is only a nickname for arbitrary power, assumed, against law, by men in arms!

This kind of despotism differs, in its foundation and essence, from the tyranny sometimes usurped by assemblies of men calling themselves deliberative bodies. The first is a "strong man armed," who, conscious of his power to enforce obedience, proclaims *his orders,* and if some presumptuous victim ask for his warrant of authority, he answers only by brandishing his sword! The second (deliberative bodies) conscious of its [their] own intrinsic weakness, and that they are nothing, without the prestige of law, always in the beginning pretend to have some lawful authority for the exercise of their assumed powers. And often they seem to prosper for a season. As long as they keep in close alliance with the armed power, and can induce it to be their minister, to carry out their decrees, under martial law, they seem to prosper, and cheat themselves into the belief that they are all-powerful. But this state of things cannot long continue. Armed men, like the unarmed, will learn the lessons that are daily taught them. And when these civil bodies, misled by their own grotesque egotism, imagine themselves supreme and above all established laws and principles, and habitually "frame iniquity into a law," the "strong man armed" soon learns the lesson thus taught him by self-conceited ambition. Out of their own mouths he convicts them, and says to them: " Yes, gentlemen, you are right; there is nothing obligatory in government but *power*, and as the power happens to be in *my* hands, and not *yours*, get you gone out of my way." Thus Cromwell answered the long Parliament of England, and Bonaparte answered the Directory and Councils of France.

No principle is better settled in the Constitution and polity of the United States than this—*the military is subordinate to the civil power*, and can act only as the minister and servant of the law. For we have no ruling sovereign but the law; and therein consists our only claim of superiority in government over the people of Europe, who, for the most part, are governed by visible, human sovereigns, in the shape of emperors and kings, in the great nations, and all the way down the scale of power to the petty princes and dukes, who reign over the inhabitants of a few thousand acres of land. This, I say, is the only claim we have of superiority over them in the matter of government, and so long as that claim is sustained by reality and truth, it is full of goodness and glory. But if that claim be falsified—if the laws of the land are no longer to rule and protect us—if we are indeed under the despotism of that *martial law*, so dear to the Convention, then I affirm that our Government is far worse than theirs, and our condition far more to be pitied. For the sovereigns of Europe (most of them) derive their place and power through a long line of descent from their ancestors, and all of them, from the Queen of Great Britain down to the Duke of Hesse Darmstadt, hope to transmit them to their posterity. In that case every conclusion of reason, and every impulse of the human heart compel the desire for stability and order. A sovereign in that condition must be not a tyrant only, but a fool, who would prefer to leave to his successor a degraded state, an empty treasury and a seditious people, rather than leave him an honorable name in history, a revenue equal to the wants of the state, and a people prosperous, contented, and loyal.

But what will be our condition if the Convention succeed in placing us under the despotism of martial law? *Our* masters will have no inducement to stability and order for the present, and no hope of continuance in the future, no rule to work by, and no law to restrain them. Without any established accountability to law, and without any fear of punishment for their misdeeds, except at the caprice of a higher tyranny than their own, ours will be worse than any hereditary despotism can be; for ours must be continually changing from one master to another. It will be despotism multiplied by republican forms.

Such, then, is martial law, so eagerly coveted by that class of Missouri politicians who are now laboring to consolidate their accidental and transient power, and who know right well that nothing short of despotism will serve their turn. In different countries and different ages of the world, despotism has taken a variety of names and forms. In some countries, the whole government was military, resting upon force alone, and consequently whoever was master of that force was master of the nation which it held in subjection, and might rule both alike by his simple orders; and it is of no importance whether we call those orders by the name of *firman*, or *ukase*, or *decree*, or *ordinance*; for, by whatever name called, they all do but express *the will of the commander*. During the time of the feudal system all Europe was governed by military power, and the sovereign ruler of each particular country—whether Kayser [*sic*], King, Prince or Duke—was the head-general of the nation, the commander-in-chief of the army. In such governments as those no question can arise about martial law, for the ruler is already despotic, and speaks to his subjects, both military and civil, only in the language of command.

If martial law be indeed *any law at all*—if it be a *rule of action*, binding upon anybody, any where, and at any time, it must have had a beginning. It did not always exist here; and if it exist now, it must be because somebody enacted it. Surely it is the simple duty of those who claim it, as the law over Missouri, and who deprecate its disuse, to inform us, the subject people, how and when it began to exist here, who imposed it, and by what pretended authority, and by what public act it is made manifest to the enslaved people. We demand of them the grounds of their tyrannical assumption, and they are silent! They leave us to infer that it has risen among us, nois[e]less and unseen, like a noxious exhalation from a putrid bog, which, as it floats away over the lands taints the vital air, and is seen and known only in the fall of its victims.

But if it should ever come to light (as, possibly, it may, for the dirty records of Missouri politics, for the last few years, *must* be scrutinized,) that some acquisitive military man has presumed to declare, by general order or otherwise, that martial law is the governing rule over this State, my answer is ready—he is a usurper! Such a declaration, divested of official form and verbiage and reduced to plain English amounts to this: " This State, to be sure, was made by law, and the people, have hitherto, lived under the protection of their own laws and the laws of the United States; but that is all changed now; for *I* have determined to abolish the laws and to govern the people *myself.* And this *I do* for the good of the people, who need my protection; and I am the sole judge of public necessity and the only guardian of public safety!" Such an insolent dictation as this, couched in language intelligible to the people, would shock the common sense of every man who ever conceived of civil liberty, and ever read the Constitution of his country; and could not fail to rouse one universal feeling of indignation against the crafty tyrant who tries to disguise and smuggle in his despotism, under the false and indefinite name of martial law. And I affirm, that no soldier, high or low, has any shadow of authority thus to revolutionize the State.

Still, it is a melancholy fact, that there are many instances in which military officers have acted in the most absolute and oppressive manner; and many other instances in which even private soldiers, taking courage from the lawless example of their officers, and from the neglect of discipline, which is sure to follow the abrogation of law, have freely indulged in wanton outrages, both on persons and property; and rarely if ever are they brought to condign punishment.

I cannot, now and here, dwell upon any of the many instances of wrong done to individuals by the military, high and low, in the spirit of lawless power. (Their turn may come hereafter.) But I cannot forbear to draw your attention to certain open, direct, contemptuous assaults upon the State itself, its dignity and its laws. It is but the other day—since the meeting of the Convention, and, I believe, since it passed that famous resolution *in favor of martial law*, that the commanding officer of a military district in the western part of the State, Col. Harding, sent *an order to the Prosecuting Attorney for the State*, young Mr. Ryland, commanding him to dismiss an indictment then pending in the State Circuit Court of a county.[8] The Circuit Attorney, it seems, had too much respect for the State and its laws, to prostitute his office by yielding obedience to such an order, and was imprisoned for his contumacy. But the Circuit Judge, one Mr. Tutt,[9] was of a more compliant temper. Intimidated, perhaps, by the dragoon boots and long sword of the bearer of Colonel Harding's order, he succumbed, and entered upon his record the humiliating *order of court*, dismissing the indictment. And thus, publicly and of record, the laws of the land bowed and did homage to the sword.

Some time ago, a year or more, a case very like this occurred under the reign of General Fisk.[10] He also suppressed an indictment in a State civil court, but I never heard that he had any difficulty with *his civil officers*. They, I suppose, were better drilled than Harding's, and yielded a prompt obedience.

I have heard of other cases similar in principle, but I cannot state them now (for I have promised to make these essays short.) I reserve them for future use, if need be. But the conclusion is obvious, that if martial law do indeed prevail here—if the military commandant may send his orders to the courts of law and enforce them by the stringent process of imprisonment, he may do the same to all other functionaries of the State. The members of the Convention when they passed that famous resolution thought, no doubt, that martial law would continue to be their servant; their tool in working out the projected revolution of the State, not in government only, but also in population and in property. But, when they find that they have gotten a master in place of a servant, I opine that some of the members would be glad of an opportunity to reconsider that resolution. But then it will be too late. Imagine their ludicrous distress, if some day, in the midst of a serious debate upon the proper oath to be required of a school mistress, or some other great constitutional question, there should stalk into the hall, a grim aid[e] or orderly, dressed in jack boots and long sword, like the one that paid Colonel Harding's compliments to Judge Tutt, and delivered to Mr. President Krekel [11] a billet, couched in the terse language of Cromwell or Bonaparte, thus:

"CONVENTIONERS!—I am the State! Take away that bauble, and cease your babbling about human rights, and your clumsy efforts at Constitution-making. Go!

By order of, &c., J. S., A. A. A. G.

[8] See *supra*, March 28, 1865.

[9] *Supra*, May 30, 1865, note 42.

[10] *Supra*, Nov. 22, 1865, note 63.

[11] *Supra*, June 6, 1866, note 46.

Colonel Krekel, President of the Convention, is better provided for, as yet, than most of his brethren, for his good services and law-abiding character have secured for him the office of United States Judge for the Western District of Missouri, though he does not live in that district. When the Convention shall adjourn, or be annulled by martial law, the colonel will at once assume his new functions of judge, and will have great advantages over most new judges. He hates conservatism, and loves martial law and the Radical party, and as Colonel Harding's command is within the western district, Judge Krekel may, from time to time, hope to receive military orders, when to act and when to forbear; and, possibly, may be furnished with opinions to be delivered from the bench, better than his own.

If there be in Missouri, a man of reputation for probity and knowledge, who denies my position, that *martial law is no law at all*, I wish he would do it in print with his name attached. But I do not think there is any such man. And, this point conceded, the second clause of my proposition follows of course, that is, " whatever may have been done under that pretense, and contrary to the laws of the land, is a personal wrong and punishable usurpation." So I waste no time on that.

I have not overlooked the shameful fact that the Convention did what it could, by way of ordinance, to insure impunity for past crimes, for themselves and their partisans, who claimed to be the executioners of martial law. I say *themselves*, because one member in his place, publicly boasted that he had burned a *woman's house*! because, as he said, she had harbored bushwhackers. And, trusting no doubt, in the crime-covering ordinance, seemed to have no fear that he would ever be called to answer for that arson. And I am pleased to be able to believe that the ordinance is as impotent for protection as the design of it was mischievous.

In my next number, I shall probably skip over my second and third propositions in order to come more speedily to the fourth, which relates to the Convention and its revolutionary character.

EDWARD BATES.

St. Louis, April 8, 1865.

Letter Number Three [12]

<I have delayed this article in order that you might have a little time to recover your equanimity after the shock caused by the horrid crime lately committed at Washington. Besides my share in the National sorrow, I had a private grief of my own, which required some indulgence. The nation has lost a chief, whom it loved and

[12] Published in the *Missouri Democrat* of April 28, 1865.

trusted; and I have lost a personal friend—a wise and good man, whom I have known for a quarter of a century, and with whom I have been closely associated for the last few years.>

In my last article, (No. 2) I treated of *martial law*, denouncing it as *no law at all*, but only despotic power, assumed against law, by men in arms. My aim was to explain to you more fully the nature and character of that sort of despotism; its capacity for infinite mischief and the certainty that it will, if its practical exercise here be continued, as demanded by the Convention, destroy all constitutional government, degrade and nullify the laws, and render insecure and almost worthless all the civil and social rights of men.

I come now to the consideration of the Convention itself, and my object is to draw your attention to some of the facts and arguments which go to prove that it is *revolutionary* in its origin, in its character and in its acts, that it has no powers *granted by law*, no *written* limitation upon its powers assumed, no rule of action but its own discretion, and no impulse to act but its own passions.

In the first place, I remark that it is our highest boast, ever since we existed [as] a nation, that we have no sovereign but law; that our government itself was created by law, can be administered by law, and may be altered by law. And in accordance with this universal American idea the existing Constitution of Missouri was framed, and it contains ample provision for its own amendment, so that the people have it always in their power to reform any abuses in the administration of their government, and to alter any features of their fundamental law whenever they may think such changes necessary to their safety and happiness—and may do it *according to law*. That being true, as it is undeniably with us in Missouri, nothing but a factious and revolutionary spirit can lead men or parties wantonly to trample down the Constitution and rush to the attainment of their ends by illegal and extra constitutional means. If the ends sought to be attained be legitimate and honest, and the legal means of attaining them ample and at hand, there can be no legal or patriotic reason for beginning by nullifying the Constitution and boldly assuming all the powers of all the departments of government? The inference is irresistible, that the ends designed were not legitimate and honest, not such as the leaders of the faction dare trust to constitutional means and to the sober judgment of the people.

To show the exemplar and the origin of this Convention, let us take a brief review of its immediate antecedents and of its own history. In 1860, the Southern conspirators (who hatched the grand treason and brought on this desolating war) had completed their plans for the dissolution of the Union. They pretended to believe that *secession* was a lawful right, belonging to every State. And in order to get a show of legality for their treason, the first grand point in their programme was to cause the Legislatures of the several States to call Conventions, for the purpose of voting the States, one by one, out of the Union. And that cunning device for cheating zealous ignorance into crime, by glossing rebellion with a show of law, was successfully acted out, in all the southeastern States, from Virginia to Texas. In that same year, 1860, the intrigues of the Southern conspirators had been so adroitly managed as to secure the official organization of this State, and its political influence, in favor of disunion and treason, by the election of secession officers, Governor, Lieutenant Governor, and a majority of the General Assembly. The Lieutenant Governor elect, Thomas C. Reynolds, went to Washington to consult with the leading spirits of the plot, (for they were there, still holding, with unexampled treachery, many of the highest offices in the nation,) to learn from them the details of the treason, in the different stages of its progress; and to receive their final orders how to execute the parricidal work. He returned, and immediately, all the machinery of revolution was put in motion. I need not dwell on the wicked measures pursued, to work upon the people at large—for they are known to our total population—such as bold falsehood to cheat the ignorant, artful cajolery to tickle the vanity of the ambitious, threats to intimidate the quiet and peaceful, and open violence to overcome the staunch and bold, who stood up for their country, in truth and loyalty, against all assailants.

But it is important to observe the conduct and policy of those traitors, as manifested by their proceedings in the General Assembly: for their proceedings have served as an exact model, in the essential particulars, for the reckless men who now rule the State. The ends respectively designed by them differ, mainly if not solely, in regard to the relations which the State shall bear to the General Government. But their policy for the internal government of the State and the means for enforcing that policy, are identical.

It was the object of Governor Jackson [13] and his rebel Legislature of 1860–'61, to form a Convention in the interest of secession, to vote the State out of the Union, and thus commit a treasonable act, against both the nation and the State. That object was as well known then, in the early winter of 1861, as it was afterwards, when the actual Convention deposed the traitors and drove them from the State; for then, many men whose principles were right, were afraid to array themselves openly against iniquity in high places. The *Radical* Convention, I admit, did not have for its object a severance of the Union; for they hoped to make the power of the nation subservient to their scheme of revolutionizing the State and insuring

---

[13] *Supra*, Jan. 9, 1860, note 15.

their rule over it. And they hoped to do this by enlisting the zeal of certain extreme Radicals of the North who were supposed to have influence in the General Government, and by using the army to break down all opposition to them, under the false pretense of martial law. But I am credibly informed that some members of the Convention and many of its partisans, were supporters of the now exploded project of a *Northwestern Confederacy!* A disruption of the Union quite as effectual, if acted out in practice as the C. S. A., and differing from it only in geographical position.

Now, let us see what the rebel Legislature actually did in order to grasp the whole power of the State, and thus consolidate and continue the rule of their party; and how exactly the Radicals acted out, step by step, the policy of the rebels (and improved upon it in one particular) and for the very same end—the aggrandizement of their party.

The rebel Legislature assembled on the last day of the year 1860, and in three weeks after, that is, on the 21st of January, 1861, passed their bill for calling a Convention, with a purpose, almost openly avowed on the face of the bill, to secede from the Union. Soon after passing that act the Legislature adjourned, perhaps supposing that their work would be accomplished by the bare act of secession, which they confidently expected, at the hands of the Convention. But that hope failed them. Our people were then true and faithful, both to the State and Nation, and elected a *Union* instead of a *secession* Convention. Then treason began to tremble for its own safety, and Governor Jackson (urged most probably by the leading conspirators in the South) hastily called together his Legislature, in an extra session, which passed that famous " act to provide for the organization, government and support of the *military forces* of the State of Missouri." By that act the whole military force of the State was placed absolutely at the disposal of the State government, then in the hands of ascertained rebels. That is what the rebels did in trying to secure to their party the control of the State. Now, let us see what the Radicals did, in trying to secure the same thing for their party. In their act to call a Convention, they copy, almost literally, the language of the rebels. The preambles of both acts, pretending to assign a reason for calling a Convention at all, fail to give any specific reason. The rebel preamble says that " the *condition of public affairs* demands that a Convention of the people be called to take such action as the interest and welfare of the State may require." And the Radical preamble is, word for word, the same, except that the Radicals say the condition of affairs *in the State* and not *public affair[s]*, generally.

Both of them had a reason for the call of a Convention, and a good reason to hide the real object from the people. The main object of the rebels was *secession*, while the control of the State was, in their eyes, a secondary consideration, desirable, chiefly, as a means to that great end. The Radicals, on the contrary, did not want secession; but they did want the control of the State, its offices, power and money.

The first sections of both of the Convention bills—the rebel and the Radical—are just alike in every essential particular. Both of them require the people, peremptorily, to vote for delegates to a Convention, and neither of them puts to the people the previous question, whether or not they chose to have a Convention. And, in both instances alike, the servants of the people assumed to be their masters.

And the Radical Legislature [h]as closely followed the example set by the rebels, in grasping all the military force of the State, for the uses of their party, as it had already followed their bad example of forcing upon the people what they call a Sovereign Convention. They passed the act of February 10, 1865, for "the organization and government of the Missouri militia," which is as effectual as the rebel act was to vacate all existing militia offices, and transfer the new appointments to their own party. But, unlike the rebel act, (which was drawn with admirable skill and cunning, to transform the militia into an effective standing army, wherewith to levy war against the United States), this act is as remarkable for the careless ignorance with which it is framed, as for its greedy clutching after power and money, and its open contempt of the settled forms of law and of the liberties of the people. Leaving to others the dissection of it before the public and the indignant criticism which its many demerits deserve, I content myself with citing a single instance. The act requires *all male inhabitants* to be enrolled in the militia—old men, tottering to the grave, and little *male inhabitants* rocking in the cradle. *All* are required to be enrolled; and, obviously, this requirement is not for any military purpose, (for the old men and the boys are, by the terms of the same act exempted from actual military duty), and as obviously it is to display their contempt for the principles of the Government and their eager pursuit of arbitrary power over the persons and property of the people. The act, in plain terms, provides that every person who neglects or refuses to enroll himself shall pay the sum of twenty dollars, "to be levied on his goods and chattels, *by order of the commanding officer of the District*, and may be *imprisoned or put to hard labor* BY SAID OFFICER *until said fine is paid!!!*" <That wise, humane and *loyal* provision may be found in the sixteenth section of the act of the last *Radical* General Assembly, entitled "An act for the organization and government of the Missouri Militia," approved February 10, 1865[.]>

Thus far the parallel is complete, between the rebel and the Radical Legislatures, in their policy for the internal government of the State, and in the means to enforce that policy; and I doubt not, that the parallel would have continued, in the action of the respective Conventions, if the rebel Legislature had succeeded, as the Radicals did, in electing a Convention like themselves. But failing to get a secession Convention, their whole scheme of revolution failed; for there was no way to get, suddenly, into their own hands, all the civil as well as all the military power of the State, but to vacate the judgeships and other civil offices, and fill the vacancies with men like themselves. Failing in that, they could not pass an ordinance to secure to themselves all power, influence and money of the civil government, as the Radicals did.

And this is the instance alluded to above, in which the Radical party improved upon the action of their prototype, the rebel party, in grasping all the powers of the State government.

They did pass an ordinance to vacate, on the first of May, all the judgeships of the State, all the court clerkships, all the offices of sheriffs and recorders, all the circuit attorneys and their assistants—in short all the offices likely to be made available to their party, by the power, influence or money attached to them. Their power to *fill* the vacancies was as ample as to *make* them—for certainly they could do neither, by any existing law. To do either required the assumption by the convention of all the powers of the State (above all constitutions and laws) over the people and their rights and properties. They did not hesitate to assume the unlimited power to *make* the vacancies; but they shuffled off upon the Governor, the delicate and odious task of *filling* them. And for this course they had several strong reasons. And *first*, at the date of the ordinance they had not gotten over their inordinate opinion of their own dignity and power. They still thought that the whole State was afraid of them, and that the Governor would be their pliant instrument to fill the vacancies, as they might indicate. *Second*, it was notoriously said, and generally believed at the time, that leading members of the Convention had parcelled out among themselves their respective shares of the spoils of the officers to be cashiered. For instance, it was rumored that Bay,[14] of the Supreme Court, was to be sacrificed to Clover;[15] Moody,[16] of the Circuit Court, to Strong;[17] and Lord,[18] of the Land Court, to some other *honorable member;* and so on through the county and the State. And under the then circumstances, they might reasonably calculate that if they stuck well together and boldly recommended each other, the Governor would

[14] *Supra,* May 18, 1865, note 18.
[15] *Supra,* Feb. 3, 1865, note 44.
[16] *Supra,* Feb. 2, 1865, note 40.
[17] *Supra,* Jan. 18, 1865, note 14.
[18] *Supra,* April 15, 1865, note 68.

hardly venture to resist their will; because he could not be so blind as not to see that the power which could, without any accusation or reason assigned, cashier the whole judiciary of the State, could cashier him! And there are strong circumstances tending to prove that that selfish scheme was entertained by many of the members, and was the motive power, without which the ordinance would not have been passed. During the discussion of the ordinance, a motion was made and debated to the effect that the members of the Convention should not be eligible to fill any of the vacancies to be made by the ordinance, and it was *voted down* by a large majority! *Third,* although the ordinance, as printed, expresses simply the arbitrary will of the Convention to dismiss those officers without any accusation of a fault or any pretense of unfitness, yet many members in debate, freely gave their reasons. They said there were some disloyal men in office, and their object was to purge them out; and as it was hard for the Convention to determine who was and who was not *loyal,* the better way was to eject them all and leave the Governor to fill their place. And they did it. During that debate, some member (in the embers of whose conscience some lingering sparks of justice still remained) suggested that it really did seem hard, that several hundred gentlemen, as fairly chosen as themselves, should be thrust headlong out of office, only because there might be found a few unworthy men among them. But the objection availed nothing. It was easily met and answered by an eminent member, (Mr. Strong, of St. Louis,) who assured the Convention that no good man would be hurt; for, said he, the Governor has told me that he would reappoint every *loyal* man among them. That was very satisfactory, especially to those members who expected a share in the spoil. They were anxious that the Governor should make the appointments, because that would relieve them from the unseemly spectacle of voting their victims out and voting themselves into their places. *Loyalty* was the Governor's only requirement for reappointment, and, at that time, the members did not doubt that the Governor's standard of loyalty was the same as theirs—that is, no man can be loyal who is not a Radical. For that bald absurdity was so often proclaimed on the floor of the Convention that the weaker members really seemed to believe it. But now that the Convention has adjourned, has abdicated its usurped sovereignty and is incapable of further mischief, Governor Fletcher will be free, like every other honest and sensible man, to judge of loyalty by the true meaning of the word and the actual conduct of the man. He knows that loyalty is true faith and allegiance to the sovereign, (whoever and whatever that sovereign is,) and not a blind devotion to a clique or a faction. He knows (every American who is not an extreme Radical *must* know) that we have no sovereign but the *law*. And I affirm that whoever is unfaithful to *that sovereign*, whoever lightly esteems the laws of the land, and wantonly tramples them down for the aggrandizement of himself or his faction, *cannot possibly be a loyal man*. By the time I shall have completed these letters I hope that you will be the better enabled to judge for yourselves whether the extreme Radicals of the Convention and the Legislature, judged by this standard, are or are not *loyal men*.

I have said that this Convention, in its origin, in its character and in its acts, is revolutionary, and I expect to be able to maintain all that I have said. But I cannot, possibly, condense into one short letter all that ought to be said, on these three branches of the subject; therefore I shall postpone the character and acts of the Convention for consideration in another letter, and, in the conclusion of this, treat only of its revolutionary origin.

This subject is not new to me. I was a member of the first Missouri Convention which sat here in St. Louis in 1820, and which erected the State and framed its Constitution; and, although young and inexperienced at the time, I still have a lively recollection of the general principles and views which actuated that Convention, and especially the reasons which led to the adoption of the mode of amendment which still stands (thank God) unrepealed. We knew that all governments are established with a view to perpetuity, and that no government, willingly embodies in its frame the means of its own destruction. And we know [*sic*] also, that, in process of time, every government may need amendment, either to correct original errors, or to change that which, by altered circumstances, has become unsuitable. We knew that, in the beginning of free, popular government, the organizing of society and the framing of government, do require conventions of the people, because, in no other way, yet found out, can the people at large, sensibly and prudently, consult with each other and make their wants and wishes mutually known. But, society organized, and government constituted, with the principle of amendment incorporated in it, reserved to the people and always in their reach, there is no need of a Convention. And (as all history proves) a Convention not needed, is always dangerous. For it is commonly called in times of heat and excitement, when the wildest spirits are sure to be evoked, and the most visionary theorists assume the places proper only for prudent statesmen and cautious legislators. Arguments like these led to the adoption of the mode of amendment which still stands embodied in our Constitution; and I still think it very good.

In the month of January, 1861, while the bill to call a Convention was pending before the rebel Legislature, I wrote a long letter to a member of the State Senate (Gen. Robert Wilson [19]) with the hope of exercising some influence against the bill. The main argument of that letter was directed against secession, which I denounced as revolution and treason. But a part of the letter was upon the subject now in hand, and from that part I insert here a brief extract: "So much for the right of secession and its revolutionary character. A word or two now about the right of our Legislature to meddle with the question. The Legislature is not the sovereignty of Missouri— it is not the People, and it no more represents the People in their sovereignty than does the Governor or the judiciary represent them. It is only one of three co-ordinate departments of Governments, and like the Judiciary and the Executive, has no powers but those granted to it by the Constitution. And what are those powers? To make laws under and in conformity to the Constitutions of the United States and of this State—for every member, by the very terms of our own Constitution, must swear to support both—and to amend our own Constitution in the manner prescribed in that instrument. It exists only in strict subordination to both Constitutions, State and Federal, and therefore of necessity, has no power to change the political status of the State, or to alter its governmental relations; and any attempt to do so is simple usurpation; and any act done in that attempt will be a legal nullity—a mere abuse of the organized functions of the State, to accomplish an end, forbidden alike by both the Constitutions.

"It is a fact often overlooked, that our Constitution makes no provision for the calling of any convention of the people for any purpose. It provides for its own amendment in a different manner; and in that manner, it has, several times, been amended. Once the Legislature tried the experiment of calling a convention to alter the Constitution. <See the act of February 27, 1843.> That convention assembled and passed an instrument which it offered, as a substitute for our existing Constitution; but when it was submitted to the people, the *people rejected it*—and so ended the only legislative experiment to alter the Constitution by extra Constitutional means." And so, the deliberate judgment of the people of Missouri, thoughtfully expressed in quiet times, condemned that first attempt to set aside the plain provisions of the Constitution, in regard to its amendment, and to cast the State and its laws, and the very structure of society, under the capricious power of a temporary assembly. And yet the act of 1843, which called that first Convention, was wise and moderate, when compared with the two Convention acts—of the rebels and the Radicals respectively. The act of 1843 provided that, at the general election in 1844, the sense of the people should be taken "upon the expediency of calling a Convention to *amend, alter or*

---

[19] *Supra*, Dec. 17, 1859, note 35.

make a new Constitution of the State." And further, if a majority
of the votes shall be in favor of a Convention, then the Governor
shall, *in the month of April*, 1845, order an election of delegates, to
be held on *the first Monday of August*, 1845—more than two years
after the date of the act calling the Convention. Thus allowing
ample time for the peaceful consideration of the subject, in all its
bearings, and time even for great changes of circumstances and of
parties. And yet the people condemned the whole proceeding, for
it disregarded the plain provisions of the Constitution and tended
to revolution. How different from the acts and the spirit of both
the rebels and the Radicals. They both assumed the power to *order*
a Convention, and both rushed with indecent haste to the consummation of their respective designs, for both of them had designs to
accomplish which would not brook delay; the rebels were eager to
get the State voted out of the Union, and the Radicals were no less
eager to clutch all the powers and interests of the State, and thus
consolidate and continue their temporary control, which originated
in social anarchy and was sustained, thus far, by martial law.
<Note—This point will be further illustrated when time will bet-
ter serve, by reference to the acts and publications of military men,
from the farewell of General Rosecrans [20] down to the circular of
Major Matlack.> [20a]

I must bring this letter to a close, lest I break my promise to be
short. Therefore I will state very briefly, the grounds upon which
I base the assertion that the Convention was revolutionary *in its
origin:*

1. The Legislature is the creature of the Constitution; and, as it
exists only by the force of that instrument, it can exist and act no
otherwise than according to its terms.

2. The Constitution has declared the method by which itself may
be amended (and that provision is as obligatory as the part which
creates the Legislature), and its creature, the Legislature, can have
no power to amend or alter it, in any other manner. For it exists
only by the Constitution, and, of necessity, can act only under and
according to it; and it can not give power to another which itself
has not.

3. The Legislature cannot legally delegate to others its own unquestioned powers; and surely, it cannot depute to any man or set
of men the power to rule the State and all its interests without limit
or definition.

This being true, it follows that the Legislature did not grant, because it could not grant, to the Convention any powers to alter or

[20] *Supra*, March 9, 1864, note 95.
[20a] See *infra*, 595.

amend the Constitution. And so in point of mere law it is obvious that the Convention was not vested with any lawful power to rule us at all. But beyond this, their election and the manner of it, may well be considered as relating to the *origin* of their pretended power. And I affirm that that election was illegal and dishonest, and brought about, not by the spontaneous will of the people, but accomplished in the midst of disorder, violence and fear, and not unfrequently by the direct application of military power. I cannot now enter into details concerning the election, but I am prepared to do it when the proper occasion shall come.

Upon these grounds I affirm that the Convention was revolutionary *in its origin*. But let no good man be alarmed because the same line of argument will prove that the Convention of 1861 was also revolutionary *in its origin*. So it was, eminently revolutionary *in its origin;* for it was plotted and contrived by traitors for the very purpose of dissolving the Union and destroying the Nation; and most of those who planned and passed the rebel Convention bill, were very soon afterwards; in open rebellion levying war against the United States. And but for the sense and virtue of the great body of the people, at that time, the revolutionary conspiracy would have been as fully accomplished, here in Missouri, as it was accomplished in the Southeastern States, all the way from the Rio Grande to the Potomac. The two Conventions were alike *in their origin*, both revolutionary; but, *in their characters and their acts*, they differ as greatly as light and darkness.

The Convention of 1861 was chosen by a great majority of a sound and true people, (I have heard the majority estimated 80,000) and consisted, for the most part, of brave and faithful men, devoted to their country and its Constitutions and laws. They found themselves in a position to try men's souls, and they rose to the level of the great emergency. The Constitutional officers, the lawful organs of ordinary power, had betrayed their trust, and raised the standard of rebellion. And they did not long hesitate to take the responsibility of resisting the official traitors, for the salvation of the Government and the people; and they did it effectually, by using against the rebels the very revolutionary weapon which they had treacherously contrived for the destruction of the nation. They were eminently *conservative*, for they conserved the State, by boldly deposing the official traitors, and filling their places with true men. loyal to the nation and the State! And is there a caitiff in Missouri who will dare to say that in doing this, they did wrong?

My next letter will be devoted mainly to the consideration of the character and acts of the Convention and some of its members.

St. Louis, April 24, 1865.

Letter Number Four [21]

I am still treating of the late Radical Convention and its revolutionary nature. I have already shown, I think, to a demonstration, that *in its origin*, it was revolutionary. And it remains for me to show that in its character and in its acts, it does but reduce to practice the revolutionary principles of its origin.

To silence all cavil, it may be well, here, to explain what I mean by denouncing the character and acts of the Convention *as revolutionary*. I mean what I say, that all acts and declarations of any man or any set of men, tending to, or having for their object the setting up of a new power, supreme and absolute, over the State, its laws and its interests, *are revolutionary*. Such a power is, in its very nature, incapable of limitation; for it is above all human law, and can have no motive to act but its own will, and no rule of action but its own discretion.

I proceed now to show that the first idea of calling that Convention was a radical and revolutionary thought, hatched in the feverish imaginations of a few restless politicians, who, in the good times of peace and prosperity, had failed to convince the people of their superior talents and worth. That class of superserviceable zealots had but little to lose, and might hope to gain much, by playing a reckless game for place, and power, and money. The nation was arduously engaged in a struggle to defend itself against a formidable rebellion, and the Government not yet practiced in the exercise of the dormant powers of the Constitution, for the use of which, happily, there had been no occasion, until called into action by this new and startling crisis. This public calamity furnished them, at once, with the occasion and the means to institute a new revolution, for their own particular benefit. And it is a sorrowful spectacle to see how many good men were unconsciously deluded to follow them, in that road to ruin. And I can only account for it by the fact that at that time the minds of many were stunned by the greatness of the shock to the State and Nation, and ready in the midst of their doubts and fears, to follow any presumptuous leader, who boldly promised to take them safely through the storm, to a place of repose and peace.

The Convention of 1861 first deposed the official traitors, Governor Jackson [22] and his Legislature. That was right—the most radical of the Radicals will not deny that. In the next place, they did what every man of thought must see was a necessity—they provided a substitute, by appointing a Governor and other necessary executive officers, in order that the civil administration of the State might still go on, and thus anarchy be avoided. But they did not undertake to

---

[21] Published in the *Missouri Democrat* of May 11, 1865.

[22] *Supra*, Jan. 9, 1860, note 15.

make their work a permanent rule for the State. They called it a *Provisional Government*, and intended it only as a temporary expediency, to conserve the State from anarchy and ruin, until the storm should pass over. That is what they did, to destroy the rebel government of the State—which was in form legal, but in fact, destructive of all the ends of good government—and to establish in its stead a faithful and patriotic government, *in form*, *illegal*, but in fact, conservative of the State, and necessary to the ends of all good government. Was not that right?

But that did not suit the eager appetite of those who had planned the new revolution; for they were in haste to seize the places, power and money incident to the control of the State; and as they could not get them by legal and civil means, they determined to break down the civil government, and substitute military despotism in its place. And to that end, they set themselves diligently to work to *make*, as they could not *find*, a pretext for destroying all civil government and superseding all law, by military power.

They denounced the provisional government, as a nuisance, and Governor Gamble [23] as a usurper and a traitor; and with persistent malignity, they persecuted that brave, good patriot, even to the grave. Still, he was not, personally, the real object of their attack, for every man of them knew, and in his secret heart acknowledged, that when he died, he left behind him, in Missouri, no man more enlightened and brave, and no patriot more faithful and devoted. But they knew also, that so long as a man of his stern integrity and absolute devotion to *liberty by law*, remained Shepherd of that flock, it would not be an easy task for the wolves and foxes of their pack to prey upon the fold. And hence their strenuous efforts, both here, at home, and at Washington, were directed for the destruction of civil government in the State, and the substitution of a reign purely military.

As to what shameful practices they resorted to here in Missouri, to accomplish that object, many of you are, no doubt, better informed than I am; but my official position at Washington enabled me to know more than you, the people of Missouri, can know about their active and continued efforts to induce the General Government to put down the State Government by the strong hand, and rule the people by the army. It is within my knowledge that the President was, for a long time, teased with applications, sometimes by delegations, and often by zealous partisans, in person and by letters, to put down Gamble and the Provisional Government, and rule the people by martial law. And all of you, I hope, remember what answer President Lincoln gave to them, on one memorable occasion. He told them, in substance, that he would not take part with either faction in Missouri;

[23] *Supra*, July 23, 1859, note 39.

that Governor Gamble and General Curtis [24] were so opposed to each other, in policy and action, that they would not co-operate for a common end; and that, as he, the President, *had no power to remove Governor Gamble*, he had no course left him but to remove General Curtis from his command. And from that time forth (until after the withdrawal of Mr. Fremont, as the Cleveland candidate for the Presidency,) President Lincoln was denounced by the faction, almost as violently as was Governor Gamble.

The faction, however, substantially gained its ends, by pandering to the vanity of such weak commanders as Fremont and Curtis and Rosecrans.[25] They were made to believe that, although they had failed to gather laurels and win renown in bloody fields, yet that they were, *at least, statesmen*, and could better govern the people *by orders* than the constituted authorities could govern them *by laws*. The faction told them so, " and they were simple and believed it "; and immediately the baleful effects were painfully visible all over the State. The law and its ministers were degraded, by being subordinated, not to " the commanding general " only, but to every petty commandant of a post, and every provost of a town. And the people were taught both by precept and example to despise the law and its ministers; for they saw them reduced by military power, ostentatiously displayed, to such pitiable impotence that they could no longer administer legal justice between man and man, according to law, in civil causes, nor punish the guilty, nor protect the innocent, in legal matters of criminal cognizance. The instances of this disloyal abuse of power are very numerous, and I have detailed accounts of many of them, from various parts of the State, but I cannot encumber this letter with their even bare statement. At this stage, therefore, I content myself with declaring that here, in St. Louis, where there is no pretense that the course of legal justice is impeded by guerrillas, and bushwhackers or other outlying thieves and vagabonds, (the false apology given for despotism, in other parts of the State,) the all-powerful District Provost habitually took control of questions of mere civil right, between man and man, and exercised absolute power over the tribunal, which had legal cognizance of such actions. A written statement has been sent me, by a responsible person of one St. Louis case (the type of many others) which marks in strong relief, the insulting wantonness with which these extraordinary powers are assumed and exercised. A landlord sued his tenant for rent, and, in due course of law, obtained a judgment for the debt; and then the Provost Marshal sent an order to the tribunal which gave the judgment, forbidding the execution of the

---

[24] *Supra*, Oct. 22, 1861, note 23.
[25] *Supra*, March 9, 1864, note 95.

judgment and all further proceedings thereon! And the Provost was obeyed, *because he was a Provost* and had soldiers under him!

And this is the martial law, so dear to the Convention, and for whose continuance, as the governing rule over this State, they have made such active efforts. And yet, in charity, perhaps we ought to attribute their conduct in this regard, at least in some degree, to the amiable sentiment of gratitude; for, certainly the members, (many of them) were indebted for their election, and the Convention was indebted for its existence, to the active interference of the military power.

And now (waiving many minor proofs, which I have not time or space to collate,) I proceed to prove the fact by very high military authority; and I vouch General Rosecrans, for my witness against them. I shall not dwell upon the humiliating story of Price's invasion,[26] last year, for all the world knows that. Let a very brief statement suffice: Price was south of the Arkansas river, with a small army, and resolved upon an invasion of Missouri, (not with any hope of conquest, but probably by way of a diversion in favor of the rebel army in Tennessee and Mississippi, and to recruit and supply his own troops). His purpose was openly proclaimed, known everywhere, and heedfully noticed by everybody, except only the military commander of this department, who, it seems, was too busily employed in regulating the government and politics of the State, to give any attention to his own official and peculiar duties. It was his duty to prevent the invasion, and save the State from the desolation and from the losses of life, property and character, consequent upon the march of two contending armies over more than half its surface. And how was this duty performed? In point of fact, Price was allowed to dominate the southeastern quarter of the State (except only the county of St. Louis); to break up the railroads, to destroy the property and conscribe the men, and to send his emissaries throughout the counties, proclaiming his power and speedy reconquest of the State, and thus reanimating the guerrilla war, by calling into action all secret and concealed foes, and turning all hesitating and lukewarm symphathizers into active enemies.

This was the upshot of General Rosecrans' military efforts to defend the State and protect the people; and he seems to think that he has atoned for the military blunder, by the excellent manner in which he discharged the "civil duties of his administration!" And for that miserable failure, he was deprived of his command, and ended his service here, both military and civil, by a farewell address, dated December 9, 1864, and entitled "General Orders, No. 221." <I wish

---

[26] See *supra*, Oct. 5, 6, and 22, 1864.

129742—33——39

every newspaper in the State would re-publish it for general information.>

The General address begins by announcing the fact of his withdrawal, and after a few words of courtesy to the soldiers, then follows this remarkable passage: "*The civil duties of my administration* have brought me into relations with the *loyal* people of the State, to whom, in taking leave, I express my sympathies," &c. I am astonished at the naivete of this short sentence, coming as it does from a Major General, who, by position, is supposed to have some little knowledge of the laws and institutions of his country. Being *military* commander of the department, he finds himself charged with "*civil duties in his administration!*" Surely the General must be a potent wizard thus to squeeze civil blood out of a military turnip, and transform martial law into a civil administration! But these *civil duties* of the General, it appears, brought him into relations (of some sort, not explained,) with the *loyal people.* That perhaps was well enough, for, "a fellow feeling makes us wondrous kind," but it is a pity that the General's *military duties* should have failed to bring him into relations of open hostility and manly contest with the *disloyal people* who, with Price at their head, were allowed to roam over and desolate half the State.

Then follows a paragraph to be admired for the innocent simplicity of its disclosures. "If (says the General) I have not been able to do for them all I desired, in relieving them from invasion," &c., . . . "I trust (resumes the General) that in what I have done to raise troops, organize citizen guards, *establish system in the administration of martial law*, defeat secret conspiracies against the State and nation, secure *outside help*, organize and direct our own forces, save our own main depots and most of the State from the hands of a formidable plundering and recruiting invasion, and bring that invasion to nought *while it gave triumph to the loyal people in the late election*, I have *done them* and the nation some good."

There now! Will any man, after reading this, presume to say that the Convention ought not to be grateful to General Rosecrans, for establishing system in the administration of martial law, (i. e. organizing anarchy,) and for giving *to them, triumph in the late election!*

Such preposterous notions of military power and such undisguised usurpation of the civil Government, being proclaimed and practiced at *Headquarters*, we need not wonder that the bad example is followed by subordinates down to the lowest grades. And, hence, our surprise is somewhat diminished, at the cool impudence of a circular address, lately published by a District Provost Martial [*sic*] in St. Louis.

The circular is dated "Headquarters, District, St. Louis, Office Provost Marshal, St. Louis, Missouri, April 17, 1865," signed L. C. Matlack, Major 17th Illinois cavalry, and District Provost Martial [*sic*]; and it runs thus: "This office has been crowded with applications from negroes, for redress of grievances and collection of claims in which white persons were parties. Attention has been given to them heretofore promptly. The inequality of the negro before the law, was alike the occasion and the justification. But all that is changed now."

The necessity which required the exercise of *civil functions by the District Provost Marshal* no longer exists. Inquiries directed to the Secretary of State, and a comparison of recent legislative with the former statutory provisions of the State of Missouri, show this.

And then, the Illinois Major, turning lawyer for the occasion, sets down several of his legal deductions drawn, no doubt, from his learned comparison of the recent, with the former legislation of the State of Missouri. And among his legal conclusions is the following general affirmation—"No law now exists to prevent the equality of the negro before the law."

And thus it plainly appears that Mr. Matlack being a major of an Illinois regiment and a District Provost Marshal in Missouri, assumes to exercise *civil functions* here! He avows it and does not pretend that it is any part of his military duty. But he does pretend that there was a necessity for him to usurp *civil functions*: and he discloses frankly what that necessity was—"The inequality of the negro *before the law* (says he) was alike the occasion and the justification."

It was not that there was any failure or defect of law, nor any ignorance on his part of what the law was, nor any want of courts to administer the law as it is written; but that the *law itself*, in Major Matlack's opinion, *was wrong!* And he being vested with supreme power in the name of martial law, thought fit to set aside the Constitution and statutes of Missouri, and himself redress all grievances, according to his own will, or as the exigencies of parties might require.

The man who sets himself up as the redressor of grievances and the collector of claims, and shows the physical power to do it, in spite of the laws of the land, is sure to have plenty of business; and so, the Major informs us that his office has been *crowded* with applications. And if the Major had not been a very loyal man, and a self-denying patriot, he might have made "a good thing of it" by retailing out his illegal justice, in the shape of grievances redressed and claims collected, by martial law.

And all this was publicly done in the city of St. Louis, the headquarters of several generals, and the law-appointed seat of several courts both of the nation and of the State; yet the Major went on as long as he pleased in the exercise of his *civil functions by military power*, and never stopped until he found out (as he erroneously supposed) that here, in Missouri, " No law now exists to prevent the equality of the negro before the law." But the Major is as much at fault in his law as he is in his politics, and ethics. Being an Illinois man, and fit to be a major, and a provost, he must know (for it is his duty to know) that the Constitution of Illinois does, in express terms, prevent the equality of the negro with the white man—for, it permits the white man to vote, but excludes the negro.

His ignorance of the laws of Missouri might find a more ready excuse, if he had not assumed, needlessly and ostentatiously, to know all about them, and to pronounce judgment upon them. And the Constitution of Missouri, now forty-five years old, is, to say the least, quite as strong as that of Illinois, in denying the equality of the negro with the white man. And even the late Convention, which above all others, affected to be the champion of *liberty, equality, fraternity*, in their draft of a Constitution, which is now on trial before the people, have carefully provided against the equality of the negro with the white man. And thus, *before the law*, as it stands, and *before the law*, as it will stand, if the people be so unwise as to adopt the proposed Constitution, the negro is not the equal of the white man, and the learned Provost made a simple blunder in making that gratuitous assertion.

All these things were notorious, and must have been known to the Convention and approved by it; and with that knowledge and in that feeling, the Convention passed the shameful resolution affirming the existence of martial law, and insisting upon its continuance, as the governing rule over the people of this State. And if all this be not sufficient to prove that the Convention was revolutionary in its character and its acts as well as in its origin, I must confess myself ignorant of the force of language, and the logic of facts.

But this is not all, nor the half, of its revolutionary spirit and action. It existed only by virtue of the act of the Legislature which called it, and that act, plainly expresses the character and extent of the powers intended to be exerted, limiting them to a few specified subjects, and requiring all its powers to be exercised in the form of *amendments of the Constitution*. And, in conformity to the act, the people voted under it, granting to their delegates no new powers, and reserving to themselves, as always in the better days of the Republic, the sovereignty of the State and the integrity of the laws.

But no sooner did the Convention meet than it defied its creators, both the Legislature and the people, and assumed the sovereignty, with all possible powers. It scorned to *amend* the Constitution, but chose rather to make a new one. It scorned to set the negroes free by *amending the Constitution*, as required by the General Assembly, but chose rather to do it by a separate act, which is said to be not an amendment of the Constitution. And, beyond this, it assumed a new and extraordinary power, not belonging to any department of the State Government, nor to all of them combined.

It assumed, by a mere arbitrary dictum without any show of law or pretense of right, to eject all the judges and other ministers of the law. This is not only without any law in its favor, but is contrary to all law. It breaks the Constitution of the United States by *impairing* and destroying the contract which each one of those officers has made with the State—a contract whereby one party is bound to serve the other for a specified time, and the other party is bound to pay him wages in money. It breaks the State Constitution in the same particular, and also in this, that it takes the *property* of the officer, for *public use*, without making any compensation. Some shallow man may say that an *office is not property;* but he is surely no lawyer, and a poor political economist; for an office is an employment and a source of revenue income, taxable by law. Moreover, a man's title to his office and to his land, are identically the same—both depend entirely upon the letter of the law. To me, it is perfectly clear, that the Convention has no more power to eject an officer who is regularly and lawfully in his place, than it has to drive me from the lot I live on, and direct the Governor to give it to some other man.

This monstrous ordinance is not only against all written law, but is original and primitive in its nature, overreaching and ignoring all pre-ordained government, and inconsistent with the existence of a legally organized society. That is eminently revolutionary; and I observe that the Convention has provided in its project of a Constitution, for a succession of such despotic tyrannies, by giving to every faction that happens to get the upper hand in a single session of the Legislature, the right to call a Convention, with the same unbounded powers.

In the course of this letter, I have spoken with some freedom of the folly of some military officers. I hope that no true soldier will take offense at that; for I am persuaded that the army itself, in its discipline, its character, and its efficiency, is as much injured by that class of offenses as are the civil institutions of the country. Such offenses are usually found to abound the most in that class of military men who are most wanting in the characteristic qualities of the true soldier. Indeed, I have noticed, throughout this war, that the commanders who were the greatest terror to non-combattants, were the least respected and feared by the embattled enemy.

EDWARD BATES.

ST. LOUIS, May 4, 1865.

Letter Number Five [27]

In my second letter I treated of Martial Law, very briefly, for so great a subject, yet, I hope, with sufficient clearness and precision to be understood by all my readers. By this time, I suppose, that you all clearly understand that there is no such *law* in existence as *martial law;* that the use of the term is only a fraudulent trick to cheat ignorant, law-loving people into the belief that they are still ruled by some sort of law, while, in fact, the law is suppressed, and there is no rule over them but the absolute will of military commanders, great and small.

In my third and fourth letters, I treated of the Convention and its revolutionary origin, character and acts. What was said on that complicated subject (though not a tenth part of what might be well said, in illustration of the theme,) I believe to be quite enough to prove the proposition with which I started, that is—" The Convention was revolutionary, in its origin, in its character and in its acts."

I come now to treat of a subject, which, if it stood alone, would require a long and laborious exposition. But as my present theme is only a part of Martial Law, only the means and machinery by which the laws of the land are silenced and suppressed, and the absolute power at *Headquarters* ramified into every corner of the State, and permeated through the whole mass of society, the particular matter in hand, is more than half discussed, under the head of Martial Law.

My distinct proposition, announced at the beginning, is this— " The government of the various sections and districts of this State by *Provost Martials* [sic] is an unlawful and dangerous anomaly "— Provost Martials [sic] are lawful and useful in their proper places. They are *military police officers*, and their authority over soldiers and camp-followers is much the same as the authority exercised over civilians by our *civil provosts* (often called *chief of police*) in our towns and cities. And the *Provost Martial* [sic] has no more authority over civilians and their affairs, than the *Provost Civil* has over soldiers, in garrison, camp or field. My objection is not to Provost Martials [sic], (any more than to captains and majors, when confined to their proper places and limited to their proper functions); but it is to the perversion of the name and uses of the office, and the gross abuse of power, openly displayed, in contemptuous defiance of the law and its accredited ministers, and in capricious tyranny over private persons and their property. The *anomalous* character of this exorbitant power is beyond dispute; for such a thing has never been heard of in this country before the present troubles; its *legality*

[27] Published in the *Missouri Democrat* of May 25, 1865.

has never been affirmed by any respected person within my knowledge; and, I venture to assert, that no publicist or lawyer of fair standing will risk his reputation by affirming it. And as to its being *dangerous* to the laws, to civil and religious liberty, and to the rights and property of individuals, all the people of Missouri know that.

And yet its very existence among us remains to this day a mystery. After frequent inquiry, both at Washington and here in Missouri, I have never been able to ascertain that the Government, acting by any of its higher functionaries, ever gave apparent sanction to the guilty subordinates, by ordering the perpetration of the outrage. It seems, on the contrary, that the mischief was done by the quiet usurpation of subordinates, backed, indeed, by bayonets, and winked at, it may be, by their superiors. And some of those superiors (negligent of their great duty, as soldiers, to resist and subdue the public enemy, to command those who were lawfully under them, and to maintain discipline and obedience to the laws,) have already suffered, in part at least, the penalty of their transgression. They have been deemed by their superiors unfit for a position whose duties they so inefficiently performed; and compelled to retire under a cloud which darkens all their future. Like the High Priest Eli, who, in his day, bore a good reputation for both patriotism and piety, yet he allowed his subordinate officers to trample upon the laws of his country and to defile the temple of God. And for this great sin of omission, his nation was deeply humiliated and his own household was destroyed. The host of Israel fled, ingloriously, before its enemies; Saul and Jonathan and Hophni and Phineas, fell in the great battle of Gilboa; the arc of God was taken by the Philistines; and Eli himself dropped dead from his seat in the gate of Jerusalem. And all these calamities were the legitimate fruits of Eli's neglect of the duties of his office, and his failure to enforce discipline among his subordinates. For (says the Holy Scripture) "I will judge his house forever, *for the iniquity which he knoweth* because his sons made themselves vile, and *he restrained them not.*"

I shall dwell no longer upon this miserable monarchic notion of governing the people of this State by District Provost, each independent and supreme in his district, without any common method of proceeding prescribed for them all, and without any law to restrain their capricious will. This is what I called, in a former letter, *despotism multiplied by republican forms.*

I proceed now to the consideration of my other propositions, the last, remaining unconsidered, of the four, distinctly announced in my first letter. It is the exact opposite of martial law, whether administered by high generals commanding departments, or by petty provosts, who dominate districts and neighborhoods. And this is my proposition: "The laws of the land (as found in the Constitu-

tions and statutes of the United States and the State of Missouri)
do confer upon the officers of Government, National and State, all
the powers which are necessary to the successful prosecution of the
war, and to the peaceful rule of the country. And any attempt to
substitute in place of the *laws*, the will of any military officer, is
not only an act of *disloyalty*, but is also a dangerous blow struck at
the Governments [*sic*] lawful power for good."

If there be any virtue in Republican Government; if civil liberty
be any benefit to a people; if it be any advantage to a nation to be
ruled by a code of laws, rather than by the fluctuating will of man:
then we are not wholly ridiculous in our habitual boasting that our
Government, as established and heretofore administered by law, is
better than most of the governments of Europe. We hear every day,
and from all classes of polititians [*sic*], that the people are capable of
self-government; and yet we are shocked with the spectacle before
our eyes, of the people of Missouri tamely submitting for a long
time to the absolute dominion of a few local military commanders
and provost marshals, who, at will, seize their property, imprison
their persons, trample down their laws and despise their courts.
And worse than all that, we have the mortal shame of beholding a
Convention, pretending to represent the people of Missouri, in the
very act of making their fundamental law, insisting upon the continuance of this tyranny, and begging a general of the army still to
rule us by martial law.

I do not deny the dogma, that the people *are capable* of self-government, but I cannot forget the teaching of all history, that nations
and men do, very rarely avail themselves, for their own good, of all
their capabilities. But of one thing I am sure, if the people be really
capable of self-government, there is but one way in which they can
exercise that glorious power—and that is by making good laws for
their own government, and causing them to be executed by their own
officers, who are responsible to the laws, and bound by legal forms
and methods of proceeding. The people can never secure their freedom by making a Dictator from time to time, (as the Romans did),
to take them through every trying emergency; nor by submitting
(as we do now) to every usurper, who pretends that there is a necessity for him to be our master. Our fathers of '76 and '89 were brave
and wise men. They knew that to win liberty they must work and
dare; and that to preserve it they must watch and guard incessantly,
and be always ready, to resist the first assaults of greedy ambition,
and to defend the ground principle of civil liberty—that is, that the
government belongs to the many, and not to one or a few. And they
laid the foundation of our system accordingly; and they built upon
it a superstructure which has challenged the admiration of mankind
for more than three quarters of a century, because it is the only ex-

ample, in the history of the world, in which the inhabitants of a large country, wisely governed by their own laws, have advanced rapidly in numbers, wealth and power, without impairing the majesty of the law or impinging upon the liberty of the people.

I said that our fathers were wise, and the truth of the saying glitters extant on every page of our history. They did not waste their labors in petty schemes for small or transient objects. They perfected a system of government, proper for a great nation, capable of indefinite extension over space, and of endless endurance. And the Constitution contains ample provision to meet all possible exigencies which may arise in all the vicissitudes of national life. Whether we be rich or poor, prospering or declining, in peace or at war, the Constitution and the laws of Congress made under its authority, do supply fit instruments to do all possible national work, and the rule to work by, and appropriate means to punish or reward the workmen, according to their works.

The Constitution does not set up any man or set of men—not even the Government itself—as our *Sovereign*, entitled to our allegiance. It requires every officer, both of the Nation and of the State, to swear that he " *will support this Constitution;* " and that is the only oath of allegiance which it does require. And it declares itself (the Constitution) to be the *Supreme Law* of the land. This, then, is our only sovereign, to which we owe fealty and obedience at all times; and whoever (setting himself up to be wiser and better and stronger than the law) usurps unlawful powers, under the pretense of serving the country, by breaking its laws, is not only a *disloyal* man, but also a presumptuous charlatan; for, to gratify his personal vanity or his party ambition, he breaks the only bond of union which holds us together as a nation, and destroys the only safeguard of individual *liberty by law*.

My proposition, I think, is fully made out. The laws, well understood and faithfully obeyed, are strong enough for the perfect accomplishment of all the honest ends of government; and all those ends may be attained, easier and far cheaper, by obeying and following the law, than by breaking and degrading it. And, in my opinion, it is only the ignorant egotism of public officers which ever makes them imagine themselves wiser and stronger than the law, and therefore, better qualified than the lawful government can be, to rule the people and save the state!

Every usurper, from Cæsar, Cromwell and Bonaparte, all the way down to the District Provost Marshal of St. Louis, conscious of the wrong he is committing, feels bound to excuse his conduct, by pretending that there is a *necessity* which impels him to act! Cæsar " asumed the purple," in order to quell the factions which had thrown the Republic into anarchy, and drenched Rome and the provinces in blood; and Major Matlack assumed the supreme judicial power here, in St. Louis, *because the laws of the State were wrong* in not equalizing all people before the law! These pretenses are always unlawful, and almost always false in fact; and not unfrequently, artfully contrived to make a show of excuse for the meditated crime, and cover up the partisan fraud with a flimsy veil of hypocritical loyalty. Of this last character is the pretense, impudently started and pertinaciously adhered to, that the laws were silenced and the courts rendered incapable of administering legal justice by the presence of guerrillas and bushwhackers in various parts of the State. To prove the absurd falsity of this pretense, it may suffice to refer to two facts: 1. General Pope,[28] in his letter to Governor Fletcher,[29] estimates the number of these outlaws at twenty to a county on the average, and surely a good sergeant's guard for each county would be enough to protect the court in the discharge of its lawful duties against such a handful of robbers. 2d. Here in St. Louis, where the commanding Generals reside; where the courts, both Federal and State, hold their regular sessions; where, to suppose the existence of guerrillas and bushwhackers is to suppose dishonor to the military power, and criminal negligence in the civil police—even here, where there is no obstacle to civil business and legal justice, but the obtrusion of armed authority, the same unlicensed and unbridled power has been used by the military, as in the most remote and exposed parts of the State. The pretense, therefore, is false in fact. And its falsehood is not its worst feature. It is a cruel contrivance, a radical measure, adopted long ago, when President Lincoln (declining to lend himself to a faction here) refused to annul the State Government, and rule the people by arms. From that moment bushwhacking became a cherished institution of radical policy, in Missouri, their stock in the trade of politics. By that false pretense they have succeeded in their first step to the comprehensive scheme of revolutionizing the State. They have succeeded in subjugating the people, and crushing their spirit, under martial law, and by those means have succeeded in electing their partisans to places of transient power. It remains to be seen whether or no they are able to carry out the whole of their destructive programme, which comprehends a thorough revolution of the State, in its principles, political, moral and religious, and also in its population and its property. I know whereof I affirm; and hold myself ready, if ever occasion should require it, to give the history, in disgusting detail, with facts, names and ancillary circumstances.

During the stress and agony of the war, when the result hung doubtful in the scales, we willingly submitted to many irregularities

---

[28] *Supra*, March 15, 1862, note 33.
[29] *Supra*, Jan. 12, 1865, note 4.

of official conduct; in fact, we were ready to submit to almost any-thing, for the sake of success in putting down the rebellion. But now that the victory is won, that the war is, substantially, ended, no pretense remains for the exercise of extraordinary powers. And the people, (breathing more freely, and looking hopefully to the future, not wholly occupied in defending against the present) will be sure to return to their first and best emotions. Their reverence for the Constitution and love for legal liberty, will revive in their hearts, and they will demand, in a voice too loud to be unheard and too strong to be unheeded, their absolute, hereditary right to be gov-erned by law, and not by the will of man. I still have undoubting faith in the theoretical perfection of our form of government, and the practical goodness of our Constitution and laws; and therefore, I do not doubt, that the law will again rise in its strength, assert its supremacy, both to protect and to punish, and put down all opposing powers.

And may we not hope that many military men, who have been made (perhaps unwillingly) the agents of unlawful power and popular oppression, seeing that the occasion is past, will at once con-fine themselves to their proper vocation, as soldiers, and cease alto-gether from troubling civil men, and from meddling with civil gov-ernment. But if, unhappily, I should be disappointed in this hope, then my advice to all the people is, to resist oppression and mis-government, by all the means which the laws authorize. Do it calmly and prudently, and taking care to keep the law always on your side; do it with unflinching courage and a fixed purpose to press the contro-versy to the end of the law. If a military officer presume to interfere with the civil courts, or to intermeddle with popular elections, have him indicted for the offense, no matter what is his rank, and prose-cuted according to law. And if any soldier, high or low, do a wrong to a private person, under the pretense of military power, let the proper civil action be promptly brought and pressed with all vigor, to a verdict and judgment for damages. My life upon it, this course, diligently and skillfully pursued, will soon bring the obstinate of-fenders to a proper sense of their subordination to the civil power.

Be not afraid of that foolish and wicked Ordinance of the Con-vention, designed to protect oppressors and to secure impunity to crime, for, I assure you, that it is powerless to protect the guilty. It is powerless—1st, because the Convention had no power to pass such a law; 2d, because the language of the ordinance (leaving the offender just where the good old law left him) does not pretend to protect the accused, unless he can show *lawful authority* to do the act complained of.

My next letter will concern the Constitution submitted by the Con-vention, in which I propose to point out certain of its radical errors, and perhaps trace their paternity to certain ultra-radical members of the Convention.

EDWARD BATES.

St. Louis, May 19, 1865.

Letter Number Six [30]

This is the last letter of the series which I proposed to address to the people of Missouri upon the unhappy condition of affairs in this State, unless I should find it proper to reply to any person who may venture to contest any of the doctrines which I have advanced or deny any of the facts which I have affirmed.

And now I propose to submit to you some remarks upon the Constitution which is offered by the Convention to be voted upon early next month—not by the people at large, but by such portion of the people only as the Convention thought qualified to pass upon the fragment of its work which alone is submitted to popular scrutiny. And in doing this I cannot well avoid the consideration of certain matters preliminary to the formation of a Constitution at all. What is the Constitution of a State? In my judgment it is the *fundamental law* of the State, and its chief function is to organize the powers of the State and govern the government thereof by dividing and distributing the power of government among the various departments and official functionaries and limiting each to its proper sphere. It is a fundamental *American* principle that " all just power in government is derived from the consent of the governed," and consequent upon that is another fundamental principle, that nobody can create a free American State or make its Constitution but the people, its component members. A power from outside, or a faction within, cannot do it so as to bind the people who compose the State. And if a Convention be deputed to organize a State and *constitute* a government, in written form, that Convention is not the State, nor the people of the State, but only *representatives* of the people. They have no powers of their own, inherent in themselves; but such powers only as may be granted to them by the people who deputed them for the special purpose of preparing the form and framework of a State Government. The making of a Constitution, then, is not a primitive act; it supposes the previous existence of society, of a community of people living together under social laws and enjoying together the common personal and social rights, such as liberty, property, contracts, marriage, family, all rights, which, indeed, make the social state, and constitute, in fact, the value of society. These need the protection of a superior law, to act as a safeguard against the greed

---

[30] Published in the *Missouri Democrat* of June 3, 1865.

and ambition of those who happen to be armed with the political powers of the community; and this (as I said before) is the chief office and function of a Constitution.

Our wise forefathers considered the *form* of government as very important, essential indeed, to civil liberty and political power in the people; and in pursuance of that idea, the Constitution of the United States (art. 4, sec. 4,) declares that " the United States shall guaranty to every State in this Union *a republican form of government.*" And what do you think they meant by that? They had already said (in the Declaration of Independence) that all just power is derived from the consent of the governed; and the people are the *governed*, for all of us are subject to the laws. By the phrase, a *republican form of government*, they must have meant—they did mean—a form of government in which *the people*, the governed, the component members of the State, should possess a controlling influence in the making and the administration of its laws. Not the *good* people only, not the favored few, not the aristocracy of wisdom and virtue, which is always a lean minority, but the body of the people, as we are found to be, in common life. No practical, republican statesman ever thought of excluding from suffrage and from office every man who could not give a satisfactory answer, when questioned sharply upon every point of the decalogue. That test would prove severe for many of the most prominent supporters of the New Constitution. If asked, " Hast thou not borne false witness against thy neighbor? " they could not help remembering, with remorse and shame, how they had denounced Governor Gamble [31] and all his colleagues in the Provisional Government as usurpers and traitors!

The majority of the late Convention indulged in the most extravagant notions of themselves and of their position—notions which would be simply ridiculous, if they were not so fraught with danger to the commonwealth. They thought (or professed to think) that a body of men, like themselves, claiming to represent the people, and called into existence for a specified purpose, distinctly stated in the call, if you will only call it a *Convention*, is, by force of that single word, armed with all possible powers! Acting under that hallucination, and in a spirit of boundless usurpation, wholly regardless of the law of its creation, the Convention has passed several ordinances, the largest of which they choose to call a Constitution—all of which are really *ordinances*, and are so declared by the Convention itself, for all of them are " ordained " by that *august body*. How they got the idea of submitting any part of their work to the revision of the people, is a wonder to me, seeing that they refused to submit the whole. They do not submit the whole of *any one of the ordinances.*

[31] *Supra*, July 23, 1859, note 39.

The long one, which they call the Constitution, is submitted to the vote of the people *only in part;* for the thirteenth article of it is declared to be already in full force, and needing no popular ratification. That *thirteenth* article requires a great deal of hard swearing of the people before they are allowed to vote upon the other twelve articles; and the friends of the New Constitution base their hopes of success, largely, upon the supposition that the terrible oath required will drive from the polls many opposers of the Constitution who are too conscientious to take that wide-sweeping oath. On this particular point, the members of the Convention may live to see themselves in a very ridiculous predicament. They say that the *thirteenth* article is now in full force, part of the supreme law of the land; now, suppose the people should reject the other twelve articles at the coming election, there stands, in *full force*, the glorious *thirteenth*, solitary and alone, a lasting monument of the folly of its contrivers.

Although the Convention was called for the only declared purpose of passing *amendments* to the Constitution, I have looked in vain through the whole new instrument without finding in the body of it any the slightest recognition of the existing Constitution of the State, or any of the amendments heretofore passed. All these are ignored by the Convention, which, claiming to have supreme powers over the State and all its interests, has made a new Constitution entire, as if we had no existing Constitution. And this is done, in open defiance of the act of the Legislature which created the Convention, and in fraud of the people who chose the members, *under and according to that act.* I do not find anything in the New Constitution which professes in terms, to repeal the old one, or any part of it; and so, even if the new one should be adopted, at the approaching election, the people may be greatly embarrassed in trying to find out what is, really, the Constitution of the State. For, if there be any part of the old Constitution which is not entirely covered and supplied, and thus superseded by the new one, such parts remain unrepealed and in full force. It is a well settled rule that to repeal an old law, *by implication merely*, the new law which is supposed to repeal it must cover the entire ground of the old law, and dispose of its entire subject-matter. And I apprehend that when questions of individual right shall arise in the courts, under the two instruments, many cases will be found to exist in which the New Constitution does not cover the whole subject-matter of the old one. And I arrive at this conclusion the more readily because, in a careful perusal of the New Constitution, I find it abounding with instances of a style of composition loose and vague, and a diction careless and indistinct; and these are clear evidences that the writer had not analysed his subject and that his mind had no distinct perception of the elements of which it was composed. Let no man fall into the mistake of supposing that this is hypercriticism—mere talk about words—for it is of the utmost importance to the people that their fundamental law—the measure, at once, of the power of their rulers, and of their own rights and duties—should be expressed in language plain and direct, and easy to be understood by " any man of ordinary intelligence." The Constitution does not belong to legislators, lawyers, and publicists. It belongs to the *people*, and if it be so ignorantly or so cunningly written that they cannot comprehend it, then it is not worth the white paper soiled by its writing.

Moreover, there is no need of a New Constitution. The Legislature which called the Convention forbade it as strongly as they could, by directing *amendment* only; the people voted for delegates *under the act of the Legislature*, without suggesting any enlargement of their powers; nobody, nobody outside of the Convention, ever asked for a New Constitution, or expected any such novelty. But the Convention, finding itself in a new position of undefined powers, became animated with a new-born ambition to consolidate its party to secure to it the continued control of the State, and to its favored leaders all the high honors, offices and emoluments which the State can bestow. That was the motive, the only motive, of this needless, gratuitous, uncalled for effort on the part of the Convention to foist upon the people a New Constitution.

I feel myself fully justified in making this assertion, not only by what I have myself advanced, but especially, by the course now openly taken by the chief advocates of the New Constitution. Both the public press and leading individuals, without one blush of shame, boldly put the question upon *party grounds*. They say that we, who oppose their monstrous plot, do it only to put down the Radical party; and they affirm (doubtless to frighten their partisans and whip them in) that the success of the New Constitution is necessary to the continued existence of that party. I hope that the last clause above written, may turn out to be true, and that the *destructive* party, that does nothing but root up and tear down the useful works of others, may sink, along with it own mischievous labors into well-merited oblivion. And as to the imputation against us, that we opposed the New Constitution *only* to defeat the Radical party, we feel bound in respect for our reputation for common sense, to deny that. We have a multitude of good reasons for opposing the New Constitution, based upon its own intrinsic demerits; and if the downfall of the destructive party, whose only business is to root up and tear down, should happen to be one of the legitimate consequences of the rejection of the New Constitution, I, for one, will be able to bear their loss with equanimity, comforting myself in the knowledge that " the wages of sin is death." But there is one circumstance connected with the New Constitution and the Radical party, which affords me great pleasure, and I think ought to be gratifying to the whole community; and that is the fact, that many of the best men in the State who ever allowed themselves to be classed with that party, are now engaged in open and strong opposition to the New Constitution. They openly denounce the extreme partisans who passed the shameful Constitution, and are trying to force it through, by shameful means, as men who degrade their party and disgrace its name.

I have not heard of a single press, or a single man, of any note or influence, who supports the New Constitution affirmatively, and on its own merits. They all admit that it abounds with errors—errors which ought not to be found in any Constitution. Yet they strenuously support it, with all its acknowledged faults; and upon the avowed ground that the extreme men who made it must share its fate, and stand or fall with it. They reject, in their own favor, the just and universal rule, that men should be judged according to their works; and in their own case, refuse to concede the simple justice, that the clumsy or dishonest workman should abide the fortune of his botched job. Alarmed for their own safety, they turn *conservative* for once, and beg to be *conserved*. Save the party, O! save *us!* though it be at the expense of the State and the people. Our Constitution, we admit, is bad, but the people will not be forced to bear it very long. We have provided for all that, by making amendments so easy that any party which gets uppermost for a year or two can change, amend or abolish the Constitution at pleasure! And so there is nothing permanent in it. The union of the States, the division of the powers of government, the right of suffrage, the trial by jury, the habeas corpus, the right to worship God as we choose, are all transient things, liable to be changed at will, as parties fluctuate in the State. Nothing is permanent. Permanence is against our creed, for we are the *men of progress*, who believe that it is beneath the dignity of a free man to acknowledge any *fixed principles* in law, politics, morals or religion! That is the substance and effect of their argument in support of the New Constitution.

But I must hasten to bring this letter to a close, by specifying some few of the many glaring objections to the Constitution. And first, as to the right of suffrage (to say nothing now of the *oath of loyalty*): I declare that I have never seen a written Constitution whose description of the persons qualified to vote was so prolix, so confused, so contradictory, so hard to be understood, as the heterogeneous provisions of this New Constitution. And I am confident in the belief that there is not a man in St. Louis, of any party, who can, off hand, and without referring to the text, recount all the qualifications, disqualifications, provisos and exceptions of a lawful voter, as set forth in the second Article of the New Constitution. Let any man try it who will; but I challenge, especially, Mr. President Krekel [32] and the leading members of the St. Louis delegation, to attempt it, in the presence of any respectable assembly of men in this city.

Of course, I shall not waste your time and mine, by attempting to analyze that second article, and thus exhibit more plainly all of its integral errors. But [I] shall content myself with stating only a few of its prominent faults. The eighteenth section of Article two begins by declaring that "*Every white male citizen of the United States, and every white male person of foreign birth*, who may have declared his intention to become a citizen of the United States, according to law, not less than one year, nor more than five years before," &c., who is over twenty-one years, and not disqualified under any of the provisions of this Constitution, and who has complied with its requirements, and has resided in the State one year and in the county sixty days before the election or the registry, *shall be entitled to vote.*

1. As to foreigners, who are all aliens until they are naturalized, and may be *alien enemies;* under this section they are allowed to vote, and thus control, it may be, the principles and policies of this country, even though at the time we may be at war with their own native country and King! and this without even being naturalized. Still aliens, under no obligation to perfect their declared intention to become citizens, and not subject by law to those civil and social duties which are required of citizens only; and in that class of duties there are several of great importance, of which the service upon juries is one. And thus the New Constitution proposes to establish among us a class of *privileged aliens!*

2. There is another class of foreigners provided for in that second Article, and put upon an easier footing than natural born citizens. It is that class of foreigners who have borne arms against us, in *any* foreign service, and afterwards have been naturalized here, and they are not required to swear that they have never borne arms against us as the natural born is required to swear. (See the latter part of Article two, section three.) And this is another class of *privileged foreigners!*

I have not observed in any of the recent discussions that any objection has been taken to this anomaly, this marked preference of the Convention for *white foreigners*, not only over *black natives*, but over *white natives*, also. Perhaps this is all right; perhaps we who have the ill luck to be born in the United States, are (both

---

[32] *Supra,* June 6, 1860, note 46.

129742—33——40

white and black) of races inferior to the *white foreigners* who are thus advanced over our heads. That seems to be the opinion of the majority of the Convention, or they blindly followed the lead of Mr. President Krekel, for he at least, declared himself openly on the subject. In a debate in the Convention on the subject of suffrage, he is reported to have declared that, in his judgment, foreigners—" and especially foreigners of his own nationality "—were well worthy to be trusted with the right of suffrage, if they had declared their intention to become citizens, and had lived *one year* in the country; and this, without any evidence of their ability to read or write, or that they were of good moral character; which literary and moral test he urged should be applied to *black natives*, if hereafter, it should be thought advisable to admit them to the right of suffrage. I do not blame Mr. Krekel for being a little proud of *his nationality*. He is a Prussian I believe, the born subject of the illustrious house of Brandenburg, a dynasty famous for a long succession of brave, prudent and wise Princes, always crescent, always acquisitive of surrounding lands, and tenacious of every acre which they got; and no less remarkable for governing their subjects with a steady, prudent, despotic hand, carefully suppressing every popular aspiration after political liberty, and every tendency towards republican ideas. I cannot imagine how Mr. Krekel could reach the conclusion that the men of *his nationality* were, especially qualified to be the precocious rulers of a Republic, in which they are still *aliens by law*. They never had a chance, in their own country, to learn, by tradition, by precept or example, any thing about Republican Government. Besides I do not think it was in good taste for Mr. Krekel to be boasting of the superiority of the men of *his nationality*, in the presence of men of subordinate, foreign nationalities—such, for instance, as the Irish, the men of Baden, the Wurtemburgers and the Hessians. But that is a matter of taste, of which, perhaps, I have no right to complain.

Mr. President Krekel seems to have impressed upon the Convention some of his own curious ideas about politics in general, and especially about the principles and doctrines of *American* public law. At first, the blatant champion of *liberty, equality, fraternity*— the absolute equality of all men *before the law*—when discussing the qualifications for Governor of the State, he was the generous advocate of the *negro's* right. The objections founded upon *race and color* were mere vulgar prejudices, which he had left far behind him, in the rapid progress of his political science. But soon, " a change came over the spirit of his dream; " the suffrage question came up, and Colonel Krekel countermarched the whole line of his boasted doctrine. *He opposed negro suffrage and equality before the law*, and the obsequious Convention, following the lead of its President, excluded " Cuffee " from the ballot box, avowedly *because he was black.* I do not *know*, but I have a strong suspicion that Mr. K.[rekel] had gotten an inkling that " our friends and fellow citizens with black skins, and of the African race " might not prove so docile as to vote, implicitly, as required by Mr. K.[rekel] and other *foreigners of his nationality.* At all events, the negro was excluded, and the hollow pretense of *equality before the law,* was exploded by the Convention. And yet, strange to say, Senator Brown[33] supports that clumsy, ragged and contradictory document, the New Constitution. And this in spite of his published letter, (called, by some irreverent persons, his instructions to the Convention.) In that letter he avows himself the advocate of the broadest and most unqualified liberty and equality of all men, and, as touching the elective franchise, he reduces his conclusions to this pithy and euphonious phrase, " Freedom and suffrage are inseparable." Every decent schoolboy knows that this is not true; for he feels that he is free, and he knows that he has not the right of suffrage. But extreme Radical politicians scorn to be such slaves to truth and sense as to be bound to say what they mean and mean what they say. In several important points of the New Constitution the instrument is, even now, supported by its chief partisans upon the avowed assumption that it *does not mean what it plainly says.* And I have no doubt that a great many self-saying *loyal* Radicals will gulp the " oath of loyalty " in spite of the notorious fact that many of them (Colonel Krekel and Senator Brown included) did all that in them lay, short of actual arms, to put down the Provisional Government of the State, and substitute it by a military despotism.

I have not sufficient time or space to treat of many of the enormous errors of the Constitution—such as its persecution of religion and its ministers; its cruel and unusual plan of taxation; its bold attempt to plunder the local school funds; its arbitrary exaction from the people of unlawful oaths, under the penalty of surrendering some of their most cherished rights, and its daring attempt to change the fundamental principle of our Government by transferring the political power from *the people* of the State to selected classes of their own choosing. These great topics are, I am happy to know, now undergoing discussion, oral and written, which, I trust, will sufficiently enlighten the public mind.

Still, I cannot close this last letter of my series without drawing your attention to one or two instances of gross ignorance or criminal negligence on the part of the Convention, as manifested in special provisions of the proposed Constitution.

[33] *Supra,* Feb. 15, 1864, note 44.

In Article II, section 9, it is provided that " the General Assembly *shall have power* to repeal or modify all ordinances adopted by any *previous* Convention."   This, if it have any force at all, puts at the discretion of the Legislature the famous ordinance of July 19, 1820, which is in fact the great original compact between the State of Missouri and the United States, and by which alone we have any legal title to—1. School lands. 2. The Salt Springs, and six sections adjoining each. 3. The Road and Canal fund. 4. The seat of Government lands; and 5. The University Lands.   Whether or not this title, unobstrusive sentence in the New Constitution was a secret contrivance, a clandestine scheme to plunder those lands and funds, I leave you to judge.

In Article 2, section 11, it is written that " Every court in which any person shall be summoned to serve as a grand or petit juror, shall require him, before he is sworn as a juror, to take said oath (a strong oath above prescribed) in open court; and no person refusing to take the same *shall serve* as a juror."   That is all upon the subject. The law has no sanctions, no *duty* to take the oath, and no punishment for declining to take it; and consequently, there can be no such thing as *compulsory* jury service.   Any man summoned as a juror can, under that section, *lawfully* evade the service by simply saying to the Judge, " Sir, I decline to take that oath *to-day*.   I have taken it many a time heretofore, and may take it hereafter, when I have nothing better to do than serve on a jury—but not *just now*, sir." And what do you think, good people, will become of our boasted *trial by jury*, under such a Constitution as that?   I fear that the jury box will be occupied by idlers and loafers, who are willing to serve for the pittance which will pay their grog bills.

My fellow-citizens, I have now finished the series of letters which I promised at the start; but I do not claim my discharge from your service.   I enlisted for the war, and am ready to spend the remnant of my life in the same good service.   So long as arbitrary power shall continue its assaults, I will continue to make the best defense I can of the only valuable inheritance left to us by our fathers— *Liberty according to law*.

EDWARD BATES

St. Louis, May 31, 1865.

INDEX

Compiled by Mary Parker Ragatz, M.A.

goes to visit his son at West Point, 402, 403; seeks release of Mrs. Mary J. Clark, a prisoner, 403; constantly appealed to, to secure pardons for prisoners, 403, 404; objects to trading with Confederacy while war is still being fought, 404–405; refers to Aristotle 405, 406, 432–433, 522; contributes to National Union Committee for the campaign (1864), 408; sends money to a Confederate prisoner, 408; opposes McClellan as candidate for the presidency (1864), 408–409; idea of, for paying the public debt, 409; on seizure of plantations in Louisiana, 411; expects the war to end, 412; Josephine Clarkson requests a pass from, to go to Virginia, 413; objects to admission of Nevada, 414; denunciation of trade between North and South during the war, 414; of Rosecrans' inefficiency in Missouri, 415; Elizabeth T. Wilson requests a pass from, to go to Virginia, 416; opinion of, called for on the question of Great Lakes as "high seas," 417; comments on Taney's character at time of the Chief Justice's death, 418; on the nature of man, 418–419; on the weakness of Democratic Party (1864), 421–422; on a Quaker sermon, 423–424; refers to Trollope's *North America*, 425; secures release of two Confederate prisoners, 426; visited by his son, Coalter, 426; on the question of blockade, 427; expresses intention to resign, 427; is told that Lincoln desires to appoint him as chief justice of Supreme Court, 427–428; resignation of, 428, 430; sale of household goods of, 428, 429; takes leave of the President, 429; leaves Washington, 429; denounces Lee for joining the rebellion, 430; praises General Curtis, 431; defines "loyalty," "radical," "convention," 431–432; quotes Guizot, 432; quotes Young's *Night Thoughts*, 433 and note 98; comments on a broadside of thoughts on the times (1864), 433–436; on "guarantees," 436–437; refers to the *Bible*, 436, 476, 521, 559, 599; opinion of, on obligations of United States in maintaining neutrality of Isthmus of Panama, 437–438; praises New Jersey, 438; writes to J. H. Ashton, 442, 481; refers to diary of Frances Burney D'Arblay, 442; to Thomas Chatterton, English poet, 442 and note 30; holds that there can be no such thing as reconstruction, 442–443; attends wedding of John Dillon and Blanche Vallé, 443; secures a dwelling in St. Louis, 443–444, 445, 449, 450, 461, 467; holds that rumors of burning of the John C. Calhoun home are false, 446; compares Radicals in

Missouri Constitutional Convention to Jacobins of France, 447; refers to Thiers' *History of the French Revolution,* 448 and note 66, 449, 451, 456, 459, 470, 478, 487; comments on character of early frontiersmen, 450; urged to write memoirs, 450; appraises his own abilities, 450; praises his grandson, Onward, 451; correspondence of, 452; denounces the St. Louis press, 455; refers to Robespierre, 456; quotes from Alison's history of French Revolution, 456; comments on the difference between a "pail" and a "bucket," 456–457; denies that martial law existed in Missouri, 457; on the difference between military and martial law, 457–458; George T. Woodson visits in home of, 462; considers writing for publication, 462, 467, 469; lists garden seeds sent to him by Isaac Newton, 463–464; is enrolled as a militiaman, 467; attends funeral of Asa Wilgus, 467; denounces Sons of Liberty organization, 469; letters by, to the people of Missouri, published in the *Missouri Democrat* (1865) 470, 471, 472, 474, 476, 477, 478, 479, 482, 486, 571–612; first and second of same republished in the *Missouri Republican,* 471, 472, 474; corrects errors of the *Missouri Republican* on his opinion, 471–472; comments on assassination of Lincoln, 473, 474, 579–580; denounces usurpation of power by the military, 475–476, 481, 482, 483, 484, 491, 496, 498–503, 547–551, *passim,* 561–562 (*see also* Military, the); subscribes to *Missouri Democrat,* 476; praises Major-General George H. Thomas, 478; praises Sherman, 478; denunciation of the Missouri Constitution of 1865, 479, 540 (*see under* Missouri); of a charge, not based on a source of information, that the Confederate Congress passed a bill for starvation of prisoners, etc., 480; of removals from office in Missouri under the "Ousting Ordinance," 480, 481, 485, 488; regrets the resignation of his son, Barton, from Missouri Supreme Court, 481; is flattered by much praise of his letters to the people of Missouri, 482; James Speed, successor to, as attorney-general, 482 and note 27, 483 (*see also* Speed, James); approves of Johnson's amnesty proclamation, 484; refers to Sir John Harrington's *Epigrams,* on treason, 485 and note 39; denounces Gov. Fletcher, 485, 488, 510, 511, 567; goes to Dardenne Prairie to visit his sister, 486; publishes a letter (June 17, 1865) in the *Evening Dispatch* to the people of Missouri, 488; refers to Lord Campbell's writings, 488, 496, 526; denounces Richard H. Dana's views on reconstruction, 490; praises the negro editor of the *Black Republican,* 492;

field and, 294; understanding between General Schofield and, necessary, 310; demands protection of the state government, 310; Radicals versus, 321; death of 328–329.

Gamble, Mrs. Hamilton R., sister of Mrs. Bates, 138, note 69.

Gamble, Joseph H., seeks a treasury agency, 400.

Gamble, May, daughter of Judge Hamilton R. Gamble, 120.

Gantt, Thomas T., of Missouri, 174, 328, 391, 531, 562.

Garat, Dominique J., member of the French Legislative Assembly, 460 and note 9.

Garcia y Tassara, Gabriel, E. E. and M. P. of Spain, 205, 374, 425, 438.

Gardenhine [?] Gen. ——, speech by, at the Jefferson City Opposition Convention, 106.

Gardens, 10, 14, 30, 104, 121, 122, 149, 443, 444, 463, 464, 506, 514, 515, 516, 520, 555, 557, 561, 562.

Gardiner, Bishop ——, 526.

Gardner, Colonel ——, 315.

Garesche, Alexander J. P., supports Douglas (1860), 90 and note 16.

Garesche, P. B., Constitutional Union nominee for the Missouri convention on secession, 174.

Garibaldi, Giuseppe, Italian patriot, 86; revolutionary activities of, 150–151.

Garrison, C. K., defends General Stone, 245; denounces Senator Baker, 245–246.

Garrison, Daniel R., St. Louis manufacturer, calls on Bates, 454, 530; daughter of, marries John N. Booth, 543; goes to Washington in behalf of Missouri railroad interests, 543.

Garrison J. L., Bates buys a house in St. Louis from, 443–444, 445, 537.

Garrison, Mary Alice, marries John N. Booth, 543.

Garrison, William Lloyd, editor of the *Liberator*, 371.

Gas, 517.

Gas lights in St. Louis, 497.

Gaston, William, of North Carolina, address of, to students of the university, against slavery (1832), 64 and note 71, 65.

Geideville, G. de, authorship of Bunyan's *Pilgrim's Progress* attributed to, 52.

George, ——, 245.

Georgetown, 210, 211.

Georgia, Joseph E. Brown, governor of, 73 and note 8; political sentiment in, (1860), 97; in the Democratic Convention (1860), 124; secession movement in, 164 and note 8; Sherman in, 364 and note 27, 367, 386, 413 and note 87, 431, 466; Governor Brown's message concerning the abandonment of the Confederacy by, 459; Sherman's

opinion on the status of, (1865), 505–506. *See also* Savannah, Ga.

Georgians, denounced by Bates, 160.

German press, 404, 476, 481.

German revolutionists, 131 and notes 23 and 24.

Germans, become legally naturalized citizens but do not become Americans, 312–313; denounce Lincoln's reply to Missouri Radicals, 327; of St. Louis County, 334; not entirely controlled by Radicals (1864), 348; and the question of negro suffrage, 445. *See* Radical German Convention.

Germany, cutting-up of estates in, 332 and note 23.

Gerolt, Baron, E. E. and M. P. of Prussia, 205, 206, 216–217, 236, 368.

Gettysburg, battle of, 300; consecration of the military cemetery at, 316.

Gibson, Charles, of Missouri and solicitor of the U. S. Court of Claims, 11, 37, 47, 50, 77, 107, 145, 211, 212, 236, 251, 279, 320, 332, 343; calls on Bates, 74, 514, 530, 543; efforts of, to prevent a split in the Opposition parties of Missouri (1859), 80; success of, in securing the nomination of Bates as candidate for the presidency (1860), by Opposition parties in Missouri, 83; dines with Bates, Henry J. Raymond, and J. H. Van Alen, 97; report of, on the Indiana Republican Convention, 102; confers with Bates, 124, 132; endorses a note for Bates, 138, 173, 175; signer of a plea for Missourians to vote for the Union, 173; accredited agent in Washington from Governor Gamble of Missouri, 201; correspondence of Gamble and, 219, 278; helps Bates in regard to placing Richard Bates, 295; letter of, to the President, 309; requests appointment of J. B. Kerr as deputy solicitor of the Court of Claims, 324; resignation of, 392; Bates regrets the waning friendship of, 528.

Giddings, Joshua R., of Ohio, 50, 129.

Giles, Mrs. ——, reference to pass secured by, to go to Richmond, 468–469.

Gill, ——, of Missouri, 34.

Gilluly, Mrs. Enid F., editor's acknowledgment to, ix.

Gilmer, John A., congressman from North Carolina, communicates with Lincoln, 167 and note 12; proposed for a Cabinet post (1860), 171.

Gilstrap, Abner L., of Missouri, 440.

Girondists, reference to the, 456 and note 93.

Gist, William H., governor of South Carolina, correspondence of Governor Hicks of Maryland and, (1860), 102 and note 87.

Glasgow, William, Jr., 10.

Made in the USA
Lexington, KY
09 December 2013